As Seen On NBC's Today Show

Baby 411

3rd edition

Clear Answers & Smart Advice for Your Baby's First Year

Denise Fields and Ari Brown, M.D.

Copyright Page and Low-Impact Pilates Workout

Saxophone, lead guitar by Denise Fields
Drums, rhythm guitar and interior layout by Alan Fields
Cover/interior design and keyboard solo by Epicenter Creative
Catering by Mark Brown and the Salt Lick
Backing harmony vocals and keyboards by Andy and Julia Brown
Percussion and additional guitar by Ben and Jack Fields
Index by New West Indexing
Band photography by Jim Lincoln and Barbara Balliette

Distribution to the book trade by National Book Network (800) 462-6420.

All rights reserved. **Copyright © 2008 by Ari Brown, M.D. and Denise & Alan Fields.** Published by Windsor Peak Press, Boulder, CO. This book may not be reproduced in whole or in part by any means without the expressed written permission of the authors. Printed in the USA.

To order this book, order online at Baby411.com or call 1-800-888-0385. Questions or comments? Please call the authors at (303) 442-8792. Or fax them a note at (303) 442-3744. Or write to them at Windsor Peak Press, 436 Pine Street, Boulder, CO 80302. E-mail us at authors@baby411.com.

The latest info on this book is online at www.Baby411.com

Library Cataloging in Publication Data

Brown, Ari, M.D.
Fields, Denise
    Baby 411: Clear Answers & Smart Advice for Your Baby's First Year/ Ari Brown, M.D. and Denise Fields
    544 pages.
    Includes index.
    ISBN 1-889392-26-X
    1. Infants. 2. Child rearing. 3. Infants—Care.

Child Care—Handbooks, manuals, etc. 2. Infants' supplies—Purchasing—United States, Canada, Directories. 3. Children's paraphernalia—Purchasing—Handbooks, manuals. 4. Product Safety—Handbooks, manuals. 5. Consumer education.
    649'.122'0296—dc20. 2008.

Version 3.0

Do you have an old copy of this book? Check our web site at Baby411.com make sure you have the most current version (click on "which version?").

Baby 411 Medical Advisory Board

Steven Adair, DDS, MS
Pediatric Dentist
Professor and Chair, Pediatric Dentistry
Medical College of Georgia

Mark T. Brown, MD, FACS
Ear, Nose, and Throat Specialist
Great Hills ENT
Austin, TX

Jose C. Cortez, MD
Pediatric Urologist
Dell Children's Medical Center
Austin, TX

Lewis First, MD, FAAP
Pediatrician Extraordinaire
Burlington, VT

Corinne Frank, Esq.
Professional Mother

Linda Hill, RN, IBCLC
Certified Lactation Consultant
Capital Pediatric Group
Austin, TX

Thomas Hughes, MD, FAAP
Pediatrician
Capital Pediatric Group
Austin, TX

Joyce Jordan, LVN
Pediatric Triage Nurse
Capital Pediatric Group
Austin, TX

Arlinda Michael, RN, CIMI, IBCLC
Certified Lactation Consultant
Infant Massage Instructor
Minneapolis, MN

Paul Offit, MD, FAAP
Director, Vaccine Education Center
Children's Hospital of Philadelphia
Philadelphia, PA

Edward Peters, MD, FAAAI
Allergist, Pulmonologist
Allergy and Asthma Associates of Austin
Austin, TX

Sidney Seidman, MD, FAAP
Pediatrician
Annapolis, MD

Karen L. Wright, MD
Pediatric Cardiologist
Children's Cardiology Associates
Austin, TX

Mark Zamutt, RPh.
Pharmacist
Dell Children's Medical Center
Austin, TX

R. Jeff Zwiener, MD
Medical Director, Pediatric Gastroenterology
Dell Children's Medical Center
Austin, TX

PRAISE FOR BABY 411

"Without a doubt, Baby 411 is definitely among the best books ever written for parents and caregivers regarding the appropriate and very logical approach to infant and child care. It is cleverly written, easy to understand, well organized, and often extremely humorous. Medical terminology and the technical aspects of pediatric care have been simplified without insulting the intelligence of the reader. Parents, grandparents, and anyone responsible for the rearing and day-to-day care of children should have this book available as a ready resource. I do!"

-Jan Drutz, M.D., Professor of Pediatrics,
Baylor College of Medicine

"Baby 411 is not only informative, it is interestingly written, contemporary and accurate. Parents overwhelmed with the rigors of raising a rugrat will be reassured . . . and it might just help them relax!"

-Carden Johnston, M.D., pediatrician

"Baby 411 is an intelligent, engaging, thoughtful romp through the science and medicine of children's health. You often hear that babies are born without an instruction book; but Baby 411 is it."

-Paul Offit, M.D., Chief, Section of Infectious Diseases,
Children's Hospital of Philadelphia, Professor of Pediatrics,
University of Pennsylvania School of Medicine

"Baby 411 is the best self help book for parents I have seen."

-Albert Karam, M.D., pediatrician

"Baby 411 is a cleverly written and comprehensive resource. I recommend it to my patients as the complete guide to raising their child."

-Barbara Huggins, M.D., Professor and Chair,
University of Texas Health Science Center, Tyler

"Baby 411 will be the book you will go to first when questions arise."
-Sidney Seidman, MD, pediatrician

"Thank you very much for an EXCELLENT resource for parents. I can honestly tell you I have used Baby 411 as a reference at least every other day, if not EVERY day. I have carried it with me everywhere we've gone, and I keep it handy at home so that I can 'consult' with you any time I have questions. I never doubt what gift to give at baby showers anymore! Baby 411 is the best gift to give a new mom."

-Kristin G., mother

YET MORE PRAISE FOR BABY 411

"One of the best guides to the first year of your baby's life. Why we like it: The comprehensive table of contents helps you flip to just the section you need, whether it's how often to clean your baby's belly button or what to include in your infant's first-aid kit."

-Parents Magazine

"Baby 411 includes a lot of practical 'insider' tips and facts that you won't get in other books that simply cover what you should expect each month. You will likely learn things that your own pediatrician hasn't told you. And I bet that new parents who read this book will need to call and see their pediatrician less often than other newbie parents."

-Vince Iannelli, M.D., keepkidshealthy.com

"Finally, a great book for new parents! Thanks for writing such a wonderful reference guide."

-James and Leanne Harvey, owners, State Street Childcare

"I have found that parents want guidelines based in science and common sense advice based in modern experience. It needs to be readily accessible for quick decisions. Parents will find it all here in Baby 411. And, it is presented in a way that will make them smile and feel like someone knows how they are feeling!"

-Arlinda Michael, RN, BSN, IBCLC,
childbirth educator and certified lactation consultant

"No parent, new or experienced, should be without Baby 411. It answers all of your questions and provides excellent tips for caring for your baby with a direct, easy to use and read, no-nonsense approach that you will not find anywhere else. Dr. Brown has a unique ability to translate medical jargon into everyday, conversational language. You will feel like your own best friend and personal pediatrician is sitting in your kitchen ready to help you at any time."

-Corinne Frank, mother of two

"I just wanted to tell you that I think your book is FANTASTIC! It is so clearly written and easy to read and understand. As a mother of a six week old baby girl, I received so many books on infant care which I found so overwhelming. Your book is the only one that covers all relevant topics and gives you advice and solutions to all the questions and fears you face as a new parent."

-Beverly S., mother

???

OVERVIEW

SECTION ONE: 3-2-1 BABY! PREPARING FOR THE NEW ONE 1

What decisions do you have to make before your baby is born? This section explores finding a pediatrician, the latest news on newborn screening and other timely topics. Next, let's talk about your baby's doctor—what are the insider tips to scheduling appointments and what to do on weekends and holidays. Finally, it's Labor Day. Your baby is here! We'll talk about your baby's first few days . . . plus how to survive the first two weeks.

SECTION TWO: CARE & FEEDING 67

How do you care for your newborn? The first part of this section explores cleaning your newborn, diaper rash and other hygiene issues. Next, let's talk nutrition and growth—what do growth charts mean? What nutrition does your baby need for the first year? We've got the low-down on your baby's nutrition, including tips on vitamin supplements, avoiding obesity and getting enough calcium, fiber and iron. Finally, we'll break down nutrition into separate chapters that focus on liquids and solids. We'll discuss breastfeeding, formula and other liquids like cow's milk. Next, we'll discuss how to tell when your baby is ready for solid foods, including advice on avoiding food allergies. The last chapter in this section is titled "The other end"—everything you wanted to know about baby poop and more!

SECTION THREE: SLEEP, DEVELOPMENT & DISCIPLINE 179

Let's talk sleep—this section will give you the scoop on your baby's sleep (or lack thereof). We'll talk about setting up good habits and look at the different sleep "gurus" that haunt the bookstore aisles. Next, we'll look at how your baby will develop, including milestones and social/emotional growth. Finally, it's a topic every parent must deal with: discipline. We'll give you advice on how to soothe a newborn, how to develop a good discipline style and dealing with temper tantrums.

SECTION FOUR: SICKNESS & HOW TO AVOID IT! 261

Here, we'll discuss vaccinations—what's required and what's optional. We'll hit the vaccines controversies head on, including the autism debate and thimerosal. This section also covers the most common infections and diseases, with separate chapters devoted to such topics as the common cold, bacterial infections and more.

SECTION FIVE: FIRST AID—TOP 12 PROBLEMS & SOLUTIONS 343

What should you do when your baby gets sick? This section will give you advice on taking your baby's vital signs and what to have in a first aid kit. We'll hit the Top 12 problems and solutions for newborns, including fever, rashes, trauma and more.

SECTION SIX: THE REFERENCE LIBRARY 397

This section includes detailed information on medicines, alternative therapies, lab tests, the glossary, references and footnotes.

ACKNOWLEDGEMENTS

So how'd a pediatrician like me end up writing a book and being on national TV? I ponder that myself every once in a while!

As we put the finishing touches on the third edition of *Baby 411*, it makes me look back on the past five years. I was perfectly content with life as I knew it prior to June 2002. I had a great pediatric practice with the nicest families I could ever dream of. And I found child advocacy for my local and state medical societies to be very rewarding.

Then I had a conversation that changed my life. Alan and Denise Fields were long-time friends and bestselling authors of *Baby Bargains*. Based on our collective experiences, we came to the following conclusion: despite the surplus of parenting books, today's parents needed help.

The Information Age led parents to more questions than answers. The Fields were experts in writing books but did not go to medical school (maybe a wise decision!). I could answer all the questions, but I didn't have the time (or so I thought) or the skill (I learned along the way) to write a book. But I had a passion to educate parents—just like I did in my office every day.

"Write a couple chapters and send them to us," said my friends.

So I did.

"We like it," said my friends/future co-author/editors/publishers. "Give us 15 chapters by Thanksgiving."

"But that's a chapter a week!" I protested.

"Yep. Welcome to the book business."

Jotting down ideas between seeing patients, pulling an all-nighter to write the sleep chapter, and missing a few bedtime stories with my own kids . . . *Baby 411* was born.

Since the first edition was published, many aspects of pediatric healthcare have changed: New recommendations to prevent SIDS . . . new studies shedding light on colic . . . new vaccines . . . new recommendations for fluoride. And that's just to name a few. It's no wonder parents are confused about what to do!

It's sad but true: any parenting book written before 2007 is already outdated. So, in retrospect, writing the first edition of *Baby 411* was the easy part. Revising the book to keep up with the pace of medicine has been the challenge. (Note to self: next time, write a book on a topic that doesn't change but every ten years.)

Life as an author, speaker, and full-time pediatrician is a bit chaotic at times, but it has taken my mission of child advocacy to a larger stage. And I wouldn't change a thing. Well, more sleep would be nice. The wonderful notes from our readers keep me energized. Keep 'em coming—we love hearing from you!

I owe many thanks to the Fields for believing in me and in this project.

Biggest thanks go to my husband, Mark, for walking down this road with me. I never could have done it without you. I also thank my sister and brothers for their grassroots marketing efforts, giving books to everyone they know, and approaching random pregnant women in Costco parking lots across the country. (I swear I had nothing to do with this idea.)

To my patients and their parents. You are my inspiration. Thank you for sharing your experiences to help other families. You teach me everyday!

I thank the citizens of Austin and the Austin medical community for their extraordinary encouragement. I am so proud to call you my friends, neighbors, and colleagues. I vow to Keep Austin Weird.

Other special folks, friends, and spiritual advisors include: The physicians and staff at Capital Pediatric Group, the stellar communications department of the American Academy of Pediatrics, Texas Medical Association and Texas Pediatric Society, the staff at Parents Magazine and Parents.com, National Association of Medical Communicators, C.S. Lewis and Co. Publicists.

And finally, I dedicate this book to Andy and Julia. I love you so much and am so very proud to be your mom.

– *Ari Brown, M.D.*

TABLE OF CONTENTS

Introduction   xvii

SECTION ONE: 3-2-1 BABY! PREPARING FOR THE NEW ONE

Chapter 1
DECISIONS

Picking A Parenting Style..4
Selecting A Medical Provider For Your Baby..................................6
Behind The Scenes: Why Is My Doctor So Late?..........................8
Circumcision Pros And Cons..15
Optional Newborn Metabolic Screening......................................18
Cord Blood Banking...19
   Table: Cord Blood Bank Options Compared............................21
Childcare..22
   Six Commandments For Balancing Work & Baby...................24
   Juggling Family & Career: 15 Tips..25
   The 5 Options For Childcare...27
Adoption..32
Making A Birth Plan..33

Chapter 2
YOU & YOUR BABY'S DOC: INSIDER TIPS & ADVICE

The Schedule Of Well Baby Checkups...35
Nine Screening Tests..36
Who Is The AAP?..37
The Difference Between A Sick Visit And A Consultation..........38
Insider Tip: The Best Time To Schedule An Appointment.........39
What To Do: Evening and Weekends..40

Chapter 3
LABOR DAY

Your Baby's First Physical Exam..44
Screening Tests, Vitamin K, And Eye Ointment..........................49
Group B Strep...50
Getting To Know You: Your Baby's 1st Days...............................51
   Does My Baby Need To Study For His APGARs?...................52
   What's THAT In My Baby's Diaper?..52
   Why Is My Baby Shrinking?...52
   Why Is My Baby Turning Yellow?...53
   When Do I Have To Use A Car Seat?......................................55
Preemie Primer..56
Special Section: The Two-Week Survival Guide.........................60
   When Can I Take My Baby Outside?.......................................60
   New Dad 411: Tips & Advice...63

The Baby Blues 64
The Handy Feeding And Elimination Table 66

SECTION TWO: CARE & FEEDING
Chapter 4

HYGIENE: THE SPA TREATMENT

The First Manicure 69
When Can I Use Diaper Wipes? 70
How Often Do I Clean The Belly Button? 70
Diaper Rash: 5 Tips & Tricks 71
Bathing Baby 72
Cradle Cap 74
Sun block And Insect Repellent 74
Eczema: Advice And Tips 75
The Boy Parts 77
The Girl Parts 78
Mouth care: Thrush, Dental Care, and Drool 79

Chapter 5

NUTRITION & GROWTH

What Growth Charts Mean 83
How Infants Grow (Height, Head Size, Weight) 84
Flat Heads & Tummy Time 86
Calories & Nutrition For The First Year 88
The Big Picture: Nutrition For The First Year 90
Feeding Schedules, Or Lack Thereof 91
Special Concerns: Dropping Down The Growth Chart 92
Does My Baby Need A Vitamin Supplement? 93
Fluoride: Is My Baby Getting Enough? 95
Overeating, Obesity, And The Body Mass Index 96
New Parent 411: How To Avoid Obesity 97
Feedback From The Real World: Avoiding The 4C's 98
Calcium, Fiber, And Iron 100
Happy Birthday! You're One! 101

Chapter 6

LIQUIDS

Breast Milk 104
   The Advantages Of Breast Milk 104
   Why Women Stop 105
   Getting Started 107
   Day-By-Day Guide 108
   New Parent 411: Anxiety At Checkout 109
   Top 10 Tips To Survive The First Two Weeks 110
   Troubleshooting: The Top 8 Biggest Challenges 113
   Engorgement 114

Sore Nipples: 7 Tips For Relief	114
Expressing Milk & Breast Pumps	116
Mom Concerns: Work, Diet, Medications	118
Special Situations: Adoptions, Twins, Preemies	124
Weaning: The Guide	126
The Big Picture: Breastfeeding For The First Year	128
Breastfeeding Problems & Solutions	130

Formula 132
- Coke Vs. Diet Coke: The Types Of Formula 132
- Soy Formula 135
- The Gourmet Formulas 137
- Powder Vs. Liquid: Which Formula is Best? 139
- Bottles: Which Are Best? 140
- Are Plastic Baby Bottles Toxic? 141
- The Big Picture: Formula Feeding For The First Year 143

Other Liquids: Water, Juice, Milk 143

Chapter 7

SOLIDS

- The Five Types Of Solid Foods 147
- How To Tell When Your Baby Is Ready? 149
- What Is Rice Cereal And Other Stage One Foods? 149
- How Do I Know If Baby Has A Food Allergy? 153
- Hidden Sources For Dangerous Foods 155
- The Big Picture For Liquid And Solid Nutrition 160

Chapter 8

THE OTHER END

- What Is Normal Newborn Poop? 162
- The Top 5 Worrisome Poops 163
- 5 Trade Secrets For Constipation Relief 164
- Older Babies: Solid Foods = Solid Poop 165
- Fun Fiber Foods 166
- Spit Up, Regurgitation, And Vomit 168
- What Is Gastroesophageal Reflux (GER)? 168
- Tricks Of The Trade: Treating GER 170
- Quiz: Does Your Baby Have GERD? 172
- Top 5 Worries About Vomit 173
- Urine And Bladder Infections 175
- Burping, Hiccups, And Gas 176

SECTION THREE: SLEEP, DEVELOPMENT & DISCIPLINE

Chapter 9

SLEEP

- The Science Of Sleep 182
- How Long Should Newborns Sleep? 183

Sleep Safety Tips: SIDS And Other Dangers	187
Deciding On Your Family's Sleep Routine	192
Family Bed: Pros & Cons	192
Solitary Sleep: Pros & Cons	194
Setting Up Good Habits	194
Top 10 Commandments For Establishing A Sleep Routine	196
Undoing Bad Habits	198
Top 10 Mistakes Parents Make With Infant Sleep	199
The Sleep Gurus: 7 Approaches Explained	202
The Ferber Technique, Demystified	204
Naps	210
Special Situations: Multiples And Preemies	212

Chapter 10

DEVELOPMENT

What Does Development Mean?	216
How Do I Know My Baby Is Developing Normally?	217
What Is The Denver Developmental Checklist?	217
Bookmark this page! Our Development Checklist	218
Failing Milestones: What To Do	218
What Is Autism And When Do I Worry?	220
Developmental Delays	224
How Your Baby Learns	225
Your Baby's Social And Emotional Growth	226
Development By Age	227
Birth to Two Months	227
Two to Four Months	229
Four to Six Months	230
Six to Nine Months	232
Nine to 12 Months	234
New Parent 411: Top 14 New Parent Safety Tips	237
Watching TV: When And How Much Is Appropriate?	238
Good Toys And Books	241

Chapter 11

DISCIPLINE & TEMPERAMENT

Getting To Know Your Baby's Temperament	244
High Versus Low-Maintenance Babies	245
The 3 Rules Of Cry Management	247
10 Tips For Soothing The Savage Beast: Newborns	247
Pacifiers: The Party Line	248
What Is Colic And What Can I Do About It?	249
A Miracle Cure for Colic?	250
Planting The Seeds Of Discipline	252
11 Tips For Developing A Discipline Style	255
8 Tried & True Discipline Techniques	256
Temper Tantrums: Hurricanes At Home	256
Special Situations: Separation Anxiety, Thumb Sucking	257

SECTION FOUR: SICKNESS & HOW TO AVOID IT!

Chapter 12

VACCINATIONS

Vaccines: A Bit Of History	264
The Top 15 Vaccine Questions	266
The 5 Biggest Misconceptions	266
7 Truths About Vaccines	267
Conspiracy theories and vaccines	273
Vaccines And The Diseases They Stop	275
The Vaccination Schedule	276
Optional Vaccines	282
Vaccine Controversies: MMR/Autism, Thimerosal & More	283
Thimerosal 411	286
Vaccine Shortages	288

Chapter 13

COMMON INFECTIONS

What Are Viruses?	292
The Common Cold	296
Humidifiers & Vaporizers	298
What Are Bacteria?	299
Telling A Bacterial Infection From A Virus	300
Antibiotic Resistance	301
When Your Child Can Return To Childcare Or Playgroup	303
Viral Infections: Flu, Croup, Chickenpox	304
Bacterial Infections: Food Poisoning, Pneumonia and more	309
Things That Make You Itch	313
Special Feature: Ear Infections	316
7 Risk Factors For Ear Infections	317
The Infection Hit Parade	325

Chapter 14

COMMON DISEASES

Eyes: Lazy Eye	327
Lungs: Asthma, Bronchiolitis	328
Heart: Murmurs	330
Blood: Anemia, Sickle Cell Disease, Iron Deficiency, Lead Exposure	332
Skin: Eczema	335
Muscles/Bones: Intoeing, Bow-Legged, Flat Feet	337
Endocrine: Diabetes	339
Allergies: Seasonal, Environmental	340
Genitals	341
What's That Smell? Unusual Odors	342

SECTION FIVE: FIRST AID—TOP 12 PROBLEMS & SOLUTIONS

Chapter 15

FIRST AID

9 Hints: Making The Most Of A Call To Your Doc	345
Your First Aid Kit	347
How To Take Your Baby's Vital Signs	347
Making A Diagnosis Over The Phone?	348
The Top Problems & Solutions	**349**
Abdominal Pain	349
Allergic Reaction	350
Bleeding And Bruising	352
How To Avoid Food-Poisoning	356
Burns	357
Breathing Problems (Respiratory Distress)	357
Everything You Wanted To Know About Croup	359
Choking Emergencies: 4 Tips	360
Cough & Congestion	361
Diarrhea	363
How To Tell If Your Baby Is Dehydrated	365
Vomiting	367
Eye Problems: Pink Eye, Blocked Tear Ducts	369
Fever: A Special Section	371
How To Take Your Baby's Temperature	375
10 Commandments To Treating A Fever	377
Poisoning	381
The Most Dangerous Household Products	381
Rashes	382
Seizures	387
Does It Need Stitches?	388
Trauma: Injuries To The Head, Neck, Back, Eyes	390

SECTION SIX: THE REFERENCE LIBRARY

Appendix A: Medications	399
Appendix B: Alternative Medicines	427
Appendix C: Lab Work & Tests	435
Appendix D: Glossary	445
Appendix E: References	469
Appendix F: Footnotes	479
Index	487
How To Reach The Authors	519
Our Other Books	522
About The Authors	Inside Back Cover

Icons

 **Helpful Hint**

 **Reality Check**

 **Bottom Line**

 **Red Flags**

 **Feedback from the Real World**

 **Old Wives Tale**

 **Insider Secrets**

 **New Parent 411**

Why Read This Book?
Intro

What's in this Chapter

◆ Meet the Authors

◆ How to use this book

◆ No ads! No plugs!

◆ Show us the Science

◆ The 6 Ground Rules for Being a Parent

Welcome to the world of parenthood. Yes, having a baby is both exciting . . . and terrifying.

Soon, you'll be responsible for taking care of this little urchin 24/7, with no time off for good behavior. We've been there—and know what it feels to stand on the edge of the new parent abyss wondering just what the heck we were doing.

Once your baby is born, your thoughts will be swimming with dozens of questions . . . from the mundane (what's THAT in my baby's diaper?) to the serious (why won't my baby stop crying? Does he have a fever? Should I call the doctor?).

That's why we are here. Think of us as your sherpa guide as you climb Mt. Everest Baby. You need detailed, up-to-date info about taking care of your baby—we've got it. You want straight answers on controversial topics like vaccines, circumcision and newborn screening—again, we're there.

Yes, we realize there are many other baby books out there, all promising to reveal the secrets to taking care of your baby. So, does the world really need another baby book? Let's put that into bold type.

INTRO

Does the World Need Another Baby Book?

Well, darn it, we think so. Yes, if you stand in the parenting aisle of your local bookstore, you'll be assaulted by an avalanche of baby books with titles like YOUR BABY'S FIRST YEAR—SECOND BY SECOND . . . and our personal favorite, WE KNOW MORE THAN YOU: WHAT CELEBRITIES AND SUPERMODELS CAN TEACH YOU ABOUT BEING A PARENT.

All that is well and good, but we found that MOST baby books miss the mark when it comes to nuts and bolts issues—like how do you clean a baby? And feed it? And what happens when something goes wrong, like God forbid, your baby gets sick?

And let's not forget about the new addition to your family—no, not your baby. We're talking about your baby's *doctor*. How do you pick a pediatrician? And how do you get along with this person? Can you call your doc at 2 am and ask a question about diaper rash? (Short answer: yes, but don't expect the doc to be real cheery on the phone).

When it comes to offering advice about medical issues with newborns, most baby books fail because, well, they aren't written by someone who's actually been to medical school. Yes, there are guidebooks written by "girlfriends" and other so-called experts . . . but for actual medical advice, we'd prefer someone who knows more about medicine than you can learn from watching *Grey's Anatomy*.

Okay, to be honest, there are a few baby books written by doctors and nurses. But we found many so boring and dry, they are listed as FDA-approved cures for insomnia. (Not that new parents will ever have that problem, of course).

And other good books on babies by respected docs haven't been updated since the Reagan administration. Sorry, the world of baby care moves at Internet speed these days, so a book published ten years ago isn't going to cut it when it comes to a topic like cord blood banking. We're proud that this book contains the very latest recommendations and controversies swirling around the world of babies. And we are one of the few baby books with a detailed web site that offers the latest updates and news on baby's health.

Finally, let's talk about our biggest pet peeve when it comes to baby books: generic advice. Too many books on babies are marred by a lack of specifics and detail.

We get the feeling that authors water down their advice and opinions so as not to offend any reader. While that's nice, it doesn't help when you want a specific answer to a question you have at 3am with your baby. As new parents, we wanted detailed, specific answers to our questions about our newborn—not bland generic platitudes.

Yes, despite all the resources available to new parents (books, magazines, the web), it is amazing how we all end up asking all the same questions as new parents: will we ever sleep through the night again? How come this breastfeeding thing is so difficult? How do I take my baby's temperature? And another 337 questions like that.

That's why we wrote this book—think of it as an FAQ for new parents.

Meet the New Authors, Same as the Old Authors

This book was created by the same team that brought you Baby Bargains—Denise & Alan Fields. This time, we've added a new twist: a co-author, Dr. Ari Brown.

Actually, Dr. Brown has written the majority of this book . . . especially the detailed medical advice. An award-winning pediatrician in private practice in Austin, TX, Dr. Brown graduated from the Baylor College of Medicine. She did her pediatric residency at the renowned Children's Hospital in Boston, under the auspices of legendary pediatrician T. Berry Brazelton. In short, Dr. Brown knows her stuff.

Denise Fields brings her 15 years of experience as a consumer advocate to *Baby 411*—as the co-author of *Baby Bargains* and *Toddler Bargains*, Fields has been featured on Oprah, The Today Show and Good Morning America as well as in articles in the *Wall Street Journal* and *New York Times*. For *Baby 411*, Denise adds in her experience as both a mom and author—many of the questions we get on our message boards hit the same hot button issues you'll see here.

As always, the secret sauce to our books is reader feedback. First, you'll notice readers of our previous books contributed to several sections of this book—you'll see their "Real World Feedback" when it comes to topics like child care, feeding and more. Second, look at the questions we list in each chapter. These are the frequent questions asked by patients of Dr. Brown and the readers of *Baby Bargains* . . . and the same questions that most first-time parents ponder.

Yes, both of the authors of this book are also mommies. They have four children between them. Best of all, the authors are from your generation—we know you want detailed info, the latest research and trends, plus handy web resources. We know you want to go online to get the latest updates, so we've created a special web site for this book (Baby411.com). There you can read any breaking news, swap stories with other parents on our message boards and sign up for a free newsletter that will provide even more insight.

How to Use this Book

Instructions: Open cover. Start reading.

Just kidding! We realize you know how to read a book, but let's go over a few details on how to get the most out of *Baby 411*.

First, let's talk about BIG UGLY LATIN WORDS. You can't discuss baby's health without whipping out the Latin. To keep the jargon from overwhelming you, we have a handy glossary at the end of this book. When you see a **BIG UGLY LATIN WORD** in bold small caps, turn to the back to get a quick definition.

Second, if you flip through the chapters, you'll note boxes with Dr. B's opinion. As it sounds, these are her *opinions* on several hot button issues. Feel free to disagree with these thoughts, but they are based on years of seeing real-world patients and talking with parents. Unlike some other parenting books, we think readers deserve to know where the line is drawn between fact and opinion. You can then decide what works for you and your family.

Finally, let's talk footnotes—we've footnoted the sources used throughout this book. These references start on page 479.

No Ads? No Plugs?

Yes, that's true—as with all our books, this guide contains ZERO ads, spam and commercial plugs. No pharmaceutical or formula company has paid the authors to plug their products in this book. Dr. Brown does NOT go on all-expense paid junkets to Aruba to learn about the latest drug or medical research (although she could use a beach vacation after writing this book). The opinions in this book are those of Denise Fields and Dr. Brown—in the latter case, based on her training and experience in the practice of pediatric medicine.

Full disclosure: Windsor Peak Press does offer a "custom publishing" program that allows companies or organizations to purchase bulk copies of our books to give away to their customers, clients or employees. These books are often specially printed with a company logo and (sometimes) a customized title page. Such arrangements do NOT imply an endorsement or recommendation of the company or its products by Windsor Peak Press, this book or its authors.

Show us the Science!

The goal of *Baby 411* is to provide you with the most up-to-date medical info on your baby. We're talking state-of-the-art when it comes to your baby's health and nutrition.

So, in the age of Internet rumors and 24/7 cable news, let's take a moment to talk SCIENCE.

When it comes to your baby's health, our mantra is SHOW US THE SCIENCE! Before we recommend a particular treatment, parenting method or medicine, we expect there to be good science behind it.

What is good science? Good scientific research is conducted by reputable researchers and published in a major medical journal, like the *New England Journal of Medicine*. Good science is based on a large enough sample to be statistically significant—and verified by peers before it is published.

Contrast this to junk science. Much of what you see online is, unfortunately, junk science—"research" done by questionable individuals who are usually trying to sell a miracle cure along with their theories. Junk science is often based on flawed studies that use too-small samples to be relevant. Just because four of your friends have babies with blue eyes does not mean there is an epidemic of blue-eyed babies on your block.

Much of the junk science you see online or read in the media is there to push a political agenda. Sure, these zealots are well meaning, but they harm their cause by hyping some obscure study from a doctor in Fiji as medical "truth."

Of course, this isn't always so black and white—sometimes good science is "spun" or hyped by groups who want to push their cause.

To put this in perspective, let's look at an example from Canada. In June 2003, the *Financial Post* newspaper in Canada reported that government

INTRO

researchers there found that most cereal-based baby foods contained small amounts of "mycotoxins." What the heck are mycotoxins? These are naturally occurring toxins that are related to molds . . . and are present in most of the world's cereal crops.

The headline in the *Financial Post* read: "Federal study finds toxins in baby food." Yet, this same story was picked up by a U.S. web site and labeled "Scientists find most baby foods toxic." Whoa! Sounds scary, no?

But let's look at what the study *really* said. The Health Canada researchers found "low levels" of toxins in baby food cereal. And the word "low" was an understatement. The Canadian scientists found a level of 32 parts *per billion* of one mycotoxin in oat-based baby cereal. That's more than "low" folks—that's infinitesimally small.

And let's face it—humans have been eating these tiny amounts of fungus in grains for centuries without ill effect. There are toxins, molds and other nasty stuff that occurs naturally in our environment.

Fortunately, there was no panic among parents that was set off by the Canadian study—perhaps CNN was too busy with the latest Lindsay Lohan news to report on this "baby food crisis." But this is an example of how "science" often gets distorted and warped as it winds its way through the meat-grinder of the web and media these days.

As your guides in Baby Health Land, we hope to steer you toward the good science when making decisions for your baby.

What's New In This Edition?

As usual, we just can't leave well enough alone! This updated and expanded version of *Baby 411* covers the latest, breaking health news on babies. Here's a quick look at what's new:

Is there a miracle cure for colic? We'll explore some promising new scientific research that suggests a simple supplement may reduce the endless crying that can drive parents to distraction.

For parents of babies that suffer from acid reflux, you'll find an expanded section in this edition, complete with a handy checklist that can help you decide how serious the problem is—plus we have practical, real-world advice on treating acid reflux.

Are plastic baby bottles toxic? We'll cover this issue in-depth, complete with the most recent findings . . . and what steps you can take to avoid this possible hazard.

This edition of *Baby 411* is also packed with new advice on avoiding flat heads and an in-depth primer for parents of preemies. Of course, you can count on our book to give you the most recent research and data on vaccines, medications and breastfeeding, autism and SIDS.

Now that you know what's new, let's go over some ground rules.

The Six Ground Rules for Being a Good Parent

I **THERE ARE NO GROUND RULES.** Well, what we mean is there are no absolute truths. Thanks to that quirky thing called DNA, every baby is different. Yes, there are "general" guidelines that will help you be a good

INTRODUCTION   XXI

parent (and we'll spend the next 400+ pages giving you those guidelines), but there are no absolute truths. Your baby will consistently amaze, surprise, frustrate and confound you. Did we mention surprise?

2 CHECK YOUR PRIORITIES AT THE DOOR. Make a list of all things that are important in your life—your friends, house, etc. Now, crunch that list up into a little ball and throw it out the window. Your baby is now priorities #1 through #17. Example: your house. Don't expect it to be clean again until 2026.

3 GO WITH YOUR GUT. Well-meaning people—friends, your parents, book authors, complete strangers—are going to try to advise you as to what's best for you and your baby. That's nice, but after a while you are just going to have figure out this parent thing on your own. Think of it like flying a plane . . . you can sit in a flight simulator all you want, but taking the controls in a 747 zipping along at 500 MPH at 30,000 feet is more like what it feels like to be a real parent.

4 SCHEDULE TIME FOR YOURSELF. Want to take a shower after your baby is born? You've got to schedule that 15 minutes. After the first couple of months (or sooner), take time OFF from being mommy and daddy. Have a friend or babysitter watch the baby and go out to dinner and a movie. Give your spouse a break once a week for an hour of "hobby time."

5 CALLING ALL FAVORS. Don't be afraid to ask for help—and feel free to lean on your friends and relatives, at least through the first few weeks.

6 BELIEVE IN YOUR CHOICES. No matter what you decide for your family (breast feeding, work, child care, etc), you're going to hear sniping from others. Often, guilt-driven folks feel defensive about what they decided for their own kids . . . so, they take it out on you. Nice, eh? The best advice: surround yourself with supportive friends who can counter any negativism.

Major Legal Disclaimer

No medical book about babies is complete without that ubiquitous legal disclaimer . . . so here's ours:

The information we provide in this book is intended to help families understand their baby's medical issues. It is NOT intended to replace the advice of your doctor. Before you start any medical treatment, always check in with your baby's doctor who can counsel you on the specific needs of your baby.

We have made a tremendous effort to give you the most up-to-date medical info available. However, medical research is constantly providing new insight into pediatric healthcare. That's why we have an accompanying website at Baby411.com to give you the latest breaking updates (and why you should also discuss your baby's medical care with your baby's doc).

Okay, enough of the introductions—let's get rolling. First up: preparing for your new baby. You've got decisions to make . . . we'll discuss this first.

Baby 411

Section 1

3-2-1 Baby!

Preparing for the New One

DECISIONS
Chapter 1

"When choosing between two evils, always choose the one you haven't tried yet."
~ Mae West

WHAT'S IN THIS CHAPTER

- ◆ PICKING A PARENTING STYLE
- ◆ SELECTING A MEDICAL PROVIDER FOR YOUR BABY
- ◆ CIRCUMCISION PROS & CONS
- ◆ OPTIONAL NEWBORN METABOLIC SCREENING
- ◆ CORD BLOOD BANKING
- ◆ CHILDCARE OPTIONS
- ◆ ADOPTION OPTIONS
- ◆ MAKING A BIRTH PLAN

Yes, your job as a parent begins the moment your baby is conceived. You will find yourself instinctively making decisions from a parent's viewpoint. Maybe it's the hormones. Or, maybe for the first time in your life, you have a sense of responsibility to a helpless little urchin inside of you. Yes, YOU are now a GROWN-UP.

This sense of responsibility will cause you to ponder the questions that all parents ponder.

> 1. Will I be a good parent? (Babysitting and pet ownership are helpful job experiences.)
>
> 2. Can I be as good a parent as my parents were? (Yes. You've learned from their mistakes!)
>
> 3. Will I handle discipline dilemmas better than my friends do? (Maybe. It's very easy to be critical when you aren't yet a parent.)
>
> 4. Will I make the right decisions for my child's health? (That's why we're here—to help point the way to the best choices for you and your child).

This chapter will address the decisions you will need to make before your baby is born. First, we'll discuss parenting styles—yep, you have to pick one BEFORE the baby is born. Then let's talk about finding the baby's doctor. Unlike most experiences you've had with doc-

tors, this one you actually pick before you need her. Next, it's on to some controversial topics like circumcision, optional newborn metabolic screening, and banking your newborn's cord blood. Yes, your parents never had to deal with all these issues.

Finally, let's talk about that endless debate: childcare. Is it better to stay at home with your baby or can you work outside the home and be guilt-free? We'll discuss the latest research and give our perspective as real-life moms. What are the options for childcare? We'll discuss the choices. Our advice: you must at least mull over this issue before baby is born—that's because other expectant parents are already putting their names on waiting lists for the hottest day care options in your community now.

If you are adopting a baby, we'll discuss the decisions you'll face in this chapter as well.

With all these decisions that need to be made, let's get rolling. In order to make some sense of this, let's start with a timeline of what you should decide and when.

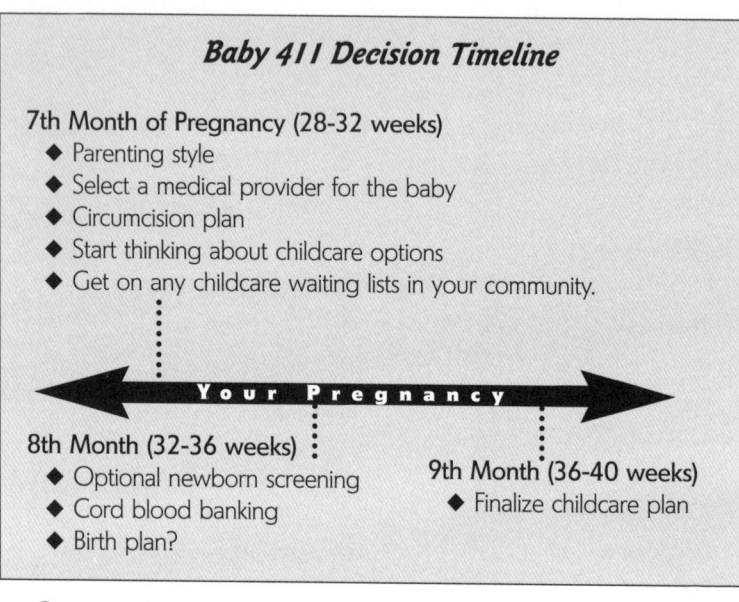

Baby 411 Decision Timeline

7th Month of Pregnancy (28-32 weeks)
- Parenting style
- Select a medical provider for the baby
- Circumcision plan
- Start thinking about childcare options
- Get on any childcare waiting lists in your community.

8th Month (32-36 weeks)
- Optional newborn screening
- Cord blood banking
- Birth plan?

9th Month (36-40 weeks)
- Finalize childcare plan

Once you have reached your seventh month, it's time to make some decisions. No, we're not talking about choosing names or wallpaper designs. Now you'll have to make choices that will affect how you raise your child together as a team (that includes moms, dads, grandparents, etc.). First and foremost is determining your team's parenting style.

We leave it up to the obstetricians to advise you on what you should be doing during pregnancy to ensure a healthy newborn. But up next are a few things that some parents also ask the pediatrician:

Picking a Parenting Style

Q. How do I pick a parenting style?

Remember Dorothy in the Wizard of Oz? She always wore the shoes she needed to take her home, but didn't realize it. You, New Parent, are wearing the shoes. You have the skills and instincts to be a great parent.

DECISIONS

THE LATEST ADVICE ON PREGNANCY

During your pregnancy, you have been warned about eating right, exercising regularly, and taking good care of yourself. Here is some up-to-date info that will keep your baby healthy while he is still inside the womb.

◆ *Toxoplasmosis screening.* This is an infection spread by cat feces, undercooked meats, and unwashed vegetables. If a mom becomes infected during her pregnancy, it can spell serious problems for an unborn fetus. If you own a cat, get it tested and keep it indoors during your pregnancy. Be sure to clean your hands well during food preparation or after gardening. You can also ask your obstetrician to test you at the beginning of your pregnancy to see if you are already immune.

◆ *Fatty acid supplements during pregnancy.* You may hear about pregnant women needing DHA/ARA or fish oil supplements. Currently, there is no official policy statement from the American College of Obstetrics/Gynecology or the American Academy of Pediatrics that recommends this practice. But there is some interesting research out there to support the idea. Some small studies show improved attention and fewer food allergies in infants whose moms had higher blood levels of DHA during their pregnancies.[1]

◆ *Avoid fishy diets.* Okay, after reading that fish oil is beneficial, you're probably wondering why pregnant moms need to avoid eating fish. In a word . . . mercury. A form of mercury from industrial waste that contaminates lakes, oceans, and rivers causes permanent neurological damage in the developing brain. The Environmental Protection Agency (EPA) and Food and Drug Administration (FDA) recommend that pregnant women eat less than 12 oz. a week of fish in general, less than six oz. a week of canned albacore tuna, and avoid shark, swordfish, king mackerel, and tilefish altogether. The same goes for breastfeeding moms.

◆ *Food allergy concerns.* Many pregnant moms are concerned about eating peanuts, fearing it will make their baby allergic later in life. Good news: there is now reliable data to show this is not true.[2]

TRUST YOURSELF.
Your style reflects your approach to certain situations. This includes food (breast vs. formula), sleep (family bed vs. crib), and discipline of your newest family member.

Every generation of parents faces "trendy" choices. Here's a newsflash: the child-rearing philosophy pendulum has been swinging back and forth for years. Sure, the names have changed, but the two basic schools of thought are the same: parent-centered (scheduled feedings, crib sleeping) versus child-centered (on-demand feedings, family bed, attachment parenting). As long as child development has been studied, experts have

DECISIONS

debated the merits (and demerits) of each school.

The take-home message: often what works for most families is somewhere in the middle. But, it is up to you to decide as a family what works for you.

You and your partner will need to discuss these issues and come to terms that are agreeable to both. Remember when you had to agree on a china pattern for your wedding registry? (Hopefully there will be fewer arguments). You *both* need to be happy about your strategy. This can be modified once you really have a baby to care for, but it helps to have some of the ground rules in place. Here are some ways to get started:

1. **Remember your own parents' style.** Besides nit-picking all the mistakes they made, consider what worked—and use it. Yes, you will hear yourself saying what your parents once said . . . and cringe!
2. **Watch other parents.** See how they respond to stressful situations with their kids (grocery store, restaurant, airplane flight). Think about what you would do. Ask your spouse how he/she would respond.
3. **Read some more books.** The parenting aisle of your bookstore is stuffed with all sorts of books on how to be a parent. Some prominent child development authors include: T. Berry Brazelton, Penelope Leach, William Sears, and Benjamin Spock. I am a Brazelton groupie, but you can decide for yourself. But beware: many parenting books preach their philosophies without science or evidence to back up their theories.

Be flexible—sometimes the best parenting style is a combination of approaches, mixing a bit of this and some of that. Your style may change over time as well. And yes, your parenting style will change out of sheer necessity when you have more than one child. You will be more confident in your skills, and you won't have time to sweat the small stuff. That's why children have certain personality traits based on their birth order.

Finally, federal law requires us to warn you of the following: you may not agree with some parts of this book. . . especially if you feel strongly about one parenting school of thought. We don't mean to be flip, but we didn't write this book to advance a political agenda. Instead, our goal is to be pro-science. We want to arm you with the best and latest medical information. Then you decide how to raise your baby.

Yep, we realize folks feel passionately about certain parenting issues (just take a look at the debate on circumcision, coming later in this chapter). But we ask you to look at our book as a whole . . . take the parts of this book that work for you and combine them with other parenting advice (from friends, other books) to create your own parenting style.

Selecting a Doctor

Q. Do I need to select a pediatrician before the baby is born? If so, why?

DECISIONS

Yes. It's helpful to meet a pediatrician (at a prenatal consultation) before the baby is born. Here are three reasons:

1. **It gives the pediatrician a chance to review any medical problems** during your pregnancy or with your family members that could affect the baby. (The doctor appreciates being prepared.)
2. **You can get advice** regarding medical decisions you'll be making in the first few days of your baby's life. (You'll appreciate being prepared.)
3. **You will be more relaxed** knowing who is examining and advising you in the hospital—yes, your pediatrician will come to visit both you and baby right there in the maternity ward. (More details in the Labor Day chapter.)

Q. So, how do I pick a pediatrician?

Ask your OB-GYN for a recommendation or consult with friends, relatives or other parents. Then, schedule a "prenatal consultation" with each candidate (keep the list short to maintain your sanity). While doctors consider this meeting a "consultation," it's really a job interview—you are considering hiring this doctor to take care of your baby, from birth to college. Consider your prenatal consultation as parent-doctor bonding time.

Q. When should I schedule a prenatal consultation?

Schedule a consult as you begin your third trimester. Don't wait any later than your 36th week. Why so early? Two reasons: first, to get some help making the medical decisions you need to make about your newborn. Second, because your pregnancy and due date are unpredictable—your baby could be early. You don't want to be shopping for a pediatrician while you are recovering from labor!

Q. Do pediatricians charge a fee for prenatal consultations?

Some do, some don't.

Pediatricians are about the only physician specialists who routinely schedule "meet the doctor" visits. Such visits aren't just for the parent's benefit—it helps give the doctor a heads up about any potential medical problems the baby may have. Don't be offended if you get a bill—it is perfectly kosher. Pediatricians are offering their time to answer parenting questions—and some parents come in with *lots* of questions! A smart move: when you schedule the appointment, ask if there is a charge for the prenatal visit.

Q. What general questions should I ask at a prenatal consultation?

If you've read any pregnancy book, you've seen a list of questions to ask at your prenatal visit. Here is some advice: ignore those cookie-cutter lists and make your own, based on the issues that are important to you. This could include:

DECISIONS

1. **Ask questions about topics you are wondering about.** You may be so overwhelmed, you can't come up with specifics and that's okay–just pick the topic and we can fill in the details. Example: allergies. You might discuss how to avoid food allergies or the history of allergies in your family.
2. **Ask questions that help you get to know the doctor.** Pretend you are on the Dating Game, and not on CSI: Miami.
3. **Ask questions about how the practice flows.** There is more to your office experience than your doctor. You need to be an informed consumer. Medical care has changed dramatically since you were a kid. We'll discuss more details on this next.

BOTTOM LINE: You don't have to ask *every* question that you have in your first meeting with your pediatrician.

Q. Okay, what smart questions SHOULD parents ask of a pediatrician?

Let us walk you through a typical prenatal visit and tell you what parents USUALLY ask . . . and what questions parents SHOULD ask instead. (Note: at the end of this section, we'll organize all these questions you should ask in one handy list).

Parent asks: What is your training?
A better question: How did you decide on pediatrics?

BEHIND THE SCENES: WHY IS MY DOCTOR SO LATE?

Do you ever wonder why your doctor is late? I'll let you in on the secrets behind the waiting room door. Let's look at a typical morning at my practice:

◆ "Dr. Brown, your 8 am well child appointment is stuck in traffic, can you see them at 8:20 am?" (Answer–"Yes.") That patient actually arrives at 8:25 am and is brought to an exam room at 8:30 am.
◆ My 8:15 am well-child appointment is brought back to a room at 8:35 am because they had new insurance that needed to be verified first (this takes my business office about 20 minutes on the phone).
◆ My 8:30 am sick child with the flu also has asthma and needs a breathing treatment. I need to go back and examine him a second time after my nurse administers a treatment.
◆ "Dr. Brown, your 8:45 am sick visit has a sister who is sick, too. Do you have time to see her?" (Answer–"Yes," . . . but now I am double booked at 8:45 am.)

So, at 8:35 am, I have five patients in four exam rooms that all need to be seen. By 9 am, I'm already 20 minutes behind and will need

DECISIONS

All pediatricians have about the same training. Just look on the wall. We spent a lot of time and money to get all those degrees. Our parents would kill us if we didn't get them framed and hung up in our office. Pediatricians complete four years of medical school and then three more years of a residency program focused only on children's medical care. Family Practitioners complete four years of medical school and then three to four years of residency that includes child and adult health care. Regardless of where a doctor trained, we will take a Board Certification Exam to prove we learned our stuff. Look for the letters F.A.A.P. or F.A.A.F.P. after our names. The "F" stands for Fellow, a distinguished title doctors get for passing our boards in either pediatrics or family practice. All pediatricians take continuing medical education courses annually and recertification exams every seven years to make sure we are keeping up with current trends in medicine.

Ask why the doctor chose pediatrics for a career, instead of say, urology. It's a more open-ended question. You'll likely hear her credentials in the answer, but you'll get a better idea of whom this person is.

Parent asks: Do you divide the sick and well waiting rooms?
A better question: How long will I be sitting in your waiting room?

Even if the practice's waiting room is divided into sick and well areas, the *patient/exam* rooms are not. Don't expect the entire doctor's office to be germ free. View your trip to the doctor like a trip anywhere else—where there are kids, there will be germs. One tip: bring your own toys and wash your hands after the visit.

I'd rather know how long I have to entertain my child before the doc-

to play catch up. It's about this time I'm dreaming of sitting on a beach somewhere with a drink adorned with a cute umbrella.

All hope is not lost. Some sick visits are simple and will take less time than the appointment slot (i.e. rashes, ear infection rechecks). Some days, there are only sick kids that are "sicker than billed" and parents that need extra handholding. I will be behind all morning.

Reality check: doctors are notoriously behind schedule because we try to address the needs of each patient, no matter how long it takes. It helps if we can anticipate those needs. If you want to discuss your child's school problems during an appointment for a sore throat, tell the appointments person. Otherwise, it's likely your doctor will ask you to schedule another appointment so there is more time to talk.

For more tips on when is the best time to schedule your baby's check ups, see Chapter 2, You And Your Baby's Doc. Finally, another point to remember: some doctors now have amazing office hours. A few are even open until 9pm each night and on Saturdays and Sundays! What a concept. Yes, these are typically larger practices in bigger cities, but they do exist. And if a practice has longer "operating hours" and more doctors, odds are the waits will be less. Again, the key is to shop around and see what is available in your community.

DECISIONS

tor sees us. You'll get an idea by how late the doctor is for the prenatal visit. We all try to be as punctual as possible, but unexpected things happen. A practice that flows well should get you and the doctor face to face within 30 minutes of your scheduled appointment.

Real world mom advice: first, call BEFORE you leave home and make sure the doctor is on schedule. If your doctor is running behind, you can prepare. Bring extra entertainment for you and your child and even snacks. Another tip: if you are sitting in the office and are not called within 20 minutes of your appointment time, it's time to find out what's going on—ask the front desk for an update on the doctor's situation. Finally, don't add to your stress—never schedule another appointment or meeting immediately after your doctor appointment. Doing so (and then running late) will only add to the frustration.

Let's talk about acceptable wait times to see your baby's doctor. On the message board for our other book, *Baby Bargains*, when discussing how to select a pediatrician, we were shocked that some parents were left waiting for up to three hours! Obviously, that was the extreme . . . we found "average" wait times to be all over the board. Some parents wait as little as ten or 15 minutes while others reported average wait times of an hour or more. In our opinion, acceptable average wait times should be about ten to 15 minutes during non-flu season. When doctors get slammed with sick patients at the height of flu season, it is understandable that wait times can slip to 30 minutes or more. Bottom line, waiting longer than an hour to see your doctor for a scheduled visit is not acceptable—you need to shop for another pediatrician.

So, what are doctors doing back there while you cool your heels in the waiting room? Are they watching CNN? Shooting the breeze over a latte with other doctors? No, there are several things that usually conspire to make a doctor run late. See the box earlier for more on this.

Parent asks: How do I schedule well child visits/sick visits?
A better question: How does your daily schedule flow? How much time is allotted for visits?

Most practices schedule well child checks in advance. A smart tip: in a busy practice, schedule the *next* well child visit when you are in the office having one. The doctor's nurse or secretary will always advise you when another well child visit is needed.

Sick visits are usually scheduled on the same day you call. Obviously, you can't predict when your child will get sick and you won't settle for

NEW PARENT 411: WELL-CHILD VERSUS SICK VISITS

Doctors divide their visits with your baby into two categories: well-child and sick visits. Well-child visits are what you might think of as a routine check-up—these are scheduled at regular intervals to check your child's general health, do vaccinations, etc. Sick child visits are when your child is, well, sick. FYI: Each of these visits is scheduled differently by most doctors. We'll discuss this later in the chapter.

>
> **DR B'S OPINION: ALTERNATIVE MEDICINE**
>
> In today's world, I tell the parent what their child's diagnosis is, explain the diagnosis, and explain the therapy that I would advise. Then the parent often quotes recent information about alternative therapies that they found on the Internet (sometimes accurate and sometimes not) and asks what I think of it. I don't mind these interactions—I find them stimulating. They keep me on my toes. As you can tell by now, I like educating parents. But not every physician is enthusiastic about this style of practicing medicine.
>
> As we discussed in the introduction to this book, our mantra on alternative medicine and therapies for your baby is SHOW US THE SCIENCE. If an alternative therapy is shown to be effective in a reputable scientific study, then we are happy to recommend it. But if it is just snake oil or an Internet myth, we won't hesitate to say so. See Appendix B, "Alternative Medicine" for more details.

waiting until tomorrow to be seen. This is probably different than what you are used to with your own doctor. I once tried to see my doctor for a sick visit and was told I could have an appointment a week later. I told the receptionist, "Thank you. I could be dead by then." But I digress.

What you really want to know is how much time you will spend with the pediatrician. Every practice varies, but well checks usually get more time than sick visits. A typical well check may be a 15-minute appointment. A sick visit may be ten minutes. If there is a chronic problem (e.g. headaches, constipation, school problem, behavior problem), we may schedule consultation appointments which are 30 minutes or longer. You'll note these time guidelines are never published or posted in a doctor's office. Why? Because doctors will take as long as needed to address the issues at hand—even if this means making other patients wait (which leads us back to the earlier discussion of why it takes so long to see a doctor). Remember appointment slots are just a framework for a doctor's day.

If you keep up with the news, you know that the U.S. health care system is under intense scrutiny. The costs of medical care and prescription drugs are on the rise. Your insurance premiums are on the rise. The CEO's salary of your health insurance company is on the rise, too. But, insurance companies have steadily *decreased* reimbursements to doctors for office visits and procedures. Yet, doctors need to keep up with our bills (overhead costs, malpractice insurance, student loans—yep, I'm still paying those off). The result? We have to schedule more patients each day.

BOTTOM LINE

Sick visits are "problem oriented." Be prepared to ask all your questions up front. If you have numerous issues or chronic issues to discuss, schedule a separate consultation. Doctors expect your list of burning questions at *well check* appointments, not sick visits. You can always call too.

Parent asks: What is your philosophy? (This one must be in some par-

enting book because everyone asks it.)
Better questions to ask: How do you approach the doctor-parent relationship? How do you feel about complementary/alternative therapies?

Doctor-parent relationships have changed since you were a child. When you went to the doctor, he told your mother what she needed to do to make you feel better. Your mother said "thank you" and did what she was told. There was no debate . . . and no "alternative therapies" mom could look up on the Internet. Doctors still wistfully reminisce about these days like a retired hall-of-famer recalls the '64 World Series.

When some parents ask about "philosophy," they really want to know about what type of medicine the doctor practices. An M.D. (medical doctor) educated in the United States is almost exclusively trained in traditional medicine. She is a scientist who learns how the body works and malfunctions and how to fix the body with medicine or surgery. Doctors also learn how scientific research is done and how to read medical studies critically. As a rule, doctors are skeptical of new therapies unless they see data and good science to support the treatment.

If you want to integrate complementary or alternative therapies into your child's healthcare, now is the time to speak up. You'll want to find a medical provider who is on the same page so you will have a good fit.

Parent asks: Do you accept our health insurance?
A better question: Do you have a list of health insurance plans you accept?

Both big and small businesses switch insurance plans as frequently as the weather changes. The result: doctors lose patients when they change insurance. There is a reasonable chance that the doctor you select now may not perform your baby's college physical. Watching your child grow is one of the most rewarding parts of any doctor's job. So, losing a family to another practice due to insurance change is something most doctors try hard to avoid. A good practice will have a smart office administrator at the helm that negotiates reasonable contracts with *many* insurance plans.

Parent asks: What hospitals do you have privileges at?
Better questions to ask: Do you have privileges at the hospital where I am delivering? Who cares for my child in an emergency hospital visit, or hospitalization?

The answers to these questions will vary significantly depending on where you live. Gone are the days of the "Do It All Doctor" unless you live in a rural area.

Although continuity of patient care is important, doctors are starting to realize they only have so many hours in a day. The current trend in medicine is to divide outpatient care (office-based practice) and in-patient care (hospital-based practice). Our patients get more specialized care and our spouses are happier with us. So, this is how some practices work:

1. **A pediatrician goes to a select number of area hospitals to see newborns.** If there is a problem with the baby at the

DECISIONS

time of delivery, there is likely to be an "in-house" pediatrician or neonatologist in the hospital to handle emergencies. If you deliver at a hospital that your pediatrician does not go to, a staff pediatrician may care for the baby until he goes home.

2. **In emergencies, your pediatrician is available by phone.** If an emergency room visit is warranted, an emergency room physician may evaluate and treat your child. That doctor will call your doctor to discuss a plan.
3. **If your child needs to stay in the hospital overnight** (an admission), a staff pediatrician (hospitalist) may be responsible for care. That doctor will call your doctor to make discharge and follow up plans.

BOTTOM LINE: You may not see your own doctor if you have an emergency or a hospital stay.

Parent asks: How are phone calls handled?
Better questions to ask:
1. Who answers your patient calls during the day?
2. Who answers emergency calls at night?
3. What is the expected waiting time for a phone call to be returned?

Phone calls during office hours are handled in a variety of ways. On one extreme, a nurse will screen and answer all phone calls. On the other extreme, the doctor will answer all calls (a rarity now, as most doctors are busy seeing patients). Most practices fall somewhere in the middle. Some practices offer a "call in hour" each day where patients can speak directly to the doctor. I'm not fond of this approach. I'd compare it to calling a radio station to win tickets for something. If you don't have auto-redial, forget it. Some high tech practices have e-mail or voicemail accessibility to the doctor. In general, most practices will have a nurse who can answer routine calls efficiently and hand the more complicated calls over to the doctor.

After office hours, practices usually have an answering service that dispatches emergency calls to the physician "on-call." The on-call doctor is usually (but not always) an associate in the practice. You will likely see or speak to all of your doctor's partners at some point in your child's life. Some practices utilize a nurse call center after hours to handle routine calls. Call cen-

BEHIND THE SCENES: CALLING YOUR DOC AT 3AM

When doctors are on call at night, we are not sitting by the phone in our offices waiting for your call. We go to sleep at home with our beepers at our bedside table. So if you talk to us at 3 am and we sound sleepy . . . we are. In our residency training (the medical equivalent of boot camp), doctors became experts at answering questions while sleep deprived. Don't expect us to have any information from your child's chart, schedule appointments, or be excited about discussing diaper rash creams at 3 am. Be a friend and save those calls for office hours.

CHAPTER 1: DECISIONS

Decisions

ters use strict protocols to manage every type of emergency imaginable. Even with a call center, the on call doctor is still available for questions.

Here are more questions to ask about phone calls:

1. What is the name of the nurse who handles phone calls? You two will be on a first name basis soon, so ask now.

2. If you want to speak to the doctor, can you? You should never feel that there is a fortress built around your doctor. You have every right to talk to your doctor directly. If it's not an urgent call, it may take until the end of the business day to get back with you . . . but it should be an option.

3. How long does it take for the nurse or doctor to return calls? You'll want to know how long to sit by the phone (you can also leave a cell phone number). If you don't hear from us in a "reasonable" amount of time you should call us back.

4. Do you charge for phone call consultations? Yes, this does happen. It is becoming more common for doctors to charge a nominal fee for phone calls. It used to be taken for granted that phone advice was a freebie. With the current status of health care, doctors are more likely to bill for services that were previously "part of the package."

BOTTOM LINE: THE 12 QUESTIONS YOU SHOULD ASK
Okay, let's sum it up again. Here are the 12 questions we suggest you ask any potential pediatrician. (See earlier in this chapter for an explanation of why we think these questions are important—and some good answers you should hear from the doctor).

1. How did you decide on pediatrics?
2. How long will I be sitting in your waiting room?
3. How does your daily schedule flow?
4. How much time is allotted for visits?
5. How do you approach the doctor-parent relationship?
6. How do you feel about complementary/alternative therapies?
7. Do you have a list of health insurance plans you accept?
8. Do you have privileges at the hospital where I am delivering?
9. Who cares for my child in an emergency hospital visit, or hospitalization?
10. Who answers your patient calls during the day?
11. Who answers emergency calls at night?
12. What is the expected waiting time for a phone call to be returned?

Q. How do I decide which doctor is right for my child?

Go with your gut instincts. Think to yourself, "Will I feel comfortable asking this person some really embarrassing questions?" If the answer is yes, go for it.

Pediatricians develop a relationship with you and your child. Doctors enjoy being a part of your family and watching your child grow with you. Unless you move or change insurance, your doctor will see your child until he moves out of your house. That means you will probably see him more than any other medical provider until you get your AARP card and senior discounts at the movies.

DECISIONS

So now that you have discussed how you will parent with your partner and chosen your child's doctor it's time to move onto some more controversial topics. If you're having (or think you're having) a son, congratulations!

With three boys between us, we authors are pretty on top of the boy thing. And one of your first decisions when you have a boy will be: circumcision or not?

Circumcision

Before we delve into this hot topic, we have a major disclaimer. Discussing circumcision is like a "friendly" discussion on abortion—this is a topic that provokes very strong reactions in some people.

We realize no matter how "fair and balanced" we are, some readers will NOT be happy (believe us, we've tried). Even a discussion of "pros and cons" of circumcision is considered blasphemy—anti-circumcision groups believe circumcision should not be an option at all. They also complain that the studies showing medical benefits of circumcision are flawed and biased.

Our goal for this section is to let parents hear both sides of the argument so you can make an informed decision on your own. Honestly, we don't have an agenda here (beyond providing a balanced look at the subject)—what you decide to do with your son's penis is your decision.

Q. Should I have my son circumcised, and when do I need to decide?

Before your son is born, you should decide whether or not you want to have him circumcised. Alternatively, you could wait and let him decide on his own, but it is a much bigger ordeal to go through circumcision as an adult (wasn't that a Seinfeld episode?). If you feel weird thinking about the future of your son's penis, join the club.

The practice of circumcision (surgical removal of foreskin) became common in the United States in the late 1800's for hygienic reasons as well as a proposed way to reduce masturbation (ha—didn't work, did it?). It has continued to be a popular choice for most American boys . . . and the subject of much controversy.

What's the right thing to do? No one in the medical community will tell you what is best. Groups such as the American Academy of Pediatrics, the American Urological Association, and the American College of Obstetrics and Gynecology (you'll understand why they are interested in your son's penis as you read on) have no official policy on circumcision. *You* have to make the call.

Circumcisions are done more for social, cultural, and religious reasons than for medical necessity.

Q. What are the arguments FOR circumcision?

In a nutshell, fewer hygiene problems, sexually transmitted infections, and risk of cancer.

1. **Better hygiene.** The foreskin of an uncircumcised penis can harbor germs (see **HUMAN PAPILLOMAVIRUS**-HPV). Compared with a

circumcised penis, it is harder to keep the uncircumcised penis clean. The foreskin can get infected and swell (see **BALANITIS**). Although balanitis doesn't occur often, it really hurts. The foreskin can also get stuck in a pulled back position (see **PARAPHIMOSIS**)—OUCH!

2. **Fewer bladder infections.** Bladder infections (see **URINARY TRACT INFECTION-UTI**) occur more frequently in girls. However, boys who are uncircumcised have a ten to 20 times greater risk of infection than their circumcised friends. This again is due to hygiene reasons. In general, boys have about a 1% risk of getting a bladder infection.

3. **Less risk of penile cancer.** Cancer of the penis is rare. A man's lifetime risk of getting penile cancer is 1 in 100,000. Compared to breast cancer (1 in 8 women) and skin cancer (1 in 75 people), it's almost not worth worrying about. But, yes, you guessed it, it happens more frequently in uncircumcised men.

4. **Reduced risk of HIV.** Uncircumcised men are more likely to have the HIV virus and infect their partners. Why? Because the area under the foreskin makes a nice spot for the virus to set up housekeeping. A recent study in South Africa found that circumcised men were 60% less likely to be infected with HIV compared to their uncircumcised peers.[3]

5. **Reduction in cervical cancer.** This is where our gynecology colleagues get involved. A recent study published in the *New England Journal of Medicine* is intriguing.[4] It showed that women involved with uncircumcised "high risk" partners (more than six previous sexual partners) had a five-times greater risk of getting cancer of the cervix compared to women whose sex partners were circumcised. The reason? **HUMAN PAPILLOMAVIRUS—HPV** (a sexually transmitted virus) loves to live under the foreskin. HPV is a known cause of cervical cancer. So, your decision to circumcise your son may affect your daughter-in-law's health someday. (Good news: with the new HPV vaccine, your daughter may reduce her risk of cervical cancer anyway.)

Q. What are the arguments AGAINST circumcision?

Like any surgical procedure, circumcision has risks:

1. **The risk of surgery.** Circumcision involves cutting the foreskin away from the head of the penis. As with any surgical procedure, there is a small chance of bleeding (1 in 3000 risk) or infection (1 in 1000 risk).

2. **Penile Adhesions.** Occasionally, the skin between the shaft and the head of the penis will get stuck together due to a collection of sticky, cream cheesy stuff called smegma. The penis will look like it is uncircumcised. Minor adhesions will resolve on their own. But, if the adhesions are really tight, they may need to be treated by using steroid cream, having a doctor pull the skin back, or having another surgical procedure ("circumcision revision"). For more details, see Chapter 4, Hygiene, and **PENILE ADHESIONS**).

3. **The Hidden Penis.** It sounds like a concealed weapon, doesn't it? Chubby baby boys have a fat roll above their genitals. It caus-

es the circumcised penis to get sucked inwards. The penis looks normal as the boys grow up, but it's always concerning to parents.

4. **Reduced sexual pleasure.** Some concerns have been raised about the removal of sensitive nerve fibers in the foreskin when a male is circumcised. Anti-circumcision groups contend that circumcision is genital mutilation. So what's the latest science on this subject? Studies that address this question report conflicting results. Some studies show a decrease in sexual pleasure; others show no difference. The data is based on men who were circumcised as adults who subjectively rated their sexual pleasure before and after circumcision.[5]

Q. Who performs the circumcision?

In most large cities, your obstetrician usually performs the circumcision procedure just before your baby leaves the hospital.

Why the obstetrician? Many pediatricians do not perform any surgical procedures—for good reason. You wouldn't want to see the way I slice my Thanksgiving turkey! Obstetricians have surgical training and are at the hospital already taking care of Mommy. But you need to check with your OB to be sure. Urologists can also perform a circumcision on your baby. This requires special arrangements, however. Urologists do not generally come to the hospital to perform routine circumcisions. You'll need to do some homework if you choose this option.

In smaller towns and rural areas, other physicians (family practitioners or pediatricians) will perform circumcisions because there is limited access to specialty care. As long as the person has been trained to do the procedure, it does not matter what the doctor's specialty is.

What if you decide to circumcise your son after he leaves the hospital? That's fine, but there is one caveat: some insurance providers will NOT cover the cost of the procedure once baby leaves the hospital.

Circumcision is performed as a religious ritual for some families. The person performing the procedure is called a mohel. Most families pay out of pocket for this service. Some savvy families have attempted to have their insurance company pick up the tab. It may be worth checking into.

DR B'S OPINION: CIRCUMCISION

While there are some medical benefits to circumcision (and the new HIV research is certainly intriguing), the benefits are not clear enough for any medical group to advocate for the procedure. One might argue that if everyone engaged in safe sexual behavior, there would be fewer sexually transmitted infections, including HIV. I think it is a very personal decision, without a right or wrong answer. And while it is hard to assess how circumcision affects sexual pleasure, I don't think either group of men is complaining.

Q. Is any pain medication used during the circumcision?

Most of the time, yes. Every doctor has her own approach. You can ask your doctor what she feels comfortable doing. Here are the options:
1. Injecting numbing medicine directly into the area (nerve block).
2. Applying topical numbing cream one hour before the procedure.
3. Giving the baby sugar water just prior to the procedure.

BOTTOM LINE: The whole procedure is relatively brief. Yes, it hurts—but using pain medication has become the standard of care. Most babies will go to sleep afterwards as a stress response and wake up happy to see you. For more information on circumcision, check out these web sites: circinfo.net and circumsicion.cjb.net.

Optional Newborn Metabolic Screening: What To Know

Once your baby is born, you'll notice that he is whisked away to get cleaned up and tested. No, not an IQ test, a blood test. Your state requires some tests and others are optional. Recently parents have become more interested in the optional tests available. Here's an idea of what's out there and how newborn screening works.

Q. Do all babies get tested for metabolic diseases?

Yes. Every state in the U.S. performs a panel of blood tests on every newborn. This can vary from three to 53 tests, depending on the state. (For details on this, see Chapter 3, "Labor Day.") To find information on required screenings in your state, go to the National Newborn Screening & Genetics Resource Center (genes-r-us.uthscsa.edu; look for the link to "Current Newborn Screening Conditions—by State"). Or simply click on the link on our website at Baby411.com.

Q. Are there more screening tests available other than those required by the state?

Yes. Many private laboratories and academic institutions offer low cost newborn screening for 25 to 60 metabolic disorders. So if you live in Kansas for instance, and your state only tests for a handful of disorders, you can get your baby tested for many more disorders on your own dime.

Metabolic diseases are disorders in which the body fails to break down (metabolize) certain products. If these products are not broken down, they start to get stored up in the body and that creates problems, including heart enlargement, mental retardation, and even death.

So, how do these tests work? When blood is drawn for the state-mandated tests, additional blood can be used for these optional tests. You can get more information from either your obstetrician or pediatrician. The cost varies, but it is usually about $25. You probably spent twice as much on a diaper bag.

Keep in mind that disorders tested for in the optional screen are quite rare (about 1 in 56,000), which is why some states compare the cost of testing and the low yield of abnormal results and opt to only test for the more common disorders.

Behind the Scenes: More on Optional Screens

Although most metabolic diseases are rare, early detection is critical to the health of an affected baby. States are beginning to expand the number of government-subsidized tests. However, some states still only offer a bare bones minimum. If your state is one of those, you can pay for additional testing on your own. FYI: If you choose to bank your baby's cord blood (see more below), you may get a "free" supplemental newborn screen to go with it. For more information, here are some groups you can contact:

1. Baylor Univ. Medical Ctr.
Web: baylorhealth.com
(800)-4-BAYLOR

2. Pediatrix
Web: Pediatrix.com
(800) 243-3839

3. March of Dimes
Web: marchofdimes.com

4. Mayo Clinic
Web: mayoclinic.com

5. University of Colorado Health Sciences Center
(303) 315-7301

6. National Coalition for PKU and Allied Health Disorders
Web: pku-allieddisorders.org
(877) 996-2723

To see which states require what screens, you can visit the web site for the National Newborn Screening and Genetics Resource Center (web: http://genes-r-us.uthscsa.edu). We also have a state by state list of required screens on our web site at Baby411.com (click on "bonus material").

Our opinion: optional newborn screening is a bargain and well worth it especially if you have a family history of these diseases.

Another amazing new option available to parents today: cord blood banking. Only recently has there been an option for parents to "bank" their baby's cord blood in case of an emergency illness in the future. So here's one more decision for parents to make.

Cord Blood Banking

Q. What exactly is cord blood banking anyway?

The era of modern medicine has given us the opportunity to store the blood from your baby's umbilical cord.
Why is this a cool idea? Well, that blood is loaded with the "seeds" (hematopoietic stem cells) that later grow into white and red blood cells. These very special cells are also found in the bone marrow of all humans. The umbilical cord blood can be used like a bone marrow transplant. These cells are currently used to treat some genetic and blood disorders and certain types of cancer. One of the advantages of using a cord blood transplant as

opposed to bone marrow transplant is that you don't have to have a perfect genetic match to the recipient and there may be less transplant rejection.

There is not much regulation of the cord blood banking biz. The Food and Drug Administration just began oversight of the banks in 2005. Yes, most companies are accredited by the American Association of Blood Banks (AABB) or licensed by the state where they're located. While state and federal regulation is minimal, cord blood banks should follow the standards set by the Foundation for the Accreditation of Cellular Therapy (FACT). Bottom line: it's still up to parents to research companies carefully. The cost of cord blood banking is high (starting at $1200 plus annual storage fees averaging about $120), so parents should be well educated about the options before investing.

Q. Is it worth the money to store cord blood?

And you thought selecting a crib was a major decision...

Here's some information to help you decide if you want to open an account at the local blood bank:[6]

◆ What are the odds your or a family member will need to use the cord blood? The estimates vary from 1 in 400 to 1 in 200,000.[7] If you already have a family member with a disease known to be treatable with cord blood, obviously the likelihood of ever needing it goes way up.

But cord blood isn't a panacea for every problem. There are some cases when a sick child can't use his own cord blood—for example, cord blood stem cells may already have pre-cancerous changes, so a child who later develops leukemia cannot use his own stored cord blood to treat it. However, the stored cord blood of a *healthy child* could be used for another family member who has a disease treatable with that cord blood.[8]

◆ The stem cells may have great potential use if "gene therapy" becomes mainstream medical treatment for genetic disorders, but that is still several years in the future. The chance you'll use it will depend on a variety of factors, like scientific advances and if the blood specimen is still viable when you are 70. At this moment, these potential uses are being tested in the research labs of academic medical centers and pharmaceutical companies. If your family has a genetic disorder, banking might be worth it for you.

◆ If you choose to bank your baby's cord blood, there are 16 companies that offer this service. The set-up cost varies between $1200 and $2050. Then you'll need to pay annual premiums of $100-$125 per year to save it.

◆ Be sure to use a company that processes and stores cord blood in their own facility. Why does that matter? Because some companies subcontract the storage to another company.

◆ If a company you're interested in does other lab work besides cord blood banking, make sure their storage facilities are intended for long-term use. Special cryogenic techniques are required to make sure the blood is stored properly.

◆ Check on the bank's collection method. Obviously, if you don't get

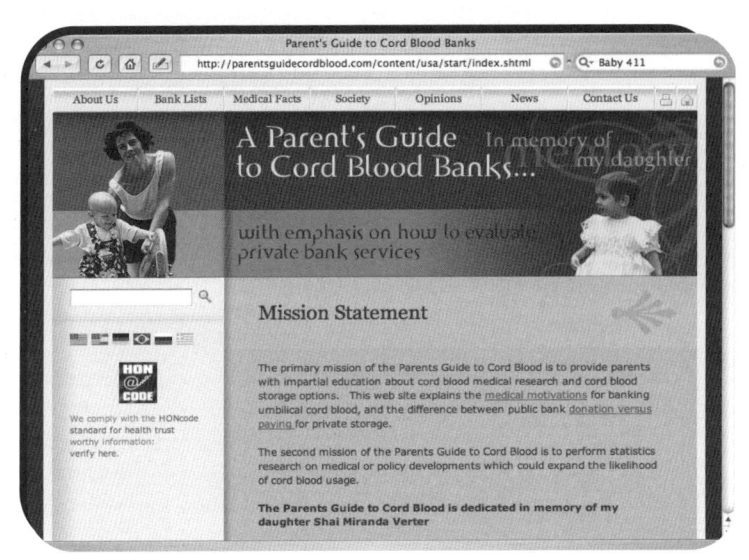

ParentsGuideCordBlood.com is a fabulous site, run by an astrophysicist who lost her own daughter to leukemia, includes a terrific sample questionnaire for parents to use when they interview cord blood banks.

CORD BLOOD OPTIONS

Here is a round up of the largest private cord blood banks—all of these banks are accredited by the American Association of Blood Banks (AABB.org):

Bank	Enrollment Fee	Annual Fee	Year Started	Comments
CorCell corcell.com	$1800	$125	1996	Discounts with some insurance plans.
Cord Blood Registry cordblood.com	$1850	$125	1995	Excellent FAQ online. Affiliated with Univ. of Arizona.
Cryobanks International Cryo-intl.com	$1750	$120	1994	Both a private bank and public donation program
Cryo-Cell International cryo-cell.com	$1595	$125	1992	Live chat and client testimonial videos online
Family Cord Blood Services MyCordBlood.com	$1420	$110	1997	Affordable option; Used to be known as California Cryobank.
LifebankUSA lifebankusa.com	$1850	$125	1998	Banks both cord blood and placenta blood.
LifeLine Cryogenics lifelinecryogenics.com	$1200	$99	2001	Most affordable. Also bank sperm, eggs, embryos.
ViaCord viacord.com	$2050	$125	1995	Detailed web site; online gift registry.

DECISIONS

> ### BEHIND THE SCENES: DONATING CORD BLOOD
>
> The American Academy of Pediatrics supports donating umbilical cord blood to a public donation bank. While we support this policy, realize that donating cord blood isn't always easy. There is no national cord blood donation bank as of this writing. For now, if you want to donate your baby's cord blood, find out if your hospital participates in the national donor program at marrow.org (click on Donor Resources).

enough cord blood, the specimen cannot be stored. The "syringe" method has a 90% success rate. The "blood bag" method has a 75% success rate. Regardless of technique, multiple births and low birth weight reduce the chance of getting enough blood.

◆ Ask about the bank's storage method. Studies show that cord blood can be preserved and used for at least 15 years. Storage in "cryovials" is optimal (versus plastic bags). The vials are more durable, versatile (the blood can be divided up several times for different uses) and resistant to contamination with germs.

◆ Be sure your obstetrician is experienced in cord blood collection. It is imperative that the blood be collected quickly (within ten minutes) and that enough blood is collected. Most companies offer training resources for doctors. Obstetricians will charge a fee ($100 or more) to collect the cord blood even if its for donation. Be sure to find out this cost in advance.

◆ For more information, check out the following non-profit sites: National Marrow Donor Program (web: marrow.org/NMDP/cord.bloodbank.list.html), and A Parent's Guide to Private Cord Blood Banks (web: parents-guidecordblood.com. See picture on previous page). Private companies are accessible if you do an Internet search under "cord blood banks." Here is a partial list of what's out there: lifebankusa.com, cordblood.com, viacord.com, cordbloodbank.com, and cryobank.com.

Feedback from the Real World
Read parent reviews of cord blood banks (or post a review of your experience) on our web site (Baby411.com, click on Bonus Material).

Okay, we realize you're a bit overwhelmed with all these decisions, but here's just one more to consider before your child is born: staying at home or going back to work. And, if you go back to work, what are your childcare options? Let's look at this topic next.

Childcare

It's probably safe to assume that if you are a woman without children, you are working outside the home while you are pregnant. And no doubt, there is an office pool going on behind your back about the odds of you returning after your baby is born.

Raising a family is one of life's major crossroads that makes you ponder which path to take. Should you drop your current career and make raising your child your new career? Can you carve out some creative combination of working part-time and staying at home with your little one? Or, will you return to the daily grind and make the most of your family time when you are able? These decisions weigh heavily on the minds of today's working moms, and for some, choosing to stay at home is not an option because their salary is paying the bills.

For those who have a choice whether or not to work, this decision can be very stressful and laden with guilt. Perhaps you've heard of the "Mommy Wars." There is no doubt: you will feel pressured about your decision from a variety of sources—your spouse, your mother, even your best girlfriends.

Our advice? Make your decision and then make the best of it. You can always re-assess down the road and change your mind.

We give you this advice based on scientific data. Research shows that *quality* time is more important than the sheer number of hours you spend with your child. Kids do best when their moms *focus* their attention, engage, and respond to them.[9]

Q. When do I need to start thinking about childcare?

Now.

I know you don't even have a baby yet, but this is something you need to think about now. Why? Because all of your buddies in your baby care class already have. Yes, it IS that competitive. The best daycares and preschools in town will have your baby's due date (instead of birth date) listed on the waiting list application.

Q. Why is my selection for childcare so important?

That seems like an obvious one—your baby is the most precious gift in the world to you. And you want to give your baby the best childcare you can find. Here are some things you should think about:

Studies have consistently shown that the first three years of life are critical times in your child's development. This is when your baby learns to trust others, function independently, problem solve, and learn the boundaries of acceptable behavior. The person/people you choose to care for your baby are incredibly important.

There are economic decisions as well. Consider what your family can afford. In tallying the cost of childcare, add the expense of a sick child. We'll explain how that issue will crop up in each scenario.

BOTTOM LINE: Your child's illness may cost you a lost workday, and the price of co-payments and deductibles when you visit the doctor.

We'll discuss the types of child care in a second; first let's talk about juggling work, family and your sanity.

Feedback from the Real World

If you plan on returning to work after your baby is born, be prepared for a fine balancing act. I suggest you strongly consider how your life will "work." For an accurate depiction of how just how stressful it is to balance career and family obligations, rent the movie *One Fine Day* with Michelle Pfeiffer and George Clooney. It was supposed to be a comedy. I didn't think it was funny at all—I felt like I was watching my life!

Just getting out the door in the morning may be more stressful than any board meeting you've attended. Getting yourself ready is the easy part. If you use out-of-the-home childcare, you will have to get your baby ready and fed, plus pack up his food for the day. This can take awhile because your baby has no idea what your schedule is, nor does he care. He also won't care if he spits up on your silk blouse or suit jacket.

Another point: be prepared for that phone call from childcare telling you that your baby is sick and needs to be sent home.

Balancing Act: Juggling work and family

How do you balance family, career—and your sanity? While the ideal situation would be to be at home for your baby 24/7, some parents find they want to work outside the home at least some of the time. For others, it is a necessity.

So, let's take a look at how moms and dads do the seemingly impossible—juggling baby, career, marriage and more. How do they do it all? To get the answers, we asked the readers of our books to share their wisdom. First, check out our Six Commandments for Balancing Work & Baby. Next, we'll look at this issue day to day, with 15 tips and tricks for juggling family and a career.

Six Commandments for Balancing Work & Baby

1 FORGET BALANCE. When we say "balance" work and family, this implies some kind of happy equilibrium. Forget it—the best you can hope for is OCCASIONAL peaceful coexistence between your family and job. Something will always be working to upset the balance, however . . . a childcare situation, sickness, job demands, etc.

2 DO THE MATH. Sit down with a piece of paper and do a serious cost/benefit analysis before returning to work. Kelly Anderson of San Diego, CA emailed her advice to moms: "Most people would be shocked to see how all the hidden costs of working outside the home add up (dry cleaning, taxes, eating out, gas, plus the fact that someone else will be essentially raising your child for you). For many people, the benefits just don't outweigh the costs." Good point: even if you have a good job with excellent pay, the cost of childcare and other hidden expenses may wipe out a good part of the earnings.

3 DUAL CAREERS, DUAL SACRIFICE. Both you and your spouse must make sacrifices for this to work. While nothing in life or marriage is always 50/50, both parents must help to make the schedule work.

4 MEET THE NEW BOSS—YOUR BABY. That means your old boss at work must adjust to your new life. "You don't want to work for a boss who does not put family first," says reader Tricia Gagnon. She's right—if your boss doesn't understand why you need to take a day off to care for a sick child, you need to find a new job.

5 **AVOID THE GUILT TRIPS.** Whatever you decide for your baby, get ready for second-guessing from friends, relatives and complete strangers. E. Moeller, Boulder, CO, wrote in to stress this important point: A happy mommy (and daddy) makes for a happy baby. "If you are fulfilled and enjoying your work and have made good childcare choices, your baby will thrive."

6 **WILL IT MATTER NEXT MONTH? OR NEXT YEAR?** When you have to decide whether to work late or another weekend, ask yourself: "How important is my job as a _____ compared to my job as a father or mother. Will this project matter next month, year or in five years?" Your child will.

Day-to-Day: Tips & Tricks for Juggling Family & Career

Sometimes it is the small details that make the difference—here are our readers' tips and tricks for balancing work and family in their daily routines:

◆ *The routine is KING.* Reader Wendy Stough emailed: "Create one that works for you and do your best to stick to it, to some degree. It cuts down on the chaos of little things like lost keys and forgotten diaper bags and allows us, as parents, to take advantage of those special moments when our children need us most. Even when chaos reigns, you'll still know where the keys are!"

◆ *Make up snacks in advance.* Reader MK Krum of Toledo, Ohio makes up snacks and even sippy cups for snack-time a week in advance. "In the morning, just grab what you need and stick it in the diaper bag and go!"

◆ *Organize your baby's closet.* One reader uses a hanging organizer marked with the days of the week. "On Sunday, we load it up with the clothes for each day and any diaper bag refills." Of course, as your baby gets older, she may want a say in what she wears, but that's another story.

◆ *Don't be afraid to ask for help.* When you feel overwhelmed, ask friends and relatives to pitch in.

◆ *Look for a local "Moms Day Out" program* to get a break once in a while. Laurie Galbreath of San Antonio emailed us this tip: "Many churches offer this and you don't have to be a member! It is also very reasonable."

◆ *Create shortcuts to make your life easier.* Example: use white boards in each room of your house to write down needed supplies. This tip was sent in by Debby Moro of Cumming, GA. She emailed: "I stuck a small write on/wipe off board on the back of every door in the house. When I was in a particular room and noticed I was getting low on some supply, I jotted it down then and there. Before I hit the store, I walked through the house, made out the list, and avoided forgetting something."

◆ *Use the web.* You have one advantage that previous generations of parents didn't—the Internet. The web is your friend . . . use it to shop for everything. Reader Area Madaras uses the web to order groceries. "It's cheaper for me to pay $10 for Albertsons.com or Vons.com to delivery my groceries than it is for me to pay a babysitter." And always consider the value of your time—it may be better to shop online and save a car trip.

◆ **Pack the car the night before.** Avoid forgetting something during morning rush by packing that diaper bag, wallet and cell in the car the night before (assuming you have a secure garage).

◆ **When you cook, double the quantity**—then freeze the extra portion for a quick meal later in the week.

◆ **Get up a bit earlier.** This will give you a jump-start on the day—many moms and dads find they can get some chores done in the 30 minutes or so before baby wakes up.

◆ **Have a "two stop" rule.** We found our children would get very cranky/hungry/(fill in blank) when we tried to do more than two errand stops. While it is tempting to try to sync errands together by stopping at X, Y and Z after work, we found there was a limit to our children's patience—usually more than two stops would make life less than pleasant for all.

◆ **Know your employer's sick leave policy.** The Family Medical Leave Act (FMLA) allows parents to stay at home with a sick child without penalty (except for lost wages).

◆ **Schedule fun time.** One mom takes ten minutes out of every morning to jump on the bed or read stories with her toddler. A few stolen moments like that can make the difference.

◆ **Cook on the weekend for the rest of the week.** "That way we always have home-cooked meals that are healthy and tasty ready to pack for lunches or to re-heat at dinner time," emailed Lori Lankey of Woodbury MN. "It saves time and energy during the week, not to mention calories and money if we ended up eating out instead."

◆ **Have a backup sitter plan.** And then get a backup for the backup. That way, if an emergency strikes, you have a plan B. And plan C.

So, let's sum it up. Here are the Top Tips to Balancing Work & Family:

1. Be organized.
2. Trust your instincts.
3. Prioritize.
4. Stick to the routine.
5. But be flexible too.
6. Ask for help when you need it.
7. Lower your expectations.
8. Control freaks need not apply.
9. Laugh! Keeping a sense of humor about EVERYTHING is key.

Q. **So what are my options for childcare?**

Your baby stays at home with someone, goes to someone else's home, or goes to a licensed childcare facility. Let's go over these options so you can get moving on this one.

1. **PARENT AT HOME.** This is not just an option for moms anymore. More dads are staying at home these days. This is the childcare choice any child development expert would recommend. But, your childcare cost is the loss of one parent's salary—which may be significant unless you already have a single-earner household. Think of your parenting job as a career change. Full time parenting is hard work, and an admirable profession. (I have great respect for stay at home parents! My job at work is much easier than my job at home.)

> **DR B'S OPINION**
>
> *"If you decide to be a stay-at-home parent, enjoy your new identity and don't look back. You will never regret being there to watch your baby grow."*

Reality Check

First babies in the household rarely get sick from birth to one year. They spend their days playing on the living room floor with their own toys. When playgroups get together (a good sanity break), the infants play independently of each other. When children start playing with each other and sharing toys (12 to 24 months), they start sharing germs. Firstborn babies who stay at home don't get sick that often.

However, your second child will get *much* sicker in his first year of life. Why? Big brother or sister brings illnesses home from preschool, Mother's Day Out, Gymboree, etc. Second babies also gets dragged around to more family activities. It's almost guaranteed that you'll have more trips to the doctor with each subsequent child.

2. **FAMILY CARETAKER.** This is when a grandparent or some other willing family member cares for your baby while you go to work.

COSTS: CHILD CARE OPTIONS

CHILD CARE	COST	MORE INFO
Au Pair	$14,000 per year or $270 per week	AuPairAmerica.com or AuPairCare.com
Nanny	$27,000 to $30,000 per year or $530 to $590 per week	Nanny.org
Day Care	$4000 to $16,000 per year or $80 to $300 per week	Naeyc.org

It is a great alternative if you have someone who is able and willing. It lets you pay the bills while your baby is at home with someone you can trust. Not only is family childcare free, but your child develops a special relationship with a family member.

Your child's frequency of illness is the same as if a parent stays at home.

Reality Check
Be sure you have a healthy grandparent! Infants require lots of lifting and time on the floor to play.

3. **NANNY/AU PAIR.** You hire someone to parent your child in your home. This may be a professional, or someone who just enjoys taking care of kids.

This is a great way to have a consistent caregiver. Your child will have a special relationship with another caring adult. Because you are paying her and she isn't your mother-in-law, you can set up the parenting guidelines you have in mind. If your child gets sick, you don't need to miss work. You'll only have a problem if your provider gets sick, needs to take a vacation or (yes, it happens) quits.

And it is the most expensive form of childcare. Some parents fear that they cannot trust someone (other than a family member) alone with their child. This option requires good instincts of both the parents and the provider.

> **DR B'S OPINION**
>
> "You won't be able to call all the shots on childrearing. It's difficult to tell your mother-in-law what to do! Set up a consistent parenting plan with your caretaker before differences in parenting styles arise. Otherwise, it could get ugly!"

Reality Check
You won't need a home surveillance system to check on your nanny. An infant will tell you if he is uncomfortable with someone—he won't be happy to see that person. Obviously, you need to do an extensive background check on a nanny BEFORE you hire them. See Chapter 10 of our other book, *Baby Bargains* (see the back of this book for details), for tips and advice on how to do a background check on potential nannies.

Tips for finding a nanny
There are various ways to find a childcare provider who will come to your home. If you put an ad in the paper or on a bulletin board in the education building of your local college, you'll need to rely on your first impression to make a decision. If you go through a nanny or au pair placement service,

---

GOOD NEWS FOR WORKING PARENTS: QUALITY TIME IS KEY

You can have a nurtured, well-adjusted child even if you and your partner both work outside the home. A recent study in the journal *Child Development* proved that "quality time" is more important than the sheer number of hours parents spend with their young children.[10]

you can pay huge sums of money to them to screen candidates for you. (They will do a police, credit, and reference background check.) Our advice: we'd recommend a trial day with your prospective provider to see how it goes before hiring her/him.

4 **IN HOME DAY CARE.** A parent has a license to care for a few children (in addition to their own kids) in her home.
This is a way to hire a mother for your child. It can be great. Your child will be around different ages of children. Often, older kids enjoy playing with the little ones. Your child may get lots of love and attention. He may also see these kids as role models. Sick child policies with in-home daycare tend to be less rigid than those in licensed daycare facilities. So, you can go to work occasionally, even if your child is ill. The cost is moderate but if your child gets sick, you may need to take off work.

Reality Check
As discussed in the stay-at-home scenario, second kids always get more illnesses. You will be adding your child to an existing household of children, so expect the same result. Also, those older kids may not be great role models. You might want to interview both the provider *and* the children she cares for before you make any decisions.

Tips for finding in-home daycare
To find these hidden gems, you'll need to start asking friends, neighbors, and co-workers for possible leads of in-home daycare providers. It's definitely a word-of-mouth kind of option.

5 **LICENSED DAY CARE FACILITY (CENTER CARE).** This is a popular option for many parents. So, I'll spend a bit more time talking about it. If you plan to have your child in daycare, you should already have done some homework. If not, put this book down right now and start!

Tips for finding a good daycare facility
Here are some quick tips on finding a good center care facility:

◆ *Look for a program that is NAEYC (National Association for the Education of Young Children; web: www.naeyc.org) approved.* This organization sets high standards for childcare facilities. If a program has been accredited, you are more likely to be in good hands. You'll be able to do a search on their site based on your zip code.

◆ *Talk to parents whose kids are in the program.*

◆ *Find out how approachable the teachers and director are.* Are modifications made if there is a problem?

◆ *Spend some time observing in the classroom.*

◆ *How do the teachers manage discipline?*

◆ *Do the teachers get down on the floor and play with the kids?*

♦ Are both the children and the adults having fun?

♦ **What are the program's policies regarding infection control (sick child policy)?** Some programs are so strict that they require a doctor's note for your child to get back in.

Center care is the most popular form of childcare in the United States. Parents have a sense of security knowing that the providers are licensed professionals. You can always check up on them. Also, good news—many daycares are trending towards a "preschool" format. Translated, they emphasize a more structured environment and learning through play.

Center daycare is relatively inexpensive as far as childcare goes. But there are hidden costs: you will have to factor in several missed workdays and doctor bills into the price tag.

Reality Check

Hopefully, you are sitting down for the following statistic: *young children have an average of eight to ten viral infections per year.*[11] Infants are at highest risk of getting respiratory infections in the first several months of daycare attendance. In fact, six-month-olds who are day-care attendees have a 79% greater risk of being admitted to the hospital for an acute respiratory infection than their stay-at-home friends (who don't have siblings).[12] Your child will be asked to leave daycare every time he gets sick and asked not to return until he is fever free for 24 hours. With each illness, expect your child to be contagious for the first two to four days of the illness.

The Monster Virus from Venus

As parents of a new baby, we got a quick lesson on daycare sickness—and it wasn't pretty. Our oldest son, Ben, was about two years old when he started a part-time program at a local daycare center. When the MONSTER VIRUS FROM VENUS struck, we didn't see it coming.

See, as parents who worked at home, the most human contact we had was with the UPS guy. And as long as he wasn't coughing on us when he made a package delivery, we were fine. Then our son started at the day care center. About a month into the adventure, he came home with a new friend—we called it the monster virus. Sure, he had a slight fever and stuffy nose—one day later, he was fine. But not Mom and Dad. Somehow, this little virus mutated and by the time it hit us it had become a cross between Ebola and the Black Plague. We were so sick, we couldn't get out of bed for three days and had to call in the emergency parent response team (that is, grandma).

The lesson: be prepare to be struck by all sorts of bizarre diseases if your baby starts daycare. And it won't only be your baby that will suffer . . . everyone in your family is going to have to deal with this!

Feedback from the Real World

There's nothing more vexing than searching for the right childcare for your child. And the "answer" is always a moving target—your childcare needs will change as your child grows. We asked our readers how they made sense of all the childcare options out there.

Here are their tips on finding the best childcare:

♦ **Look for a referral service.** MK Krum of Toledo, Ohio emailed that the YMCA in her area "offers a referral service for about $25 per year. You tell them what kind of daycare you are interested in (center, provider's home, your home, etc) and they match it up to you by zip code." Each year the providers are required to resubmit their info along with letters of recommendation. "It gave us several options both close to work and home."

♦ **Evaluate your commute.** You may find it makes more sense to use a day care close to your home or work, depending on the circumstance.

♦ **Look for red flags when you visit a childcare facility.** Do children seem unattached to their caregivers? Or vice versa?

♦ **Consider going slow to ease the transition.** Instead of dropping your child in to a new childcare situation cold turkey, take it slow. "Bring her for a few hours one day while you're with her," said one mom we interviewed. Or do a new program part-time for a week or more to ease the transition.

♦ **Get on those waitlists early.** It's a fact of life—the best childcare in your town will probably have a wait list. A word to the wise: get on the waitlist NOW, while you are still pregnant. Waiting to arrange childcare usually means having to go with your third or fourth choice—or worse.

♦ **Don't make any firm decisions about childcare until AFTER your baby is born.** Now that sounds like a contradiction with the previous tip, but it isn't—getting on a waiting list for a popular childcare alternative in your town does NOT mean you have to take the spot. Meanwhile, many parents advise waiting until after baby is born before you make your decision about whether to go back to work. Deb Steenhagen, Muskegon, MI emailed her advice: "You may feel completely differently once the baby is born. Give yourself as much time for maternity leave as possible, it helps to bond with the baby strongly before you go back to work and then you'll have those memories to hold onto after you do go back."

♦ **"If you can find one, go with an in-home provider,"** emailed E. White of Maple Grove, MN. "They are much cheaper. The different centers I looked at cost twice as much as in-home daycares."

BEHIND THE SCENES: IS DAYCARE SICKNESS GOOD?

From a health standpoint, it's not all bad that your child gets exposed to infections. A recent study showed that children who were in daycare/center care from birth to at least one year of age had fewer allergies at age two than their "sterile" stay-at-home peers. It's called the "Hygiene Hypothesis." [13] Hygiene Hypothesis or not, I admit having a personal bias on babies and daycare. If someone can stay at home with your baby for his first year—do it. He'll be less likely to see me!

◆ **"Talk to friends and co-workers about what they did.** You might stumble upon a great nanny referral or a nanny share option. My co-worker turned me on to a great service (non-profit organization) in our area that links parents to home daycare providers. While I was leery of home daycare providers (because they have no standards governing their behavior), these particular providers are subject to rules and regulations set by the non-profit organization. Now our son is being watched after by a wonderful woman and we could not be happier!" T. Ross, Arlington, Virginia.

◆ *"In Texas, some of the best center care to be found is provided by churches, which don't advertise heavily like private day care centers.* Ask around, visit lots of places, and ask the tough questions." L. Alvarado, Houston, TX.

◆ **Consider an au pair.** Au pairs are authorized cultural exchanges—a young woman in her 20's comes to live with you to do childcare. Pros: you have one person who takes care of your baby in your home and the au pair becomes part of your family instead of just hired help. Downsides: you have to have a separate bedroom because you have a new family member and they must leave after two years. For more info, go to AuPairAmerica.com.

◆ **Accept the fact that your babysitter or nanny will do things differently than you do.** As long as your child is content and healthy, that is just fine. Don't try to micro manage day care.

◆ Laura L. of Hot Springs, AR says **getting some help cleaning your house was critical to her sanity**: "Hiring a housekeeper, even one that comes every two weeks, is worth every penny you pay. Amazing how much more time it gives you with your baby and family to have that help, even if your budget is already strained!"

Adoption

Having a child is quite an exciting experience, no less so for parents who choose to adopt. In their case, there's more to it than just picking up their new baby and heading on home. Here are some topics for adoptive parents to consider while you're waiting to adopt.

Q. I plan on adopting a baby. Is there anything special I should know?

It depends on the age of the baby at the time of adoption, and from whom you are adopting the baby (for example, international adoption). Here are some considerations:

1. If you are adopting the baby in infancy, adoptive mothers can try to stimulate their breast milk production with a prescription medication. If this is something you are interested in, contact your doctor.

2. It is helpful to know the medical history of the birth parents (if possible). Parental drug use and high-risk sexual activity are important to find out. For all babies, screening tests for HIV, Hepatitis B and syphilis are encouraged.

3. For infants adopted internationally, additional testing is suggested including the following:
    - Stool culture for intestinal parasites.
    - TB (tuberculosis) screening test.
    - Tests routinely done in U.S. on state metabolic screens (thyroid, phenylketonuria, sickle cell disease, etc.). You can also opt for the expanded metabolic screening.

4. Vision, hearing, nutrition status, anemia testing, and developmental milestones can be assessed when your baby meets the pediatrician.

5. If the baby's immunization status is unknown, he is presumed NOT to be immunized and will start the series at the beginning.[14] If there is any doubt about the quality of the country's vaccine supply, it is better to err on the side of repeating the entire vaccination series.

Q. Are there special doctors who care for children who are adopted?

Because adoption is an increasingly common choice for families, most pediatricians and family practice doctors feel comfortable taking care of these children.

However, there are some physicians who have an additional level of expertise in the field. For a listing of these physicians and general info on adoptions, check out the AAP website (www.aap.org/section/adoption/). Another good site is calib.com/naic.

The Birth Plan

Strangely, the last topic we're going to discuss in this chapter is the birth plan. What, you might wonder, does this have to do with pediatrics? You probably thought the birth plan was just for the nurses and doctors who deliver babies. Not so as you'll see in this section.

Q. I am writing a birth plan for my baby's delivery. Do you have any advice? How does my decision regarding pain medication during childbirth affect my baby?

It is currently en vogue for first time parents (notably second-time parents skip this) to create a birth plan. This means that you sit down with your partner before D-Day (Delivery Day) and discuss how you want to manage the pain of childbirth. This includes interventions you want and don't want at the hospital. This list of demands is posted in your labor room for every medical provider to abide by. Some parents get very detailed about the experience they want—down to what color wallpaper they prefer in the labor room (I'm not kidding—I had someone do this.)

Thoughts on Creating a Birth Plan

◆ *Having a baby is a beautiful, amazing experience.* Medical providers who work in the baby making/caring field chose this profession for a reason—they like to participate in that experience. They also want it to be as wonderful as possible. Doctors and nurses will ask you what you need and you should feel free to speak up. Times have changed since the 1950's.

◆ *You don't need written orders* to demand dim lights, music, extra pillows, or just to be left alone for a while.

◆ *For the person giving birth: don't ever let your partner decide for you what pain relief you will have.* You're the one in pain; you decide what you want and when you want it. For the partner: don't be disappointed that your partner chose pain relief. It's easy for well meaning friends, relatives and partners to armchair quarterback when it comes to pain. But until you've been there, you know not of what you speak!

◆ *You can use as many breathing techniques as you want.* When you beg for pain medicine, the staff will give it to you. No one will sneak pain medicine into you—even though you'll be wishing they could. Here's another true story… one family of mine typed up their birth plan. It stated, "No pain medication until we ask for it." During the delivery, that line was crossed out in ink and in bold letters was handwritten, "NOW PLEASE!!"

◆ *Seasoned parents rarely make birth plans because they know that having a baby is an unpredictable event.* You pray for the best and put yourself in the hands of people you trust.

Reality Check

It is your decision whether or not to use pain medication during labor. Despite urban legends, pain medication does *not* have harmful effects on your baby. Mom-to-mom advice: prepare a *backup* childbirth plan. That is, you should learn breathing techniques, etc., even if you want an epidural and you should be prepared to handle having a C-section even if hypno-birthing was your Plan A.

ENJOY the birth of your child, without any guilt.

You & Your Baby's Doc

Insider Tips & Advice

Chapter 2

"There is no such thing as fun for the whole family."

~ Jerry Seinfeld

What's in this Chapter

- ♦ The schedule of well baby checkups.
- ♦ How and why to schedule a sick visit appointment.
- ♦ The difference between a sick visit and a consultation.
- ♦ Insider tips for booking appointments.
- ♦ What to do in the evening and on weekends.
- ♦ Getting in touch: phone calls, voicemail, email, and fax.

Welcome to your baby's second home—the doctor's office. Now that you've picked the person you want to be your baby's doctor, it's important to understand how their office works—and the insider tips and tricks to making your time here as smooth as possible. Let's take a walk around.

Q. Does my baby need to be seen by a doctor regularly?

Yes. These appointments are called well-child visits or well baby checkups.

Bringing your child in at regular intervals is an important part of his health care. These visits let your doctor evaluate your child's health, growth, and development. It lets you address issues that concern you. Smart advice: make a list of questions to discuss at each appointment. At the first few visits, your list may be quite lengthy (up to several pages!). But by the one-year well check, your list will probably fit on a sticky note. That's when you know you have graduated to professional parenthood.

Q. Is there a standard well child visit schedule?

Yes. Most pediatric practices follow the guidelines of the American Academy of Pediatrics (AAP) for routine well child checks. At every visit, we examine your child head to toe. Some visits involve screening tests and immunizations. Below is a standard well child visit schedule up to age five. Note: the immunization schedule has some variability, but this gives you a rough idea of what to expect.

Age of Visit	Screening Tests	Immunizations*
Birth	Metabolic screen, hearing	Hep B
2 weeks	Metabolic screen	
2 months		DTaP, IPV, Hep B, HIB, Prevnar, Rotavirus
4 months		DTaP, IPV, HIB, Prevnar, Rotavirus
6 months		DTaP, HIB, Prevnar, Rotavirus
9 months		IPV, Hep B
12 months	Hematocrit, Lead screen First dental visit	MMR, Varicella, Prevnar, Hep A
15 months		DTaP, HIB
18 months		Hep A
3 years	Blood pressure	
4-6 years	Hearing, vision, Urinalysis, PPD	DTaP, IPV, MMR, Varicella

* What the heck is a DTaP? IPV? HIB? Yes, the world of immunizations has a language all its own. We'll explore the topic of immunizations (and decipher these codes) in Chapter 12, "Vaccines."

Screening Tests

- ◆ ***Metabolic Screen.*** This is a blood test performed at 24 hours of life and repeated at two weeks of age. The number of tests varies by state, but at the minimum includes screens for (big words alert) phenylketonuria, congenital hypothyroidism, galactosemia, sickle cell disease, and adrenal gland insufficiency. (See Chapter 3, "Labor Day" and the glossary.)

- ◆ ***Hearing Screen.*** The AAP recommends all newborns have a hearing test before leaving the hospital. This simple test identifies children with congenital deafness (Again, see Chapter 3, "Labor Day" and BAERS in glossary). A hearing screen is often repeated before starting kindergarten.

- ◆ ***Hematocrit.*** This is a blood test performed at one year of age to determine if your child is anemic. This test may be repeated as necessary.

- ◆ ***Urinalysis.*** A urine sample is obtained at age four to five to evaluate for diabetes and kidney function. This test may also be repeated as needed.

- ◆ ***PPD*** *(Tuberculosis or TB test).* This skin test demonstrates exposure to tuberculosis, an infectious lung disease. Routine testing is performed in high-risk areas, and many schools require one TB test before school entry.

- *Vision screen.* A vision test is performed at age four to five and may be repeated as necessary. If your school district screens annually, this may be omitted from your child's physical exam.

- *Lead Screen.* This blood test demonstrates exposure to lead. High levels can cause anemia and neurological problems. Routine testing is performed in high-risk areas. If you live in a house built before 1978 that has peeling paint or has been renovated, notify your baby's doctor.

- *Cholesterol screen.* This blood test identifies children who have elevated levels of fat that can lead to heart disease. Routine testing is not performed in children. If someone in your family has had problems with high cholesterol, or heart problems before the age of 55, inform your baby's doctor.

- *Immunizations.* This is a whole chapter unto itself, literally. (See Chapter 12, "Vaccines.")

Q. What kind of appointment do I schedule if my baby is sick?

A sick visit. This is a problem-focused appointment. Your child has a problem (fever, ear ache, rash) that needs to be evaluated. Your doctor will focus on the issue and likely do a physical exam limited to the problem. We point this out so you can appreciate the difference in appointments.

BEHIND THE SCENES: WHO IS THE AMERICAN ACADEMY OF PEDIATRICS (AAP)?

Just who is the AAP? And why are their "policy statements" so important? The AAP is an organization of 60,000+ pediatricians who are "dedicated to the health, safety, and well being of infants, children and adolescents in North, Central, and South America."

This active group makes recommendations (called policy statements) that allow doctors to maintain the highest standard of care for their patients. The policies are reviewed and updated frequently. You can check the AAP's policy statements online at www.aap.org.

Doctors who bear the letters, F.A.A.P. after their names are pediatricians who are Fellows of the American Academy of Pediatrics. Fellowship is granted after passing a standardized board certification exam and learning the secret handshake (just kidding on that last one). Fellows must take recertification exams every seven years to remain board certified. Look for the FAAP designation from your pediatrician. This means your doctor is not only trained in her specialty, but also has proof of her competency.

Reality Check

Your baby can get his vaccinations at his well child visit even if he is sick. Many families cancel a well child visit if their baby wakes up ill on the day of his appointment. This causes delays in getting the baby immunized. Unless your baby has a fever of 102 degrees or greater, he can still get his shots. There are also lots of other things to do at a well baby check besides shots. Bottom line: keep your well child appointments!

Q. What kind of appointment do I schedule if I have several/chronic issues I want to discuss?

See if your doctor schedules consultations.

Many doctors offer longer office visits for patients with chronic medical problems or several involved issues. Typically these concerns are behavioral issues, sleep problems, school problems, or medical problems that have been occurring for more than three or four weeks. If the appointment is scheduled this way, your doctor can provide ample time to assess these problems.

Insider Tips: How To Make Friends With The Office Staff

Bringing cookies is helpful. Just kidding! Seriously, here are five tips to make a nice impression in the doctor's office:

1. **Bring your insurance card.** Most doctors' staffs verify proof of insurance at *every* office visit.
2. **When you come for your first office visit, arrive 30 minutes before your appointment time.** You'll need to fill out a lot of paperwork and the office staff need to verify your insurance (that often takes 20 minutes on the phone with your insurance company). The same is true if you have changed insurance plans.
3. **If you are an established patient, come a few minutes early for well child visits.** You will soon understand why. You will need to completely undress your baby to take his measurements. This itself can be an event. Then, inevitably, the baby will either poop or pee on the measuring scale, which then further delays the measurements being taken. Multiply this experience by two if you have twins.

NEW PARENT 411: WHEN DOES MY CHILD STOP GOING TO THE PEDIATRICIAN?

It depends on the child. Some teenagers wouldn't be caught dead in their pediatrician's waiting room. Other teenagers never want to leave the nest. Most pediatricians feel comfortable seeing their patients until the age of 18-21 years, if they still want to see us. (My pediatrician kicked me out after he performed my physical examination for medical school.)

Family practice physicians are comfortable seeing teenagers. Internal medicine physicians (internists) are not. They often limit their practice to age 18 and up.

DR B'S OPINION: WELL CHECKS

Don't try to squeeze in a well-child visit when you come in for a sick visit. Busy families frequently bring their baby in for a sick visit and ask, "So, can't you do a well check today since we are here?" I usually say no, unless my schedule is light. I need time to do a complete exam and evaluation. Doing a quick once-over isn't doing justice to the importance of a well-child visit.

4. **If you have more than one child that needs to be evaluated by the doctor, schedule an appointment for each of them.** It shows that you respect your doctor's time. If everyone would follow this mantra, there's no doubt that wait times to see your doctor would decline.
5. **If you are running late for an appointment, call your doctor.** Most medical offices can modify their schedule if they know when you are coming.

Insider Tips: The Best Time To Schedule Appointments

Let's make an analogy to an airport. Your baby's doctor's office is a bit like La Guardia Airport. When is the best time to fly? In the early morning, before delays set later flights back.

When is the worst time to fly? Monday mornings, Friday afternoons, and national holidays.

Now let's look at some trends in the doctor's office. Because many doctors' offices are closed on the weekends, parents tend to bring their sick kids in either before the weekend or after enduring a long weekend with them. Translation: *peak volume days are Mondays and Fridays*.

Seasons also cause volume trends. Cold and flu season (October through April) is the highest patient volume all year. Christmas Eve is always busy because no good parent will allow his or her child to be ill on Christmas. National holidays are popular times to visit because many parents have the day off from work.

In the summer (June through August), our older patients keep us busy with well child visits because they don't have to miss school. They also need camp or sports physicals.

May and September are the slowest months of the year (that's when I usually take a vacation!)

If you want to visit your doctor when the office is quieter (or running less behind) here are some tips:

1. *Schedule well baby visits on Tuesdays, Wednesdays, or Thursdays.*
2. *Try to get the first appointment of the morning or afternoon to avoid delays.*
3. *Schedule well baby visits that occur in the winter months far in advance.* There are often fewer well child visits offered to make room for the sick visits.

4. If you want to avoid the rush for school or camp physicals, consider booking in May or September.
5. See if your doctor offers weekend hours. Then you can avoid the Monday/Friday crunch.

Q. Who will I meet in the doctor's office?

Let me introduce you to the office staff. Practices vary a great deal, but these are the usual folks that you will encounter.

- *The medical provider or "primary care provider:"* This is the person responsible for your child's medical care. This may be a pediatrician or family practice doctor, depending on whom you select. Their initial medical school training is through a certified medical school (M.D.) or a school of osteopathic medicine (D.O.). Their specialty training is either in children's healthcare (pediatrics) or a combination of both adult and children's healthcare (family practice). When all is said and done, either type of provider will have at least seven years of training beyond college before they have their own office.

- *Mid-level providers:* These people have been popular additions to busy offices. Nurse practitioners (NP's) and physician assistants (PA's) help with straightforward sick visits and well child visits. They can evaluate patients, make decisions, and treat patients with the supervision of a medical provider. Nurse practitioners have at least two years of training beyond their bachelor's degree in nursing (B.S.N.). Physician assistants complete a two-year program after completing at least two years of college.

- *Nursing staff:* The staff may have a variety of degrees. The head nurse may have either a R.N. (registered nurse) or L.V.N. (licensed vocational nurse) degree. Many pediatric offices utilize medical assistants who are trained to administer shots and perform screening tests.

Q. What do I do if my baby gets sick in the evening or on the weekend?

It is Murphy's Law that your baby will only get sick when the office is closed.

Be prepared for this and have a game plan. Some offices offer limited evening and weekend hours. Find out the specifics for your doctor's office.

If the office is closed, the next option is a minor care center or an emergency department of your local hospital. Ask your office for their recommendation. The most convenient location may not be the best place to go.

BEHIND THE SCENES: CONFIDING IN YOUR BABY'S DOC

If you found yourself struggling with depression after your baby is born, who would you turn to for help? A doctor? Friends? The 'net?

A recent study looked at mothers of young children and whether or not they felt comfortable discussing their "emotional health" with their pediatrician. Although pediatricians could be a resource for help, many moms said that discussing stress with their pediatrician would be admitting failure. (Hello? Isn't stress part of the job description?) Moms relied on breastfeeding groups, postpartum groups, playgroups, and the Internet as sources of support. Yet, over 50% of pediatricians feel it is their responsibility to recognize postpartum depression.

Bottom line: test the waters next time you visit with your child's doctor—you might be pleasantly surprised at the results.

BOTTOM LINE: Always call your doctor first before you go running anywhere. What may seem like an emergency to you may not be. Your phone call might save you a trip in the middle of the night.

Q. What is the best way to contact my doctor's office?

Ah, the age of technology. So many options—email, IM, voicemail...

Despite the digital age, the most effective way to contact the office is by picking up the phone. Doctors' offices anticipate numerous calls during office hours and have systems in place to answer the calls efficiently.

Some offices are more progressive and have started accepting questions via email. However, most offices still rely on the telephone to communicate with patients. One reason for the resistance to change is for medical privacy issues. The U.S. Government has enacted a program to protect medical information (HIPAA). The act is subject to interpretation by individual medical offices. Thus, some offices now prohibit transmitting medical records via fax or email, or leaving medically sensitive information on answering machines or voicemail. Although this may seem like a hassle, these restrictions are meant to protect you.

Reality Check

If you find yourself lying to your baby's doctor to avoid an unwanted discussion, you probably need to find a doctor you are more comfortable with.

Notes

Labor Day

Chapter 3

"Giving birth is like taking your lower lip and forcing it over your head."
~ Carol Burnett

What's in this Chapter

- **The details of your baby's first physical examination.**
- **Screening tests, Vitamin K, and eye ointment.**
- **The significance of Group B Strep.**
- **Why is your baby shrinking?**
- **What you will see in your baby's diaper.**
- **Jaundice.**
- **Car seats.**
- **Preemie Primer.**
- **Special Section: The Two-Week Survival Guide.**

Labor Day is finally here—the most incredible day of your life. You have prepared the nursery and taken the birthing class, breastfeeding class, and baby care class. You've bought too many childcare and parenting books. Hopefully, you've also met with your pediatrician (see Chapter 1, "Decisions"). So you're ready, right?

There is no way anyone can prepare you for this, but this chapter will guide you through your baby's first day at the hospital.

Let's leave the giving birth part to the pregnancy books . . . ask your obstetrician if you have any questions on this. Instead, we'll focus on what happens once your baby is born. Many people are not aware of this, but pediatricians and family practitioners examine their patients for the first time in the hospital. Why, you may ask? Because entering the world is a big transition. Babies who are still inside the womb may have certain medical problems that do not show themselves until they take their first breath of fresh air. It is very helpful in the world of modern day medicine to have ultrasounds, lab tests, and amniocentesis to get a glimpse of potential problems in your baby—but they don't cover every problem.

When the hospital calls your doctor to notify her of your baby's birth, she will be out to examine her new patient and visit with his mom and dad (that's you—has a nice ring to it) within 24 hours of the birth.

If there is an emergency at delivery, or

urgent problems with your newborn, the hospital may ask a neonatologist (newborn intensive care specialist) or a pediatrician who is present in the hospital to care for your baby immediately.

Q. Tell me about the baby's first exam. What are you looking for?

Bear with us—this stuff is a little dry, but we think it will help you to understand what your doctor is doing. It will also make you appreciate how fortunate you are to have a baby who makes an A+ on his first exam!

Vital Signs
This includes heart rate (pulse), breathing rate (respiratory rate), body temperature, and weight. Abnormalities can indicate infection, dehydration, and heart/lung abnormalities. These are checked at least every eight hours. Babies are weighed daily. Input (length of breast feeding/amount of formula) and output (number of pees and poops) are also documented.

The Head
- Shape of the head. (Your baby will not be a permanent member of the Conehead family—it rounds out after a few weeks).
- Bruises from the trauma of delivery caused by forceps, vacuum, pushing on your pelvic bones for 2+ hours). Big bruises can take 6-8 weeks to resolve (see **CEPHALHEMATOMA**)
- Soft spot. The soft spot (**FONTANELLE**) in the middle of the skull is open with room for the brain to grow. (see **CRANIOSYNOSTOSIS**)

The Eyes
- Red reflex. Doctors use a special light to see the baby's red reflex (the "red eye" you see in flash photography pictures). **CATARACTS** and eye tumors (see **RETINOBLASTOMA**) are two problems doctors are trying to catch here.
- Tear ducts. Many newborns get clogged tear ducts (see **NASOLACRIMAL DUCT OBSTRUCTION**). The ducts are narrow and cause the tears to get goopy and make the eye look infected. This can come and go for your baby's entire first year of life. We'll cover this issue later in Chapter 15, "First Aid."

Reality Check

Newborns can only see 8 to 12 inches in front of them. They can see you if you bring their face up close to yours. They frequently look cross-eyed for the first two months. Most newborns are born with blue eyes—we can't predict their true eye color until about six months of life.

The Ears
- Eardrums are checked, as well as abnormal formations of the outer part of the ears (see **PREAURICULAR PITS, SKIN TAGS**).
- A hearing test is performed on all newborns. No, we don't ask them to raise their hand when they hear the beep. The baby wears headphones and we measure the electrical activity of the brain when a noise is made. (see **BAERs**)

Reality Check

The American Academy of Pediatrics recommends hearing screening for *all* newborns. Thirty-seven states require the testing by law. However, not all states enforce their legislation by requiring insurance companies to foot the bill for the test. Even if a hearing test is not a covered benefit, however, you should have the test done. Congenital hearing loss occurs in 3 per 1000 newborns. Early detection can make a considerable difference for a child's language development.[1]

The Nose
- Can baby breathe through his nose (see **CHOANAL ATRESIA**)? By the way, all babies have stuffy noses at birth and continue to have nasal congestion for the next four to six weeks (see **NEWBORN NASAL CONGESTION**).

The Mouth
- Formation of the mouth. A doctor will check to make sure the roof of the mouth (palate) has formed and the funny thing hanging in the back of the mouth (uvula) is there (see **CLEFT LIP** and **CLEFT PALATE**).
- Tongue. Your baby's tongue is checked for a forked tip or any trouble in moving it. This is called a tongue tie or a tight frenulum (see **ANKYLOGLOSSIA**).
- Gums. Some babies are born with white pimples on the gums (see **EPSTEIN'S PEARLS**) that go away on their own. These are not teeth—the first tooth usually comes out between six to 12 months of age.

The Throat
- Breathing. Occasionally, babies make unusual noises when breathing. Some babies are born with floppy breathing tubes (see **LARYNGOMALACIA**) that they will outgrow. This sound concerns parents, but is usually of no consequence.

The Neck and Shoulders
- These are checked for any unusual lumps, bumps, or cysts (see **BRANCHIAL CLEFT CYST**).
- If birth was difficult (big baby, small mommy), the collarbone can break (see **CLAVICLE FRACTURE**, **SHOULDER DYSTOCIA**).
- Can your baby turn its head to each side? Some babies will have a stiff neck muscle that limits head motion (see **TORTICOLLIS**).

The Chest
- Doctors look for any signs of difficulty breathing (see **RESPIRATORY DISTRESS**). Adults breathe 12 times per minute at an even rate. Newborns breathe 30 to 40 times per minute and have episodes of **PERIODIC BREATHING**. So, your baby will breathe rapidly several times, p-a-u-s-e, then breathe again. That pause will seem like an eternity to you. It is normal. Signs of respiratory distress are:

    1. A pause between breaths that lasts 15 to 20 seconds (see **APNEA**).

2. Baby is consistently breathing over 60 times per minute. (see **TACHYPNEA OF NEWBORN**)
3. Baby's ribs are sucking in at each breath, nostrils are flaring, grunting noises are heard (see **RETRACTIONS, RESPIRATORY DISTRESS**)

The Heart and Circulation
- Murmurs (unusual noises), irregular heartbeats, fast or slow heart rate, unusual discoloration (pale or dusky blue). Many heart problems, especially severe defects (see **CONGENITAL HEART DISEASE**) are now detected on fetal ultrasounds. However, doctors listen carefully with their good old stethoscopes to pick up abnormalities.
- Baby's pulses are carefully checked, particularly those in the groin area (femoral pulses). The main blood vessel (aorta) supplying oxygen rich blood to the body can have kinks and narrowings (see **COARCTATION OF AORTA**) causing a weakened pulse in the groin.
- A normal, benign murmur is often heard in the first 24 hours of life, as the newborn's circulation transitions from that of the fetus. This murmur, often called a "**TRANSITIONAL MURMUR**" resolves within the first few days and does *not* represent a problem.
- Purple hands and feet (see **ACROCYANOSIS**) are due to newborn circulation. Your baby is merely attempting to adapt to life outside the womb. This is normal and can last from weeks to sometimes months, especially after exposure to cold, or following a bath.

The Abdomen
- Your doctor will feel your baby's belly to check the size of her liver and spleen. The belly should be soft and not hurt to touch. Abnormally large body organ size can be caused by problems metabolizing foods (see **METABOLIC STORAGE DISEASE**) or poor heart function (see **CONGESTIVE HEART FAILURE**). Abnormal fullness or distention alerts doctors to look for **ABDOMINAL TUMORS**.
- Firm or full bellies may be a sign of abnormal intestine formation (see **MALROTATION, DUODENAL ATRESIA**). An abnormal exam and problems feeding—that is, vomiting, especially bile, will be a tip off to investigate things further.
- A baby is expected to pass one stool called **MECONIUM** in the first 24 hours of life. A delay in pooping will make us evaluate for abnormal anus formation (see **HIRSCHSPRUNG'S DISEASE, ANAL ATRESIA**) or poor stool formation that can be seen in cystic fibrosis (see **MECONIUM PLUG, CYSTIC FIBROSIS**).
- Sometimes the belly button (umbilicus) pops out. This is the extreme form of an "outty" (see **UMBILICAL HERNIA**) and often resolves on its own.

Old Wives Tale
Placing a coin or a Band-Aid on the belly button will help the "outty" belly button go in. FALSE. Time is the best therapy.

The Genitals
BOYS
- For boys, your doctor makes sure both testes are in the scrotum. Occasionally, one or both testes will not make the pilgrimage south (see **UNDESCENDED TESTES**).
- For boys, the fullness of the scrotum is also checked. Many boys are born with extra fluid in the scrotum that goes away over the first six months of life. (see **HYDROCELE**) The other thing that causes fullness is a hernia—part of the intestine that has pushed into the scrotum. (see **INGUINAL HERNIA**). Cool doctor trick: we can tell the difference by shining a light on the scrotum. Fluid (hydrocele) is light and intestine (hernia) is dark.

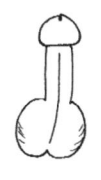

Normal penis

- For boys, your doctor will make sure the opening (urethra) is at the tip of the penis. The opening can abnormally develop on the undersurface of the penis shaft (see **HYPOSPADIAS,** see picture at right) or on topside (see **EPISPADIAS**). Boys with this problem are not routinely circumcised because the foreskin is needed to surgically correct it around six months of age.

Hypospadias

GIRLS
- For girls, the vagina and urethra (the holes tucked inside the lips) are checked. The lips (labia minora) can be stuck together (see **LABIAL ADHESION**). Usually, you see some white mucousy fluid (see **VAGINAL DISCHARGE**). This is normal. Occasionally, newborn girls also have some vaginal bleeding (see What's That in My Baby's Diaper? question). Dads—you need to learn how to clean this area well. (See Chapter 4, "Hygiene" for details.)

BOTH SEXES
- When the clitoris looks too large, or the penis looks too small, your doctor will evaluate for problems with the baby's hormones or chromosomes. (see **AMBIGUOUS GENITALIA**)
- For both sexes, the breasts can be swollen due to Mom's hormones passing through to baby. It is temporary and they shrink back down on their own.

The Kidneys and Bladder
- Expect the baby to pee (urinate) once in the first 24 hours of life. We start investigating if this does not occur.
- Abnormal formation of the passageway from the kidneys to the bladder (see **VESICOURETERAL REFLUX**, **POSTERIOR URETHRAL VALVES**) can occur in rare occasions. An evaluation for this is done if a baby develops a bladder or kidney infection. (see **URINARY TRACT INFECTION**, **PYELONEPHRITIS**)

The Spine and Nervous System
- Your doctor will look for dimples or tufts of hair near the buttocks. Abnormalities on the skin can be a clue to a spine abnormality

underneath the skin (see **SACRAL DIMPLE**, **NEURAL TUBE DEFECT**, **SPINA BIFIDA**).

- Also checked: the newborn's unique reflexes that fade over the first six months of life. It tells us their brain and nerves are coordinated. (see **CEREBRAL PALSY**) These reflexes include: *Rooting* (turning the head when the cheek is rubbed), *Sucking* (automatically sucking on objects placed in the mouth), *Palmar Grasp* (closing fingers on object placed on the palm), and *Moro* (body startles when head is dropped back).

The Arms and Legs (Extremities)
- Do both arms move? A weakness of the nerves causes a limp arm. (see **ERB'S PALSY**)
- Many people are familiar with purebred dogs with hip problems. Humans can have similar problems. We check the hips by rotating them in and out. If there is a concern, we'll order an ultrasound to look at the hips. Breech babies have a slightly increased risk of this disorder. (see **HIP DYSPLASIA**)
- Rarely, babies will have extra fingers and toes, and some that are fused together (see **POLYDACTYLY**, **SYNDACTYLY**).
- A severe deformity (see **CLUB FOOT**) makes the bottoms of the feet face each other and requires casting. This occurs in about 1 in 1000 births.

The Skin
- Brown birthmarks: Moles (see **CONGENITAL NEVUS**) and light brown oval shaped areas (see **CAFÉ AU LAIT SPOTS**) are permanent markings and rarely are related to other medical problems.
- Purple birthmarks: These marks (see **PORT WINE STAINS**) are permanent and can be quite large. If they are located on the face, your doctor will look for other medical problems (see **STURGE-WEBER SYNDROME**).
- Red birthmarks: These marks (see **STRAWBERRY HEMANGIOMA**) may be seen at birth, or by the first month of life. They start out flat, grow much larger and become raised. These particular marks shrink and go away by the age of ten.
- More red birthmarks: Red marks known as stork bites and angel kisses (see **NEVUS FLAMMEUS**, **FLAT ANGIOMATA**) are on the back of the neck or eyelids and fade over the first few months of life. When your baby gets mad at you, you will see them turn even redder.
- Blue, bruise-like marks: These spots (see **MONGOLIAN SPOTS**) are found on the buttocks of dark skinned babies. They fade over several years.
- Yellow skin: This is a whole topic in itself—see section on **JAUNDICE**.

Go to our web site Baby411.com for pictures of all of these common birthmarks. Click on "Bonus Material".

Reality Check
Newborns are really rashy. Most rashes will come and go. You'll have a window of "photo opportunity" from two to three weeks

of age when their skin is clearer. Then more rashes crop up at four to eight weeks of age. These are all due to fluctuating hormone levels. No matter what you do, they will go away. A good thing to remember is your baby could care less. The names are listed below. For details, refer to the glossary. (see **ERYTHEMA TOXICUM, MILIA, MILIARIA, NEONATAL ACNE, PUSTULAR MELANOSIS**). For pictures of these rashes, check out our web site Baby411.com (click on "Bonus Material.")

Q. What is the PKU/Newborn Screen and why does my baby need to be tested?

This is a test required by all 50 states to check for serious diseases that would otherwise go undetected in the first several weeks to months of life. The number of screening tests varies from state to state but all include: **HYPOTHYROIDISM, PHENYLKETONURIA (PKU)**, and **GALACTOSEMIA**. These tests are done once at the hospital, and again at two weeks of age. Some states also test for **SICKLE CELL ANEMIA** and **ADRENAL GLAND INSUFFICIENCY** (see glossary for details of diseases).

Although the risk of any of these diseases is quite low, the benefit of making an early diagnosis is tremendous. Children with undetected hypothyroidism were permanently mentally retarded prior to the era of state newborn screening programs.

FYI: We've posted a list of which states require what screens on our web site Baby411.com (again, click on "Bonus Material").

Q. Why do all babies get a shot of Vitamin K?

Vitamin K is essential for blood clotting. Babies who are born with a Vitamin K deficiency can have significant bleeding into vital organs (such as the brain, see **HEMORRHAGIC DISEASE OF THE NEWBORN**). Since time is of the essence, it makes more sense to give all babies the vitamin K than to test them all and find out too late who needed it.

Q. Why do all babies get eye ointment?

Having a baby is messy. Some mothers carry bacteria that can lead to serious eye infections in the baby. Again, it makes more sense to treat every baby immediately than to test every mother at delivery and figure out which baby needs it. Antibiotic ointment has low risk with great benefit.

NEW PARENT 411: WHY DO ALL THESE TESTS?

Some parents feel uncomfortable with all the poking and prodding their newborn endures. Trust us—there is a method to the madness. Your doctor wants to make sure you are taking home a healthy baby! Remember the key rule to all these tests: if it wasn't important, we wouldn't be doing it!

LABOR DAY

Q. Will my baby's blood type be tested?

Sometimes. Blood types are not routinely tested in the hospital. This might worry some parents, who are concerned that not knowing their baby's blood type immediately is dangerous. You should know that any person with a medical emergency (such as a car accident) that requires a blood transfusion gets type O negative blood regardless of his or her blood type. O negative blood is compatible with ALL blood types. When a blood transfusion is less urgent, a person's blood type is tested and numerous tests are done to find a donor blood match.

Your baby's blood type will be tested if Mommy has O blood type because blood type incompatibility (i.e. baby is A or B) can lead to problems with jaundice. See Jaundice section (**ABO INCOMPATIBILITY**).

Group B Strep: All You Ever Wanted to Know & More!

Q. What is the significance of the Group B Strep or Beta Strep test?

Mothers are routinely screened at the 35th to 37th week of their pregnancy for the presence of a bacteria that lives harmlessly in the genitals and intestines of some healthy women. This bacteria, called Group B Strep, can infect a newborn as he passes through the birth canal.

If Mom is a carrier for Group B Strep, she is given intravenous (IV) antibiotics during labor to suppress the growth of this bacteria. If Mom goes into labor before 37 weeks, has her water broken for more than 18 hours or has a fever greater than 100.4 degrees, she also gets IV antibiotics because of the risk of Group B Strep infection. (Women who have planned C-sections don't have to worry about this stuff).

Doctors get worked up about Group B Strep because it can cause blood infection (bacteremia), pneumonia, and meningitis in newborns. All newborns are watched closely, but those babies with moms who test positive for Group B Strep are watched even more closely.

It is standard protocol to get a complete blood count and blood culture on a newborn *if* mom is Group B Strep positive and she didn't get pretreated with antibiotics (which happens with quick labor), the baby is born sooner than 35 weeks gestation, or if a baby starts misbehaving (temperature instability, labored breathing, etc.).[2]

> **Reality Check**
> Don't be too alarmed if you carry Group B Strep. This does not mean you are Typhoid Mary. Most babies with Group B Strep positive mothers do not get sick—they are just at a slightly higher risk.

Q. Are there any other tests on mom done during pregnancy that the pediatrician needs to know about?

Yes! It is a standard of prenatal care to obtain blood tests looking for previous infections in the mother. This panel of tests includes Hepatitis B exposure (see **TORCH INFECTIONS**). If Mom received prenatal care, her lab work should be on the baby's chart at the hospital.

This wasn't in the birth plan!

While most full-term deliveries and post-partum days go smoothly, your newborn may throw you a curve ball. While we don't mean to freak you out, here are some of the more common complications that might happen:

- *Group B Strep.* As we discussed in the section above, your baby may have blood tests done in certain situations to look for infection.

- *Blood sugar testing.* If your baby is very large (over eight pounds), very small (under five pounds), feeding poorly, jittery, cold, or very sleepy, he will have his blood sugar tested to be sure that his level is high enough (usually that magic number is 40 mg/dl). Blood sugar is also routinely tested in babies whose mothers have diabetes or gestational diabetes. Be aware that some hospitals will test at-risk babies several times in the first couple of days. If your baby's blood sugar is low, you may need to supplement with formula for a day or two, even if breastfeeding is your long-term plan.

- *Meconium.* Babies who are stressed prior to or at delivery may pass their first poop before they leave the womb. That poop can be seen in the amniotic fluid. If the meconium enters the baby's lungs, it can cause inflammation and problems breathing. So, it's important to clear the baby's airway before he takes his first breath. If your water breaks and your OB sees the meconium, a neonatal team is called to attend the delivery. Yes, even more people get to see you naked—you won't care at that point, trust us.

- *Labored breathing.* Babies who are delivered by C-section don't get their fetal fluid squeezed out of their lungs like those who get pushed out through the birth canal. As a result, some babies may have temporary labored breathing for the first few hours after delivery (called Transient Tachypnea of the Newborn, or TTN). Occasionally, babies delivered vaginally will have this too. If your baby has TTN, he will be monitored for a little while in the nursery before getting his first snuggles with you.

- *Fever.* Your baby's body temperature will be watched closely during the first two days. If your baby runs a fever of 100.4 (taken rectally), he will have lab tests done to rule out infection.

- *Jaundice*: See the section below for details.

Getting to Know You: Your Baby's First Few Days

After your baby passes his first exam, the fun is just beginning—it's time for you the parent to get to know your little guy or gal. Let's talk about what you'll experience for the first few hours . . . and days. This section will cover Apgar tests, changing those first diapers and more.

LABOR DAY

Q. Are there any vaccinations given to the baby at the hospital?

The Hepatitis B vaccine is recommended for all newborns as part of the universal immunization series. Infants usually get the first of three doses between birth and two months of age. It is ESSENTIAL to get the first dose at birth if Mom tests positive for Hepatitis B to prevent infection in the newborn. For more information see Chapter 12, "Vaccines."

Q. Does my baby need to study for the Apgar test?

No. He probably won't score a perfect "10" either—those foreign judges are so critical of the dismount. Just kidding. The Apgar test determines which babies need extra help adjusting to life outside the womb. They are given a score from zero to ten. Your baby's **A**ppearance (color), **P**ulse (heart rate), **G**rimace (reaction to stimulation), **A**ctivity (tone), and **R**espiration rate are assessed at one minute of life and again at five minutes. Babies who endure difficult deliveries often have low (less than five) Apgar scores at one minute then perk up (greater than seven) at five minutes. The babies that don't rise in their scores may need observation and assistance by medical staff. Rest assured, low Apgar scores do NOT correlate with low SAT scores and future intelligence.

Q. What's THAT in my baby's diaper?

We've got an entire chapter with accompanying pictures on our website dedicated to poop (exciting, no?), but let's give you a brief primer on what you'll be seeing in those first few diapers.

◆ *Black tar poop.* The official name is **MECONIUM**. Doctors expect one of these poops in the first day of life. If you see more, congratulations—you're on your way to being a diaper changing pro. See Chapter 8, "The Other End," for details.

◆ *Brick dust.* Babies should urinate (pee) at least once in the first day as well. If your baby is hovering around that 10% weight loss (see later box, Why is My Baby Shrinking?), you may see a red-orange brick dust spot in the diaper (see **URIC ACID CRYSTALS**). You'll think it is blood, but take a closer look. Blood gets absorbed into the diaper since it's a liquid. The crystal powder sits on the surface. It just means your baby needs to drink. See Baby411.com's "Bonus Material" (visual library) for a great picture.

> **NEW PARENT 411: WHY IS MY BABY SHRINKING?**
>
> The shrinking baby phenomenon! No, it's not a headline ripped from the tabloids. Babies travel out of the womb with extra baggage. They have about 10% more fluid than their bodies need. Over the first few days of life, they will lose 10% of their birth weight, then quickly gain about an ounce a day once they start eating (about their third day of life). This is sure to cause you anxiety, particularly if you are breastfeeding. For details, see Chapter 5, "Nutrition."

- **Blood.** Baby girls will have a "period" thanks to Mom's hormones. Don't worry, they don't get the PMS to go with it! This should only happen in the first month of life and not again until puberty.
- **Gel balls.** This did not come out of your baby. It is your super absorbent diaper. When the volume of urine (pee) exceeds the diaper absorbency, the gels rise to the surface. Your baby is not an alien and it is not a health hazard.

Q. Should I "room-in" with my baby at the hospital?

Yes. It is the latest recommendation from the American Academy of Pediatrics to help make breastfeeding successful. This will allow you to learn your baby's hunger cues and nurse before your baby is screaming and demanding to be fed.

However, we should warn you that babies are very noisy sleepers. Try not to obsess over every squeak your baby makes. You need sleep to recover from the delivery and produce milk.

If you are formula feeding, it is your call. The nursery staff is happy to baby-sit for a few hours while you get some shut-eye.

Q. My baby sleeps all the time. Were my prayers answered?

Wait until the baby gets home…you will find out then! All babies sleep through their first two days of life. They have been through the same experience as their Mom. They realize they have left the womb about the exact moment you take them home. It is not the magic of the nursery nurse's touch (although you will feel inadequate when faced with a screaming baby). Newborns don't have the skills to pull it together and settle down. You will need to figure out what soothes your baby. For details, see Chapter 9, "Sleep."

Q. Why is my baby turning yellow? What is jaundice?

Here's the 411 on jaundice. While it sounds scary, there are two types of jaundice when it comes to newborns: NORMAL jaundice and ABNORMAL jaundice. Yes, you read it right—there is a form of jaundice that is NORMAL in newborns.

So what is jaundice? Short answer: it's body garbage that hasn't been

NEW PARENT 411: BIRTH TRAUMA

This is what happens when your baby is larger than your pelvis can handle or just simply doesn't want to leave the womb. Your newborn's head may be pressed against your pelvic bones for 2 hours or he may have had forceps or a vacuum applied to his head. The result: a huge bruise on his head caused by bleeding just under the skin that clots and looks rather dramatic. (see baby411.com for a great picture).

Because the skin is also injured, a scab will form and peel off (like a sunburn). The blood clot will get hard and leave a lump for up to eight weeks. Not to worry, none of this is permanent.

eliminated yet. Long answer: humans make body garbage called bilirubin. Bilirubin breaks down in our livers and comes out in our poop. The problem: a newborn's liver is not working at full speed yet, nor are his intestines.

So, for most newborns, the body garbage (bilirubin) will start to collect in the skin. This is normal jaundice. Bilirubin has a yellow pigment, causing the whites of the eyes and skin to yellow. The level of yellow (jaundice) correlates with how far down the yellow gets on the body (increasing from head to toe.) The level will continue to rise until baby is eating and pooping regularly (day four to five). You will notice that the poop changes from black to a yellow/green/brown color at that time.

Again, by day four or five of life, bilirubin *normally* comes out in the poop and no longer collects in the skin.

What about abnormal jaundice? See the following red flags.

RED FLAGS: Abnormal Jaundice.

These are signs for ABNORMAL jaundice (see the previous discussion of normal versus abnormal jaundice):

- Jaundice is seen in the first 24 hours of life
- Jaundice persists more than five days of life
- Level of jaundice descends below the belly button
- When mom and baby's blood types are different (mom is O and baby is A or B). Mom's blood can potentially mount a response that destroys some of baby's red blood cells. This leaves the baby with even more bilirubin to break down.

Q. How is jaundice treated?

The best way to get rid of bilirubin is to eliminate it in the poop. The more the baby eats, the more he poops. For a majority of babies, the bilirubin level peaks around day four of life. This is precisely the time that mom's milk comes in and babies are interested in eating.

For various reasons, some babies either have a delay in eliminating the

YELLOW BABY 411: JAUNDICE

Although most newborns turn a little bit yellow, pediatricians monitor all babies closely for a rare, but preventable form of brain damage (see **KERNICTERUS**) caused by excessive bilirubin levels. Levels of bilirubin (see **JAUNDICE**) start to rise just as babies go home from the hospital at 48 hours of life. The levels usually peak between 3-5 days of life. Breastfeeding can be a risk factor for jaundice if the baby is not feeding at least eight times a day or there is a delay in mother's milk coming in.

The American Academy of Pediatrics wants to improve identification of any babies at risk for brain damage. The AAP recommends that parents ROUTINELY schedule an appointment with their baby's medical provider at three to five days of life—even if that means an appointment on a weekend! And if your baby starts to look like a pumpkin, don't wait to call your doctor.

bilirubin, or produce higher levels than their bodies can eliminate effectively. They need some help for a few days to get rid of the bilirubin. One or more of the following interventions are used to reduce the bilirubin load:

1. **Supplementation with formula until Mom's milk comes in.**
2. **Phototherapy.** This technique uses blue light to breakdown the bilirubin. Babies either rest with a lighted blanket around them or under a bank of lights similar to a tanning booth.
3. **Intravenous fluid.** Dehydrated babies have more trouble with jaundice.

FYI: It is NOT recommended that you lay out poolside with your newborn, or place him by a sunny window to treat jaundice. It's not that effective and can overheat him.

Q. I am getting a lot of different advice from nurses and lactation specialists—who is right?

Everyone, sort of. You will meet many health care professionals in your baby's first few days. They will all have different approaches to the same child health issues. To avoid frustration and confusion, realize that there are many ways, for example, to position a baby to nurse. Just take it all in, then figure out what works for you and your child. P.S. If you feel like you have NEW PARENT stamped on your forehead, you do!

Q. When will I need to use a car seat?

Every time you take your baby with you in the car! This includes your trip home from the hospital. It's the law, folks. Here's what you need to know:

- All 50 states require that infants under one year of age be restrained in an approved car seat. Laws vary from state to state beyond a year of age. However, the American Academy of Pediatrics advises that children be in a safety restraint (convertible car seat and then a booster seat) until they weigh 80 pounds.
- Infants must be facing the rear of the car until they are 20 pounds AND at least one year of age.
- Kids under age 12 should be in the back seat of your vehicle. Front air bags deploy right at the level of a child's head, which can be fatal.
- So, what do you need to buy now? Newborns can sit in either an infant car seat (0-20 pounds) or a convertible car seat (0-40 pounds). You can conceivably use only a convertible car seat and save money. But most parents choose the more expensive option of getting the infant car seat (knowing they'll have to get the convertible car seat after their baby outgrows the infant seat) because it's portable. When your baby falls asleep in the car, you'll find it's worth the investment. For more details on buying a car seat including reviews and recommendations, see our other book, *Baby Bargains* (for more information see the back of this book).
- Practice using the car seat *before* game day so you don't feel foolish. You may need an engineering degree to figure out how your particular car seat works, especially if you bought a fancy

Swedish one. The hospital nurses will help you get the baby strapped in, but you'll need to do the rest. Our advice: get your seat safety checked BEFORE the baby is born to make sure it is correctly installed.

- Where to get help: The National Highway Transportation Safety Administration is the government entity that regulates car seat restraints. They have a helpful web site at www.nhtsa.gov including info on finding someone to check for proper car seat installation (click on "car seat inspections"). Check out www.chop.edu/car seat for a virtual car seat demonstration sponsored by Children's Hospital of Philadelphia.
- New trend: hospitals are now testing premature and small babies in their car seats to be sure they can breathe properly while restrained. Ask your healthcare provider about this simple test if your baby is born before 37 weeks or is under six pounds.

Special Section: The Preemie Primer

Premature babies (before 37 weeks gestation) make up 12.5% of all babies born in the United States each year.[3] While this is certainly not in the master plan for any pregnancy, it could become reality with little notice.

Instead of that special bonding time with your newborn post-delivery, your baby may be whisked away to a neonatal intensive care unit (NICU). Scary? Yep. What a way to be initiated as a new parent! Keep your chin up—most parents graduate from the NICU with healthy babies . . . it just may take a while.

While we don't have enough room in this book to go over all the medical issues you may face with a premature baby, there are two books we'd recommend for further reading: *What to Do When Your Baby is Premature*, by Joseph Garcia-Prats, M.D. and Sharon Hornfischer, R.N. and *Preemies: The Essential Guide for Parents of Premature Babies*, by Dana Linden.

Once you are ready to head home with your preemie graduate, here are some key issues. You'll also find more preemie advice scattered throughout the rest of this book.[4]

Neurologic/Developmental
Intraventricular hemorrhage

If your baby was born before 34 weeks gestation, he's probably had at least one ultrasound to rule out bleeding in the brain (**INTRAVENTRICULAR HEMORRHAGE** or **IVH**). If an abnormality was detected, you will need to follow up with a pediatric neurologist.

Eye exams

If your baby was born before 32 weeks gestation or weighed less than three pounds, a pediatric ophthalmologist has already seen him at the hospital, looking for immaturity of the eyes (**RETINOPATHY OF PREMATURITY OR ROP**). Premature babies are also at risk for **AMBLYOPIA**, **STRABISMUS**, and **REFRACTIVE ERRORS** (see Chapter 14, "Diseases" for details). Your baby will need to have his vision checked periodically by the eye doctor once you go home.

Hearing tests

A routine hearing screen is done on all newborns. Babies who are born prematurely have a ten to 20 times greater risk of hearing loss than full term babies. If an abnormality is detected or concerns arise later, you should follow up with an ear, nose, and throat specialist and an audiologist.

Developmental assessment and therapy

Babies who are born prematurely will be developmentally delayed compared to their peers who are the same age. To know where your child's milestones should be tracking, subtract the number of months missed in pregnancy from the baby's current age to determine the "adjusted age." For example, your four-month-old baby who was born two months early will be expected to have the milestones of a two-month-old.

Preemies should catch up on their milestones by two years of age. However, very low birth weight babies (under three pounds), are at risk for language, motor, and learning delays. All premature babies should be assessed by developmental assessment program (often referred to as "Early Childhood Intervention") in your community.

Respiratory

Apnea of prematurity

If your baby has trouble remembering to breathe (**APNEA OF PREMATURITY OR AOP**), your doctor may prescribe medication (caffeine) and a breathing monitor. Parents will need to download data from the monitor periodically and review those findings with a lung specialist.

Chronic lung disease

If your baby has chronic lung disease (**BRONCHOPULMONARY DYSPLASIA OR BPD**), you will also need to consult with a lung specialist.

Infectious Diseases

After being a NICU veteran, you have learned the art and science of good hand washing. Keep up the good work at home. No doubt the NICU nurses have instilled the fear of God in you when it comes to infections (especially **RSV**–see below).

RSV/Synagis injections

Depending on the time of year and the age of your baby, she will probably get an injection of Synagis, a medication that contains antibodies to a virus called **RESPIRATORY SYNCYTIAL VIRUS or RSV**. Your baby will need to continue to get Synagis injections on a monthly basis during the peak time RSV hits your community (usually the fall/winter/early spring). You may need a referral to a community resource that administers this injection—many pediatric offices do not routinely stock it. For more information on Synagis, see the Medications section in the Appendix A.

Flu shots

If you are bringing baby home during flu season, be sure your entire household has received a flu shot.

Gastrointestinal

Gastroesophageal reflux

If your premature baby has **GASTROESOPHAGEAL REFLUX** (**GER**), he may be on a prescription medicine even after you come home. The therapeutic dose of that medication is based on his weight. Since he'll be growing like a weed, be sure to ask your pediatrician to re-calculate his dose based on his weight each time you visit the doctor.

Growth/Nutrition

Catch up growth

Your baby will be doing catch up growth for several months. Full-term newborns gain 3/4 to one ounce a day. Ideally, your baby should grow *at least* one ounce a day for the first four months of life. Consider buying or renting an infant scale to weigh your baby once a week for at least the first four to six weeks. Alternatively, you can pop in and borrow your doctor's scale. For information about preemie growth, see the special growth chart for premature babies at the back of this book.

Breastfeeding a preemie

Many preemie grads go home on a diet of both breast milk and high-calorie premature formula (which has 22 calories per ounce).

If you are breastfeeding, you'll probably find that your little one gets tired out long before he fills his tummy. And since your baby is small or weak, he may not be able to rev up your breast milk supply with his demand. Therefore, it's a good idea to pump after nursing sessions to improve your milk production. You may be doing a combination of feeding at the breast, and supplementing with expressed breast milk from a bottle. Our advice: it's wise to meet with a lactation consultant to make sure breastfeeding is successful. If you are exclusively breastfeeding, your baby may need "human milk fortifier" added to expressed milk to increase his calcium, phosphorous, and caloric intake.

Babies who were less than three pounds at birth (very low birth weight or VLBW) and those who had poor growth in the NICU should probably get at least two bottles of high-calorie premature formula a day. This should continue until the baby is nine months old (adjusted age) to improve bone growth.[5]

Premature formula

Whether you are breastfeeding and adding human milk fortifier, breastfeeding and supplementing with high-calorie premature formula, or exclusively formula feeding with high-calorie formula, there is no magic age or weight at which you can discontinue fortifying or switch to the regular (and cheaper) formula. As we discussed above, very low birth-weight babies (under three pounds at birth) should probably remain on the premature formula until nine months adjusted age. For bigger preemie grads, there's less consensus on when to make the switch.[6]

Vitamin supplements

Premature babies may benefit from a daily multivitamin and iron supplement, depending on what they are eating (breast milk/formula). If your baby is sent home from the NICU on these supplements, you can continue them for the first year of life.

Feeding schedules

Your baby was probably on a rigid feeding schedule of every three hours in the NICU. Once you are home, if your baby sticks with that routine, great. Depending on how old your baby is when he leaves the NICU and how he is growing, you may be able to relax that schedule a bit, and even let him sleep at night if he wants to—be sure you have the green light to do this from your doc, however.

Dental

Premature babies are at increased risk of poor development of tooth enamel (**ENAMEL HYPOPLASIA**) as well as cavities. Be aware of these potential problems. You should visit a dentist at your baby's first birthday.

Sleep

You may still need to wake your baby up at night for feedings, depending on his age and growth.

But even if your doc gives you her blessing to let him sleep through the night, your baby may have his own ideas. As you will see in our chapter on sleep, the ability to sleep through the night is based on a baby's neurological maturity. So, if your baby is six months old, but was born three months early, he's really only three months old (brain-wise) ... don't expect miracles.

Safety

You may not be able to use a standard infant car seat to transport your child home from the hospital. Why? Infant car seats do not fully recline so you may find your baby's head plops forward when placed in the car seat causing a blocked airway. For situations like this, you can purchase a car bed, a seat that allows your child to lay flat but still be protected in case of a crash. See our *Baby Bargains* book for more information on car beds. FYI: your child will be given a car seat test before leaving the NICU to be sure you have the appropriate safety seat.

Another tip: parents and caretakers should all take an infant CPR course before going home.

So, let's sum up your to-do list with a preemie:

- Follow-up eye exam.
- Assessment by developmental assessment program (often called Early Childhood Intervention).
- Monthly Synagis injections.
- Flu shots for the entire household.
- Rent/buy infant scale or weigh regularly with pediatrician.
- Get help with breastfeeding. Use human milk fortifier.
- Feed or supplement with high-calorie formula made for premature babies.
- Continue multivitamin and iron supplement, if prescribed.
- Do car seat test before checkout.
- CPR Class for Mom and Dad.

LABOR DAY

The Baby 411 Two-Week Survival Guide
a.k.a. What Do I do NOW?

Okay, now you are ready to take your baby home. Without the luxury of the nursery nurses right down the hall, you are probably scared to death.

Hopefully, this book will be helpful in answering all those questions you have. But remember, your pediatrician or family practitioner is only a phone call away. We've covered the basics in this section, but each chapter in this book has information pertinent to newborns. We'll refer you to those sections for more details.

Q. When can I take my baby outside?

Whenever you feel like it. Let's review some Old Wives' Tales...

- *The baby will catch pneumonia if he is out in the cold weather.* FALSE!
- *The baby will get an ear infection if the wind blows in his ears.* FALSE!

It is perfectly fine to go out for a stroll with your baby at any age. Dress him in the same layers you would wear.

NEW PARENT 411: GERM-O-PHOBIA

Many new parents (especially parents of premature babies) have a mortal fear of germs. And we can understand that. As a doctor, I recommend avoiding crowd scenes and airplane travel for the first four weeks of your baby's life. Why? If your baby catches a bug and develops a fever of 100.4 or more during his first 28 days of life, he must be admitted to a hospital. Yes, even if it is just a cold.

Of course, that doesn't mean you must live in fear and never have contact with the outside world! Here is a Q&A with some practical suggestions to limit your newborn's exposure to germs . . . without going overboard.

- *Can your newborn go for a stroll around the neighborhood?* Yes.
- *Can a few family members and friends come over to your house and hold the newborn?* Yes. But, ask them to wash hands first and not visit if they are sick.
- *Can you hold your newborn if you are sick?* Yes, but wash hands, don't touch your face, and try not to breathe on her! If your spouse can take over the baby chores, go for it. Yes, you can and should continue breastfeeding.
- *Can your newborn be around other children?* Yes, as long as they are not sick. You can have a rule that the children can touch baby's head or feet, but not her hands or mouth.

However, I recommend avoiding crowded restaurants, grocery stores, and airplanes in the wintertime until your baby is four weeks old (if possible). This minimizes exposure to cold and flu viruses that are spread from respiratory droplets (coughs and sneezes). For details, see Chapter 13, "Common Infections."

Next: our detailed two-week survival guide. We've divided this advice into five areas: breathing, feeding, elimination, sleep and skin. Let's go:

1 Breathing. As adults, we breathe about 12 times per minute at an even rate. As we discussed earlier in this chapter, newborns breathe 30 to 40 times per minute and have episodes of *periodic breathing*. This means that your baby may breathe rapidly several times, p-a-u-s-e, then breathe again. This pause can last several seconds (less than ten seconds). This is normal, but is bound to freak you out.

Nasal congestion is normal in the first several weeks of life. Use saline nose drops to flush the secretions

RED FLAGS: Breathing
- When a pause between breaths lasts 15 to 20 seconds.
- If your baby is panting, or breathing over 50 to 60 times per minute.
- If your baby's rib cage sucks in (*retractions*), nostrils flare, or he makes grunting noises.

2 Feeding. Whether you breast or bottle-feed, your newborn will be very sleepy for the first few days. The result? He may fall asleep during a feeding, sometimes after only a few minutes. Encourage your baby to stay awake by rubbing his head, playing with his feet, or unwrapping him and placing him away from your warm body.

How often does a newborn eat?
- A breast-fed baby usually eats every two to three hours (at least eight times in 24 hours).
- A formula-fed baby eats about two to three ounces every three to four hours. (six to eight times in 24 hours)

Either way, your baby should wake up spontaneously and eat frequently. In the first two weeks of life, *do not let your newborn go more than 5 hours without eating.* You need to wake him up to feed him if this occurs. (Note: after two weeks of age, if your baby wants sleeps longer and is gaining weight appropriately—let him!)

Mom's breast milk usually arrives on the baby's third to four day of life. Until then, the baby gets antibody rich (but lower-calorie) colostrum when he nurses. This is all your baby needs right now.

Spitting up some milk is normal. It can look fresh or curdled. Both are normal. Vomiting up large volumes at every feeding is not normal.

RED FLAGS: Feeding
- You consistently have to awaken your baby to eat.
- Your baby is consistently vomiting large volumes of milk (i.e. the whole feeding)
- If nursing, your milk has not come in after three or four days.

For more information on this topic, check out Chapter 5, "Nutrition and Growth," Chapter 6 "Liquids" and Chapter 8, "The Other End." See the end of this section for a handy guide to keep track of feedings.

3 **ELIMINATION**. Your newborn's body is just learning how things work initially. In the first 24 hours of life, he may pee (urinate) and poop (stool) only once. When he really begins to take food in, things should start to come out. This is a good way to tell if your infant is eating enough, particularly if you are nursing. Your hospital may give you a diary to keep track of intake and output.

Urine: By the third day of life, your baby should pee at least four times a day. By one week of age, six to 12 wet diapers a day is normal.

Stool: The first few poops are called **MECONIUM** and are black and *tarry* looking.

RED FLAGS: Elimination
◆ Your baby is not urinating at least every six hours.
◆ Your baby's poop looks red, mucousy, or does not change from the black meconium.
◆ Your baby's poop looks like yours.

For more information, check out Chapter 8, "The Other End" as well as our website at Baby411.com for pictures!

4 **SLEEP.** Your baby sleeps 17 to 20 hours a day, but rarely more than four to five hours at a time. He may be very hard to console initially and force you to walk with him or rock him to sleep. *You can't spoil a newborn.* Do what it takes to get him to sleep. Bad habits happen AFTER two months of age.

RED FLAGS: Sleep
◆ Your baby consistently needs to be awakened to eat.
◆ Your baby is completely inconsolable for over three hours straight.

For more information, check out Chapter 9, "Sleep."

5 **SKIN.** Your newborn may have a few bruises from delivery that will fade with time. He may also have a few rashes—also normal.

As we discussed earlier in this chapter, a yellow appearance to the skin,

NEW PARENT 411: DR. BROWN'S STOOL RULES

1. Once your baby starts to eat, his poop will change colors and texture.
2. Breastfed babies often have yellow, watery, seedy poop.
3. Formula fed babies often have green, pasty strained-peas poop.
4. Any shade of yellow, green, or brown is normal.
5. Stool frequency can vary from once every feeding to once a week. The frequency is not an indication of constipation— the texture is.
6. *All* babies turn red and grunt when they poop, not just yours.

called *jaundice*, is often normal, but is something that should be followed. Your baby's liver is just starting its job of breaking down a body waste called bilirubin. Until this happens, the skin on the face may be a little yellow as a result of the bilirubin's pigment. That's okay. What is NOT normal: if you see this in the first 24 hours of life, or if the yellow color descends below your baby's waistline.

The umbilical cord takes one to four weeks to fall off. Until then, the stump is gooey. This is normal. If the skin around the cord is getting infected (see **OMPHALITIS**), the area is red, tender, and foul smelling.

RED FLAGS: Skin

◆ Jaundice occurs in the first 24 hours of life or below the waistline once you get home.

◆ Redness of the skin around the umbilical cord, or pus draining from it. *See Chapter 4, "Hygiene" and the glossary for more information.*

NEW DAD 411: 4 TIPS FOR NEW FATHERS

Hello Dads! Yes, we know you read baby books too—so let's go over a few specific new dad tips to help out in those first days.

1. BYOW. That is, Bring Your Own Wipes. Surprise! You, Daddy-o, will be doing most of the diaper changes at the hospital—especially if your spouse had a C-section. But as we discussed earlier, those first poops will not be pretty (meconium, that black, tar-like stuff). Now, the hospital will probably give you gauze pads and water for this task . . . and that frankly won't be up to the job. Our advice: bring in your own baby wipes. If for some reason your baby's skin is super sensitive, you can go back to the gauze if necessary.

2. Pay attention to the lactation consultant (LC). If your spouse is breastfeeding, you will need to watch how the baby latches on to the breast (that's where a LC works her magic). After the LC departs, you may need to help position the baby's mouth on mom's nipple (it sometimes takes four hands to maneuver this in the early days). *You will be the lactation consultant at home, so take notes!*

3. Sleep when you can. The first few days of your baby's life is so exciting. Well-wishers are calling and visiting you throughout the day. Guess what—that's when your baby is sleeping! You will then be up all night with the little rugrat. So, take advantage of daylight hours to catch a nap and encourage your spouse to do the same. Turn off those cell phones and Blackberries.

4. Smile, nod and be supportive. Your partner will be on a hormonal roller coaster after delivery. That will equate to laughter one moment and tears another. Be on the lookout for something above and beyond normal emotions. (See the discussion on baby blues and postpartum depression on the next page.)

Labor Day

6 FEVERS. We'll discuss fevers in-depth in Chapter 15, "First Aid." For now, read the red flags below for the basics.

RED FLAGS: Fever

From birth to three months of age, *any* fever can be a sign of a serious infection. You need to call your doctor immediately if your baby has a temperature greater than 100.3 F taken *rectally*. (See the section how to take a rectal temp in Chapter 15, "First Aid").

Ear thermometers tend to be unreliable and since a fever in an infant is so concerning, these are not recommended for use.

Fever medications should not be used for infants under three months of age unless recommended by your doctor (for example, when your baby is vaccinated).

Q. **My mother/mother-in-law will be helping me for the first couple of weeks at home. Do you have any suggestions to keep my sanity?**

Baby Blues

Here is a newsflash for you...your life will never be the same. I know, everyone has told you this during your entire pregnancy. But by now reality has hit you like a sledgehammer. Becoming a parent is the most amazing experience of your life—so why are you crying right now?!!

Let's see. Your physical body feels like it was run over by a truck. Your hormone levels are off the charts. You haven't had a good night's sleep since the baby was born. You understand why sleep deprivation is used as a form of torture in POW camps. You find it difficult to make rational decisions, or any decisions for that matter.

Here's another newsflash for you . . . you are normal. No matter how wonderful it is to become a parent, it takes time for your body and mind to adjust to it.

RED FLAGS: When Mom has Postpartum Depression

The Baby Blues are short-term feelings of sadness that subside after a few much needed breaks provided by supportive family and friends. Postpartum depression doesn't go away that easily. Here are the clues that professional help is needed:

1. Frequent episodes of crying or weepiness.
2. Flat "affect" (Mom won't smile).
3. Lack of interest in the family or activities.
4. Loss of appetite.

Mothers who experience postpartum depression often don't recognize the clues. If a family member expresses concerns about you, be smart and let them get you some help!

Some people get along with their parents and in-laws better than others. But even if you have a terrific relationship, a newborn makes things more stressful. New moms are sleep deprived, healing from childbirth, and off-the-charts hormonally. Throw in a well-meaning grandmother who wants to share her sage advice—which often is interpreted as criticism—and it takes you over the edge.

So, before the fireworks start, think about *how* you and your mother (or mother-in-law) will spend time together. A few suggestions:

♦ *Baby chores.* If you are breastfeeding, put grandma in charge of everything else baby: diaper changes, rocking, bathing. It will be her pleasure to do it.

♦ *Household chores.* Don't be a control freak. Let her cook, clean, or even run a few errands.

♦ *Ask for advice on small matters.* "How did you swaddle your babies?" It will make her feel important—and that her opinion is valued.

♦ *Avoid conflict.* If you run into conflicting parenting approaches, feel free to quote your pediatrician's advice (feel free to blame any controversial decision on your doc).

On the next page, we have a feeding and elimination chart—this will help you track your newborn's pee and poop for the first seven days. After day eight, you'll be an old pro.

Tech-savvy families can track these items on a software program called Baby Manager by Babblesoft (web: babblesoft.com). The program works on PC and Pocket PC-based PDAs. Or if you're a techie, you can create your own little Excel spreadsheet to keep track of things.

New Parent 411: The Newborn Hold

If you have never held a newborn, keep reading. Newborns have poor control of their neck muscles, and thus, cannot hold their relatively large heads up. If possible, hold your newborn with two hands, one supporting the body, and one supporting the head. If you don't have two free hands, cradle her head in the crook of your arm (kind of like a football, dads). With a little practice, you'll be an old pro in no time.

LABOR DAY

Handy Feeding & Elimination Table: The First 7 Days

Instructions: Circle the hour your baby nurses.
Circle W for wet diaper (urine). Circle S for soiled diaper (poop).

Day 1
Goal 6-8 feedings
Diapers: 1 wet, 1 soiled

12am 1 2 3 4 5 6 7 8 9 10 11 12pm 1 2 3 4 5 6 7 8 9 10 11

W   S   (black, tarry)

Day 2
Goal 8-12 feedings
2 wet   2 soiled

12m 1a 2 3 4 5 6 7 8 9 10 11 12pm 1 2 3 4 5 6 7 8 9 10 11

W W   S S   (black/brown)

Day 3
Goal 8-12 feedings
2 wet   2 soiled

12m 1a 2 3 4 5 6 7 8 9 10 11 12pm 1 2 3 4 5 6 7 8 9 10 11

W W   S S   (green, yellow)

Day 4
Goal 8-12 feedings
4 wet   3 soiled

12m 1a 2 3 4 5 6 7 8 9 10 11 12pm 1 2 3 4 5 6 7 8 9 10 11

W W W W   S S S   (yellow)

Day 5
Goal 8-12 feedings
5 wet   3 soiled

12m 1a 2 3 4 5 6 7 8 9 10 11 12pm 1 2 3 4 5 6 7 8 9 10 11

W W W W W   S S S   (yellow)

Day 6
Goal 8-12 feedings
6 wet   4 soiled

12m 1a 2 3 4 5 6 7 8 9 10 11 12pm 1 2 3 4 5 6 7 8 9 10 11

W W W W W W   S S S S

Day 7
Goal 8-12 feedings
6 wet   4 soiled

12m 1a 2 3 4 5 6 7 8 9 10 11 12pm 1 2 3 4 5 6 7 8 9 10 11

W W W W W W   S S S S

Baby 411

Section 2

Care & Feeding

Hygiene

The Spa Treatment

Chapter 4

"Ray! You take that diaper off your head, you put it back onto your sister!"
~ Raising Arizona

What's in this Chapter

- ◆ The first manicure
- ◆ Yes, it's okay to use diaper wipes
- ◆ How many layers of clothing your baby really needs
- ◆ What to do about diaper rashes
- ◆ Belly button/cord care
- ◆ Soaps, cremes, and detergents
- ◆ Cradle cap
- ◆ Sunblock and insect repellents
- ◆ The Boy parts
- ◆ The Girl parts
- ◆ Thrush, dental care, and drool

You survived nine months of pregnancy, Labor Day and the hospital food after your baby was born. Now the fun begins—it's time to take baby home.

Due to budget cutbacks at the federal government, babies are no longer sent home with personal butlers or detailed care instructions on cleaning and hygiene. Just kidding! They never used to do that. You are expected to know about this stuff on your own. Consider this chapter your baby care primer.

So first, let's talk candidly about diaper rash. No it isn't pretty, but there are several steps you can take to stop it. Next, it's on to belly button care. Also, we'll discuss the topic of dressing your baby as well as tips on cradle cap, sun block, dental care and more. And let's talk about your baby's private parts—you've got questions and we've got the answers, handily divided into boy and girl sections.

Q. When can I clip my newborn's nails?

Around three to four weeks of life.

The fingertip and nail are stuck together for the first few weeks. Attempts to use a nail clipper will result in drawing blood. For now, you can use a nail file and give your baby a manicure.

Helpful Hint
You can place socks on your baby's hands if he is scratching his face and you want nice pictures.

Q. When can I use diaper wipes?

Now.

Most hospital nurseries use gauze pads soaked in water for diaper cleanups. This is done to prevent potential skin irritation. The truth is that most babies have no problem with typical diaper wipes.

Helpful Hint
Some parents like to keep antibacterial hand sanitizer at the changing table (for mom and dad's hands). It's not a bad idea, since you need to keep your hands and your eyes on your baby.

DR B'S OPINION

"Bring your own diaper wipes to the hospital. If your baby's skin gets irritated, then you can use water and gauze pads. After your first diaper change cleaning meconium (see Chapter 8), you will understand why I recommend using diaper wipes."

Q. How many layers of clothing does my baby need to wear?

As many as you do.

Babies live at the same body temperature as we all do. They will be comfortable in the same number of clothes as you are. It is true that your baby loses heat a little more quickly than you, so keep an eye on him in cooler weather.

Reality Check
Parents often dress their babies for an arctic freeze in July. Then they wonder why their baby has a heat rash.

Old Wives Tale
My baby will catch pneumonia if he gets cold.
Your baby's body temperature will drop if he is outside in cold weather for a prolonged period of time and is not dressed for it. Pneumonia is an infectious disease. It does not infect people who are cold; pneumonia infects people who *have* a cold.

Q. How often do I clean the belly button?

While the idea of cleaning your baby's belly button may seem a no-brainer, there is actually quite a bit of debate about it. According to the American Academy of Pediatrics, "no single method of umbilical cord care has proved to be superior in preventing...disease (that is, infection of the belly button)."[1] Therefore you may find some variability in what hospital nurseries do. Some apply antibiotic solutions, "triple-dye" (an antiseptic) or alcohol to the cord. The current trend among hospitals, however, is moving AWAY from these treatments. Why? Some research suggests the stump may heal faster if simply left alone.[2] Your doctor will probably have his or

HYGIENE

TREATING DIAPER RASH: 5 TIPS & TRICKS

There are basically two kinds of diaper rashes:

Irritated skin. Flat red rash caused when poop and pee break down the skin, causing redness and irritation.

Yeast infection. Raised, pimply rash surrounds an area that looks like raw meat. (Yeast likes the diaper area because it is dark, warm, and moist.)

Curious to see exactly what these different rashes look like? Check out our web site at Baby411.com (click on Bonus Material). For basic skin irritation, creating a barrier to protect the skin from further insults is key. Here are our tips:

1. **Use petroleum jelly** (Vaseline) **or zinc oxide** (store brand: Balmex, Desitin) at every diaper change. Avoid powders—baby can inhale the powder into his lungs when it is poured out. Creams are a better bet.
2. **Let your baby "air dry."** If you are feeling brave, let your baby go bare bottomed for a while. For the less ambitious types, use a blow dryer on a cool setting and dry the diaper area after cleaning.
3. **For more severe rashes,** try Dr. Smith's Diaper Ointment, Triple Paste, or Boudreaux's Butt Paste. These products are a little thicker and more protective. Although they are available over-the-counter, you may have to ask your pharmacist to order some for you.
4. **Use pure lanolin** (Lansinoh). Many women use this for cracked nipples caused by breastfeeding. It's very expensive to recommend as a first line of defense against diaper rash, but if you have it in the house, use it.
5. **If the rash looks like yeast, try an over-the-counter antifungal** (e.g. Lotrimin AF)—the package will say it's for jock itch and athlete's foot. Don't be alarmed. Apply twice daily for a week.

If none of these tricks work, check in with your doctor. Most pediatricians and family practitioners have additional tips for stopping diaper rash.

her own preference.

So what do you do with the umbilical cord stump once you get home? Well you can't just pretend it's not there and ignore it! Check on it at diaper changes, and clean it at least once a day. Keep an eye out for infection too. Infection clues: redness and swelling around the cord, continued bleeding, yellowish pus and/or foul smelling discharge from the area.

How should you clean the belly button? You have two choices: sterile water or rubbing alcohol. The time-honored method is alcohol. But we now know that using rubbing alcohol does not prevent infection or make the cord fall off any faster. The only benefit to using alcohol on the cord stump is to keep the belly button from getting stinky. Alcohol should be applied to the BASE of the belly button, where the gooey stuff is—exactly where you are afraid to go.[3]

The alternative: you can spot clean the cord with sterile water on a gauze pad if it gets dirty. Whichever method you choose, just make sure the cord stump stays clean.

RED FLAG: Belly Buttons

A foul smelling belly button with pus draining from it and surrounded by red skin indicates infection (see **OMPHALITIS**). You need to call your doctor immediately.

Q. When will my newborn get his first bath?

Your baby will get cleaned up shortly after delivery. Most hospitals will sponge bathe newborns and recommend parents do the same at home until the umbilical cord falls off. Babies don't get that dirty and sponge bathing minimizes heat loss.

Sponge-bathing also keeps the umbilical cord dry until it falls off. You can sponge bath your baby with soap, water, and a washcloth every few days. Once the cord falls off, you can give him his first real bath.

Feedback from the Real World

Some hospitals have changed their bath procedures for newborns. For example, Hoag Hospital in Newport Beach, CA has abandoned the age-old tradition of sponge-bathing and are now immersing their newborns in a full bath right after delivery. The Association of Women's Health Obstetric and Neonatal Nurses supports this practice, so you may see it popping up in a hospital near you in the future. We should point out that while your hospital may do an immersion bath, we advise a sponge bath until the umbilical cord stump falls off.

Q. How often should I bathe my baby?

As often as you wish.

You can bathe your baby every day if you like. Many parents and babies enjoy the time together. On the other hand, your baby does not make body odor or play in the sandbox yet. You can bathe him as infrequently as two to three times per week.

Q. What soap products should I use on my baby?

We like Dove soap, because it is perfume and dye free. Plus, it has a moisturizer (particularly good for babies with eczema). And it's cheap. Johnson and Johnson's hypoallergenic baby shampoo is fine.

Helpful Hint

A good rule for baby products—if it smells good or has a color, don't use it on your baby.

Q. Can I put lotion on my baby's dry skin?

Sure. Just be sure it is perfume-free and dye-free.

Most newborns have dry skin from swimming around in water (technical term: amniotic fluid) for nine months. We personally recommend hydrated petroleum jelly (Creamy Vaseline is one brand name). When it comes to dry skin, the greasier the better. One warning: there are products claiming to be "hypoallergenic" or "natural" that contain food products which are highly ALLERGENIC. Avoid products that contain milk, almond, or peanuts (or arachis oil) in their ingredients. If you don't already read labels, get used to it now. You should be careful about anything that goes in your baby's mouth or on her skin.

Q. My baby has acne. Should I buy some Oxy 10?

No. Do nothing and it goes away by eight weeks of life.

Acne develops from your baby's rapidly changing body hormones. It is the worst from age four to eight weeks. Putting creams and lotions on the skin only makes it worse. Most importantly, your baby is not bothered by it.

Q. What laundry detergent do I use to clean baby's clothes? Do I really need to wash everything before I use it?

It depends on the baby.

Stick with the perfume-free and dye-free rule, especially for babies with

BATHING BABY 411: THE 10 STEP METHOD

Never bathed a baby before? Relax. Here is your 10 step how-to guide for a sponge bath:

1. **Get everything ready first.** Have two baby towels, washcloth, a bowl of warm soapy water and a bowl of warm water for rinsing, baby comb, shampoo, fresh diaper, and clean outfit.
2. **Place a towel in the infant tub** (you won't be filling the tub with water).
3. **Put naked baby onto the towel in the tub.** Cover all body parts not being cleaned at the moment.
4. **Expose one body part at a time (starting head to toe) and wash with soapy water except eye areas.** Rinse.
5. **Take the other towel and dry the area that has been cleaned.**
6. **Be sure to get into the creases,** especially under the chin/neck.
7. **Shampoo hair, rinse, and dry quickly.**
8. **Move baby from the towel he is sitting in and dry him completely with the other towel.**
9. **Diaper and dress.**
10. **Clean up mess later.**

sensitive skin. But, that does NOT necessarily mean that your baby's laundry needs to be washed separately with his own expensive detergent. The whole family's laundry can be done with a product like ALL Free and Clear or Tide Free.

For the baby with sensitive skin, pre-wash items that will be touching him. It may also be helpful to double rinse the laundry. And remember to avoid dryer sheets (they all contain perfume).

Helpful Hint

Have a spray bottle of stain remover next to baby's laundry basket. You'll probably need it for the shoulders on all of your shirts, too. For more laundry tips, check out our other book, *Baby Bargains* (see back of the book for details). Another seasoned parent tip: if you've been thinking about getting a new washing machine, now is the time. Newer, front-loading washers really do clean clothes better. Considering the time you and your washer will be spending together, it is probably worth the investment.

Q. What is the scaly stuff in my baby's hair?

For twenty points, Alex, what is cradle cap?

Cradle cap (see **SEBORRHEA**) is caused by baby's hormonal changes and possibly due to yeast. It makes the scalp and eyebrow skin get dry, flaking patches. It can last for several months.

Because it is similar to dandruff, it can be treated the same way. Anti-dandruff shampoos (Head and Shoulders, Selsun Blue, Sebulex) work well if used two or three times a week. You can also massage vegetable oil into the areas and lift the scales up with an old toothbrush. Some doctors will use an anti-yeast product like Nizoral AD shampoo (over the counter) for resilient cases.

Eyebrows can be treated with 1% Hydrocortisone cream (over the counter) twice daily for a week.

Reality Check: Cradle cap may bother you, but it doesn't bother your baby.

Q. Does my baby need a waxing? She has hair on her ears and on her back.

Nope. We know it is cosmetically undesirable (especially for those baby girls), but it's not permanent. What's not normal: pubic hair or armpit hair—time to call your doctor if you see this before puberty.

Q. When can my baby start using sunblock?

Now. Sunblock can be applied to newborns.

The AAP *previously* recommended that sunblock be used only in infants over six months of age (because of the potential for skin irritation). However, the risk of skin cancer (1 in 75 over a lifetime) has outweighed concerns over potential skin irritation. Suncreen is critical because sun damage and sunburn at an early age is correlated with a higher risk of skin cancer later in life. Translation: use the suncreen on that baby. Any product with a SPF of 30 is fine; anything higher is a waste of money. Other tips:

try to keep baby out of the sun, especially from 10am to 4pm every day, apply sunscreen liberally (at least a half ounce each time) and reapply frequently (every two hours).

What sunscreen is best? Check out our other book, *Toddler Bargains* (see back of this book for details) for a discussion on sunscreens and which ones we found work best. Also: *Consumer Reports* has a report on suncreen on their web site (www.consumerreports.com) that includes product tests, ratings and more.

The key to preventing sunburn is to RE-APPLY the sunblock frequently—don't buy the combo sunblock and bug repellent (we'll explain why next).

ECZEMA: ADVICE ON DEALING WITH DRY SKIN

Some babies develop dry, scaly patches on the skin (see **ECZEMA**). It gets worse when the skin is dry. The key to keeping it in check is using a moisturizing soap and frequent applications of moisturizing cream. For some reason our family (the Fields) has been unlucky enough to be plagued by eczema. Perhaps its thanks to the ultra-dry climate here in Colorado, where the relative humidity is often measured in single digits. Mom, Dad and both boys have had it, including one child with severe, chronic eczema. Here are our tips for living with this itchy-scratchy skin condition:

1. **Baths:** Avoid bubble baths, oils, perfumes, dyes, and detergents. Try Dove bar soap (not the liquid), Aveeno, or Cal-Ben's Seafoam liquid soap (available online or at natural food stores)

2. **Moisturize constantly.** As a side benefit, this is a great way to bond with your baby when you massage lotions or creams into his skin frequently. A room humidifier will help introduce moisture as well.

3. **Avoid detergents.** If your baby has severe eczema, this family commitment may be worth the effort. Detergents may break down already sensitive skin. Avoid all detergents in the home—yes that means dishwashing, laundry, and personal hygiene products. Try Cal-Ben's products: Seafoam Dish Glow, Gold Star Shampoo, and Seafoam liquid soap (www.CalBenPureSoap.com). Another option: www.soap-flakes.com.

4. **Observe** whether eczema shows up when you start adding new foods to baby's diet. Eliminating the offending food will obviously help. And if it happens frequently, you should consider seeing a food allergy specialist.

5. **Don't be afraid** to get a referral to a dermatologist if your baby's eczema gets really bad. Dermatologists are skin experts with knowledge of the newest treatments.

Old Wives Tale
Dark skinned people do not need to wear sunblock.
All humans who have skin need to wear sunblock. While it is true that darker-pigmented people have less risk of skin cancer, there is still a risk and prevention is easy.

Q. My spouse and I are both African-American and our newborn looks white! Is this normal?

Yes. The skin pigmentation, called melanin, develops as the baby grows. Babies born with light skin may get significantly darker with time.

Q. When should I apply insect repellent on my baby?

When your baby is at least two months of age.

Mosquitoes and ticks are known carriers of illness. The most notable diseases in the United States spread by these bugs are West Nile Virus (mosquitoes) and Lyme Disease (deer ticks). The safest option to avoid mosquitoes is to stay inside at dawn and at dusk, when they are out in greatest numbers. It's also a good idea to wear light colored clothing, long sleeves, and long pants when your baby is outside.

As far as insect repellents go, the most effective products contain DEET, picaridin (sold as Cutter Advanced or Off Skintastic), or Oil of Lemon Eucalyptus. While Oil of Lemon Eucalyptus is effective, it is not recommended for kids under three years of age.

Many parents want to avoid using harsh chemicals on their child's skin and have turned to citronella-based repellents. A recent study, however, showed that products containing citronella repelled mosquitoes for a mere 9.6 minutes, while 23% DEET will repel mosquitoes for five *hours*.[4]

The problem with DEET is that it can be absorbed into the body via the skin and cause "neurotoxic effects" like dizziness (and rare, more serious adverse effects in massive doses). Therefore, you should wash the DEET repellent off once returning indoors. Here are some additional safety tips for using insect repellents on your baby:[5]

1. **Don't use DEET repellents on infants under two months of age.** It's fine AFTER two months of age. Picaridin has had no toxic effects on any human of any age (that we know of).
2. **Young children should not apply repellent themselves—** that's mom and dad's job.
3. **Don't apply repellent under clothing or to wounds. It goes on exposed skin**—yes, that means ALL exposed skin areas, not just the arms or legs.
4. **Don't put any repellent near children's mouths or eyes—** and avoid getting it on their hands.
5. **Insect repellents come in several forms**—the liquids, sprays, washcloths, and lotions are effective. Exception: The DEET wristbands don't work.
6. **When you come back inside, WASH your baby's skin.**
7. **DEET products with a concentration of 30% are as safe as those with 10%.** 30% DEET lasts for five hours, 10% just two hours.

8. **How much DEET should you use?** That depends on how long you plan to be outdoors—10% is fine for less than two hours, etc.
9. **DEET should only be applied once a day.** Picaridin based products should be re-applied every 3–4 hours.

The Boy Parts

Q. When can I stop using gauze around my newborn's circumcision?

This question usually comes up at the two-week well baby check. The nurses at the hospital will show you how to apply a gauze dressing and Vaseline. The skin starts to heal around three or four days after a circumcision procedure is done. It starts to look gross with a yellowish scab. You will think it looks infected, but it's not. When it looks like that, it no longer needs gauze to protect it.

> **Helpful Hint**
> A parent remarked to me, "You need to tell me the endpoint for certain things. Otherwise I'll think I'm just supposed to keep doing it." If you are still putting gauze on your six month old, you have gone above and beyond the call of duty! Bottom Line: If you don't know when to stop, ask your doctor. It will save you a lot of time and labor.

Q. How do I care for my son's circumcised penis in the long term?

Make sure you always see a definite separation between the head and the shaft of the penis.

When you change your baby's diaper, gently pull down at the base of the penis and clean the area where the head meets the shaft. This area collects dead skin (this is called smegma; memo to Seattle-area musicians, this would be a great band name). If the smegma remains there, it can cause the head and shaft to adhere together (see **PENILE ADHESION**; second memo to Seattle bands—this is NOT a good name).

Q. My son's circumcised penis is stuck and I can't see the head. Now what do I do?

There are a few options to "Free Willy" (a patient's father gets the credit for coining this term). If the skin on the shaft is stuck to the head of the penis (see **PENILE ADHESION**), it can be unstuck. The options: applying a prescription steroid cream, manually pulling it apart, or having a surgical procedure to correct it. Check in with your doctor to decide on the best plan. If the adhesion is minor, it may even un-stick on its own.

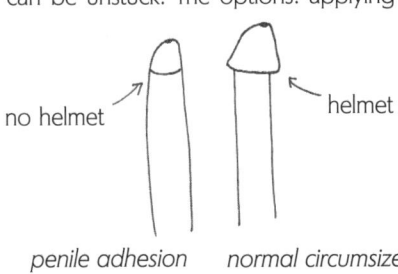

no helmet   *helmet*

penile adhesion   *normal circumsized penis*

Q. How do I care for my son's uncircumcised penis?

Here are four rules:

1. Do NOT forcefully pull the foreskin back to clean the penis.
2. Dead skin (smegma) collects under the foreskin and will come out on its own.
3. Once the foreskin pulls back on its own (usually by age five years), clean under the foreskin one or two times per week with water. Always push the foreskin back down after pulling it up to clean it.
4. Teenagers need to clean under the foreskin daily.

The foreskin is attached to the shaft of the penis with tight tissue called adhesions. Most of the time, these adhesions loosen up by the age of five. Some boys, however, may have adhesions into their teen years and this is still okay (but check it out with your doctor).

Rarely, the foreskin remains tight and hard to pull back (see **PHIMOSIS**). The foreskin can also get pulled back and unable to be manually brought back down (see **PARAPHIMOSIS**).

BOTTOM LINE
If your son has a red, swollen penis, or an abnormal stream of urine, call your doctor.

The Girl Parts

Q. How do I clean my daughter's private parts?

Front to back, and in every crease. Dads—time to pay attention.

Poop has bugs in it (bacteria). Pee (urine) does not. If the poop ends up in the opening to the bladder (urethra), the bacteria will climb in and grow there (see **BLADDER INFECTION/UTI**). This is a bad thing.

Look at your daughter's private parts. Gently separate the lips (labia). You will see two holes. The top hole is the urethra; the bottom hole is the vagina. These areas, including the lips, need to be poop-free zones. Wipe from the top of the genitals, down to the anus. Never go backwards and use several wipes if you need to.

BOTTOM LINE
Don't ever hesitate to change your daughter's poopy diaper, even if it isn't your turn. Delay can lead to a bladder infection.

Q. When can I get my daughter's ears pierced?

Although ear piercing is a safe procedure for your infant, there is no consensus on the right time to do it. Here are some things to consider:

- *Infection*: Inserting a needle through the skin carries a small risk of infection. You might want to wait until your baby is at least four months old.

- *Allergy*: Some people are allergic or sensitive to the metal in the posts or backing. Use either surgical steel or 14k gold products.
- *Scarring*: Some people have poor wound healing where a thickened area of skin forms at the break in the skin. If a family member has this problem, you might want to wait and let your baby decide if she wants to take this risk.
- *Cosmetic result*: Babies can be moving targets. Be sure the person performing the procedure is comfortable with infants or you could end up with uneven results!

Mouth Care

Q. Why is my baby's mouth coated in white? Is that milk?

It is either milk or thrush (a yeast infection in the mouth).

When babies are toothless, their mouths don't have many bacteria (germs) living there. Teeth provide a home for bacteria (that's what plaque is). Remember the yeast diaper rash? Yeast likes dark, warm, wet places that don't have other germs around. A newborn's mouth is a perfect locale.

How do you tell the difference between milk and thrush? Milk wipes off and is only on the tongue. Thrush collects on the gums and inner cheeks and can't be wiped off.

Thrush requires a prescription anti-fungal mouthwash to be treated. Call your doctor.

Helpful Hint

If your baby gets thrush, you need to sterilize any products that go in baby's mouth (rubber nipples, pacifiers), as yeast will continue to grow on these items. Breastfeeding moms frequently develop a yeast infection on their nipples when their baby has thrush. See Chapter 6, "Liquids," for top tips to treat yeast infections.

Q. When do baby's teeth come in?

Around six to 12 months old. There are some kids whose teeth come in earlier or later, though. Universally, the first tooth to erupt is a bottom, middle one. The rest come in randomly. See the chart on the next page for more info on which teeth come in when.

New Parent 411: Baby toothpaste

Let's talk baby toothpaste. Fluoride-free "kid" toothpaste is okay to use for infants, but the sweet taste encourages your baby to suck on the toothbrush as soon as you get it in his mouth. Bottom line: special baby toothpaste is not really necessary—it's expensive and it's hard to maneuver the toothbrush with the baby sucking on it.

HYGIENE

Reality Check

Drool is not a reliable indicator of teething. All four-month-olds are drooling and usually toothless. Why? The salivary glands are getting revved up at this age to start digesting solid foods.

Baby Teeth

Tooth	Age Tooth Comes In (mo)
Upper Central incisor	9.6
Upper Lateral incisor	12.4
Upper Cuspid	18.3
Upper 1st primary molar	15.7
Upper 2nd primary molar	26.2
Lower 2nd primary molar	26.0
Lower 1st primary molar	15.1
Lower Cuspid	18.2
Lower Lateral incisor	11.5
Lower Central incisor	7.8

Q. How can I tell if my baby is teething?

Babies have a lower coping threshold and trouble settling down. The pain of throbbing gums can usually be forgotten when a baby is busy playing.

First-year molars come in somewhere between 12 to 18 months old, even if the more central teeth are not in yet. Don't be fooled when your baby starts pulling on his ears—it's most likely not an ear infection. Look in his mouth. It's often the jaw pain from the molars that causes the ear pulling. It will save you a trip to the doctor.

Feedback from the Real World

Seth Silber, a seven-month-old from Austin, TX likes to gnaw on frozen celery when he is teething. His dad claims it works like magic.

Helpful Hint

Acetaminophen (Tylenol) is the safest and most effective medication choice for teething pain at bedtime. For daytime, try frozen mini-bagels or a cold teething ring to gnaw on. Teething gels (Numzit, Oragel) are short lasting and can have unwanted side effects. Homeopathic teething tablets, considered "safe" by poison control, do contain trace amounts of belladonna (a toxin) and caffeine.

Q. When do I start cleaning baby's teeth?

According to Steven Adair, DDS, MS, Professor and Chair of Pediatric Dentistry at the Medical College of Georgia, you should wipe your baby's mouth with a soft cloth after every feeding even before he has teeth.

Start regular tooth care when your baby's first tooth comes in. Use a wet washcloth or soft bristle brush to wipe the teeth, at least twice daily. You absolutely need to clean your baby's teeth AFTER the last feeding of the night. Otherwise, you will promote tooth decay (cavities).

Personally, I do not recommend using the fluoride-free tooth gels because babies like to suck on it and it interferes with your ability to get into their mouths and clean. Water and wiping/brushing is sufficient. I usually recommend using a pea-sized amount fluoride toothpaste when your child can spit it out (around age three years). Some dentists will recommend starting fluoride toothpaste earlier, depending on your child's individual risk of cavities and his daily fluoride intake.

Q. When is the first trip to the dentist?

For children who are at higher risk of tooth decay, the American Academy of Pediatrics recommends a dental visit at one year of age. Those babies that fall into the high-risk category include kids:

- Whose mothers have cavities.
- With special medical needs.
- With teeth who sleep with a formula bottle or breastfeed throughout the night.
- With plaque buildup on their teeth.

However, even if your baby doesn't fall into a high-risk category, pediatric dentists think (and we agree) it is a good idea for ALL kids to have an initial dental visit around their first birthday so you can establish a "dental home." You'll then have a point person if you have questions or a dental emergency. Your child can visit the dentist every six months after that. While a professional cleaning may not happen until your child is two years old, these early visits can provide guidance and direction.

FYI: Tooth decay is contagious. Plaque is bacteria that can be passed from person to person. So it is NOT recommended that parents share food utensils or clean pacifiers by using their saliva (that's kind of gross if you think about it, anyway).[6]

Q. My baby has a snotty nose. What can I do about it?

All newborns have nasal congestion for four to six weeks after birth. It's not a cold.

Some congested babies are extraordinarily loud. They may snort, snore, cough, and sneeze. It is all normal. If the congestion interferes with feedings or sleep, use saline nose drops to clear the mucus.

Saline is just salt water (1/2 tsp salt to 8oz water). You can make it or buy it. It is impossible to overdose and can be used any time your baby has thick mucus or congestion. Shoot several drops in each nostril before feedings. *You don't need to suck it out with a bulb syringe.*

The saline will either make your baby sneeze or loosen the mucus enough for the baby to swallow it.

BOTTOM LINE
Leave the bulb syringe at the hospital!
Bulb syringes can irritate a baby's nostrils to the point of nosebleeds. And if you don't evacuate the air in the bulb before sucking out the snot, you may get some unpleasant results. One family I know tried this…the baby was shocked and held its breath. The parents were shocked and called 911. Saline drops are a more effective and less traumatic way to deal with baby snot.

Notes

Nutrition & Growth

Chapter 5

"A baby is an inestimable blessing and bother."
~ Mark Twain

What's in this Chapter

- **What growth charts mean**
- **How infants grow (height, head size, weight)**
- **Teeth**
- **Calories & nutrition for the first year**
- **Feeding schedules, or lack thereof**
- **Vitamin supplements**
- **Overeating, obesity, and the Body Mass Index**
- **Calcium, fiber, and iron**
- **Once your child turns one**

Welcome to the world of food. This section of *Baby 411* is dedicated to growth and nutrition—first, we'll look at the general questions you might have about your baby's growth, like what those ominous-looking growth charts really mean. We'll also discuss HOW your baby will grow (height, head size, weight), as well as the needed calorie and nutrition for the first year. Should you put your baby on a feeding schedule? We'll hit that hot-button issue here, as well as discuss vitamin supplements, obesity and your baby's needs for calcium, fiber and iron.

The next two chapters (six and seven) will get into the nuts and bolts of nutrition, as we discuss liquids (breast milk, formula, juice) and solids (baby and table foods). But first things first—let's dive into Baby Nutrition 101.

Infant Growth

Q. At my baby's well checks, my doctor charts her growth on a chart. What's this for?

Growth charts help your doctor follow the trends of your child's growth.

Your baby's height, weight, and head size are checked at every well child visit. (Weight is usually checked at sick visits too, to assess the severity of an illness—for example, dehydration—and in case medication needs to be prescribed). Most doctors currently compare your child's statistics to standard charts provided by the Centers for Disease Control (CDC). These charts were created in 2000. The percentiles on the charts compare your child to other children the same age and gender in America. (For example, a boy in the 75th percentile for height is taller than 75% of boys his age.)

As a side note, the World Health Organization (WHO) created new growth charts in 2006 that may be phased in over the next few years. Why new charts, you may ask? The WHO's charts are based on how a *breastfed* baby should grow, regardless of what country she lives in. Breastfed babies gain slightly less weight than their formula-fed counterparts from four to six months of life—and therefore may look like they are not thriving on the CDC's charts. Breastfed babies also weigh less than formula-fed babies at their first birthdays.[1] See Appendix E for CDC growth charts (birth to 36 months) for boys and girls; see our web site (Baby411.com, Bonus Material) to find the WHO growth charts.

The key issue: is your baby's growth consistent? In other words, if your child is at the 50th percentile for height at three months, he should roughly be at the 50th percentile at six months. What if your child's height and weight percentiles are significantly different? We'll address the issue with a discussion of the Body Mass Index later in this chapter. Also later: what if you child's head size is growing too fast or too slow? We'll cover that too.

Q. How much weight can I expect my baby to gain in his first year?

Here are some general guidelines. Babies double their birth weight by four to five months of age. They triple their birth weight by one year, and quadruple their birth weight by age 2. After age 2, kids gain about four pounds a year until they hit puberty.

For example: A seven-pound newborn should weigh about 14 pounds at five months and 21 pounds at one year.[2]

Q. How tall will my baby grow in his first year?

Your baby will grow ten inches in his first year, and another four inches by age two. After that, he'll grow three inches a year from ages three to five, then two inches a year until he hits his growth spurt at puberty (rule of thumb is 10-4-3-3-2 inches per year).[3] For example: A 20-inch tall newborn should be about 30 inches tall at one year.

PREEMIES & CATCH-UP GROWTH

Babies born prematurely experience a phenomenon called **CATCH-UP GROWTH**. Most preemies catch up to their peers by the age of two. Your baby's measurements can be plotted on the term baby growth chart both by *chronological age* (determined by birth date) and by *adjusted age* (determined by due date).

The head catches up the fastest, followed by weight, then height.[4]

NUTRITION

Q. Can you predict how tall my baby will be?

For boys: Add five inches to Mom's height and average that number with Dad's height.

For girls: Subtract five inches from Dad's height and average that number with Mom's height.

This number is your baby's growth potential. Of course, some people exceed their potentials and some people never reach their potentials.

The first fairly accurate height predictor is the measurement taken at age two years. Kids have established their growth curves by then. A good rule of thumb is that kids are half of their adult height at age two.

Q. Why do you measure my baby's head size?

Because your baby's brain is also growing at a tremendous rate. Most of this growth occurs in the first two years of life. We want to make sure this is happening, and that the skull is providing enough room for this to happen (see **CRANIOSYNOSTOSIS**).

Some babies have huge heads (see **MACROCEPHALY**) and some babies have tiny heads (see **MICROCEPHALY**). Most of the time, this is thanks to their gene pool. The apple doesn't fall far from the tree. A baby's head size percentile may be completely different than his height or weight percentiles—and that's okay.

The average newborn head size is 35 cm. It grows 12 cm in the first year, and then only 10 cm more for an entire lifetime![5]

Q. My baby has a flat head. Will he need to wear a helmet?

Unlikely. Save the helmet for his first bicycle.

Changes in infant sleep position recommendations have done wonders to reduce the risk of sudden infant death syndrome (SIDS) by 40%. (See Chapter 9, "Sleep" for more discussion of SIDS.) However, many babies have flat heads (official name: **POSITIONAL PLAGIOCEPHALY**) as a result of being placed to sleep on their backs. In most cases, the head shape improves once kids begin to move and reposition themselves during sleep. Helmets are recommended as one of a few treatment options for *severe* flattening, and effective if used only between four and 12 months of age.[6] See the next page for more on this issue.

Q. When does the soft spot (fontanelle) close?

Anywhere between nine to 18 months. The fontanelle gives the brain the growing room it needs.

Pediatricians rely on that soft spot to provide clues for fluid status (dehydration), infection (meningitis), and problems inside the skull (brain tumors, hydrocephalus).

Q. When will my baby's teeth come in?

Anytime between five and 12 months.

Teeth may erupt as early as two months, but that is a rare event. And all you should expect is one tooth by a year of age.

As a rule, the first teeth to erupt are the bottom middle teeth (medial incisors). After that, it's anyone's guess. There is no order to further eruptions. Frequently, a baby's one-year molars will come in before the middle or eye teeth (incisors/canines).

By the way, once the teeth arrive, you need to clean them! See Chapter 4, "Hygiene" for teeth cleaning tips and a handy visual aid to explain which teeth are which.

Flat heads and tummy time!

Why do some babies wear helmets? Why is it important for babies to have tummy time? And what the heck is tummy time, anyway?

Before we answer that, here's a quick 411 on your baby's skull: newborns have skull bones with soft tissue between them (sutures) and a couple of bigger gaps or soft spots (anterior and posterior fontanelles). This skull structure allows the baby's head to squeeze through the birth canal and the brain to grow rapidly in the first two years of life.

By the time the child is two years old, her skull has hardened and those gaps and sutures have closed.

A newborn's malleable skull can put her head at risk for some really odd shapes after delivery. Later if a baby spends much time on her back (or in one position), the skull may flatten. While most newborn heads will eventually round out and look normal, here are some things to be watching for:

◆ *Molding*. Some newborns look like they have a "cone head" because the skull compresses as it goes through the birth canal (more common in vaginal deliveries than C-sections). Babies who have had vacuum- or forceps-assisted deliveries may have pretty dramatic molding or even a large bruise (**CEPHALHEMATOMA**) that can harden and leave a lump on the skull for several weeks. These irregular head shapes are present at birth and resolve by six to eight weeks of life.

◆ *Positional Plagiocephaly.* Yes, we know this is a mouthful—it literally means "oblique (flat) head." Babies who spend significant time lying on their backs or leaning their heads back (sleeping, sitting in a car seat or in an infant swing) are at risk for a flat head. This odd head shape becomes noticeable after eight weeks of life. In most cases, the flattening is mild or moderate, and rounds out over the first year. You can try to avoid this problem by following the tips at the end of this section.

◆ *Torticollis*. A tightening, shortening, or bruising of a neck muscle when baby's head favors in one position for a long time. This becomes a vicious cycle, because the baby then develops a preference for turning his head to one particular side. The result? The skull flattens on one side and the facial structure starts to look asymmetric. **TORTICOLLIS** can be present at birth or begin during infancy. Aggressive neck stretching exercises are required to fix this problem.

◆ *Craniosynostosis*. This is a premature closure of one of the suture lines that sits between the skull bones. Unlike some of these other problems,

CRANIOSYNOSTOSIS is not something that is preventable—it's an uncommon disorder that just happens to some kids. Early closure not only causes a funny looking head shape, but also interferes with the brain's ability to grow. If untreated, these babies can be at risk for vision defects and increased pressure within the skull. Surgery is required to fix this problem.

Now you know how your newborn's skull will change and what problems to look for. But let's look at the most common cause for head-shape problems: sleep position.

Ever since safety advocates recommended infants sleep on their backs, babies have spent an increasing amount of time in that position. Add in time spent in car seats and swings—and you can understand why positional plagiocephaly (flat head) is an increasing concern. Of course, there is a simple answer: tummy time.

So, what is tummy time? Simply put, tummy time is an opportunity for your baby to lie on his belly while awake and practice lifting up his head. This will develop neck and other muscles for head control and rolling over. Tummy time also keeps the pressure OFF the back of baby's head by altering his position.

Here are some simple guidelines for tummy time. For babies age birth to eight weight weeks, offer at least five minutes of tummy time a day. For older babies (two months and up), do tummy time five minutes or more *at least three times a day*.

What if your baby hates tummy time? One idea: have him lie on your chest and he will work to lift up his head. Or get on the floor with baby so it doesn't seem so lonely down there. To help baby lift up his head, you can use a rolled-up receiving blanket under the chest.

What else can you do to prevent a flat head?

◆ Alternate which direction you do diaper changes so your baby has to turn his head both ways to look at you.
◆ Alternate turning your baby's head from left to right on his back when he is sleeping.
◆ Play "airplane" with your baby and let him lift his head to look at you.

What to do once your baby has a flat head or torticollis:

1. Aggressively work on **neck stretching exercises** at home. See Chapter 14, "Common Diseases," for specific advice on exercises you can do.
2. Hire a personal trainer (okay, really it's a **physical therapist**) to help with neck exercises.
3. **Encourage your baby to spend more time holding his head up**—see the tummy time tips above.
4. **Check in with your doctor** every month so she can monitor your baby's progress.
6. If the head is significantly misshapen and not improving with exercise, **consult with a neurosurgeon** and consider a helmet. Again, your doctor should be able to give some guidance.[7]

NUTRITION

Infant Calorie and Nutrition Needs

Q. How quickly will my newborn grow on a day-to-day basis?

Faster than you want him to.

After you look at the following stats, you will never buy newborn clothes as baby gifts again. You can also understand why babies need to eat all the time. It takes a lot of caloric energy to grow that much.

On a day-to-day basis, here is what you can expect:

- *Birth to four days old:* A weight LOSS of 5-10%. As we discussed earlier, babies are born with extra baggage for the trip out into the world.
- *Four days to three months:* A weight GAIN of about 2/3 to one ounce a day (1/2 lb a week). Note: newborns should be back to birth weight by their second week doctor visit.
- *Three months to six months:* A weight gain of about 1/2 to 2/3 ounce a day (1/2 lb every 2 weeks).
- *Six months to 12 months:* A weight gain of about 1/4 to 1/2 ounce a day (3/4 to 1 lb per month).

Q. How many calories does my baby need to eat?

It depends on her age.

The calculations are listed on the next page, but please don't get too wound up about these numbers. Do NOT do calorie counts on your baby. As you can see, your baby's calorie needs will increase as she grows.

Real mom tip: baby's appetite can vary from day to day. This advice also applies to older children. Focus on what your child eats over the space of a week, not every meal. Obsessing over every ounce of milk/formula or spoonful of rice cereal isn't healthy for you or your baby.

That said, here's how many calories a baby typically needs to eat per day (given your baby's weight in kilograms): For babies birth to six months they should consume 110-115 calories per kg in 24 hours. Babies six to 12 months need 100-105 calories per kg in 24 hours. Don't know your baby's weight in kilos? To convert pounds to kilograms, divide the weight in pounds by 2.2. For example, a baby weighing seven pounds would weigh 3.2 kilograms.

Now that we have all the formulas, let's figure out how many calories a seven-pound newborn will need each day to grow normally. Your little

NEW PARENT 411: GROWTH SPURTS

Babies will have growth spurts and their appetites may seem insatiable at times. These episodes usually occur at three weeks, six weeks, and occasionally later in the first year. They may last a couple of days or a week. If you are breastfeeding, do not be alarmed that you can't satisfy your baby. His appetite will ramp up your milk supply.

Common Conversions

For the mathematically challenged (that is, us writers) and for those who have forgotten the metric system, here are the common conversions you'll need to digest this chapter:

cc (cubic centimeter) or ml (milliliter) are ways of measuring fluid volumes.
1cc = 1ml
5cc or 5ml = 1 teaspoon
15cc or 15 ml = 1 tablespoon
3 teaspoons = 1 tablespoon
There are 30cc per ounce, or 2 tablespoons per ounce (oz).
There are 16 ounces (oz) in 1 pound (lb).
There are 2.2 pounds in 1 kilogram (kg).

There will be a quiz on this next Tuesday.

---

bundle of joy needs 368 calories per day (3.2 x 115). Breast milk and formula have 20 calories per ounce. So divide 368 by 20 calories per ounce and you'll find that your baby needs to consume about 19 ounces a day. But, once again, obsessing over every ounce will only give you an overwhelming need for Zantac.

A word on preemies: Premature babies have higher calorie needs to catch up on their growth. Some babies go home from the Neonatal Intensive Care Unit (NICU) with a higher calorie diet requirement. This is achieved with either a higher-calorie formula or a special human-milk fortifier that is added to expressed breast milk.

Q. Can you show me how a baby's calorie needs change for the first year of life?

Okay, here is an example, but remember these are ballpark figures:[8]

Age	Weight (lbs)	Weight (kg)	Calories (per day)	Range (cals/day)	Breast milk or formula per day
Newborn	7 lbs	3.2 kg	368	350-700	19 oz
1 month	8 lbs 4 oz	3.75 kg	432	"	22 oz
2 months	10 lbs 2 oz	4.6 kg	530	"	26 oz
3 months	12 lbs	5.5 kg	630	500-850	31 oz
4 months	13 lbs 14 oz	6.3 kg	720	"	36 oz
6 months	16 lbs 8 oz	7.5 kg	787	600-1000	40 oz
9 months	19 lbs 8 oz	8.9 kg	930	700-1200	liquid + solid food
1 year	21 lbs	9.5 kg	1000	"	liquid + solid food

BOTTOM LINE

Do NOT calculate your baby's dietary needs at every moment. You will drive yourself, your spouse (and your doctor) nuts. This is especially challenging to do if you are breastfeeding and can't see the volume. It's just helpful information to help you gauge things.

The Big Picture: Nutrition For The First Year

The details will become clearer to you as you read through the next couple of chapters, but here is the big picture:

1. **Babies need either formula or breast milk exclusively for the first six months of life.**
2. **Any solid food offerings from four to six months of age should not be considered nutrition.** There's so much debate about this, even two advisory committees of the American Academy of Pediatrics cannot agree on when is the right time to start offering solid foods. However, most pediatricians agree that there is no rush to start and that solid food plays no role in nutrition before six months of age. If you (or grandma) choose to sneak in some solid food from four to six months of life, view it as a treat. In other words, offer a taste or two of solid food when it is *not* feeding time. The exceptions: families with a high risk of food allergies as well as preemies should hold off on any solid foods until six months of age. (for details see Chapter 7, "Solids").
3. **From six to nine months of age, a baby begins eating solid foods,** so he cuts back on liquid nutrition volumes.
4. **From nine to twelve months of age, a baby usually eats three solid meals a day** and takes 20 to 30 oz of breast milk or formula.
5. **After a year of age, breast milk/formula is replaced by whole milk,** with a goal of 16 oz. or dairy serving equivalent a day. Solid food intake becomes three solid meals and one to two snacks per day. Families may choose to continue breast feeding after one year of age, but kids need additional sources of nutrition.

Reality Check

When it's your first baby, you can't wait to start solid food. When it's your second or third child, you'll avoid it as long as possible! Why? Solid food becomes yet one more chore you have to do—and it's really not that much fun. Because there's no real benefit to getting started, you might as well just wait. We personally think holding off until six months of age is fine for all babies.

So let's sum this up in chart form:

AGE	LIQUIDS	SOLIDS
0-4 months	breast milk or formula only	none
4-6 months	breast milk or formula, about 40 oz/day	none
6-9 months	yes, but cutting back	solids becoming more important
9-12 months	breast milk or formula, 20-30 oz/day	3 solid meals a day
12 months +	switch to cows milk, 16 oz per day	3 solid meals plus 1-2 snacks

See later in this chapter for information on calcium and dairy requirements at one year of age. For a more detailed chart of liquids and solids, see Chapter 7, "Solid Foods."

Reality Check

Babies have "off" days and growth spurts. So, your baby may not be as predictable as you would like when it comes to meals. Occasionally, he will be less interested in feedings. And sometimes, he will seem like he hasn't eaten in days.

Feeding Schedules

Q. I've heard about putting my newborn on a feeding schedule. How do I do it?

You don't. Your baby does it for you.

The phrase "newborn feeding schedule" is an oxymoron. Newborns are learning how life works outside the womb. Before birth, they were on a 24/7 feeding schedule. Now, your newborn will have to rely on her innate sense of being hungry when her body needs energy. However, she will not have a neat and tidy schedule.

Newborns need to eat about eight to 12 times in a 24-hour day. This may be every 1 1/2 hours for a few cycles, then four hours later, then two hours, etc. Somehow, in 24 hours, they do it. This is called "ad lib" or feeding on demand. Ideally, parents (and their doctors) would like their baby to have "'cluster feeding'" of every 1 1/2 hours during the day and a nice four hour stretch at night. But, short of divine intervention, there is little that can be done to *make* this happen.

For parents of preemies: Premature babies *really* need those feedings frequently. Their smaller tummies, and need for catch-up growth often require feedings every two to three hours until they are at least four months old. (That is, four months from the original due date, not the actual birth—their so-called adjusted age).

**DR B'S OPINION:
BABYWISE OR BABY FOOLISH?**

As a new parent, you'll probably hear about a book called *On Becoming Babywise*. Released in 1995, this best-selling guide instructs parents to rigidly schedule their newborn's feedings (called "parent directed feeding"). The result? Babies were showing up in their doctor's offices malnourished—and falling off of their growth charts. The American Academy of Pediatrics was so concerned they issued a media alert about the teachings of this book. The AAP advised parents that "newborns should be nursed whenever they show signs of hunger, such as increased alertness or activity, mouthing, or rooting….Newborns should be nursed approximately eight to 12 times every 24 hours until satiety."[6]

Here's the take-home message: Lower your expectations. Yes, your baby IS in charge of your house right now. That'll change in about 18 years. Or 26.

BOTTOM LINE

Although newborns can't be put on a schedule, by four months of age, your baby WILL BE capable of regular feeding and sleeping patterns. Some lucky moms and dads will have a baby that falls into a predictable feeding/sleeping pattern by two months of age.

Q. My six-week-old seemed to have somewhat of a feeding schedule . . . but now seems insatiable. Is my milk drying up?

No. Babies often have growth spurts at three weeks and six weeks of age. They will have feeding frenzies during those periods of time. As your baby's demands increase, so will your milk supply. (For details, check out Chapter 6, "Liquid Nutrition").

Old Wives Tale
Adding rice cereal to formula or expressed breast milk will make your baby sleep through the night.

The truth: Only if your baby has heartburn. Let's think about this in a scientific way. Formula has 20 calories per ounce. If your baby is taking a six oz bottle, he gets 120 calories. A teaspoon of rice cereal flakes has about five calories. It's not providing any calories to fill them up. But it is heavier. If your baby has acid reflux, he will be happier but he still won't sleep through the night!

Special Concerns

Q. My 6 month old has dropped his weight percentiles from 75% to 25% since his four-month visit. What happened?

Did he start solid food? Solid foods contain *significantly* fewer calories than formula or breast milk. When babies are given solid foods *before* their milk, it reduces the amount of formula or breast milk they drink. Don't get carried away with feeding your baby solid foods until he can take one or two jars (two to four oz. of solids) at a sitting. What many parents don't realize is that your baby will tell you when he or she wants more. If your little one is finished, you'll know it. And until she's asking for more, don't push the solid food. See more on solid foods in Chapter 7.

If your baby is exclusively breastfed, you may want to check out the World Health Organization's growth charts. Remember, the CDC's charts may not reflect a breastfed baby's growth curve from four to six months. If your baby is tracking fine on WHO's curves, that's all the reassurance you need (www.who.int/childgrowth).

Q. My nine month old seems to be dropping on his growth percentiles. Is he malnourished?

Probably not.

Babies these days are born much bigger than they used to be (good for them, bad for Mom's pelvis)—thanks to good prenatal care. But not all babies turn out to be sumo wrestlers. Their genetic makeup (i.e. Mom and Dad) determines their ultimate size. Big babies that have more average sized parents start to plateau, showing their truer growth curves as they approach a year of age.

Your doctor will check for iron deficiency anemia at this age, as this can also be a cause of poor growth (a drop in growth percentiles). If your baby is dropping off the growth charts, your doctor should perform a thorough evaluation to see what's wrong.

Q. My baby has dropped off the growth charts for his weight. What is wrong with him?

No, your baby hasn't begun the South Beach Diet behind your back. The official term for this problem is **FAILURE TO THRIVE.**

Babies whose weight percentiles started off fine, then plateau or fall below the third percentile need to be evaluated. The causes are various and include: poor feeding routines, incorrect formula preparation, gastroesophageal reflux, malabsorption of food from intestinal problems, kidney disease, metabolic disease, hypothyroidism, and anemia.

An extensive medical evaluation is usually performed, unless a cause is found easily. If no cause is identified, a higher calorie diet is initiated and baby's weight is checked frequently.

Vitamin Supplements

Q. Does my baby need a Vitamin D supplement?

It depends on whether your baby is breastfed, formula fed, or doing a combination of both.

Breast milk is perfect nutrition with one caveat. Frequently, there is not enough Vitamin D in breast milk for your baby's growth (primarily because most mothers are deficient in Vitamin D themselves). While Vitamin D is present in some foods (cod liver oil, salmon, sardines, fortified milk), we get most of our Vitamin D from the sun's rays. Mother Nature planned on children producing Vitamin D in their skin after sun exposure. She did not plan on the creation of sun block that blocks UVB rays—an essential component of Vitamin D synthesis. Vitamin D deficiency causes **RICKETS**, a bone malformation (see glossary).[9,10]

Because it is impossible to determine the amount of sunlight every baby needs to make enough Vitamin D (skin color, sun block, and the latitude you live in complicate the equation), the American Academy of Pediatrics issued guidelines for Vitamin D supplements in April, 2003.

Vitamin D supplements of 200 IU per day are recommended by two

> **DR B'S OPINION: SUPPLEMENTS**
>
> I recommend Tri-Vi-Sol (a three vitamin solution that includes Vitamin A, D, and C). Use one dropper-full for the baby, once a day. Tri-Vi-Sol is available over the counter or from web sites like DrugStore.com. I also suggest that Mom stay on her prenatal vitamins. This isn't for the baby—it's for Mom's health.

months of age for:
1. Babies who are exclusively breast-fed.
2. Babies who are breastfed and receive less than 500 ml (17 oz) of supplemental formula daily.
3. Babies who are formula fed but eat less than 500ml (17oz) of formula daily (preemies).
4. Children who have little sunlight exposure and drink less than 500ml (17 oz) of Vitamin D fortified milk daily.

FYI: Babies who are at the greatest risk of Vitamin D deficiency rickets are those with darkly pigmented skin living above latitude 40 degrees (that's Iowa and north). However, breastfed babies in Texas and Georgia have been found to have rickets too.

Q. Does my baby need an iron or vitamin supplement?

There are a few kids who will need this.

Iron is needed to carry oxygen (on your red blood cells) throughout your body. Babies are born with a large iron bank, thanks to Mom. As withdrawals are made from the bank, the supply needs to be replenished via baby's nutritional intake. By six to nine months, the original stores are gone and baby is on his own. So, it becomes important for baby to get iron in the diet. Formula fed babies get the right amount in their iron-fortified formula. Breast fed babies, after six months of age, need an additional source of iron. The easiest way to get it is in iron-fortified cereal (all baby cereals contain iron). That's why we recommend starting solid food by six months of age (see Chapter 7, "Solid Nutrition" for details).

Iron deficiency causes **ANEMIA** (see glossary). Anemia causes fatigue, poor weight gain, and poor intellectual functioning. We routinely check for iron deficiency anemia at either the nine-month or one-year well check. If your baby is anemic, we'll recommend an iron supplement.

Babies who eat a relatively "balanced" diet do not need multivitamins. So, we don't routinely recommend iron or multivitamins for all babies.

BOTTOM LINE: If you are formula feeding your baby, DO NOT BUY A LOW IRON FORMULA. Your baby needs the iron to grow. (see Chapter 6, "Liquid Nutrition," for more details)

Helpful Hint

If your doctor prescribes an iron supplement for your baby, do not give it with a dairy product (e.g. breast milk, formula, whole milk). The calcium and iron compete for absorption in the digestive tract and will decrease the amount of iron that the body gets.

PREEMIES & IRON SUPPLEMENTS

Premature babies go home from the hospital on iron supplements because their rapid rate of growth requires it. Depending on your doctor's recommendation, your baby may continue on iron supplements through the first year of life. Also: most preemies head home with a multivitamin recommendation as well.

Q. I've heard about fluoride supplements. Does my baby need this?

Fluoride is proven to prevent tooth decay. So, our kids need fluoride, right? Well, yes. But we want them to get the *right amount* of it. Too little, and you risk tooth decay. Too much, and you risk fluorosis (a permanent stain on tooth enamel). Fluorosis occurs only in teeth that are developing under the gums—the teeth are not at risk once they have erupted. So, the greatest risk of fluorosis is in kids under three years of age.

Therefore, it's important to know how much fluoride your baby is getting in his diet. You can contact your local water department or public works agency to find out the fluoride level in local tap water.

Fluoride is usually measured in parts per million or "ppm." A safe level of fluoride is about 0.7ppm to 1.2ppm. Be aware that some communities (particularly in Texas, Oklahoma, South Carolina and Virginia) have water supplies with high levels of naturally occurring fluoride—above 2 ppm. Some towns have 4ppm or more of fluoride in their water, which is clearly a concern.

Here is the latest advice on excess fluoride and babies, courtesy of the American Dental Association (ADA):

◆ *Breast-fed babies.* Babies who are breastfed for the first year of life are not at risk for excessive fluoride intake.

◆ *Formula-fed babies.* As you'll read in the next chapter, there are three general types of baby formula: ready-to-feed, powder and liquid concentrate. Ready-to-feed formula is just that—you simply pour it into a bottle for baby to drink. If you live in an area with high levels of fluoride in the tap water, the ADA recommends this type of formula (which is very expensive, unfortunately).

As for less-expensive powder or liquid concentrate (which you mix with tap water), the ADA recommends using "low fluoride" tap water (less than 0.3ppm is probably okay), or bottled water. FYI: Bottled water companies are *not* required by the government to label fluoride content. In general, most bottled water contains less than 0.9ppm of fluoride unless specified on the bottle. To find low-fluoride bottled water, look for bottles labeled "purified, demineralized, deionized, distilled or reverse osmosis filtered."[11] You can also use a home water treatment system that removes fluoride from your tap water (reverse osmosis filtered).

Now, let's talk about the MINIMUM level of fluoride a baby needs. (We realize this is confusing, but stay with us).

Babies *over six months* of age need 0.25 mg fluoride a day. We wish we could give you a concrete number on exactly how much water your baby needs to drink to get the right amount of fluoride, but we can't. Fluoride is not only found in your tap water, but also in things you cook with water, and commercially produced beverages, etc. What we can give you is a ballpark of what is safe and adequate fluoride intake. So, let's sum up our recommendations for babies over six months of age:

1. **If you are breastfeeding or using ready-to-feed formula**, your baby should also drink fluoridated tap water daily. Again, the safe level is 0.7ppm–1.2ppm.

2. **If you use powder/liquid concentrate formula:** continue mixing it with low/no fluoride water. *HOWEVER,* your baby should also drink your fluoridated tap water (0.7ppm–1.2ppm fluoride) on a daily basis.
3. **Which children need a fluoride supplement?** If your baby is over six months of age, and is drinking water that contains LESS than 0.6ppm fluoride for whatever reason (filtered tap water, well water, etc), your doctor or dentist can prescribe a fluoride supplement. Be sure to ask about it! For yet more details on fluoride supplements, see Appendix A, "Medications."

Overeating, Obesity, And The Body Mass Index

Q. I am concerned that I am overfeeding my baby. Is that possible?

It is unlikely, but it can happen in rare cases.

Let's look at this rationally. Most infants do not think, "I'm full, but that dessert looks pretty good." That is a *learned* behavior in our society. Most infants will eat until their tummies are full and stop. If they do overindulge, they usually just throw up.

But, it is a good idea to learn your child's cues. Some new parents think their baby needs to eat every time he cries. This becomes a set up for obesity.

It's a good idea to institute new "House Rules" in your kitchen as your baby approaches a year of age. See below for some astounding facts on the childhood obesity epidemic and ways to prevent it.

The Rise In Childhood Obesity

The United States is super-sized, to paraphrase an article in *U.S. News and World Report* (Aug. 19, 2002). A startling fact: the number of overweight school-aged children has *doubled* in the past 20 years. Why? Here are the reasons:

1. **Lack of activity.** Children are spending more time (about three hours a day) watching TV and playing on computers than ever before. Whatever happened to the good old days of playing outside?
2. **Eating out and take-out food.** 34% of our calories are eaten outside of the home. Restaurant food has more fat, salt, and sugar than home prepared meals.
3. **Larger serving sizes.** Super-size servings have become the norm at all types of restaurants, not just fast food outlets. This trend toward giant portions has even crept onto our own dinner tables.
4. **Too many sugar drinks.** This starts in toddlerhood. Don't let your child become a juice-a-holic. Kids graduate from juice to soft drinks. Believe it or not, the average teenage boy drinks *three* sodas a day.

Q. How can I find out if my child is overweight?

There is a calculation called the **BODY MASS INDEX (BMI)** that compares your child's height to his weight. The formula is applicable to children ages 2-20 years of age. The ranges vary for gender and age (because the BMI varies as kids grow).

NEW PARENT 411: AVOIDING OBESITY

Set up the right routines while your baby is an infant and toddler. Here are our tips:

1. Keep your child physically active.
2. Make restaurant food a treat. McDonald's should be a once a month treat—not a weekly outing.
3. Offer appropriate serving sizes. Start with two tablespoons per serving. Offer seconds on fruit and vegetables.
4. Banish the "Clean Plate Club." Don't force your child to eat. Yes, there are starving children in India, but they won't be eating your leftovers.
5. Make juice a low-priority item.
6. Keep the four C's out of your pantry: cola, chips, cookies, and candy. If you have to go out of the house to get these items, they will truly be a treat.
7. Be a good role model. Your child is watching what you are eating.
8. No TV while food is being served. Watching the tube while you eat encourages that couch-potato thing. Don't watch the news during dinner—set the Tivo and watch it after the kids go to bed.

One of the realities of being a parent is that you often end up eating what your kids eat. That's how you end up at the end of baby's first year still wearing those prenatal pounds. What to do? Change your eating habits now and everyone in the family will benefit.

Next, buy healthy, yet good snacks: cereals like Rice Chex and Cheerios are great (see box on the next page for more snack ideas). And if you are going to buy juice, stick with 100% juice products. An example: Vruit, a vegetable and fruit juice combination with no added sugar (see their web site at AmericanSoy.com). It comes in individual boxes, too, for easy transport. And be a good example to your kids. Don't drink soda in front of them day and night. Instead opt for milk or here's a crazy thought: water!

In the end, an outright ban on cookies, soda, chips and candy can backfire. As we said earlier, these can be occasional treats. Otherwise, you're going to have a kid who sneaks out to a neighbors' to indulge or spends his allowance on the sly to buy candy bars.

NUTRITION

Here's the formula:

$$\frac{\text{Weight in lbs.}}{\text{(height in inches)} \times \text{(height in inches)}} \times 703 = BMI$$

For children, the risk for obesity is a BMI of 85-95%. An overweight child has a BMI of 95% or higher. To check your child's BMI, go to www.KeepKidsHealthy.com (click on "Useful Tools" and then the "BMI Calculator"). The BMI range for ADULTS is based on the number derived from the

FEEDBACK FROM THE REAL WORLD: AVOIDING THE 4 C'S

You've seen the statistics and you're worried. You don't want your child to be one of them. We're talking about overweight and obese children. They are a statistic on the rise and if they start out overweight, most likely they'll be overweight adults. You've also seen the incredible array of snack foods on the shelf at your local grocery store. So it's time to ask our experienced moms for tips on keeping your baby off the junk and excited about healthy snacks.

1. **It takes a family.** Julie DeCamp Palmer of Seattle, WA spoke for most of our readers when she said, "It takes the whole family eating a healthy diet." So lead by example and don't stock the four C's (cola, chips, cookies, candy) in your home. For those of us who want a little of the forbidden items ourselves, eat them when your child is not around or when you're out and about without him.

2. **Presentation is important.** Healthy snacks can still be exciting to a child when they are presented with enthusiasm. One reader Tiffany Johnson from Vancouver, WA, who is also a daycare provider noted that "children like anything that isn't called what it is...i.e. celery sticks with cream cheese and raisins becomes much more appealing when you call it ants on a log. Cottage cheese with raw fruit or veggies is a hit when you make it into a face and call it clown food."

3. **Moderation.** Yes, an occasional cookie as a treat is just fine. In fact, S. Von Lengerke had a great story about her own childhood where the four C's were completely banned: "I believe everything in moderation is OK. I was raised in one of those families where we could never have soda or sweets, so my brother and I chose our friends based on their snacks. We were chubby kids. I think having some access to sweets, rather than forbidding them, makes them less of an allure to kids and the children, in turn, will have a healthy regard for snacks."

4. **Go with the flow.** "One item I think many parents forget is that kids' eating often ebbs and flows. Kids will be starving and eat more than Dad at one meal and turn up their noses at even

calculation above:

Healthy BMI   18-25
Overweight BMI 25-30
Obese BMI   Greater than 30

For more information on body mass indexes for both children and adults, check out the Centers for Disease Control's website at: www.cdc.gov/nccdphp/dnpa/growthcharts/bmi_tools.htm

favorite foods the next. It's not easy, but we offer a variety of healthy and favorite foods at meal- and snack-time and let the kids decide if they are going to eat or not. We don't take it personally and trust that our children will eat when they are hungry. Not always easy, but usually very successful." –Wendy Stough

Not only did our readers have great tips on avoiding the four C's, they also offered food recommendations on what snacks work best in their households. Here are a few suggestions:

1. **Veggie Booty and Pirate Booty.** Manufactured by Robert's American Gourmet (web: robscape.com), the veggie variety of this puffed rice snack food is sprinkled with a blend of spinach, kale, cabbage, carrots and broccoli. Pirate Booty is a cheddar version of the snack and there is a fruit version as well. Readers report their kids love them.

2. Another reader recommended dehydrated vegetables from a company called **Just Tomatoes** (web: justtomatoes.com). Crunchy and salt- and fat-free they don't spoil like fresh food so they're great to pop into your diaper bag.

3. Other readers recommend **rice cakes, whole grain crackers,** or organic products from Hain (web: hain-celestial.com), including their all-natural animal cookies.

4. **Yogurt pops:** Several brands come in those easy to transport squeeze tubes (hint: pick the brands with the least sugar). One mom recommended freezing the tubes for a popsicle treat!

5. **Fresh fruits and veggies are the ultimate snacks.** Bananas, peaches, avocados, or pears are easy to pack and then cut up at snack time. Cooked peas or soft-cooked carrots are also easy to transport and make for great finger foods.

When you find a great product, check to see if they have a web site. We discovered that they are full of nutritional information, fun games and even e-coupons for their products.

Calcium, Fiber, And Iron

Q. Are there any nutrients that children eat too little of?

Calcium, fiber, and iron. Let's take a look at each:

1. **CALCIUM.** The requirements change as children grow. For ages one to three years, children need 500 milligrams per day (mg/day). Kids ages four to six need 800 mg/day. Kids ages seven to 14 need a whopping 1300 mg/day. If your child has a milk intolerance or allergy, try calcium fortified orange juice, broccoli, rhubarb, or tofu as alternative calcium sources. If you are looking for a vitamin supplement that contains calcium, get one with Vitamin D added (it helps the body absorb calcium better).

Calcium Content Of Foods

Food	Calcium content (mg)
8 oz cup of milk	250 mg
1 slice of cheese	200 mg
1 cup of ice cream	175 mg
4 oz cup of yogurt	200 mg

Note: As you can see, milk is the most efficient way of getting calcium. But don't lose sleep if your child has a milk allergy. Calcium fortified beverages have comparable absorption to dairy products and the calcium in green leafy vegetables is absorbed better than milk (that is, if you can get your kid to eat kale).

2. **FIBER.** The fiber requirement for children is calculated by: Age in years + 5 = Number of fiber grams/day. Example: a two-year old needs seven grams of fiber day. However, there are no established guidelines for children under one year of age.

Adults need 25-30 grams of fiber per day. The average American diet doesn't come anywhere close to our daily needs. Not only does fiber make your child a regular guy or gal, it also has potential benefits to reducing heart disease. So, make it a little family project to increase everyone's fiber intake.

The best way to get a kid to eat fiber is through the bread and grains food group. Green leafy vegetables, while high in fiber, are not the most popular food items for kids. Also, many parents don't realize that the source of fiber in many fruits is the skin, which usually gets peeled off before a child gets to the fruit.

For details on fiber foods, see Chapter 8, "The Other End."

3. **IRON.** We have already chatted about this one. It's important to have a daily intake (10 mg/day) for growth and brain function.

Good Sources Of Iron

Meat, poultry, fish, bread, enriched pasta, dark green vegetables (spinach, broccoli, kale), legumes (dried beans, soybeans, lentils), eggs*, nuts/seeds*, peanuts and peanut butter**, dried fruits (raisins, etc)*, cereals (infant as well as grown up breakfast cereals are iron fortified). *Note: Eating iron in combi-*

nation with Vitamin C (orange juice, etc), helps the body absorb iron.

*Items only for kids over one year of age.
**Because of risk for lifelong and life threatening allergy, consider avoiding until at least three years of age. See discussion of peanut allergies in Chapter 7, "Solids."

Happy Birthday, You're Turning One!

Yes, your child is turning one! How exciting, no? No doubt you've heard about the new food pyramids launched by the federal government in the past year. Unfortunately, the new pyramid (www.mypyramid.gov) starts at age two. There is no specific pictorial guidance for one year olds. However, the following servings should help you determine the proper diet for your child.

Food Guidelines for a One Year Old

The serving size is listed beside the food item.
The average calorie intake for a 1-3 year old is 1300 calories.

Breads/Grains	**4-6 servings/day**
Whole wheat bread	1/2 slice
cooked cereal, rice, pasta	1/4 cup
cold cereal	1/2 cup

Fruits/Vegetables	**4 servings/day**
	(1 Vitamin A/ 1 Vitamin C)
Vitamin C	
citrus, berries, melons, tomatoes, broccoli, potatoes, cauliflower	1/4 cup
Vitamin A	
peaches, carrots, peas, green beans, melons, apricots	2 Tbsp
Other	2 Tbsp

Milk/Dairy	**4 servings/day**
Whole milk	1/2 cup
Cheese slice	1 slice (1 oz)
Yogurt	4 oz
Ice Cream	1/2 cup

Meat/Protein	**2 servings/day**
Beef, chicken fish, pork	2 Tbsp
Egg	1 egg
Beans	1/4 cup

Fats	**3 servings/day**
Butter, mayo, ranch dressing	1 tsp

NUTRITION

Q. My one year old is on a hunger strike. Help!

Very few one year olds have a world cause they support that passionately!

The *toddler diet* appears as your baby approaches one year old. The typical toddler eats well once every three days or eats one good meal in 24 hours. The food that is loved for seven straight days will be refused shortly thereafter. A good strategy is to offer three food choices in a meal. Pick one that is sure to be a hit—the others are trial offerings. If your child refuses everything, *do not make another meal for him*. Mealtime is over. Don't worry, your child will eat at the next opportunity.

All humans have both a hunger and thirst drive that compels us to fulfill our calorie and fluid needs.

Now that you have the low down on your baby's nutrition, let's get specific: next up is a discussion of both liquids (breastmilk, formula, milk) and solid foods. We'll start with the liquids.

LIQUIDS
Chapter 6

"In short, breastfeeding occurs above the eyebrows as much as or more than it occurs in the mammary glands."
~ Judithe A. Thompson

What's in this Chapter

Breast milk
- The advantages of breast milk
- How long to do it
- Why women stop
- Getting started
- Troubleshooting
- Where to get help
- How to pump and store breast milk
- Considerations for Mom (diet, going back to work, etc.)
- Introducing a bottle
- Special situations
- Weaning

Formula
- Formula options
- Bottle management

Other liquids
- Water, Juice, Milk

For the first six months of your baby's life, you have only to make one decision about her nutrition: breast milk or formula. You can guarantee that decision won't occur in a vacuum: friends, neighbors, relatives and complete strangers at the grocery store will want to weigh in on what's "best." But you are the only one who can make that decision for your baby.

This chapter will offer you the pros and cons of both breast milk and formula. We promise we won't make judgments about your choice. But, we do admit one bias: we'd like all babies to be breastfed. As such, we will do our best to convince you to breastfeed and to stick with it—with lots of tips and handholding along the way. Without question, human breast milk is the perfect nutrition for human babies. But if breastfeeding doesn't work out, at least you gave it a good try!

If you decide to go with formula, you should never feel guilty about that and we'll teach you what you need to know about your formula options.

Besides breast milk and formula, you'll be addressing the question of what other liquids to serve your child. These include water, juice and cow's milk. We'll discuss these other liquids in this chapter as well.

Breast Milk

Q. I have heard that breastfeeding is best for babies, but what are the real advantages?

There are advantages for both baby and mom. Let's take a look at each:

Breast-Feeding Advantages for Baby:
Mother's milk:
1. **Has the ideal ingredients for a human body.** Formula is an approximation of the real thing. Breast milk is living food.
2. **Carries the mother's antibodies to protect baby from various infections.**
3. **Reduces the severity of certain infections, like stomach viruses and the common cold.**
4. **Is hypoallergenic.** It is rare to be allergic to human milk.
5. **Contains products that stimulate brain development.** Breast milk naturally contains nutrients (called DHA and ARA, more on this later) known to stimulate brain and vision development.
6. **Reduces risk of diabetes, inflammatory bowel disease, and some forms of cancer later in life.**

Breast-Feeding Advantages for Mom:
1. **It may be the easiest way to lose those pregnancy pounds and still eat like you are a professional wrestler.**
2. **It is always ready to serve, at the perfect temperature.**
3. **It is free.** Formula can cost $1200 or more for the entire first year of life.
4. **It reduces your risk of breast cancer.** A study published in the journal *Lancet* showed that for every two years spent breastfeeding, a woman's lifetime risk of breast cancer goes down by 5%. Currently, one in eight women will get breast cancer.
5. **It is a wonderful way to feel close to your baby.**
6. **It can be a form of birth control,** but don't rely on it exclusively (unless you want a toddler and a newborn in the house!)

BOTTOM LINE: Breastfeeding is worth the effort it takes to learn how to do it.

Reality check

You may hear that breast milk is contaminated with rocket fuel, dry cleaning fluid, and other environmental toxins. Truth is, there are many environmental hazards our kids are exposed to today—whether they are breastfed or not. Hopefully, more steps will be taken to protect our kids as more information on these health hazards come to light. The take home message: Despite all the alarming things you might hear that may or may not be in breast milk, it is still safe to drink.

Q. How long should I breastfeed my baby?

The American Academy of Pediatrics recommends breastfeeding for at

> ### ENCOURAGING BREAST-FEEDING: NEW GUIDELINES
>
> In order to promote breastfeeding, the AAP recently released guidelines for parents and doctors. Here are the highlights:
>
> - Encourage "rooming-in" with your newborn at the hospital to learn baby's cues.
> - Trained caregivers should formally evaluate breastfeeding (latch, position, etc) at least twice daily while newborns are at the hospital. (If that doesn't happen, speak up!)
> - Supplements (water, sugar water, formula) should not be given to a breastfed newborn unless ordered by the baby's doctor for a medical reason.
> - Pacifiers are discouraged until breastfeeding is going well.
> - Breastfed babies should see their healthcare provider at three to five days of life and again at two weeks of age to assess breastfeeding.
> - "Complementary foods" (solid food) should be introduced at SIX months of life. (Good luck convincing your mother about this one!)
> - Babies should sleep in close proximity to their moms to encourage breastfeeding. (Note the word choices here—the AAP is not recommending a family bed with this statement.)

least the first year of life. The latest statistics show that 75% of American babies go home from the hospital breastfed. But only 30% are still breastfed at six months of life. The numbers are even lower for babies who are breastfed until one year of age.

Why Women Stop Nursing . . .

There are many reasons why women choose to stop nursing. Most of the time, it is NOT due to poor milk supply. Here is a run-down:

1 POOR TECHNIQUE. Breastfeeding is a learned process. It's not as natural as you might think. Babies know how to suck, and Mom's body knows how to make milk. But the technique of getting the baby latched on correctly requires a great deal of patience and sometimes *four* hands. Throw in a hormonal roller coaster after delivery and you'll understand why many women give up. Learning how to breast-feed is analogous to learning how to drive with a manual transmission.

2 ENGORGEMENT. Mothers who survive the technique test get to move on to the engorgement phase—this is what happens when the milk actually comes in. Your breasts may be more impressive than your neighbor's boob job. Your husband will want to take pictures. *You* will wish that it is a bad dream and hope that your old breasts will be back when you wake up—engorgement often means tenderness, pain, sore nipples and more. This too shall pass. If you make it to the two-week mark, you are on cruise control. That should be your goal. You may need a great deal of moral support to get to two weeks, however.

DR B'S OPINION: GRANDPARENTS & BREASTFEEDING

There are some things about babies that will never change. But there are many things we have learned in the past 20 or 30 years that are different than what our parents were taught (like using car seats, for instance). Learn grandparents' trade secrets for soothing your crying baby because they have been there and done that. Learn the 411 on current pediatric trends in this book.

3 **LACK OF SUPPORT.** And speaking of support . . . the newly crowned grandmothers arrive on the scene in the first few weeks of your baby's life. Since most of them fed their babies formula, they feel helpless. They will watch you struggle with breastfeeding and throw in little zingers like, "It's so much easier to formula feed—I never had this trouble." Put Grandma to work cooking dinner, changing diapers, and soothing your baby. She is an expert in those categories. And this will give you the freedom to concentrate on breast-feeding your baby.

A poignant comment from one mom we interviewed: "If everyone would just leave the baby and I alone, we could figure it out!" Truer words were never spoken. However, if you are at wit's end, utilize your pediatrician and a lactation consultant. Lactation specialists (IBCLC's) are medical personnel certified to handle breastfeeding challenges. We suggest you ask your obstetrician or pediatrician for a recommendation. Lactation consultants who have a relationship with your doctor are likely to be "team players." It is helpful to have everyone working towards the same goal: your success!

4 **LACK OF MILK SUPPLY.** It doesn't happen that often, but some women cannot produce enough milk to meet the demands of their baby. Trying to rev up mom's supply takes a lot of effort, medication, and persistence. And even then, the milk might not come in for some moms. The reasons: advanced maternal age, some types of breast surgery, hormonal issues. Watching a hungry baby scream at the breast 24/7 can make any mom want to throw in the towel.

5 **RETURNING TO WORK.** Working moms, in general, have trouble finding time to pump. To completely keep up with your baby's demands, you need to pump every three hours (nearly impossible, right?). But remember, to pump *some* breast milk is better than none at all. This is not an "all or nothing" situation. Some moms can only pump once while at work, and continue to nurse while at home. Your body can adjust to many different feeding patterns . . . which means you can continue some level of breastfeeding even after you head back to work.

Despite all these challenges, it is well worth the effort to make breastfeeding successful. Breastfeeding is kind of like running a race, with the hardest hurdles up front. Many moms don't realize that they will be coasting the rest of the way if they just make it past the first mile.

THE FACTS OF LIFE—A.K.A. SCIENCE OF BREASTFEEDING

Keep in mind these four tips on the "science" of nursing your baby:

- Breast milk production is a supply and demand phenomenon. You should have no trouble making enough milk if the demand is there. Nursing at least eight times in 24 hours promotes a good supply.
- Colostrum, the first milk, is all your baby needs for the first few days of life. Mature milk, the high fat stuff, arrives when your baby needs it—around the fourth day of life.
- ALL babies are exhausted by the birth process and are not very interested in eating for the first 48 hours. They latch on, get cozy…and fall asleep after five minutes. This behavior will change (at almost the same moment you leave the hospital!)
- Babies are born with 10% extra baggage to carry them through the first few days of life. They will lose 5-10% of their birth weight—expect that. Do not think you are failing at breast-feeding because your baby is losing weight.

Denise's Opinion: Sometimes, the criticism you get about your decision to breast-feed comes from unlikely sources. Exhibit 1: grandparents. The generation of parents from the 60's and 70's seldom breast-fed their babies—it just wasn't fashionable. And, the idea of baring your breast in front of them (especially grandfathers) makes them squeamish to say the least. Here are some suggestions for how to deal with their objections.

1. **When in your own home, you have a right to nurse in your living room.** It's your house, your rules. But your dad will probably appreciate it if you either cover yourself with a shawl or warn him before you whip out your breast.
2. **At their house, be discreet.** Try nursing in a bedroom if you know it makes them uncomfortable.
3. **When they ask, "Why can't we just give baby a bottle so we can participate in feedings,"** promise that they can when your baby's nursing is well established and you can pump a bottle or two.
4. **When they ask you why you're still nursing your baby at ten months,** calmly inform them that the American Academy of Pediatrics recommends that babies breast feed for at least a year of age.

Getting Started Breastfeeding

First, some definitions to help you understand breastfeeding lingo:

1. **Colostrum.** The first milk that your breasts produce. Some women start making (and leaking) it before the baby is even born. It is a high protein drink, filled with mom's antibodies that provide an immunity boost to the newborn. It has fewer calories than mature milk because of a lower fat content.

> ### BREASTFEEDING MOJO: LINDA'S TIPS
>
> Before we delve into our breastfeeding tips, we'd like to give a special shout out to a special expert here at *Baby 411*: Linda Hill. Linda is a registered nurse and a certified lactation consultant (IBCLC). Linda works with Dr. Brown in her Austin, TX practice and we appreciate her sharing her thoughts and advice. Look for "Linda's Tips" throughout this chapter.

2. **Mature Milk.** The milk that arrives on the third or fourth day after birth. It is about 50% fat.
3. **Foremilk.** The milk that comes out in the first several minutes of feeding. In general, it contains slightly less fat. Babies who "snack" end up getting mostly foremilk, leading to more frequent feedings (and possibly, fussy moods).
4. **Hindmilk.** The milk that comes out in the later part of a feeding. It is slightly higher in fat than foremilk. Babies who drain a whole breast in a feeding tend to be more satisfied, for good reason.
5. **Engorgement.** When mature milk is produced initially, mom's breasts may feel full, tender, lumpy, and hard.
6. **Plugged ducts.** An area of the breast has obstructed milk flow, creating a hard, tender lumpy area. These areas are at risk of getting infected (mastitis—ouch). See tips below for more info.

And some info on breastfeeding gear...

- **BREAST SHELLS.** Plastic devices that pull out inverted nipples.
- **NIPPLE SHIELDS.** Plastic devices that protect sore or cracked nipples. Unfortunately, they can limit the amount of milk that flows to the baby's mouth.
- **LANOLIN.** A thick emollient that helps heal cracked nipples. Brand names: Lansinoh, Pur-lan. Available at breastfeeding boutiques, and even Wal-Mart.

Linda's Tip: Cracked Nipples. If you don't have any lanolin around your house and you are desperate, try putting olive oil on your nipples to heal the cracks.

Q. What do I need to know about my baby's first few days of breastfeeding?

Let's break this down, day by day...

First Day of Life (0-24 hours old):
1. Nurse your baby for the first time within an hour or so of his birth. He will be awake, alert, and interested.
2. At two hours of life, he will be exhausted and hard to arouse for several (three to four) hours. Don't get too worked up about trying to nurse right now. Take a nap yourself.
3. Frequency goal: six to eight feedings in the first 24 hours of life.

4. Your baby will probably fall asleep at the breast after a few minutes of nursing. An acceptable feeding session for today is five to ten minutes per breast.

Second Day of Life (24-48 hours old):
1. Today's goal is working on your technique. It may take a second set of hands to position the baby while you hold your breast. You will fly solo eventually. See tips to survive the first two weeks later in this chapter.
2. Frequency goal: eight feedings in 24 hours. Do not let your baby sleep more than four hours at a stretch or you will have trouble meeting this goal.
3. Length of feedings goal: at least five to ten minutes per breast. Do not take baby off the breast at ten minutes if he is still actively sucking.
4. If your nipples are cracked and bleeding, you need help with your technique.

Third Day of Life (48-72 hours old):
1. Your baby is suddenly awake and sometimes, insatiable. As long as your baby has lost less than 10% of his birth weight (and has no other risk factors-see below), keep your chin up and resist the temptation to supplement with formula. Your baby's demand is precisely what your body needs to create the supply of milk.
2. Make sure your technique is okay and you are comfortable when your baby latches on.
3. Frequency goal: eight feedings in 24 hours (it should be an easy goal to reach today!)
4. Length of feedings goal: at least ten minutes per breast.

NEW PARENT 411: ANXIETY AT CHECK OUT

You will go home from the hospital with a shrinking baby and no "mature" milk in your breasts. Understandably, this often creates great anxiety for new parents. Your baby will do just fine with colostrum as long as your breast milk comes in around the fourth day. The circumstances that interfere with this perfect plan are:
1. Jaundice (elevated bilirubin).
2. Prematurity or small gestational age (small for dates).
3. Loss of more than 10% of birth weight.
4. Delay in milk's arrival.

The AAP recommends follow-up appointments for babies at the fourth or fifth day of life to make sure things are heading in the right direction.

It's a good idea to keep a breastfeeding diary (see our handy two week survival guide earlier in Chapter 3) that tracks both feeding and elimination for the first two weeks. If the milk is going in, it will come out the other end. If you are still uncertain of how things are going, schedule an appointment!

LIQUIDS

Top 10 Survival Tips for The First Two Weeks

And now, from the home office here in Austin, TX, our top 10 list of advice for breastfeeding success in the first two weeks:

1. Make sure your baby is latched on to your areola and not just the tip of your nipple.
2. If it hurts for more than a few seconds, take your baby off your breast and reposition him. Do not be a martyr.
3. If the position you are using is not working, try another one. See page 112 for more comments on positions.
4. Have a spouse or willing volunteer get the baby's open mouth to your breast while you hold your breast. Have this person pull down your baby's chin gently with their finger.
5. Ask for a nipple shield (a plastic covering with a hole) if your nipples are too tender or cracked to nurse comfortably. This is a controversial option because the volume of fluid coming to baby is reduced. But it may make the difference for some women if used for a day or two. If you choose this option, schedule a follow-up appointment with a lactation consultant.
6. One word: LANOLIN. Various brands (such as Lansinoh) of this ointment are sold to provide comfort to healing nipples. It's also great for baby's bad diaper rashes.
7. Use both breasts during each feeding to stimulate milk production. Once your milk supply is established at four weeks, it is fine to nurse on one breast per feeding. One exception: veteran moms may have plenty of milk to accomplish this sooner.
8. Sleep when your baby sleeps. Your baby should not sleep more than a four-hour stretch in the first two weeks.
9. Don't be afraid to ask for help.
10. Don't give up. The first two weeks can be rough, but then it will all be worth it!!

5. You may feel that your baby is on your breast non-stop. If that is the case and your nipples are sore, take a break if you have nursed for more than 45 minutes. Let someone else have a chance to soothe your baby. (Letting baby suck on someone's finger may be helpful.)

Fourth Day of Life (72-96 hours old):

1. Hello milk! There is usually little question of whether or not your milk has arrived. How will you know? Your breasts will be much larger, heavier, and tender. You should feel full before you nurse, and softer after you nurse. You should also see milk when you burp your baby (and sometimes when you shower). Your baby's poop will also tell you the milkman has arrived. See Chapter 8 "The Other End" for more.
2. If your breasts are rock hard and your areola (the darker colored ring around your nipple) are flattened against them, you are offi-

cially engorged. This lasts for a day or two. See troubleshooting tips below.
3. Frequency goal: eight feedings in 24 hours. Do not let your baby sleep for more than a four hour stretch.
4. Length of feedings goal: at least ten to 15 minutes per breast. Once your milk supply is well established (around four weeks of life), some women prefer to nurse with one breast per feeding. For now, use both at each feeding as it stimulates your milk production.
5. You should be on your way now. Your baby should be gaining about an ounce a day.

Looking ahead…

The Two Week Mark: If your full term baby is at or above birth weight at his check up, you have my blessing to let your baby sleep as long as he wants at night.

The One Month Mark

Your baby should be more efficient at feeding sessions. You may prefer to nurse on one breast only and alternate at each feeding. Some babies prefer this because they are more likely to get to the richer hindmilk and are more satisfied. Your body makes enough milk for one complete feeding in each breast. You can start expressing (pumping) breast milk now that your supply is well established. See more about pumping later in this chapter.

Helpful Hint

When you are told that babies feed every two to three hours, time is measured from the BEGINNING of one feeding until the beginning of the next. If the feeding session itself lasts 45 minutes or an hour, that may leave less than an hour before it's time to nurse again. Your goal is to nurse at least EIGHT TIMES a day. This may be every two to three hours or it may be a series of cluster feedings every 90 minutes, followed by a four-hour stretch. As long as the number of feedings add up to eight in a 24-hour period, it is fine.

Old Wives Tale

"My doctor told me I didn't have enough milk."

The truth: Doctors in the 1960's thought breast milk was supposed to come in immediately after birth—and hence when it didn't appear in day one or two, panic bells went off. We now know that it is Nature's Way to have colostrum first and milk later. This is one of the reasons why our mothers did not breastfeed us.

BOTTOM LINE: Be prepared for the 72 hour Colostrum Zone. Your mature milk will arrive soon enough.

RED FLAGS

Check in with your baby's doctor if:
1. You don't have a dramatic change in your breasts by the fifth day of life.
2. You don't hear your baby swallowing when he is at the breast.

3. Your baby's poops have not changed from black tar (meconium) to a yellowish color by the fourth day.
4. Your baby does not have at least four wet diapers on the fourth day.
5. Your baby is sleepy and hard to arouse for feedings.
6. Your baby is nursing non-stop.

Breastfeeding positions

♦ **Cradle hold:** Baby's head rests on Mom's forearm with his belly next to Mom's.

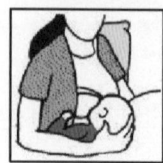

♦ **Football hold:** Baby's head rests on Mom's hand with his body coming underneath Mom's armpit. (Good for after a C-section, large breasted moms, preemies, and twins.)

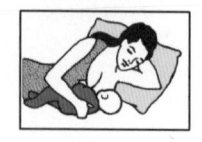

♦ **Side-lying:** Baby and Mom lie sideways and face each other. (Popular at night feedings)[1]

Linda's Tips: Positioning.
- Mom should be comfortable with her arms and back supported.
- Mom should not lean over the baby. Instead, use a breast-feeding pillow—a firm pillow that wraps around Mom's waist and allows baby to rest supported (see our other book, *Baby Bargains*, for more info on breastfeeding pillows).
- Baby should directly face the breast without having to turn his head.
- Baby's stomach should be pulled in close to Mom.
- Baby's ear, shoulder, and hip should be in a straight line.

Helpful Hint

To take your baby off of your nipple without causing excruciating pain, place one of your fingers into the corner of his mouth and break the suction seal. Pulling down on his chin also works. If the seal doesn't break, slip your finger deeper into his mouth to relax his jaw.

Infant Feeding Behaviors

Newborns can be divided into five types of feeding styles. Identifying what type your baby is may help you understand how to help him feed better. The types listed below were characterized by a study done in the 1950's, but are still relevant today:

1. **The Barracuda.** This little guy attacks the breast and gets down to business. Mom's nipples sometimes pay the price for this style. Be prepared.
2. **The Excited Ineffective.** Yes, this is the baby who is so excited to eat that he loses his latch. Calming, then reattempting to latch

helps until baby figures out the routine.
3. **The Procrastinator.** The baby who waits until the milk lets down to bother with eating. There is no rush. Be patient and keep trying.
4. **The Gourmet.** She must mouth the nipple, have a taste test, then begin the meal. Again, there is no need to rush. Let her do her thing.
5. **The Rester** (similar to a cow who grazes). He takes his own sweet time. He eats for a few minutes, rests, then continues. He will eventually finish the meal and eat well but you can encourage him by rubbing his back or head.[2]

Trouble Shooting:

When breastfeeding goes wrong, these are the usual suspects:

1. **Poor position.** There are several positions that keep you and your baby comfortable. If one is not working, try another one. See list above.
2. **Poor latch.** You should hear your baby swallowing/gulping. Clicking is NOT a sound you should hear. Get your baby to open wide, with curled lips. Make sure his nose and chin are next to your breast. Don't let go of your breast until your baby is securely latched on. Poor latch leads to problem #6 (sore nipples). If your nipple looks like a lipstick tube, you have a problem (see picture at right). Cracks and open wounds are also a dead giveaway for a latch issue (ouch!)

   Normal nipple

   Lipstick nipple
3. **Houston, we have a nipple problem.** Flat and inverted nipples pose a challenge. The football hold may help get baby latched on. Stimulating inverted nipples to stand out prior to nursing may help. Breast shells (see page 108) also help inverted nipples. Lactation consultants are very helpful for this situation.
4. **Mouth problem.** Babies with tongue thrusting and tongue tie can have poor technique. See more about tongue tie below. Babies who thrust their tongues forward while nursing can be taught how to suck correctly (with a lot of patience and professional help).
5. **Poor milk supply.** Remember, milk supply is based on demand. If your baby is not stimulating you enough, use a breast pump to help rev up the supply. Pump for a few minutes after each feeding session.
6. **Sore nipples**. See box on the next page for tips.
7. **Engorgement.** See below for tips.
8. **Plugged ducts.** Equate this to a clogged pipe. The milk backs up and causes a hard, lumpy, tender area. Massage these areas while you nurse. Use moist heat before feedings and ice afterwards. Nurse or pump frequently (at least every three hours). Beware of any redness on the skin or fever. Plugged ducts are the precursor for a breast infection called mastitis (see later in the chapter for more info).

SORE NIPPLES: 7 TIPS FOR RELIEF

Experienced breast-feeding moms share these tips:

1. *Good hygiene is key.* Let nipples air dry and change nursing pads frequently. Cotton bras let more air through.
2. *Make sure you have a good latch and position.* That's what probably got you where you are right now. You don't want to continue to injure your nipples.
3. *Lanolin.* Using a protective cream will help the healing process. Apply *after* feedings.
4. *Acetaminophen (Tylenol) is fine to use*
5. *Nipple shields.* As we have already discussed, these are controversial because they inhibit the flow of milk. Use for a limited time only—until the thought of nursing doesn't make you want to cry anymore.
6. *Shorter feeding sessions are more tolerable.*
7. If you need to use a pump and express your milk temporarily, *use a hospital grade pump*. (For details on pumps, see below.)

Linda's Tip: Plugged ducts. Try nursing your baby with his chin pointing to the plugged duct—the suckling motion will massage the area and perhaps help unplug the duct.

Helpful Hint

Sometimes a baby has a poor sucking technique because he has a slight tongue tie (**ANKYLOGLOSSIA**). This leads to cracked, painful nipples in Mom and poor intake because baby has trouble compressing the nipple. If you think this may be a problem, let your pediatrician know about it. The thin piece of tissue causing the problem can be easily clipped (this procedure is called a frenulectomy).

Engorgement

Q. My breasts look like I have had implants and my baby can't get latched on. Help!

Welcome to engorgement. Don't worry, this is only a two or three day experience at most.

When your body first starts making milk, it sometimes gets carried away. This also happens if your baby takes less volume or suddenly starts sleeping through the night. Here are some ways to feel better:

1. **Pump or manually express for a few minutes before getting baby latched on.** Your nipple will stand more upright, be soft, and compressible.
2. **Pump or manually express only to soften the breast.** Pump off after feedings only if your baby is unsuccessful in nursing. Otherwise it can create an even greater supply of milk.

3. **Wear a bra 24 hours a day for support.** No underwires, ladies.
4. **Take a hot shower and massage breasts to encourage let down.**
5. **Cabbage leaves.** Yes, they can help. Try this: wear washed, chilled, crushed cabbage leaves in your bra. Replace wilted leaves every fifteen minutes for a total 45 minute experience, three times daily. Reality check: your baby may refuse the breast due to the cabbage flavor. Try another method if this happens!
6. **Put a bag of frozen vegetables** on your breasts for ten to 20 minutes before nursing if your breasts are hard and not leaking. Some women feel better using ice packs after nursing, too.
7. **Encourage your baby to nurse at least ten minutes on each breast.** This is the time women usually get desperate and wake their babies up to relieve their own discomfort.
8. **Take some ibuprofen (Motrin).** Yes, it's safe to use while breastfeeding.[3]

Reality Check

Speaking of implants…yes, you can nurse even if you have breast implants. However, certain types of reconstructive or breast reduction surgery may interfere with your ability to breastfeed exclusively. Get professional help from a lactation consultant.

Breastfeeding Books

Among the best is *The Nursing Mother's Companion* by Kathleen Huggins, R.N. It will hold your hand and give you 25 different ways to relieve engorgement. Also good: *The Womanly Art of Breastfeeding* by La Leche League.

Reality Check
Pacifiers and breastfeeding

Babies are soothed by sucking. In the first two months of life, sucking on a pacifier may be the only thing that reliably settles your baby. However, giving a breastfed baby a pacifier is controversial. Some experts argue that pacifiers create confusion for babies who suck pacifiers differently than the breast. It can interfere with your ability to decipher your baby's cues to eat. And a recent study showed that pacifier use shortens the duration babies are breastfed.[4]

In our opinion, breastfeeding and pacifiers are not mutually exclusive—pacifiers are NOT evil. But it is wise to wait on introducing a pacifier until your baby is a confident breastfeeder (between one and four weeks old). And, we recommend the "Soothie" brand (green with a long nipple; web: soothie-pacifier.com) as it is more similar to the human nipple than other brands. A reasonable alternative to the pacifier is a parent's finger. The other obvious alternative is to offer your breast for comfort nursing. This may or may not be for you.

Note: as we'll discuss in Chapter 9, "Sleep," pacifiers have been shown to reduce the risk of SIDS in babies under six months.

BOTTOM LINE

If you opt to use a pacifier, we suggest getting it out of your baby's life by six months of age when he no longer needs to be soothed by sucking. For more information, see Chapter 11, "Discipline."

Expressing Milk

Q. Why do some women express their breast milk (that is, pump)?

Many mothers pump to survive engorgement. You can pump off the excess milk to get more comfortable and baby can have an easier time getting latched on. For working moms, it's essential to pump to maintain breast milk supply. For stay-at-home moms, it allows you to escape your house for a little while.

Q. How do I pump and store my milk?

Here's is what you need to know:

- Wash your hands.
- Clean all breast pump apparatus thoroughly.
- Freshly pumped breast milk will last eight hours at room temperature and 24 hours in a cooler with blue ice.
- Use sterilized opaque plastic bottles (polypropylene) or polyethylene disposable bags for collection of milk. See below for a discussion of disposable bottle bags.
- Expressed milk can be refrigerated and used within five days.
- Expressed milk can be frozen for up to six months in the back a standard freezer (with a separate door from the refrigerator). It stays fresh in a freezer within a refrigerator for about two weeks. Avoid storing breast milk on the bottom of a freezer, as that area may warm up during a defrost cycle.
- Expressed milk can be frozen for up to 12 months in a deep-freezer.
- Remember to put a collection date on the bottles or bags! Use the oldest milk first.
- Yes, you can combine expressed milk from different pumping sessions together in one container. Just keep it going for a full day, then divide the milk up into individual servings.
- Start with four oz servings of milk to freeze. Store six to eight oz servings when your baby is three months old. Leave room in the container. Fluids expand when frozen.
- Newly expressed breast milk can sit out at room temperature for up to eight hours. So you can take freshly pumped milk with you when you are out and about without keeping it on ice.[5]

Reality Check

Plastic disposable bottle bags are very convenient for storage. You can pour the milk directly into them, put on a twist tie, and freeze. For use, immerse the bag in a bowl of warm water to thaw it out.

Here is the downside: many of those great antibodies in Mom's milk stick to the bags and don't get to baby's mouth. Most lactation professionals prefer the soft polypropylene bottles (frosted or colored plastic) for breast milk storage because the antibodies in the breast milk won't stick to these bottles as much.[6]

Another reality check: Breast milk can be different colors (white, yellow, blue, brown, black) and that's okay. Once it is frozen, it can smell kind of like soap. If it smells rancid, scald (not boil) your future freshly expressed milk, then quickly cool it and put in the freezer. It's not spoiled—use it.

Q. How do I serve my expressed breast milk?

Warmed and gently shaken. Some tips:

1. Thaw frozen milk in the refrigerator overnight.
2. Warm it up by placing the bottle into warm water.
3. Do not microwave it! It may lead to hot spots that can burn baby's mouth.
4. The milk will separate into water and fat. Mix the bottle up before serving.
5. Once the milk has been thawed, it will last in the refrigerator for up to 24 hours.

THE LOW DOWN ON BREAST PUMPS

You can rent a hospital grade pump, purchase an electric pump, or purchase a manual pump.

A smart move: rent a pump when you go home from the hospital. Renting lets you figure out whether you need a pump long term, without making a serious financial commitment. Most hospitals offer rentals or at least provide a list of medical supply companies in the area that rent pumps.

Moms who are returning to work but still want to pump have two options: rent a pump for an extended period of time or buy a pump. We recommend a hospital-grade dual pump. You can control the speed and pressure, which less expensive models don't allow. For working moms, efficiency is key. You can pump both breasts simultaneously in 15 minutes with a high-grade pump. A Medela brand "Lactina" or "Symphony" will cost $30-75 per month to rent. It pumps 50 cycles per minute (baby sucks about 60 times/minute) at a comfortable pressure.

You can purchase a hospital grade equivalent product (example: Medela "Pump In Style") for about $300. Another good brand: Ameda Purely Yours for $150. Both are decent double pumps. If you are looking at less expensive models, remember to look at the cycle speed and pressure.

You might get a manual pump as a shower gift. This is convenient for emergencies or travel. The mechanism is similar to operating a bike pump. Your arm may get tired out long before your breasts have emptied.

FYI: For an in-depth discussion on buying a breast pump (including brand name reviews) as well as the best milk storage options, check out our other book *Baby Bargains* (see back of this book for details).

6. Thawed (defrosted) milk is good for one hour at room temperature.
7. An unfinished (fresh, not defrosted) breast milk bottle can be placed back in the refrigerator and used within four hours. It's okay to reheat it.

Reality Check
Very few insurance companies will cover the cost of a breast pump or a private lactation consultation, despite the obvious medical advantages for both.

Q. When can I introduce a bottle?

Ideally, introduce one bottle a day of expressed (pumped) breast milk at two to four weeks of age. Why?
- Dad gets involved.
- Mom can go out to get her hair cut (remember you are nursing every 2-3 hours).
- Baby learns that food comes in different packages.

A common mistake is waiting until the end of maternity leave or when you want a date with your spouse to try a bottle. Once a baby is in the breast-only mode, he is less flexible about change.

Linda's Tip: Introducing a Bottle. Keep the bottle more horizontal when you are feeding a breastfed baby. That way, the baby has to actively remove milk from the bottle, just like at the breast. Don't let him chug it or he may not want to work at the breast.

Q. My baby is refusing to take a bottle. Help!

Babies are smarter than you give them credit for. They can see and smell Mom if she is anywhere in sight. Get out of the house and let someone else feed your baby the bottle.

Babies have thirst and hunger drives. No matter how stubborn your baby is, he will eventually accept a bottle of your breast milk if he is not given an option.

This is not cruel or unusual punishment.

Considerations for Mom

Q. I've heard I need to restrict my diet while I am breastfeeding. Is this true?

Not really.

Human milk is remarkably uniform despite differences in women's diets. It is always a good idea to eat healthfully for both you and your baby, though. There

DR B'S OPINION

"It is very healthy for your marriage to leave your baby at home with a loving family member or friend! I frequently prescribe this form of mental health therapy to my families. Dinner or a movie (you won't have time for both) is much cheaper than marital counseling."

DIETARY RESTRICTIONS FOR CERTAIN CIRCUMSTANCES

Two and a half percent of all newborns have a hypersensitivity to cow's milk. Occasionally, babies with a milk allergy can have problems if their breastfeeding moms have milk products in their diet (see "I Give Up" story below). For more information on food allergies, see Chapter 7, "Solid Nutrition."[9]

are actually very few restrictions. Here are the recommendations, according to the Institute of Medicine:

1. Avoid diets that promise rapid weight loss.
2. Eat a wide variety of foods including breads/grains, fruits, vegetables, milk and dairy, meats or meat alternatives daily.
3. At least three servings of milk products daily. But see below for details on milk protein allergies in babies.
4. Specifically eat Vitamin A rich foods: carrots, spinach, greens, sweet potatoes, cantaloupe.
5. Drink water when you are thirsty.
6. Caffeine-containing products (cola, coffee) are suggested in moderation (two servings or less per day). The caffeine enters the breast milk—so nurse first, and then have your coffee.
7. Avoid eating shark, swordfish, king mackerel, and tilefish because they may contain high levels of methyl mercury which can interfere with neurological development.[7]
8. It's okay to eat 12 ounces or less of shellfish, canned fish, small ocean fish, or farm-raised fish (and less than six ounces of canned tuna) per week.[8]

Feedback from the Real World: "I Give Up"

One of our readers sent us a note, in desperation, regarding her baby's problems. The mom had been exclusively breastfeeding her baby. She wrote, "it breaks my heart to hear her scream all the time… to have your child be so obviously unhappy and/or in pain all the time is the worst feeling in the world…I think it's time for me to give up (breastfeeding) because nothing else I've tried seems to work." A milk protein allergy was ultimately diagnosed.

Our response: You are not alone. Babies who suffer from this problem leave both baby and parents in misery. But do not fear—your child will not be like this forever. Some babies outgrow this problem by six months of age, and over 80% outgrow it by age five. Babies who are breastfed and have a milk protein allergy can still have problems because mom's milk/dairy intake can end up in the breast milk. If you want to continue breastfeeding, you need to avoid ALL products containing milk or dairy. There are often hidden dairy sources, so it's not only the obvious dairy products you need to avoid. Check out the web site FoodAllergy.org for more information.

FYI: Babies with classic milk protein allergies have blood streaked poop/diarrhea.

When your doctor gives you the green light to reintroduce dairy into your diet how will you accomplish this? After all, you don't want to start drinking a half-gallon of milk a day with extra-cheese pizzas and such. Here is a reasonable approach to introducing dairy gradually:

◆ Step 1: Start with small amounts of hard cheeses (cheddar, swiss) or yogurt for the first week.
◆ Step 2: If baby does well, try soft cheeses (gouda, cottage cheese) for week two.
◆ Step 3: If baby does well, try butter, ice cream, and cooked dairy products for week three.
◆ Step 4: If baby does well, have a glass of milk.

Of course, if your baby shows allergy symptoms again, it's back to the dairy free diet for you.

Old Wives Tale
You need to drink excessive amounts of water when you are nursing.

The Truth: Your body will increase its thirst drive to accommodate for your fluid needs. You don't need to go overboard.

FYI: Your daily caloric needs will be higher if you are breastfeeding. The average recommended daily allowance for non-pregnant women is 2100 calories. With breastfeeding, the recommendation is 2700 calories.[10] Don't bother counting calories, though, unless you are losing too much weight or having a problem producing enough milk.

DR B'S OPINION

"Babies will get what they need from breast milk, at the expense of Mom's body. I recommend continuing your prenatal vitamins if you are nursing."

Old Wives Tale
You need to avoid gassy foods like beans because it will make the baby gassy.

The truth: You may want to avoid gassy foods because other people might not want to be around you. Your baby is unaffected by this food choice.

Q. Is there any truth that some foods in my diet will make my baby fussy?

Yes, but there is no reason to restrict your diet unless you identify a problem. Foods that *might* cause a problem: cabbage, turnips, broccoli, rhubarb, apricots, prunes, melons, and peaches.[11]

Linda's Tip: Funky food, fussy baby? Is your baby fussy because of something you ate before nursing? Remember it takes anywhere from four to 24 hours to notice the effect. So, if your baby is acting unusually fussy, think about what you ate in the past day.

Q. Should I take DHA (Omega 3 fatty acids) supplements while I am nursing?

Maybe. DHA is an essential fatty acid found in fish oils. DHA is found in breast milk, but the amount varies depending on the nursing mother's diet. DHA is known to promote brain and vision development in infants. As a result, companies are promoting DHA supplements in prenatal vitamins and supplements for moms who are nursing. In a way, they have a point. Because the FDA has issued warnings about limiting fish consumption (tuna, mackerel, shark, swordfish, tilefish), nursing moms may be getting less fish oil in their diet. However, neither the American College of Obstetrics and Gynecology nor the American Academy of Pediatrics currently recommends DHA supplements. Bottom line: Ask your doctor for his/her opinion.

Q. Can I eat sushi while I am nursing?

Yes. Just be aware that consumption of raw fish (whether you are nursing or not) carries a slight risk of food-borne infection. And the FDA recommends that you eat less than 6 oz a week of tuna. So, order less toro and more unagi.

Q. Can I eat peanuts and peanut butter while I am nursing?

Yes. With the increase in people with peanut allergies, there has been quite a bit of research on this subject. A study in the *New England Journal of Medicine* looked at the diets of breastfeeding women and later development of food allergies in infants. The results: there was no association or prevention of peanut allergy even if mom avoided these foods in her diet. Interestingly, infants did show a sensitization to peanuts when skin products containing peanut oil were applied to irritated skin! Translation: kids with eczema or irritated skin may develop a peanut allergy from creams and lotions containing peanuts. Be careful to read the ingredients of those "natural" skin care products.

Q. Can I drink any alcoholic beverages while I am nursing?

Yes, in limited amounts.

Alcohol enters the bloodstream and the breast milk anywhere from 30-90 minutes after ingestion. The levels in the milk drop quickly. Each individual's metabolism is slightly different. So, a good rule of thumb is to avoid nursing for at least two hours after drinking. And, don't nurse if you feel tipsy!

I'd suggest you limit your intake to one alcoholic beverage, sporadically, if you are nursing.

Old Wives Tale
Drinking alcohol improves your milk supply.
The truth: Drinking alcohol may help relax an over-stressed mother, but it does not improve breast milk volumes or let-down reflexes.

Q. Are there any medications I need to avoid while I am nursing?

Yes, lots of them.

The short answer to this question is, always inform your doctor that you are breastfeeding. That way, a medication choice for you can be made safely. You can always call your child's doctor, or your pharmacist to double check.

See Appendix A, "Medications" for more information.

Q. I love exercising. Any problems with that while I am breastfeeding?

If you exercise vigorously then nurse, your milk may have a sour taste that your baby may not like. Exercise produces lactic acid in your body, which goes into your breast milk. It's not harmful, it just tastes funny. There have also been anecdotal reports of infant fussiness up to six hours after Mom's exercise/nursing session. Here are some suggestions:

- Pump or express for a minute or two before nursing.
- If your baby gives you a strange look, use some stored breast milk for that feeding!

Reality Check
While we are on the subject of sour tasting milk…your breast milk may change flavors during your period (if you have one). And it may not be a flavor your baby likes, according to lactation expert Dr. Ruth Lawrence.

Q. I am going back to work after my maternity leave. How am I going to make this breastfeeding thing work?

Setting aside time, having a progressive workplace, and being committed.

Some women are able to go back to work AND provide breast milk to feed their babies. It may take some trial and error to figure out what works for you, but here are some ideas.

1. Leave for work a little early and pump BEFORE you start working.
2. Invest in a high-powered, double pump. You can successfully pump in 15 minutes with one of these models.
3. Let your boss/co-workers know of your intentions. You may be surprised at how understanding people are.

DR B'S OPINION: MEDICATIONS AND BREASTFEEDING

Mothers frequently call me about medications they are taking and if they are okay to use while breastfeeding. Although I sound smart knowing all the answers on the phone, I find the answers in a book called *Medications and Mother's Milk* by Thomas Hale, Ph.D. If you are planning on nursing for the long haul, or have a chronic medical condition, it might be worth having this gem on your bookshelf at home. (Find it at www.iBreastfeeding.com or 800-378-1317.)

4. Think about where you will be able to pump and how often.
5. Think about where you will *store* your expressed milk until you get home. It can sit in a cooler with ice packs if you don't have access to a refrigerator.
6. Start stockpiling expressed milk BEFORE maternity leave is over.
7. Be prepared for being exhausted the first few weeks. It does get better.
8. If you don't have enough breast milk for the whole time you are away, supplementing with formula is okay. Your baby will benefit from any milk you can provide.

Q. I have a fever, can I still breast feed?

Absolutely!

Your body is producing antibodies to whatever infection your body is fighting. Those antibodies are going directly to your baby. If you have a cold or upper respiratory infection, not breathing on your baby would be helpful!

Contact your doctor (obstetrician, preferably) if you have a fever shortly after the birth of your baby. You could have a bladder infection, womb infection, or mastitis.

Q. So, what is mastitis?

A breast infection due to raw nipples and germs from your baby's mouth.

New mothers often have trouble with their baby's latch initially, leading to raw and cracked nipples. This lets baby's mouth germs enter Mom's breast. Symptoms include fever, chills (like you have the flu), pain/swelling/redness of the breast. Women are usually afflicted with this one to four weeks after delivery.

Treatment requires antibiotics (you need to call your OB for this) and continued elimination of breast milk from the breasts. Yes, this means you either need to continue nursing or pumping through this unpleasant experience. Your baby will not be harmed—it's *his* germs that did this to you!

If you take antibiotics, we suggest you also take probiotics (also known as acidophilus or lactobacillus). These are good germs (found naturally in yogurt) that will help prevent you from getting a yeast infection on top of everything else!

What causes mastitis?

1. Cracked nipples (mostly from poor latch technique)
2. Plugged milk ducts (from incomplete emptying at a feeding, tight clothes)
3. Missed feedings (lack of nursing or pumping for several hours)
4. Stress and exhaustion
5. Rapid weaning (lack of nursing)

If you notice that you have a tender, painful area on your breast—do something about it ASAP. Massage the area while you nurse or pump to unclog the duct. Apply a warm compress to the area. Nurse or pump every two to three hours. And, get some sleep![12] If your symptoms persist or worsen, call your OB.

Q. My nipples are burning every time I nurse. Why?

This is likely to be a yeast infection.

Pediatricians try to stay out of Mom's medical care, but parents often ask their opinion. Yeast infections also come from your little one's mouth. Babies (who are toothless) have some bacteria in their mouths, but not nearly as much as we do (because plaque goes along with teeth). Yeast likes dark, warm, moist, low bacteria places. So, newborns often get yeast or **THRUSH** infections in their mouths. It looks like curdled milk that can't be wiped off the gums, cheek lining, and roof of their mouth.

If your nipples burn or itch and you experience shooting pains every time your baby nurses, check your baby's mouth, and check with both your obstetrician and pediatrician. A family practitioner should be able to handle both of these problems.

Your baby can get an antifungal mouthwash and you can get an antifungal cream or oral medication.

There is evidence to show that the yeast clears more quickly if both mother and baby are treated, even if only one party is showing symptoms of infection. And some yeast infections get passed back and forth for what seems like forever. If that is your situation, see below.

Linda's Tips: Top 10 Tips to Beat Yeast
- Wash hands with hot, soapy water and dry with paper towels before and after nursing, toileting, and changing baby's diaper.
- Use bath towels once and then wash.
- Wash laundry in hottest water possible. Add a cup of white distilled vinegar to final rinse.
- Avoid powders or deodorants that contain cornstarch.
- If you have intercourse, use condoms to prevent cross-infection.
- Boil all pacifiers, bottle nipples, pump flanges daily for five minutes, or place in dishwasher on hottest setting and add white distilled vinegar to the rinse.
- Do not freeze breast milk while being treated. But it is OK to nurse and pump for daily use.
- Change bra pads as soon as they become moist.
- Wear a clean bra each day.
- Eat yogurt/take probiotics daily.

Special situations

Q. I am adopting a baby. I have heard that I can take a medicine to stimulate my milk supply. Is this true?

Yes. There is a medication called metoclopramide (the brand name is Reglan) that helps some women produce milk. This is also used for women who have trouble producing enough milk for their babies. While there are natural remedies to stimulate milk production, there is no scientific data on how effective these are. A good web source for info on this top is AskLenore.info.

Q. My milk supply is low. Can I do anything to improve my production?

Yes, some women do not make enough breast milk to feed their baby. Here are some suggestions to pump up the volume.

1. Try pumping with a high-efficiency breast pump AFTER nursing sessions. An empty breast signals the body to make more milk.
2. Try herbal supplements. Fenugreek (three pills, three times daily) and blessed thistle (three pills, three times daily) or a tincture called Mother's Milk Plus appear to be safe and may improve milk supply.
3. Try Reglan (metoclopramide). This medication requires a prescription from your doctor and may have some undesirable side effects.
4. Eat and sleep more. Your milk production depends on you taking good care of yourself.
5. Try eating a combo carbohydrate/protein snack just before or during nursing. This increases your prolactin hormone level, which in turn, increases milk supply.

Q. I am unable to breast-feed, but I want my baby to be breast-fed. Is there some place I can buy breast milk?

Yes. There are several programs across the country called Mother's Milk Banks that sell breast milk, primarily to ill, premature babies. The donors are rigorously tested to be certain they are free of infectious diseases like Hepatitis B and HIV. And, the breast milk is pasteurized. If a bank has excess supply, they will sell it to healthy newborns. It's quite pricey ($3 per oz). Check with your area hospital's lactation services or the La Leche League to see if there is a program near you.

On the flip side, if you have more milk than your freezer can handle, consider making a donation!

Reality Check

Certified milk banks check donors and their milk rigorously for infection before the milk is sold. It is becoming trendy for moms to purchase breast milk from neighbors, friends, and even wet nurses via the Internet. Let the buyer beware—this is probably not the safest idea for your baby.

Q. I have twins and want to breast feed. How do I make it work?

The key is getting both babies fed at the same time. Otherwise, it will be a challenge to get any sleep. Start this routine from day one and you will have more success.

When it comes to multiples, you will do a little more scheduling and a little less feeding "on demand." If you are able to get some hired or volunteered help around the house, things may be less chaotic for you.

The football hold and/or the cradle hold work well for simultaneous feeding sessions. It's probably wise not to have one breast exclusively designated for one baby. That way, they will accept either breast in the long run. And, just in case one breast produces more milk than the other, one baby won't get short-changed.

Q. I have a baby who was born prematurely. Anything special I need to know about breastfeeding?

Yes—it's even more important to breast-feed these little ones. Here are some special considerations:

1. Many premature babies get tired easily while nursing. If you no longer hear your baby swallowing, take him off the breast and burp him. Then return to feeding.
2. Many premature babies have poor technique (sucking, latching). Get professional help (from a lactation consultant) if you are having trouble.
3. You may be supplementing with formula or expressed breast milk for a while. Don't give up.
4. Rent a hospital grade pump for the first month because you will need to pump eight times daily to protect your milk supply until your baby is feeding well at the breast. A rental pump is the fastest, easiest option when pumping this often.
5. Weigh your baby once or twice weekly to make sure he is gaining, ideally, an ounce a day. Eventually you can stop doing this—check with your doctor.
6. The football hold works well for little preemies. That way you have better control of positioning and latch.
7. Give baby skin to skin time. This stimulates your milk production (and promotes bonding!)

Q. I need to leave my baby for a few days. Do you have any tips?

Leaving your nursing baby can be anxiety producing for both mom and baby. Some ideas to make life easier are:

- Start stockpiling expressed breast milk in the freezer a few weeks before the trip.
- Take an electric breast pump and a hand held one if you have a long flight.
- Offer breast milk in a bottle once daily before your travel begins.
- Take a picture of baby with you to inspire you to let down.
- Leave your slept-in nightie or another clothing item with your scent on it for your baby.
- Know that your baby will be just fine while you are away and happy to see you when you return.

Weaning

Q. When should I wean my baby off of breast milk?

When one or both of you is ready.

The American Academy of Pediatrics recommends breastfeeding for at least a year, with the addition of "complementary" solid food by six months. Hopefully, both you and your baby will enjoy nursing for at least that long. Some nursing teams (mother and baby) opt to continue even after one year.

So, the right time to wean is when one or both of you thinks it is time to stop. That time may be when your baby refuses the breast, when you decide you want your body to yourself, or when your ten-year-old asks for your breast by name. It is really a personal decision.

Reality Check

Americans tend to nurse their babies for less time than many other cultures. In some cultures, women nurse one child until the next one arrives. These same women have lower rates of breast cancer. Food for thought.

Q. I am planning to wean my baby. How do I do it?

Slowly and methodically.

If you stop breastfeeding abruptly, your body will be unhappy with you. Milk ducts get clogged (and infected). With that said, here is a typical strategy:

1. Create a timetable for the projected target date of nursing completion.
2. Eliminate one nursing session every three to four days, two to three weeks before your target date. The length of time for the entire weaning process depends on how many times a day you are currently nursing.
3. If you are weaning prior to one year of age, replace that feeding with either previously expressed breast milk or formula.
4. Eliminate the first morning and last evening feeding at the end of the weaning process.
5. Once you have completely stopped nursing, you may continue to leak milk for a week or two.
6. Wear an old bra (non-nursing), even though it is a little binding.
7. If your breasts feel so full that they are going to explode, pump or manually express just enough milk to get comfortable.
8. Taking Sudafed during the day, Benadryl at night, and/or drinking three cups/day of sage tea may also help.

Q. I want to continue breastfeeding, but my nine-month old seems to be weaning himself. Is that okay?

Yes, but you may gently encourage him to continue. Babies go on strike (from formula or bottles, too) for various reasons.

- Some babies get distracted during feeding sessions when they realize the world is pretty interesting. Nurse in a boring, dark, quiet place. Or nurse while he is sleeping.
- Some babies don't want to suck if they are teething. Try using acetaminophen to relieve teething discomfort.
- Ear infections and nasal congestion can also discourage a baby from nursing. Check in with your doctor.

If none of the advice above helps, transition to formula in a bottle or a cup (depending on your baby's age and skills). Transition to whole milk if your baby is over a year of age.[13]

Q. If I stop breastfeeding before my baby is one year old, what do I offer him instead?

Commercial-brand formula is the acceptable substitute for breast milk in the first year of life.

Note: whole milk, soymilk, goat's milk, and rice milk are NOT substitutes for breast milk in the first year of life.

The Big Picture: Breastfeeding for the First Year

Okay, let's sum up this breast-feeding section with an overview of nursing for your baby's first year:

Birth to 2 weeks: (18-24 ounces/day)

Breast fed newborns tend to eat every two or three hours. That adds up to eight to 12 times in a 24-hour day. They may cluster feed as frequently as every 1 1/2 hours (that's from the beginning of one feeding to the beginning of the next). If you are expressing breast milk and feeding via a bottle, your baby will probably take two or three ounces at a feeding.

Babies who try to nurse more frequently than every 90 minutes are nursing for comfort—BEWARE OF BEING THE HUMAN PACIFIER. Babies have no other way of consoling themselves. They can't just pull it together and settle down. Sucking is extremely soothing. So, if it has been less than 90 minutes since the beginning of the last feeding, try using your finger to let him suck. Your breasts will thank you. Note: If your baby is truly nursing non-stop, go get your baby weighed. Make sure you have enough milk supply.

On the flip side, your baby may take a four-hour stretch before feeding again. In the first two weeks of life, do not let your baby go more than four hours without feeding. Why?

- ◆ Breast milk is a supply and demand phenomenon. To get your supply established, the demand must be there.
- ◆ Your breasts will feel like they are going to explode. If that four-hour stretch is during daylight hours, you are in for a long night of cluster feedings.

2 weeks to 2 months: (20-32 ounces/day)

Once your baby is two weeks old, you can relax a bit. Your milk supply will be better established and your baby will have regained his birth weight. If he sleeps through the night, let him! You may need to pump to get comfortable during the night, but don't wake a sleeping baby. By the way, this is unlikely to happen. If it does, don't tell your friends about it. They will hate you.

This feeding "pattern" goes on for at least the first two months of life. While this seems a bit erratic, it is normal for a newborn is to be irregular with her feeding (and sleep patterns).

2 to 4 months: (30-40 ounces/day)

Your baby will start to have some regularity! He will have more predictable wakeful periods and sleep periods. Hopefully, you will be down to one or two night feedings. If you are returning to work and pumping, plan on four ounces per feeding at two months of age and up to eight ounces per feeding at four months. *Babies usually max out at 40 oz per day at four months of age.*

4 to 6 months: (36-40 ounces/day)

You can look forward to five or six breast feedings a day. You should be able to get an evening stretch of six hours without nursing. Six hours is considered "sleeping through the night", although this is probably not your definition.

6 to 9 months: (28-36 ounces/day)

Your baby will nurse four or five times per day. You should be done with night feedings. If you are not, do some problem solving with your doctor. You may enjoy those cuddly moments nursing in the middle of the night, but these are not a necessity. Your baby is comforted and used to feeding at night. Frequently, so is Mommy. If both of you are enjoying this situation, keep doing it. If one of you (Mom) is not enjoying it and wants more sleep, read Chapter 9, "Sleep."

You will be introducing solid foods at this point (see the next chapter on solid nutrition). Initially, solid food is dessert. Your baby needs the same volume of breast milk until he takes large volumes of solid foods.

9 to 12 months: (20-30 ounces/day)

Babies are well into solid foods and start to wean—that is, their volume and frequency of nursing decline. Your baby may nurse three or four times per day.

By one year of age, babies wean to 16 to 24 oz per day. At this point, you deserve a gold medal of honor. If you and baby are ready, you can stop breastfeeding.

We recommend switching to whole milk with Vitamin D added at one year of age. The goal is two cups of milk per day (or dairy serving equivalents). Remember, breast milk is low in Vitamin D and iron. So, if you want to go beyond a year of nursing, find other nutritional sources for these nutrients.

Now that you've learned more than you wanted to know about breastfeeding, let's talk about formula. But before we launch into that topic, the chart on the next page explores the top 8 biggest breastfeeding problems . . . and solutions.

Insider Secrets: Top 8 Breastfeeding Problems...

Sure, you know that breastfeeding is best for your baby ... but if something goes wrong? Don't give up! Here are the top eight breastfeeding problems and how to solve them.

Problem	Solutions
#1 Underproduction ◆ *Newborn*: less than three poops a day by Day 3 of life, poop not yellow/seedy by Day 5 of life, less than six wet diapers a day by Day 4 of life, no weight gain by Day 5 of life, birth weight not regained by Day 14. ◆ *Day 5-4 Months*: weight gain less than 5 oz/week. ◆ *4 Months-1 Year*: weight gain less than 3 oz/week.	◆ Continue nursing and pump with hospital-grade pump after each feeding ◆ After nursing, feed baby with expressed breast milk or formula ◆ Check baby's ability to get milk at the breast and discuss options to increase milk production with a certified lactation consultant.
#2 Overproduction ◆ *Baby*: coughs or chokes while nursing, excessive weight gain, green frothy poops. ◆ *Mom*: always feels full, milk shoots out forcefully.	◆ Nurse on one breast per feeding and return to that same breast if baby wants to nurse within two hours. ◆ Manually express or pump off for a minute before having the baby latch on (don't overdo it, or you will have even more milk production!) ◆ Lean back while nursing to reduce the flow.
#3 Engorgement ◆ *Baby*: has trouble latching on. ◆ *Mom*: has severe fullness and pain, nipples are flattened.	◆ Increase milk removal by nursing more often or pumping. ◆ Cold packs for 10-15 minutes after feedings. ◆ Ibuprofen. ◆ Should get better in 1-2 days, if not, visit a lactation consultant.
#4 Nipple Pain ◆ *Mom*: nipples/areola are red, cracked or bleeding, look like a tube of lipstick after nursing, look blanched after nursing, or have blebs (white cysts).	◆ Check baby's mouth and chin (tongue tie or a recessed chin can cause a latch problem). ◆ Have a lactation professional assess how baby is latching on. ◆ Have a lactation professional assess mom for a nipple infection.

...And solutions!

#5 Nipple Bacterial Infection
- *Mom:* nipples are cracked, painful during latching, draining pus or has golden crust.

- Mom's doctor can prescribe an antibiotic cream until nipples are healed.

#6 Plugged Duct
- *Mom:* localized area of a breast is painful, red, and tender usually before nursing, decreased milk production, fever free or temperature below 101.3F.

- Breastfeed frequently, always starting on the affected breast.
- Position baby with chin pointing towards the affected area.
- Massage the area while nursing or pumping. Apply heat before and ice after feedings.
- See a lactation consultant for more help.

#7 Mastitis
- *Mom:* Fever, body aches, redness or red streak on breast(s), decreased milk production

- Milk is safe to use. Nurse frequently on the affected breast.
- Use a hot pack on the breast for four minutes before each feeding (if breast is not feeling hot).
- Alternatively, if the breast feels hot, use ice pack before and after feedings.
- Mom's doctor can prescribe an oral antibiotic that's ok to use while nursing.
- Mom can take probiotics while taking antibiotics to prevent a yeast infection.

#8 Yeast infection
- *Baby:* may be symptom free, or may have white adherent plaques on the tongue, inside of cheek, inner lip, and gum line.
- *Mom:* may be symptom free or may have sharp/shooting/burning pain while nursing, shiny/red areola, cracked/ easily bleeding nipples, painful or itchy nipples/breasts throughout the day.

- Mom and baby should be treated for infection, even if only one party has symptoms.
- Baby: doctor can prescribe oral antifungal medication.
- Mom: can use over-the-counter antifungal cream on nipples or doctor can prescribe oral antifungal if pain is deep. Take probiotic supplement.
- Boil all pacifiers, teething toys, pump parts, breast shells, bottle nipples for five minutes daily.
- Good hand washing before and after breastfeeding.[14]

This chart is adapted with permission from Physician's Breastfeeding Triage Tool Kit, developed by Diana West, IBCLC, for International Lactation Consultant Association, Copyright August 2006.

LIQUIDS

Formula

Q. Is it okay to feed formula to my newborn?

Yes.

Although it is wonderful to breastfeed, it is also acceptable to feed your baby infant formula for the first year of life. But consider these points:

1. **It's expensive.** Expect to pay $500 for the first six months (and up to $800 during the first year) if your baby tolerates the least expensive cow's milk based product (hypoallergenic formula costs $1000).
2. **Prep time.** It isn't a pretty sight—your baby screaming at you at 2 am while you frantically mix a bottle of formula. Of course, your efficiency at preparing formula will improve over time, but the prep time is still a significant factor.
3. **Intolerance.** Human milk is made for human babies—it makes sense that it is more easily tolerated. It's more likely your baby will have a problem with formula. But, most babies do just fine.

Q. I have chosen to feed my baby formula. What formula do you recommend?

The cheapest cow's milk based formula with iron you can find. Get a warehouse club membership now, if you don't have one already. In general, the cheapest formula is the generic or store brand sold at discount stores like Wal-Mart and Target. Buy in bulk to get the maximum savings.

Here is an overview of these products. Dr. Lewis First, Chief of Pediatrics at the University of Vermont, deserves credit for the explanations below. He classifies formula into three categories: Coke, Diet Coke, and Caffeine

---

THE HISTORY OF BABY FORMULA

1700's: "Wet nurses" were paid to breast feed infants who could not be fed by their mother.

1800's: Milk from other animals was used as a substitute.

1838: The ingredients of animal milk and human milk were analyzed. We learned that cow's milk had a higher protein and lower sugar content which could cause problems for infants trying to digest it. This led to the first chemical "formula" that was added to cow's milk.

1870's: Nestle made the first infant formula that only required water to be added. It was very expensive and therefore quite unpopular.

The inventions of evaporated milk (1883), pasteurization (1890), and the refrigerator (1910) allowed parents to make infant formula in the comfort of their own home.

Free Diet Coke. We'll also provide you the brand names for each type in the following list:

◆ **Coke =** Cow's Milk Based Formula with iron. This is the formula tolerated by most babies and recommended first by most doctors.
   Name brands include: Enfamil Lipil*, Similac Advance*, Nestle Good Start Supreme*, Earth's Best. There are also generic or store brand cow's milk formula found at Wal-Mart, Target, and your grocery store.
   * These products contain DHA and ARA fatty acids. We'll discuss what that means later in this chapter.

◆ **Diet Coke =** Soy Protein Formula with iron. Some doctors recommend soy protein formula for babies who seem intolerant to cow's milk formula. (Note: this intolerance is NOT an allergy to milk protein, which is addressed with the formula type discussed next). "Intolerance" is a vague term for extremely gassy babies, or those who throw up more formula than they keep down. About 25% of American babies are fed soy formula. Soy formula is also an option for parents looking for a vegetarian-based alternative to cow's milk-based formula.
   Name brands include: Prosobee Lipil* (by Enfamil), Isomil Advance* (by Similac), Nestle Good Start Supreme Soy*. As you might guess, there are also generic/store brand soy formulas sold at Target and Wal-Mart as well.
   * These products contain DHA and ARA fatty acids. We'll discuss what that means later in this chapter.

◆ **Caffeine Free Diet Coke =** Protein Hydrolysate Formula with iron. The Dom Perignon of formulas, these are for babies with a **MILK PROTEIN ALLERGY**, not merely an intolerance to regular milk-based formula. Babies who are allergic to cow's milk protein have diarrhea with blood and/or mucus in their poop. Occasionally, babies with milk protein allergy also have a soy protein

---

1940-1960: Parents made infant formula out of evaporated milk, water, and corn syrup or sugar. The elaborate process of making formula daily provides much of the basis for the Old Wives Tales you hear about formula today.

1900'S → **PRESENT DAY**

1960's: Commercial formulas become popular due to a reduction in cost and ease of preparation. Breastfeeding rates drop sharply.

1970's: Only 25% of newborns left the hospital breastfeeding. As a result, the parents of this generation are the most formula fed babies in recorded history.

1980's and 90's: New scientific studies that point out the benefits of breastfeeding over formula spur a renaissance in nursing.

2003: 75% of babies go home from the hospital breastfeeding, but only 30% are breastfed beyond six months of life.[15]

DIFFERENCES BETWEEN BREAST MILK & FORMULA

To understand the differences, you need a brief chemistry lesson here. Milk contains fat, protein, and sugar. Use the following table as a reference:

	Human Milk	Cow's Milk formula	Soy Formula	Protein Hydrolysate
Calories	20 cals/oz	20 cals/oz	20 cals/oz	20 cals/oz
Protein % of calories	5%	10% Nonfat milk, whey	10% soy protein	10% of calories casein hydrolysate
Fat % of calories	54%	50% Vegetable oil	50% Vegetable oil	50% of calories Vegetable oil
Carbohydrate % of calorie	41% Lactose	40% Lactose	40% Corn syrup/ Sucrose	40% of calories Corn syrup/ Sucrose
Live cells Antibodies	Yes	No	No	No
DHA, ARA	Yes	Yes	Yes	Yes

Special notes:
1. Human milk has lactose sugar.
2. Soy formulas replace cow protein with soy protein and are lactose free.
3. Protein Hydrolysate formulas are the most hypoallergenic because the protein is pre-digested.
4. All formulas in the table contain the recommended daily iron requirement for babies. Avoid low-iron versions of formula unless specifically directed by your doctor.
5. Note that 50% of the calorie intake comes from fat.
6. The major formula companies are adding very long chain polyunsaturated fatty acid derivatives of Omega-3 and Omega-6 (DHA and ARA). These are present in breast milk and some studies suggest they promote vision/brain development. (For more on this topic see DHA below).

allergy. Some babies need this formula for the entire first year—but, based on a family history of food allergies and the severity of the baby's reaction to milk protein, your doctor may attempt a trial of soy formula before one year.

Name brands include: Nutramigen Lipil* (by Enfamil), Alimentum Advance* (by Similac).

* These products contain DHA and ARA fatty acids. We'll discuss what that means later in this chapter.

Helpful Hint
Do not switch formulas without asking your doctor. Most babies who are gassy and fussy will be gassy and fussy for the first three months of life no matter what they are eating. (For details, see Chapter 11).

BOTTOM LINE

All marketed formulas are tested extensively and required by law (Infant Formula Act 1986) to contain minimum levels of 29 different nutrients.

Soy Formula

Considering soy formula? The American Academy of Pediatricians (AAP) recommends soy formula for the following reasons:

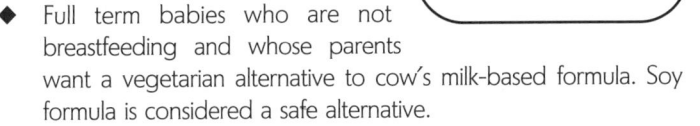

- Full term babies who are not breastfeeding and whose parents want a vegetarian alternative to cow's milk-based formula. Soy formula is considered a safe alternative.
- Full term babies with galactosemia or hereditary lactase deficiency.
- Full term babies with documented (diagnosed) transient lactase deficiency.
- Babies with documented (diagnosed) IgE-mediated allergy to cow's milk.

The AAP does NOT recommend soy formula for:
- Preterm infants with birth weights less than 1800g (4 lbs).
- Prevention of colic or allergy.
- Infants with cow's milk protein-induced enterocolitis/enteropathy (i.e. food allergy causing blood in stool)[16]

DR B'S OPINION

"Although we encourage you to breastfeed your baby for obvious benefits, your baby will be fine if he is formula fed."

Q. What are "comfort proteins" and "gentle formulas"? Should I believe claims that some formulas are easier to digest?

The cynic in us says: beware of another marketing ploy. But there are some minor differences you may want to know about. The Infant Formula Act requires a standard AMOUNT of protein in formula, but the TYPE of protein (the whey to casein ratio) can vary a great deal. Whey and casein are two types of protein found in milk. (Whey is acid soluble, casein is not).

Human milk has a whey to casein ratio of 60:40. Cow's milk has a ratio of 18:82. Because of the casein, cow's milk is much harder for a human baby to digest. Cow's milk based formula makers alter the ratios so the product is more easily digested. Enfamil and generic products have a 60:40 ratio. Similac has a 48:52 ratio. Nestle Good Start, however, is 100% whey, and the whey is pre-digested (hydrolyzed).

Both Enfamil's new "Gentlease Lipil" and Wal-Mart's Parent's Choice "Gentle" formulas contain partially digested whey protein in

DR B'S OPINION

"If you think Coke and Pepsi have an intense rivalry, check out the competition between formula companies. Despite the hype and personal preferences, the products are basically equivalent in each category."

the 60:40 ratio with reduced levels of lactose (milk sugar).

Do any of these formulas actually make babies happier? Maybe or maybe not—there is no good scientific data to prove that these are superior products.

Q. So which is better, cow's milk formula or soy formula?

The consensus here: cow's milk. Why? Cow's milk-based formula is a better source of protein than soy, according to research studies. But neither are without controversy . . .

Q. I heard that cow's milk formula causes diabetes?

A recent article in the *Wall Street Journal* pointed out "some researchers suspect cow's milk formula may increase the risk of type 1 diabetes in certain children, although the science behind this theory is far from conclusive." Again, the science is NOT there to draw any conclusions on this.

Soy formula also is somewhat controversial. Some researchers think soy formula may interfere with reproductive or immune functions when given in high doses to infants. Why? Soy formula contains phytoestrogens, which is a plant version of estrogen. While this chemical has shown to lower the risk of certain cancers in adults, it is unclear what effect it is has on infants. Again, however, there is NO proof that soy formula is harmful to babies. In 2006, the Center for Evaluation of Risks to Human Reproduction reviewed all the concerns regarding soy formula. One committee member said it best, "After 40 years of soy exposure we haven't seen a blip on the radar screen. Right now, we don't have a problem."

We don't mention these controversies to scare you, but you should be aware of them as you might hear discussion of this online and among parents. Just because a researcher has a *theory* about a particular product, it should NOT inspire panic in parents.[18]

As always, we'll track these controversies and put the latest updates on these issues on our web site at Baby411.com (sign up for our free newsletter for breaking news items).

WHAT ARE DHA AND ARA? LIPIDS?

DHA stands for Docosahexaenoic Acid. ARA stands for Arachidonic Acid. DHA and ARA are also called "lipids." Walk into your grocery store and you'll see lots of formula cans hyping their added lipids. So, what is this stuff? Lipids (DHA/ARA) are polyunsaturated fats that occur naturally in breast milk. They are also found in fish oils, egg yolks, and algae/fungal oil.

There has been a fair amount of research done on these fatty acids because they are present in nerve tissue and the eyes. Some studies show improved vision and scoring on infant developmental testing when babies have DHA and ARA in their diets.[17]

While the major brand-name formulas have lipids (these brands have phased out their non-DHA/ARA products), the generic formula brands still offer a choice. If you are trying to save money, we'd suggest buying the generic formula with the added lipids. We think your baby's formula should be as close to breast milk as possible.

Reality Check
I've heard that soy formula causes Attention Deficit Disorder (ADD). Is this true?

No. This fear stems from a study that purported to show a link between one ingredient in soy formula (manganese) and neurological disorders like ADD. But let's take a closer look at that study. Researchers fed baby rats extremely high doses of manganese—some 38 times greater than the level found in formulas. Surprise! These toxic doses caused developmental problems in the rats. The bottom line: Soy formula has been around for over 40 years and is considered acceptable by both the AAP and the Food and Drug Administration. If you give toxic doses of anything to rats (or people), bad things happen to them![19]

Q. I have seen other formulas on the shelf at the grocery store. What are they used for?

These would be classified as the "gourmet formulas." Most are made for babies with particular problems. A few are made as optional products, which are not based on a medical necessity. See the following section for more on gourmet formulas.

The Gourmet Formulas

1. Lactose Free Formula

Lactose intolerance occurs in older children and adults. Babies are rarely born with this problem. Lactose intolerance can occur temporarily after an infant has a stomach virus. Some stomach viruses break down the human enzyme "lactase" which digests the lactose sugar, creating a temporary intolerance. This can go on for one to six *weeks* after the virus.

When babies are allergic to formula, it is usually the milk *protein* that is the problem, as it is the most allergenic part of the food. It is rare for a baby to have a problem with the milk sugar (lactose). Human milk has lactose in it and it is perfect nutrition.

2. Isomil DF

This delicacy is made for babies who are experiencing a stomach virus. Not only has the lactose sugar and cow's milk protein been removed, but 6 grams of fiber are added per liter of formula. You're thinking, why give fiber to a child with the runs? Believe it or not, fiber actually bulks up watery stools. This formula can be used for the duration of a stomach bug to cut down on the water loss that occurs with intestinal infections.

3. Low Iron Formula

Most low-iron formulas have been taken off the market. Iron is the key ingredient in red blood cells. Iron carries oxygen to your whole body. Formula companies used to sell low-iron formula as an alternative product, but put a disclaimer on the package that babies needed iron supplementation if they were eating this stuff. Huh? Parents who turn to this product believe their baby is constipated from iron-rich formula—and hence expect that the low-iron stuff will solve the problem. Bottom line: steer clear of generic formulas that still offer a low-iron formula.

The American Academy of Pediatrics sees no role for the use of low-iron formulas in infant feeding and recommends that all formulas fed to infants be fortified with iron (more than 6.7mg/100kcal–this is present in standard formulas with iron).[20]

Old Wives Tale
Iron is constipating.

The truth: If your baby is constipated, he needs more fiber in his diet, not less iron. If you doubled your size in four or five months, you'd need that much iron, too.

4. Enfamil AR / Similac Sensitive RS

All babies spit up a little. But babies who suffer from heartburn (a.k.a. gastoesophageal reflux), look like the Exorcist. Thickening the formula can help keep it from coming back up. So pediatricians often recommend parents add a teaspoon of rice cereal to each bottle to make the formula heavier. After trying this at home, however, I can tell you that the formula gets clumpy and it requires minor surgery on the rubber nipple to get it out of the bottle. No fun.

Enfamil AR solves this problem by adding rice starch to their regular cow's milk formula. This is much easier to use, reducing your frustration. You will still need to use bottle nipples with a larger hole to get the formula to flow, however.

It is an old wives' tale that adding rice cereal will make your baby sleep through the night. But those old wives would be correct if they are speaking about babies with reflux.

5. Organic Formulas

These are the certified "antibiotic, pesticide, and growth hormone free" products on the market. Brands include: Earth's Best, Similac Organic, Parent's Choice. Are these organic formulas worth the hefty price tag? It's your call. The good news: stores like Wal-Mart now sell generic organic formula at lower prices.

6. Formula with probiotics

As of this writing, Nestle Good Start Supreme is the only formula that contains active living bacteria cultures like the stuff found in yogurt. Good Start has Bifidus lactis, a "good germ" similar to what resides in the guts of babies who are breastfed. The potential benefits include fewer illnesses, less severity/frequency of diarrhea, and maybe even less colic. And there do not seem to be any significant risks with this type of formula.[22]

Are the health benefits worth the added cost? Maybe, but only time

FORMULA FOR PREEMIES

There are higher calorie formulas made especially for babies who are born before 34 weeks gestation or less than four pounds. These formulas have more calories, more protein, more calcium, and more phosphorous than standard formulas. Some babies will switch to standard formula, but the premature formulas can be used for a whole year if necessary for growth.[21]

and more research will tell. A cheaper option: Buy a probiotic supplement like L reuteri and toss it into whatever your baby is eating once a day. (see Appendix B, Alternative Medications, for details)

FYI: If you use a probiotic-enhanced formula, be sure to mix it with water less than 100 degrees or you will kill all those little good germs!

7. Nestle Follow-up and other "toddler" formulas

According to Nestle, their Follow-Up formula is designed for babies from four to 12 months of age. This product contains more calcium (120mg per 5oz) than its competitors' standard infant formula (78mg per 5oz). The manufacturer's theory: babies over four months have a higher calcium requirement than those under four months of age.

Other formula companies have tried to jump on this bandwagon as well, with "next step" products for 9-24 month olds and "toddler formulas" designed for one to three year olds. The formulas, with added vitamins, are pitched to parents as an allegedly better substitute for cow's milk.

Is any of this necessary? We say no. Follow-up (for four to 12 month olds) and toddler formulas (for one to three year olds) are generally a waste of money. The calcium content of standard infant formulas is appropriate for birth to 12 months of age. After one year of age, a baby can drink whole milk—at a savings of 80% compared to the cost of toddler formula! The American Academy of Pediatrics Committee on Nutrition concurs. They do not recommend using toddler follow-up formulas for healthy children who have low risk of nutritional deficiency.[23]

Q. Do you have a preference of powder, concentrate, or ready-to-feed?

In previous editions of this book, we told our readers to pick the cheapest formula option: powder. But this answer is now a bit more complicated. Here's why:

The American Dental Association suggests using ready-to-feed formula to avoid excess fluoride intake (see discussion of this in the previous chapter).

Powdered formulas are heat-treated but cannot be commercially sterilized like ready-to-feed formula. Thus, powdered formulas contain low levels of microorganisms. One particular germ, Enterobacter sakazakii, can cause serious infections in babies who are low birth weight, born prematurely, or immune compromised.[24]

Given those concerns, we have revised our recommendations: while we STILL recommend powder formula as the best option for baby, we do so with the following caveats:

1. Mix powder formula with purified, demineralized, deionized, distilled, or reverse osmosis filtered water.
2. Use the prepared formula within 24 hours of preparation.
3. Don't use a blender to prepare it—blenders can harbor bacteria.
4. Don't use powder formula if your baby was low birth weight, premature, or is immune compromised.

It's perfectly fine to use liquid concentrate or ready-to-feed formulas, but they are significantly more expensive.

FYI: the nutrients are the same for all types of formula!

LIQUIDS

Old Wives Tale
The ready to feed formula is easier to digest.
The Truth: The ready to feed is convenient, a little thicker, and a lot more expensive. All products are digested exactly the same way.

Q. Do I need to sterilize the bottles, boil water, or use bottled water to mix the formula?

No, no, and yes.

You don't need to sterilize bottles. Yes, we do suggest a run through the dishwasher when you first open the packages. Thereafter, you can clean bottles with warm, soapy water. That's clean enough. Your baby isn't sterile once he leaves the hospital nursery anyway, and is exposed to real world germs on a daily basis.

You don't need to boil the water you use to mix formula because the American water supply is pretty clean. Formula companies have instructions to boil the water on the package because their products are distributed worldwide. Note: if you have well water, you need to get your water tested before your baby arrives to make sure it isn't contaminated.

Sterilizing bottles and boiling water are all based on the kitchen chemistry our mothers and grandmothers followed to prepare formula in the olden days.

Yes, we do recommend bottled water to mix formula—see the above discussion in the previous question for more details. We also discuss this issue (fluoride and formula) in the previous chapter, Chapter 5, "Nutrition."

Helpful Hint
Look at the mixing instructions on the formula can. Powder requires one scoop per two ounces of water. Liquid concentrate is one ounce of formula per one ounce of water. Ready-to-feed is ready to go (DON'T ADD WATER). This may seem obvious to you. But if you screw up, your baby gets either half of the calories he needs or rocket fuel.

My mother-in-law (who is a very bright woman) mistakenly bought ready-to-feed formula for her third baby (my future husband) and added water because she thought she had purchased concentrate. Her astute pediatrician identified the problem at the baby's two-week well check when he wasn't gaining weight. Sure, this baby ended up nearly six feet tall as an adult, but we figure he could have topped Shaq's height if this mistake was caught earlier.

Q. Which bottles/nipples do you recommend?

There are so many products out there. You'll end up trying a few out to discover your baby's preference. Some have advantages that may be appealing to you: disposable bottle bags, curved bottles, air free mechanisms (an example: Dr. Brown's bottles—no relationship to the author of this book). The nipple manufacturers all claim to be the most like Mom's nipples—Playtex and Avent are the most popular in this category. As you will read below, there's currently a bit of controversy regarding clear, hard plastic bottles made of polycarbonate. That may or may not influence your bottle selection.

Lactation consultants we've interviewed seem to like the Avent nipples best. They believe there is less nipple confusion when they are used.

Lactation consultants also recommend holding the bottle in a more horizontal position so babies have to work a bit harder to get the milk. Why? Bottles are usually much easier to feed from so babies get "lazy."

Note: There are newborn nipples (low flow), older baby nipples (higher flow), and cross cut nipples (highest flow). You can switch to the older baby nipples at four months. The cross cut nipples are better for babies with reflux who drink thickened formula.

For an in-depth discussion of bottles (including brand reviews and money-saving tips), check out our other book, *Baby Bargains*. See the back of this book for details.

Q. Are plastic baby bottles safe? I've heard they release harmful chemicals.

Psst! Hey, buddy! Want to buy a baby bottle?

No, we're not making this up: in San Francisco, selling a plastic baby bottle could someday bring you a $1000 fine and six months in jail.

What's all the fuss about?

Clear plastic baby bottles (as well as some food containers and water bottles) are made of polycarbonate, which contains a chemical called Bisphenol A (BPA). It is the BPA that makes the hard, clear plastic bottles . . . well, hard and clear.

So why did San Francisco ban polycarbonate baby bottles in 2006? Well, BPA's chemical bond with polycarbonate breaks down over time, especially with repeated washing or heating of the bottle. As a result, BPA leaches out of the plastic and ends up in the liquid—that is, the breast milk or formula.

As you can imagine, there are some potentially serious health concerns here. BPA may mimic the natural female sex hormone, estradiol. While most data about BPA comes from animal research, these studies show even low level exposure of BPA *may* be linked to everything from early puberty and breast cancer, to attention and developmental problems.

Yet, like many other environmental health issues, we don't know all the answers about BPA—the research is evolving . . . and contradictory. A 2003 study of BPA linked huge doses of the chemical to chromosomal abnormalities in mice. *But there have been no studies to prove these chemicals cause any harm to humans.*

Adding fuel to the baby bottle debate was the recent release of a study by the Environment California Research and Policy Center, a left-leaning advocacy group. The center independently tested the best-selling clear, hard, plastic baby bottles (Avent, Dr. Brown, Evenflo, Gerber, Playtex). All of them leached between 5-10 ppb (parts per billion) of BPA. These levels are higher than those known to cause health problems in animal studies.[25] This report, however, contradicts an earlier scientific study that did *not* find levels of BPA leaching from baby bottles that exceeded EPA standards.[26]

And even Europe has backed away from calling BPA harmful—the European Union's Food Safety Authority (EFSA) recently released a report that reaffirmed BPA's safety. The same report criticized the methodology of the rodent/BPA studies as unreliable.[27] Even San Francisco has had second-thoughts about its bottle ban: the city repealed law in April 2007 and instead called for more testing. But, the city vowed to reconsider the ban if the California state legislature doesn't take up the issue this year.

Meanwhile, the lawyers have joined the fray—baby product manufacturers and retailers have sued San Francisco, saying the ban is unnecessary. And other lawyers have filed a class action lawsuit against bottle makers that use BPA. For the record, bottle makers like Avent dispute the notion that BPA-containing bottles pose any health risk.

When will we find out if BPA (and poly-carbonate) baby bottles are a danger? Well, the National Institute of Health/National Toxicology Program has assigned an independent panel to evaluate the rising concerns of BPA—answers may be forthcoming later in 2007.[28] We'll keep you posted on the results of this study on our Baby 411 blog and E-newsletter. Be sure to sign up for it at our website, baby411.com.[29]

So what's the take-home message for the time being? *Until we get more definitive answers about their safety, we do NOT recommend using polycarbonate (hard, clear plastic) baby bottles.*

What if you've already bought $100 worth of Avent bottles? Instead of throwing them away, follow these safety precautions:

- Limit the number of times you boil those bottles or put them in a dishwasher.
- If you do use a dishwasher, skip the "heated dry" cycle.
- Buy new bottles every time you have a new baby.

If you want to avoid BPA altogether, you have several options:

- Use glass bottles. Obviously, there is a risk of injury to baby or mom if the bottle is dropped, so glass isn't a perfect alternative.
- Use bottles made of opaque plastic. These bottles (made of polyethylene or polypropylene) do not contain BPA. (Note polycarbonate-containing bottles have a #7 on their recycling label).
- Consider a BPA-free plastic bottle. Born Free makes a BPA-free clear plastic bottle (Newbornfree.com) sold at Whole Foods. But these cost about $10 each, twice the price of Avent bottles.
- Use a drop-in system. For example the Playtex Drop-in System is BPA free (that is, the bottle liners do not contain BPA).
- Avoid store-bought baby food in metal or plastic containers.

(Consistency alert: we realize the above advice contradicts what we wrote in our other book, *Baby Bargains*. In that book, we said polycarbonate bottles were fine to use. However, that book went to press BEFORE the release of the most current BPA studies and concerns. We apologize for any confusion and we will update the *Baby Bargains* book as soon as we go back to press).

Again, we will post the latest news on BPA (including the latest research) on our blog (Baby411.com, click on News/Updates).

Reality Check

Feeder bottles (solid food dispensers) are unnecessary. Your baby needs to learn how to eat, *not drink* his solid food. (See the next chapter for more).

The Big Picture: Formula Feeding for the First Year

Birth to 2 weeks: (18-24 oz)
Newborns tend to eat two to three ounces every three to four hours. For the first two weeks, wake your baby if it has been more than four hours since the last feeding. Once baby has regained birth weight, he can sleep as much as he wants (good luck)!

2 weeks to 2 months: (20-32 oz)
You will see a gradual increase in volumes at feedings. By two months, babies usually take around four ounces per feeding, about every three hours.

2 to 4 months: (30-40 oz)
Your baby will eat six to eight ounces per feeding, and *max out at about 40 oz per day at about four months of age.*

When the volumes go up, the number of daily feedings go down. So, a baby who chugs 8oz at a feed can eat five times a day and sleep through the night. Parents often ask if they can space out the frequency of daytime feedings. NO! Use common sense here—if your baby eats every two to three hours during the day, you will all be sleeping at night.

Babies who take smaller volumes at each feeding will need to eat more often. These tend to be babies who suffer from heartburn (**GASTROESOPHAGEAL REFLUX**). We'll have more on this in Chapter 8, "The Other End."

4 to 6 months: (40 oz)
Babies continue to take a ballpark of 40 oz per day of formula. *There should be no reduction in the volume of formula.*

6 to 9 months: (28-36 oz)
You will be introducing solid food. Initially, you should view it as dessert. Your baby will start to wean—decreasing volumes of formula as his intake of calories from solid food increases.

9 to 12 months: (20-30 oz)
Your baby will decrease drinking formula to a minimum of 24 oz per day. At one year of age, your baby will usually drink three 8 oz bottles. This will then be replaced by whole milk that is Vitamin D fortified. *The goal is 16 oz a day (which is two cups a day) of milk.* The equivalent of dairy products is also fine.

It's time to kick the bottle habit at a year. Don't get stuck here. You don't have a baby anymore. You have a toddler. If you want a baby in your house, go have another one. Yes, your child will be quite capable of drinking via a cup, sippy cup, or cup with a straw. He will not go thirsty.

Other Liquids

Q. Does my baby need any water?

Not until six months of age.
The reason: your baby is already getting water. It's naturally mixed in

breast milk and artificially mixed in to prepare formula. Your baby gets plenty of water. After six months of age, your baby should start to drink some water every day. How much? Even though there is no official guideline, we think four to six ounces of water a day is adequate.

No matter what other liquid babies are drinking or how it is prepared (breast milk, ready-to-feed formula, or powder/liquid concentrate formula), babies *over six months of age* should all drink some fluoride containing water (0.7ppm–1.2ppm) on a daily basis. Again, four to six ounces a day is our best estimate on what is needed.

If your baby has no source of fluoride-containing water in his diet for whatever the reason (using fluoride-free bottled water, reverse osmosis filtered tap water, etc), then you should discuss getting a fluoride supplement with your doctor or dentist. For details on this whole fluoride issue, check out Chapter 5, "Nutrition."

Reality check: Bottled water is not any safer than tap. A Dutch study compared bottled water from 16 countries. 37% of the samples were contaminated with bacteria and 4% were contaminated with fungus.

Q. When can I give my baby juice?

What's the rush?

Pediatricians, as a general rule, are not very enthusiastic about juice. Sorry, juice producers of America. Here are the reasons:

1. *Juice provides little nutrition.* Vitamin C has to be added to many juices to give them any nutritive value. Otherwise, juice is just a form of liquid sugar.
2. *Juice is filling,* which decreases a child's appetite for more nutritious foods.
3. Drinking juice throughout the day (especially in a bottle) causes sugar buildup on the teeth. This, in turn, creates **high dental bills**.
4. *A sugar-loaded diet causes diarrhea.*

BOTTOM LINE: Children with poor weight gain, chronic diarrhea, or rotten teeth often are juice-a-holics. The American Academy of Pediatrics recommends no more than six oz of juice a day for 1-6 years of age.

Helpful Hint

A sneaky way to get those vegetables in: drink them. Although we aren't big fans of juice, combination carrot-orange juice is a tasty option most kiddos like. And it's an excellent source of Vitamin A and C. Tropicana Healthy Kids Orange Juice also contains Vitamin A, C, E, and has calcium added. Another great product: Vruit (web: americansoy.com). A blend of both fruit and vegetable juices, they are 100% juice and come in kid-sized boxes.

DR B'S OPINION

"If you are going to offer juice, do it after six months of age. Offer no more than six ounces per day. Diluting it half and half with water is even better. I also suggest introducing juice in a cup not a bottle."

Q. When can my baby drink from a cup?

Any time after six months of age.

Your long-term goal is to have your baby drinking from a cup at his first birthday. Babies usually get the hang of it between six and 12 months.

> **Reality Check**
> *Once your baby has teeth, you need to wipe them or brush them after the last feeding (before bedtime).* Your baby shouldn't be falling asleep while he is eating by the time he has teeth anyway. (See Chapter 9 "Sleep" for details.)

Q. When and how do I switch to cow's milk?

At one year of age, cold turkey.

Your baby still needs a high fat diet because his brain development is on overdrive. The American Academy of Pediatrics recommends whole milk until *two years of age*.

After the second birthday, your child should drink what the rest of the family is drinking. This should be *skim milk*, everyone. The fat will clog your baby's arteries just like it clogs ours.

Q. What do you think of alternative dairy products compared to cow's milk?

While some products have nearly the same calories as whole milk, less of those calories come from fat (and 12 to 24 month olds still need the fat). The preferred dairy beverage of choice is whole cow's milk. Here is a comparison:

8 OUNCE SERVING	WHOLE MILK (3.5% FAT)	SKIM MILK (0.1% FAT)	SOY MILK	RICE MILK
Calories	150 calories	80	100	130
Total fat	8 grams	0	4	2
Sodium	115 mg	125	140	105
Carbohydrate	11 grams	12	22	26
Cholesterol	35 mg	0	0	0
Protein	8 grams	9	7	1
Vitamin A	yes	yes	yes	yes
Vitamin C	yes	yes	no	no
Vitamin D	yes	yes	yes	yes
Calcium	50%	50%	60%	<10%
Other nutrients			iron	B12

Q. What do you think of organic milk?

It's expensive.

Some families prefer to buy organic, pesticide free products. Others don't. There is no public health group that recommends the use of organic milk over store brand cow's milk. Some parents have concerns about bovine growth hormone in "regular" milk causing precocious puberty. Currently, medical evidence is lacking to support this claim. It's your call.

> ### DR B'S OPINION: SIPPY CUPS
>
> Yes, I know they are popular: the no-spill sippy cup. Yet, I have never been a fan of these because the sucking mechanism to get the fluid out is similar to a bottle. Dentists dislike sippy cups because the flow of liquid heads straight to the back of the top front teeth. In short, sippy cups can promote tooth decay.
>
> I'd prefer to have your baby drinking from a straw if he hasn't quite mastered the art of drinking from a cup.

Q. Is it okay to use formula after a year of age?

It is not the appropriate diet for a child over age one. For babies who are failing to thrive, your doctor might recommend a dietary supplement (such as Pediasure, Carnation Instant Breakfast). Using formula for convenience when you are out and about isn't harmful, but is unnecessary. Using formula for nutrition is a waste of money.

Solids
Chapter 7

"Raising kids is part joy and part guerrilla warfare."
~ Ed Asner

What's in this Chapter

- **How to tell if your baby is ready to eat solid food**
- **What is rice cereal?**
- **Stage 1 or first foods**
- **Making your own food**
- **Food allergy**
- **Food intolerance**
- **The big picture—how much to offer and when**
- **Food labeling**

This is the chapter you have been waiting for! After months of feeding your baby a liquid diet, you're looking forward to those photos with peas all over your baby's cute little face. And friends and relatives can get into the act of feeding baby too.

You are allowed to read this chapter at any time, but know that solid food is not part of your baby's dietary needs until six months of life. Although some doctors recommend experimenting with solid food between four and six months, it's NOT meant to be nutrition, but rather, dessert. If you are breastfeeding, the AAP recommends holding off on *any* solid food until your baby is six months old.

When your baby is taking larger amounts of solid foods (seven to nine months of age), solid food will start to replace some of the nutrients that liquid nutrition offers.

Before we get going, let's define some baby food lingo:

- **Stage 1 Food.** The first solid food given to babies. Pureed. Most easily digested, least allergenic. Examples: rice cereal, fruits, vegetable, except for berries and citrus.
- **Stage 2 Food.** More complex to digest, more allergenic solid food. Chunkier texture. Examples: oatmeal cereal, barley cereal, mixed cereal, meats, pastas, dairy, papaya, mango, guava.

- **Stage 3 Food.** Most complex solid food. Very chunky. Comparable to table food.
- **Finger foods.** Food your baby can feed to himself. Good for independence, fine motor skills. Examples: teething/biter biscuits, small pieces of fruit/vegetables, crackers, pasta wheels, Cheerios, ground meat, canned chicken.
- **Table food.** What you eat.

Babies progress through the solid food experience based on four issues:

1. Food allergies. Start with the least allergenic foods first.
2. Oral motor skills. See what your baby can do. Babies cannot eat solid food until they know how to swallow it.
3. Texture complexity. Start with pureed foods, move up to chunks, then pieces. Babies cannot move up to pieces of food until they know how to gum it or chew it before swallowing. Some babies develop preferences for certain textures (or lack of texture).
4. Volume. Start with a tablespoon or two once a day. Your baby will work his way up to several ounces of solid food at a "meal," three times daily from six to twelve months old.

We'll cover all of these issues in detail later.

Q. My mother wants to feed my two-month-old solid foods. I've heard this is a bad idea. Help!

Your mother will tell you that she fed you rice cereal at two months of age and you did fine. Here is your ammunition to keep the baby spoon out of Grandma's hands:

1 **STARTING SOLID FOODS WILL NOT MAKE YOUR BABY SLEEP THROUGH THE NIGHT.** Most babies start sleeping through the night by four months of age. It is not because their tummies are full of rice cereal, but because they are developmentally able to by that age.

2 **INTRODUCING SOLID FOODS AT AN EARLY AGE (BEFORE BABIES CAN DIGEST THEM) MAY RESULT IN FOOD ALLERGIES.**

3 **SOLID FOOD IS SPA CUISINE.** As you already know, breast milk and formula are the only items that should be on the menu for babies from birth to at least four months. These products contain 50% fat and thus, are loaded with calories (20 calories per oz). So unless you are serving lard for dinner, you will never get that many calories in solid food! For example: rice cereal has 60 calories per 1/4 cup (5 calories per tsp) and a jar (2 1/2 oz) of "Stage 1" carrots has 25 calories. Your baby would need to eat almost 3/4 cup of cereal or six whole jars of carrots to replace one bottle or breastfeeding session. You'll be lucky if your baby eats two tablespoons of cereal or 1/2 jar (1 oz) of carrots in a feeding session.

4 **TELL GRANDMA THAT YOUR DOCTOR TOLD YOU NOT TO START SOLIDS UNTIL AT LEAST SIX MONTHS OF AGE.** Use your doctor as an excuse any time. We don't mind.

PREEMIES & SOLID FOOD

Because eating solid food requires a certain level of oral motor skill, many premature babies are not ready to eat solid food until their adjusted age (based on due date) is at least four to six months old. Also, preemies tend to need lots of extra calories for catch up growth. Liquid nutrition is a much better source for calories than solid food.

Q. My baby is four months old now. Is he ready to eat solid foods?

It depends. Here are the key questions: Is he exclusively breastfed? Does your doctor suggest it? Does your baby know what he is doing when you put a spoonful of cereal on his tongue?

The World Health Organization and UNICEF both recommend starting "complementary foods" (that is, solids) at or about six months of age. And that timeframe is similar to the AAP's recommendations

Yet, the advice on this topic can be confusing. Even the AAP doesn't agree with itself on when to start solid foods. The Breastfeeding Committee of the AAP says to wait to start solids until six months if you are breastfeeding. The Nutrition Committee of the AAP says you can start at four to six months of age when the baby is showing signs of readiness (see below). As you can see, the advice is a little muddled, but here is the bottom line: It never hurts to wait.

From an allergy standpoint, he can probably tolerate "Stage 1" foods (see below). It's a matter of knowing what to do with a bit of food on the tongue (**ORAL MOTOR SKILLS**). Some babies are ready at four months; some aren't ready until six months. Your baby will tell you if he is ready. Try putting a spoonful of rice cereal on his tongue. If he swallows it, he's ready. If he spits it back out at you, put the box away and try again next week. Again, the take home message: *there is no hurry to start solids.*

BOTTOM LINE: There is a great deal of variability amongst babies (and their doctors) about when they are ready to eat solid food. But remember, solid food before six months of age is just for fun. And once you get the green light to start solids, remember that solids are "complementary foods," not the main source of your baby's nutrition. Breast milk/formula is still the priority.

First Foods and Beyond

What are Stage 1 foods? Stage 2? We'll give you the answers below. Before we get rolling, however, let's answer that age old question: IN WHAT ORDER do you introduce these foods? The answer: there is no right answer. All Stage 1 foods are fine to introduce to a baby who is at least six months old—these foods are the LEAST allergenic. That changes a bit with Stage 2 foods (more on this later in the chapter). Why are Stage 2 foods, well Stage 2? That's because babies start with pureed foods (Stage 1, such as oatmeal) and need to figure out how to deal with textures and bite-sized pieces (crackers, for example, are a Stage 2 food).

SOLID FOODS

FYI: We don't list Stage 3 foods here because most are just a combination of the first two stages (that is, turkey and rice dinner).

Bottom line: start with Stage 1 and see what happens. Once a food has been introduced and tolerated by your baby, you can include that food in combinations or recipes.

Fruits and Vegetables, Stage 1:
- Applesauce
- Apricots
- Asparagus
- Avocados
- Bananas
- Broccoli
- Carrots—cooked, pureed
- Green beans
- Guava
- Mashed potatoes
- Mango
- Melons
- Nectarines
- Papaya
- Peaches
- Peas
- Pears
- Plums
- Prunes
- Pumpkin
- Squash
- Sweet potatoes *(alone or sneak into pancake mix for Stage 2 food)*

Fruits and Vegetables, Stage 2:
- Bell peppers
- Blueberries
- Grapefruit
- Kale and other greens
- Kiwi
- Oranges
- Pineapple
- Rhubarb—cooked
- Spinach—cooked
- Strawberries
- Tomatoes

Dairy, Stage 1:
- Whole milk yogurt
- Cheese
- Yogurt smoothies

Grains, Stage 1:
- Rice cereal
- Barley cereal
- Oatmeal cereal
- Wheat cereal
- Millet cereal
- Quinoa cereal

Grains, Stage 2:
- Cheerios/Oatios or generic
- Cornmeal: *polenta, cornbread, corn tortillas*
- Oat bran cereal/muffins
- Pasta such as wagon wheels
- Puffed kashi
- Rice cakes
- Whole grain pancakes
- Whole grain waffles
- Whole wheat crackers

Meats and Beans, Stage 1:
- Beans: *red, kidney, white, black-eyed, navy, etc*
- Beef
- Chicken
- Garbanzo beans: (hummus spread)
- Lamb
- Lentils
- Pork
- Split peas
- Tofu
- Turkey

Meats and Beans, Stage 2:
- Edamame
- Egg yolks: *(no egg whites until after first birthday)*
- Sunflower seed butter

SOLID FOODS

Q. What is rice cereal?

You will find it in the baby food aisle in a box.

Rice cereal is often the first food a baby eats. You buy it in a box as dry flakes. Mix it with either expressed breast milk or formula (otherwise it tastes like cardboard). Be sure you read the packaging. *Some rice cereal already has formula added.* This can be a problem for a baby with a cow's milk allergy. Make sure the cereal is pretty watery—not the thick texture you would eat. Make about two tablespoons worth. You can always make more.

Offer it as a snack *after* baby has had breast milk or formula. If you try to feed him solid food when he is hungry, you won't be able to shovel it in fast enough. By six months of age, your baby could probably win a chugging contest with the speed he guzzles down 160 calories (eight ounces of liquid).

Try one feeding a day of rice cereal for four days before embarking upon other foods. Cereal should be offered daily because it is a great source of iron. If your baby is at least six months old, you can experiment with tastier cereals (oatmeal, barley, and other grains).

Q. What other foods should I offer first?

Rice cereal and Stage 1 foods are the first foods to introduce. Stage 1 foods include carrots, sweet potatoes, mashed potatoes, squash, green beans, peas, bananas, peaches, pears, plums, prunes, and applesauce. (See previous page). All of these foods must be pureed.

Q. How often do I introduce a new food?

After your baby has mastered rice cereal, forge ahead and introduce one new Stage 1 food every three to four days. You are introducing foods slowly because you are looking to see if your baby has any food allergies (see a discussion on this topic later in this chapter).

Q. How often do I feed my baby solid foods?

Here is a ballpark figure: one solid meal daily at six months, two at seven to eight months, and three solid meals daily by nine months of age.

Start with one feeding a day and work up to three feedings a day (by nine months old).

DR B'S OPINION: BABY FOOD COOKBOOKS

I bought a baby food cookbook for my husband, our chef, when our first child was born. (Being in the kitchen actually makes me nervous!) The recipes amused him. The recipe for carrots was:

1. Steam carrots. 2. Puree. 3. Serve.

My advice—don't bother buying a baby food cookbook. Just use a food processor or blender and puree your home cooking. You can pour the food into ice cube trays (perfect serving size) and freeze them. It's easy to thaw out and serve.

Always feed your baby his breast milk or formula first. Then offer solid food as a between meal snack. Remember, until your baby eats several jars of food, he's drinking his calories. When your baby is only eating rice cereal, one feeding a day is fine. When he has a repertoire of foods, you can feed him three times a day.

Old Wives Tale
Introducing fruits before vegetables will give your baby a sweet tooth.

The truth: Your baby will either like vegetables or not. The order of introduction has nothing to do with it. When your baby is a toddler, he won't eat *anything*.

Q. My six-month old started solids and now his skin is turning yellow—HELP!

You are what you eat!

Babies are often first introduced to a series of yellow vegetables (carrots, squash, sweet potatoes). All of these vegetables are rich in Vitamin A (carotene). This vitamin has a pigment that can collect harmlessly on the skin producing a condition called **CAROTINEMIA**. The difference between this condition and jaundice (high bilirubin level) is that jaundiced babies have a yellowing in the whites of their eyes. Sweet potato lovers don't have that. See Baby411.com (click on "Bonus Material") for a great picture.

Q. Can I make my own baby food?

Absolutely. There is nothing special about prepared baby foods, other than being prepared. It's actually preferable to offer food from your table. That way, your baby will get used to your cooking!

Q. What do you think of organic baby food?

It's a lifestyle choice.
As we have discussed, some parents feel this is important. Others don't.

BEHIND THE SCENES: WHAT IS "ORGANIC"?

The USDA has recently regulated the labeling of all of these "natural" products so that people know how natural a product really is. Organic products are meats, poultry, eggs, and dairy products made from animals that did not receive antibiotics or growth hormones or fruits and vegetables grown without pesticides or petroleum based fertilizers. Organic farms are certified by a government inspector. Here are the rules:

- *100% Organic* must have a USDA seal on it.
- *Organic* is made of 95% to 100% organic ingredients.
- *Made with Organic Ingredients* is made of at least 70% organic ingredients.

What does the science show? There is no consensus in pediatric medicine that recommends organic foods over other prepared baby foods. If you are interested in organic foods, it's much cheaper to prepare your own baby food from organic fruits and vegetables.

All processed Stage 1 foods (Gerber, etc.) are preservative and additive free. The Stage 2 and 3 foods do add other ingredients, so you may want to check the packaging.

Q. How do I know if my baby has a food allergy?

Look for an impressive rash, profuse vomiting, or horrible diarrhea.

Allergic reactions are not subtle. If your baby has a few dots of a rash or a diaper rash, it's not because of the food you just introduced.

Allergic responses occur within minutes or at most four hours after an exposure. A chemical in the body called **HISTAMINE** is released in massive quantities with an allergic reaction. Histamine can cause a tingling or itchy mouth, mouth or lip swelling, shortness of breath, and dramatic diarrhea. You may also see hives (raised borders of red plaques that look like mosquito bites with circles around them). See our web site at Baby411.com (click on "Bonus Material") for a picture.

The extreme scenario is called an **ANAPHYLACTIC REACTION.** This is when loss of consciousness and airway swelling occurs—obviously, this is life threatening and you need to call 911. This is very unlikely to ever happen, particularly with a Stage 1 food—they are extremely well tolerated.

Infants who are more at risk for food allergies are those with parents who are very allergic. These babies' risk of having a food allergy may be as high as 20%. Compare that to the general population, which has about a 2% risk of food allergies. Children who have asthma have a higher risk of having a more serious allergic reaction if they have a food allergy.

Q. What is food intolerance?

This term refers to an adverse reaction to a food or food product, not an allergic response.

Allergic reactions produce histamine. Food intolerances do not. If a baby has intolerance to a food, he might have stomach cramps or bloating. You'll probably avoid that food in the future, but he'll never have a life-threatening (anaphylactic) reaction if he is exposed to it.

(Example: An adult with lactose intolerance gets diarrhea when he drinks milk, but doesn't get hives).

Q. What foods are more likely to cause food allergies?

1. *PEANUTS/Peanut Butter.* We'll discuss this in detail next.
2. Egg whites. (the *white* part—egg protein is the problem)
3. Shellfish (crab, lobster, shrimp, scallops, oysters).
4. Fish.
5. Tree nuts (walnuts, cashews, etc).
6. Wheat.
7. Cow's milk.
8. Soy.
9. Citrus fruits, berries.
10. Cocoa.

Food Allergies Stats

- 2.5% of newborns have a cow's milk allergy. 80% outgrow it by age five.
- 1.5% of children are allergic to eggs.
- 0.5% of children are allergic to peanuts, but of those with the allergy, only 20% will outgrow it.
- Most food allergies occur in the first three years of life (6% of all children).
- Only 2% of adults have a food allergy, and of those, 50% are allergic to either peanuts or tree nuts.[1]

Q. Can my baby have a milk protein allergy if I am breastfeeding?

Yes. Food proteins are passed into mom's breast milk, and cow's milk protein is no exception.

Babies with a milk protein allergy may have blood streaked poops, diarrhea, and poor growth. The problem may be seen in the first few weeks of life with a baby fed cow's milk based formula. In breastfed babies, it may not be a problem for a few months.

Q. So when can I feed my child a peanut butter and jelly sandwich?

Okay, let's talk peanuts and peanut butter.

Here's the scary fact about peanut allergy: it is life threatening. That's right, kids with a peanut allergy can die from ingesting less than one peanut. Another scary fact: only 20% of kids who have peanut allergy will outgrow it!

Here is the party line from the American Academy of Pediatrics on peanuts: for families with NO history of food allergies, the AAP suggests your baby can eat peanuts or peanut butter after one year of age. For "high risk" families (that is, those with a history of food allergies), the AAP says you should avoid the top allergy foods (including peanuts) until age three.

However, you may find some variability of opinions amongst pediatricians and allergists. After having personal experience with this one, we'd suggest ALL children avoid peanuts and peanut butter until after age THREE—or longer if possible. Since peanut allergies are life-long and so dangerous, it doesn't pay to roll the dice on this one. And studies show that when you introduce peanuts LATER in life (like after age three), there is a much lower chance of developing this allergy.

What about avoiding TRACE amounts of peanuts? You probably don't have to worry. Some products have warnings that they MAY contain trace amounts of peanuts because they are processed on machines that also process products made with peanuts. Bottom line: While you should stay away from peanuts and peanut butter until age three, eating food that MIGHT contain a trace of peanuts is kosher after a year of age.

Feedback from the Real World: Ben's Story

Want to hear something really scary? How about the story of Ben, (Denise's son), and how we discovered his life threatening peanut allergy. When Ben was one year of age, we decided we could add peanut butter into his life. Being a confessed peanut nut (I've searched the Southern U.S. for the best peanut butter pie–haven't found it yet but I'm still looking), we thought this would be a tasty addition to his diet. Besides, most parenting books say you can add peanut butter at age one and we had no history of severe food allergies in our families.

Shazam! He immediately swelled up like a tomato. This was our first experience with an allergic reaction. Hives hit him like a ton of bricks. We practically threw him in the car and raced down the mountain (yes, we did live in the mountains at the time) to the doctor's office. There we were informed that he was allergic to peanuts. After treating the hives, the doctor mentioned that this would probably be for life and the next time could be life-threatening anaphylaxis (after eating one peanut he could stop

HIDDEN SOURCES FOR DANGEROUS FOODS

You've got your peanut radar set to high—as a parent, you know to avoid peanuts for your child until he is three years old (or even better, five years old). And obviously, that means no peanut butter or peanut M & M's. But are you aware of how peanuts and other potential food allergy dangers are hidden in other products? Candy and cookies, as well as fresh baked goods, are a flash point—undeclared soy, wheat, nuts, and eggs are common in baked goods. Today most processed foods are required to list allergy facts, but some products still are not covered by these laws.

And let's talk about restaurants. Unfortunately, there is no law requiring restaurants to disclose the use of allergenic foods as ingredients. As a parent, you have to take charge: inform the waiter of your preference to avoid peanuts (or a child's allergy) and ask what dishes are a problem. If you get a blank stare in return, ask to see the manager. Ditto for quick-serve restaurants.

Watch out for stealth uses of allergenic foods like peanuts—for example, some Chinese restaurants seal their egg roll wrappers with peanut butter!

Now, we're not trying to make you overly paranoid here. But as a parent, you have to be vigilant—especially when your child goes over to friends' or relatives' homes. If in doubt, speak up and don't forget to warn all your friends and relatives every time you drop off your child. In fact, it may be a good idea to get a MedicAlert bracelet for your child when he gets older. It reminds him of his allergy as well as the adults he's with for the day. For more information, check out the web. Food Allergy Network's website (FoodAllergy.org) has a brochure you can download called "Preventing or Delaying the Onset of Food Allergies in Infants." It also provides an FAQ, alerts and school resources.

breathing and die). We next visited with an allergist who confirmed the diagnosis with a "peanut challenge" test.

So what now? Well, we see the allergist once a year. And we have to carry an epinephrine injectable pen with us everywhere we go. In fact, there is an Epi-Pen at school, at Nanna's, at our house and in my purse. We had to teach Ben to read labels on food, never share at school and never, ever take food samples without first checking with us (Sam's Club is a nightmare sometimes!). It's no wonder a recent study showed that kids with a peanut allergy suffer from more stress than kids with diabetes.

The good news: scientists are developing a vaccine (TNX-901) that may someday save my son and other peanut allergic kids from an accidental ingestion. But until then we're amazingly careful about everything that goes in his mouth. My wish, however is that no other parent have to deal with this scary allergy. That's why my recommendation, as discussed above, is to avoid nuts altogether until your child is at least three years old. And longer if you can. It's worth waiting a bit for that PBJ experience.

Helpful Hints

1. *If your baby does have a food allergy, get educated about hidden sources of the problem food.*
2. **Know how to read an ingredient label.** Products containing milk include: casein, sodium caseinate, whey, or lactoglobulin.
3. **Be a detective.** Deli slicers are often contaminated with milk because both cheese and lunchmeat are sliced on the same machine. Many candies without peanuts are processed in the same location as those with peanuts.

Q. What is the best way to avoid food allergies?

Good question. Answer: introduce more highly allergenic foods later.

There is a lot of research to prove that early exposure to these risky foods lead to more food allergies—some that can last a lifetime.

Since human milk is made for human babies, it is the least likely to be problematic for a baby. Babies can have food allergies to both cows' milk protein and soymilk protein.

There has been some research done on nursing mothers eliminating highly allergenic foods from their diets to prevent "sensitizing" their infants. The reasoning: the breakdown products of these foods end up in breast milk. The current thinking, however, is that this does *not* trigger food allergies. But for families with a *significant* history of food allergies, it may be a good idea for breastfeeding moms to avoid peanuts and tree nuts in their diet.[3] Even though there is no research to back this up, there is no downside to eliminating these items during nursing. If there is no family history of food allergies but allergy symptoms are discovered in the baby, removal of milk, eggs, fish, peanuts, and tree nuts are suggested.

Q. Okay, so when can I try these high allergy foods with my baby?

For *low risk* babies, egg whites, shellfish, fish, and tree nuts can be introduced after the first birthday. But, even in low risk families, we suggest starting peanuts after three years. For *high risk* babies (family history of food allergies, asthma), wait on all five of the foods listed above until three years old.

SOLID FOODS

FOOD ALLERGIES AND ECZEMA

Food allergies are one of the key precipitating factors for eczema. 37% of kids with severe eczema have a food allergy. The eczema improves when the food offender is eliminated from the diet. The vast majority of food offenders are the top 8 foods on the list earlier.[2]

BOTTOM LINE

For high-risk allergy families, the AAP recommends:
1. Breastfeeding to reduce the incidence of food allergies.
2. Introduction of solid food after six months of age.
3. Introduction of peanuts, tree nuts, and seafood after three years of age.
4. Introduction of eggs at two years of age.
5. Introduction of milk and soy products at one year of age.[4]

Q. What is a good reference if my baby does develop a food allergy?

Check out the Food Allergy Network at www.foodallergy.org. Or call, (800) 929-4040.

How Food Allergies are Tested

There are four basic ways to test for a food allergy, but be aware that there is no perfect science:

1 ELIMINATION DIET. Eliminate the food from the diet for three to six weeks; see if there is an improvement in symptoms (i.e. eczema, diarrhea, etc).

2 SKIN TESTING. Skin prick tests detect a true allergic response (see IgE below) to a food. If skin testing shows an allergic response, RAST testing can be done for confirmation.

3 CAP-RAST TEST. Blood test detects an elevation of the body's IgE antibodies (an allergic response chemical). RAST testing is useful because it can identify some food allergies. However, not all food allergies cause an elevation of IgE levels. The newer CAP-RAST tests have been shown to be 95% predictive in food allergies for milk, eggs, peanuts, and fish.

4 FOOD CHALLENGE. When a person is known to be allergic to a certain food, periodic (annual) RAST testing may show a decrease in allergy response levels. A person can try a certain food again in a controlled medical setting to see if he is still allergic to a particular food. (This does not mean at your kitchen table).[5]

Can you outgrow a food allergy?

Most kids outgrow food allergies to milk, eggs, soy, and wheat by the time they are five years old. Over 50% of kids will outgrow their food allergies by the age of one. The foods that tend to be lifelong problems are peanuts, tree nuts, fish, and shellfish.[6]

Q. Are there any other foods my baby shouldn't eat?

Yes. Here are three:

- *Honey*: Wait on honey until your child is one year old. Honey contains *clostridium botulinum* spores that can cause botulism in an infant. (Infants' digestive systems are relatively sterile compared to ours and can't kill the spores).
- *Choking Hazards:* Raw carrots, celery, popcorn, potato chips, nuts, hard candy, hard meat, fruits with seeds, raisins, hotdogs, and grapes (unless cut lengthwise). Wait on these foods until your child is really good at chewing (two to three years).
- *Artificial sweeteners:* There is no official party line on this one, but there is no reason to offer these products to babies.

Q. My baby is six months old now. What can he eat?

Start at Stage 1 foods. Then advance to Stage 2-3 Foods and start feeding him off of your plate.

If your child is doing well, expand his diet. You will work your way through the different food groups and textures, while increasing the volume of food as your baby demands it.

Now is the time to start good eating habits, and give your baby a feeling that mealtime is enjoyable. (That means, don't worry about making a mess.) Solid foods should still be a supplement and not replacement of calories. Your baby will tell you he is done by turning his head, spitting out his food, and/or throwing it on the floor.

Once you get through Stage 1 foods, move on to Stage 2 and Stage 3 foods. Beware, your baby may not like the textures. They are chunkier than the Stage 1 pureed foods. These foods are complex grains (wheat, barley, oats), dairy, and meats. Remember: Avoid egg whites, peanuts/peanut containing products, fish/shellfish, and nuts (the Top Five). Everything else is fair game.

So, if the food on your plate looks good to your baby, let him try it. This includes a variety of safe ethnic foods. You will know he is ready because he will be watching every spoonful that goes into your mouth. Don't worry about herbs and spices you use in seasoning. Your baby needs to get used to your methods of food preparation.

See our handy list earlier in this chapter for fun food ideas.

Helpful Hint

It's good to offer cereal daily. Babies older than six months old need to have a source of iron in their diets. Check the previous chapter for a list of foods that are good sources of iron.

Q. My baby is nine months old. What can he eat now?

Almost anything (except the Top 5 high-allergy foods; see list earlier). This includes "finger foods."

Your baby is ready to feed himself when he uses his index finger and thumb to grasp things, otherwise known as the ***pincer grasp.*** Finger foods include: Cheerios, pieces of banana, pieces of pears or peaches, small pieces of cheese, whole wheat toast, soft meats (my personal favorite is the chicken in a can—it's next to the canned tuna fish at the store), wagon wheel pasta, graham crackers, and teething biscuits. And you thought solids were messy before…do not make a big deal out of it—just clean it up. Kids sense frustration and will have mealtime anxiety if you make it an issue. Your child can be toothless and enjoy solid and finger foods. They can gum just about anything.

As far as amounts, your baby should be taking enough solid food at a sitting to cut back on the volume of liquid nutrition. Aim for three solid meals per day (eight to 14 ounces of solid food). See the "Big Picture" table at the end of this chapter.

Helpful Hint

Now is a good time to take that CPR class you have been meaning to take. It's unlikely you will ever need to utilize your skills, but it's always good to be prepared.

Q. My nine month old refuses any food that has a texture to it. Help!

This is called **TEXTURE AVERSION.**

Some babies prefer smooth, pureed foods well into their second year of life. If he is otherwise developing normally, I'd consider your baby a little eccentric, but normal.

Babies with texture aversions, adverse reactions to sensory stimulation, and developmental delays may be worth talking to your doctor about (see **PERVASIVE DEVELOPMENTAL DISORDER, SENSORY INTEGRATION DYSFUNCTION**).

Q. My one year old refuses to let me feed her, but can't use utensils yet. Any ideas?

One way is to let her use a spoon while you shovel in the food with your spoon. If she clues in to this trick, try letting her dip foods. Yogurt, applesauce, guacamole, and beans will stick easily to a cracker that your baby can lick off.

Remember, getting your toddler to eat anything is a real challenge.

CELIAC DISEASE: A RARE CAUSE OF CHRONIC DIARRHEA

As babies start to eat cereal grains (wheat, barley, and oats), a rare disorder can become apparent—celiac disease. Other names for this disorder are celiac sprue or gluten sensitive enteropathy. There is a particular protein called "gluten" found in all of these grains. People with Celiac Disease form an immune response to the protein gluten that causing injury to the intestinal lining. The result: chronic diarrhea, failure to thrive, vomiting, and bloating to name a few symptoms. This is a genetic disorder; so more than one family member may have this problem.

If you have a family member with this disorder, or notice a change in your baby after introducing these foods, check in with your baby's doctor.

Solid Foods

Q. What are the food expectations for a one-year old?

To join the family at the dinner table, and eat what the family is eating. The goal is for your child to graduate to table foods (what you eat) at one year of age. He should eat three meals and two snacks per day. He should drink whole milk (16 oz or dairy serving equivalent), juice (less than six oz per day), and water out of a cup. Say goodbye to bottles.

Q. Is it okay for my one year old to eat fish?

Yes. The few restrictions are: shark, swordfish, king mackerel, and tilefish. These fish contain high levels of mercury, so the Food and Drug Administration has recommended that these be avoided for young children. It is also recommended to contact your local health department about any warnings on fish caught in area lakes. Canned tuna is okay in small amounts (less than six ounces/week).

The Big Picture For Liquid And Solid Nutrition

Age	Liquid Nutrition	Solid Nutrition	Solid serving size
4-6 months	32-40 oz 5-6 meals	Maybe cereal* Maybe fruit/vegetable* 0-1 feeding/day	2-4 Tbsp (1-2 oz) 1-2 items at each meal 0-8 oz/day Pureed foods.
6-9 months	24-32 oz 4-5 meals	Cereal Fruit/vegetable Meat Grains Dairy (limited amt) 1-3 feedings/day	2-4 Tbsp (1-2 oz) Two or three items at each meal, or a whole Stage 2 jar. 8-14 oz/day More textures.
9-12 months	20-30 oz 3-4 meals	All of the above Table foods 3 meals/day	3-4 Tbsp (2 oz) Three items at each meal, or a Stage 3 jar. 10-15 oz/day Bite size pieces.

*Solid nutrition from 4-6 months is completely optional.

Key Points To Remember

- Prepared baby food jars: Stage 1= 2oz serving. Stage 2 = 4 oz serving. Stage 3 = 5-6 oz serving.
- Remember that breast milk and formula have 20 calories per ounce. A 2.5 oz jar of Stage 1 carrots has 25 calories.
- Do not reduce the amount of liquid nutrition until your baby eats enough solid food to replace the calories. This gradual taper begins somewhere between six and nine months. This is when a solid meal is at least a four to six ounce serving.
- Every baby is different!

The Other End

Chapter 8

"Gil, why are you standing there?"
"I'm waiting for her head to spin around."

~ Parenthood

What's in this Chapter

- **Normal newborn poop**
- **The top 5 worrisome poops**
- **Trade secrets for constipation relief**
- **Fun fiber foods**
- **Spit up, regurgitation, and vomit**
- **What is gastroesophageal reflux (GER)?**
- **Top 5 worries about vomit**
- **Urine and bladder infections**
- **Burping, hiccups, and gas**

This chapter addresses a subject taboo at most dinner tables. We are going to have a candid discussion about poop (as well as gas, burps, pee and spit up, too). Why spend a whole chapter on poop? Let's be honest—you'll have LOTS of questions about this subject. And you'll be looking at lots of it too! The average baby goes through 2300 diaper changes in the first year alone.

Parents have concerns because baby poop does not look like theirs. If it does, your baby has a problem. And as you might imagine, changing at least eight diapers a day also results in a pre-occupation with diaper contents.

Before we go too far, it's a good idea to go over the terminology we'll be using in this chapter:

- **Stool.** Your digested food garbage that is eliminated through your anus. Stool also has bacteria germs in it (these germs help us digest our food). Just so we're on the same page—it's also known as poo, poop, feces, caca, Number 2, bowel movement... for this book, we will use the term **POOP**.

- **Urine.** The garbage that your kidneys clean out of your bloodstream that is eliminated through your urethra (the hole in the penis or the hole above the vagina). Urine is sterile (germ free). Otherwise known as pee, pee-pee, wee-wee, wet diapers...for this book, we will use the term **PEE**.

♦ **Gas.** The air inside the intestines that is a by-product of the food transit through it. When babies eat 24 hours a day, their intestines move 24 hours a day, *and* make a whole lot of gas. The gas slows down when the intestinal transit slows down, around six weeks.

♦ **Burps.** The air that gets swallowed comes back out of the esophagus. Because babies exclusively suck and swallow their nutrition for the first four months of life, burping feels good after a big meal. Some babies suck very aggressively and ingest a large air bubble. When this air bubble comes up, often so does the whole meal.

♦ **Hiccups.** This is caused by a muscle spasm of the diaphragm (the muscle that divides the chest and abdomen). All babies have some hiccups, a few have a lot of hiccups. This sometimes is a sign of sensory overload (i.e. over stimulation). There is nothing wrong with your baby. You may just want to soothe him.

Newborn Poop

Q. What should my newborn's poop look like?

Black tar.

In the first 24 hours of life, your baby should pass a poop called **MECONIUM**. This has the color and texture of black tar. It looks like this because the baby has swallowed some blood while inside the womb. The black tar contains some digested blood. (Good to remember if you ever see poop that looks like this again from your baby or a family member).

As your baby starts to eat breast milk or formula, the poop will change color and texture. This happens on about the fourth day of life. (Remember, they don't eat much the first few days.)

Q. My newborn is breastfed. What should his poop look like?

Grey Poupon (or crab mustard, as my Baltimore friends would say).

Breast milk poop is very watery. In fact, many parents worry that their baby is having diarrhea if they have never changed a breast-fed baby's diaper before. It's watery because the breast milk is so easily digested, it goes right through the intestines and leaves very little solid garbage to be pooped out.

Parents often wonder how they will know when their baby is having diarrhea. The answer is the *frequency* of poop increases. Breastfed babies often poop with every feeding for the first six weeks of life. Some babies will poop less frequently than that, sometimes only once every few days. Do not worry unless the consistency of the poop looks like yours.

The color is often yellow. But, ***any shade of yellow, green or brown is okay.*** Florescent green is okay too.

DR B'S OPINION: GREEN POOP AND FOREMILK?

Some mothers hear that green poop is a sign that their baby is only getting the foremilk and not the richer hindmilk. (For a discussion of foremilk and hindmilk, see Chapter 6, "Liquids"). While this may be true, a better way to tell if a baby is getting hindmilk is to look at the feeding patterns and growth charts, not the poop color. Babies who get foremilk only tend to be snackers who eat frequently (they don't fill up as well). They also gain less weight if they miss out on the fatty hindmilk.

Q. My newborn is formula fed. What should his poop look like?

Strained peas.

Formula poops tend to be greener than breast milk poop. But, as we mentioned, any shade of yellow, green or brown is okay.

Formula poops are also thicker and pastier than breast milk poop. It takes longer to digest formula in the intestines, so more water is absorbed before the "final product" comes out.

Q. How often do formula fed babies poop?

Formula fed babies poop less often because the "transit time" through the intestines is longer. These babies may poop three or four times per day or once every couple of days. The frequency slows down even more at six weeks of life.

RED FLAGS: Worrisome Poop

If you see/note any of these, call your doctor immediately:

1. Your baby doesn't poop in the first 24 hours of life (see **MECONIUM PLUG OR ILEUS**).
2. Your baby's poops look bloody, tarry, or mixed with mucus (see **BLOOD IN STOOL**)
3. Your baby's poop looks like yours. (see **CONSTIPATION**)
4. Your baby has a stomachache and poop that looks like grape jelly (see **INTUSSUSCEPTION**)
5. Your baby's frequency of poop doubles or triples (see **DIARRHEA/GASTROENTERITIS**)

Q. My baby grunts and his face turns red when he poops. Is this normal?

Yes.

Try lying down and pooping some time. See what your face looks like. This does NOT mean your child is constipated. There is actually a term for this phenomenon—The Grunting Baby Syndrome.

THE OTHER END

Q. My three-week-old usually poops with every feeding. Now, he hasn't gone in 24 hours. Is he constipated?

No.

Please read this carefully. Constipation is diagnosed by the FIRMNESS of the poop, NOT THE FREQUENCY (or infrequency) of pooping. *Concerned parents often think their baby is constipated when they are not.* Newborns to six week olds usually poop several times a day. Occasionally, though, they may take a day off. That's when you call the doctor in a state of panic. The answer is, "Be prepared for the Mother Load." Some babies may poop once or twice a week. That's fine, as long as it is soft when it comes out.

Your baby is constipated when the poop looks like logs, rock balls, marbles, or deer pellets. See below for tricks of the trade for relieving constipation.

Old Wives Tale
The iron in formula causes constipation. My mother-in-law told me to switch to a low iron formula.

The truth: There isn't enough iron in formula to make a baby constipated. And without the iron, your baby won't grow. Don't switch formula. Try some of the tricks below and read the formula section in the Chapter 6, "Liquids."

Trade Secrets For Relieving Constipation

1. **RECTAL THERMOMETER TRICK.** If your baby is straining and not having any success, insert a rectal thermometer in his anus for about a minute. Trust me—this is the most dispensed phone advice by any pediatrician's office. You can read the exact details on how to insert a rectal thermometer in Chapter 15, "First Aid." This usually provides the inspiration your baby needs to get moving. (And no, they don't mind having it done like you would!)

2. **PRUNE JUICE COCKTAIL.** If your baby is regularly irregular, he may need some extra fiber to move things along. Try one teaspoon of prune juice per feeding (mixed in formula or given separately to breast fed babies) until you get the desired consistency of poop. You can adjust the volume to what your baby needs (that is, anywhere from one to five teaspoons a day). Prune juice has both fiber and sorbitol (sugar) that pull water into the poop to make it softer.

   Hint: Buy store brand prune juice—not the stuff in the baby food section. Baby prune juice is mixed with apple juice and is very expensive by comparison.

3. **KARO COCKTAIL.** Some pediatricians recommend using karo syrup instead of prune juice to pull water into the stool. I don't use it because there are some anecdotal reports of botulism spores in karo syrup (similar to the concerns we discussed about honey in the feeding chapter).

4. **WASH IT OUT.** Sometimes, babies need drink a little water to soften up the poop. I wouldn't offer more than an ounce or two, though, to an infant under six months of age.

5 **THE GLYCERINE BULLET.** For immediate relief, use a glycerine suppository to get dramatic results. These suppositories can be purchased without a prescription at the grocery store or pharmacy. Frequently, the label will read "infant" suppository. The suppository looks like a bullet made of soap. Insert it directly into the anus. It dissolves as you push it in. Be prepared for the fireworks.

If these tricks don't work, call your doctor. Pediatricians always have a few more tricks like this up their sleeves!

Q. My six-week old breastfed baby used to poop at every feeding. Now she only goes once a day. Should I be worried?

No. This is normal and you should be thankful.

Babies are born with intestines that work 24/7. They work that way to keep the nutritional juices flowing. By six weeks of age, things start to slow down. This is called slower intestinal transit time. Mature breast milk is also mostly digested, so there is very little garbage to eliminate.

As long as the poop is soft, your baby is fine. So be grateful you have fewer diaper changes!

Solid Food Equals Solid Poop: Older Babies

Q. My six month old started rice cereal and now she is constipated. Help!

Rice cereal has this effect on some babies. Offer only one feeding a day of rice cereal and introduce higher fiber foods sooner rather than later. Pureed prunes are a Stage 1 food and add both fiber and taste to rice cereal. See below for more fun fiber foods.

Q. How much fiber does my child need to eat?

The equation is Age in Years + 5 = Total daily fiber requirement (in grams)

This equation doesn't apply for babies under a year of age. Breast milk contains no dietary fiber, thus there are no requirements for babies from birth to six months. From six to twelve months, fiber is introduced in the diet via solid foods. The daily needs varies from baby to baby and there are no established guidelines. But studies have shown that children who are constipated eat significantly less fiber than their "regular" peers.[1]

Reality Check
You, Mom and Dad, need 25 to 30 grams of fiber per day no matter how old you are. Most Americans do not eat enough fiber. The way to get your child to eat fiber is for you to have it in the house and eat it yourself. If you don't realize this yet, your baby is watching every move you make!

Q. Which foods are high in fiber and more importantly, which ones will my child eat?

THE OTHER END

This is my favorite fiber food list. Some foods will be off limits under a year of age and are designated with an asterisk (*)—these are choking hazards. Kids usually find the bread/grain category the most appealing. Take careful note of serving sizes. The sizes listed below are sometimes more than even a one year old will eat. We've noted in bold print the highest fiber foods (or the ones that pack the biggest fiber punch).

Product	Serving Size	Fiber grams/serving
Bread/Grains		
Whole wheat Bread	1 slice	2 grams
White Bread	1 slice	0
Pepperidge Farm HeartyWheat Crackers	3 crackers	1 gram
El Galindo Wheat Tortillas	**1 tortilla**	**9 grams**
Hodgson Mill Whole-wheat pasta	2 oz	6 grams
Brown Rice	1/4 cup	0.9 grams
Cereal		
Baby Rice	1/4 cup	0
Baby Oatmeal	1/4 cup	1 gram
Baby Mixed	1/4 cup	0
Cheerios	1/2 cup	1.5 grams
Quaker Oat Bran	1/2 cup	2.4 grams
Quaker Oatmeal Squares	1/2 cup	2.5 grams
Kellogg's Nutragrain bars	1 bar	1 gram
Wheat germ	**1 Tbsp**	**1 gram**

(I like wheat germ because you can sneak it into food and your child might not even notice)

Fruit (raw)
Note: The peel is often the part of the fruit that contains the fiber. Since most kids hate the peels, the fiber ends up in the garbage disposal and not in your child.

Apple (with peel)	1/2 medium	1.8 grams
Apricots	1/4 cup	0.8 grams
Banana	1 whole	2.7 grams
Blackberries	1/4 cup	1.8 grams
Dried Cranberries*	1/4 cup	1.5 grams
Grapefruit	1/4	1 gram
Grapes	1/2 cup	0.5 grams
Orange	1/2	1.5 grams
Pear (with peel)	1/2	2.1 grams
Prunes	**1/4 cup**	**3.5 grams**
Raisins*	1/4 cup	2 grams
Raspberries	1/4 cup	2 grams
Strawberries	1/4 cup	0.8 grams
Watermelon	1/2 slice	0.5 gram

Product	Serving Size	Fiber grams/serving
Vegetables (Usually unpopular with children, however.)		
Broccoli	1/4 cup	1.4 grams
Corn	1/4 cup	1 grams
Green beans	1/4 cup	0.7 grams
Green peas	1/4 cup	2.2 grams
Lima beans	1/4 cup	3 grams
Pinto beans	1/4 cup	3.7 grams
Refried Beans	**1/4 cup**	**3 grams**
Squash (baked)	1/4 cup	2 grams

Q. Now that my nine month old eats a large amount of solid food, what should his poop look like?

Soft and solid.

The more your baby eats like you do, the more his poop will look like yours. It should always be easy for your baby to pass. It has a cow patty appearance when your baby sits on it after he poops.

By the way, some foods don't get completely digested as they pass through the intestines. It's normal to recognize last night's corn, carrots, etc. in your child's poop.

RED FLAGS: Worrisome Poops For Older Babies

1. **Streaks of blood.** If the streak is on a hard, firm poop, it's probably due to a tear in the anus as the poop was passed. Worth checking out, though.
2. **Streaks of blood/mucus.** More concerning for infection, particularly if poop is loose/diarrhea. Be prepared for a homework assignment (providing your doctor with a fresh poop specimen). This can also be a sign of a food allergy.
3. **Clay (white) colored poop.** Also known as **ACHOLIC STOOL.** This can occur in conjunction with a stomach virus. But worth checking out with the doctor.
4. **Looks like meconium again.** Black, tarry poop can be a sign of bleeding in the upper part of the intestinal tract (because the blood has had time to get digested). This may indicate irritation and inflammation in the intestines. Your doctor will do a test to check for blood in the poop.
5. **Grape Jelly poop.** The doctor term for this is actually "currant jelly stool." This is a medical emergency. It is a sign of **INTUSSUSCEPTION** where the intestines have kinked.
6. **Bulky, REALLY stinky, greasy, floating poops.** This may indicate difficulty with absorption (see **MALABSORPTION**).

Helpful Hint

Pepto Bismol makes poop look black like meconium. Pepto Bismol is *not* currently recommended for infants. Just thought you'd be interested for your own sake.

THE OTHER END

Q. My baby just had a BLUE poop. Help!

Your baby is not an alien. It's either natural or artificial food coloring.

To the best of my knowledge, blue poop is never a sign of illness. Blue colored kid juices (Hi-C) and kid yogurts are often the culprits.

Beets cause a dramatic red hue in both poop and pee.

Q. I am interested in toilet training my baby. Is it too early to think about this now?

Yes. Your baby will be in diapers for a long time.

Being toilet trained is a developmental milestone, just like learning to talk and walk. Milestones can be encouraged, but the child has to achieve it on his own. Your child needs to be able to sense the urge to pee and poop (not just after he has gone). His only incentive to be toilet trained is the desire to be clean (regardless of how many toys you buy him). If he runs around in a poopie diaper and could care less, he is miles away from this milestone.

Girls usually train around 2 1/2 years of age. Boys train around 3 or 3 1/2 years. There is no need to purchase a potty seat any time soon. All it will do is collect dust in your bathroom. Good news: we cover this topic in depth in the sequel to this book, *Toddler 411* (see back of this book for details).

We should note there is another school of thought on this topic: Elimination Communication (EC). Proponents say babies give subtle clues that they need to poop or pee and it is up to the parent to respond to those cues. These babies go diaper-less, and parents put them on the pot every time they think their kid needs to go. If you want to learn more about this method, check out DiaperFreeBaby.org. We admit our skepticism about EC—it seems that the parent is potty-trained, not the child.

Spit Up, Regurgitation, And Vomit

Q. My newborn spits up all the time. Should I be worried?

No. Most babies spit up after meals. They are born with a loose muscle between the esophagus (swallowing tube) and the stomach. This muscle, called the *lower esophageal sphincter* (see picture at right), will tighten up by about six months of age. Until then, liquids travel down into the stomach. Then some will return into the esophagus and mouth. By definition, most babies have **GASTROESOPHAGEAL REFLUX (OR ACID REFLUX, GER)**. They spit up effortlessly and with small volumes.

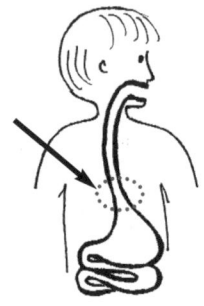

GER is not a problem (other than forcing you to spot treat all the shoulders on your shirts). According to Dr. R. Jeff Zwiener, Medical Director of Pediatric Gastroenterology at Dell Children's Medical Center of Central Texas, GER only becomes a problem called **GASTROESOPHAGEAL REFLUX DISEASE (GERD)** if it leads to these unpleasant consequences:

- ◆ irritation of the esophagus (esophagitis), making babies irritable or fussy.

- respiratory/airway problems that make babies wheeze, gag, choke, or have trouble breathing.

RED FLAGS: When to worry about acid reflux

1. If your baby spits up large volumes consistently, he won't gain weight (see **GER TREATMENT**).
2. If your baby cries or arches after feeding, with or without spitting up. The stomach acid is irritating his esophagus. (See **GER TREATMENT**).
3. If your baby has Exorcist-style, projectile vomiting after every meal, call your doctor immediately. (see **PYLORIC STENOSIS**).

Q. My baby is four-months old now and is spitting up more than he did when he was younger. Should I be worried?

No.

It takes six months for the sphincter muscle to tighten up. As your baby takes larger volumes of breast milk/formula, larger volumes will come up. Hence, it gives the appearance that your baby's reflux is getting worse instead of better.

Q. Okay, my baby is nine-months old and still spitting up. Should I be worried?

No. You're just at the end of the bell curve. Most babies will have graduated from spitting up by six months, but there are a few stragglers.

Reality Check

No, it's not just your baby who is an Olympic-caliber spitter. Consider this:
Of all babies 0-3 months of age, 50% spit up.
Of all babies 4-5 months of age, 67% spit up.
Of all babies 6-7 months of age, 21% still spit up.
By 12 months of age, less than 5% of babies are still spitting up.[2]

Q. How can I tell if my baby is suffering from acid/gastroesophageal reflux?

Everyone is usually miserable from this. Your doctor can help you make the diagnosis on this one.

This is usually the problem behind fussy, "colicky" infants. Most parents are convinced that their infant either has horrible gas pains, a milk allergy, or colic. They also think that they are inadequate as parents because their baby is always fussy and they haven't figured out how to make her feel better. Some adventurous parents will unsuccessfully try Mylicon drops (an over-the-counter medicine which makes big gas bubbles into little gas bubbles), switching formulas, or eliminating dairy from breastfeeding Mom's diet before scheduling an appointment with their doctor.

How do we make the diagnosis? We look at the time the fussiness occurs, and what seems to make it worse. *The first rule: babies with reflux*

THE OTHER END

TRICKS OF THE TRADE TO TREAT ACID REFLUX

If your baby is uncomfortable from the heartburn associated with acid reflux, or is not gaining weight, there are many options to reduce the severity of the symptoms. Start by using the following tricks at home. If that doesn't work, consider a medication (which will require a prescription).

1. Keep your baby upright for 20 minutes after feedings. This lets the food travel out of the stomach into the small intestine before moving baby around.

2. Let your baby plan his mealtimes. Babies often figure this out themselves. They have more discomfort with large meals, so they learn to become snackers. It's not great for parents' schedules, but is more comfortable for baby.

3. Have your baby sleep in an inclined position. Keeping the head upright 30 degrees keeps food going downwards instead of upwards. Consider buying a Tucker Sling (tuckersling.com) that allows your baby to be inclined safely and securely for sleep. While some babies under three months do well in their car seats, some reflux babies actually have more problems because they slump down, increasing the pressure on their bellies. For infants *over* three months of age, you can prop up the crib mattress with a purchased wedge or pillow UNDER the mattress. It's not terribly effective, though, because many babies roll all over their crib.

*4. For formula fed or expressed breast milk babies: Add one teaspoon of rice cereal to each bottle (*or use Enfamil AR—see Chapter 6, "Liquids" chapter). Thicker milk is heavier and stays down better. You will see the same effect with solid food.

5. Medications. Babies use the same antacids as adults. Many products are over the counter for adults, but are by prescription-only for kids. Some products are not approved by the FDA for use in children, but are routinely used by both pediatric gastroenterologists and pediatricians. The options are listed below. (For details, see Appendix A on medications.):
  Histamine 2 Receptor Antagonists: Zantac (Ranitidine), Axid (Nizatidine)
  Proton Pump Inhibitors: Prilosec, Zegerid (Omeprazole), Prevacid (Lansoprazole)

If you reach the point that your baby needs medication, he likely has a pretty irritated esophagus lining from constant stomach acid burns. The medication prevents further insults, but it takes at least a week for the irritation to heal. So, don't expect a miraculous change in your baby's behavior after just one dose of medicine. Give the medicine for a week, then see if it is working.

Helpful hints: The medication is dosed based on your baby's weight. In some cases, if your baby gains a pound or two, he may no longer be getting a therapeutic dose of his meds. Remind your doctor to recalculate his dose every month or so. And medications like Prilosec that have to be specially mixed (compounded) may separate after a couple of weeks. Get a two-week supply and refill it frequently. Parents are often leery of giving medication on a daily basis to their babies. Understandable. However, these medications are safe to use daily, as a general rule. Once your baby outgrows the problem (about six months old), the medicine is no longer needed.

don't always spit up–(spitters are really easy to diagnose). Some babies experience heartburn when the stomach acid comes up into the esophagus with the milk. If it doesn't make it all the way up to the mouth, you won't see it. Babies with heartburn often cry during and shortly after feedings. They can also cry when lying down (for example, on the changing table) because this lets the acid to come up. They may try to arch their backs or thrust their heads back to alleviate the pain. This happens around the clock, making a very unhappy baby.

Colic is ruled out by the frequency of the behaviors. Babies with colic are also unhappy. However, they are only unhappy for three hours a day (say, around 5 pm to 8 pm). Colic starts at three weeks of age and lasts until three months of age. If your baby has been fussy since two weeks of age and is always fussy, it's probably not colic and most likely acid reflux. (See the next chapter on sleep for more about colic).

Milk allergy or intolerance is ruled out by exploring some details about baby's poop. A true milk allergy causes mucus and/or blood in loose poop. If you have a fussy baby with normal poop, the food is not the problem. A therapeutic trial of changing formula or Mom's dairy elimination will not improve a reflux baby's symptoms.

Q. Can't we just do a test to look for acid reflux?

Yes, tests are available. Here's an overview:

An Upper GI or "barium swallow imaging study" (see Appendix C, Lab Work and Tests) can be done to rule out other problems that cause regurgitation. If the baby happens to reflux while the test is being done, you have an answer. But having a "normal" barium swallow can simply mean your refluxing baby didn't do it during the test.

An esophageal pH probe can be inserted through the baby's nose to his esophagus and acid levels can be monitored for 24 hours. While the test is about 70% accurate, performing the test on all babies is impractical for obvious reasons—keeping this lovely tube in a baby's nose for a day is no fun, nor is the time baby isn't allowed to eat (several hours).

Then, there's always the option of doing an endoscopy. That involves anesthesia—a tube with a camera at the end of it that is inserted through the baby's mouth and throat to look at the esophagus. Biopsies (tissue samples) can also be taken at the same time to make the diagnosis. This test is 100% accurate, but very expensive.

Given the unpleasant and imperfect nature of these tests, most doctors rely on a simple examination of baby (and parent reports) to make an acid reflux diagnosis.

What's your baby's I-GERQ score?

Here's a free and painless way to assess for reflux in your baby. It's called the I-GERQ score. If your baby scores 7 or more, he has a greater than 90% chance of having at least mild heartburn (**ESOPHAGITIS**).[3]

The test is on the following page.

THE OTHER END

QUESTION	POINTS
How often does the baby usually spit up?	
One to three times a day	1
Three to five times a day	2
More than five times a day	3
How much does the baby usually spit up?	
A teaspoon to a tablespoonful	1
A tablespoon to an ounce	2
An ounce or more	3
Does the spitting up seem to be uncomfortable?	
Yes	2
No	0
Does the baby refuse feedings, even when hungry?	
Yes	1
No	0
Does the baby have trouble gaining enough weight?	
Yes	1
No	0
Does the baby cry a lot during or after feedings?	
Yes	3
No	0
Do you think the baby cries or fusses more than normal?	
Yes	1
No	0
How many hours does the baby cry/fuss each day?	
One to three hours	1
More than three hours	2
Do you think the baby hiccups more than most babies?	
Yes	1
No	0
Does the baby have spells or arching back?	
Yes	2
No	0
Has the baby ever stopped breathing while awake and struggled to breathe, or turned blue or purple?	
Yes	6
No	0

Again, if your baby scores 7 or more, he has a greater than 90% chance of having at least mild heartburn (**ESOPHAGITIS**).[3]

BOTTOM LINE

Most babies outgrow their symptoms of acid reflux when the esophagus muscle tightens up (around six months of age). A few babies will continue to have problems up to their first birthdays. Babies who suffer with daily reflux symptoms from 6-12 months of age are more likely to have feeding problems in their second year of life (even if the reflux is gone).[4]

Reality Check

Your baby does not have acid reflux because your Great Uncle Harry has acid reflux. Nor will your baby develop a hiatal hernia because of acid reflux. The acid reflux that adults suffer from has the same symptoms, but for different reasons. Your baby has acid reflux because he is a baby.

Insider Tip: Acid Reflux . . . a reason for wheezin'

Some babies with acid reflux have respiratory symptoms such as chronic cough and wheezing. This happens because the milk is coming up and irritating the baby's airway. Again, even babies with severe reflux may not be spitting up large volumes of milk. If a baby is having this much trouble with reflux, doctors are pretty aggressive about a treatment plan (for good reason!).

The flip side: if your baby wheezes and a diagnosis of asthma is being considered, get him evaluated for acid reflux (GER)—that may be the reason he wheezes.

Q. **Occasionally, my baby will throw up his whole feeding. Should I worry?**

No.

When babies eat aggressively, they suck in a lot of air. When that big air bubble comes back up with burping, often the whole feeding does too. Unlike adults, babies often throw up and then want to eat again.

The only time to worry is when the whole feeding gets thrown up at *every* feeding. This is a red flag for **PYLORIC STENOSIS** (see picture at right). This is a medical emergency caused by a narrowing of the muscle between the stomach and small intestine (called the *pyloric sphincter*). It usually occurs at six to eight weeks of age because the muscle seems to narrow over time.

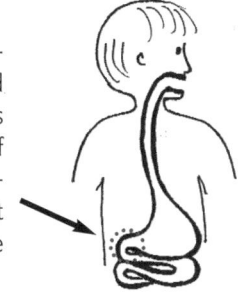

RED FLAGS: Vomiting

1. **Vomiting bile.** Bile is a fluorescent green/yellow color that can indicate a blockage in the intestines. It is especially worrisome if associated with stomachache or a bloated looking tummy, or fever. Call your doctor ASAP.

2. **Vomiting blood or "coffee grounds."** In newborns, blood in

baby's spit up is often from Mommy's cracked and bleeding nipples. Beyond that time, blood in vomit warrants a call to the doctor. Blood that has been partially digested by the stomach looks like coffee grounds when it is thrown up. Both of these symptoms can be caused by bleeding in the esophagus or stomach.

3. **Vomiting repeatedly over six hours.** Excessive vomiting can be caused by stomach viruses (see **GASTROENTERITIS**), food poisoning (see **BACTERIAL ENTERITIS**), or an intestinal blockage (see **ACUTE ABDOMEN**). Most of the time, it's a stomach virus. It's time to check in with your doctor after six hours because your baby can get dehydrated.

4. **Vomiting associated with fever and irritability.** This is how meningitis presents in a baby. Babies have a unique "window" to the brain with their soft spot (fontanelle) on their heads. A full, bulging soft spot occurs with meningitis. Call your doctor immediately.

5. **Morning vomiting.** Babies don't get morning sickness. It's incredibly rare, but vomiting exclusively in the morning is a symptom of increased pressure in the skull. This can be caused by abnormal fluid collections or a mass (i.e. **HYDROCEPHALUS, BRAIN TUMOR**). Both of these abnormalities cause a full, bulging soft spot (fontanelle). This definitely needs to be checked out.

Q. What should I feed/let my baby drink while he is vomiting?

Nothing.

When your baby is actively vomiting, give him nothing to eat or drink unless you want to see it come right back out.

Wait until it has been at least an hour since the last vomit to test the waters. Start with Pedialyte, which is basically Gatorade made specifically for babies. Give one teaspoon every five minutes. Don't let your baby chug as much as he wants. He will be very thirsty. If he takes a full bottle worth on an unsettled stomach, it's destined to be thrown up. He'll get about two ounces an hour for the first couple of hours. If the Pedialyte test fails (more vomiting occurs), call your doctor.

Once the Pedialyte stays down, resume formula or breast milk.

Q. What are the signs of dehydration?

Lethargy, dry skin and lips, sunken soft spot (fontanelle), and decreased urination (less than three wet diapers in 24 hours—or no wet diaper in eight hours).

Another measure is weight loss, which is checked in the doctor's office. If your child is vomiting and/or having diarrhea, *start tallying how many wet diapers your baby is having.* Your doctor will ask you that question when you call or come in for an appointment. For more info, check out Chapter 15, "First Aid."

Pee/Urine

Q. My newborn urinated only once in his first day of life. Is this normal?

Yes.

All you can expect is one wet diaper on baby's first day. We just want to know that the pipes are working. Your baby might pee twice on his second day of life. The wet diapers will start to accumulate once your baby is drinking more. By day four of life, you should get at least four wet diapers. This should reassure you that your baby is getting something to drink when you are breastfeeding.

Q. These diapers are so absorbent, how can I tell if my baby has urinated?

Put a tissue in the diaper and you can see the pee.

In the first week of life, keep track of wet diapers. This information is also useful if your baby is vomiting and has diarrhea.

Another hint: diapers with pee in them feel heavier than dry ones.

Q. My newborn looks like he has blood in his pee. What is it?

Take a closer look. Does it look like brick dust? Is it powdery and on the *surface* of the diaper?

If the answer is yes to these questions, it's not blood. These are **URIC ACID CRYSTALS**. When newborns are a little dehydrated (in the initial 10% weight loss mode), the pee is more concentrated and less watery. This causes one of the ingredients of pee, uric acid, to separate out. That's what you are seeing. Uric acid crystals are nothing to worry about if it is just one newborn diaper. Call your doctor if this is persistent or you see it in an older baby. For a picture of this, see Baby411.com.

Q. My newborn looks like she has blood in her diaper. What is it?

This is the equivalent of a menstrual period. It's not in the pee.

Baby girls' bodies respond to their mother's hormones. There is frequently some bleeding and vaginal discharge in the first few weeks of life. This is normal.

Q. I've heard that baby girls are prone to bladder infections. How can I prevent them?

Good hygiene.

A brief anatomy lesson here. Girls have a very short tube (urethra) that attaches the bladder to the outside. The urethral opening sits just above the vagina. Just below the vagina is the anus. Remember that poop has bacteria in it and urine is sterile. If the poop ends up in the nooks and crannies surrounding the urethra, the bacteria (usually E.coli) can climb into the urethra and grow in the bladder causing a bladder infection. Girls in diapers are particularly prone to infections. The best ways to prevent infection are:

THE OTHER END

- *Change a baby girl's poop diaper ASAP.*
- *Wipe "front to back."* Dads—this means start cleaning your daughter at the urethra and wipe downwards to the anus. Never go the other direction! Gently separate the labia and be sure to clean well in there.

Boys rarely get bladder infections because the urethral tube is much longer from the bladder to the opening (the urethra tube is inside the penis and the opening is at the tip). It's much harder for those bugs to travel that far.

Q. How do you diagnose a bladder infection in a baby?

Foul smelling urine, cloudy urine, and particularly, *fever in a baby with no obvious symptoms* (i.e. no runny nose, cough, or diarrhea).

This is one of the top reasons why we want to hear from you if your baby under three months of age has a fever. *Untreated* bladder infections can quickly lead to kidney infections (and even meningitis) in infants under six months of age.

If your baby is in diapers, and has a fever with no obvious symptoms, your doctor will need a urine sample to look for infection.

Q. Are some babies more prone to bladder infections than others?

Yes. There is an uncommon abnormality of the urinary system that causes urine to flow backwards into the kidneys called **VESICOURETERAL REFLUX (VUR)**. See pictures at right.

Any pre-pubertal child who has a bladder infection needs to be tested for this abnormality. There is also a hereditary factor. Siblings of affected children may get screened as well. Three to five percent of all girls and 1% of boys will get a bladder infection before puberty. Forty percent of these children have vesicoureteral reflux. Take home message: It's worthwhile to be tested for VUR.[5]

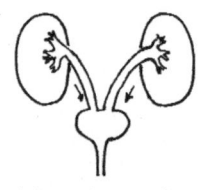

Normal urine flow.

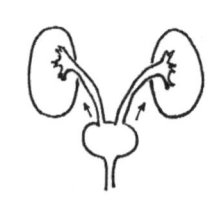

Vesicoureteral reflux.

Reality Check
There is a 60% chance of a child having vesicoureteral reflux if a parent has the disorder. There is a 30% chance of having VUR if a brother or sister has the disorder.[6]

Burping

Q. Do you have any tips on burping my baby? I spend 20 minutes trying to burp him and nothing happens.

It's either going to happen or it won't. It's not your technique or patience that does the trick.

Burps are the result of swallowed air during feedings. Once your baby is an efficient eater (by four months old), he's also likely to be an efficient burper.

For the first few months of life, stop in mid-feed to burp your baby. There are basically three techniques.

1. Baby is upright on your shoulder, and you rub upwards on her back.
2. Baby is sitting in your lap, upright, and you rub upwards on her back.
3. Baby is lying face down on your lap, and you rub upwards on her back.

If it has been more than ten minutes, the burp ain't happening on your watch. Unfortunately, your baby may sleep for 20 minutes, then wake himself up when he burps. Welcome to parenthood. Just do what you can.

> **DR B'S OPINION**
>
> *"Note that the burping technique involves rubbing. I watched my brother burp his twins once and considered reporting him to child protective services. Patting and hitting aren't really necessary!"*

Hiccups

Parents ask a lot of questions about hiccups. Here is what you need to know:

1. Hiccups don't hurt.
2. Hiccups are not a sign of an underlying disorder.
3. Don't worry about hiccups—doctors don't.

Gas

A nice way to exit this chapter.

Q. My baby has more gas than me. Should I be worried?

No.

Your baby has more gas because he sucks in a lot of air and because his intestines are on high alert 24 hours a day.

Most of the time, babies don't really care that they have gas. And don't be embarrassed, it's the only time in your child's life when people will think it's cute when he toots.

Q. What can I do about my baby's gas? Are Mylicon drops okay to use?

Not much, and sure, it won't hurt.

Gas is one of the biggest obsessions of newborn parents. Some parents believe it is the root of all evil . . . the reason that the baby is unhappy . . . the reason why nobody is sleeping. The truth is—IT'S NOT THE GAS. But, if you feel compelled to do *something* (which is a common feeling of all parents), it's okay to try those Mylicon (simethicone) drops. See below for gas tips.

The good news; the gassy phase will pass by age two or three months.

THE OTHER END

NEW PARENT 411: HELPING YOUR BABY PASS GAS

Here are three tips from seasoned parents:

1. Infant massage. This is a comforting way to help your baby relax. Pressing gently on baby's belly sometimes gets the gas out.

2. Warm bath. This also works by relaxing your baby.

3. Mylicon (simethicone) drops. This over the counter medication is safe for babies, including newborns. It makes big gas bubbles into little gas bubbles. Some parents swear by it, others see absolutely no difference in their baby's demeanor. Gripe water, a combo of ginger and fennel, is also a popular remedy.

Q. I'm breastfeeding. Will eliminating high fiber foods from my diet fix my baby's gas problem?

No, but it will give you, Mom, a constipation problem.
This is rarely the cause of baby's gas. You can try an elimination diet, but it's usually not the problem.

Q. My baby is colicky. Is it because of gas?

No. Gas gets a bad wrap.
See Chapter 11, Discipline and Temperament, for information on colic. Eliminating gas won't solve your colic problem.

Baby 411

Section 3

Sleep, Development & Discipline

Sleeping Like A Baby

Chapter 9

"Whoever coined the phrase, 'sleeps like a baby' never slept with one!"
~ Anonymous

What's in this Chapter

- ◆ The science of sleep
- ◆ Newborn sleep issues
- ◆ Sleep safety tips
- ◆ Deciding on your family's sleep routine (family bed vs. solitary sleep)
- ◆ Setting up good habits
- ◆ Undoing bad habits
- ◆ Top 10 Mistakes parents make
- ◆ The Sleep Gurus
- ◆ Naps
- ◆ Special situations—Multiples and Preemies

Who needs sleep?
well you're never gonna get it

Who needs sleep?
tell me what's that for

Who needs sleep?
be happy with what you're getting
There's a guy who's been awake since
the Second World War
— Barenaked Ladies

New (and veteran) parents struggle with their baby's sleep habits—it's a fact of life. Everyone warned you about it, but you weren't buying it. At first, the excitement of being a parent gives you the momentum to make it through the first few weeks of sleep deprivation. Then, the novelty begins to wear off. You are exhausted and desperate for a good night's sleep. You'll ask friends and relatives for tricks that worked for their babies. It's no wonder that books on infant sleep are a booming section at your local bookstore.

If you are reading this chapter before your baby is born, good for you. You will be prepared for what lies ahead. If you are already in the desperate category—don't worry—we can help you, too.

Before we give you all of our sage advice on this subject, it is *essential* that you understand the science of sleep.

Knowing the basics will help you appreciate the advice and avoid the common mistakes parents make.

The Science Of Sleep

Q. Do newborns have the same sleep patterns that adults do?

NO. That's why you cannot expect them to sleep like we do. Here are four important concepts you need to understand:

1 TYPES OF SLEEP. There are two basic types of sleep: REM and Non-REM. REM stands for **R**apid **E**ye **M**ovement. Here are the differences between the two.

	NON-REM SLEEP	REM SLEEP
Muscle movements	relaxed	active (stretches, sucks, vocalizes)
Brain activity	relaxed	active (dreams)
Occurrence	1st part of night, PM nap	2nd part of night, AM nap

Newborns spend 50-80% of their sleep in REM sleep while adults spend only 25% of their sleep in REM. The result: babies are very active when they are asleep. And that pattern continues even now. Your baby will be noisy and moving around, but he is not awake.

BOTTOM LINE: Your baby's sleep activity and noises do not mean you need to feed or help him.

2 SLEEP CYCLES. Humans go through a series of sleep cycles throughout an evening's rest. Adults tend to bunch all the Non-REM cycles first, and then go through REM cycles. Babies do more flip-flopping of Non-REM and REM cycles. Each sleep cycle has a beginning and an end, where a person goes from light sleep to deep to light again, before entering the next cycle. Humans recheck their environments and body comfort at that time. At the end of each sleep cycle, a partial wakening occurs. Babies may whimper or briefly cry out during this time.

BOTTOM LINE: Leave your baby alone when he has a partial wakening. He will enter into his next sleep cycle if you leave him alone. If you intervene, you will wake him up. As the saying goes, let sleeping babies lie.

3 LENGTH OF CYCLES. The average adult sleep cycle lasts 90 minutes. The average newborn sleep cycle lasts 60 minutes.

BOTTOM LINE: Your baby has shorter sleep cycles than you. It can take several months until he has mature sleep patterns like an older child.

4 CIRCADIAN RHYTHM. The human body has a biological clock that registers 24.5 to 25 hours in a day. This is called a circadian rhythm. It is affected by both light exposure and a body chemical called melatonin. Babies follow their mother's circadian rhythm in the womb probably because of melatonin levels. Once outside the womb, they have exposure to light and must form their own circadian rhythm.

BOTTOM LINE: It takes several weeks for a baby to get their circadian rhythm sorted out. If you lived in the dark for nine months, you'd probably be a little confused too.

Newborn Sleep Issues

Q. Okay, now I understand why my newborn has erratic sleep patterns. But, how can I get my baby to sleep at night instead of during the day?

This is called Day-Night Reversal. It usually takes three or four weeks to resolve.

The best way to help your baby through this is to stimulate him during the day and keep things low key at night. Talk to your baby during daylight hours and encourage any wakeful periods he has. At night, do your feeding routine with little interaction. Only turn the lights on if you have a poopy diaper to clean. If your baby decides he wants to have a slumber party, he can party on his own. You don't have to entertain him.

These nocturnal habits usually resolve by three to four weeks of age. See "Sleep Tips" below in this chapter for more advice on the first couple weeks of life.

Q. How much should a newborn sleep?

About 16 to 18 hours total a day.

But here's the cruel part: most newborns will not sleep more than four hours at a stretch. They need to eat frequently and their little bodies know it.

Check out the table in the setting up good habits section later in this chapter to get an idea of how sleep changes through the first year of life.

BOTTOM LINE: Most newborns have six or seven stretches of sleep every 24 hours. Feedings occur in between these stretches.

Helpful Hints
Three Sleep Tips for the First Two Weeks of life
♦ *Wake your newborn up if he has slept longer than three hours during the day.* When your baby has day-night reversals, he may have his one long stretch of sleep in the middle of the day. Discourage this! Otherwise, you will be in for a long night of cluster feedings.

♦ *Do not let your newborn sleep more than four hours straight during the night.* He needs nutrition to grow. He also needs to stimulate your milk supply to come in if you are breastfeeding. Once he has regained his birth weight and your doc gives you her blessing, you can let the baby sleep at night (he won't, but it's fine if he does).

♦ *Your job is to sleep when baby sleeps.* Become nocturnal. Don't even think about doing laundry when your baby crashes in the afternoon. Go to bed!

Q. When can I expect to sleep through the night?

Now that you are an expert in "sleep-ology," you can appreciate the following fact: it takes (on average) *17 weeks of life* for an infant to develop mature sleep patterns. Yep, that's about four months. Think about that for a moment.

The definition of "sleeping through the night" is six hours of uninterrupted sleep. That will feel like a great night's sleep by the time you get there![1]

FYI: Even parents with school-aged kids will be awakened by middle-of-the-night announcements ("I just had a nightmare, Mom"...... you get the picture). The concept of "sleeping through the night" is only a fuzzy and abstract concept that exists for childless couples.

Old Wives Tale
Giving your baby rice cereal helps him sleep through the night earlier.
The truth: Food has nothing to do with it.

DR B'S OPINION

"If your full term, healthy baby is still not sleeping six hours straight by six months of age, it's not your baby's fault. It's probably yours. Read the section 'Undoing Bad Habits' later in this chapter."

Q. My friend says that their baby slept through the night at four weeks of age! That's not fair! How can this be?

Odds are, your friends are lying—or will soon be proved wrong when their baby reverts back to a normal sleep pattern (that is, waking up during the night). Sure, lightning sometimes strikes and a one month old will sleep through the night . . . for one night. Or even a month. But then, as we'll discuss later, she may relapse into waking up during the nighttime.

Another explanation for these wild claims: dads. When we hear about a baby that miraculously slept through the night from birth, this claim usually comes from the proud new dad. Of course, the baby wasn't sleeping but daddy was—mom still had to get up several times a night!

By the way, some babies *will* sleep up to 12 hours a night as early as two months of age, but it's not the norm. If your baby is a terrific sleeper, don't brag about it—you'll jinx yourself for the next baby!

Q. How do I get my newborn to fall asleep? He seems to have trouble relaxing.

It would be nice to have the baby who awakens to feed and then goes right back to sleep. More likely, you have the baby who eats and then fusses until you help him return to the Land of Nod.

After you and your baby get to know each other better, you will figure out what helps him settle down.

Newborns are born with immature nervous systems. That means, they don't have the ability to pull it together, relax, and fall asleep. The most reliable way babies know how to settle down is to suck. See the next box for our Newborn Sleep Tips.

NEW PARENT 411:
TOP 5 TIPS FOR GETTING A NEWBORN TO SLEEP

1. **Suck to soothe**. If you are so inclined, your breast may become the human pacifier. If this approach is not for you, use your finger or a pacifier in your baby's mouth to encourage sucking. This is fine for the first two months of life (more on pacifiers later in this chapter).
2. **Move around.** Rocking, swaying, and bouncing (you will have the veteran-parent-bop down quickly) are effective.
3. **Sing**, in or out of tune.
4. **Snug as a bug.** Swaddling, sleeping in a bassinet, or even sleeping in a car seat may do the trick.
5. **Go for a car ride.**

Q. How long should my newborn sleep in a bassinet?

Two or three months max.

You are not setting up any permanent habits the first two months of life. Babies become aware of their surroundings around three to four months of age. That's when you need to set up a permanent routine.

For now, newborns prefer to be snug. They like to sleep in bassinets or even their infant car seat (both are fine) until they decide they want to stretch out. I recommend transitioning over to the crib by three months of age. Another factor: some playpens with a bassinet insert have weight limits that are usually exceeded by two or three months of age.

Old Wives Tale
Too much holding and rocking will spoil your baby.

The truth: You cannot spoil a newborn. Remember, babies don't have the ability to settle on their own. Do what it takes to get your baby to sleep. *However, you need to grow as your baby does. Your six-month-old will be quite capable of settling down on his own.*

Reality Check
Many babies will sweat while they are asleep. Don't be alarmed if your baby awakens in a pool of water (well, you might want to check the diaper, too).

Q. My baby will only sleep on me. If I put him down anywhere (bassinet, etc.) he wakes right up. What do I do?

Remember, babies are not born with self-soothing skills. They are used to being snug, warm, and next to your heartbeat. While you can simulate that environment (you can even buy a device that makes heartbeat noises), your baby may still do his best sleeping when he is skin to skin with you.

During the day, it's fairly easy to do this. Wearing your baby is very stylish. In fact, there are some beautiful fabric slings out there these days. Just continue your daily activities with your baby in tow.

During the night, it's a bit more of a challenge. You'll need to come up with a safe way for both of you to get some sleep. One solution: a co-sleeper bed that attaches to your mattress. That way, each of you will sleep in your own space, but you are still next to each other.

You are not setting up any bad habits. By two or three months, your baby will want to stretch out and won't need to be a fashion accessory anymore. You're welcome to continue using the sling as long as you'd like for transportation or nursing, but we'd suggest discontinuing its use as a sleep aid at three months.

Q. How do sleep patterns and needs change as baby grows?

Check out this information as well as the handy sleep requirements chart on the next page for details.

◆ **Birth to two months.** Newborns sleep 16-18 hours a day. They have day-night reversals, and rarely sleep for more than a four-hour stretch at a time. Yes, you have our blessing to do whatever it takes to get your baby to fall asleep and stay asleep. Swaddling, rocking, nursing to sleep, wearing your baby as an accessory (in a sling), going for a car ride, using a pacifier, etc. You are not spoiling your baby or setting up any permanent bad habits. Remember: your baby does not have the neurologic maturity to pull it together, relax, and fall asleep on his own yet.

◆ **Two to four months.** On average, babies sleep 14-16 hours a day. They are usually taking three naps per day. If you are lucky, your baby may sleep for a six-hour stretch at night. It is still too early to train your baby to sleep. What you should be aiming for now is to set up *healthy sleep routines*. We'll have more on this subject later in the chapter.

◆ **Four to six months.** The average four to six month old sleeps a total of 14-15 hours a day, with two naps included. Your baby should be sleeping AT LEAST six hours at night. Some babies will sleep up to 12 hours at night.

Sleep requirements, birth to 2 years (in hours)

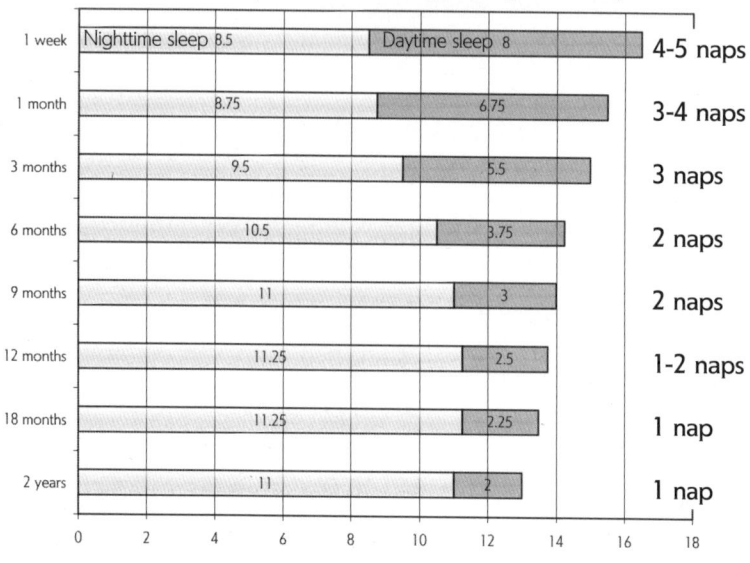

Age	Nighttime sleep (hours)	Daytime sleep (hours)	Naps
1 week	8.5	8	4-5 naps
1 month	8.75	6.75	3-4 naps
3 months	9.5	5.5	3 naps
6 months	10.5	3.75	2 naps
9 months	11	3	2 naps
12 months	11.25	2.5	1-2 naps
18 months	11.25	2.25	1 nap
2 years	11	2	1 nap

Yes, everyone in the house should be getting sleep by now...but if this is not happening, you need help. Do not be convinced that your baby NEEDS to be up at night. In fact, everyone will be happier if your child is sleeping at night. Sometimes parents aid and abet their baby's bad sleep behaviors. We'll discuss the reasons why babies this age continue to wake at night later in this chapter.

◆ **Six to 12 months.** On average, these babies sleep 13 to 14 hours per day, with two naps included. Most babies sleep ten to 12 hours straight at night. Yes, your prayers were answered! If your baby is still waking up for night feedings or comfort, you need help. See "Undoing Bad Habits" later in this chapter.

Sleep Safety Tips

Q. I've heard about sudden infant death syndrome (SIDS). What is the official recommendation about infant sleep position?

The "Back to Sleep" Campaign is promoted by the American Academy of Pediatrics and various other health organizations. The official recommendation is that babies sleep on their backs from birth to at least six months of age to reduce the risk of SIDS (90% of SIDS cases occur in babies under six months old).

Our own parents put us on our bellies to sleep. Any grandparent will tell you that babies sleep better on their tummies. They are right. However, numerous studies have proven that this sleep position significantly increases the risk of sudden infant death. It seems to be caused by the infant smothering himself—a pocket of carbon dioxide forms around the baby's face when she is face down in a mattress or soft bedding. Babies don't have the neck muscles to move their heads and, sadly, that's how some SIDS deaths occur.

Before the Back to Sleep Campaign began in 1992, 5000 babies died per year in the U.S. from SIDS. Today, that number is down by over 40%. Let's take a look at a graph that shows how the SIDS rate plummeted as parents stopped putting baby to sleep on their stomach:

US SIDS rate versus the % of babies sleeping on their stomach

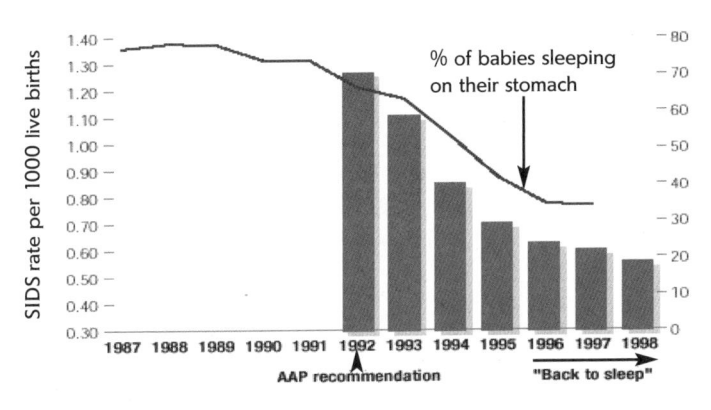

Source: Contemporary Pediatrics, Vol 17, No. 9

Memo to Grandparents: Back to Sleep

Here's a scary fact: babies who are used to sleeping on their backs and are placed on their sides (and roll over) or stomachs to sleep have a significantly greater risk of SIDS than those babies who are used to sleeping on their tummies.

The message: make sure that your childcare provider or occasional grandparent-as-babysitter puts your baby on his back to sleep. They may have missed the memo on the Back-To-Sleep Campaign.

Q. Are there any other known risk factors for SIDS?

Yes. Here are the top six:

1 ROOM TEMPERATURE. The cooler the room, the better. SIDS occurs more frequently in the winter months when babies are bundled and the heat is on. Believe it or not, the recommended "safe" room temperature to reduce SIDS risk is 68 degrees.

2 SOFT BEDDING. All those beautiful bedding sets need to stay out of the crib. The heavy quilts, pillows, and blankets cause the ambient temperature of the crib to go up. Babies can also smother themselves in the bedding.

3 SMOKING. Babies whose parents smoke have a higher risk of SIDS. So, if you can't do it for yourself, stop smoking for the most important thing in your world.

4 ETHNICITY. Native Americans and African Americans have a much higher risk of SIDS than other babies. New research suggests a genetic defect may be passed on in certain ethnic groups who carry the gene.

5 FAMILY HISTORY. There may be a higher incidence of SIDS when a previous family member has had it.

6 BRAIN ABNORMALITY. A recent study showed several babies who died of SIDS have dysfunctional neurotransmitters that control certain body functions. The abnormality may explain why some babies quit breathing (instead of awakening or turning their heads) when they're sleeping face down and not getting enough oxygen. The problem is more common in boys. While this research is touted as a major advance, there's no practical way of testing babies for this disorder right now.[2]

Obviously, there are risk factors on this list that you cannot control. But try to avoid the ones you can—like bedding, sleep position, and smoking.

Reality Check: Pacifiers Reduce SIDS Risk

Believe it or not, there is substantial evidence to show that pacifiers actually reduce the risk of SIDS. It is unclear why, though. It may be that the pacifier keeps a baby's airway open. Or, sucking on a pacifier prevents a baby from forgetting to breathe. But whatever the reason, not using a pacifier during sleep may increase the chances of SIDS (90% of SIDS cases occur between one and six months of life).[3] For a quick look at the latest recommendations to avoid SIDS, see the chart later in this chapter.

Helpful Hints

◆ **What should you do with that baby quilt you got as a gift?** Use it as a wall hanging. Or buy a special quilt rack for your baby's nursery. You can always use it on the floor as baby gets older. Put a few toys out and encourage some supervised tummy time. Another alternative: some crib bedding makers are substituting lighter-weight blankets for thick quilts in their sets.

◆ **Don't borrow a crib older than a 1990 model.** The safety standards changed in 1989. The width between crib slats in older cribs was more than 2 1/2 inches apart, creating an entrapment hazard.

Q. What bedding items are acceptable to place in the crib?

A fitted sheet and a light receiving blanket. Of course, you don't even have to use a blanket—baby can just sleep in a sleeper or be swaddled. Or consider a new alternative: the sleep sack (pictured here is the SleepSack from HALO Innovations, web: www.halosleep.com). These "wearable blankets" provide warmth but cut the SIDS risk, as babies can't crawl under them or become entrapped. Again, the key goal here is to not over-heat your baby—putting your child in a sleep sack and cranking up the thermostat is a no-no.

What about crib bumpers? Suffice it to say, these are a controversial item. We have a long discussion of the pros and cons of bumpers in our other book, *Baby Bargains*. To sum up, we believe crib bumpers are purely optional. One important point: if you decide to use them, remove the bumpers before your baby can pull herself up to a standing position. Why? Babies who can stand can use those bumpers to escape from the crib! Take the bumpers out by six months of age.[4]

Pictured here is the Consumer Product Safety Commission's suggestion for how baby should sleep in their crib. Note there are no bumpers or other soft bedding in the crib. The thin blanket is tucked in the mattress at one end of the crib to keep it from moving around.

Q. Is it okay to swaddle a baby in his crib?

Yes.

Newborns like to be snug for the first couple months of life. Think about it. They are used to being in a confined space. Your friendly nurses from the hospital probably taught you the "burrito wrap" technique of swaddling your baby. If not, see the box on the next page. Swaddling works well for the first six weeks of life, until baby wants to stretch out.

A good tip if Baby Houdini lives with you: The Miracle Blanket ($30). This is one blanket your baby will not be able to squirm out of. Check out their website at www.miracleblanket.com for product info.

Q. Okay, I put my baby on his back to sleep. What do I do if he rolls over?

Let him sleep!

Your baby probably won't figure out how to roll over until he is at least four months old. Once he starts doing it, you can't stop him. The next morning, you will find him in a completely different position than the way you left him!

If it makes you feel any better, once babies are good at clearing their nose and mouth by turning their heads, the risk of SIDS is lower.

Q. I'm concerned my baby might choke if he sleeps on his back. Should I be?

No.

Babies have a gag reflex that protects their airway when they vomit (all humans do). There is no increased choking risk.

As a side note, babies with gastroesophageal reflux do better with their heads elevated 30 degrees (the angle of a car seat). They experience less heartburn that way. (That's the way I sleep, too, after overindulging on Tex-Mex food). These babies sleep better with a wedge under their mattress (an example is the Tucker Sling, tuckerslign.com, discussed in Chapter 8, "The Other End"), or may sleep in their car seats for the first several weeks of life.

Q. Can I cheat, and let my baby sleep on his side?

We can't recommend it. Babies who sleep on their sides may accidentally roll onto their tummies. And babies who are not used to being tummy sleepers have an 18 fold increased risk of SIDS if they end up sleeping that way.

Q. Can I buy one of those breathing motion detectors and let my baby sleep on his stomach?

These products are not worth the expense—a gadget can't prevent

---

HOW TO SWADDLE A BABY—AKA BABY BURRITO WRAP

And now, the six steps to swaddling your baby:

1. Take a square receiving blanket and turn it diamond shaped on a flat surface.
2. Take the top corner and fold it towards the center of the blanket. You now have a horizontal line at the top.
3. Place your baby on the blanket with his neck at the level on the horizontal line.
4. Bring the bottom corner up to the baby's belly button.
5. Bring one side corner over the baby and fold over the other side of the belly.
6. Bring the other side corner over the baby and fold over on the other side.

Voila!

SIDS. It leads to more parent anxiety and disrupted sleep when the alarm goes off accidentally. The motion detectors you buy at the store are not the same as "apnea monitors" that some premature infants use after they are sent home from the hospital.

Q. My baby has a flat head and a bald spot on the back of her head from this sleep position. Is this permanent?

No. This is called **POSITIONAL PLAGIOCEPHALY** and most kids do not need helmets to fix the problem. As your baby starts to roll over, the head shape will round out. All babies lose their hair around four months, and then grow new hair in.

You can help with the head shape issue by scheduling daily tummy time. This also promotes neck and back muscle strength. And, it helps them learn how to roll over. (It's easier to roll from stomach to back than the reverse). For details on tummy time and positional plagiocephaly, see Chapter 5, "Nutrition & Growth" and Chapter 14, "Common Diseases."

Q. Is there any greater or lesser risk of SIDS with a family bed?

While the risk of SIDS with the family bed is controversial, we know the family bed increases the risk of smothering and entrapment. Both can be fatal. Waterbeds, comforters, and pillows in the family bed are suffocation hazards. If you choose the family bed option, here are some safe methods to try:

◆ Use a co-sleeper mattress that hooks up to yours so baby has his own space.
◆ Move the crib next to your bed and take the side rail down.

BOTTOM LINE
Here are the latest American Academy of Pediatrics recommendations to prevent SIDS:

1 **NO TO SIDE SLEEPING.** Babies who sleep on their sides are more likely to roll onto their tummies and increase their risk of SIDS. And infants who are used to back sleepers that sleep on their tummies increase their SIDS by 18 times.

2 **NO TO CO-SLEEPING.** The risk of smothering or entrapping an infant is greater when parents and baby share a bed.

3 **YES TO ROOM SHARING.** The AAP encourages room sharing to support breastfeeding and reduce SIDS risk.

4 **YES TO PACIFIERS.** For unknown reasons, the binky is protective. Just know when to start (after breastfeeding is well established) and when to stop (when the risk of SIDS is over) using it.

Top Ten Take-Home Messages on Sleep Safety

1. Put your baby to bed on his back.
2. Keep soft bedding out of the crib.
3. Keep the room temperature cool (68 degrees).
4. Don't over bundle your baby with too many clothes. Swaddling in one light blanket is okay. No need for a hat or cap.
5. No smoking.
6. Use a crib made after 2000.
7. Buy a new, firm crib mattress.
8. Make sure the mattress fits into the crib snugly, without gaps.
9. Take bumper pads out of the crib by six months old.
10. Lower the mattress height to the lowest level *before* your baby starts to pull on the railings to stand up.

Deciding On The Family's Sleep Routine: a.k.a. The Family Bed vs. Solitary Sleep Debate

This debate is worthy of an introduction before we get to the details. Where your baby sleeps is completely your decision. There is no right or wrong answer—the right answer is what works for *all* of you. There are advantages and disadvantages, whichever choice you make. We'll give you the information to make an educated decision about what is best for you.

Here are the options:

- **The Family Bed (Co-sleeping):** Parents and children sleep together in the same bed.
- **Solitary Sleep:** Each child sleeps separately in his own bed.
- **The Desperation Move:** Parents prefer that their baby sleep in his own bed, but end up having him in their bed out of sheer exhaustion and frustration with their inability to get their baby to sleep in his crib. (See undoing bad habits section later in this chapter.)

Q. What are the advantages of a family bed?

The main advantage is convenience.

For a breastfed newborn, it's very easy to eat at night. As soon as he stirs, his mother is there for him. This is also convenient for Mom, who might fall asleep shortly after (or during!) those middle-of-the-night feeds. Recent data suggest that co-sleeping babies nurse more frequently and take larger volumes of breast milk at night than their solitary sleeping peers.[4] The American Academy of Pediatrics, as of 2005, recommends that breastfed babies sleep "in proximity" to their moms to improve breastfeeding success. They choose their words carefully, though, because of safety concerns (more on this below).

Family bed advocates claim there are other advantages to co-sleeping. These include: better parent-infant attachment, sense of security, sense of trust, and protection from SIDS.

> **DR B'S OPINION**
>
> "Having a well-adjusted and happy child has nothing to do with where he sleeps!"

But there is no statistical data or scientific proof to back up these claims.

Many parents choose this option simply because it feels good to snuggle up with their baby.

Just a bit of trivia: in the U.S., 12.8% of infants sleep in a family bed regularly. The percentages are higher in ethnic and lower-income groups.[5]

Q. What are the disadvantages of the family bed?

Potential for SIDS and smothering risk.

The American Academy of Pediatrics policy position warns against the family bed, cautioning families to AVOID co-sleeping.

Solitary sleep advocates argue that co-sleeping families get poor sleep and prolong the time before a baby starts sleeping through the night. They also feel that co-sleeping interferes with a baby's ability to become an independent being.

One way to address this issue is to use a hybrid method of co-sleeping—putting the baby in a co-sleeper (pictured). This port-a-crib attaches to the adult bed, allowing a parent to easily reach the child for feedings or comforting. But the baby really is in its own space instead of sleeping in the bed.

DR B'S OPINION: THE FAMILY BED

Despite the AAP's warnings, some families still opt for the family bed. If you choose this option, make sure EVERYONE sleeping in the family bed is happy with that arrangement. If the answer is yes, go for it—but do it safely. The right answer for where your baby sleeps is what works for your entire family.

But after caring for countless families, I am compelled to point out some realities about the family bed.

One of my colleagues used to say, "The family bed is a wonderful form of birth-control." Be honest with yourself. Many women lack the energy and interest in sexual relations after the baby is born. Don't use the baby in your bed as an out. It's important that BOTH parents want baby in bed with them. *The truth is, Dad often ends up on the couch to get some sleep.* Don't sacrifice your marital relationship to any sleeping arrangement. Your baby needs happy parents.

Also, remember the discussion about babies having mostly REM sleep? Babies are noisy and mobile a good portion of the night. If you are a light sleeper, the family bed may not be for you. And let's be honest—even if you are a heavy sleeper, having an infant cry/fuss/feed every two hours is enough to wake the dead. Although the concept may be appealing to you, the reality may not be. One mom told me, "I am getting kicked awake every hour even if I am not getting up to feed her."

That said, for many families, the family bed works just fine. The take home message: it doesn't matter WHERE your baby sleeps as long as it is safe and the entire family is happy with it.

BOTTOM LINE
An eighteen-year study on parent-child bed sharing:
A landmark study came out recently that evaluated children who slept in a family bed as infants and young children and compared them to their solitary sleeping peers. These children were studied from birth through age 18 years. *The data showed that co-sleeping had no statistically significant problems or benefits.*[6]

Q. What are the advantages of solitary sleep?

Better and safer sleep.

As stated above, breastfed babies who co-sleep are up more often at night to feed. According to the AAP, the crib is a safer place for baby to sleep.

Q. What are the disadvantages of solitary sleep?

Consistency is required.

A baby who is used to sleeping alone in his own bed may have more sleep disruptions when families travel or sleep away from their home. It also requires taking a portable crib on trips or making arrangements to borrow one at your destination.

Babies who sleep alone need a consistent sleep ritual and often a transitional object (the proverbial security blanket) to wind down.

Q. With all of these night feedings, my baby ends up falling asleep on me. I don't want a family bed—will this be a problem in the future?

For the first two months, do anything that buys you some sleep.

Babies are very malleable for the first two to three months of life. You are not setting yourself up for having a five-year-old in bed with you. If your baby nurses and falls asleep on you, try to put him into his bassinet afterwards.

Your goal should be to have a consistent sleep routine by four months of age.

Setting Up Good Habits (Two to Four Months)

For the first two months of life, when it comes to you and your baby's sleep, you gotta do what you gotta do—nursing, rocking, infant swing, a car ride, etc. You know the drill.

Guess what? Your baby is now nearly four months old. It's time to stop those old habits.

Why? Your baby is becoming more aware of her environment. She will respond better when things are *predictable*, anticipating what is next. She will also start to form sleep *associations*. That means your baby will rely on certain routines to fall asleep. Those routines are the good sleep habits you want to keep. And now is the time to punt the bad habits. Think about it—you really don't want to be rocking your five year old to sleep every night, do you?

For the nitty gritty on forming good sleep habits, check out our Ten Commandments for establishing a sleep routine in the box on page 196.

Q. When can I start to schedule my baby's naps and bedtime?

Between two and four months of age, your baby will start to have some regular sleep and feeding patterns (finally). Keep a sleep/feeding diary for a week and you'll know your baby's preferences.

Then you can put your baby down for naps and bedtime *before* she shows you that she is tired (cranky, rubbing eyes—you've seen it all before). The key word in that previous sentence is BEFORE. Once you see those sleepy signs, she is actually overtired.

Start your wind down routine before that happens by aiming for nap/bedtime about 20 minutes earlier than what your sleep diary shows. Not only will you have some idea how to schedule your day, but you'll give your baby the best shot at falling asleep on her own.

You're in the driver's seat now and can put your baby on a schedule she already likes—yes, YOU have the power!

Q. My three month old only falls asleep while feeding. How do we change that habit?

You will be walking a fine line between two and four months of age. Your goal is to *separate* the eating experience from the sleeping experience. Your baby may not need to eat to fall asleep, but you won't know until you try! And if you fail the first time, try again the next week. Your baby is maturing at the speed of light. At this stage, a week older is a week smarter.

In the middle of the night when you hear your baby cry . . . walk, don't run, to your baby's bedside. She might just go back to sleep without your intervention.

You can also try soothing your baby without offering food if you have frequent night wakenings. Your baby may not need to eat every time and is just relying on you to help him get back to sleep. If you are breastfeeding, let Dad try to be the soother. There will be less expectation of food if he shows up. But if it has been more than four hours or so since the last feeding, you will probably have a hungry baby on your hands who needs to eat.

Q. My four month old still needs help falling asleep. What do I do?

You can gradually cut the virtual umbilical cord. Your goal is for your

> **DR B'S OPINION:**
> **FOUR MONTH OLDS AND SLEEP**
>
> Your four-month old baby is aware of his surroundings. If he falls asleep in your arms and you sneak him into bed, he will awaken at the end of his sleep cycle (every 90 minutes) looking for comfort. If your child is awake when you leave the room, he will fall asleep alone and content. You'll hear him on your baby monitor discussing his day with inanimate objects. Your baby is growing up—it's time to accept that change and adapt to it.

baby to fall asleep on her own—without feeding or rocking her to sleep.

Now that she is four months old, set up a consistent sleep ritual. If she falls asleep during the feeding, wake her up before putting her in bed so she is aware of where she is going.

Give her at least ten minutes to try to fall asleep on her own. Yes, she will protest (code word for cry) and that is okay. She is learning how to self-soothe. If she cannot fall asleep, go back in and do as little as possible to relax her. Try patting, singing to her, and cuddling her for a few MINUTES (not hours). Rocking her until she is dead weight on your shoulder or nursing her to sleep is the last resort.

The exact method of transitioning to a better sleep pattern varies for each baby. Basically, you do as little as possible and give your baby more time to work things out on her own. Thirty minutes is a reasonable amount of time by five months of age.

If your baby still cannot fall asleep on her own by five months, use the Ferber or Weissbluth methods (more info later in this chapter). The same rules apply for frequent night wakings.

INSIDER SECRETS: TOP 10 COMMANDMENTS FOR

1. TEACH YOUR BABY TO FALL ASLEEP ON HIS OWN. Remember those sleep cycles? The cycle consists of light to heavy to light arousal before entering the next cycle. At the end of each cycle, humans re-check their environment and change body position (move a pillow or blanket, roll over). By three to four months of age, your infant will be aware of his world. If he falls asleep on a parent's shoulder and gets moved to a crib, or falls asleep when he is drinking or sucking a pacifier, that is what he will be expecting when he arouses at the end of his sleep cycle. Translation: be careful of sleep "crutches" like the pacifier. Put your child in a crib or bassinet when he is sleepy . . . but before he falls asleep. If the child always falls asleep on your shoulder, he will expect to see that shoulder at the end of every sleep cycle.

2. BE CONSISTENT. KIDS DO BEST WITH ROUTINES. Predictable is comfortable. You will learn that rapid transitions and unexpected activities promote anxiety and outbursts in your child (see Chapter 11 "Discipline & Temperament" for details). Have a routine for both nap and bedtime and stick with it by the age of four months.

3. YOUR CHILD SHOULD ALWAYS SLEEP IN THE SAME PLACE FOR NAPS AND NIGHTTIME. That's not the car seat or the infant swing anymore. Reality check: yes, every now and again your child may fall asleep in a car seat, especially after a long trip on the weekend for example. That's OK on an occasional basis. But when you are at home, keep the sleep place the same.

4. NAP TIME AND BEDTIME SHOULD BE APPROXIMATELY THE SAME TIME EVERY DAY. That goes for vacations, visits to relatives, etc.

Consistency is key. Do the same ritual for both nap and bedtime. And, give your baby a chance to figure things out—two to three minutes of protesting doesn't count as a chance.

Q. I've heard babies are more likely to sleep through the night if their tummies are full. What do you think of "dream feeds"?

For newborns, feeding and sleep patterns are intimately related. Babies under two months of age need to eat frequently, usually every two to three hours day or night. That means they can't sleep very long because they get hungry. Babies start to stretch out feedings at night (and give parents a small break) at two to four months.

However, as babies get older, their ability to sleep through the night has more to do with their brains than their guts. Your four month old is capable of sleeping at least six hours without needing to eat. Don't let her fool you. The key to Mr. Sandman's house resides in your ability to teach your

ESTABLISHING A SLEEP ROUTINE (2 TO 4 MONTH OLDS)

5 **ALWAYS FOLLOW YOUR SLEEP RITUAL.** Bath, feeding, (teeth brushing), story-time, songs, prayers...you might do the Cliff's Notes version of a book or song if it has been a long day, but still do it.

6 **START YOUR SLEEP RITUAL BEFORE YOUR CHILD IS TIRED.** Don't wait for the yawns and eye-rubbing to begin the routine.

7 **EARLY TO BED, LATE TO RISE.** Sounds like it wouldn't work this way, but it does. Babies actually sleep better when they go to sleep early. An "overtired" baby does not sleep longer —so, you are not buying time to sleep in by putting your baby down later in the evening. Trust me on this one.

8 **GET RID OF THE PACIFIER BY FOUR TO SIX MONTHS OF AGE.** Your baby is very aware of his world. If he falls asleep with a pacifier in his mouth, he will cry when it falls out. At 3am. And 5am.

9 **BABIES NEED REFRESHER COURSES ON SLEEP ETIQUETTE AFTER TRAVEL, ILLNESS, OR TEETHING.** When consistency is broken, it takes a few days to get back on track. If you don't remind your baby of what to do, he will remain on a disrupted sleep schedule.

10 **DON'T TREAT YOUR FOUR MONTH OLD LIKE A NEWBORN.** Your baby will take advantage of your naiveté. Many four month olds are capable of falling asleep on their own if given the opportunity to do so.

baby self-soothing skills . . . not stuffing her full of milk.

For a full-term, healthy thriving baby (who doesn't have acid reflux), here are some helpful feeding parameters:

- Four month olds: Can sleep SIX hours without needing to eat.
- Five month olds: Can sleep NINE hours without needing to eat.
- Six month olds: Can sleep TWELVE hours without needing to eat.

Some parents will try to feed a sleeping baby (a.k.a. Dream Feed) before they go to bed, hoping to catch that six-hour stretch during the hours they want to actually sleep. For example, instead of your baby fasting from 8 pm-2 am, he fasts from 11 pm-5 am. While this sounds great in theory, I am not a big fan of this strategy. I think it sets up a habit of feeding a child when he isn't hungry, and it in no way guarantees you'll sleep until 5 am. Second problem: cavities. Many parents continue night feedings long after their baby has teeth (around six months of age). Unless you plan on brushing your child's teeth after that dream feed, you will be paying for your dentist's kids to go to college.

If your baby learns how to soothe himself, you'll have better odds of sleeping through the night.

Undoing Bad Habits (Four to 12 months and beyond): Solving the Sleep Problems That Parents Create

If you have a baby who is still not sleeping at least six hours a night, or you are bringing your child to bed with you out of desperation (and not choice), this section is for you. Admitting you have a problem is the first step!

The International Pediatric Sleep Education Task Force met in 2005 to discuss cross-cultural infant sleep issues. The most amusing conclusion: 25% of ALL parents report problems with their baby's sleep patterns......no matter what country they live in. You are not alone.[8]

Behind the Scenes
Is there a correlation between parents' behavior and infant's sleep?

A recent Canadian study showed that many infant sleep disorders were based on parents' excessive intervention in comforting

Continued on page 200

DR B'S OPINION: BEEN THERE, DONE THAT

I am a parent of young children. I have walked in your shoes. I know that irrational thoughts seem rational at 3 am. It SEEMS EASIER to just bring your baby in bed with you or nurse them to sleep. But it is not the right answer anymore.

Once you are on the other side (sleeping through the night), you'll say, "What was I thinking?" I am happier and so are my children when we have all slept at night.

THE TOP TEN MISTAKES PARENTS MAKE WITH INFANT SLEEP ROUTINES

1. Sneaking baby into bed. Your baby falls asleep in your arms, and then you sneak him into his crib. Compare this to the following scenario.[9] You fall asleep on the couch in front of the TV. Your spouse picks you up and carries you into your bed. When you wake up in your own bed, you are disoriented and alarmed. Your baby feels the same way—and hence, wakes up and wants your arms back!

2. Falling asleep while eating. Your baby falls asleep when he is drinking (breast or bottle). When he stirs, he is in a different place and not eating anymore.

3. Falling asleep with a pacifier. Here is the comparison: You fall asleep with your head on your pillow. In the middle of the night, your spouse steals your pillow. When you wake up, you are confused and probably annoyed.[10]

4. The Trained Night Feeder. Your baby gets used to eating a snack or a meal in the middle of the night, so he continues to be hungry at that time. Equate this to working the nightshift and having your lunch break at 3 am. Yes, your body will work up an appetite if you are used to it. Stop eating at 3 am, and your body will no longer be hungry. Parents frequently continue these feedings well beyond six months of life because they don't know any better and their babies continue to demand it.

5. Inconsistent schedules. Babies are creatures of habit. Adjust your schedule as much as possible around your baby's. Don't change your baby's bedtime because you got home late from work and missed spending time with him. Pushing back your baby's bedtime for selfish reasons is always a recipe for disaster. Tomorrow is another day.

6. Missed naps. The better your baby sleeps during the day, the better he will sleep at night. Being overtired actually creates sleep disturbances. So, don't run errands when it is your baby's naptime.

7. Late to bed equals EARLY to rise. This is really true, even though you would think the opposite. As we've said, overtired babies sleep poorly.

8. Interventions at partial wakenings. Just because your baby stirs at night, does not mean he needs your help. We all stir at the end of each sleep cycle (every 90 minutes). If you go in "to help," you will wake your baby up. If these partial wakenings are waking you up, turn off the baby monitor. If your baby really needs you, you will hear him.

9. Bringing baby into bed when you don't want him there. Babies get used to routines. If you consistently bring your baby into your own bed when he cries, this is what he will expect. He will continue to cry until he gets what he wants. If the expectation is not there, the behavior won't exist. Make a plan between BOTH parents and STICK WITH IT.

10. Not letting your baby learn how to self-soothe. The ability to soothe one's self is a learned skill. This skill can be mastered by six months of age, if your baby is given the opportunity. Yes, both thumb sucking and comfort objects (see below) are acceptable. Those Old Wives are correct about "spoiling" if you coddle your *older* baby.

them to sleep. These parent behaviors with their five month olds included:

1. Putting a baby in bed *after* he was asleep.
2. Remaining in the room *until* the baby was asleep.
3. Taking the baby out of his bed to comfort him.
4. Parent feelings of inadequacy.

A significant percentage of these babies continued to have sleep problems well into their third year of life.

BOTTOM LINE: Don't just wait for your baby to outgrow his sleep issues—it may be a long time waiting. And the issues may belong to the parent and not the baby.[7]

Q. My baby started sleeping through the night at three months old. She is five months old now and waking up in the middle of the night again. Help!

Babies who are early to start sleeping through the night (less than three months old) frequently start up again when they become aware of their surroundings.

These are babies who never needed the sleep rituals before. They just fell asleep eating and were placed into bed. Now, they are alert little beings and need to learn how to fall asleep on their own.

When your former perfect baby starts having night wakenings, it will be at the end of a sleep cycle (a multiple of 90 minutes after bedtime). That's when you know the sleep routine you have created has backfired on you. Start using a sleep ritual that lets your baby fall asleep on his own.

Q. My baby uses a pacifier to fall asleep. When should we stop offering it?

By four to six months of age.

In the first two or three months of life, babies have very few ways to soothe themselves. Parents usually figure out within the first few days of bringing their baby home that a pacifier buys everyone some sleep. This approach is fine for the first few months.

BUT, do not use a pacifier beyond six months of life. Trust me. This is the time when you need to set up the routines you plan to keep. What if someone stole your pillow while your were sleeping? If the pacifier falls out in the middle of the night, your baby will be looking for it.

You don't want to have a baby who is capable of sleeping through the night waking *because* the pacifier is out. If the pacifier isn't there to begin with, he won't be looking for it. See Chapter 11, "Discipline and Temperament" for more details.

Helpful Hints

♦ Don't place dozens of pacifiers in your baby's crib so he can find one on his own.

♦ Don't go in every 90 minutes to put a pacifier back into your baby's mouth.

♦ Don't buy a glow-in-the-dark pacifier so your baby can find it at

night. I promise that your six-month-old can fall asleep without the pacifier.
- Don't get stuck treating your older baby like a newborn!

Q. My eight month old can only fall asleep nursing/taking a bottle. When will he outgrow this?

Your baby has been capable of it since four months of age. But he will continue to do it much longer if you let him. Feeding has become his crutch to fall asleep.

Again, for the first two months of life, anything goes. The optimal time to change this behavior is by four months. But if you missed the window of opportunity, it's not too late. Babies are resilient and adaptable. If he falls asleep while feeding, wake him up just enough so he knows he is getting into bed and you are leaving the room. Be prepared for some protesting the next few nights, but he will adjust soon.

It's much easier to change these behaviors now. Your child isn't going to wake up one morning and move on from this routine—you need to actively change it. (I once consulted with a family whose five YEAR old still drank milk to fall asleep every night. Don't let this be your kid!)

Q. Are comfort objects okay to use?

Yes.

Comfort objects are also called transitional objects because they help a baby transition from needing their parents 24/7.

Use a little blanket or *small* stuffed animal that can go to bed with your baby starting at six months old.

Q. My nine month old still has a middle of the night feeding. Is there something wrong with him?

He is a trained night feeder. There is nothing wrong with him. You've just allowed him to get part of his nutritional needs met during the night beyond when he needs them. Healthy, full term babies are all capable of fasting for up to 12 hours at night by six months of age. As long as your baby is growing well, read on.

Stop the night feeding and he will stop being hungry. That's easy to say, right? Offer water at 3 am and see what happens. It's likely to be rejected the first night. And yes, your child will protest. The second night, offer water again. The protesting will be less lengthy. By the third night, your baby won't bother to wake up.

Reality Check
It's likely that your nine-month old has at least one tooth. Therefore, offering milk at night without brushing his teeth afterwards may be a set up for cavities (milk has sugar in it). Be honest—you aren't getting out the toothbrush at 3 am after your child has crashed on your shoulder. The answer: STOP THE NIGHT FEEDING.

Q. What sets off disrupted sleep patterns?

Travel, teething, and illness. Any change in routine will disrupt a child's perfect sleep pattern.

Q. How do I get my baby back on track after a disrupted sleep schedule starts?

A quick refresher course in nighttime etiquette is helpful.

Your baby will have a protest rally in his crib. Yes, it really works and is unpleasant to hear. If you continue to intervene, that will become your baby's new "normal." See below for a discussion of the Ferber method.

Q. My nine month old sleeps through the night, but she likes to start her day at 5 am. Can we change that?

You can adjust it somewhat, but some kids are early risers. Here are a few tips:

First, pick a reasonable time to start the day–like 6 AM (sorry about that!). When you hear your little one making noise at 5AM, wait until 5:15 or 5:20 before going to her. The next morning, wait until 5:45. By the third morning, you can begin the day at 6 AM.

Next, try to put her down a little earlier at night. Early to bed often means late to rise-the opposite of what you might think.

Finally, try putting a few board books in her crib. She can look at them for a while until the sun comes up. Some babies will decide to play, others will go back to sleep. But let her decide what to do. Your presence signals the beginning of the day.

Helpful Hint

A baby's bedtime should fall between 7pm and 8:30pm. Just because your baby or toddler is bouncing around the living room doesn't mean it isn't time bed. Don't fall for this trick!

Q. There are so many books written about infant sleep. What do you think about them?

If you are looking for more information, there are a few books that are worth reading.

Here are our opinions of the leading sleep authors and their books. First, the table on the next page sums up the background and theory of each guru. Then below we offer a more detailed description of each.

SOLVE YOUR CHILD'S SLEEP PROBLEMS, FERBER. *Theory*: "What parents view as abnormal wakenings in the night are actually normal. What they do to treat the 'abnormal' wakenings—namely going in to help their child go back to sleep—is actually causing the disturbance."

For the first four months of life, parents need to create positive sleep associations, routines, and rituals. If your baby is not sleeping through the night (six hours of uninterrupted sleep) by five or six months of age, it is time to train or untrain (break bad habits) your baby to stop the night wakenings.

Note: Babies under four months of age are not neurologically mature enough to settle and console themselves. This method is not intended for that age group.

SLEEP

The Sleep Guru Table

Author/Book	Background	Theory	Grade
Ferber Solve Your Child's Sleep Problems	M.D.-Director of Sleep Lab, Boston Children's Hospital, Harvard	Ferber method. Intervals of intervention extinguish night wakenings.	**A+**
Weissbluth Healthy Sleep Habits, Happy Child	M.D.-Director of Sleep Disorders Program Children's Memorial Hospital, Chicago	Sleep deprivation creates a vicious cycle. Break cycle cold turkey.	**A**
Mindell Sleeping Through the Night	PhD, Director of the Sleep Disorders Center at Children's Hospital, Philadelphia	Ferber with a dash more reality—finding that "golden moment" by setting limits	**A**
Hogg Secrets of the Baby Whisperer	Nurse	E.A.S.Y. Eat, Activity, Sleep, Your Time	**B**
Sears The Baby Book	Pediatrician	Attachment parenting. Babies belong in contact with parents 24/7—asleep and awake.	**B-**
Pantley The No Cry Sleep Solution	Mother of 4	Pantley method. Comfort baby until he is almost asleep.	**C**
Ezzo/Bucknam On Becoming Babywise	A pastor and his friend, an obstetrician turned pediatrician	Parent-directed feeding. Don't let the baby dictate when it is time to eat.	**F**

Ferber Method, in a nutshell:

1. Do not let your baby fall asleep feeding, rocking, or being stroked by you.
2. Provide the identical sleep ritual (books, songs, cuddling) at nap and bedtime.
3. Have your baby sleep in the same place for naps and bedtime.
4. Avoid crutches. (i.e. pacifiers)
5. Put your baby down relaxed, but not asleep.
6. If your baby protests, make brief appearance at increasing intervals (add five minutes *each* time) to reassure your baby that you have not abandoned him. This is NOT intended to console your baby. In fact, he will yell louder. Eventually your baby falls asleep on his own.

Pros: This method works! And it works quickly—in three or four nights. Dr. Ferber is truly one of the world's experts on sleep disorders in children. His book thoroughly explains the science of sleep at a level that parents can understand. He explains his method clearly with good detail and examples.

This book also addresses the gamut of all childhood sleep disorders, not just infant sleep problems. It is an excellent reference for night terrors, bed-wetting, sleep walking, etc.

Cons: Yes, your child will cry. Yes, the first night will be ugly. The second

THE FERBER TECHNIQUE, DE-MYSTIFIED

1. Be consistent with your sleep routine at nap and at bedtime.
2. No falling asleep rocking, eating, or sucking a pacifier.
3. Comfort object/Lovie is allowed after four months of age.
4. Get your child relaxed, put him in his crib, and say goodnight.
5. Your child will start complaining.
6. Wait five minutes before returning to the nursery.
7. When you enter the nursery, make your response short and sweet (no more than 60 seconds). Tell your child you love him and say goodnight. Do NOT pick him up, rock him, or feed him. Leave the room. The purpose is for you to see that your baby is just fine and for your baby to know you have not gone to Brazil.
8. Your baby cries louder. (No surprise here.)
9. Wait ten minutes before returning.
10. Repeat step 7.
11. Your baby sounds possessed.
12. Wait 15 minutes before returning.
13. Repeat step 7.
14. Wait 20 minutes before returning...

This process lets your baby know that you haven't abandoned him, and requires *him* to do the work to fall asleep (yes, he is quite capable). The first night will be very difficult to tolerate. You may reach the "Wait 30 minutes" mark (which will be almost two hours of intervention) before your baby falls asleep. **Don't back down.** That will only convince your baby that if he cries long enough he will get what he wants. When your baby wakes up the next morning, he will be happy to see you.

The second night is much easier. The night's events will last half as long as the first night.

The third night may last only ten minutes. By the fourth night, your baby will have adjusted to his new sleep schedule.

Some final thoughts:
1. This technique only works when your baby is old enough to have the neurological maturity to settle on his own (five or six months old).
2. I always recommend doing this over a weekend. Otherwise, you will be cursing Dr. Ferber and me the next day at work.
3. You can't give in or give up once you start.
4. Buy Dr. Ferber's book. It's worth every penny.

night is less ugly. The third night is manageable. The fourth night, your baby has a smile on his face and so do you. Your baby will be fine. Parents are always guilt-ridden when they hear their baby crying. More on this later.

As in every method, there are occasional setbacks. Illness, teething, and travel create sleep disturbances. Kids need an occasional refresher course (shorter than the initial training) to remind them what they are supposed to do at night.

Grade: A+

Reality Check

Dr. Ferber's most recent book (2006) explains that there is no one-size-fits-all approach to infant sleep training. But his key point remains the same: babies thrive on consistency and routines. And, setting up good sleep habits up front prevents sleep problems down the road.

2 HEALTHY SLEEP HABITS, HAPPY CHILD, WEISSBLUTH. *Theory*: Good sleep is critical to good behavior and functioning. Overtired children have a lower frustration tolerance (short fuses), more behavior problems, and more difficulty falling asleep. Parents perpetuate their child's poor sleep habits unintentionally with their actions. These mistakes are thoroughly explained.

Weissbluth Method, in a nutshell:
1. Set an earlier bedtime to get baby down BEFORE he is overtired. This may limit the evening playtime after a working parent comes home, but makes for a happier child.
2. Naptime should be preserved at all costs.
3. Let your baby learn the process of falling asleep by letting him do it on his own.
4. If your baby is already in a vicious cycle of being overtired, end this cycle abruptly by letting him 'protest cry' until he falls asleep on his own (after four months of age). This is called Plan A, and it takes one night to accomplish.
5. Plan B is a more gradual approach offered for parents who can't handle Plan A.

Pros: This method works quickly—in one or two nights. Dr. Weissbluth provides an understandable, in-depth discussion of sleep physiology. His philosophy makes a lot of sense.

The author provides true stories that will hit home with many of the parents that read this book. There is even a chapter written by a psychiatrist that is very insightful about parenting styles and how these styles impact a child's sleep routine.

Cons: Can be one very long night of crying (both on the part of the baby and the parent). Many parents don't have the stamina to let their child cry for more than 15 minutes, even if it is in their child's best interest. (See why parents can't let their child cry later in this chapter).

The author spends 200+ pages explaining sleep and he does it beautifully. But it takes a while to get to the brief action plan.

Grade: A

3. Sleeping Through the Night, Mindell.

Theory: Ditto Ferber and Weissbluth, sprinkled with a bit more reality.

Mindell Method, in a nutshell:
"All you want is that golden moment when your child falls asleep independently. How you get there doesn't really matter."
1. Set up a sleep routine and be consistent about it.
2. Allow your child to fall asleep on his own.
3. Check on your baby as frequently or infrequently as you and your baby can tolerate.
4. Resist the temptation to resort to past sleep crutches like rocking or nursing to sleep once you've started to let your baby self soothe.

Pros: Mindell's method gives a bit more wiggle room for parents who are squeamish about the whole crying thing. But, her take home message is essentially the same. As she says, "Setting limits for your child is part of being a good parent . . . it's a tough job, so don't feel guilty when your child doesn't like what you just told him to do." Her writing style is warm and engaging.

Cons: Mindell gives the green light to prolonged pacifier use (up to age four!) and dream-feeds. Since I don't really care for either of these sleep crutches, we'll have to agree to disagree on these points.

Grade: A

4. Secrets of the Baby Whisperer, Hogg.

Theory: Parents should control bedtime.

Baby Whisperer Method, in a nutshell:
1. Identify your baby's tiredness cues.
2. Put baby to bed before he is overtired.
3. Put baby down when he is relaxed, but not asleep.
4. Give the baby a "dream-feed" before parents go to bed. (Baby is asleep and parents feed him).

Pros: Ms. Hogg has a charming way of explaining sleep behaviors and parent mistakes. Her whole plan is to teach parents how to find their baby's window of opportunity to fall asleep. The author supports the appropriate foundations for good sleep without pretending to be a sleep authority.

Cons: If you miss the "window of opportunity," you are screwed. Ms. Hogg then sticks parents with the unpleasant alternative—several hours of patting and soothing until baby is finally relaxed enough to fall asleep. I also disagree with the "dream-feed" concept.

Grade: B

5. The Baby Book, Sears.

Theory: Babies need positive sleep associations. To Dr. Sears, this means your baby should be skin to skin with you during sleep. Dr. Sears once said in a Child magazine interview (1998), "Why would a parent want to put her child in a box with bars in a dark room all by herself?"

> ### DR B'S OPINION: WHICH SLEEP METHOD IS BEST?
>
> By far, my patients' families have had the most success with Dr. Ferber's technique, known as "Ferberizing." Weissbluth's method also works—it really depends on the parents' ability to cope. Some parents prefer to go into the nursery to check on their baby (Ferber). Some parents prefer to avoid seeing the drama unfold (Weissbluth). Either way, the baby learns to self-soothe.
>
> *In my opinion,* the Ferber method is the most rational way of setting up good sleep habits. Some parents read a negative review of the book or hear how the Ferber technique failed one parent . . . and believe it can't work for them. Other exhausted parents say "I just can't let my child cry" or "I tried it and it doesn't work." Sometimes, these parents have never read the Ferber book . . . or have not followed the technique correctly. So, we'll try to de-mystify Ferber (see box on page 204).

Method: The family bed fosters attachment parenting. There is no reason to force your baby to sleep through the night or discontinue night feedings.

Pros: Many cultures use the family bed. If this is your plan, this is the guidebook. Attachment parenting, for those who desire it, is rewarding for both parents and baby.

Cons: Co-sleeping should be a choice both parents vote for. Sometimes, only one parent is in favor of the family bed (the mother). Dad agrees to the family bed because his wife is exhausted from the frequency of having to get up for breastfeeding sessions. Eventually, Dad moves out to the couch or the spare bedroom to get some sleep. There is also a safety concern with the family bed, as we discussed earlier.

There is no one-size-fits-all approach to infant sleep training. Our reservations about the Sears' sleep advice: parenting should be guilt-free.

Grade: B-

6   THE NO CRY SLEEP SOLUTION, PANTLEY. *Theory:* Babies develop associations with sleep that become a crutch (co-sleeping, feeding to fall asleep). Pantley says breaking these bad habits by letting the baby cry is insensitive and cruel. The focus is on establishing good routines and earlier bedtimes before missing the window of opportunity.

Method: Author provides 20 ideas that promote good sleep associations and routines. She tested her method on 60 families with infants.

Pros: Some families just can't listen to their baby crying. This book provides some ideas for establishing sleep rituals.

We agree with many of the author's comments on establishing sleep routines, although none of them are unique to her book. She does a nice job of addressing how to transition a co-sleeping child to his own bed.

She suggests that parents compile data on their own child and then make a personal plan for addressing their child's sleep disturbances.

Cons: Author admits that following her approach may take up to *eight weeks* to be successful. Perhaps a prescription for Prozac could be included for the parents when they buy her book. Most sleep-deprived parents are at the end of their rope at week ONE!

Ms. Pantley focuses on families who choose attachment parenting and the family bed. Her answer to reducing night feedings is to pretend to be asleep—not very realistic.

Grade: C

7 ON BECOMING BABYWISE, EZZO AND BUCKNAM.

Theory: Parents create a high need baby by having a "child-centered universe" approach to family life. The authors promote a family-centered lifestyle whereby the baby must adapt to the needs of the family. It is up to the parent to schedule feedings, wake time, and naptime.

Babywise Method, in a nutshell:
1. From birth to eight weeks of age, feed the baby every three hours during the day. At night, let the baby sleep.
2. If the baby awakens before the scheduled "first morning feeding," wait to see if he will fall back asleep without feeding.
3. If the baby must eat, readjust the feeding schedule for the day—but try not to make a habit of it.

Pros: According to the authors, 98% of their babies are sleeping through the night at eight weeks of age. (Yet the authors offer no scientific proof that their method really works.) One message we like: the importance of nurturing the family relationship.

Cons: This book is so contrary to mainstream pediatric practice that the American Academy of Pediatrics issued an alert regarding their concerns with this book. When parents followed this method to the letter, some babies became dehydrated and did not gain weight appropriately (termed failure to thrive). Setting up a routine for your four month old is healthy. Setting up a routine for your newborn is not.

Memo to the authors of the *Babywise* book: Newborns need to eat frequently (yes, sometimes even MORE than every three hours) because their body metabolism functions that way. If you doubled your weight in four months and your brain size in a year, you would eat all the time, too! Messing with Mother Nature can be dangerous.

Grade: F

Q. If the Ferber technique is so successful, why doesn't it work for every parent?

Most parents are unsuccessful because they do not follow the technique correctly or are not committed enough to endure the three-night experience. And although most babies adapt very quickly, there are a handful of kids who may not be ready for this approach.

Here is my pep talk to give you the incentive to persevere.

1. What you are doing currently is not working.
2. Nothing is medically wrong with your child.
3. Nothing will happen to your child if he cries.
4. Your child will not hate you or feel you have abandoned him. Your baby will be HAPPY to see you the next morning and you'll be happier to see him.
5. Your infant is currently in charge of your house! It's time to change that.

Now, we realize number five sounds a bit like the *Becoming Babywise* book we discussed earlier. But let's separate the subjects—the Ezzo's mantra is a rigid *feeding* schedule intended to eliminate night feedings and wakings with *newborns*. We think that's dangerous. Dr. Ferber does not suggest using his method until your child is five or six months old and is actually capable of self-soothing at night and no longer requires night feedings for nutritional needs.

Feedback from the Real World

One parent wrote of her nine-month-old twins:

"You'll be interested to know that they slept through after the second night. I guess they were as ready as I was."

Q. I know I am being a wimp, but I don't think I can listen to my baby cry.

Letting your baby cry may not be something you personally feel comfortable with. There is light at the end of the tunnel, but it may be a very long time to see it. If you are completely miserable, please read on.

Think to yourself, "There is nothing wrong with my child."

Yes, your baby is mad that he is not getting his way. You will see a lot of this behavior in the years to come (a preview of the toddler and teenage years)! Remember when you were 16 and your parents didn't let you borrow the car? Did you still love them? Your child will still love you, even when you set limits on his behaviors (including sleep).

For the long three nights ahead of you, I prescribe:

1. Planning your next vacation.
2. Renting some videos.
3. Making love with earplugs—a novel idea, I know.

FIVE REASONS PARENTS CAN'T LISTEN TO THEIR BABY CRY

1. You feel like you are helpless and not 'doing anything' for your baby (not true).
2. You are a working parent and feel guilty (don't).
3. You think you will cause your baby to have long-term emotional scars (you won't).
4. You think you are an inadequate parent if you can't get your baby to settle down (you aren't).
5. You think something must be wrong with your baby (probably not).

You get the idea. Find something else to do other than lie there in your bed listening to the drama going on in the nursery. Be strong. You can do it. Sweet dreams.

Feedback from the Real World

From Helen G. in Austin, TX: If you are really bothered by letting your baby cry without seeing what is going on, buy a video baby monitor. That way you will know if there is a serious problem (his leg is stuck between the crib slats) . . . or if he is just testing you.

So now that we've picked apart all of the sleep gurus, it's our turn to summarize our approach to sleep. Yes, it's the BABY 411 SLEEP PLAN. Drum roll please . . . we've cleverly used the acronym S.L.E.E.P. (Heck, you all are so exhausted, it would be hard to remember otherwise!)

S **Set up a sleep routine.** Babies and kids thrive on consistency. Follow the SAME routine at naps and bedtime. Make it short and sweet. Example: one book, one song, one minute of rocking, bed.

L **Less is more.** The less you intervene, the more everyone sleeps. Babies who learn to self-soothe won't need you to help them fall asleep or go back to sleep after every sleep cycle.

E **Empower the child.** Babies (by four to six months) are capable of going to sleep, and falling back asleep on their own . . . if you let them!

E **Earlier bedtime.** Babies who are overtired have more trouble falling asleep. The earlier they go to bed, the better and longer they sleep.

P **Plan together and stick to it.** Make a plan *with* your spouse that you BOTH agree to follow. And then don't cave at 3am. If you need to do a sleep "intervention," start it over a weekend so no one has any excuses.

Nap Schedules

Q. How much should my baby be napping?

Here's the timeline:

- *Birth to two months:* three to four naps per day (mostly waking up to eat and going back to sleep)
- *Two to four months:* Three naps per day
- *Four to 12 months:* Two naps per day

Babies usually cut back to one afternoon nap a day shortly after their one-year birthdays. Some will keep that nap until kindergarten. Most (like my own kids) give it up by three years old.

Q. When will my baby be on a nap schedule?

By four months, maybe earlier. Follow your baby's lead.
At two months of age, you will have more predictability in your lives.

Your goal, at this point is to start having a schedule by four months of age. You follow your baby's plan and work around it. In general, babies are awake for a couple of hours and then it's time for a nap.

Naptime can begin within 30-45 minutes of your daily goal. But try as much as you can to be consistent. Overtired babies are not exactly the life of the party. Things happen and delays sometimes are unavoidable. Just be prepared. . . you will pay for it!

Remember, from birth to two months, anything goes. If your baby falls asleep in the car, that's fine. This is a popular parent trick. But by four months, avoid it.

Put your baby down awake and follow your same sleep routine as at bedtime. View naptime as your baby's downtime. If he chooses to talk for 30 minutes instead of sleep, so be it.

By six months, you should have the nap thing down. If you don't, it's time to Ferberize. The only difference with the Ferber nap technique is that if your intervention goes on for more than an hour, that is the end of naptime. That may equate to a baby who is not actually sleeping during naptime for a period of three days.

Q. How long are naps supposed to be?

Thirty minutes to three hours.

It depends on the child. By four months of age, your baby should have two or three naps per day. One is likely to be a catnap in the morning. The afternoon nap may be a three-hour marathon.

By a year of age (12-21 months), the morning nap is lost, and your baby will take a 90-minute to three-hour afternoon siesta.

Q. My baby never naps at daycare and comes home cranky. Help!

Some babies just don't do well with group naptime. They prefer solitude.

See if your daycare center is willing to put your baby in a private area to take his naps. If this is not a possibility, you may need to rethink your childcare options.

Q. My nine month old talks and plays during his second nap of the day and rarely falls asleep. Is it time to cut that nap out?

It's reasonable for naptime to last one hour. What your baby chooses to do with it is up to her. She is having downtime (and likely, so are you). She may look at books, talk to her dolls, or complain. But she still needs that opportunity to rest or sleep. The second nap is usually dropped around 12-21 months.

Q. I have an older child that is in school. My baby's naptime falls right at the time I pick him up from school. He either misses his nap or falls asleep in the car, only to be awakened when we get home.

Naps are an important part of your baby's schedule. Enough that it is worth looking into carpool options. Perhaps you could drive in the morning and a friend could pick your child up from school. Don't sacrifice that nap if you can help it.

Q. **My baby takes a late afternoon nap and then wants to stay up all night. I don't. What should I do?**

It's wise to *end* that afternoon nap by 4 pm or 5 pm at the latest. Otherwise, your baby won't be tired enough to go to sleep at a reasonable hour. Try putting your baby down for the last nap of the day by 1pm or 2 pm. If your baby plays in his crib for an hour and then finally falls asleep, you will probably need to wake him up to stick to the game plan.

Beyond The First Year

Q. **How long will my baby sleep in his crib before graduating to a big bed?**

As long as he still likes it.

That can be as old as three years of age. We don't recommend toddler beds or convertible beds because they are a waste of money. When your child starts trying to climb out of his crib, take the mattress out and put it on the floor. Put up a safety gate in front of his doorway. That way, he'll have free reign of his room, but not the whole house.

Q. **We have a one year old and are expecting again. Should I take the older baby out of the crib when the new one arrives?**

No.

A bassinet will buy you a couple of months with the newborn. Then, see if the older child still likes his crib. If the answer is yes, borrow or buy a crib for the younger baby until the older one graduates. (see information above about purchasing a new mattress)

Otherwise, you are asking to have a toddler roaming free around your house at night.

Q. **Can we use a small travel pillow in the crib?**

After a year of age, it's okay.

Special Situations

Q. **I have twins. Is it okay to let them share a crib?**

Yes. Until they start waking each other up.

For the first two months, both babies will sleep snugly and not get in each other's way. After two months, it's probably wise to give them the space they need to move around—that means two cribs. It's fine to have them share a room.

Q. **Do you have any recommendations for how to get both babies to sleep through the night?**

The answer is the same as for single babies. Set up the right routines and rituals.

The only difference is with feeding times. See Chapter 6, "Liquid Nutrition" for how to coordinate night feedings with multiples.

Q. **I have a baby who was born prematurely. Will it take longer for him to sleep through the night?**

Yes. It may be as long as 17 weeks beyond your baby's *due date*, not his birth date.

Premature babies are neurologically immature. They also need more calories for "catch up growth." Night feedings will be necessary for a longer period of time than full term babies need.

Q. **My baby has acid reflux (GER). Will this make any difference in his ability to sleep through the night?**

Yep. Babies with reflux take longer to sleep through the night for a few reasons. For starters, their heartburn symptoms are worse at night when they are lying down. You can't really blame them for having trouble falling asleep. If your baby is taking medication to control the symptoms, be sure he hasn't outgrown his dose of medication (get the dose re-calculated by your doctor every month). You don't want your child lying there in misery.

And crying can make the acid reflux worse. So it's probably not the best idea to let your baby cry it out for an hour. It's okay for five or ten minutes, but not for the duration an otherwise healthy baby would cry. The good news: most kids outgrow reflux by six months of age. Get the green light from your doc or gastroenterologist, and then proceed with your sleep plan.

BOTTOM LINE

Some final thoughts: the National Sleep Foundation released a study in 2004 reporting that infants and young children are not getting enough sleep (and neither are their parents—but you already knew that). Infants aged 3-11 months, on average, are getting 12.7 hours a day even though they need about 14-15 hours. Tired kids are not only cranky, but they are less interested in learning new information. Make sure both you and your baby get enough sleep!

Notes

DEVELOPMENT
Chapter 10

"I have found the best way to give advice to your children is to find out what they want and then advise them to do it."

~ Harry S Truman

WHAT'S IN THIS CHAPTER

- **WHAT DOES DEVELOPMENT MEAN?**
- **HOW DO I KNOW MY BABY IS DEVELOPING NORMALLY?**
- **WHAT IS THE DENVER DEVELOPMENTAL CHECKLIST?**
- **FAILING MILESTONES AND EARLY CHILDHOOD INTERVENTION**
- **AUTISM**
- **INTELLECTUAL (COGNITIVE) DEVELOPMENT**
- **SOCIAL & EMOTIONAL DEVELOPMENT**
- **FOSTERING DEVELOPMENT**
- **KEEPING KIDS SAFE WHILE THEY EXPLORE**
- **DEVELOPMENTALLY APPROPRIATE TOYS AND BOOKS**

Okay, you've heard the conversations on the playground: "Janey was walking at only ten months." "Well, my little Henry was saying his first words at four months." You know—competition starts early. Now if you're pregnant as you read this you're probably wondering when they should start walking and talking. If you have a child already, you may be one of those quiet moms who doesn't join in the above boasting conversation. But, you may still be wondering if your baby is behind. That's what this chapter is here to tell you.

When can your child roll over, when should he, and when is he developmentally delayed? And what is important to worry about and bring up to your doctor during well check visits? This chapter provides the key to understanding how your child's brain works. Knowing what to expect will help you know how to respond to your child's needs as he is growing. This is required reading before you get to the next chapter, "Discipline and Temperament." We'll refer back to this stuff, so don't jump ahead.

Your first lesson: DO NOT COMPARE YOUR BABY TO OTHER CHILDREN. We know, you just can't help it. You watch other kids in playgroups, at the park, and in your own family and then look at your baby. Don't do it. Every child reaches her developmental milestones at her own pace. Yes, there is a certain timeline to reach these milestones, but there is a broad range of "normal."

DEVELOPMENT

Q. What does development mean?

The way a child evolves in muscle skills (large and small muscles), language skills, social and personality skills, and intelligence. This is different from the term "growth" which refers to physical body changes. We'll define some key terms on this topic next.

1. Gross Motor Development. This refers to using large muscle groups to function (i.e. arms, legs, torso). *Milestones:* rolling, sitting, crawling, climbing, walking, running, throwing, and kicking a ball. *FYI: Gross motor development is mastered in a "Head, shoulders, knees, and toes" direction. Remember these milestones by the numbers 3-6-9-12:*

- Three-month-olds have achieved *head* control. (no more head bobs)
- Six-month-olds have *shoulder* and trunk support. (rolling over, sitting up)
- Nine-month-olds have *knee* control and can stand up holding on, and walk with support.
- 12-month-olds have control of their feet and *toes*, standing alone and taking steps.

2. Fine Motor Development. This skill involves using small muscle groups to function (i.e. fingers). *Milestones:* batting with hands, grabbing, picking up objects, feeding oneself, holding food utensils, holding writing utensils, coloring, and writing.

3. Oral Motor Development. The ability to use mouth and tongue muscles. *Milestones:* swallowing, chewing, and talking. Newborns only have the ability to suck, swallow, and cry.

4. Language Development. This refers to the ability to communicate with others. The pre-requisites for language development are oral motor development and the ability to hear and process language (see receptive language skills below). *Milestones:* cooing, babbling, stringing sounds together, imitating noises, and using words purposefully. There are two sub areas of language development:

- *Receptive language skills.* The "input" that babies get in the form of words is understood long before they start talking. Babies can follow directions (if they are in the mood) before they say any words.
- *Expressive language skills.* This is language "output." When people refer to a child having language delays, it is usually an expressive language delay (i.e. they aren't talking yet). If there is a concern for an expressive language delay, your doctor should always check to be sure there is not a receptive language delay, too (a hearing problem, or an **AUDITORY PROCESSING DISORDER**).

5. Social-Emotional Development. This is how a child adapts to his world. *Milestones:* smiles responsively, knows parents, asks to be held, laughs, imitates, plays peek-a-boo, anxiety towards strangers, anxiety from being separated from loved ones, seeks independence.

Social skills are a learned process. And, parents are the most important role models for a child. Children interact in social situations quite differently at different ages.

6. Cognitive (Intellectual Development). This refers to how a child figures out his world. Babies are like a big sponge. They absorb vast quantities of information on a daily basis and learn how to decipher it all. And you thought your learning curve was steep with this new parent experience. Imagine what your baby's brain is going through!

Milestones: follows people and objects in field of vision, expresses needs, explores toys, prefers routines, knows how to get people's attention, understands cause-and-effect (that is, banging this toy makes noise), object permanence (things still exist even if not in view), remembers frequent visitors, limited problem solving skills.

Q. How do I know that my baby is developing normally?

You come to visit the pediatrician or family doctor for well baby checks.

Many parents think that well baby checks are "just for shots." They're not. At every well baby check, your doctor will ask a series of questions to be sure your baby is developing all five types of skills at an appropriate pace. Don't expect these questions to be asked at sick visits because these are "problem-focused" appointments.

If a delay in any of the developmental areas is detected, it may be followed for a period of time to see if your baby "catches up" or a referral may be made to a specialist in that particular field.

This is an extremely important part of both the parent and doctor's job description. If you have concerns about your child's development, don't be shy about it. There is never a downside to getting your concerns checked out.

Early intervention makes the greatest impact in lifelong outcomes. For more on this, see the section "Learn the Signs. Act Early."

Q. I've heard the term "developmental milestones." What does it mean?

These are individual skills that your baby progressively masters as he matures.

The series of questions your pediatrician asks are based on expected milestones at specific ages. Some babies will show off and demonstrate their new tricks in the office. In most cases, however, doctors rely on your descriptions for the rest. Remember, there is a range of time for when milestones are achieved.

Q. Can I have a milestone checklist so I can follow along?

Yes. The Denver Developmental Checklist is considered the gold standard to assess milestones. We have included the test items in a box on the next page.

Remember, no obsessing over this list. Do not tape it to your baby's crib and check off his accomplishments. This is by no means a perfect test, but it is a helpful guide for doctors to screen for developmental delays.

There is a very low criterion to "pass" a test so that children with normal skills are not falsely considered delayed. In light of this, if a child does "fail" a test on the Denver Checklist, it is quite likely he has a developmental delay in a certain area. In such a case, the doctor will investigate this further either in her office or via referral to a developmental specialist.

Q. What is the significance if my child fails in his milestones?

BOOKMARK THIS PAGE! THE BABY 411 ALL-IN-ONE

Developmental checklists are designed to identify developmental delays in infants and young children. In general, the areas are divided into the following categories:

- Gross motor skills (large muscle groups)
- Fine motor skills (small muscle groups)
- Language including all forms of communication (indicating wants, facial expressions, understanding language, and vocalization)
- Personality/intellectual development

Because children accomplish these milestones at a range of ages, mastery of a particular milestone will vary over a period of time (i.e. walking may be mastered between 9-15 months of age). The cutoff for 'normal' is at the level where over 90% of children have achieved a milestone at a particular age.

For babies born prematurely (if your child was born before 36 weeks gestation and your child is under 2 years old): Subtract the number of months missed in pregnancy from the baby's current age and check at the adjusted age.

Gross Motor:	Age achieved:
Lifts head	0 to 2 months
Holds head steady	1.5 to 4 months
Pushes chest up while lying on stomach	2 to 4 months
Rolls over	2 to 4.5 months*
No head lag when pulled to sitting position	3.5 to 6 months
Bears weight on legs when held in standing position	3 to 7.5 months
Sits alone	5 to 8 months
Stands holding on to something	5 to 10 months
Pulls self up to standing position	6 to 10 months
Gets to sitting position independently	6 to 11 months
Walks holding on to furniture ("cruises")	7.5 to 12.5 months
Stands alone briefly	9 to 13 months
Stands alone	9.5 to 14 months
Walks alone	11 to 14.5 months

*Note: Rolling over is a less reliable milestone now that babies spend most of their time on their backs with the anti-SIDs campaign.

*Note: Crawling is not listed on the developmental checklist because many children skip crawling and are developmentally normal.

Development

Maybe something, maybe nothing.

This is a non-committal answer, but it is the truth. Some children will have an isolated delay in one particular developmental area (that is, just motor skills, just expressive language skills, etc.). With a little help and encouragement, these kids catch up to their peers and you might never notice a problem later on. For others, it may always be an issue. For

Development Checklist

Fine Motor:	Age achieved:
Brings hands together	1.5 to 3.5 months
Grasps objects	2.5 to 4.5 months
Reaches for objects	3 to 5 months
Transfers objects hand to hand	4.5 to 7.5 months
Grabs objects with whole hand ("rakes")	5 to 8 months
Able to feed self a cracker	4.5 to 8 months
Grabs object between thumb and finger ("crude pincer grasp")	7 to 10.5 months
Bangs objects together	7 to 12 months
Mastery of pincer grasp ("fine pincer")	9 to 14 months
Drinks from a cup	10 to 16.5 months

Language/Communication:	Age achieved:
Eyes focus on objects in front of them	0 to 1.5 months*
Eyes follow objects to the sides	0 to 2.5 months*
Baby regards person's face	0 to 1 month*
Baby smiles in response to person smiling at them ("social smile")	0 to 2 months*
Responds to loud noise	0 to 1.5 months
Makes happy noises	0 to 2 months
Laughs	1.5 to 3.5 months
Makes squealing noises	1.5 to 4.5 months
Baby smiles without prompting	1.5 to 5 months
Turns to someone's voice	3.5 to 8.5 months
Says "dada" or "mama" but doesn't mean it	6 to 10 months
Imitates speech noises (baby talk/jabber)	6 to 11.5 months
Says Dada or Mama and means it	9.5 to 13.5 months
Indicates wants non-verbally ("point & grunt")	10.5 to 14.5 months
Says 3 or more words besides Mama/Dada	11.5 to 20.5 months

*Note: A newborn's vision is 20/200. They can only see about 8 to 12 inches in front of their faces. So, to test these items, you need to be very close to your baby's face.

Personality/Intellectual development	Age achieved:
Plays peek a boo	6 to 9.5 months
Looks for hidden object	5 to 8 months
Initial shyness with strangers ("stranger anxiety")	5.5 to 10 months
Plays pat a cake	7 to 13 months
Plays ball with someone	9.5 to 16 months

Development

WHERE TO GET HELP

♦ *Head Start and Early Head Start programs:* www.ehsnrc.org
♦ *Parent training:* www.patnc.org
♦ *Early Intervention for children birth to three years:* www.nectas.unc.edu

instance, a child with gross motor delays may grow up to be a non-athletic kid. A child with expressive language delays may turn out to have a learning disability. Both of these children might also be a varsity football player or the valedictorian. It just might take a little more work for that kid to succeed in those areas.

The children we are most concerned about are those with delays across the board, termed "global developmental delays." These children are more at risk to never catch up to their peers. When children continue to have global delays by the age of three years old, they are ultimately diagnosed with mental retardation. There is a range from mild to severely affected children. Doctors evaluate these children for genetic and metabolic (the way the body breaks down certain chemicals) defects when they are diagnosed.

Autism

Q. I've heard a lot about autism in the news. What is it, and when do I worry?

AUTISM SPECTRUM DISORDER (ASD) is the umbrella name for several disorders that range from mildly to severely affected social skills, communication skills, and repetitive or obsessive traits. These disorders include **PERVASIVE DEVELOPMENTAL DISORDER (PDD), ASPERGER'S SYNDROME**, childhood disintegrative disorder, and Rett's Syndrome.

There is a very broad range of severity within ASD. A child may have normal intelligence and language, but be socially awkward and have panic attacks if his sandwich is cut in triangles instead of squares. Or a child may appear out of touch with reality and spend his entire day rocking and flapping his hands. Both children may carry a diagnosis of ASD.

Children are usually diagnosed by 18-24 months of age when language delays are obvious.

However, clues to the diagnosis appear long before that time. Some early clues include: not smiling back at people, poor eye contact, not imitating, not gesturing (waving bye-bye), not responding to being called by name, and not trying to communicate/connect/engage with other people by one year of age.

There are also some unusual behaviors. Cuddling may not be soothing. In fact, an autistic child may get very upset by being touched. Bright lights and noises often bother them. Because of their repulsion of sensory stimuli, they may turn inwards and perform repetitive self-soothing behaviors (rocking, head banging, spinning). Autistic children may have little interest in playing with toys. Or they may play in an odd way—such as using a phone as a comfort object.

DEVELOPMENT

> **LEARN THE SIGNS, ACT EARLY.**
>
> The Centers for Disease Control recently launched a campaign called "Learn the Signs. Act Early." It empowers parents with information on what is normal child development and what isn't. The key point: early diagnosis and intensive therapy leads to the best developmental outcome for the child. Kids who get help before age three (and earlier is even better) have the best chance of overcoming developmental challenges. You can access their info at www.cdc.gov/actearly or at 1-800-CDC-INFO.

Be aware that there is a broad spectrum of developmental abnormalities that all get grouped into Autism Spectrum Disorder. Some children have very subtle symptoms, and some have very severe problems.

BOTTOM LINE: Children with autism have autism long before their first birthdays, even though their "official" diagnosis usually occurs in their second year of life. Remember this fact when we discuss the measles (MMR) vaccine controversy. (see Chapter 12, "Vaccines" for details).

Q. My baby bangs his head frequently. Does he have autism?

No.

Many babies have behaviors that they perform repeatedly. The repetition is soothing for them. It becomes a red flag (see below) when the behavior goes on all day long and replaces meaningful play. And with autism, there are other also other atypical behaviors (lack of social skills, poor language, etc.). By the way, babies have the same self-preservation instincts that we do, so they really won't hurt themselves by head banging.

RED FLAGS for Autism

Although autism is usually diagnosed by age two or three, clues are apparent much earlier. Here are some things to be watching for by a child's first birthday.

- Lack of eye contact. Babies should make eye contact (and smile back at you) by two months of age.
- Failure to respond to name by first birthday.
- Constant repetitive behaviors (hand flapping, etc).
- Preference for unusual comfort objects (that is, not a doll or blanket).
- Lack of symbolic play or imitation—pretending to talk on the phone or use the TV remote.
- No babbling by first birthday.
- No gesturing by first birthday.
- Lack of social skills. Babies should try to engage and get someone's attention.

Insider Tip: Testing

All children who are being evaluated for autism should have chromosome testing done (karyotyping). There is a chromosomal abnormality called Fragile X Syndrome that can manifest itself with symptoms similar to autism.

Q. Is there a test for autism?

There's currently no blood test or imaging study that detects autism. An autism diagnosis is based on the symptoms that a child displays (and lack of findings/results that would suggest a different diagnosis). Your pediatrician can do an assessment in her office. If autism is suspected, then consider a consultation with a developmental pediatrician or multidisciplinary assessment program. Ask your doc for a referral.

Q. I have a friend whose child is autistic. She said he was a normal child until he was about 18 months old. Does this happen?

For starters, do some children have normal developmental milestones and suddenly lose them? Yes. Is their diagnosis autism? Probably not. There are a small number of metabolic and genetic disorders that manifest themselves this way. If a previously normal 18 month old walked into my office with loss of milestones, I would be on the phone with my local metabolic specialist pronto. Before you panic, these disorders are very rare.

Some parents report that their autistic child spoke a few words and then "lost" the ability to say them. If you delve a bit deeper, the children may have randomly said a few things, but were not consistently using words like *juice* or *daddy*.

There is growing research in language development that looks at brain anatomy. Primitive brain parts control early language development from birth to 18 months. At 18 to 24 months, the mature brain parts turn on and language takes off. With autistic children, the language does not take off. But, from a parent's perspective, it may look like a loss of skills.

And again, children with subtle atypical behaviors may be harder to diagnose early on. Reviewing home movies of a child once the diagnosis is made often shows that early signs are overlooked.[1]

Q. I have heard that the MMR vaccine causes "regressive" autism. Is this true?

What you need to know: there does *not* appear to be a new or distinct form of autism where children lose their developmental milestones after being vaccinated with the Measles-Mumps-Rubella combination vaccine. Yes, parents of autistic children may report a loss or "regression" of milestones (see question above). But the frequency that parents report this has not changed in decades and is not directly correlated to the timing of vaccination.[2]

(We have included information on this topic in the vaccine chapter as well, so feel free to pop over to Chapter 12 for further insights.)

Q. Okay, so what causes autism?

The million-dollar question.

In the 1980's, one in 10,000 kids were diagnosed with autism. Today, one in 150 American eight-year-olds have some form of autism. Boys outnumber girls four to one. The U.S. is not the only country seeing this trend. Denmark also reports a disconcerting rise in the past decade. And curiously, 13 states in the U.S. have seen sharper rises in autism rates than others.

Part of the increase in autism may be the fact that we are getting better at diagnosing it. Prior to new diagnostic criteria for autism in 1987, autistic kids were previously diagnosed as having developmental delays or mental retardation. In 1991, laws for special education services changed to improve services for these kids—it actually benefits children to be labeled autistic.[3] Also remember that "Autism Spectrum Disorder" is really a hodgepodge definition of several disorders that have some similarities. But in the worlds of school special education or insurance-billing, any child along the spectrum gets the same label or code.

Another possible reason for the increase of autism: the trend of parents having babies at a later age. Moms who conceive after the age of 40 have a 30% increased risk of having a child with autism. Dads who conceive after the age of 40 have a 50% increased risk of having an autistic child.[4]

Genetics also plays a role. Studying twins is an obvious way to detect genetic disorders. If one identical twin has autism, 60-90% of the time, so will the other twin. To date, the exact "autism" gene has not been identified, but it may reside on the X chromosome, which might explain the prevalence in boys.[5]

A scientific effort to find the specific genes that cause autism (the Autism Genome Project) recently reported some interesting new data: kids with autism have defects on Chromosome 11 and dysfunctional neurexin 1 protein. Of course, the big question mark is how these detected abnormalities affect fetal and infant brain growth. This is a hotbed of research—genes that control how nerves grow.

Although autism's cause is unknown, we do know autistic children have problems with brain growth. Babies are born with immature brains that grow rapidly and make nerve connections called synapses . . . like an information superhighway. In the normally growing brain, some branches of this superhighway get "pruned." In the autistic brain, this pruning process seems to be defective. This may explain why babies who are autistic have abnormally rapid head growth under one year of age.

Is there some environmental exposure that sets off abnormal brain development in a genetically predisposed baby? Maybe. Researchers and scientists have taken a long, hard look at vaccines—and there is conclusive evidence that vaccine exposure is NOT the turn-on switch for autism.[6]

Follow our website at Baby411.com for new information on this topic.

Q. My child may be autistic. What therapy do you recommend?

The first place to start with is your child's medical provider. He/she can help with both diagnosis and referrals locally in your community. National resources to help you get started include:

The Centers for Disease Control: www.cdc.gov/actearly
American Academy of Pediatrics: www.aap.org
Autism Society of America: www.autism-society.org

Early, intensive therapy with developmental specialists is key. Please beware of unproven (and possibly dangerous) therapies that promise a cure for autism. We realize that parents will do anything to help their kids. But we also know that leaves them prey for unscrupulous folks selling snake oil.

Q. If my child has a developmental delay, where can I get help?

Want to use a service that makes house calls?

There is a government program called Early Childhood Intervention (and, like many other government programs, it has seen cutbacks). Every town has an agency. Look yours up in the phonebook. Your child's development will be screened over the phone. If he qualifies as having a delay, a specially trained physical therapist (large muscles), occupational therapist (small muscles), or speech therapist (language, mouth skills) will show up at your doorstep and do a formal assessment. If help is needed, a regular therapy schedule will be set up.

The other option is to get a referral from your pediatrician to a private specialist in your area. Easter Seals also has a national program that provides services based on ability to pay. You can contact them at www.easter-seals.org or at (800)-221-6827.

Denise's opinion: We've all been at the park and noticed a child who seems to be "hyper" or "slow" or "aggressive" or non-communicative. But no matter how tempting it is, keep your opinions to yourself. Besides, behavior problems on the playground probably have more to do with kids who are tired or hungry than with some kind of serious brain dysfunction.

As the parent of a learning disabled child, I can tell you that no outsider would have known he was anything but normal until he got closer to school age. And kids who *seem* to have delays and problems often sort them out and have no issues by the time they reach kindergarten.

But if you notice your child doesn't seem to be keeping up with other kids his age physically or socially, be sure to bring it up to your doctor at the next well visit. If you don't say anything, your doctor may not notice subtle signs in a ten or 15-minute visit.

Feedback from the Real World
Special babies, Extraordinary Parents: Meredith's Story

"When we first learned of Meredith's diagnosis (developmental delays) our first worry was that there would be nobody to take care of her in the future when we were gone. We now realize that dwelling on that is giving up any hope for the present. When Meredith was finally able to throw a ball, we celebrated all the years in therapy that got her to that moment. When she was able to catch the ball, we marveled that it happened the very next day."—Sarah Barnes and Jim Hemphill, parents of Meredith Hemphill, age 6 (diagnosis: agenesis of the corpus callosum).

DEVELOPMENT

Q. My baby was born prematurely. Does the same developmental checklist apply to him?

Yes, but not at first.

Babies born more than five weeks early have some catching up to do from both a growth and development standpoint. Your baby's chronological age will be adjusted by subtracting the number of weeks born prematurely. So, the expectations will be lower initially. Babies will catch up with their peers developmentally by one year of age.

Now that we've talked about general developmental milestones and delays, we want to explain a bit about intellectual development and social/emotional development. We'll explore theories from two prominent doctors with their thoughts on the stages your child will go through throughout his life.

How Your Baby Learns

Ever wonder how your baby learns all the amazing things she does? How does she go from being a little lump at birth to a smiling, talking, walking dreamboat by her first birthday? Dr. Jean Piaget, the father of the major accepted theory for cognitive (intellectual) development, believes that a child's brain processes and understands information in different ways at different ages. As a parent, it's helpful to know what "stage" of brain development your child is at, because *your child's reasoning will be different than yours*. And if you are educated about those differences, hopefully, you'll be less perplexed and frustrated by them.

So here is the big picture, stage by stage:

Sensory-Motor: Age birth to two years

Babies learn by hearing, feeling, tasting, smelling, moving, and manipulating (that is, using their Five Senses). Babies are **EGOCENTRIC**. In their minds, the world revolves around them. They continue to think this way until about age six or seven years old (although you might think that some adults haven't outgrown this stage yet!).

◆ *Birth to one month:* A newborn comes equipped with immature reflexes (sucking, rooting, grasping). He will learn how to use and coordinate them. Newborns have no concept of "self."

◆ *One to four months:* Babies realize that they have body parts, and can control them. If you see your baby staring at his hand, it's because he has discovered it.

◆ *Four to eight months:* Babies are more interested in the world. They realize their actions can make other people do things. They start to manipulate objects and explore with their mouths. But, people and things don't exist unless they are within a baby's visual field. They do well with routines and predictable events with their limited memory banks.

DEVELOPMENT

◆ *Eight to 12 months:* Babies grasp the concept of *object permanence*. A baby realizes that a person still exists even when he leaves a room. The same goes for toys, food, etc. A baby this age has a limited repertoire of techniques to explore a new situation. He uses his *memory* of what worked in the past to approach something unfamiliar.

◆ *12 to 18 months:* Toddlers have more sophisticated approaches to problem solving (although it won't feel that way to their parents). They experiment systematically. Toddlers go through a trial and error method of attack. Things are explored more with hands than with mouths. They CAN follow directions. (It's a matter of whether or not they CHOOSE to).

◆ *18 to 24 months:* As these kids approach two years of age, they can do "trial and error" in their minds, and figure out the solution to a problem (i.e. simple puzzles). They will figure out language, and start to pretend.

Pre-Operational: Age two to seven years

Kids have the concept of symbols representing things (i.e. language, pretend play). Their level of reasoning is based on *their* viewpoint. They are not capable of taking someone else's perspective. They have primitive logical thinking. For example, a full juice cup will look like it has more in it than a half-full water glass.

Concrete Operational: Age seven to eleven years

Kids this age can think logically, order and classify items, compare, and sequence information. But, everything is black and white—there is no *gray* zone.

Formal Operational: Age 12 to Adulthood

This is the age of abstract reasoning— when a child can "think outside of the box." A teenager can take a hypothetical situation and reason it out.[7]

Your Baby's Social and Emotional Growth

As one of the most influential psychologists of the 20th century, Erik Erikson continues to influence our view of social and emotional development today. His theory suggests that personality development rests on how a person deals with a series of stages in his life. A person's sense of identity depends on the outcome of eight crises or conflicts. If a person does not successfully resolve a particular conflict, the unresolved issue persists in later life.

People can also regress to prior stages during times of stress (that is, a four-year-old returns to the Terrible Two's when a baby sister is born).

Again, the big picture....

Trust vs. Mistrust: Birth to 18 months

Infants learn to trust their parents. They learn that their needs are met. Babies who do not get appropriate care have a sense of distrust and apprehension around others.

Autonomy vs. Doubt: 18 months to three years

Children are seeking independence and are trying to gain confidence in their abilities. This happens while parents are trying to set limits on inappropriate behaviors. (This meeting of the minds is also known as the Terrible Two's). Children need a certain autonomy to rely on their own skill, or else they will begin to doubt themselves.

Initiative vs. Guilt: Three to six years

Children thrive on decision-making and accomplishments. If parents do not support these experiences, the child feels guilty for trying to be independent.

Industry vs. Inferiority: Six to 12 years

Children gain confidence in their skills and want to learn. With failure or lack of support, children feel inferior to others.

Identity vs. Role Confusion: 12 to 18 years

Simply put, teens either figure out who they are and what they want (sense of self) or they are confused and reliant on their peers.[8]

Now you know the theories behind how babies develop. So you're probably wondering how to put them to work. This is the section for you. Here we're going to discuss how to foster appropriate development for each age and stage. Keep in mind the idea is not to "train" your child to be the next Beethoven, Mary Cassat or Bill Gates.

Birth to Two Months of Age

Q. So what is a general idea of how my baby will develop in the first two months?

Here is a thumbnail sketch.

You may think that your newborn spends his whole life eating and sleeping, but he is actually learning a great deal. Babies are born with an immature nervous system (brain, spinal cord, nerves). So, most of what you see develop is not dramatic in the first two months of life. Instead, development is happening with a baby's neurological system. *Milestones:*

- ◆ **Newborn reflexes.** Babies suck and turn their head instinctively when you rub their cheeks. They will also grasp anything placed in the hands. If you gently drop their heads back, they will flail their arms out and open their eyes. These reflexes should go away by six months of age.

- ◆ **Motor skills.** Babies are born with poor head and neck stability. Over the first two months of life, they gain better head control. They should move both arms and legs equally well. A dominant side or hand preference is NOT normal.

- **Vision.** Newborns have 20/200 vision. They are not blind. But, they can only see clearly about eight to ten inches in front of them. Putting your face right up to theirs is very entertaining for them. Babies like contrasts (hence, all of the black and white toys at trendy baby stores). By the time your baby is two months old, he will be able to see one to two feet in front of him. He should also be able to fix his eyes on an object and follow it side to side.

- **Hearing.** Newborns are born with normal hearing. They startle to loud noises. Babies recognize their parents' voices. They have heard you inside the womb.

- **Social.** Newborns are interested in your face. By two months of age, if you smile at your baby, he will smile back (called a social smile). Under six weeks of age, any smiling is a mere coincidence, or gas.

- **Language.** Initially, babies cry to express all of their needs. As they approach two months, babies will start to "coo" (ooo and ah noises). They may even start to laugh and squeal.

Q. What kind of developmental stimulation should I provide my birth to two month old?

Give them lots of time with you. Here is a breakdown:

1. Sensory-motor:
- Give your baby interesting things to follow with her eyes (your face, colorful toy).
- Listen to music; play with rattles, music boxes.
- Let your baby touch different objects (your face, your hair, the dog).
- Give your baby short (five minutes) bursts of time on her tummy (a.k.a. Tummy Time) to work on shoulder and stomach muscles. Not only does it strengthen neck and shoulder muscles, it also prevents the flat head issues we discussed earlier in the book (**POSITIONAL PLAGIOCEPHALY**).

2. Language:
- Start a *reading ritual*. Set aside reading time EVERY day until your child packs up and goes to college. There is a great deal of research that proves infants who are read to at early ages have stronger language and cognitive skills than their peers.
- Infants respond best to rhymes and good illustrations. See the end of this chapter for a list of good books for kids age birth to one-year-old.

3. Social:
- Spend time talking and smiling at your baby.

Q. My newborn does not have good head control yet. Is it okay to use an infant baby carrier (Snugli/Baby Bjorn)?

Yes. Holding your baby in your arms 24/7 gets old quickly. These carriers provide enough head support and allow you to use two hands to get something done.

Q. My two month old's eyes cross frequently. Should I worry?

No. A baby's eye muscles are weak initially and frequently are not in sync with each other.

Doctors start testing for lazy eye muscles (see **AMBLYOPIA**) from six to nine months of age. If you notice that one eye turns in, turns out, or only one eye has a "red eye" effect in photographs, let your doctor know. Note: a two month old can follow your face as you move it in front of him. A three month old can follow it for a full 180 degrees.

Old Wives Tale
Letting an infant bear weight on his legs will make him bowlegged.

The truth: Babies like to bear weight on their feet with your support. It's fun—and it won't make them bowlegged.

Two to Four Months of Age

Q. What milestones should I expect my two to four month old to achieve?

- *Gross Motor.* Your baby should have good head control by three months of age. If you lift his body from a lying position, his head should come up at the same time and not lag behind. He may or may not roll over. By four months old, he should bear weight on his legs if you stand him up. Most babies can lift their heads up when lying on their stomachs.

- *Fine Motor.* Your baby will start to realize that his hands are useful. At first he will bat at objects, then start to grab successfully around four months. (This is when moms usually stop wearing

NEW PARENT 411: READING PROGRAMS

Reach Out and Read (reachoutandread.org) is a national program that encourages 15-20 minutes a day of reading to young children. In participating doctors' offices, books are given free of charge at well child visits from infancy to five years of age. This allows parents to build a developmentally-appropriate reading library in their homes.

You can also seek out local libraries and national bookstore chains that offer free story times for both infants and toddlers.

The benefits of reading to children at an early age are clear. Set aside special time everyday for reading with your little one!

hoop earrings and pull their hair back). Your baby should also be able to bring his hands together.

- *Language.* Babies are really experimenting with their voices at this age. They will move on from cooing to laughing and squealing. They may start to "blow raspberries" (spray saliva). This is particularly fun at mealtime. They also experiment with the volume of their voice.

- *Vision.* Your baby's vision improves to about 20/40 by four months of age. So he will be able to see you across the room.

- *Social/Personality.* Your baby will try to imitate social contact with you. Smiling, tickling, and laughing are very entertaining for your baby.

Q. What developmental stimulation can I provide for my two to four month old?

- *Motor.* Give your baby more tummy time (five to ten minutes) several times a day. He will let you know when it's time to turn over. Activity gyms are fun because they can start to bat and grab at the objects.

- *Language/Social.* Keep that reading ritual going. When you are out and about, talk to your baby. He is your companion, so treat him like one. Tell him where you are going and what you are doing. You may feel silly telling him what you are putting in your grocery cart, but all those vocabulary words will be recorded in his growing brain.

Reality Check
A recent study looked at three-month-old babies' brain activity in response to hearing simple phrases. Guess what? Their little brains lit up when they heard phrases they had heard before! While you may not hear your baby talk back to you for a while, there is a lot going on in there. This study validates the importance of talking to your baby early in life.[9]

Four to Six Months of Age

Q. What developmental milestones will I see with my four to six month old?

- *Gross Motor.* Your baby will sit up with your assistance, then "tripod sit" with his hands supporting him between his legs. Eventually, he will sit up without support.

- *Fine Motor.* Your baby has mastered grabbing. He will start to use his fingers more than just his hands. He will "rake" objects to get them into the palm of his hand by six months. He will also start to transfer objects from one hand to the other by six months old.

DEVELOPMENT

> ### ⚠ RED FLAG: AVOID WALKERS
>
> The American Academy of Pediatrics strongly discourages the use of walkers. Canada went so far as to ban walkers in 2004. Why? Babies drive these things without taking a driver's ed course. Walkers allow babies to get places that their knees or feet would never take them. This sometimes means falling down a flight of stairs.
>
> New walkers now have some safety devices built in meant to keep them from falling down stairs. Because of the new safety requirements, there has been a marked decline in the number of injuries caused by walkers. However, the Consumer Product Safety Commission reports that there were still 3700 injuries from walkers that required a hospital visit in 2003 (the latest year stats are available as of this writing).
>
> Pediatricians see numerous head injuries every year as a result of walkers. Even if a child doesn't fall down the stairs, she can still run into low tables and chairs and knock items off tables (like hot drinks and glass vases, for example). And older, used walkers without the new safety devices are definitely death traps.

- ◆ *Oral Motor.* Your baby will figure out how to maneuver his tongue to swallow solid food by six months of age (see Chapter 7, "Solids"). This is one reason why it is not recommended to offer solid food before this age.

- ◆ *Language.* Your baby will start making the first recognizable sounds of language. Consonant sounds usually progress from B's to D's to M's. This means, you'll first hear "ba-ba" then "da-da" then "ma-ma". The "Ba-Ba" occurs around six months of age. Your baby should also turn to you when you are talking to him by six months.

- ◆ *Social/Cognitive.* Your baby is very aware of his surroundings. He knows his family and friends. He knows his room and his crib. Four month olds already thrive on the routine and the expected. But even at six months of age, your baby will not have the concept of "object permanence." So, if you leave the room or a toy leaves his sight, it no longer exists.

Q. My six-month-old is sitting up but he never rolled over. Should I be worried?

No. Welcome to the anti-SIDS generation.

It is easier to roll from tummy to back, than from back to tummy. Babies of our generation spend significantly less time on their tummies because of the "Back to Sleep" campaign to prevent Sudden Infant Death Syndrome. As a result, babies these days often master rolling over about the same time as sitting up (or skip rolling over entirely). Rolling over used to be a four-month milestone. Sitting up is a six-month milestone.

Q. What can I do to foster my four to six month old's development?

- *Gross Motor.* Because babies of this age group aren't quite sitting alone yet, the stationary Exersaucer toys are great. They give babies a sense of independence, and free up their hands to play. However, we don't recommend using them for more than ten or 15 minutes at a time. Some studies have shown that babies who can't see their feet and legs because of the trays on these toys can have delays in walking. Also, be sure to give babies lots of floor time to work on rolling and balancing.

- *Fine Motor.* Give your baby large plastic or plush toys to grab, manipulate, and mouth. Yes, mouth is used as a verb here. Everything your baby examines will go into his mouth to test out. Toys that make noise are fun. The plush caterpillars that have different sounding objects in each segment are popular.

- *Language.* You know the drill by now. Read to your child on a daily basis. Use board books and those designed for tub time (that is, they're waterproof)—these give your child a tactile experience as well. But, for safety reasons, no chewing on vinyl books.

- *Social/Personality.* Babies are keenly aware of facial expressions. Get a cheap plastic mirror for hours of fun—your baby will sit there and stare at himself.

Six to Nine Months of Age

Q. What are your expectations for a six to nine month old?

- *Gross Motor.* The main milestone over these three months is locomotion. Your baby will figure out how to get where he wants to go. That may be achieved by rolling, crawling, or "cruising" (walking while holding onto furniture). Some babies skip crawling. Because of this, if you look at the Denver Developmental Checklist, you'll notice that crawling isn't listed. Meanwhile, your baby should also be able to get from lying down to sitting, and from sitting to standing up (holding on to something).

- *Fine Motor.* Your baby will refine his reaching and grabbing skills. The crude "raking" will change to a "pincer grasp" (picking things up between index finger and thumb). Things like lint and dirt on the floor will suddenly become very interesting. This correlates with the ability to self-feed (see finger foods in Chapter 7, "Solids").

- *Oral Motor.* Your baby should be able to maneuver his tongue and chew food with teeth (or gums).

- *Language.* Your baby should be progressing into the D's and M's. We expect a nine month old to say "Dada" and "Mama", but don't expect them to know the meaning of those words until about 14 months. Everything you are saying is recorded in your little one's big brain. His receptive language is quite good (that is, he understands what you are saying). *Your nine month old understands the word, "No." Whether he chooses to respond to it is another story.*

♦ *Cognitive/Social*. Ah, the light has turned on. Somewhere between six and nine months, your baby will have achieved *"object permanence."* This is a MAJOR concept. He realizes that people and things still exist, even if he can't see them anymore. So, if you leave the room, he will look for you. This, understandably, creates some anxiety (see "separation anxiety" in the next chapter).

♦ *More social issues.* Another concept that arises is *stranger anxiety*. Not only will your baby want to know your every move, but he won't want to hang out with anyone but you. Don't get too frustrated. When your baby is so independent that he wants nothing to do with you, you will look back fondly at these days. Your baby also is picking up social cues. He will smile to engage others. He might wave bye-bye by nine months of age. He also is starting to figure out how to express his needs non-verbally. Finally, your baby will start testing the limits of his world. At nine months old, your real parenting job begins. You need to set limits on your baby's behaviors STARTING NOW (see Chapter 11, "Discipline").

♦ *Vision*. Your baby's vision is 20/20 by six months of age.

Old Wives Tale
A baby who skips crawling and walks first won't be able to do higher math.
The truth: Where did this one come from? I crawled before I walked and still couldn't figure out calculus—so there. It has no bearing on intelligence.

Q. What developmental stimulation can I provide for my six to nine month old?

♦ *Gross Motor*. Provide a SAFE environment for your baby to move around in (see safety section below). Your house is now his playground.

♦ *Fine Motor.* Provide SAFE toys for your baby to feel, touch, maneuver, and taste. Babies explore with their hands first, then their mouths. If you are buying toys, pick ones that make sounds or lights when manipulated. Before you rush to Toys R Us, look around your kitchen. Old measuring cups, Tupperware, seasoning bottles (sealed shut), pots, pans, and wooden spatulas are often a hit with this age group. If you actually venture to a restaurant, those individually wrapped crackers are a real crowd pleaser until your meal arrives.

♦ *Language*. Do you have a bookstore frequent buyer's card yet? Get one. Use your local library as your baby gets older, but for now buy some cardboard books (called board books) of your own. Your baby's library will double as his teething toys.

- ***Even More Language***. When you speak to your baby, use single words and short phrases. Otherwise, you will sound like the teacher in the Peanuts cartoon to him. Your baby will start to show you what he wants. Instead of saying, "Oh, do you want the rubber ducky?" say, "Duck?" That will teach him the vocabulary word he is looking for. The same language rules apply for discipline. Instead of saying, "Oh, no, Honey, don't bite Mommy's shoulder!" say, "No biting." (Yes, there is more coming on this in the next chapter).

- ***Social/Personality***. Your baby is a social being and is very responsive to family members. Your baby will imitate the way you respond to situations. He follows your lead. Be a good role model. Since your baby now has object permanence, playing peek-a-boo is fun. It's also fun to hide toys under a blanket and let your baby look for them. How easy it is to amuse a child this age!

Nine to Twelve Months of Age

Q. What are the developmental milestones for a nine to 12 month old?

- ***Gross Motor***. Your baby should definitely have his sea legs. He should be able to stand holding on to someone's hand or a piece of furniture. He probably will be able to pull up to stand and get back down to a sitting position. One day, you'll go into the nursery and be shocked to find your baby standing up in his crib grinning at you. Your baby may or may not be taking his first steps at his birthday party. It's still within developmental limits to be walking by 15 months old.

- ***Fine Motor***. Your baby should be good at picking up small items. He will also start banging objects together. Babies this age get really good at pointing.

- ***Oral Motor***. Your baby should learn how to drink liquids from a cup. Ideally, she will be able to drink from a real cup, but most parents seem to prefer the no-spill sippy variety. Drinking from a straw is also something that works well for a child this age. By one year of age, your baby should graduate from a bottle to a cup (see Chapter 6, "Liquids" for details).

- ***Social/Personality***. As your baby approaches his birthday, he will be very good at expressing his needs non-verbally. There is a universal "point and grunt" that babies around the world know how to do. As his expressive language improves, there will be less frustration due to communication barriers.

- ***Anxiety***. Separation anxiety peaks at nine to 12 months, then again at 15 to 18 months. Remember that anxiety stems from the fear that you are leaving permanently. Ease these fears by kissing your baby goodbye and telling him when you will be back. Keep it short and sweet, and make your exit.

- *Language.* From nine to 12 months, your baby may start to say "Mama" and "Dada" and mean it. He may also say a word or two (but it's more likely to happen if you have a girl). Regardless of sex, your baby will speak with great confidence in some foreign language. If you listen to him (via monitor) in his crib at night, you should hear a whole monologue going on. This singsong intonation of speech is called "jabbering." Even though there aren't any vocabulary words, you know your baby has been listening to you.

Babies start to imitate their parents' activities. You may catch him pretending to dust and sweep. You may have a cleaning buddy!

Your baby will make it clear that she wants to be in charge and independent (in simple terms, it's her way or the highway). *It is important to begin discipline and setting limits.*

Your child will have conflicting moods. He may happily leave you behind, but then call for your help. Your availability as a consultant teaches your child to turn to adults for problem solving. Your child's sense of self (ego) is developing. Praising your child for small accomplishments gives him confidence.

Q. My one year old son isn't talking yet. All of the girls in his playgroup are yakking up a storm. Should I be worried?

Girls are talkers. Boys are walkers.

There is no question that girls learn language skills more quickly than boys. And once we start talking, you can't shut us up! Boys tend to reach motor milestones more quickly than girls—hence the roughhousing and athletic skills that you see later on. It's very interesting to watch. Clearly, parents have some hand in the way children develop along gender lines, but a lot of it is pre-determined.

However, if your one year old son or daughter has no signs of non-verbal communication skills (babbling, pointing/grunting), it's time to get it checked out.

New Parent 411: Car Seats & Head Control

Babies need to be at least one year of age to be forward facing in the car seat. Their neck support is not good enough to sustain the impact of a collision in a forward facing position until that age. Even if your baby is at least 20 pounds AND one year of age, you can still keep them rear-facing in a seat (as long as you aren't near the limit)—in fact, safety advocates recommend keeping baby rear-facing as long as possible. Most convertible seats go to 30 pounds rear-facing today—that's quite a while beyond the first birthday for most children.

Q. We speak two languages in our house. Will our child learn both?

Yes. She will have excellent receptive language skills in both languages (that is, she'll understand both) long before she speaks either language.

Q. What can I do to foster my baby's development from nine to 12 months?

- *Gross Motor.* Offer a wide-open space for your child to roam. Start playing with a ball. Toys that can be pushed are fun for babies who are walking (lawn mower, grocery cart, baby buggy).

- *Fine Motor.* Play pat-a-cake. Offer toys that your baby can bang together. It's also fun to get "cause and effect" toys (your baby pushes a button that causes a toy to move or make a noise; Jack-in-the-Box). Now is the time to buy "the classics." These toys are called stacking cups (plastic cups of various sizes) and shape sorters (cylinder with plastic shapes and matching holes in the top). Toys that can be filled and dumped are also entertaining.

- *Social.* Let your child participate in activities of daily living. While you are cooking dinner, let your baby "cook" his own meal on the floor with old pots and pans. While you are cleaning up, give him a towel, too. Start reviewing body parts with your child as a part of his vocabulary. You can also begin giving jobs to your baby. He should be able to follow one-step directions (such as "Bring me the ball.")

- *Language.* Books, books, and more books. Picture books with a single picture and word on each page encourage vocabulary words. Remember to converse with your child as your companion. Continue to identify items in single words and short phrases. Singing songs helps with language skills, and helps pass the time in traffic. Your baby doesn't mind if you can't carry a tune.

If you're looking for a great resource on the best toys to buy for your child, check out the *Oppenheimer Toy Portfolio* (web: toyportfolio.com). The book and accompanying web site rate and review toys, books, videos, software and music for kids. You can find age appropriate toys that are geared toward stimulating your child's development.

Don't forget friends' toys. When you take your child to another kid's house for a play date, they get exposed to a whole other set of toys. Some parents even get together and toy swap so their kids get different toys but don't have to spend oodles of money on them. Not to mention the social interactions baby will experience in a new environment.

Q. When should I buy shoes for my baby?

When he is a good walker.

There is no medical reason to wear shoes. Most babies use their toes to grasp the floor when they are trying to walk. For this reason, we encour-

NEW PARENT 411: TOP 14 SAFETY TIPS

Now is the time to make your home safe. Put this one on the Honey-Do List.

Children start to explore their world as a natural part of their development. Make their world safer so they can accomplish their goals. Here are the Top Safety Tips:

1. *Safety gates need to be at the top and bottom of the stairs.* The best and safest option is to permanently install gates (instead of using pressure gates).
2. *Electrical outlets need to have plastic safety covers.*
3. *Get down on the floor* and look at the world through your child's eyes. Electrical cords and telephone cords need to be moved behind furniture.
4. *Toxic cleaning products in lower cabinets need to be moved.*
5. *Cabinet locks on cabinets* with knives, glass containers, and china.
6. *Coffee tables and fireplace hearths with corners need safety bumpers.*
7. *Anchor bookshelves to the wall.*
8. *Get toilet lid locks so your baby cannot fall in.*
9. *Set your hot water heater to 120 degrees or less.*
10. *Get cord shorteners* or wall brackets to avoid dangling drapery cords.
11. *Remove any toys hanging over the crib* by the time your baby is five months old.
12. *Keep medicine out of reach.* Be especially watchful of grandparents who come to visit. They are more likely to a) be taking a medication and b) be leaving it out on a bathroom counter.
13. *If you drop something, pick it up.* Otherwise, your baby will do it for you and stick it into his mouth.
14. *If you are a gun owner* (remember I live in Texas, y'all), *lock 'em up.* Guns should *never* be accessible to children.

For more safety advice and which safety products are best, check out our other book *Baby Bargains* (see back of this book for details).

---

age your baby to travel the house in bare feet. If you are out in public, by all means, put shoes on your child. You don't need to buy expensive shoes. But, it is a good idea to get your child's foot measured when you buy that first pair of shoes to ensure proper fit.

The hottest trend: Robeez. These are soft leather moccasins meant for protection and flexibility. Did we mention, pricey? Does your baby NEED these shoes? No. They are not a medical miracle. But they are a nice alternative to socks if your child will be exiting his stroller on your travels.

Helpful Hints

◆ *Take a CPR course* and have any caregivers who are taking care of your child take one, also. The biggest potential problem for a child after nine months is choking. Kids this age do not get the famous Heimlich maneuver— they get back blows to force out the foreign object. You'll want to find out how to perform this if you don't know already.

◆ *Have Poison Control's phone number by your kitchen phone.* The national number is: 1-800-222-1222. You can find your local Poison Control number from the American Association of Poison Control Centers' web site at aapcc.org. Always call poison control first if your child has ingested something. FYI: It is no longer recommended to have syrup of Ipecac in your medicine cabinet. Not all toxic chemicals should be removed by vomiting because they can burn the esophagus and mouth when coming back up.

Q. Where can I get information about toy safety? I have heard about baby product recalls.

Check out the U.S Consumer Product Safety Commission Hotline on the web at cpsc.gov or toll free at 1-800-638-2772.

Q. When can my baby start watching TV?

The American Academy of Pediatrics says *avoid* TV for kids under two years of age. Once children turn two, the AAP recommends limiting total screen time (including videos and computers) to two hours a day.[10] Despite that recommendation, 43% of kids under age two watch TV every day and 26% even have a TV in their bedrooms.[11]

Why are the experts so negative on TV? What's the harm, you say? Sure, we know that a 30-minute educational DVD might buy you time to take a much-needed shower. And don't educational DVD's and television programs help kids learn?

Here's why TV is bad for babies under age two:

1 TV IS A LOW ENERGY ACTIVITY. If the TV is on, your child is sitting down (unless you are doing an aerobics video). The average school age child watches an astounding three hours a day. Yep, that's three hours sitting on their butts. Do you want to start this couch-potato habit in infancy?

2 IT'S ONLY EDUCATIONAL WHEN YOU CAN UNDERSTAND IT. Studies have shown that educational programming is beneficial for kids... BUT only for children who understand the content. The magic age to understand TV is two years old. While there are some very bright 18 month olds who "get it," the majority of kids don't, and thus do not gain any knowledge by watching. The reality: those baby videos that *claim* developmental stimulation have no data to back up those claims (heck, why spend money doing a study when the product sells like hotcakes). Bottom line: even Sesame Street, which is an educational show, is not appropriate for your baby to watch.[12]

3 TV DISPLACES OTHER ACTIVITIES. TV has become a scapegoat for everything from the obesity epidemic, the rise of Attention Deficit Disorder (ADD) and the increase in autism. (None of these theories have panned out, by the way). Sure, the ads for junk food on kid's TV probably have something to do with obesity . . . but one thing we do know for sure: the time kids are watching TV is time they are not spending with their family, engaging in conversation, playing with someone, or playing independently. These are important activities for kids of all ages.[13] *That* is the harm of TV for babies.

4 **MANY PROGRAMS ARE INAPPROPRIATE FOR CHILDREN.** For instance, the evening news can be very graphic and disturbing (and don't think your baby/child isn't watching because it's "your" show). Even children's programs can be problematic. Have you watched a cartoon lately? The average cartoon has 20 violent scenes per hour. The violence that occurs does have an impact. Studies have shown a direct influence on children's behaviors after watching cartoons.[14]

So, here are some suggestions:

◆ *After your child turns two or older, limit the amount of time your child watches TV a day.* Have house rules and stick to them.

◆ *Know what your child is watching.* Any PBS show is usually a good bet. Cartoon Network shows require a parent preview. Yes, that means sitting down and watching "Jimmy Neutron" without your child to see if that show is appropriate.

◆ *Watch TV WITH your child.* Talk about what you are seeing. Stress to your child the "make believe" part. As your child gets older, explain the advertisements.

◆ *Have a family TV.* One in five American children have a television in their bedrooms. That means there is no supervision of what kids are watching. You need to be the V-chip—don't put a TV in your kid's room.

DR B'S OPINION: BABY SIGN LANGUAGE

We know that children are capable of understanding language and communicating non-verbally long before they are able to speak. So, teaching an older baby or toddler hand gestures to communicate makes sense. And there is scientific proof that signing is beneficial. One study found that infants and toddlers that were "sign talkers" spoke earlier and performed slightly higher on IQ tests at age eight that their non-signing friends.[15]

While your baby may only learn a few signs, sitting down with your child to learn any new skill has its merits. You don't need to buy a book to learn sign language. You can create the hand gestures on your own (remember *Meet the Fockers*?). If you choose not to teach your child sign language, do not fear…your child will master the universal "point and grunt" skill to tell you what he wants.

◆ *Don't watch TV at meal times*—no exception for kids' shows OR the news. This not only interferes with important time together as a family, but it also encourages people to continue eating after they are full.

BOTTOM LINE

Many baby videos have clever marketing pitches—watch THIS video and your child will be smarter! Stronger! Wealthier!

The truth: your baby will be smarter if *you sit down for 15 minutes and play with him*—no DVD required. Children learn much better when they are actively participating in a learning activity. No video will make your child an Einstein or a Mozart.

Q. But I just need 15 minutes to take a shower or prepare dinner. Is it okay to pop in an educational DVD to entertain my child?

We hear you—as parents of four children ourselves, we know there are times you just want to take a shower. Or cook dinner. Yes, this means taking your attention away from your child.

But what is your child to do during this brief period of time? We know the simple answer is to turn on a kid TV show or DVD as a babysitter. While there are no studies that suggest this will leave a permanent scar on your child, here is an alternative:

It's called *independent play*. Crazy, eh?

Yes, you have our blessing to let your child find something to do with his time! And yes, it stimulates your child's creativity and problem solving skills. He can be sitting in the bathroom while you take a shower. Or on the floor in the kitchen with some age-appropriate toys (plastic bowls and wooden spoons do nicely).

We'd argue this is time well spent. Our kids have become the Entertained Generation—if they aren't plugged in, they're bored. The take home message: you do NOT have to entertain or find entertainment for your child 24/7. Let them play on their own.

Q. What do you think of "Mommy and Me" and other community programs for babies?

For babies, these are a mixed bag. For the most part, Mommy gets more out of these programs than babies less than one year of age. Look for programs that focus on singing, story time, and finger plays. The more

NEW PARENT 411: FINDING THE BEST TOYS

The best place to find great toys are to look in your own home. Old bowls, wooden spoons, measuring cups, and Tupperware can entertain a child more than you think.

But, if you are in the market for toys, it is worth doing a little research. The *Oppenheimer Toy Portfolio* is a great resource (it's both a book and web site). Visit their website at www.toyportfolio.com.

motor oriented programs (Gymboree, Little Gym) are more appropriate for toddlers (over one year in age). One tip: watch a class or two before you sign up so you aren't wasting your time.

Q. What books do you recommend if I want to learn more about child development?

Touchpoints by Dr. T. Berry Brazelton. He has a beautiful style to approaching development, developmental stimulation, and the challenges within these topics. Brazelton has a "cup is half full" way of viewing your child's struggles with growth and independence.

BOTTOM LINE

The most critical developmental stimulation for your baby is *the time you spend with him*. You don't need to buy expensive toys or "developmentally appropriate" DVD's. Nor do you need to enroll your baby in a special preschool program. We'll discuss preschool at length in our *Toddler 411* book (see the back of this book for details). For now, just concentrate on spending time with your baby.

Q. Can you give me some ideas for age appropriate toys for babies?

Here are some guidelines:

Infants birth to six months:
Look for: bright primary color, clear lines, features, human faces
Fine Motor (manipulatives): soft blocks, rattles, squeeze toys, keys on a ring, activity gyms.
Other sensory activities: Tape recordings of you singing or reading a story, music boxes, mobiles, mirrors, hand held puppets

Infants six to 12 months:
Look for: things safe to go in the mouth, things to stack, pour, dump, things to push, turn, or press, things to open and shut
Gross Motor Play (large muscles): Push toys, Low climbing platform
Fine Motor: soft blocks, easy puzzles, squeeze-squeaky toys, pop-up boxes containers to empty and fill, nesting cups, water toys
Other sensory: music boxes songs, tapes, tapes of you

This list is derived from The Consumer Products Safety Commission guide called *Which Toys for Which Child: A Consumer's Guide for Selecting Suitable Toys, Ages Birth Through Five.* Check out their website at cpsc.gov for your own copy.

Recommended books for birth to age one

We suggest buying the board book versions if you can find them. Not only will your baby enjoy listening to the stories, but he'll want to help turn the pages. He's also likely to use them as a teething toy at some point (as we discussed earlier). If you want the books to have a decent lifespan, go cardboard.

Here are some favorite titles:

Margaret Wise Brown: *Good Night Moon, Runaway Bunny, The Big Red Barn*
Eric Carle: *The Grouchy Ladybug, The Very Busy Spider, The Very Hungry Caterpillar*
Eric Hill: *Where's Spot?*
Bill Martin, Jr.: *Brown Bear, Brown Bear, What Do You See?*
Golden Books: *Pat The Bunny, The Pokey Little Puppy*
Nancy White Carlstrom: *Jesse Bears' Yum Yum Crumble*
Dr. Seuss: *Mr. Brown Can Moo! Can you?*
Sandra Boynton: *Barnyard Dance!*
Tedd Arnold: *Five Ugly Monsters*
Jan Pienkowski: *Little Monsters, Oh My a fly!*
Paul Strickland: *Dinosaur Roar!*
Stephen Losordo: *Cow Moo Me*

Discipline & Temperament

Chapter 11

"Any child can tell you that the sole purpose of a middle name is so he can tell when he's in trouble."

~ Dennis Fakes

What's in this Chapter

- ◆ Figuring out your baby's temperament
- ◆ The high maintenance baby
- ◆ Tips for soothing the savage beast
- ◆ Pacifiers
- ◆ Colic
- ◆ Infant massage
- ◆ Tips on planting the seeds of discipline
- ◆ Separation anxiety
- ◆ Masturbation
- ◆ Thumb sucking
- ◆ Biting and being bitten

Every parent will go through it. You can see it coming. Your son snuck out last night to hang with his buddies after you explicitly told him he couldn't. So he's grounded. You took the car keys. He has to bum a ride to school or, worse, take the bus. Maybe you remember when you did exactly that or something like it.

Okay, so you don't have to worry about this scenario yet, but you do need to set up the foundation for what seems like a lifetime of discipline. And now that you know all about child development, you can take all that knowledge and apply it to guiding your child's behaviors today and into the future.

But before we get to discipline, we'll need to discuss temperament. Call it the "getting to know the real you" section of the book. Once you figure out your little angel's temperament, you can tailor your discipline issues to fit him like a glove. Or at least that's the theory.

Believe it or not, your baby's doctor may be a good resource to help you sort through these issues. If she doesn't have all of the answers, she can point you in the right direction to get the answers.

Temperament and discipline issues are the toughest part of your job description. Here is a general list of what you will be facing this first year:

DISCIPLINE

AGE	FUN CHALLENGE
0-3 months	Learning your baby's temperament
	Colic
3-4 months	Night feeding/sleep issues
9 months	Separation anxiety
	Stranger anxiety
	Night wakenings
	Limit setting
12 months	Aggressive behaviors (biting, hitting)

Adapted from the Harriet Lane Handbook, 2002

Temperament: Getting to know YOUR baby

Every baby is different. We know that's not news to you. No matter how much advice you get, or how many books you read, no one can tell you what YOUR child's emotional needs will be. You will realize when you have a crying baby on your hands that you'd better figure out your child ASAP . . .or check into the nearest mental health facility.

Q. What are the typical temperaments of babies?

Landmark research done in the 1970's described the three main types of temperaments. Every child doesn't fit into only one category all the time, but here are the groups:

1 EASY CHILD. Surprisingly, 40% of kids fit in this category. These babies have regular eating, sleeping, and elimination habits. They are usually happy and easy going. They are interested in exploring new things and don't mind change.

2 DIFFICULT CHILD. Only 10% of kids fit in this category—although if it happens to you, it is 100%! These babies have more irregular eating, sleeping, and elimination schedules. They have trouble with change, transitions, and new experiences. These babies are intense.

3 SLOW TO WARM UP CHILD. About 15% of kids fit here. These kids are also difficult because it takes them a while to adjust to change in environment or care provider. They hide in their shells when they encounter a new situation.

4 THE REST. Thirty-five percent of kids don't fit into any of the above categories and have "mixed" temperaments.[1]

BOTTOM LINE

Figuring out what type of baby you have will help you to *anticipate* how your child will react to certain situations. Plus, you'll have a better idea on how to make his world (and yours) a better place. For example, a difficult baby needs extra time getting into his car seat without a fight. Plan extra time in your schedule for coaxing if you have some place you need to be.

Real world parent story: It always amazes us to watch our child-less friends decide to go somewhere (like a restaurant). They just pick up their keys, lock the door and poof! they're gone. For parents of children, it is a 20 (or 30 or 40) minute odyssey that first involves finding shoes/socks, coats, toys, books, etc. Then someone has to have a diaper change. It then takes more time to buckle in the car seat, only to discover a child has forgotten their toy and then the process repeats. As a parent, outings require the pre-planning that usually goes into staging a small-scale military invasion—remembering to bring that diaper bag (honey, do we have any wipes?), wallet, purse, keys . . . as well as your sanity. Then add in a "difficult" baby and you may as well just stay home.

> **DR B'S OPINION**
>
> *"View your baby's temperament . . . as a cake mold. While you can't break the mold, you can control how the cake is baked. How you interact with your baby can positively impact his future!"*

Q. When will I be able to figure out my child's temperament?

By the time a baby turns one, most parents have his number—you know what kind of child you have on your hands.

Of course, some temperaments are more difficult to live with than others. But all have their strengths. When you are feeling frustrated with your baby, think about how successful he will be in the future with those traits!

Here are seven questions to help you understand your child's temperament:[2]

1. *Adaptability*: How does your baby respond to change or new situations?
2. *Regularity*: Does your baby follow a schedule with sleep and mealtimes?
3. *Mood*: Is your baby's attitude positive or negative about life?
4. *Persistence*: Does your baby persist at activities or give up easily?
5. *Sensitivity*: Is your baby sensitive or oblivious to environmental changes (like noises, smells, tastes, lights)?
6. *Intensity*: Is your baby laid back or intense?
7. *Energy*: Is your baby energetic or quiet?

Q. As a doc, what is your view of infant temperament?

There are high-maintenance babies and low-maintenance babies. If you are blessed with a high maintenance baby, recruit family and friends to help out.

High-maintenance babies require more physical and emotional strength from their parents. These babies get walked around, rocked, and soothed more than their low maintenance friends. Parents of these babies are exhausted and frequently at wits end. They have irrational thoughts about giving their baby up for adoption. Don't worry—you are not alone.

Low-maintenance babies need little intervention, and therefore need little discussion here.

DISCIPLINE

Q. Can you predict a child's future personality based on their temperament as an infant?

Yes.

Elements of a child's temperament will persist through a lifetime. However, all humans adapt to succeed in the face of life's challenges. The way you respond to your child has a *tremendous* impact on your child's personality. It's that heredity vs. environment thing—both have an influence on behavior.

Q. I have an extremely active baby. Can you tell if he has Attention Deficit Disorder (ADD)?

No.

Attention Deficit Disorder is a diagnosis based on the shortened attention span of a child compared to peers his age. All babies under one year of age have fleeting abilities to pay attention to anything for very long. It's virtually impossible to make a diagnosis of ADD in a child less than three years of age.

Will your very active baby ultimately have ADD? Only time will tell. As we discussed in the previous chapter, armchair quarterbacks (namely, other parents at your local park) may be quick to offer a diagnosis for your child on this subject. Don't listen to them!

Q. Why is my baby crying?

Because he can't talk. The average baby cries one to four hours a day.

If you had no other way of communicating you'd be crying, too. Babies are trying to tell you something when they cry. It's your job to play detective and figure out what it is. Yes, there are certain types of cries (I'm hungry, tired, in pain), and that will give you some clues. The truth is, when you spend 24 hours a day with your crying baby, you will get each other figured out—we have no doubt about it. Welcome to Hell Week—you are about to be initiated as a parent.

Read the next box for a reasonable cry management approach.

> **Reality Check**
> A recent study done at a clinic for babies with colic showed that two-thirds of the babies referred actually had gastroesophageal reflux (that is, heartburn).[3]

> **BOTTOM LINE**
> The mistake most parents make is that they give their newborn more credit than they deserve. Newborns have simple needs.
>
> Your baby is not nearly as sophisticated as the baby in *Look Who's Talking*. They don't cry because you are a bad parent, because they are lonely, or because you have gone back to work and they are mad at you.
>
> Most of the time, your baby just can't pull it together to fall asleep and needs some soothing. Depending on your baby's temperament, that may mean a little—or a lot—of soothing.

New Parent 411: The 3 Rules of Cry Management

Rule #1: DON'T PANIC—the most important advice!

Rule #2: Go through your baby's To Do List. Is your baby crying because she:

- Needs to eat?
- Needs a diaper change?
- Is overtired and having trouble falling asleep?
- Is a high-maintenance baby and doesn't know what she wants?

Rule #3: Rule out medical causes if crying persists over two hours straight. A good rule of thumb is that medical reasons for crying are generally not fixed by holding and rocking your baby. For example, your baby may be saying:

- I'm having heartburn. (This is probably the most common medical reason—see **GASTROESOPHAGEAL REFLUX**).
- I have colic. I do this every night. (See later in the chapter for more discussion on colic.)
- I have a fever. (If your baby is under *three* months old, call your doctor ASAP.)
- I have gas, constipation, or milk intolerance (Memo to new parents: usually this is NOT the cause, but every parent is convinced that this is the problem).
- I have a really serious medical problem (also rare, but that's why you should call your doctor).

Old Wives Tale

Picking your newborn up every time he cries will spoil him.
The truth: Your newborn does not have a neurological maturity to relax and settle down on his own. You need to do the work to comfort him—*given his age*. From birth to two months, you do whatever it takes. There is no such thing as spoiling a newborn. As babies reach four to six months of age, they are quite capable of self-soothing. Wait to see if your baby can settle on her own before intervening.

Top Ten Tricks for Soothing a New Baby (under four months of age)

1. **LET YOUR BABY SUCK ON YOUR FINGER.** Sucking is incredibly soothing for newborns. Pacifiers are okay, too. (More on this below).

2. **DO THE BABY BURRITO WRAP.** Swaddle your baby in a receiving blanket. They are used to being snug in the womb, without limbs flailing around. See Chapter 9, "Sleep" for details on how to do this.

3. **ROCKING.** Either sitting in that expensive rocking chair you bought, or walking around and gently swaying baby back and forth in your

arms. (Much as YOU would like to be sitting in that chair, babies often prefer you to walk around.) Singing or humming is also helpful.

4 **GO FOR A WALK IN THE STROLLER.** A change of scenery often helps baby and parent.

5 **GO FOR A CAR RIDE.** When parents call me about prolonged (over two hours straight) crying, I tell them to go for a car ride. If a few trips around the block don't make the crying stop, I'll tell them to keep on driving to the nearest emergency room.

6 **USE A VIBRATING INFANT SEAT OR INFANT SWING.**

7 **TAKE A TRIP TO THE LAUNDRY ROOM.** Put your baby in his car seat and place on top of the dryer. Turn on the dryer. Vibration is particularly helpful for colicky babies. Don't leave your child unattended, however.

8 **GIVE YOUR BABY A BATH.**

9 **TRY SOME INFANT MASSAGE.** (see below for more info)

10 **PUT YOUR BABY IN BED AND LEAVE HIM ALONE.** If you have tried everything and now you are crying, too, it's time to let your baby cry it out. They are truly exhausted at this point and will fall asleep on their own.

Q. Is it okay to use a pacifier?

In our opinion, pacifiers are okay to use for babies *under six months of age*. Let's look at this in a developmental way.

- Newborns are neurologically immature.
- Newborns are soothed by sucking.
- If babies don't find their own thumb, or suck on your finger, they will use Mom's breast as a pacifier. *Remember, it's Mom's choice whether or not to accept this role.*

Here is why should you *stop* using a pacifier by six months of age:

1. Babies over four to six months of age have many other ways to console themselves.
2. Pacifiers become a crutch for naptime/bedtime, car rides, etc. If the pacifier falls out during these times, you will have a crying baby. If the pacifier isn't there to begin with, you won't have a problem.
3. Prolonged pacifier use and thumb-sucking (for over a year) can cause

DR B'S OPINION

"I cringe when I see a three-year-old walking around the mall with a pacifier in his mouth. In fact, my husband gets great joy in pointing these kids out to me to see my reaction."

altered bite position and cross-bite in preschoolers.[4]
4. Pacifiers encourage perpetuation of the "oral exploration" phase of childhood. As children approach their first birthdays, they stop exploring everything with their mouths and start using their hands. If they continue their oral fixation using a pacifier all the time, they continue to mouth everything well into their second year of life. If your child is in daycare, you are asking for illness when shared toys are going into your child's mouth.
5. Pacifier use increases the risk of having ear infections.

BOTTOM LINE: The longer the pacifier remains in your baby's world, the harder it will be to kick the habit. A six-month old will forget about that old pacifier within a day or two and move on.

Reality Check

If you are breastfeeding, it's probably wise to wait until things are going well (at least four to seven days) to introduce a pacifier. Why? Your baby learns good sucking etiquette at your breast first. For the same reason, we recommend Soothie pacifiers (www.soothie-pacifier.com)—they are shaped the most like a human nipple. "Orthodontic" pacifiers are flanged and teach the baby to chomp on your nipples (undesirable, trust us).

Q. What is colic?

If I had the answer (and the solution) I'd be rich.

This problem is known as the Rule of Threes. A three-week-old baby with colic cries for about three hours straight daily until he is three months old. This occurs in about 15% of babies. The crying usually occurs in the early evening time, just when your spouse is coming home from work and you are attempting to eat dinner.

The problem seems to be related to immaturity of the gastrointestinal system. Through the years, pediatricians have tried medications to reduce gas, relax the intestine muscles, or cause sedation. None of these medications help although a new treatment option, probiotics (see below for more info) may be beneficial. For now, the best medicine is time—all babies eventually outgrow colic.

BOTTOM LINE: The difference between a baby with colic and one with heartburn (gastroesophageal reflux) is that colicky babies act this way for specific periods during the day. Babies with heartburn do it all day long.

Q. I heard that white noise can help soothe babies who have colic. But then I heard about a study that said white noise can damage a baby's hearing? What's up with that?

Yes, it seems conflicting to us too. Here's the scoop: a recent study published in the journal *Science* showed that rat pups exposed to white noise (such as radio static or an air conditioner's hum—no words or varying sounds involved) led to developmental delays in the hearing center of the brain.[5] Extrapolate that to humans and some scientists think that those white noise machines are a bad idea. The other side of the debate:

researchers point out that white noise is similar to what babies hear when they're sloshing about in the womb—and that noise runs 24 hours a day! So at least for the first few weeks, listening to white noise can help an infant cope with all the silence outside the womb.

Our opinion: white noise is NOT a bad thing, especially in moderation. If white noise is helpful for a baby who has real colic, by all means use it. But don't expose your baby to white noise constantly—and turn it off once your baby falls asleep. Wean him off the sound once the colic goes away (at about three months of age).

Q. I heard about a "miracle cure" for colic—probiotics. Is it too good to be true?

Sold in capsules or powder, probiotics are the good germs in your body that help improve intestinal function. Babies are born germ-free and then acquire good germs in the gut to help digest food (you have millions in your adult gut as you read this).

So here's the theory: could an "immature" gut cause colic? And if babies take probiotics (good germs), could this kick-start their digestive system and "cure" colic?

A 2007 study published in *Pediatrics* provided some answers: researchers gave "good germs" to babies. They compared 90 exclusively breastfed babies with colic. Half received over-the-counter gas drops (simethicone) and the other half got one capsule a day of a probiotic containing the germ Lactobacillus reuteri (commonly known as L. reuteri).

The results? Pretty darn impressive......the gas drops group saw a 7% reduction in crying. *The probiotics group had a 95% reduction in crying.* No, that isn't a typo. *Babies who cried two to three hours a day were crying less than an hour after one month of treatment.*

So, are docs ready to recommend probiotics for every colicky baby? Not yet—more research needs to be done. This was only one, relatively small study. But this may be a reasonable way to reduce the misery of colic and certainly less expensive than hiring a babysitter every night for two months! A two-month supply of L. reuteri is about $12.

In my practice, we sell a powder form of L. reuteri from Nature's Way. The dose is a half-teaspoon a day, immersed in a few drops of water (or mixed in expressed breastmilk or formula).

If you decide you want to try this colic remedy, please consult with your doctor first.

Q. What can I do about colic?

The eternal parent question. We are always compelled to do *something* to make our babies feel better. In this case, YOU may need more help than your baby.

You think I'm kidding, but I'm not. Your baby is screaming, but he will be fine. You need an escape before you go over the edge. Moms are already sleep-deprived and hormonal. Throw in an inconsolable baby—*daily*—for eight to ten weeks and you'd be justified in asking for the jumbo size bottle of Prozac at this point.

Here is what you should do:

Discipline

1. Recruit loving friends and family to come over from 5 to 8 pm a night or two a week. You leave.
2. If #1 isn't an option, put your baby in his crib and step outside for a few moments.
3. Put your baby in a sling or carrier and run the vacuum cleaner. You probably haven't had a chance to clean the house in a while anyway. We're not being cruel, just realistic here.
4. Seek professional help for yourself if you can't take it anymore—this is not a sign of weakness or poor parenting skills.
5. For those parents who are really desperate, and will spend any amount of money to stop the crying, there is a product called "Sleep Tight" which attaches to the baby's crib to simulate the vibration and noise of a car going 55mph. For a mere $140, it can be yours. Check out www.colic.com or call 1-800-NO COLIC. Another idea: those vibrating bouncer seats ($30 to $40) have been the savior of more than one parent of a colicky baby.

Tips and tricks for dealing with colic could fill an entire book—and, in fact, one doctor has already written an excellent book on this. Dr. Harvey Karp, a retired pediatrician in Santa Monica, CA, has developed a terrific method for soothing colicky babies. His *Happiest Baby on the Block* book (Bantam, $13.95) focuses on five steps to mimic the baby's experience in the uterus: swaddling, side/stomach position, shhh sounds, swinging and sucking. We highly recommend Karp's book.

Reality Checks

◆ *A common parent thought is, " I can't listen to my baby cry."* That is exactly the way nature intended it to be. All animals have a certain noise that is disturbing to their elders and that prompts them to take action. As a doctor, I listen to children cry all day long in my office and completely tune it out. When I get home and my own children cry, it drives me nuts. Parents (including me!) need to learn to take their own emotions out of the picture. View crying as a form of self-expression and it won't raise your blood pressure. Remember this rule: Most of the time, YOUR CHILD IS FINE.

◆ *Parents at the end of their rope need to walk away from their baby. NEVER SHAKE a baby.* Babies who are colicky or high maintenance have a significantly higher risk of being abused. A baby's brain is very fragile. If he is shaken, the motion can lead to blindness, brain damage, or death.

Q. **What do you think about infant massage?**

Everyone benefits from a massage.

The power of touch has known therapeutic value. Not only are babies soothed, but parents are too. Learning infant massage teaches parents how to feel more comfortable holding

> **DR B'S OPINION**
>
> "Spouse massages are also very important. Often our energies get focused on the baby and our spouses get treated like chopped liver."

and handling their babies.

Infant massage classes are a popular trend. Check with your local hospital or parenting magazine for information in your area.

Q. When should I encourage my baby to have a favorite toy?

The official term is *transitional object*. Six months of age is the perfect time to introduce it.

Remember that *object permanence* concept? Babies start to realize that parents still exist when they leave their viewing field between six and 12 months of age. The transitional object or toy is the friend that travels with your child when you aren't there. They are making an emotional "transition" to seeking an alternative source of comfort. The object may be a doll, blanket, or even a piece of parent's clothing.

Your child will likely have his comfort object for a while. He will give it up before going to his first slumber party (age seven to eight years is normal).

Helpful Hint

Try to pick a transitional object you don't mind carrying around everywhere. One of my patients clung to his mother's satin nightie. Another important point: buy EXTRA objects. Once your child has a favorite "lovie" (such as a stuffed animal or blanket), be sure to buy extra identical ones. Odds are, the lovie will get lost or destroyed—and that isn't a pretty scene. Having back-ups is important for everyone's sanity. Also: be careful when you attempt to wash a lovie—a much-loved stuffed animal can easily fall apart in a washing machine. Hand washing or using the delicate cycle (and not drying) is important.

If you've ever seen those kids who seem to have their parents wrapped around their little finger (think Veruca Salt from *Charlie and the Chocolate Factory*), you know you want to avoid that fate. But how can you prevent that future behavior in your cute little baby? Even though you now know how your baby's brain works, you still may not have all the right answers in every discipline situation. Why? Because your child is really smart and has figured YOU out. So let's move on to setting up a good discipline foundation that can hopefully take you through the tougher times to come.

Planting The Seeds Of Discipline

Q. At what age should I start to discipline my baby?

By nine months of age.

Planting the seeds of discipline is CRITICAL. From birth to eight months, your parenting job is easy. It is physically exhausting but doesn't require too many mental strategies to succeed. At about nine months old, you will start playing chess with your child and will continue to play for a lifetime. Here are the rules of the game:

Discipline is the process of teaching your child to be an independent being. Your job is to give your child a **SUPER-EGO**. This is a Freudian term that refers to a person's internal control that limits inappropriate behavior from occurring (that is, self-control). In other words, your discipline implants a device in your child's hard drive that he will carry with him wherever he goes. That way, your child will do the right thing even when you aren't around.

Let's review your child's development. A nine to 12 month old is exploring, not purposefully destroying, his environment (your house). He uses his memory of what has worked before to approach the unfamiliar, so everything ultimately ends up in his mouth (and hence, a safety hazard). He has figured out how to get other people to repeat behaviors (if you scream when he bites you, he will bite you again). He is egocentric—the world revolves around him (how could a phone call be more important than him?) He wants independence, but doesn't quite have the motor skills to accomplish his goals (refusing to let you feed him). He has developed a sense of trust with his parents and caretakers. He doesn't want anyone to leave him, even to go to the bathroom (separation anxiety). Are we having fun yet?

When the baby I just described is *your* baby, it's time to get to work.

BOTTOM LINE

Consistency is the key to making a discipline plan work. If there is an adult who ignores a behavior that other adults reprimand, the behavior will continue to occur. Grandparents are usually the worst in this department— and kids know it! It's like having a substitute teacher.

Q. What should be included in our House Rules?

Anything dangerous or potentially painful to the child or others.

These are behaviors that are *never* acceptable. These include pulling on cords, touching the stove, putting fingers in electrical outlets, turning on bathtub water, biting, hitting the dog and so on. Look around your house and add to your list.

Q. What is a discipline management plan?

How adult caretakers will respond to inappropriate behaviors.

Everyone has his or her own style. Most parents will think back to their own parents' approach and remember what worked. You and your spouse need to come up with a uniform strategy that both of you feel comfortable enforcing.

NEW PARENT 411: PLANTING THE SEEDS OF DISCIPLINE

1. Make your house kid safe, so you don't have to say "No" to everything your child touches.
2. Make up a set of "House Rules" that all caretakers enforce.
3. Make up a discipline management plan with consequences—again, that all caretakers enforce.
4. Know that your nine-month old understands the word "no", but wants to be sure you really mean it. Yep, this is called *testing limits*.

DISCIPLINE

Q. Do you think it's okay to spank my child?

No.

We never recommend using physical force to punish a child. Your child learns from you. If you are violent when you are angry, your child will be that way, too. We know that your first reaction when your child hits you is to hit back—DON'T. You're older than your child remember?

BOTTOM LINE: The goal of discipline is to *teach*. If you want a well-behaved child, you need to be well behaved as their role model.

Q. At what age does the Terrible Two's start? My one year old is already acting terrible.

The Terrible Two's is a misnomer. It actually starts when your child declares independence from you.

We usually see this behavior start around 18 months and last until age three, but some kids are ahead of their time.

My advice is to have a glass of wine at dinner for the next two years. Just kidding—sort of. My other advice is to give your child the opportunity to feel like he is in control of his world. You are really in charge, but he doesn't need to be reminded of that 24 hours a day. When there is an opportunity for *him* to choose something, let him (picking out a snack, a toy to play with, etc.). Also, don't bother to discipline for minor infractions. It's not worth it and limits the amount of conflicts that arise.

Q. What is a temper tantrum and how should I respond to it?

A physical release of anger. You need to let it happen.

Tantrums are frequently seen in toddlers, but some kids like to start early. When your child is at the end of his rope, he may have an emotional breakdown. This involves kicking, screaming, crying, and flailing around on the floor.

Your job is to give him a safe place to have it out. Do not respond to your child while he is in the midst of this performance. When he is done, you can scoop him up and discuss things.

Just for fun, as parents, we also like to rank our children's temper tantrums much in the way scientists score hurricanes. There are Category 1 and 2 fits, which like minor hurricanes involve a minimal amount of damage. Then there are the serious tantrums—up to and including the big ones we like to call Category 5.

Once we took our two year old to a train show, something he absolutely loved. Until it was time to go. They were closing it down and turning out the lights (we had been there for an hour or more). Suddenly, our son launched into the most amazing Category 5 tantrum—a one-hour screamfest. You just had to marvel at the intensity of it all. Of course, at the time, we wanted to give back our parent license and go into the Federal Parent Witness Protection Program.

11 Tips For Developing A Discipline Style

1. **Avoid as many conflicts as possible.** Make your house kid safe. Don't push your child past his threshold. For example: running too many errands, missing naptime, waiting forever at a restaurant. For eating out, we have a ten-minute rule—if the wait is over ten minutes, it's time to go elsewhere. Obviously, eating early is a good way to avoid lengthy waits for a table.

2. **Anticipate conflicts.** If you see your child heading towards the stereo, move him elsewhere or offer him a toy. Obviously, parents develop a sixth sense for this—soon, you'll be able to scan a room and predict the future (that is, zeroing in on your baby's next conflict).

3. **Anticipate attention-seeking behavior.** Be prepared for trouble when your attention is turned elsewhere. If your child gets into trouble when you are cooking dinner, let him "cook" on the kitchen floor.

4. **Pick your battles.** Saying "No" twenty times a day loses its effectiveness. Believe it or not, I had a parent tell me her child thought his name was "No." Categorize behaviors into major errors, minor ones, and those too insignificant to bother with. Minor infractions are negotiable with an older child.

5. **Act Immediately.** Discipline when the behavior occurs, not after the fact. Otherwise, your child won't remember what he is getting in trouble for. Never say: "Just wait till your father/mother gets home!"

6. **Make your comments short and sweet.** Speak in short sentences such as "No hitting." This is much more effective than, "Johnny, you know it's not nice to hit the dog." Believe us, you lost Johnny right after "you know."

7. **Focus on the behavior, not the child.** Be sure to state that a particular behavior is bad. NEVER tell your child that HE is bad.

8. **Remind your child that you love her or him.** Always end your intervention with a positive comment. It reinforces the reason that you are teaching her how to behave.

9. **Use age-appropriate and temperament-appropriate discipline techniques.** You need to adapt to your baby and find a discipline style that works well with your individual child. What works at nine months might not work when your child is two. He's had time to figure out your strategy!

10. **Don't yell.** It's not the volume of your voice, but the tone that gets your point across. Remember *The Godfather*? He never needed to yell. Some of the most effective discipline we've ever seen has been whispered.

11. **Catch your child "being good."** Praise for good behavior is so important and helps encourage more of it. Think of it as fertilizer for her conscience.

Reality Check

A word of caution: If you give in to a situation when your child has a tantrum, you have just taught him that a tantrum is an effective way to get what he wants. Be strong!

Q. What sets off a temper tantrum?

Anything and nothing.

Look at your child's world through your child's eyes. He has poor language skills and can't tell his parents everything he needs and wants. He hasn't mastered all his motor skills to accomplish certain tasks. He isn't sure where his activity boundaries are and is told "no" numerous times a day. Add in an egocentric perspective that Mom and Dad can read his mind (if he thinks it, everyone must know what he is thinking). Finish with the unattainable goal of complete independence.

Being tired, bored, and hungry are also contributors to ugly behavior.

So, when you pick out the wrong pajamas at bedtime and your child explodes, don't think it's just the P.J.'s.

8 Tried & True Discipline Techniques

Here are some tips to keep the peace in your house and foster your child's self-control.

1. **Ignore**. If it's not a major infraction, ignore the behavior. If your child doesn't get a rise out of you, she will stop doing it.

2. **Redirect**. Move your child to a different activity. Children repeat the same inappropriate behavior to see if they can get away with it. It often takes numerous times and consistent redirection of the same misbehavior until you can eliminate it. Don't give up.

3. **Use Humor**. It works beautifully with power struggles. Instead of digging in to the trenches and holding your ground on the situation, change to an upbeat approach. Your child will do the same.

4. **Time Out**. Yes, it really does work. The premise is that your child is removed from his play and must sit out for a period of time. Your child gets one minute for every year of age. Kids under age two rarely sit in isolation for the time requirement. Little ones can sit facing away from you on your lap. You do not talk to them or interact. Time out is reserved for particularly inappropriate behaviors and it should be used every time the behavior occurs.

Special Situations: Tips & Tricks

Q. How do I deal with separation anxiety? Can I just sneak out of sight?

Before, you could leave the room and your baby might not have cared. Now, if you leave the room, he wants to know where you're going. This is about the time you will keep your bathroom door open so your baby does not panic every time you answer nature's call. (That bathroom door often remains open for the next several years. I have to remind myself when we have company to close mine. But I digress). It is CRITICAL that you tell your baby where you are going. You will think it is better to "sneak out" of the house when you leave, so your baby doesn't cry. But, you are NOT helping your baby with his anxiety—you only make it worse. He doesn't know if you are leaving for a minute or for a lifetime. If your baby is prepared for your departure, he will protest for a few minutes and then move on.

Q. My child freaks out with strangers. How do I make him more comfortable?

Be patient. All babies, but especially the slow-to-warm-up ones, are afraid of strangers. They need some time to check out these people and make sure they are okay. And "strangers" to a baby might include a grand-

5. **Positive Reinforcement**. Catch your child being good. Tell your child how proud you are when they are behaving well. This will pay off.

6. **Avoid Unintentional Reinforcement**. Any attention (good or bad) that you pay a child is attention. So behaviors that cause a reaction from you (even a negative reaction) are likely to be repeated by your child. What you are doing is reinforcing a behavior you don't want to see. Think before you react.

7. **Give Choices/Teach Consequences**. As your child gets older, he (who is seeking independence) will appreciate being given choices. Instead of getting into a power struggle, let him pick the consequence of his actions. Example: If your child insists on picking out his pajamas (which might take a long time), then he will opt not to read books that night. One real world parent tip: LIMIT the number of choices any baby is offered. Too much choice can be overwhelming.

8. **Loss Of Privileges**. As your child gets older, he will appreciate that certain activities are special. You can reinforce consequences of actions by withholding special activities for misbehavior. The most important activity in your child's world is special time with a parent (not TV time, dessert, etc). Use this to your advantage. Bottom Line: Whatever discipline style you use, BE CONSISTENT. If your child knows he can get his way if he persists, he will.

parent who lives out of town.

To help the situation, let your baby watch this person before handing him over. Then, stay in your child's view for a while after the hand off.

It's probably a good idea to have consistent caregivers while your child is in his stranger anxiety mode (nine to 15 months).

Q. My baby is playing with his genitals. How do I make him stop?

He is normal and you don't need to stop him.

The official term is **MASTURBATION**. It is amazing how quickly babies find these body parts, and yes, it does feel good to touch them. P.S. Erections are also normal.

For now, there is little you can do to limit this behavior. As your child gets older (18 months) you can start explaining to him that it's okay to touch down there, but only when he is at home/in his room. This is a good segue into a discussion that no one else touches or looks down there except for Mom, Dad, and Doctor.

Masturbation is in the same category of self-soothing behaviors as thumb sucking. You won't be able to eliminate these behaviors, but you can limit where and when they are occurring.

Reality Check

Boys aren't the only ones exploring their pleasure zones. I had a female patient who would ride the high chairs at restaurants. Needless to say, her parents didn't take her out to eat much.

THE QUIET ZONE—WHEN YOU ARE REALLY IN TROUBLE!

When our oldest son became a toddler, we had our share of discipline problems. In hindsight we think he was a pretty well behaved guy. But we learned one important tip we wanted to pass along to all you first time parents: if your rambunctious child is unusually quiet, check it out quickly.

You see, Ben normally exhausted us and once, when we were sitting in the living room resting from a particularly long day, we began to notice how quiet the house was. Hmmm, should we investigate? Boy it was hard to give up the couch, but eventually we pried ourselves loose and meandered to the kitchen. There we were presented with the sight of our son Ben covered head to foot (no exaggeration) with flour. We immediately turned around and walked back to the living room to laugh our heads off. And of course we took lots of pictures. But then we all had a sit-down to explain exactly why Ben wouldn't be doing that again.

So even to this day, if the house seems too quiet, we are quick to check things out. And while most of the time all is okay, you never know when your oldest child will be using every inch of tape to turn his little brother into a mummy.

DISCIPLINE

Q. My nine-month old enjoys having food fights in our kitchen. Help!

A budding John Belushi. Children start to play with their food when they are no longer eating it. When the food starts to fly, mealtime is over. Your child will quickly learn that he is excused from the dinner table when more food ends up on the floor than in his mouth.

Q. My one year old sucks his thumb. How can I stop it?

You can't. The thumb goes everywhere your child does. This is another self-soothing activity. As your child gets to be around 18 months, you can reason with him about where it is appropriate to thumb suck (in his bedroom) and where it is not (out in public). This will limit the behavior to certain times when your child needs to have some down time.

Q. My child holds his breath when he gets angry. What do I do?

Nothing. At worst, he will faint. It is human nature not to inflict harm on oneself. If your child holds his breath long enough, he will lose consciousness and start breathing spontaneously. This sounds really cruel, but a *breath-holding spell* is potent ammunition for a little kid to get his way. If you want to win the battle, you can't give in.

Note: If your child has numerous breath-holding spells, check in with your doctor. Occasionally, this can be related to iron deficiency anemia.

Q. My child is biting me. What do I do?

Don't bite back. And whatever you do, don't scream.

When babies are teething, they often start to gnaw on whatever is available. This may be a parent's shoulder or Mom's nipple (OUCH!). It's not malicious. But, if you respond dramatically, it will encourage your baby to bite again.

Your response: Take your baby off your body and place him on the floor. Calmly and sternly say, "No biting." Do not pay any attention to your baby for one minute. Your baby yearns for your attention so this is a good punishment. Lick your wounds later, out of sight from your baby.

It may take 20-30 times before your baby gets the message, but he will.

Q. My child is biting/being bitten at daycare. What do I do?

Talk to the daycare director and do an observation in the classroom.

There is a biter or hitter in every room. A good childcare program will be constantly watching the children and be able to prevent Hannibal Lecter, Jr. from successfully drawing blood from another child.

Reality Check

My son's kindergarten teacher had a wonderful motto. "If I'm doing my job, I don't have to discipline these kids." The point is, children who have the opportunity to bite or hit are those that aren't being watched closely enough by an adult caregiver. If your child is biting, do an observation in the classroom.

DISCIPLINE

Q. We are traveling with our baby. Do you have any tips?

For starters, lower your expectations. Then you can be pleasantly surprised when things go smoothly. How your baby does with a travel adventure depends on his temperament.

Regardless of the mode of travel, bring a "goodie" bag packed with old favorites and new toys/books to explore. Remember the New Toy Rule: whipping out a special new toy your child has never seen before can provide a valuable distraction. It still works on our babies and one of them is in middle school now. If your baby likes music, take an iPod with some fun songs.

And try to travel at off-peak times—traffic delays and delayed flights make the experience that much more challenging.

For air travel:

- Get a seat for your baby, if possible. The National Transportation Safety Board recommends that kids under age two be restrained in their own seats while in the air, but the FAA does not require it. Check to see if your airline will discount that seat—it's rare but worth a try.

- Feed baby on takeoff and landing. Babies don't know that yawning will equalize pressure in their ears as cabin pressure changes. Drinking works the same way as yawning.

- What about drugs? Parents often ask about giving Benadryl (diphenhydramine) to make their babies sleep through the flight. If your baby is under six months old or your flight is less than six hours long, I don't suggest it. If you are taking an international flight, it is a consideration but check with your doctor first.

- Can my baby fly with a cold or ear infection? Yes. For either issue, using decongestant nose spray (see Appendix A, "Medications") before takeoff reduces nasal secretions and makes cabin pressure changes less unpleasant (see Chapter 13, "Infections" for more info).

Finally, here's when you know you're getting through to your kids: My four-year-old was watching a football game on TV with my husband. One of the teams called time out. My daughter astutely asked, "Daddy, why is the team in Time Out?"

Baby 411

Section 4
Sickness & How to Avoid it!

Vaccinations
Chapter 12

"No man is an island, entire of itself; every man is a piece of the continent, a part of the main..."

~ John Donne (1572-1631)

What's in this Chapter

- **The Top 15 Vaccine Questions**
- **The vaccination schedule**
- **Vaccine preventable diseases**
- **Optional vaccines**
- **Controversies and Misconceptions**
  - MMR and Autism
  - Rotavirus
  - Thimerosal
  - Vaccine shortages
- **Where to get more information**

It's time to jump right into the deep end of one of the most controversial subjects you'll find in parent circles—vaccines. Nothing seems to stir the blood these days more than a good ol' fashion debate on vaccinating your child.

Before we get to our take on this debate, let's go back in time a bit. Well, more than a bit. How about three million years? While watching the Discovery Channel show *Walking with Caveman* with our kids, a thought occurred to us—why did we survive while other early humans didn't?

Hundreds of thousands of years of human evolution boiled down to this: survival meant more than making tools and finding food more efficiently. The "cavemen" that evolved into our ancestors had one crucial advantage—they had imagination. They could plan for the future. And it was the evolution of imagination and our ability to anticipate the future that made the crucial difference. What resulted was a sense of responsibility . . . to ourselves and to our society.

We don't think we ever appreciated that responsibility more than on September 11, 2001. We suddenly felt closer to every person in this country, and we felt stronger about our civic duty to work together as a community.

So, what's all this pontificating have to do with vaccines? It's that responsibility issue again. Just look at a bit more recent history: in the 1890's, people would have seven or eight children in their families and only half of them would survive childhood. Just go to an old graveyard some time and look at the ages listed on the headstones. Many of the diseases that killed those children are now prevented by vaccination. It's a fact: vaccinations, single-handedly, have increased the life expectancy of our nation's children.

Again, you might say "so?" Well, the key to a vaccine's success is that *everyone* in the community gets vaccinated. Think about that for a minute. As a society, we are often taught to think just about ourselves—and to be suspicious of the Establishment. Or the Government. Yet, vaccines won't work if a large number of folks just choose to opt out of the system and their responsibility. Germs are rather simple creatures . . . they just look for a new person to infect. They don't play politics.

A Bit of History: Smallpox

So where did the idea of vaccinations develop? It took centuries of observation as well as trial and error. (And sometimes, error meant death.) The first real step was describing the disease, in this case, smallpox. Smallpox was a deadly disease that, historically, wiped out entire civilizations. The earliest descriptions can be found as far back as the ninth and tenth centuries among Turks. In fact, "inoculation" or the infecting of a person with the disease in hopes of introducing a mild form and then creating immunity was practiced first in Asia. In the 1700's an English aristocrat, Lady Mary Wortly Montagu, was living in Constantinople and learned of the practice of inoculation (known then as variolation). She had her son inoculated and subsequently, brought the practice back to England.

At about the same time, an English country doctor, Edward Jenner, made an interesting connection: farmers who had been exposed to cowpox (a common disease in cattle at the time) never seemed to get smallpox infections during epidemics. He began to study the idea that vaccinating humans with cowpox virus would make them immune to smallpox. In 1798 he published a paper on his idea and called it "vaccination." Not to say, by the way, that Dr. Jenner's idea was accepted with completely open arms. In the nineteenth century there did emerge a group opposed to vaccination led by Mary C. Hume. See, even the anti-vaccination lobby has been around a long time! Of course, in those days, you could be prosecuted for refusing to vaccinate.[1]

People were inoculated with a small amount of cowpox virus on their arm. It caused a localized infection at that site (hence, the scar that we thirty-somethings and above bear). And true to Dr. Jenner's hypothesis, it provided protection against smallpox disease. In 1972, the United States stopped vaccinating against smallpox because it was no longer a threat to the population. In 1977, the last case of smallpox occurred in Somalia. In 1980, the World Health Organization declared the world free of smallpox, thanks to a global effort to immunize all children.

The success of the smallpox vaccine and other scientific discoveries led to the evolution of many vaccines. These new, safer vaccines are extremely effective in preventing diseases and epidemics that our grandparents and parents can still remember.

Today's Paradox—Have Vaccines Been Too Successful?

As you can see, vaccinations are one of the greatest achievements in medical history. Above all other advances in public health, vaccinations have significantly decreased infant and childhood mortality. Yet, amazingly, doctors have to convince many of today's parents that immunizing their child is extremely important, not "optional." Most parents have not spent a night in a pediatric intensive care unit with a child who has HIB meningitis, watched a child gasping for breath with whooping cough, or seen a child die with a Strep infection as a complication of chickenpox. Sadly, every pediatrician has had one of these experiences and has known that the child's illness or death could have been prevented by vaccination.

That's the bitter irony of today's vaccine "debate." As a vaccinated society, we've made diseases like whooping cough so rare that parents have no idea today how devastating it was and still can be. Hence it is easy to pontificate about real or imagined risks with vaccines when you don't see the real devastation the original disease created.

Reality Check

The concept of "public health" has been around since antiquity. Obviously, rulers had a vested interest in keeping their subjects healthy so they had a society to rule. Through the years, governments have been responsible for managing numerous programs. The most important advances in public health have been vaccination programs, water purification, and waste disposal/sanitation systems. The only way for public health to work, though, is for all members of the community to follow the same rules.

BOTTOM LINE

The decision to vaccinate your child impacts the health of other children in the community. Choosing NOT to vaccinate your child is choosing to put your child AND your community's children at risk. This is a public health issue, not just a personal one. As a parent, you want to make the right choices for your child to protect

OUTBREAK: IT COULD HAPPEN TODAY

Let's get even more serious here. European settlers who came to the New World had a very effective (yet unintentional) way of clearing locals off the land they intended to settle. They brought their germs from the Old World and infected Native Americans. In some cases, entire groups of native peoples were wiped out by disease. Why? They had no immunity.

Fast forward to the present day. One obvious real-world example: SARS (Sudden Acute Respiratory Syndrome). Here's a new virus that in a matter of weeks spread around the world and killed hundreds. Thanks to today's modern air travel system, a bug can go from a regional problem to a worldwide epidemic in a blink of an eye. SARS, like many of the diseases we vaccinate for, is a VIRUS. There is no medication to stop the spread of infection—despite our scientifically advanced world.[2]

them. We want you to ask questions. We want you to be informed. And we want you to get your child vaccinated. YOUR decision impacts OUR children.

There are two critical points for vaccination to work:
1. *You need to be vaccinated.*
2. *Your neighbor needs to be vaccinated.*

This concept is called herd immunity. And yes, you are a member of a herd. When 90-95% of "the herd" is protected, it is nearly impossible for a germ to cause an epidemic. Think of germs as rain. Vaccination is a raincoat. Even with a raincoat on, you can still get wet. You need an umbrella, too. The umbrella is "herd immunity." Those who don't vaccinate expect someone to share their umbrella when it rains. But society can only buy umbrellas TOGETHER. And raincoats aren't made for newborns—they need umbrellas!

The Top 15 Vaccine Questions

1 WHAT ARE VACCINES? Vaccines are materials that are given to a person to protect them from disease (that is, provide immunity). The word vaccine is derived from "vaccinia" (cowpox virus), which was used to create the first vaccine in history (smallpox).

Modern medicine has created many vaccines. Vaccines PREVENT viral and bacteria infections that used to cause serious illness and death.

2 HOW DO VACCINES WORK? Here is your microbiology lesson for today. Your immune system is your body's defense against foreign invaders (viruses, bacteria, parasites). Vaccines prepare your body to recognize foreigners without getting infected. A vaccine revs up your immune system to make antibodies (smart bombs with memory) for the signature of a particular germ. So, if your body sees the real germ, voila! You already know how to fight it off.

There are three types of vaccinations: inactivated, live attenuated, and inactivated bacterial toxins.

FIVE BIGGEST MISCONCEPTIONS ABOUT VACCINES

Pop online to any of the anti-vaccine web sites out there today and you'll find a plethora of misconceptions, untruths and worse about vaccines. Here are the top five we hear most often:

1. Diseases disappeared before vaccines were introduced. *No!*
2. Vaccines cause illness and death. *Reactions are very rare.*
3. Vaccine preventable diseases are rare. *No!*
4. Multiple vaccines overload the immune system. *No!*
5. There is a government conspiracy to inject cancer-causing agents into our children. *Dr. Strangelove, check your messages!*

Source: CDC and Dr. Brown's patients.

- *Inactivated vaccines* do not contain any living germs. An immune response forms against either a dead germ, part of the germ (recombinant DNA), or a protein or sugar marker that sits on the outer layer of the germ (its signature). Very cool. These vaccines are safe to give to immune-compromised people. The only down side is that several doses of the vaccine are needed to provide full, lifelong protection against disease. Some of these types of vaccines include: *Flu, Hepatitis A & B, HIB, Pertussis (whooping cough), Inactivated Polio, Prevnar.*

- *Live attenuated vaccines* are weak forms of the germs that cause infection. An immune response occurs just as if your body had the infection. So one or two doses of vaccine gives you life-long protection. These vaccines are not given to immune compromised people because they can make them sick. Examples include: *MMR, Oral Polio, Smallpox, Tuberculosis, Varicella (chickenpox), Rotavirus.*

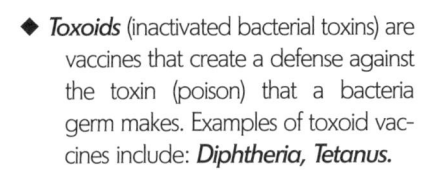

- *Toxoids* (inactivated bacterial toxins) are vaccines that create a defense against the toxin (poison) that a bacteria germ makes. Examples of toxoid vaccines include: *Diphtheria, Tetanus.*

3. What are the diseases we are protected against with vaccination?

Good question. You are probably unfamiliar with most of these diseases since we don't see them much anymore in the U.S. After you see this list, thank your parents for immunizing you.

As you read through the list, note that some diseases are viruses. Antibiotics kill bac-

> **DR B'S OPINION**
>
> "I consider my patients to be my own children. I would not sleep at night if I knew they were not protected against preventable disease. If a parent chooses not to vaccinate their child, it is their responsibility . . . and risk. But, it is not one I will share with them."

Seven Truths About Vaccines

Let's contrast those misconceptions about vaccines with these truths:

1. Vaccines save lives. They have single-handedly reduced infant mortality rates.
2. Lower immunization rates mean higher disease & mortality rates.
3. Misinformation is everywhere—the web, media, and playgroups.
4. The decision NOT to vaccinate is a decision to accept the consequences of the disease.
5. The decision NOT to vaccinate is a decision to put your community at risk for epidemics.
6. Vaccines are not 100% safe.
7. Your parents have respect for vaccinations because they have seen these diseases.

teria only. Doctors have no medications to cure the viral infections. See section on "vaccine specifics" for details on all of these diseases and the vaccines.

Deaths drop by 99%!

Doubt the effectiveness of vaccines? Let's look at the facts. Here is a chart that compares the annual deaths by vaccine-preventable diseases in 1901 compared to 2003 in the United States.[3]

Disease	1901 Deaths	2003 Deaths	Type of germ
Smallpox	48,164	0	virus
Diphtheria	175,885	1	bacteria
Tetanus	1,314	4	bacteria
Pertussis	147,271	11	bacteria
Polio	16,316	0	virus
Measles	503,282	1	virus
Mumps	152,209	0	virus
Rubella	47,745	0	virus
Congenital rubella	823	4	virus
HIB	~20,000	5	bacteria
Hepatitis B	200,000	685	virus
Hepatitis A	unknown	54	virus
Chickenpox	unknown	16	virus

Rather amazing, no? Diseases that used to kill *thousands* (if not hundreds of thousands) now only harm a handful of people—thanks to vaccines.

4 HOW ARE VACCINES TESTED TO MAKE SURE THEY'RE SAFE? Vaccines are researched extensively for an average of 15 years before being approved for use.

A pharmaceutical company conducts medical research trials in a series of stages. Once safety is proven, the vaccine is tested in several thousand volunteers to make sure the vaccine actually works. These volunteers are followed for at least one year to be sure that no serious side effects occur.

Nothing in this world is 100% foolproof, including vaccine science. But the research trials that occur before licensing are very rigid. If you think there are a lot of vaccines on the market, imagine how many didn't make it through the research phase of development.

The Food and Drug Administration (FDA) governs this whole process. The FDA is the watchdog for any medication that is sold over-the-counter or by prescription. There are extremely high standards that must be met before any product is allowed for human use.

After a vaccine is approved for use, long-term follow-up studies are done to assess for side effects, adverse reactions, and potency over a lifetime.

Reality Check

Given the recent track record of the FDA with medications (remember Vioxx?), you may be skeptical about trusting the government when it comes to vaccine safety. But in truth, the system is in place to protect consumers. Although conspiracy theorists might disagree, the FDA really is on our side.

To improve drug and vaccine safety, the Institute of Medicine has called for an overhaul of how the FDA works—in the future, the FDA will do more ongoing safety reviews of medicines (not just before they are approved). And the FDA will also make all clinical study results public. This should help boost public confidence in the FDA.

5 WHY IS MY CHILD GETTING MORE SHOTS THAN I DID? Because vaccinations are one of the most important advances in modern medicine. There has been a tremendous effort to create more vaccinations because they are so effective in preventing serious infections.

Many of the vaccine preventable diseases are viruses. These viral infections cannot be treated with medicine once an infection occurs (for example, Hepatitis B).

Vaccines that protect against bacterial diseases are often serious ones, and resistant to many antibiotics (for example, Prevnar).

6 CAN MY BABY'S LITTLE BODY HANDLE FOUR OR FIVE DIFFERENT VACCINATIONS GIVEN AT ONCE? Yes, probably better than you!

On any given day, your baby is exposed to literally thousands of germs (it doesn't matter how spotless your house is). Exposing your child to five to eight different germs in the form of vaccines is a spit in the bucket.

Young children have better immune responses to vaccines than adults and older children. So they will form adequate immune responses to various vaccines *simultaneously*. (This is studied extensively before a vaccine is licensed). Even if your baby got 11 shots at the same time, he would only need to use about 0.1% of his immune system to respond to them.[4]

Also, the diseases that the vaccines protect against are the most severe in infants and young children. Your doctor wants to get those vaccinations in as quickly and as efficiently as possible.

Q. **Can't you just give one big shot that has all the vaccines in it?**

Medical science is working on it!

There have been a few combination vaccines licensed for use. The largest combination vaccine is called Pediarix. Pediarix includes DTaP, IPV, and Hepatitis B. The problem is that some vaccines are less effective when they are sitting together in a solution. Even if your doctor uses the Pediarix shot at the two, four, and six month visits, the HIB and Prevnar vaccines are administered separately.

More combination vaccines are on the horizon.

Helpful Hints
Top Five Tips to Make Shots Less Painful

1. Distraction. Blow in your child's face, or pull out a new toy.

2. A spoonful of sugar. Put a little sugar water on a nipple or pacifier. It is a known pain reliever (analgesic).

3. Acetaminophen (Tylenol). It's a great pain medicine. Be sure to check with your doctor for the correct dose for your baby's weight.

4. Numb it. There is a prescription anesthetic cream called EMLA that can be applied one hour before shots are administered. The downsides: a) Pain is not just from the needle going through the skin but also from the fluid injected into muscle. b) You may not know where to place the cream.

5. Freeze it. There is a cold "vapocoolant" spray that can be placed on the skin just before the injections. A few doctors use it. It works slightly better than the distraction technique.[5]

7 **WHAT GROUP MAKES DECISIONS ABOUT VACCINATIONS FOR CHILDREN?** There are four governing panels of experts in infectious diseases that make recommendations for vaccinations. These smart folks include: American Academy of Pediatrics (AAP), American Academy of Family Physicians (AAFP), Advisory Committee on Immunization Practices (ACIP), and the Centers for Disease Control (CDC). Because there are several groups involved in this effort, there is some variability in vaccination schedule recommendations.

8 **MY BABY HAS A COLD. SHOULD I HOLD OFF ON VACCINATIONS?** No! This is a common misconception of parents. We cannot stress how important it is to get your child vaccinated in a timely manner. Unless your baby has a fever of 102 or higher with his illness, he can get his vaccinations when he is sick.

9 **CAN I CHOOSE NOT TO VACCINATE MY CHILD?** Yes, but we wouldn't advise it. Choosing not to vaccinate is choosing to expose your child to potentially serious infection. It's also choosing to expose other children in society to serious, preventable diseases. Remember, your decision impacts the welfare of others. And if you think your child will be safe

---

REASONS NOT TO VACCINATE

There are very specific medical reasons to discontinue or hold off on certain vaccinations:

1. *An immune-compromised patient or family member.*
2. *Had disease (for example, if you've had chicken pox, you don't need the vaccine).*
3. *Encephalitis or degenerative brain disorder.*
4. *Allergy to vaccine or an additive in vaccine.*

If your baby has a food allergy to eggs or gelatin, or an allergy to antibiotics (such as Neomycin, Streptomycin, Polymyxin B), notify your doctor before any vaccinations are given. Several vaccines are grown in chick embryo cells and therefore contain a small amount of egg protein: flu vaccine (Flushield, Fluzone, Fluvirin), MMR, rabies (RabAvert), and yellow fever vaccine (YF-VAX). The MMR vaccine also includes gelatin.

Rabies, MMR, Chickenpox and Polio vaccines include several different kinds of antibiotics to prevent contamination of the vaccine itself. Check with your doctor if your child is allergic to any antibiotics.[6]

If your child has a food allergy to eggs, it is recommended that your child be observed for allergic reaction for 90 minutes after receiving the MMR vaccine at one year of age.[7] The flu vaccine is NOT advised for people with egg allergies.[8]

because everyone else vaccinates his or her kids, you'd be wrong (and very selfish, we might add).

You can also choose not to stop at a stop sign, but we wouldn't advise it!

Reality Check

Vaccine requirements for school entry vary by state. There is no one consistent policy. All 50 states allow vaccine exemptions for medical reasons, 48 states allow exemptions for religious reasons and about 16 states allow exemptions for philosophical reasons.[9]

10 I'VE HEARD THAT GETTING A DISEASE PROVIDES LIFE LONG IMMUNITY AND VACCINATIONS MIGHT NOT PROVIDE LIFELONG PROTECTION. WOULDN'T IT BE BETTER TO GET THE DISEASE? ISN'T THAT A MORE "NATURAL" WAY OF CREATING IMMUNITY?

No.

The diseases we prevent by vaccination are not minor illnesses (this includes chicken pox). For instance, would you rather have your child get meningitis and die or get the vaccine? Getting chickenpox or any other disease the "natural way" does not create any more immunity than using a vaccine. And just think of the discomfort, pain and perhaps serious injury that come with getting any of these diseases.

It is true that some vaccinations require a booster dose to keep antibody levels high. That is why we need to get a tetanus, diphtheria and pertussis booster every ten years.

11 WHAT WOULD HAPPEN IF WE STOPPED USING VACCINATIONS? That's an easy one. The diseases would come back.

Vaccinations keep us from getting sick from these infections. But, all of the infections we protect against are alive and well in our world. As of today, the only disease we have completely eliminated is smallpox. And when it was eliminated, we stopped vaccinating for it. (However, "eliminated" may be too strong a word. Smallpox still exists in laboratories in the U.S. and Russia as well as potentially in rogue countries.)

Anyway, it's a simple fact: when immunization rates drop, epidemics occur. Just look at states with lower immunization rates—their rates of pertussis (whooping cough) are twice the number seen in states with higher percentages of immunization rates.[10]

Reality Check

◆ In 1990, low immunization rates led to a measles epidemic of 55,000 cases and over 100 preventable deaths in the U.S.

◆ In 2003, UNICEF sent a team to Iraq to vaccinate five million children against measles and polio prior to the second Gulf war. Why? Because these diseases flourish in cramped housing conditions (such as refugee camps). It is estimated that there could have been 10,000 deaths of Iraqi children from measles, a vaccine-preventable disease.[11] The team also went to post-Tsunami Sumatra for the same reason.

12. WHAT ARE THE TYPICAL SIDE EFFECTS OF VACCINATION?

Fever, fussiness, redness or lump at the site of the injection.

Inactivated vaccines cause an immediate immune response. The body mounts a response to the foreign invader as if it were being infected. The result, typically, is a fever within 24 hours of vaccination. Babies sometimes feel like they are coming down with a cold or flu (body aches, pains). Some babies prefer to sleep through the experience; some choose to tell you how they feel (fussiness, crying). All of these symptoms resolve within 24 to 48 hours of vaccination.

Live attenuated vaccines (MMR, Varicella) cause a delayed immune response. This occurs one to four *weeks* after the vaccination is given. Long after the doctor's visit, your child may wake up one morning and have a fever. This may be accompanied by a rash that looks like measles (pimples) or chickenpox (clear, fluid filled pimples). The rash can sometimes be dramatic. Both the fever and the rash tell you that your baby is forming an immune response to the vaccination. Babies are not contagious and aren't too bothered by the rash. You don't need to call your doctor. This reaction is expected.

Redness at the injection site is common. In particular, the fifth booster dose of the DTaP (at age five years) can cause a huge area of redness. This happens because our bodies already recognize these germs pretty well. Doctors get many phone calls on this reaction.

A firm lump may develop at the injection site if some of the fat in the arm/leg gets nicked as the needle goes into the muscle. This is called **FAT NECROSIS**. It usually goes away within six to eight weeks. It doesn't hurt.

RED FLAG

If your baby has a fever *more* than 24 to 48 hours after being vaccinated, it's not from the vaccination. You need to call your doctor. The only exceptions are the MMR and chickenpox vaccines given at one year of age.

Reality Check

It's okay to give your baby acetaminophen (Tylenol) to help reduce the fever and discomfort of vaccinations. The dose is not listed on the package of infant drops. It says to "consult a doctor." That's because doctors don't want you giving this medicine to a baby *three months or younger* with a fever without checking in first. Other than with shots, you need to call your doctor about fevers in this age group—see Chapter 15, "First Aid" chapter.

13. WHAT ARE THE WORST REACTIONS TO VACCINATION?

These are called adverse reactions. This is the equivalent of an allergic reaction to a medication—and fortunately, they are all quite rare. With each generation of newer vaccinations, the risk of serious reactions is almost eliminated. Adverse reactions include:

1. Death.
2. Encephalitis.
3. Fever related seizure (convulsions).

Both the CDC and FDA keep close tabs on adverse reactions to vaccines via a Vaccine Adverse Event Reporting System (VAERS). Both doctors and patient families may submit a VAERS form if any adverse reaction occurs.

Keep in mind that medical illness reports do not prove an association of a particular illness with a particular vaccination. The job of both the CDC and FDA is to review each report that occurs and see if there is a pattern of subsequent illness after vaccination.

While we would be remiss if we didn't tell you that vaccinations have some risks associated with them, we want you to remember that the risk of adverse reaction is *significantly* lower than leaving your baby unprotected.

In 1989, recognizing that there are rare, serious reactions that occur as a result of vaccinating children, the U.S. Department of Health and Human Services created the Vaccine Injury Compensation Program. This program attempts to determine whether adverse reactions from vaccines are responsible for injuries or death and then to provide the victim with compensation. Since 1989 there have only been 2250 claimants. Considering there are four million babies born each year (or 68 million since the program started) and most have been vaccinated, the odds of an injury are staggeringly tiny.

Another statistic to mull over: 1.9 billion doses of vaccine were given in the U.S. from 1991 to 2001. Only 2,281 cases of allergic reactions were reported.[12] (Compare that statistic to one in 50 adults who have a food allergy!)

We agree that an adverse reaction only has to happen to one child for it to be heartbreaking. But if we look at the big picture, we can point to the millions of children who might have experienced illness, disfigurement and death if diseases like smallpox or polio were not controlled by vaccinations.

RED FLAGS

Call the doctor if your baby does the following after a vaccination:

1. Inconsolable crying over three hours.
2. Fever over 105 degrees.
3. Seizure activity.
4. Extreme lethargy.

Q. How do I know that the CDC and FDA are on "our" side?

Again, the government conspiracy theory.

In the past, some members of vaccine advisory committees had ties with vaccine production. These people were invited to the table because they brought a wealth of knowledge with them (example: vaccine research scientists).

Today, no one working for the vaccine watchdogs (CDC, FDA, AAP, ACIP, or AAFP) receives any grant or research money from pharmaceutical companies. So there is no real or perceived financial incentive to allow a bad vaccine to stay on the market. If there is concern about a vaccine, it will be pulled from the market immediately (see the example of the rotavirus vaccine later in this chapter).

To further ensure unbiased recommendations, the National Immunization Program (NIP) and the Vaccine Injury Compensation Program (VICP) parted ways in 2005 so there would be no perceived "conflict of interest."

Here is another consideration: Why would these groups want our nation's children to suffer chronic illness, pain, or even death? Think about it. It is in *nobody's* interest to increase infant morbidity and mortality rates.

VACCINES

14 **WHO KEEPS A RECORD OF MY CHILD'S VACCINATIONS?** You and your doctor. Your doctor keeps a record of vaccinations in your child's records. If your doctor retires or dies, you may find it difficult to locate your records. If another doctor buys the practice, the records are kept. And some states have an immunization registry that also keeps records of vaccinations.

But ultimately, YOU need to have a copy of these in your personal medical record file. You will need proof of vaccinations for many things. Any childcare or school program requires this information. Summer camps and athletic programs want the records too. If your child becomes a healthcare professional, joins the military, or is a food handler, he will also need this information.

Helpful Hint
It's a good idea to have a medical passport for your child. This should include an immunization record, growth chart, list of medical problems, list of surgeries, drug allergies, and name and dosage of any medications that are used regularly (such as asthma medicine).

Q. How do I know when my child needs booster shots?

Your doctor will remind you at each well child visit.

We wish pediatricians were more like dentists or veterinarians. Most do not usually send out reminder cards to let you know your child is due for shots. What most practices do is provide the schedule in an information packet at your child's *first* visit. Your doctor will tell you at each well check when to return. This system works pretty well unless you start missing well-child visits. Then your child gets behind on his vaccination series. You can try to catch your child up on shots when he is in for a sick visit if this happens.

Reality Check
Wanted: a national immunization registry.
There is no uniform system of tracking immunization status and sending reminder cards to patients' families. One solution: a national immunization registry. Advocates of this plan feel it will improve our country's poor immunization rates. Those opposed to the plan think it invades personal privacy and creates a government health care tracking system. So, like most governmental decisions, it may take years to resolve.

15 **WHAT VACCINES ARE REQUIRED AND WHICH ONES ARE OPTIONAL?** The answer varies state to state. It also varies depending on the frequency of disease in particular counties within a state. We have provided a table of the most recent requirements in the U.S. on our web site Baby411.com (click on "Bonus Material").

Q. Can I take my baby out before she gets her first set of shots?

Yes, just be smart about it.

Pediatricians usually recommend limiting human contact with babies under four weeks of life. Why? Because if your newborn gets any fever (of 100.4 or greater), that is an automatic ticket to the hospital for two days (see Chapter 15, "First Aid" for details). Even if your baby has the cold that the rest of the household has, we still need to rule out a serious infection.

That said, you aren't quarantined, but use discretion when planning your outings. In cold and flu season, avoid crowded places for the first three months of life.

With respect to an unvaccinated baby, the biggest threat these days is whooping cough. Whooping cough is spread by cough and sneeze droplets of an infected person. Babies get a series of four shots over the first two years of life to protect them from whooping cough. To keep everyone inside that long is crazy! But being cautious until she gets her first shot at two months isn't a bad idea.

Vaccination Schedule

The schedule for vaccinations is on the following page. For details on these specific vaccines, see the next section. Note: If you want to know what shots your baby is due for, use the CDC's free Immunization Scheduler. Go to: www.cdc.gov/nip/scheduler_le and just type in your baby's birth date!

Disease And Vaccine Specifics

Let's talk specifics—here is a breakdown of the vaccines and the diseases they are designed to stop. View our website at Baby411.com for a visual library of these diseases (click on "Bonus Material").

Diphtheria, Tetanus, Pertussis

◆ **Diphtheria**: This is a *bacteria* that causes a serious throat infection. It invades the tonsils, kills the tissue, and creates a thick pus lining that can block off the airway. It also produces a toxin that enters the blood and injures the heart, kidneys, and nerves. It is spread by respiratory droplets (coughs and sneezes). There is a 10% mortality rate from infection, even today. *Before the vaccine, 200,000 Americans had this disease every year—and 20,000 died per year.*

◆ **Tetanus**: This is a *bacteria* that causes wound infections. It is not contagious person to person. Tetanus bacteria produce spores that are found in the soil and dust around the world. These are resilient little germs, so we will never eliminate them. Tetanus spores can enter open wounds (especially puncture wounds, animal bites, and umbilical cord stumps) and make a toxin that attacks nerves. The affected nerves cause muscles to spasm (called "tetany"). These spasms prevent breathing and swallowing (lockjaw). There is a 30% mortality rate from infection.

◆ **Pertussis (Whooping Cough):** This *bacteria* causes irritation and inflammation of the throat. This swelling prevents mucus from being coughed up and creates a blocked airway, particularly for those with the smallest airways (infants). Pertussis infection initially looks like the common cold. Over time, infected people have coughing fits or spasms. As a person tries to get a breath in, he makes a characteristic "whoop." Infants, who have smaller airways, are unable to breathe at all. So instead of whooping, they stop breathing and their faces turn red or purple. Children often throw up during a coughing fit. In Asia, this illness is known as the "100 Day Cough." The infection is spread by respiratory droplets. *Prior to vaccine development, there were 200,000 cases a year in the U.S. There were 10,000 deaths annually, mostly in infants.*

Reality Check

Boulder, Colorado has three times more whooping cough cases than the entire state because fewer children are protected by vaccination. Why? A large number of parents in Boulder and other similar communities believe vaccines are at best, a personal lifestyle choice (like nose piercings).

Here is a typical riff on vaccines that was published in the *Boulder Weekly* (May 15, 2003): "Some vaccinations are tied to serious side effects and come with a range of contraindications. Parents who think they must immunize their kids aren't likely to do the research necessary to find out if immunizations are right for their child." No surprise: Boulder ranks 13th in the U.S. for least vaccinated counties.[13]

Again, the emphasis is that vaccines are purely optional—and after a little web surfing, the educated parent may decide that vaccinations might not be "right" for their child. But what is right for the community as a whole? Sadly, states like Colorado give such parents an easy out by letting them sign an exemption, which enables them to enroll an unvaccinated child in public school.

Here's the ultimate irony: today's skeptical parents were vaccinated themselves as kids, but now they are denying the same protection to their kids. Which one of your child's friends or classmates isn't vaccinated? You can't tell, unfortunately.

Sure, you can argue that unvaccinated children make up a small part of the population. In fact a recent study noted that only 0.3% of kids are not vaccinated by parental choice. BUT, remember this: when you have a high

VACCINATION SCHEDULE

Vaccine ▼ / Age ▶	Birth	1 month	2 months	4 months	6 months	12 months	15 months	18 months	19–23 months	2–3 years	4–6 years
Hepatitis B[1]	HepB	HepB			HepB					HepB Series	
Rotavirus[2]			Rota	Rota	Rota						
Diphtheria, Tetanus, Pertussis[3]			DTaP	DTaP	DTaP		DTaP				DTaP
Haemophilus influenzae type b[4]			Hib	Hib	Hib[4]	Hib		Hib			
Pneumococcal[5]			PCV	PCV	PCV	PCV				PCV / PPV	
Inactivated Poliovirus			IPV	IPV		IPV					IPV
Influenza[6]						Influenza (Yearly)					
Measles, Mumps, Rubella[7]						MMR					MMR
Varicella[8]						Varicella					Varicella
Hepatitis A[9]						HepA (2 doses)				HepA Series	
Meningococcal[10]											MPSV4

Range of recommended ages

Catch-up immunization

Certain high-risk groups

concentration of unvaccinated kids in one community (say 10 or 20 children at one school), this can create a perfect storm for epidemics.

Q. What is the DTaP vaccine? I've heard that it is safer to give than the DTP.

This is the vaccine that protects against **D**iphtheria, **T**etanus, and **P**ertussis (whooping cough).

The combination vaccine has been around since the 1940's. The older vaccine (DTP) was called a "whole cell" vaccine because the vaccine was derived from a whole dead whooping cough germ. This vaccine was effective, but caused a significant number of high fevers and convulsions. A newer formulation is called the "acellular" vaccine or DTaP vaccine. The immune response is formed to a piece of the bacteria (its signature). This safer vaccine came out in 1991 and our babies are a lot happier with us.

The primary vaccination series is five total doses. The fourth and fifth booster doses are more likely to cause a fever or redness at the injection site because our bodies recognize it and have an immune response ready to go. After the fifth dose of DTaP, boosters are given every ten years.

The immunity, particularly to pertussis, wears off over time and leaves adults as reservoirs of infection to expose infants who aren't fully protected yet. So it's important for moms, dads, and other adult caretakers (under age 65) to get their DTaP boosters!

Q. Is it true that whooping cough epidemics still occur?

Yes. In fact, whooping cough is alive and well in the hometowns of both authors of this book (Austin, TX and Boulder, CO) as well as other communities. What do these towns have in common? LOW immunization rates. There is no question that whooping cough is on the rise. There were 11,647 cases reported in 2003, 25,847 cases in 2004, and 25,616 cases in 2005. We've hit a 45-year high for this vaccine preventable disease. Most troubling of all, babies still die from this disease.[14]

Here are some things you should know:

1. Whooping cough epidemics occur about every three to four years.
2. Immunity to whooping cough wanes in teens and adults despite vaccination. The good news: a whooping cough vaccine for teens has been FDA approved and is now available.
3. Many cases of whooping cough are undiagnosed and untreated in older people. Have you ever had a cough that just "hung on" for several weeks? You may have had whooping cough and not known it.
4. Dropping immunization rates allow the disease to spread quickly through a community.
5. Infants are given their first whooping cough (pertussis) vaccination at two months of age. Yes, it is the youngest children who are the most susceptible and have the highest risk of serious illness and death.

BOTTOM LINE: If you or anyone in the family has a chronic cough, get it checked out. It's important for you and your baby. And please get your baby vaccinated.

Polio

This *virus* attacks the spinal cord and brain. It has particular affinity for the nerves that control leg muscles and the diaphragm muscle (that helps you breathe). Polio infections leave people paralyzed, or needing a machine to breathe for them. Prior to our modern day ventilators, people survived the illness by living in iron lung machines. The virus spreads through the stool of infected people. This was a common summertime epidemic, and whole households would get the infection. Before the vaccine, there were 20,000 cases of paralysis per year in the U.S. Since 1979, there have been no cases of naturally occurring polio infection in the U.S. There were a few cases annually of vaccine associated polio disease when the live (oral) vaccine was used. In 1997, doctors switched to an all-inactivated vaccination series (IPV; that is, not live). IPV does not cause polio disease.

Q. Why do we still give the Polio vaccine? I thought we got rid of polio disease.

Because the infection is an airplane flight away.

Polio infections occur in 30 countries around the world. There has been an extraordinary effort to eradicate the disease, like smallpox. While this may happen in our lifetime, polio is still a threat.

In the U.S., we give the inactivated form of the vaccine (a shot). The vaccine that was given from 1963-1996 was a live vaccine (a drink) that carried a small risk of acquiring vaccine-associated polio disease. As mentioned above, this is no longer used.

Haemophilus Influenza B (Hib)

This is a *bacteria* that causes a potentially fatal throat swelling (epiglottitis) and **MENINGITIS** (infection of the brain lining). Despite the name, there is no relationship to influenza, the flu virus—yes, we realize that is confusing. HIB is spread by respiratory droplets (sneezing, coughing). Prior to vaccine development, there were 20,000 cases of HIB infection annually in the U.S. and 500 deaths. Most infections occurred in children less than five years old. Survivors of meningitis may be permanently deaf, blind, or mentally retarded. The development of the HIB vaccine is a true success story of modern-day medicine. The vaccine was licensed in 1985. By 1992, HIB infections were virtually eliminated (less than 200 cases per year).

Q. Does the HIB vaccine need to be given separately? My doctor uses something called Comvax.

The HIB vaccine can be given either individually (in three or four doses) or in a combination product. Examples of such combo vaccines include Comvax (which combines Hepatitis B and HIB) or Trihibit (which combines DTaP and HIB). Children form a good immunity with any of these products.

Measles, Mumps, Rubella

◆ *Measles:* This is a *virus* that infects the entire body. Infected people start out with cold symptoms and pink eye. It causes a dramatic head to toe rash, then spreads to other organ systems. These include the intestines (diarrhea), lungs (pneumonia), and brain (encephalitis). The highest rate of these complications is in children under age five. The virus is highly contagious and is spread through respiratory droplets. Measles was as common as chickenpox used to be. *Before the measles vaccine, there were an amazing four million cases per year and 500 deaths per year in the U.S.* Measles is more common in other countries, but international travel easily brings it to our home. Twelve children adopted from China had measles infection when they landed on U.S. soil recently. And an unvaccinated American student brought a measles infection back as a memento from a trip to Romania in 2005 that led to one of the largest measles outbreaks in the past decade.

◆ *Mumps*: This is a *virus* that attacks the salivary glands. Mumps infect the glands located along the jaw line and causes a marked swelling. It also infects other body parts that swell up, including the testicles, ovaries, and brain. Mumps attacks the brain (meningitis) about 15% of the time. It can cause deafness and mental retardation in survivors. Like measles, mumps is spread through respiratory droplets. *Before the mumps vaccine was developed, there were 200,000 cases per year. We usually see fewer than 600 cases a year in the U.S.* However, 2006 saw a mumps epidemic with over 4000 cases in 12 Midwestern states.

◆ *Rubella* (**German measles**): This is a highly contagious *virus* that causes mild infection in children, but fatal or disabling infection in unborn fetuses. Rubella spreads through respiratory droplets and causes a runny nose, swollen glands, and a rash in children. If a pregnant woman gets rubella, the fetus can die in the womb (miscarriage) or be born with severe mental retardation, deafness, or blindness (called congenital rubella syndrome). *An epidemic in 1964 (prior to the rubella vaccine) affected 20,000 babies.* The good news: the CDC took rubella off the U.S. disease "threat list" in 2005 because only nine cases were reported in 2004. But we need to continue vaccinating since this disease is not eliminated worldwide.

The vaccines for measles, mumps and rubella are given together as the MMR vaccine. As an alternative, there is also an MMR–V vaccine that also includes varicella (chickenpox).

Hepatitis A

This virus attacks the liver. And there is a vaccine to prevent it. It's spread through infected poop, contaminated water and food. It spreads rapidly in childcare centers due to all the kids in diapers. Fortunately, children infected with Hepatitis A have a relatively minor illness. Some children don't even have symptoms. Adults, however, get very sick. There are over 150,000 cases per year in the U.S.

The Hepatitis A vaccine was approved in 1995. It is a required vaccine in some states, and optional in others. We'd suggest (as the AAP does) that your child get the vaccine whether your state requires it or not. If it is optional in your state, during outbreaks it will be required for all children in childcare/school settings.

Kids may get the vaccine starting at age one. It is a series of two doses given at least six months apart.

Hepatitis B

This is another *virus* that attacks the liver. There are various types of Hepatitis. The most noteworthy are A, B, and C. Each type of virus is spread differently. Hepatitis B is spread through blood and body fluid (saliva, vaginal discharge, and semen) contact. It is extremely contagious. Yes, it is spread primarily by sexual contact and by exposure in the health-care field. However, children are most at risk of exposure to Hepatitis B during birth if their mother has the disease.

The infection causes skin to turn yellow because the liver is unable to metabolize bilirubin as it should (see earlier in this book for a discussion of bilirubin). It causes stomach upset and lack of appetite. Some people with Hepatitis B recover quickly, while others die. Others have a chronic infection that goes on for 20 years until they die. And some people become carriers of the disease once they survive the infection.

Reality Check

There are *1 million* Hepatitis B carriers walking around the U.S. If this isn't enough to convince you to protect your child, Hepatitis B also is a known cause of liver cancer. Yes, the Hepatitis B vaccine is the first cancer vaccine. Before the vaccine became part of the childhood immunization series, 30,000 children were infected with Hepatitis B annually in the U.S.

Q. I thought Hepatitis B was a sexually transmitted disease. Why does my baby need to get it?

Don't think of this disease as one that only happens to IV drug users or people with several sex partners. 30% of people who get Hepatitis B have neither of these risk factors.

Giving the vaccine as a part of the childhood immunization program ensures that your child gets immunized and has lifelong protection (yes, someday your child will become sexually active). Babies born to mothers who have Hepatitis B need to get the vaccination within 12 hours of birth to prevent infection.

Varicella (Chickenpox)

This is a *virus* familiar to most of us. Prior to the development of the chickenpox vaccine, 3.7 million people got chickenpox every year in the U.S. So most of you reading this book probably remember having this illness. *What most of you don't know is that chickenpox also led to 10,000 hospitalizations and 100 deaths annually.*

The varicella virus spreads by respiratory droplets and by the fluid found in the skin lesions. It is incredibly contagious. The virus attacks the whole body via the bloodstream. Infected people feel tired and run a fever, then break out in classic clear fluid-filled blisters that arrive in clusters. The average number of skin lesions is 350. Does it make you feel itchy just thinking about it? People are contagious for seven days, on average.

The virus itself can cause pneumonia and encephalitis. Even more problematic is that Strep bacteria have a field day with the open wounds when the blisters pop. These secondary infections can be deadly.

DR B'S OPINION: CHICKENPOX CAN BE DEADLY

During my residency, I cared for a five-year-old patient with chickenpox who came to our emergency room with a secondary Strep infection—she died two hours later. That experience has left an impact on me. When parents perceive that chickenpox is just a minor illness, I tell them that story.

Reality Check
Even if a child has a minor case of chickenpox, he cannot return to childcare/school for seven days. This has an obvious economic impact for working parents.

Helpful Hint
The American Academy of Pediatrics and Centers for Disease Control changed their recommendations in 2006 regarding the varicella vaccine. Two doses of vaccine are now recommended. The first dose is given at 12–15 months and the booster dose is given at 4–6 years in preparation for kindergarten. School aged kids who have only gotten one dose of vaccine will need to catch up and get a booster.[15]

Insider Tip
There is a combo MMR–V vaccine that includes Measles, Mumps, Rubella, and Varicella. If your doctor stocks it and your insurance covers it, it will save your child a couple of needle sticks.

Strep Pneumoniae (Prevnar Vaccine)

This is a *bacteria* that is in the Strep family. It is not the Strep that causes Strep throat. It's a distant cousin. This bacteria causes meningitis, pneumonia, blood infections (sepsis), sinus infections, and ear infections. The Prevnar vaccine protects against the top seven strains of Strep pneumoniae (there are 90 total) that cause serious infection.

Respiratory droplets spread the bacteria. Once the bugs get in, they head for the respiratory system (ears, sinuses, lungs) or the brain. They travel via the blood en route to these places. Infected people run a high fever when the bacteria are in the bloodstream. Fortunately, many infections are treated before meningitis occurs. *Prior to the Prevnar vaccine, there were over 500,000 cases of serious Strep pneumoniae infections a year in the U.S. and 11,000 deaths. In babies, Strep pneumoniae is the #1 cause of bacterial meningitis.* The highest risk groups for serious infection are infants and the elderly.

Prevnar is recommended as part of the routine immunization schedule by the American Academy of Pediatrics. There has been an 87% reduction in serious Strep pneumoniae disease (meningitis, blood and pneumonia infections) since the immunization program began in 2000. Interestingly, we have also seen a 50% reduction in pneumonia in the elderly since there is less Strep out there.

VACCINES

> **Reality Check**
>
> There are antibiotics to treat Strep pneumoniae, however, doctors are seeing more drug-resistant strains. It's survival of the fittest for germs—and these germs are some of the smartest around. Twenty percent of the Strep pneumoniae strains in the vaccine are resistant to Penicillin. Ten percent are resistant to three OR MORE types of antibiotics. Daycare children are at higher risk for Strep pneumoniae infection, particularly the drug-resistant strains.

Rotavirus

Rotavirus is a *virus* that comes to visit every winter.

Doctors always know rotavirus has arrived in a community. The littlest patients come into the office with so much watery diarrhea that parents cannot keep up with diaper changes. The vomiting part is pretty miserable, too. Because there is so much water lost in the poop, infants are at high risk of becoming dehydrated.

Rotavirus infection causes about 50,000 hospitalizations of young children every winter. There are also about 30 deaths per year in the U.S. from rotavirus. Worldwide, rotavirus kills 440,000 kids every year. You can see why docs have long wanted a vaccine for this disease!

The FDA approved the rotavirus vaccine (called Rotateq) in February 2006. It's a live, attenuated vaccine given in the form of oral drops at two, four, and six months of age. While it is an optional vaccine in all states, we STRONGLY recommend your child get the vaccine (especially if he attends daycare, where rotavirus infections spread like wildfire). Another rotavirus vaccine (Rotarix) will likely get FDA approval soon.

The most common side effect of the rotavirus vaccine is mild diarrhea within a week. Past rotavirus vaccines had a nasty side effect in some cases: bowel obstruction (intussusception); see the controversies section later in this chapter. However, since this new vaccine came out, 3.5 million doses have been given and results are promising—the risk of bowel obstruction is no greater in vaccinated babies than in the general population. Nonetheless, parents should be looking out for severe abdominal pain/irritability or blood in the poop/grape jelly poop after vaccination.

One word of caution: rotavirus vaccine is a live vaccine. If your baby or any caretaker is immune-compromised (for example, on chemotherapy) there is a theoretical risk of an adult getting the disease from the vaccine (or exposure to the vaccinated baby's stool). Let your doc know and you can discuss your individual situation.

Other Vaccines

Influenza

Q. What are the recommendations for the flu vaccine?

Here are the latest recommendations.

The flu shot is *recommended* for people who are:

1. 50-years or older.
2. Immune-compromised (weak immune systems)

3. Suffering from chronic illness (asthma, heart disease, diabetes), age six months old or older.
4. Health care workers.
5. Pregnant women during flu season (November-March).
6. Children ages six months old to five years old.

The flu shot is *encouraged* for:
Household contacts and caretakers of ANY child aged birth to five years.

The flu vaccine currently used for kids under five years of age is an inactivated vaccine, in the form of a shot. They won't get the flu from it. It provides immunity after two weeks of getting the vaccine. The vaccine is effective for one year. The particular influenza virus strain that shows up every year is different, so we have to get vaccinated for the new bug in town each autumn.

Kids under nine years of age who get the flu vaccine for the first time need two doses given one month apart. One cautionary note: children with egg allergies should first consult their doctor about the flu vaccine (see page 270).

Currently, there is only one flu vaccine that is "preservative free" and allowed for use in infants as young as six months old. It's called Fluzone (Aventis Pasteur). The other flu vaccines contain a trace amount of thimerosal (0.025 milligrams per dose) however, the acceptable limit of exposure is over 12 times this dose (0.2-0.4mg). See the section "Controversies" later in this chapter for more information on thimerosal.

Insider Tip

There is a live inactivated flu vaccine nasal spray called Flumist, currently FDA approved for healthy children ages five years and up. Flumist may get FDA approval down to one year of age in the near future. The nasal spray vaccine provides better protection than the injectable one—and it doesn't hurt. Stay tuned to our website and sign up for our helpful eNewsletter for updates.

Smallpox

Q. Will my baby get the smallpox vaccine?

No. The World Health Organization declared the world "smallpox-free" in 1980 (a major accomplishment). We no longer vaccinate for this disease.

Currently, there is no plan to resume smallpox vaccination. If bioterrorism becomes an increasing concern, we may hear about this vaccine again. Check our website at Baby411.com for more info and updates.

Controversies

Let's face it, controversy sells newspapers and drives TV ratings. No one is interested in hearing about things that work as they should—and vaccines are a good example. As you might guess, vaccines have made the news lately. Unfortunately, rare adverse events and theoretical concerns tend to make more headlines than the remarkable success story of vaccinations. These problems are then seized on by vaccine opponents and spread online through the web like a, well, virus.

VACCINES

So, let's address this head on. Here are the controversies you might hear about with vaccines:

Does MMR Cause Autism?

Q. I've heard news reports that the MMR vaccine might cause autism. Is this true?

As far as we know, no.

Parents also hear that vaccinations cause multiple sclerosis, diabetes, asthma, and SIDS. None of these are caused by vaccination. The government operates a safety monitoring system (VAERS, FDA, CDC)—watching for any possible adverse effects from vaccines. *No one wants to increase autism rates.*

One small study of only eight patients in 1998 led a research group to feel that the combination MMR vaccine might cause autism.[16] But in March 2004, ten of the 13 researchers of the study withdrew their claim of having found a possible connection between MMR and autism. They said, "In this paper, NO CAUSAL LINK was established between MMR vaccine and autism as the data were insufficient......now is the appropriate time that we should together formally retract the interpretation of the data suggesting a link."[17]

Numerous major studies (at least 17 so far) have been done *since* and soundly refute this theory. The most prominent: the Institute of Medicine's 2004 report clearly dispelled any link of MMR to autism.

Q. If the MMR vaccine doesn't cause autism, why is the diagnosis made around the same time as the vaccination?

One of the criteria used to make a diagnosis of autism is a language delay. Because children do not have significant expressive language under a year of age, doctors have to wait until 15 to 18 months to confirm a language delay and make the diagnosis. That's about the same time as the MMR vaccination, which leads some parents to wonder about autism and vaccination.

Q. Why don't we just give the MMR vaccine separately?

A reasonable question.

Yes, the vaccines are produced separately but most doctors' offices just stock the combination MMR vaccine (instead of the individual doses). My practice has checked into this for a few families (usually about one patient a year asks for it). The individual vaccines can be special ordered from the manufacturer—If you really want to do this, plan ahead and order it before the one-year well check.

It is not the recommendation of the AAP to administer the shots separately because there is no additional risk when the vaccines are given in combination. It is also easier to ensure that children have received all the shots they need by using the combination MMR vaccine.

Rotavirus

Q. I've heard about a vaccine that was taken off the market. What was the problem with it? It makes me nervous about other new vaccines.

The original rotavirus vaccine was approved in August 1998 after a study was done on 10,000 individuals. It looked like a safe vaccine. That vaccine was then given to 1.5 million children over a period of nine months. During this time, there were 15 reports of bowel obstruction (intussusception) that occurred within a week of being vaccinated. There were no deaths. The CDC immediately pulled the vaccine off the market and initiated an investigation.

Although this was certainly a setback for new vaccinations, it proves that the adverse events reporting system (VAERS) works. Modifications have been made to the license process as a result of the rotavirus vaccine. This was the first vaccine recall in over 20 years.

As we mentioned earlier in the chapter, a new rotavirus vaccine has debuted—it was studied in 70,000 infants in Latin America and Europe before getting the nod by the FDA. After a year on the market and over 3.5 million doses administered, this new vaccine appears to be very safe. But given the history of the previous rotavirus vaccine, the FDA is being cautious and closely monitoring reports for any cases of bowel obstruction.

The Thimerosal (Mercury) Controversy

Q. I've heard there is mercury preservative in the vaccines. Is this true?

Not anymore. It was removed from all required childhood vaccines by 2001. This deserves repeating: *YOUR baby will not be getting required vaccines that contain mercury (thimerosal) as a preservative.*

Despite the fact that vaccines are mercury preservative-free now, speculation persists about vaccines **previously** containing mercury and links to autism. This speculation continues even after the Institute of Medicine published a conclusive report in 2004 negating any association between vaccines and autism. (The IOM spent four years studying both the mercury question and the MMR combo vaccine question and published a series of eight reports on the subject).

Because of ongoing concerns, we present to you: more than you ever wanted to know about thimerosal!

BOTTOM LINE: Thimerosal will remain in the news, the legislature, and in the courts. But the preservative does not remain in any of the required vaccines that YOUR child will get.

Q. I heard that I should still ask my doctor if the vaccines for my baby are thimerosal-free. What do you suggest?

I think you should ask as many questions as you need to feel comfortable. Remember that since 2001, the entire childhood vaccine series went thimerosal (mercury) preservative-free. If your doctor has a 2001 vintage vaccine vial sitting on the shelf (that would be quite rare), he needs to re-stock. To give you some perspective, Dr. Brown's practice buys its vaccine supply on a *monthly* basis.

However, you do need to be aware of the specific regulations regarding thimerosal use. The FDA required manufacturers of *routine* childhood immunizations to stop using thimerosal as a *preservative*. Flu vaccine manufacturers get around this because technically, flu vaccine is optional and not routine. Hence, some flu shots (not the flu nasal spray) contain thimerosal. Ask your doctor for a thimerosal-free flu vaccine if you are concerned. Soon, the flu nasal spray (which, again, is thimerosal free) will be approved for use in young children—that may help end concerns about this issue.

FYI: a couple of other vaccines, Pediarix and Engerix B, are made with thimerosal in the *production process*—but then the thimerosal is extracted

THIMEROSAL 411

Preservatives and stabilizers are used in vaccines so that the vaccinations remain potent and uncontaminated. A popular preservative *used* to be a chemical called thimerosal, which contained trace amounts of *ethylmercury*. Thimerosal use began in the 1940's.

A quick chemistry lesson: Certain compounds have completely different properties even though they may be related. For instance, take the alcohol family. *Methanol* is anti-freeze; *ethanol* is a Bud Light. Keep this in mind when we discuss mercury. We are all exposed to small amounts of mercury. The type of mercury that has raised health concerns is called *methylmercury*. High concentrations of methylmercury can be found in tuna, swordfish and shark from contaminated waters. The information known about mercury poisoning comes from unfortunate communities that have experienced it. Example: there is a large amount of data from the Faroe Islands, near Iceland. The people there would eat whale blubber contaminated with toxic levels of methylmercury and polychlorinated biphenyls (PCBs). Children, especially those exposed as fetuses during their mother's pregnancy, seemed to have lower scores on memory, attention, and language tests than their unexposed peers. (They were *not* diagnosed with autism or Attention Deficit Disorder, however.)[18]

Chronic exposure to liquid mercury causes Mad Hatter's Disease, named for hat makers who used liquid mercury in the hat-making process. The disease consists of psychiatric problems, insomnia, poor memory, sweating, tremors, and red palms. Chronic mercury poisoning also impairs kidney function.

Because of the increased number of vaccinations that children get, the potential *cumulative* exposure to mercury became a concern in 1999.

There are three federal groups that set standards for acceptable daily mercury exposure (Environmental Protection Agency, Food and Drug Administration, Agency for Toxic Substances and Disease Registry). When the exposure was calculated, the cumulative dose was higher than acceptable levels set by the EPA only (the other groups' standards were higher). The Food and Drug Administration mandated the removal of thimerosal at that time for concerns extrapolated from data on methylmercury.

Vaccines still contain other preservatives (more on this in the additives section later in this chapter).

DR B'S OPINION: MMR & AUTISM

I follow the developmental milestones of all my patients carefully. I have concerns for autism and mental retardation long before a patient turns a year of age. But I keep these concerns to myself because many of these worrisome children ultimately catch up developmentally. It is only when I am sure of the diagnosis do I sit down with my families to discuss these lifelong developmental disorders.

I have never had a developmentally normal patient come in for his one year well check, get his MMR vaccine, and come back at his 15-month checkup as an autistic child. The 15-month-old who is autistic is a child I was worried about long before the one-year well check.

In another study, doctors noticed the same results. Developmental specialists viewed footage of children's first birthday parties (who had not received the MMR vaccine yet). The specialists accurately identified the children who were later diagnosed as being autistic.

---

before the final product is bottled. Therefore, thimerosal is not used as a preservative in these vaccines because it is removed before your child receives the vaccine.

However, because of they way these vaccines are produced, both Pediarix and Engerix B vaccine vials will state that they may contain *trace amounts* of thimerosal. There is probably little to no thimerosal in the finished product, but the manufacturer must declare it.

Confusing, we know. Bottom line: It's fine to use the Pediarix or Engerix B vaccines because they are safe. But if you are completely freaked out about the thimerosal thing (despite the evidence that these vaccines are safe), there are other alternatives to these specific vaccines.

The FDA has a chart online that tracks thimerosal in vaccines—we have a link on our web site Baby411.com.

Reality Check

One 5.6 oz. can of tuna has about 0.115mg of mercury. A thimerosal-containing flu vaccine has about 0.025mg of mercury. Computation: There is five times more mercury in a tuna fish sandwich.[19]

Q. Does thimerosal cause autism?

No. The Institute of Medicine reached this conclusion in 2004. What proof do we have?

1. Thimerosal has been removed from vaccines since 2001, but the rates of autism are still skyrocketing.
2. Mad Hatter's Disease (mercury poisoning) and Autism are very different disorders. See chart below.

DR B'S OPINION

"We have spent a lot of money studying vaccines. Now let's spend our research dollars on finding a cause for autism.

"A colleague of mine, Dr. Jill Nichols, said it best: 'This is not the case of two sides to every story. It is a case of fact vs. opinion.'"

3. A study of 100,000 kids in England compared those receiving thimerosal containing vaccines to those who did not. The ones who had the t-free shots had HIGHER rates of autism.[20]

Does thimerosal cause autism? Notice the differences between autism and mercury poisoning:

	AUTISM	MERCURY POISONING
Motor	Repetitive movements	Wobbly, shaky gait
Vision	Normal	Impaired
Speech	Delay, repetitive sounds	Articulation problem
Sensory	Hyper-responsive	Loss of sensation
Psychiatric	Aloof, likes sameness	Psychosis, depression
Head size	Large	Small

Reference: Nelson K. Pediatrics, Vol 111 (3), 2003: 674-678

Q. Are there other additives in the vaccines?

Yes. And you should know about them.

As we have already discussed, vaccines contain the active ingredients that provide immunity. But there are inactive ingredients that improve potency and prevent contamination. Below is a list of additives and why they are there. These products are present in trace amounts and none have been proven harmful in animals or humans.[21]

- Preservatives: Prevent vaccine contamination with germs (bacteria, fungus). Example: 2-phenoxyethanol, phenol, (thimerosal, prior to 2001).
- Adjuvants: Improve potency/immune response. Example: Aluminum salts.
- Additives: Prevent vaccine deterioration and sticking to the side of the vial. Examples: Gelatin, Albumin, Sucrose, Lactose, MSG, glycine.
- Residuals: Remains of vaccine production process. Examples: Formaldehyde, Antibiotics (Neomycin), Egg Protein, Yeast Protein.

See our web site (Baby411.com, click on "Bonus Material") for a list of ingredients for the routine childhood vaccination series.

Vaccine Shortage

Q. I've heard there is a vaccine shortage. Is this true, and why did this happen?

Yes, our country has had shortages in many of the childhood vaccinations. Most vaccines are available now, though.

Now that you have read about removing thimerosal, VAERS, and the rotavirus vaccine, would you want to be a vaccine manufacturer? There used to be 15 pharmaceutical companies that made vaccinations. Now there are only four. When the others left the market, the remaining companies were forced to increase production for the needs of our entire country.

The biggest problem was the tetanus booster. We had such a shortage that state health departments kept emergency doses under lock and key. That shortage is over now.

Prevnar vaccine also experienced a shortage. This optional meningitis vaccine has been so popular since it came out in 2000, the company had trouble keeping up with the demand (1.4 million doses per month). The shortage is now over.

Helpful hints
Where to get more information

Our advice: don't type in "vaccinations" in a Google search. You will end up with inaccurate information from concerned groups who do a great job of creating parental anxiety. The following sites will provide *accurate* information:

- *CDC's National Immunization Program*
  www.cdc.gov/nip, (800) 232-2522
- *American Academy of Pediatrics*
  www.aap.org, (800) 433-9016
- *Immunization Action Coalition*
  www.immunize.org
- *Vaccine Education Center, Children's Hospital of Philadelphia*
  www.vaccine.chop.edu

There are also two excellent reference books written for parents:

Vaccinating Your Child: Questions and Answers for the Concerned Parent. Humiston, S. Atlanta: Peachtree, 2000.

Vaccines: What You Should Know. 3rd Edition. Offit, P. New York: MacMillan, 2003.

Feedback from the Real World
Ryan's Story

Frankie Milley, a founder of Meningitis Angels (web: meningitis-angels.org), offered up this heartbreaking story about vaccines:

On June 22, 1998, a vaccine preventable disease called Meningococcal meningitis took the life of my only child, my son, Ryan. Thousands of children will develop meningitis each year and many will die. But death isn't the only outcome: children who survive are often left with limb amputations, organ damage, and the list goes on.

The two types of meningitis that are most common are meningococcal and pneumococcal (Strep pneumoniae). There are vaccines for both.

This vaccine preventable disease took away my identity, my right to ever be the parent at a wedding, to hold a grandchild, and to have the comfort of a child in my old age. We must work together in the United States to protect our children from epidemics which other parts of the world see everyday. Because epidemics are a plane ride away. And vaccinations save lives.

Notes

Common Infections

Chapter 13

"A family is a unit composed not only of children but of men, women, an occasional animal, and the common cold."

~ Ogden Nash (1902-1971)

What's in this Chapter

- **What are Viruses?**
- **What are Bacteria?**
- **Antibiotic Resistance.**
- **What you always wanted to know about the Common Cold.**
- **When your child can return to childcare or playgroup.**
- **Germ Hit Parade.**
- **Special feature—Ear infections.**

This chapter answers that age-old parent question: "So, when can my child go back to child care/playgroup?" Yes, it's time to take a look at the germs that like to invade us. Infectious diseases are a large part of pediatrics. Adults have their share of infections, but the numbers pale in comparison to kids (a.k.a. human culture dishes). FYI: diseases that are not caused by infections are covered in the next chapter, "Common Diseases."

Common infections are usually caused by one of two issues—viruses and bacteria. We'll cover both in this chapter.

Most infections that your child will get are viruses. These are infections that go away on their own, without medication. One of the advantages of being a pediatrician is that in the case of viruses we do nothing, and our patients usually get better! Many parents don't understand what viruses are and feel compelled to DO SOMETHING. It often takes more time to explain to a parent that their child will get better without a prescription, than it takes to diagnose the ailment.

You will be an honorary microbiologist after reading this chapter. It will prepare you for the numerous infections coming your way. We'll go over viruses and bacteria since those are the biggies. Fungi, mites, lice, and parasites are discussed in "Things that make you itch just thinking about them" in this chapter. Fun, no?

INFECTIONS
Viruses

Q. What is a virus?

These are tiny germs that need our body cells (called the "host") to survive and prosper. Viruses are like little copy machines. Their genetic coding allows the virus to reproduce quickly in the host.

Most viruses enter our bodies, reproduce for a few days, then leave to infect someone else. Examples include the cold virus and hand/foot/mouth diseases (see the table at the end of this section for a complete run-down of viruses with their common and scientific names). A few viruses like to stick around, lie dormant, and then reactivate to torture us again, such as herpes and chickenpox. Rarely, a virus kills their host—one example is HIV.

Here's some cocktail party trivia for you: according to the International Committee on Taxonomy of Viruses (7th Report, 2000), there are more than 1550 virus species, divided into 56 families. Within each family, there are sometimes thousands of relatives for each virus. These identified viruses are just a small portion of what is actually out in the world.

Q. Where do viruses live when they aren't infecting someone?

Viruses can be airborne or live on surfaces for a period of hours to days. Germs live on surfaces called **FOMITES**. Fomites include door handles, grocery carts, gas pumps, changing tables, shared toys, etc.

BOTTOM LINE: Your mother was right—WASH YOUR HANDS!

Q. Is anti-bacterial soap a good defense against disease?

We have mixed feelings about this kind of soap. A Columbia School of Nursing study, funded by the National Institutes of Health, found that anti-bacterial soap, when used for normal daily washing did not destroy more bacteria than regular soap. "We found antimicrobial or antibacterial soaps provide no added value over plain soap, " noted Elaine Larson, associate dean of research at the School of Nursing.

The Center for Disease Control, on the other hand, recently recommended anti-bacterial soaps for patient care settings such as hospitals and doctors' offices. They said that it reduces the number of infections transmit-

---

> **NEW PARENT 411: WHY EVERYONE IN THE HOUSE GETS SICK WHEN A CHILD HAS A VIRAL ILLNESS**
>
> Everyone gets sick because of what families do in their own homes. We hug, kiss, share drinks, touch door handles, touch hand towels, etc. We also wash our hands less in our homes than when we are out in public.
>
> **BOTTOM LINE:** Think twice before you decide to finish what is left over on your child's plate. Is that half-eaten chicken nugget really worth it?

ted by health care providers. They even went so far as to recommend it for surgeons prior to surgery, replacing the age-old tradition of "scrubbing."

Finally, what about the possibility that anti-bacterial soaps are "too much of a good thing?" Some health care professionals fear that the use of anti-microbial and anti-bacterial soaps may help create new breeds of bacteria that are harder to kill.

Ultimately, the decision is up to you. You may decide to keep some anti-bacterial soap for when you are out and about or at the diaper changing table. But in most other circumstances regular soap will do just fine.

Denise's opinion: On a personal note, we have found that in the Fields' household, anti-bacterial soap aggravates our chronic dry skin (we live in a very arid climate) and eczema. We stick to regular Dove soap and wash frequently. Also those alcohol based hand sanitizers like Purell are very painful if you have cracks from eczema. We avoid them as well.

Q. Do we pass viral infections back and forth in our house?

No. Once everyone is infected, everyone is immune to that particular germ.

Q. Why is my child always getting sick?

Because he is being exposed to infectious germs he has no immunity to.

There are literally millions of germs out there. Every time your child gets an infection, he creates antibodies to a specific bug. But until your child has a large immune memory in his body's "hard drive," he will get almost every illness that comes down the pike. Most infections are spread through respiratory droplets (snot and cough secretions), saliva, and poop. Babies don't have good manners. They cough and sneeze on each other. They also explore toys in their mouths, leaving the germs behind for someone else.

Reality Check
Babies begin to get sick when they start venturing out in the world. Here are some astounding statistics:
- ◆ The average number of viral infections per year for kids under age five is EIGHT. Yes, you read that right.
- ◆ Each illness lasts seven to ten days.
- ◆ Most infections occur between October and April.
- ◆ That's 80 days of illness packed into six months of the year.

BOTTOM LINE: That's right, expect an infection every other week in the winter. And that's just the AVERAGE. If you win the sick kid lotto, you could be in for more. Astounding, eh?

Q. Why is my second child sicker than my first?

Because your older child is bringing home infections to share.

Firstborns often live in a bubble for their first year of life (unless they are in childcare). Second babies don't have that luxury. They get carted around to big brother or sister's activities. And big bro/sis share whatever infections they have acquired with the little ones. So, it is natural for a second child to get more illnesses earlier in life than the first.

INFECTIONS

Q. Why do we only see the flu virus in the wintertime?

Viruses prefer certain times of year to attack.

When a virus arrives in a community, it spreads in an epidemic fashion for a period of weeks, then disappears. Doctors know what virus has arrived because every patient has the same illness for a few weeks. Yep, it's a fact of life—viruses are always coming to town, it's just a matter of when they arrive every year. Here are the seasonal patterns of viral epidemics:

> *Summer*: Coxsackievirus (hand/foot/mouth), Enteroviruses (stomach, skin, respiratory, eye)
> *Fall*: Parainfluenza (croup), Rhinovirus (common cold)
> *Winter*: Influenza (the flu), Rotavirus (stomach flu), RSV (bronchiolitis)
> *Spring*: Parainfluenza again, Varicella (chicken pox)

What causes these seasonal patterns? There are various factors that influence the annual epidemics of these viruses. Scientists have been studying this for years. It seems to be a combination of atmospheric conditions and host (that's us) behaviors that lead to the perfect conditions for a virus to attack. Interestingly, viruses can be found infecting people in their "off-season," but not at epidemic levels.[1]

Q. How do viruses cause infection?

Remember, viruses need us to survive. They jump at the chance to enter any body orifice (eyes, nose, mouth, anus, vagina, urethra). Most often, they are spread via the nose or through cough droplets, saliva, poop, or sexual relations.

Garden-variety viruses enter our body, replicate, and leave. This makes it hard to detect a virus or use a medicine to stop a viral infection—by the time you realize you have been attacked by a virus, the virus itself may have moved on.

The symptoms we experience are due to our immune response to the infection. For example, the common cold virus (rhinovirus) attacks the nose. Our immune system sends white blood cells there to fight the infection. The result of the bug/white blood cell battle is mucus production.

Once we have symptoms, the virus has already replicated numerous times in our body. It's usually too late to do anything. Fortunately, most viral infections are not serious and our bodies recover from the invasion.

BOTTOM LINE: Think of a virus as a speedboat. It zips in and out of our body.

Q. How do doctors know that a child has a viral infection?

Your baby's doctor will make a diagnosis based on symptoms (the problems/complaints you describe) and the signs of infection (the abnormal findings on physical examination). *Most experienced physicians are able to accurately make the diagnosis of a typical viral infection on this information alone.*

Q. Are there any tests that can detect a viral infection?

For the most part, no. Most testing looks for signs of a *bacterial* infection. The problem with viruses is that they are extremely small. We can't see them with a regular microscope. And often, the virus is already out of the body so it can't be caught. Lab work that tests for specific viral infections look for an immune response to a particular virus (antibody levels).

Can't your doctor just do a blood test to see if your baby has a virus? If a complete blood count is done on a child with a viral infection, the results are usually normal. The white blood cell count does not rise in response to a virus. In fact, some viruses cause a decrease in the number of cells that fight infection (termed *viral bone marrow suppression*). Influenza is classic for causing a low white blood cell count. White blood cells can be further differentiated by their shape under a microscope. The types of white blood cells that mount an immune attack to viruses are predominantly *lymphocytes*. Seeing a high number of lymphocytes is one of the only useful bits of information in a blood count to diagnose a viral infection.

BOTTOM LINE

Lab work and x-rays are rarely necessary to diagnose a virus in your baby. If a child does not improve as expected, though, doctors need you to call or follow up to explore things further.

Q. Are there any anti-viral medications?

Yes. There are a few available. But all of these medicines must be given within the first 24 to 48 hours of symptoms because they act by inhibiting the replication of the virus. It is useless to take an anti-viral medicine more than three days into a viral illness.

For most viruses, there is no anti-viral medication available to clear the infection. The ones that ARE available include:

1. Tamiflu (Oseltamivir) for influenza A and B
2. Symmetrel (Amantadine) for influenza A
3. Zovirax (Acyclovir) for chicken pox, shingles, or herpes
4. AZT, Abacavir for HIV infections
5. Formvirisen for CMV eye infections

Q. How long do most viral infections last?

You can expect a typical virus to cause symptoms for seven to 14 days.

Usually a fever is present for the first two to four days of illness. While there is a fever, your child is contagious. The virus is actively growing/replicating. The fever stops when the virus stops replicating. But our bodies will feel the impact of the infection for about a week.

Q. Is there any way to prevent a viral infection?

Yes—with vaccination.

We are fortunate to have vaccinations to prevent some of the most serious viral infections known to civilization: smallpox, polio, hepatitis B, measles, mumps, rubella, rotavirus and chickenpox.

INFECTIONS

The Common Cold

Q. What is the common cold?

Answer: a viral infection usually caused by our friend, rhinovirus ("rhino" is the Latin word for nose.)

Here is what you need to know:
1. The virus enters the host body through the nose and goes to work.
2. Fever and body aches occur when the virus starts reproducing.
3. Snot (mucus production), cough, with or without sore throat follows.
4. Symptoms last for up to 14 days, with day three or four being the worst.
5. The snot can change from clear to green and still be just the same old virus (not a sinus infection, which we'll discuss later in this chapter).

So, how long with cold and flu symptoms last?

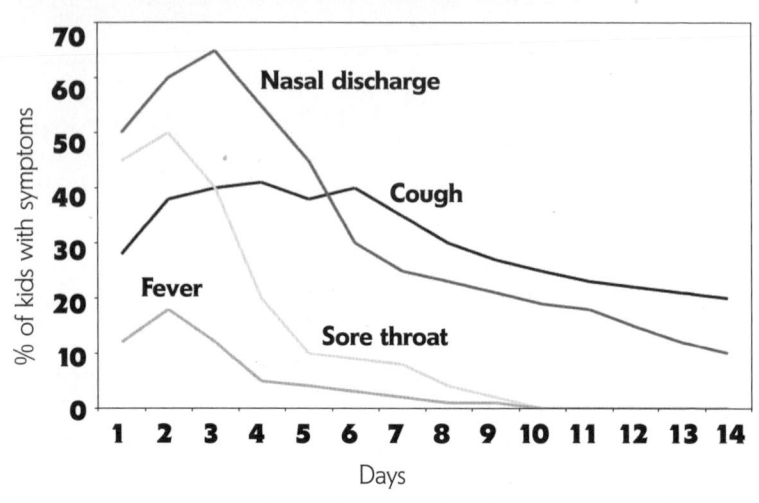

Source: Dr. S. Michael Marcy & Kaiser Permanente from data presented in JAMA

Q. How is the common cold diagnosed and treated?

A cold virus or upper respiratory infection is diagnosed based on the symptoms that the patient has. There is currently no test for it.

For babies, the best treatment is to use saline nose drops as much as needed. Saline is salt water. (See home remedies in medications, Appendix A.) A mist or two in each nostril before feedings and bed helps loosen the

**DR B'S OPINION:
COLD MEDS AND INFANTS**

I do not recommend using over-the-counter cough and cold preparations for babies under six months of age. Infants under six months of age can have a paradoxical reaction to antihistamines (instead of sedating a baby, these medicines can leave your child wired). The decongestants used in most of these medicines can act similarly to caffeine. I personally would rather deal with a snotty sleeping baby than a snotty awake baby.

mucus and often makes babies sneeze. The beauty of saline is that it is safe and nearly impossible to overdose on it!

Remember, antibiotics will not cure a cold.

Top Remedies to Treat a Cold

◆ Saline nose drops.
◆ Running a humidifier in baby's room to help loosen the mucus.
◆ Having baby sleep in car seat or with head of mattress elevated (place a pillow or wedge *under* the mattress).

> **DR B'S OPINION: VAPO-RUBS**
>
> Some parents love to use this stuff. There is no proven scientific benefit and it makes the baby smell stinky! But if it makes you feel better doing something for your baby, go for it. It is not harmful to place it on the baby's chest. See Appendix B "Alternative Medicine" for information on menthols/peppermint oil.

Reality Check
There are over 100 rhinoviruses. Once your child has a rhinovirus infection, he is immune to that one. But there are 99 more that he isn't immune to. Get the picture?

Q. I can feel a rattling in my baby's chest. Are you sure the infection isn't in his lungs?

Yes. It's air moving through snot that you hear and feel. See transmitted upper airway noise info in Chapter 15, "First Aid."

Q. How long is a baby contagious with a cold virus?

In general, the first three days of illness.

With viruses in general, people are contagious while they have a fever. The infection is spread via hand-to-hand contact with snot (mucus). It is also spread from cough and sneeze droplets.

Q. When my baby has a cold, he has a runny nose for almost two weeks. I'm afraid to take him back to playgroup because the other moms seem upset. When is he no longer contagious?

With the common cold virus or upper respiratory infection, the virus is spread in the first three or four days of illness (usually when kids have a fever). After that, it's just snot. You can return to playgroup.

Q. My baby has swollen glands. What is that?

Lymph nodes. Our bodies have chains of lymph nodes that look like a string of pearls. These chains are located throughout the body, but mostly

Humidifiers & Vaporizers: Cold vs Warm Mist Debate

A humidifier and vaporizer both do the same thing—they add humidity to dry air. Vaporizers have a place to add medicine to the mist but this feature is rarely used today. Kids who have asthma and need breathing treatments have a high-tech machine called a nebulizer.

Warm mist humidifiers are unnecessary and they make the nursery feel like the Bahamas. There is also a risk of an older baby burning his hand on a warm mist machine.

Bottom Line: Buy a cheap, cool-mist humidifier. It loosens up mucus so babies can sleep when they have a cold.

For a discussion of which humidifier models are best, ratings and buying advice, see the web site for our other book *Baby Bargains* (BabyBargains.com; click on "Bonus Material").

---

in the neck, armpits, and groin. Each area works to protect a particular body area. For instance, the neck nodes are dedicated to the head, ears, nose, and throat. These tiny glands are jam packed with the cells that fight off infection. When there is an active infection in the body, these glands rise to the occasion, swelling to several times their normal size. They can be tender and can remain enlarged for up to six weeks after the infection is gone.

Swollen lymph nodes point us in the direction of where an infection is located.

Q. What is the significance of green snot? I always thought that it meant a bacterial infection.

Bacterial sinus infections cause green nasal secretions, but green snot alone does not diagnose sinusitis. The nasal secretions are a result of our immune system (white blood cells) fighting with either a virus or bacteria. The discoloration tells us that the battle has been going on for a while.

The change from clear secretions to yellow/green secretions WHEN ACCOMPANIED by fever, headache, fussiness, or prolonged symptoms (over two weeks of illness) is suspicious for a bacterial sinus infection.

The difference between a cold and a sinus infection

Key: --- Fever — Green Snot

Common cold | **Sinus infection**

The common cold causes a short lived fever with several days of snot. A sinus infection causes prolonged fever and prolonged snot.

Bacteria

Q. What are bacteria?

These are much larger germs than viruses. These bugs can live on their own without a host. Most bacteria do not cause illness, and live in harmony with us. Some bacteria cause infection only in susceptible humans (those that are "immune compromised"), or when they end up in places they don't belong (e.g. intestinal bacteria in the urinary tract causes a bladder infection). And there are only a few bacteria that live to hurt us.

Q. I have heard about "good bacteria." What are they?

The bacteria that live in and on our bodies are called *normal flora*.

These bacteria live on our skin, and in our mouths, nostrils, vagina, and intestines. Babies are born relatively sterile (bacteria free). But it only takes a day or two in the real world to become colonized with bacteria. Here are the typical bacteria that are in you and your baby's body:

- *Skin bacteria:* Staph and strep
- *Nostril bacteria:* Staph and strep
- *Gut bacteria:* lactobacillus and e coli, among many others
- *Vagina and gut bacteria:* Group B strep
- *Mouth bacteria:* too numerous to mention here

Q. How do bacteria cause infection?

They enter through any body opening under favorable conditions. These conditions include open wounds, mucus in the nose from viral infection, fluid in Eustachian tubes with a common cold virus, poop and bacteria pushed into the urethra/bladder opening. Other bacteria get in via respiratory secretions, saliva, or sexual activity.

Then they grow and fester in our bodies. Unlike viruses, they like to stick around.

Bacteria either invade our body tissues or produce a toxin (poison) that injures our bodies. Each bug has a particular body part they prefer to hang out in (throat, intestine, bladder, eye, etc)

Q. I have heard the term "secondary bacterial infection." What does it mean?

Bacteria often capitalize on a person who already has an active viral infection.

The viral infection is the *primary* infection. The bacteria that come in later are termed *secondary* infections. This is an important concept to understand why a) you are at risk for bacterial infections when you have a cold or flu, b) you don't often get bacterial infections when you are well, and c) why many bacterial infections are not contagious to others.

BOTTOM LINE: Think of bacteria as tugboats. They are slower moving than viruses. Their lack of speed and tendency to stick around make them susceptible to antibiotics.

Old Wives Tales

◆ **Going out in the rain causes pneumonia.**

The truth: Having a viral infection (cold or flu virus) predisposes a person to getting a secondary bacterial infection (pneumonia is a bacterial infection in the lungs). The weather has nothing to do with it.

◆ **The wind or ceiling fans cause ear infections.**

The truth: If your baby has a cold (or any viral infection), she is more susceptible to getting an ear infection (or another bacterial infection). Like the old wives tale about the rain and pneumonia, the wind has nothing to do with ear infections.

Q. Are bacterial infections contagious?

It depends on the bug and the host.

Not all bacteria jump from person to person. Some just set up shop in one body and grow until they are killed off.

And some bacteria will only cause infection in people who are susceptible (either because they already have a viral infection or their immune systems are compromised—such as premature infants, the elderly, people on chemotherapy, AIDS patients).

As a general rule, assume your child is contagious if he has a fever. The fever tells you that the body's immune system is actively fighting the bug.

But your doctor can tell you if the particular bacterial infection is contagious to others (or read the final section of this chapter) For example, strep

---

HOW A DOC CAN TELL A BACTERIAL INFECTION FROM A VIRUS

1. **Your child is sicker.** Bacterial infections, in general, make people sicker than viruses.
2. **Your child's fever lasts longer than four days.** Viral illnesses usually cause fever for three to four days maximum (except influenza which last up to a week).
3. **Your child's fever is really high (over 105).** Viruses cause high fevers, too. But there is a greater chance it's a bacterial infection when you could fry an egg on your child's back.
4. **Your child has a localized area of infection.** Bacteria pick a body part to live in. The most common bacterial infections in childhood include: ear, sinus, throat, eye, lung, bladder/kidney, lymph node, intestine, blood, or the brain.
5. **Your child has abnormal lab work.** If there is not an obvious source of infection on examination, and he looks really sick with or without prolonged or high fever, some tests will be done. A complete blood count shows an elevation of the cells that fight infection (total white blood cell count over 15,000, and a high percentage of **NEUTROPHILS**—see lab section in Appendix C for details). Or, white blood cells in urine, spinal fluid, etc. indicate that infection is there (white blood cells are never found in normal urine or spinal fluid).

throat (Group A strep) infection IS contagious. An ear infection caused by strep pneumoniae is NOT contagious.

Q. Can you find out which bacterium is causing an infection?

Yes.

Because bacteria don't leave the body, doctors can potentially catch the bacteria and identify them under a microscope or grow them on a culture plate. Blood, urine, stool, spinal fluid, eye discharge, ear discharge, throat pus, sputum (mucus coughed up), and vaginal discharge to name a few, can be examined. Bacteria living in our bodies can grow on a culture plate in about 48 hours.

> **DR B'S OPINION**
>
> "If you can get a child over three months old to smile at you, he isn't that sick. There is a scientific study that has proven this. In practice, I can tell you it's true."

The only problem is that we can't always get a specimen from the location of the infection (like an ear infection). Fortunately, a limited number of bacteria cause certain infections. Once the source of the infection is identified (eye, ear, sinus, lung, etc.), doctors have a pretty good idea which bacterium is wreaking havoc.

Q. How do doctors know which antibiotic will kill a bacterial infection?

Doctors select an antibiotic that kills the bacteria most likely causing the infection. Antibiotics are not all the same. They are each potent against specific families of bacteria. (See Appendix A, "Medications.")

If bacteria grow on a culture plate (from an available specimen), doctors get exact information for antibiotic selection. The growing bacteria are placed on several "sensitivity" plates. These plates contain a growth medium and an antibiotic. If the bacteria can't grow on a particular antibiotic plate, the right medication to keep the infection from growing in the body is found.

Antibiotic Resistance

Q. I've heard a lot about drug resistant bacteria/antibiotic resistance. What is it?

Darwin's Survival of the Fittest.

Bacteria adapt to survive. There is a constant challenge to create more anti-microbials (antibiotics) to kill off the smart drug-resistant bugs.

Many people don't understand the concept of antibiotic resistance. They think that a *person* who is taking antibiotics will develop a drug resistance. *Drug resistance refers to the bugs.* When so many antibiotics are being used in the community, the bugs know our ammunition. Those that survive are drug resistant. The idea is that we can't overuse our weapons—otherwise we will be left with no defense. We need to use our antibiotic weapons judiciously.

Reality Check

Penicillin resistant strains of bacteria, particularly one called strep pneumoniae (see Prevnar in the last chapter on vaccines) began emerging in 1991. Now 20% of strep pneumoniae strains are resistant to Penicillin and 10% are resistant to at least three types of antibiotics. Strep pneumoniae cause five to seven million ear infections annually.

Q. What can be done to stop drug-resistant bacteria?

- Give the Prevnar vaccine to children at high risk of getting strep pneumoniae infection (children under age two).
- Use a higher dose of the first-line antibiotic (Amoxicillin).
- Save the big gun, broader spectrum antibiotics for persistent infections.
- Only use antibiotics when it is really necessary.

Q. When should antibiotics NOT be prescribed?

1. The common cold or "upper respiratory infection."
2. A sore throat caused by a virus (as opposed to strep throat which is caused by a bacteria).
3. Green snot (see the common cold section earlier in this chapter).
4. Because someone else in the house is on antibiotics.

The abuse of antibiotics

Here are a couple of startling stats: In 1980, four million prescriptions were written for Amoxicillin (a popular antibiotic).

In 1992, over 12 million prescriptions were written for Amoxicillin.

It is clear that doctors over-prescribe antibiotics. Want to know the number one reason doctors site for over-prescribing? Parent expectation that an antibiotic will be prescribed!

Truth be told, it's not just the parents' fault. A recent study showed that doctors often misperceive what a parent expects at an office visit (and try to satisfy them).[2]

Old Wives Tale
I am on an antibiotic for an upper respiratory infection. My child is sick, too. He needs antibiotics.

DR B'S OPINION: CAN WE TALK?

Parents and doctors need to communicate better. If a bacterial infection is diagnosed, an antibiotic is in order. Viruses are not cured by antibiotics.

Doctors need to do a better job of explaining viruses. Parents need to do a better job of accepting the fact that their child will get better on their own. And this may mean missing work to take care of a sick child. A miracle "pill" isn't always available to restore your child to perfect health in mere hours.

The truth: Not everyone with a cold develops a sinus infection. That is probably why you are taking an antibiotic. Your child should be checked for a secondary bacterial infection if he has a fever, crankiness, or prolonged symptoms (beyond ten to 14 days). It was common 15 to 20 years ago that if one person in a house had a strep infection, then doctors prescribed antibiotics for the ENTIRE family. Now, we realize that is NOT the answer. Giving antibiotics to healthy folks only strengthens the bugs' resistance to drugs.

When can Johnny go back to childcare/playgroup?

DISEASE	TREATMENT	RETURN TO CHILDCARE?
Common cold	None	When fever is gone.
Influenza	+/- Anti-viral Rx	When fever is gone.
Croup	+/- Steroid Rx	When fever is gone.
Hand-foot-mouth	None	When fever is gone.
Herpes stomatitis	None	When lesions are healed.
Conjunctivitis/Pink eye	None if viral infection	When eyes are clear.
Bacterial conjunctivitis	Antibiotic eye drops Rx	After 24 hrs. of treatment.
Stomach virus	None	When poop is formed.
Viral rashes	None	Depends on the infection.
Chickenpox	+/- Antiviral Rx	When all lesions crusted (1 wk).
Fifth disease	None	Not contagious once rash appears.
Impetigo	Antibiotic Rx	After 24 hours of treatment.
Food poisoning	Depends on the bug	When poop is formed.
Giardia	Anti-parasitic Rx	When poop is formed.
Ringworm	Anti-fungal Rx	After 24 hours of treatment.
Scabies	Body wash Rx	After 1 treatment.
Head lice	OTC shampoo	After 1 treatment.
Pinworms	Anti-parasitic Rx	After 1 treatment.[3]

KEY—Rx: prescription medicine; OTC: over-the-counter medicine

Putting it all together...

Now you know the usual suspects. Here is how doctors put it all together. When a child has a fever, your doctor looks for infection. (There are other causes for fever, but infection tops the list). The symptoms IN ADDITION TO the fever are what lead to the diagnosis. (Vomiting, diarrhea, cough, runny nose, decreased appetite, rash...) The constellation of symptoms and findings on physical examination are often enough information to make the call. Lab work and x-rays are sometimes needed to help figure out the source of infection.

Viral infections for the most part do not require any medication and are fought off by our body's immune systems. Bacteria, fungi, mites, and parasites respond to medication, which helps eliminate the infection. The medication selection is often based on the usual suspects for a particular illness. If an infection doesn't clear up or the patient is pretty sick, cultures can help identify the particular bug and the right medication.

Bacterial infections are frequently secondary infections that capitalize on a weakened immune system that is fighting a virus (ear infections, sinus infections/adenoiditis, pneumonia). Doctors worry about secondary infections when a child with a viral infection suddenly gets worse (i.e. new fever, new green snot, new irritability, new respiratory distress).

NEW PARENT 411: ANTIBIOTICS

Just because YOU are on an antibiotic, does not mean your child needs to be on one. Whole families can get infected with a virus. But not everyone gets a secondary bacterial infection from the virus. Remember that secondary infections are not contagious. So, even if you now have a sinus infection, your baby most likely will still have just a cold.

Viral Infections

And now, for your listening pleasure, the viral hit parade! In just a bit, we'll have a special section on ear infections. But first, here's an overview of the viral infections that most impact babies:

1. Respiratory Viruses

The Flu (Influenza)

Disease: Respiratory illness caused by either influenza A or B. A different strain causes epidemics every year. Influenza causes more severe respiratory illness than the common cold. There is a higher risk of secondary bacterial infections in infants, people with chronic lung disease, or other chronic diseases.

Symptoms: High fever, body aches, and chills. Then runny nose, cough and sore throat.

Diagnosis: Based on symptoms. White blood cell count is low (less than 4,000) with mostly lymphocytes. Rapid flu assay is available, but may not be covered by insurance.

Treatment: Tamiflu (Oseltamivir), an anti-viral, can be given to children over one year old if diagnosis is made within 48 hours of becoming ill.

Contagious: From 24 hours before symptoms start, and while person has symptoms. Spread via respiratory droplets, fomites.

Incubation period: 1-3 days after exposure

Season: Winter

Prevention: Annual flu vaccine offered each November. Now recommended for children ages six months to five years old, and other high-risk groups.[4]

Bronchiolitis (RSV)

Disease: RSV stands for Respiratory Syncytial Virus. (Or, as one of my patient's dads says, "Really Sucky Virus".) It can infect anyone, but causes more severe illness in infants, especially babies born prematurely. As opposed to the common cold or upper respiratory infection, RSV attacks the tiny branches of the lower lung airways (bronchioles). Swollen bronchioles make the air flow turbulent through them, creating a wheeze with inspiration, similar to the mechanism of asthma. In 2002, over 200,000 kids were hospitalized with RSV infections.[5]

Symptoms: Fever, runny nose, breathing faster than normal and wheeze, but no "distress." Infants and premature babies may have more "**RESPI-**

RATORY DISTRESS" (see glossary). *About 30% of children who wheeze with an RSV infection will have asthma.* The cause is debatable. Does the RSV infection causes long term damage to the airways, predisposing to asthma; or are the kids who wheeze with RSV really asthmatics with sensitive airways? Regardless, damage to the bronchioles from RSV takes a long time to heal. Symptoms can go on for *weeks*.

Diagnosis: Based on symptoms. A rapid assay test is available, usually only in hospitals.

Treatment: Some kids respond to asthma medication (Albuterol) via a nebulizer machine to aerosolize the medication. Some kids need oxygen, which requires hospitalization.

Contagious: 3 to 8 days, but sometimes up to 3 weeks. Spread by fomites, respiratory droplets.

Incubation period: 2 to 8 days.

Season: Winter, early spring

Prevention: For children under age 2 who were born prematurely (less than 32 weeks gestation) or who have chronic lung disease, RSV-Antibody (Synagis) provides immunity for one month. The medication is a shot given monthly through RSV season. (It's about $1000 a shot, and the series is usually six injections). (See Appendix A "Medications" for details on Synagis.)[6]

Croup

Disease: A viral infection that attacks the voice box area. The smaller the child, the smaller the airway tube, the more problematic when the airway is swollen.

Symptoms: Fever. Cough is a classic "bark", like a seal. Always worse at night when lying down. This is a three *night* illness. With babies, significant swelling can occur. A squeal is heard. Persistent squealing (**STRIDOR**) more than five to ten minutes is a medical emergency. Adults with croup have laryngitis instead of a bark because adults' airway tubes are larger.

Diagnosis: The bark is usually enough to prove it. A neck x-ray is occasionally done to identify the swollen area.

Treatment: Turn on the shower in a closed bathroom. The steam works well. Humidifier in room. For more severe cases, steroids (taken by mouth or a shot) help reduce the airway swelling. A breathing treatment (racemic epinephrine) also relaxes the airway for kids with stridor.

Contagious: 4 to 7 days. Spread via direct contact, fomites, respiratory droplets.

Incubation period: 2 to 6 days.

Season: Fall.[7]

2. Mouth And Tonsil Viruses

Hand-Foot-and-Mouth (Coxsackievirus)

Disease: A virus that causes ulcers in the back of the mouth, and sometimes a rash on the palms, soles, and around the anus.

Symptoms: Fever, lack of interest in eating. Rash can be flat red dots or raised like pimples. Ulcers in the *back of mouth*.

Diagnosis: The ulcers in the back of the mouth are classic. No diagnostic testing is done.

INFECTIONS

Treatment: Avoid citrus and salt. Acetaminophen (Tylenol) or Ibuprofen (Motrin) for discomfort. Make up a concoction of Benadryl and Maalox (1 tsp of each), then give about 0.8 ml of the mixture before feedings. This coats the ulcers.
Contagious: Up to 7 days. Spread through saliva, poop, and fomites.
Incubation period: 3 to 6 days.
Season: Summer, fall.[8]

Oral Herpes Stomatitis

Disease: Viral infection caused by HSV Type 1. (Type 2 is genital herpes—a completely different infection). Once a person is infected, the HSV-1 lies dormant for life and can re-activate as a cold sore. Cold sores appear on the outer lip and last for a week. Cold sores spread HSV-1 to others. The worst case scenario is a newborn who contracts HSV infection (75% of these are from genital herpes type 2, but 25% are HSV-1). These babies are at high risk of getting an infection of the brain (**ENCEPHALITIS**) from HSV.
Symptoms: Fever over 102 for a week. VERY poor fluid and food intake (at risk of dehydration). Numerous ulcers in mouth, gums, tongue called **GINGIVOSTOMATITIS.** The pain is so severe, some children avoid swallowing their saliva. These kids feel awful.
Diagnosis: Can be made just by looking at the mouth lesions (very impressive looking). Can also be grown (takes 3 days) in a culture by taking a specimen from the ulcer base. It's not always cultured because by the time the culture grows out, it's too late to treat the infection.
Treatment: FLUIDS. Acyclovir, an antiviral, is used for newborns. The gingivostomatitis is usually diagnosed too late (after two days of illness) to use an antiviral medication. Cold sores can be treated with anti-virals.
Contagious: VERY! For 7 days. Spread via saliva and direct contact with the lesions.
Incubation period: 2 to 14 days.
Season: Year round.
Prevention: Avoid contact with child if someone has an active cold sore.[9]

Reality Check

If Great Aunt Suzy has a cold sore, kindly ask her not to hold your newborn. If you have a cold sore, don't touch your lips and don't kiss your family members.

3. Viral Sore Throat

Disease: A viral infection that causes the tonsils to be swollen. Caused by many different viruses. Adenovirus often causes pink eye (***viral conjunctivitis***), runny nose, and ear infections in addition to a sore throat.
Symptoms: Fever, decreased appetite, redness or pus (white patches) on tonsils.
Diagnosis: Based on age group and associated symptoms. No lab test. Strep test rarely done because it is rare for babies under age two. It is extremely rare for babies under age two to get strep (bacterial) throat.
Treatment: To treat the symptoms only. Acetaminophen (Tylenol) or Ibuprofen (Motrin), lots to drink.

Contagious: While child has a fever. Spread by direct contact, respiratory droplets, fomites.
Incubation period: 2 to 14 days.
Season: Winter, spring, summer.[10]

4. Gastrointestinal Viruses

There are many types of viruses that are known collectively as the "stomach virus." They are all treated the same way—lots of fluids to prevent dehydration. The most notorious one of all is Rotavirus. It comes every winter.

Viral gastroenteritis (Rotavirus)

Disease: Rotavirus enters the stomach and intestines. Almost all kids get this infection by three years old. (And you can get it more than once). The kids at greatest risk are infants. They lose so much water in the diarrhea that it's hard to keep the fluid intake greater than the losses. That's why some babies get admitted to the hospital for IV fluids.
Symptoms: Fever, vomiting, and extremely watery diarrhea (often more than 20 times a day). This lasts for about a week.
Diagnosis: Usually obvious by the volume of diarrhea! Assay test is available.
Treatment: Lots of fluids. See Diarrhea section in Chapter 15, "First Aid."
Contagious: VERY. FOR THE WHOLE TIME YOUR CHILD HAS DIARRHEA. Spread via contact with infected poop, fomites. Spreads like wildfire through childcare centers and households.
Incubation period: 1 to 3 days.
Season: Winter (starts southwest and moves northeast every year—the opposite of birds)
Prevention: Rotavirus vaccine, given at two, four, and six months of age.

5. Viral Exanthems (viruses that cause rashes)

See rashes section in Chapter 15, "First Aid" for more info on treatment.

Roseola (Herpes virus 6)

Disease: A virus that the entire world population over one year of age has had. Because it is a Herpes virus (this is NOT genital herpes HSV 2), it stays in our bodies forever. We all shed this virus in saliva and respiratory droplets daily. Mom's antibodies (immunity) are passed to baby and provide protection against illness for 9 to 12 months. When immunity wanes, babies get this infection. The only time you see a roseola "epidemic" is if you hang out with a bunch of one year olds.
Symptoms: Fever over 102 for about four days with no other signs of infection. Kids are usually in good spirits. *When the fever breaks, the rash comes out.* The rash can be subtle or dramatic. It is mostly flat, with some raised areas. Red, blotchy. On chest, back, arms. Not itchy, goes away within hours to a few days.
Diagnosis: Obvious after the rash comes out. The fever often prompts lab work (CBC, urinalysis) to prove that there is not a bacteria causing the fever.
Treatment: None. Acetaminophen (Tylenol) or Ibuprofen (Motrin) for the fever.
Contagious: We are all contagious because we shed the virus for a lifetime once we are infected.

Incubation period: Ten days.
Season: When is your baby's first birthday?

Chicken pox (Varicella)

Disease: Caused by Varicella-Zoster virus, another type of Herpes virus. Like all Herpes viruses, it lies dormant forever in previously infected people. Because chicken pox can cause serious infection and death, vaccination became the standard of care in 1995. The vaccine is given to all children at one year of age and anyone (including adults) who has never had chickenpox. The vaccine is not 100% effective in preventing infection. But people who get infection despite vaccination have a very mild form of the disease. Babies under three months of age are usually protected via Mom's immunity (as long as she had chickenpox). Both immunized and infected kids can get Zoster (shingles) infection later in life (reactivation of Varicella). Shingles infects only one group of nerves (called a dermatome). A group of lesions come up in one patch. These blisters are more painful than itchy. They contain the virus and are contagious.

Symptoms: A full blown case causes fever, body aches, and a rash of tiny fluid filled blisters (called **VESICLES**) that appear in crops. New crops come up over a period of 3 to 4 days. The average number of pox is 350. Very itchy. Secondary strep skin infections can occur. Watch for red areas surrounding pox, or a new fever after the initial fever breaks.

Diagnosis: Classic rash. Virus (found in vesicle fluid) will grow in culture in 2 to 3 days.

Treatment: Acyclovir, an anti-viral, can be given within 48 hours of illness. It will shorten the course of illness by a couple of days and reduces the total number of lesions (not dramatically though)

Contagious: VERY. FOR ONE WEEK. Child is contagious for 24 hours before the rash comes out and until all lesions (which contain the virus) are crusted over. Spread via respiratory droplets and direct contact.

Incubation period: 10 to 21 days. If you know when your child has been exposed, look for infection 10 days later and for the next 11 days. If you make it out of that window, you are safe.

Season: Winter, early spring

Prevention: Vaccination.

Slapped Cheek (Parvovirus)

Disease: Also known as **FIFTH DISEASE** or **ERYTHEMA INFECTIOSUM**. Occurs more in school age children. Questions arise more with exposure in pregnancy than anything else. The biggest problem with this infection is that it can cause miscarriage. If a pregnant woman (usually in the first 20 weeks) is not immune to parvovirus and gets the infection, her fetus is at risk. Unfortunately, by the time we know a child has had parvovirus (i.e. the rash appears), he has already exposed everyone.

Symptoms: Mild or even undetectable when a child is contagious. Low fever, body aches, or headache. Ten days after the infection is gone, a classic rash erupts. The red cheeks look as if someone slapped them plus a lacy, mostly flat, red rash on chest, arms, and legs. The rash can last several weeks. When older kids and adults get infected, they may get joint pains that last for weeks.

Diagnosis: Easy once the rash has erupted. Antibody levels can be checked

for evidence of recent infection.
Treatment: None.
Contagious: Hard to know when contagious because often there are no symptoms. Spread via respiratory droplets, blood products.
Incubation period: 4 to 21 days.
Season: Winter, spring.

Bacterial Infections

1. Sinus Infections

Disease: Caused by the same bacteria that cause ear infections. Sinus infections are a secondary bacterial infection after a person has a common cold or flu. The virus sets up fluid in the sinus cavities behind the cheeks and above the eyes. More common in older children.
Symptoms: Prolonged runny nose over 14 days. New onset of discolored nasal secretions (snot) after 10 to 14 days of illness. New fever. Nighttime cough.
Diagnosis: Mostly by examination. Occasionally sinus x-ray is helpful.
Treatment: Same antibiotic choices as for ear infections, but often needs longer course.
Contagious: No.

2. Lung Infections (pneumonia)

Disease: Lung tissue inflammation that can be caused by bacteria or a virus. Bacterial pneumonia is a secondary infection after a viral illness (cold or flu).
Symptoms: High fever, wet cough, respiratory distress, vomiting. Child is getting worse instead of better with an illness, or new fever after initial fever resolved from an upper respiratory infection.
Diagnosis: Abnormal lung exam, chest x-ray, elevated white blood cell count
Treatment: Antibiotics. Rarely hospital admission—for respiratory distress, need for oxygen.
Contagious: Depends on the bug.

3. Skin Infection (Impetigo and cellulitis)

Disease: Skin infection caused by bacteria that normally live on the skin that get under the skin. Bacteria capitalize on open wounds (bug bites, raw nostrils, burns).
Symptoms: Wound gets red with a golden, crusty, weeping discharge over it with impetigo. The skin is red, warm, and tender with cellulitis.
Diagnosis: Based on symptoms. Bugs can also grow in a culture if drainage from wound is obtained.
Treatment: Impetigo can be treated with prescription antibiotic cream. Extensive impetigo and cellulitis are treated with antibiotics given by mouth.
Contagious: Impetigo—yes. Spread by direct contact with wound. Not contagious after 24 hours of antibiotic therapy. Cellulitis is not contagious.
Incubation period: 7 to 10 days.
Season: Year round.

INFECTIONS

Special alert: Drug-resistant staph infection. "MRSA" (Methicillin Resistant Staph Aureus) is a bacterial skin infection that is a real problem to treat.

Disease: Skin infection caused by staph (bacteria) that is resistant to several antibiotics and can spread through the whole household.

Symptoms: Infections look like spider bites, boils, or red, tender areas.

Diagnosis: Suspicious looking lesions can be lanced to drain as well as obtain culture to check for the germ and its susceptibility to antibiotics.

Treatment: Topical or oral antibiotics, IV antibiotics for serious infections. People who are carriers (not infected) may harbor MRSA in their noses. They can be treated with topical antibiotics to the nose.

Contagious: Yes. Spread via carriers of MRSA, or those infected with it spread to another person's skin.

Prevention: Wash hands thoroughly with soap and water or alcohol based hand sanitizer. Keep cuts/scrapes clean and covered with a bandage until healed. Avoid contact with other people's wounds or bandages. Do not share personal items like towels, washcloths.[11]

Season: Year round.

4. Eye Infections "Pink Eye" (Bacterial conjunctivitis)

Disease: Infection of the eye lining. Can be caused by either viruses or bacteria. Bacterial infections usually cause yellow or green eye discharge. Viral infections usually cause watery eye discharge. One bacteria, Haemophilus influenza, causes pink eye, sinus infections, and ear infections at the same time. About 30% of babies under age two with bacterial pink eye will also have an ear infection to go with it.

Symptoms: Red, itchy eyes with discolored thick fluid draining or matting the eyes shut.

Diagnosis: Based on exam. Occasionally, a culture is done of the fluid.

Treatment: Antibiotic eye drops if infection is bacterial. No treatment for viral pink eye.

Contagious: VERY. Spread by direct contact with eye discharge. Use separate hand towels.

Incubation period: Varies. For viral pink eye, 2 to 14 days.

Season: Year round.

5. Food Poisoning (E. coli, Salmonella, Shigella, and others)

Disease: Bacterial infection spread through contaminated food (and infected people's mouths and poop). Salmonella bacteria is the most common cause of food poisoning (80% of the time). E. coli Type 0157: H7, although less common, can be particularly serious. This bug releases a toxin/poison that causes **HEMOLYTIC UREMIC SYNDROME** (HUS). HUS causes severe anemia, low platelet count, and kidney failure. It is a reversible condition, but can be fatal. These kids are *really* sick with abdominal distention, pain, bloody diarrhea, and **PETECHIAE.** E. coli 0157 comes from cow and deer poop. Ground meat can have bacterial contamination throughout. Because of that, the meat needs to be cooked thoroughly to kill any of these bugs. Whole muscle cuts are only contaminated on the surface of the meat, which are always cooked well. (The poop gets spread to the meat during hide removal or evisceration).[12]

Symptoms: Vomiting, diarrhea mixed with blood or mucus. Fever. Body aches. Abdominal pain.

Diagnosis: Stool culture, blood and white blood cells in poop, some blood test abnormalities.

Treatment: FLUIDS to avoid dehydration. Some bacterial infections need antibiotics to clear. Some bacterial infections should NOT be treated with antibiotics as it causes the person to remain a "carrier" of the infection.

Contagious: Spread through contaminated food/water (poultry, undercooked eggs, alfalfa sprouts, unpasteurized milk, undercooked hamburgers), breast milk, fomites (e.g. raw meat on countertop), direct contact with infected poop, saliva. Salmonella is also spread via pet iguanas and turtles, who are carriers. People, especially infants, who get Salmonella will often remain carriers for months after the infection.

Incubation Period: Varies on the bug, usually 6 to 72 hours.

Season: Year round.

Prevention: Never eat a hamburger that can moo back at you (it needs to be well done). Avoid fresh fruit/vegetables and water when traveling to developing countries. Drink only pasteurized milk and apple cider. Be careful in the kitchen. Food preparation should be separated from baby products (bottles, nipples, etc.). Avoid pet iguanas or turtles.

Reality Check

There was an E. coli outbreak in 2005 blamed on petting zoo exposure. Kids touched animals that had rolled around in cow manure. The kids later touched their mouths with their contaminated hands. Note: wash your child's hands thoroughly after going to a petting zoo.

6. Bladder Infections or Urinary Tract Infections (E. coli and others)

Disease: A bacterial infection caused by intestinal bacteria that get into the bladder. Bacteria (e.g. E. coli) routinely come out in our poop. They only cause infection when they creep into our bladders. Babies who are in diapers are susceptible to bladder infections (especially girls) because the poop collects where the opening to the bladder sits (urethra). Some babies are prone to bladder infections because of an abnormality called **VESICOURETERAL REFLUX.**

Symptoms: Fever, fussy mood, lack of other symptoms to explain fever

Diagnosis: Abnormal urinalysis, urine culture grows bacteria. All pre-pubertal kids with bladder infections have an evaluation done of their urinary tract system to rule out abnormality.

Treatment: Depends on the age and severity of infection. Babies under six months of age are hospitalized because of a higher risk of kidney infection and meningitis from infection.

Contagious: No.

Prevention: Clean poopie diapers as soon as possible. Wipe girls front to back.

7. Meningitis

Disease: Inflammation of the tissues that line the brain. This can be caused by viruses or bacteria. Bacterial meningitis is a life threatening illness. There are different bacteria that cause meningitis in various age groups. Meningitis can be caused by more than one type of bacteria. The top two that you need to know about are discuss below:

INFECTIONS

Group B Strep

Disease: With a newborn, the bacteria you will hear the most about is **Group B strep.** This bacteria is normal flora in the intestines, bladder, and the vagina of mothers. It uniquely causes infection in newborns as they pass through the birth canal. Pregnant women are routinely screened at 35 to 37 weeks to check for the presence of Group B strep (GBS). If Mom is a carrier, she is given IV antibiotics during labor to suppress the growth of this bacteria. If Mom goes into labor before 37 weeks, has broken her water more than 18 hours, or has a fever greater than 100.4, she also gets IV antibiotics because of the risk of Group B strep infection. (Women who have planned C-sections don't have to worry about this stuff.) Doctors watch all newborns closely, but those with GBS-positive Moms get watched even more closely. A standard protocol is to get a complete blood count and blood culture on a newborn if Mom is GBS-positive and didn't get pretreated with antibiotics (i.e. a quick labor), baby is born less than 35 weeks gestation, or if a baby starts misbehaving (temperature instability, respiratory distress). There is also potential for a late onset GBS infection up to three months after delivery.

Diagnosis: Bacteria can be seen in blood or spinal fluid under a microscope (see Gram stain in lab section). Blood or spinal fluid cultures give the definitive answer in 2 to 3 days.

Treatment: IV antibiotics. Penicillin works well.

Contagious: Spread via birth canal.

Incubation period: 0-3 months.

Season: N/A.

Prevention: Prophylactic antibiotics to Mom while in labor.

Strep pneumoniae

Disease: This type of strep is also known as *pneumococcus* (very confusing). This bacteria is THE number-one cause of bacterial meningitis in infants. (It also causes ear infections, blood infections, sinus infections and pneumonia). Strep pneumoniae has developed resistance to many antibiotics. This is why the Prevnar vaccine (for strep pneumoniae) has been a welcome arrival. Since the vaccine was introduced in February 2000, we have seen an 87% disease reduction in bloodstream (bacteremia) infections and meningitis.

Symptoms: High fevers (usually more than 103), *without obvious symptoms*, irritability. If the infection is caught early while it is in the blood, treatment prevents travel to the brain (meningitis).

Diagnosis: Blood infections (bacteremia) by an elevated white blood cell count over 15,000 (often over 20,000) and a blood culture which may grow the bug. Meningitis is diagnosed by an abnormal spinal fluid (white blood cells in it) and a culture that grows bacteria.

Treatment: Blood infections get treated with an antibiotic shot initially, then oral antibiotics. Meningitis requires IV antibiotics and hospitalization.

Contagious: Spread by respiratory droplets. Strep pneumoniae lives everywhere. Some people are carriers. Children get infected when they already have a viral upper respiratory infection.

Incubation period: 1 to 3 days.

Season: Winter mostly

Prevention: Prevnar (PCV-7 strains) vaccine for infants and children under five who are high risk. There is also a Pneumococcus vaccine (23 strains) for high risk children and elderly people. High risk: sickle cell disease, children with no spleen, kidney disease, immune compromised, HIV.[13]

Things That Make You Itch Just Thinking About Them

Fungal Infections

Disease: Fungi are plant relatives (yeast, mold) that don't need light to live. Fungi prefer places where there is little competition (i.e. low bacteria levels). And, some fungi thrive on people whose defenses are down (i.e. immune compromised). We get infected in the following ways:

1. Fungus infestation. These are the accidental tourists. These fungi thrive on our skin, but don't go any deeper than that (**RINGWORM, ATHLETE'S FOOT, JOCK ITCH**). They are passed from person to person, or via a pet. These fungi just happen to be at the right place at the right time.

2. Opportunistic infection. These fungi grow when other factors alter our body defenses to fungi. Infants are susceptible to fungal infections (**THRUSH, YEAST DIAPER RASH**) because their bodies are relatively free of bacteria flora. Kids are also at risk for yeast diaper rash after having a course of antibiotics because the antibiotic not only kills the bad bacteria, but also the good normal flora. Other fungal opportunities include people on chronic steroids or with diabetes.

3. Invasive infection. This virtually never happens to normal, healthy people. A fungus invades the blood or lungs after its spores are inhaled.

Diagnosis:
Ringworm. Classic circular area with raised red border, and central scale. Fungus visible under microscope. Culture will grow in 2 to 3 weeks.
Ringworm of scalp. Patch of hair loss with overlying scale, or dots of hair loss with stubs of broken hair, or big ugly pus pockets (kerion) in the scalp. More in African American kids (fungus likes the hair texture). Culture grows in 2 to 3 weeks.
Thrush. Classic white plaques on a red base in the cheeks, gums, tongue. Looks like milk you can't wipe off. Diagnosis based on examination.
Yeast diaper rash. Raw meat red area with satellite pimply dots. Won't improve with Desitin. Found often when thrush is present in the mouth.

Treatment:
Ringworm. Anti-fungal cream for 2 to 4 weeks.
Ringworm of scalp. Anti-fungal medicine by mouth for 1-2 months. (cream won't kill it). The fungus imbeds in the hair follicle and is very hardy. We see some drug resistant strains.
Thrush. Anti-fungal mouthwash for 1 to 2 weeks. Sterilize all nipples, pacifiers.
Yeast diaper rash. Anti-fungal cream for 1 to 2 weeks.

Contagious: Until treated for 24 hours with anti-fungal medicine.
   Ringworm. Direct contact with infected person or animal (itchy dogs). Fomites too.
   Ringworm of scalp. Direct contact with combs, hairbrushes, bed sheets.
   Thrush. Direct contact with infant's mouth (spreads to Mom's nipples)
   Yeast diaper rash. Opportunistic infection. Not particularly contagious.[14]

Scabies (Mite Infection)

Disease: An infection caused by mites. Mites are tiny bugs that are somewhere between parasites and ticks. The female scabies mite burrows into our skin and lays her eggs. She lays 200 eggs in eight weeks. When the eggs hatch, the babies burrow into our skin and start eating. This is the ITCHIEST rash ever. Even after treatment, people are itchy for weeks afterwards.

Symptoms: The mites usually burrow between our fingers, elbow creases, armpits, belly button area, and genitals. In infected kids under two years old, they prefer the neck, palms, and soles. What you will see is a streak made out tiny bumps—they start out gray, but are usually red by the time medical attention is sought.

Diagnosis: If the rash is classic, diagnosis is made on examination alone. For unclear cases, a scraping of a burrow can be done. It may reveal the mite, mite egg, or mite poop under the microscope.

Treatment: A scabicidal body wash (Elimite-5% Permethrin) is available by prescription. ALL FAMILY MEMBERS GET TREATED. Clothing and bedding used for four days before treatment need to be washed and dried on the hot cycle. Disinfecting the house is a waste of time.

Contagious: Until treated with Elimite. Spread by direct contact, especially by holding hands. Co-sleeping is also an easy way for the whole family to get infected with scabies. Mites cannot survive off of humans for more than 24 hours.

Incubation period: 4 to 6 weeks.

More mite facts:

Chiggers are mites who like pores and hair follicles of people. These are self-limited infestations, but are also very itchy.

Dust mites do not cause infection. They feed off of the dead skin that we slough off on a daily basis. Some people are allergic to dust mite poop and have chronic nasal congestion as a result of it (see environmental allergies).[15]

Lice

Disease: Infection by a human louse. Head lice enjoy feeding on us via human hair. They don't have wings. They migrate from one head to the next by crawling over. They can't survive away from hair for more than 24 hours. The adult females lay eggs in the hair shafts (less than 1/4 inch from the scalp). Adults live about one month. The eggs become thriving nymphs in about one week. Head lice prefer the straighter hair of Caucasian people. Outbreaks happen more in school age children, but younger kids can acquire lice at childcare centers.

Symptoms: Itchy scalp, white flakes that are firmly adherent to the hair shaft.

Diagnosis: Adult lice are brown and visible with the naked eye—but they move quickly. The diagnosis is made most often by finding white nits (empty eggshells). Nits stick firmly to the hair shaft close to the scalp. Dandruff is rubbed off easily, nits are not.

Treatment: An over-the-counter shampoo called Nix (1% permethrin) kills adult lice and the eggs. Two treatments, one week apart (to kill any baby lice that survived the first round). Since the nits are empty eggshells, removing them is more of a cosmetic issue than a therapeutic one. The phrase "nit-picking" comes from the tedious task of removing the sticky nits that are close to the scalp. Some little lice are resistant to treatment.

Contagious: Until treated. "No-nit" policies in childcare facilities are not necessary.

Incubation period: 6 to 10 days.

Creative treatment for resistant head lice: If living *adult* lice are found (not nits), then re-treatment is in order. The list of alternatives include prescription 5% Permethrin (Elimite), Malathion (a pesticide), Bactrim (an antibiotic), and products that smother the lice (Vaseline, olive oil, mayonnaise). A combination of tea tree oil, eucalyptus oil, and olive oil (1 teaspoon of each mixed together) applied to the scalp may also prove effective for kids over age three.

For more information on lice: www.headlice.org

Pinworms

Disease: Pinworms live in our intestines and lay eggs on the outside of the anus. Infection is spread when worm-ridden Johnny scratches his bottom and plays in the sandbox. Suzie plays in the sandbox later and picks up the eggs on her fingers. Her fingers go in her mouth, and voila! Suzie has pinworms too!

Symptoms: The female pinworm comes out to the anus at night and lays her eggs. This causes a symptom called pruritus ani (Latin for itchy tushie). Itchy vagina also happens from pinworms.

Diagnosis: Often based on symptoms alone. Parents can go on a worm hunt. The female comes out of the anus about two hours after a child is sleeping. Put clear Scotch tape on a toothpick and obtain a specimen.

Treatment: Two doses of Vermox (Latin for worm-out) prescription, given two weeks apart. Doctors often treat the whole family. Bathing in morning helps remove the eggs.

Contagious: Until treated. Infected people often re-infect themselves by scratching their anus and ingesting more eggs.

Incubation period: 1 to 2 months (egg is ingested, then matures into an adult egg-laying female in 1 to 2 months).[16]

Parasites

Another stomach infection is called Giardia. This is a parasite spread via water. Yes, this includes swimming pools, hot tubs, and area lakes. Someone with the infection who is swimming in the water can share it. It frequently haunts childcare centers. Prolonged or foul-smelling diarrhea deserves to be tested for parasites.

Special Feature: Ear Infections

Is your child earning frequent flier miles at the doctor's office? Are you exhausted by the constant ear infections your poor baby has had to endure? Then this section is for you.

Q. Why is my baby prone to getting ear infections?

Thanks to your baby's facial structure, her Eustachian tubes are not working right.

The Eustachian tubes equalize pressure changes in the ear and clear the fluid created from infection or allergies. Babies are born with round heads to get through the birth canal. As a result, the Eustachian tubes (connection between the ears and the back of the nose) *lie horizontally* in kids until three years of age. This keeps the tubes from draining effectively. As a child grows, his head and face elongate. The Eustachian tubes ultimately slant downwards (and work better).

When a child gets a cold or upper respiratory infection, the virus causes the lining of the Eustachian tubes to swell, making the tubes even more inefficient. Bacteria like to grow if the fluid sits there long enough. The body's immune response to the bacteria creates pus, and that is the definition of a middle ear infection (**ACUTE OTITIS MEDIA**). Older children and adults rarely get ear infections because their Eustachian tubes drain more effectively.

Your Baby's Ear, in a nutshell

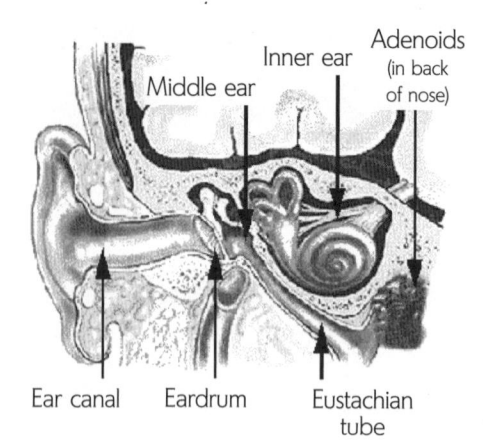

Notes:

1. The ear is divided into three parts—the inner, middle, and outer areas.
2. The Eustachian tubes attach to the middle part of the ear.
3. The eardrum (tympanic membrane) is a piece of tissue that separates the middle and outer ear.
4. The eardrum protects the delicate middle ear bones and nerves.

Ear Infection Facts

- By the age of three, 75% of all children have had at least one ear infection.
- 40% of all antibiotics prescribed for children are for ear infections.
- The peak age of ear infections is six to 18 months of age.
- 90% of ear infections are caused by bacteria. 10% are caused by viruses.

Q. What is the difference between an ear infection and swimmer's ear?

An "ear infection" generally refers to a *middle* ear infection (**ACUTE OTITIS MEDIA**). The pus/infection sits behind the eardrum (see diagram on the previous page). A "swimmer's ear" (**OTITIS EXTERNA**) refers to an infection of the skin lining the *outer* ear (the canal where Q-tips don't belong!).

Middle Ear Infection (Acute Otitis Media)

A normal looking eardrum is grayish and translucent. The bones that control hearing (the ones you learned about in junior high science class) are visible behind it. An infected eardrum has pus behind it and is swollen and red. The pus and swelling obscure the view of the middle ear. *Think of the infection as being a zit.* It has to drain before it gets better. It can either rupture the eardrum and drain (undesirable) or drain down the Eustachian tube (desirable). The use of antibiotics taken by mouth clears the pus and decreases the chance of the zit bursting (**PERFORATED EAR DRUM:** see more on the next page).

TOP 7 RISK FACTORS FOR EAR INFECTIONS

Parents often ask if there is anything that can be done to prevent an ear infection from happening. Here are the risk factors:

1. **The common cold/upper respiratory infection.** By definition, fluid must be present in the Eustachian tubes to allow bacteria to grow. Having a cold is the perfect set up for fluid accumulation in the sinuses and Eustachian tubes.

2. **Daycare.** Children get more cold viruses when they are around other kids. Naturally, kids in daycare will get more colds, thus more ear infections. And the bacteria that live there are more likely to be drug resistant bacteria.

3. **Second hand smoke.** Smoke is irritating to the whole respiratory tract, from the nose down to the lungs. Irritation of the Eustachian tubes causes swelling of the tissues and inefficiency in clearing fluid.

4. **Pacifier use.** Constant sucking seems to create a backup of fluid in the back of the throat and Eustachian tubes.

5. **Bottle propping.** Babies who lie down and hold their own bottles allow fluid from the back of the throat to end up in the Eustachian tubes. The fluid is a set up for infection.

6. **Native American.** The facial structure of this ethnic group predisposes them to Eustachian tube dysfunction.

7. **Cleft lip/palate.** This facial structure predisposes them to Eustachian tube dysfunction.

If you're looking for more information on common ear, nose and throat problems in childhood, check out the web site of the American Academy of Otolaryngology Head and Neck Surgery at www.EntNet.org/kidsent/.

Swimmer's Ear (External Otitis)

This is a skin infection caused by either water that chronically collects in the ear canal or skin irritation from being scratched (from a Q-tip). Both situations allow bacteria to penetrate the skin and cause infection. *Swimmer's ear causes extreme pain with touch or movement of the outer ear* (the part you can see). There is swelling, redness, and sometimes debris in the canal. The eardrum is normal. These infections usually clear up with antibiotic eardrops.

Q. My baby's eardrum popped! Will he have permanent hearing damage?

No. Perforated eardrums heal like a piece of skin that has been cut.

Remember the zit analogy? The eardrum is under pressure with all that pus behind it. When the pimple pops, it lets the pus drain out. The perforation hole is usually small and not completely ruptured. The ear feels better if this happens. The infection still needs to be treated, though. The doctor may prescribe antibiotic drops and oral antibiotics if this occurs. It should heal up without any long-term consequences as long as the infection is treated.

Q. Will my child get an ear infection from lying in bath water?

No.

Bath water is fairly clean and very little collects in the outer ear canal. But it's a good idea to wipe the water out of the ears. It's not a major player in causing swimmer's ear. And it has absolutely nothing to do with middle ear infections (which happen on the other side of the eardrum).

Q. My child was just in the doctor's office two days ago. Now he has an ear infection. Didn't the doctor see it then?

Back to the zit thing. Ears can go from normal to bulging with pus in a matter of hours.

Q. Can I buy one of those ear scopes (otoscope) and examine my own child's ears?

Sure. But you might not know what you are looking at.

An acute middle ear infection may present itself in one of several ways. The obvious bulging red ear is one you'd be able to diagnose. But not all of them look like that. They are more subtle. It doesn't just take the light of an otoscope to make the diagnosis. It takes the experience of looking at thousands of ears for comparison.

Don't be disappointed if you buy an otoscope, feel sure that you have diagnosed an ear infection, and find that your pediatrician has a different opinion.

Q. I've heard that not all ear infections require antibiotics to go away. Do we have to treat every ear infection with antibiotics?

Not all middle ear infections require antibiotics.

A small percentage (10%) of ear infections are caused by viruses. And up to 60% of bacterial ear infections will clear on their own without any consequences. However, bacterial ear infections clear more quickly with antibiotics.

In Denmark, ear infections are treated differently than in the United States. Doctors in Denmark diagnose an ear infection and send a child home without a prescription. They tell the parent to give their child a pain medication and come back the next day for a re-check. If the ear looks worse or unchanged, they prescribe antibiotics. If the ear is improved, no therapy is required.

Q. What happened in the days before antibiotics when children had ear infections?

Some children did just fine. Others did not.

Untreated bacterial infections can lead to *hearing loss* (from chronic fluid accumulation, chronic infection, and chronic ear drum perforations), *mastoiditis* (infection invades the skull bone), and *brain abscesses/meningitis* (infection extends to brain and spinal fluid). In the old days before antibiotics, 80% of ear infections would go away on their own. But the last 20% of ear infections that were untreated led to these significant complications.[17]

Q. What antibiotics are typically used to treat ear infections?

The right drug for the bug.

The most common bacteria that cause middle ear infections are:

NEW PARENT 411: NEW & IMPROVED GUIDELINES

The American Academy of Pediatrics revised their treatment guidelines for ear infections in March 2004. Here's a look at the new rules:

Infants under six months of age with acute middle ear infections will still get treated with antibiotics. They are more likely to suffer complications from ear infections.

Kids ages six months to two years with clear cut infections are also treated, but when the diagnosis is in question, a wait and see approach is in order. Your doctor may ask you to return for a followup visit or have you fill a prescription in a couple of days if your child's symptoms don't improve.

The guidelines attempt to limit antibiotic use in kids with mild to moderate symptoms and avoid use when the diagnosis itself is in question (not all ear infections are so black and white).

Ask your doctor for his or her opinion about this issue. Record his thoughts here:

- Strep pneumoniae (now less common thanks to Prevnar vaccine).
- Moraxella
- H. Influenza *non-typable* (a cause of pink eye with an ear infection)
- Group A strep

There are basically four antibiotic classes that kill all of these bugs. As a general rule, doctors prescribe Amoxicillin (in the Penicillin class) as their first choice. It is a broad-spectrum antibiotic that is well tolerated by most kids, has been around for a long time, and is relatively inexpensive (about $10 for generic). It works about 85% of the time, depending on the amount of drug resistant bacteria living in your neighborhood. That's a pretty good track record.

If it has been *less* than 30 days since a previous ear infection, doctors may select a different class of antibiotics because the bacteria may be resistant to the Amoxicillin (that is, the same bug may have grown back after being off medication).

If there is pink eye associated with an ear infection, there is a good chance that H. influenza is the bug. This bug is resistant to Amoxicillin about 50% of the time (again, depending on your neighborhood). So, a doctor may choose a different antibiotic in this situation.

Q. My child was on Amoxicillin before and it never works.

Your child is not resistant to Amoxicillin—the bacterium he is being infected with is resistant. Children in daycare settings tend to have more ear and sinus infections with drug-resistant bacteria. That does not mean that Amoxicillin will *never* work. For instance, Group A strep (which causes strep throat) is almost always cured with Amoxicillin.

Q. My child is pulling on his ears. Should I be worried about an ear infection?

No. It's not a reliable indicator.

Parents frequently rely on ear pulling as a sign of an ear infection. There was an excellent study done on this suspicious behavior that showed ear pulling predicted ear infections only 5% of the time. 95% of the time, babies pull on their ears because they can![18]

Q. Why do I have to bring my child back for an "ear check" after he has been treated?

Because infants can't tell you that their ears are better.

The antibiotic prescribed should kill the bacteria. But there are smart, resistant bugs that will survive. That's one reason why the doctor wants to see your child back two to three weeks after the diagnosis.

The other reason is that residual sterile fluid (**SEROUS OTITIS MEDIA**) can remain for a long time after the bacteria is gone. This is basically pus that is dissolved, but not dried

DR B'S OPINION

"I always pick the least potent antibiotic that will work in a given situation. The only way to have the 'big gun' when you need it is to avoid using it when you don't need it."

up. The fluid is not infected, but can create two problems:

- It puts a child at risk for getting another middle ear infection down the road.
- It inhibits sound waves from getting through the middle ear (**CONDUCTIVE HEARING LOSS**). It's like walking around with earplugs in all day long. Chronic fluid (more than three months duration) is a problem for a child who is trying to learn his native language (**EXPRESSIVE LANGUAGE DELAYS**).

Q. My child feels better after just a couple of days taking Amoxicillin for his ear infection. Why do we have to continue the medicine for ten days?

Antibiotics start to clear an infection within 48-72 hours. However, it can take five to ten days to kill off all of the bacteria. Stopping an antibiotic early allows a germ to re-grow and cause infection (and pain) to return. Doctors are trying to shorten the course of antibiotics because of the growing number of antibiotic resistant bacteria. If you doctor prescribes a shorter course (five days) of medicine, be sure to follow up with an appointment to make sure the infection has cleared.

Q. We are flying with our baby tomorrow and he was just diagnosed with an ear infection. Should we cancel our trip?

No. Go have fun.

As anyone who's traveled on a plane knows, the pressurized air in the cabin requires you to "clear" your ears (by chewing gum, yawning, etc). Babies have the same needs—their middle ear must accommodate to the pressure change. When a child has an acute ear infection, pus fills in the middle ear space and the eardrum cannot move. The ear won't hurt. In fact, the pressure change might make the drum pop to release the pressure (and that's okay—see perforated eardrum earlier in this chapter).

It is more problematic when an ear infection is starting to clear up. Then there is both air (normal) and fluid (not normal) in the middle ear. The

---

RESIDUAL EAR FLUID

The pus from the ear infection gradually dissolves and gets reabsorbed by the body. The name for this sterile (bug-free) fluid is called **SEROUS FLUID** or serous otitis. 70% of children will still have serous fluid two weeks after an ear infection. Up to 40% of kids will still have serous fluid one month later, and 10% have fluid three months after infection.[19]

The serous fluid does NOT need to be treated with antibiotics to clear up. However, kids with residual fluid need to be re-evaluated to make sure the fluid goes away. As mentioned earlier, chronic fluid in the ears interferes with language development (in the short term).

If a child has chronic fluid in the ears, over three months duration, an Ear/Nose/Throat specialist may want to drain the fluid by popping the eardrum with a needle. Frequently, if the drum is popped, a PE tube is inserted to prevent further accumulations of fluid.

eardrum will try to accommodate to the pressure change and will be only partially successful. This HURTS. Don't cancel your trip; just be prepared for some discomfort on take off and landing. Nursing, feeding your child a bottle or sucking on a pacifier can help relieve the pressure.

Q. How many ear infections are too many?

Great question. For this answer, we've recruited Dr. Brown's husband, Mr. Dr. Brown (an Ear, Nose, and Throat specialist) for some advice:

"Most kids outgrow the problem of ear infections by about three years of age. (See earlier for information on why this is). So theoretically, we can all wait until your child turns three. But there are some important considerations that compel doctors to take a more active approach." Here are some key questions:

1. **How many courses of antibiotics are too many?** Antibiotics can have unpleasant side effects like diarrhea and yeast infections. Being on antibiotics frequently leaves a child susceptible to bacteria that are smarter (the drug-resistant strains) and allows bacteria in the community to see our weapons. From an economic standpoint, every ear infection costs parents a visit to the pediatrician, missed work, and another round of antibiotics.
2. **How old is the child?** If a child is in the midst of language acquisition (nine months to age two), it's critical for him to hear what people are saying to him. Otherwise, the infections can contribute to short-term expressive language delays. In the long run, these kids do catch up and have normal language skills.
3. **How miserable is the child?** Ear infections hurt. That leads to disrupted sleep for the whole family. This important point tends to get overlooked by both parents and doctors.

Reality Check

It's important to look at what is in the best interest of the child. There is some variability amongst doctors, but a reasonable answer to what is "too many" is the following:

- Four infections in the peak (winter) season
- Three infections in the off peak (summer) season
- Three months of persistent residual fluid (serous otitis media)
- Three back-to-back courses of antibiotics for the same ear infection.

Too many ear infections buy your child a trip to see the Ear, Nose, and Throat specialist. These doctors assist in decision making for children with recurrent ear infections. If necessary, they can place pressure equalization tubes in the eardrum to reduce the number of ear infections (we'll discuss this more in detail later in this chapter).

Ear infections occur mostly in cold and flu season. (Remember, bacteria are secondary infections for a child with fluid in his ears already). So, it's expected that more infections will happen then. Kids who get middle ear infections in the off-season are time bombs for the winter.

Q. How can I prevent ear infections from happening?

There are a few things you can do:

1. **Feed your baby in an upright position.** Milk can get into the Eustachian tubes if a baby is lying horizontally while eating.

2. **Avoid pacifiers after six months of age.** There is some good data to suggest this is a risk factor for ear infections.[20]

3. **Don't smoke.** Smoking is a respiratory irritant—both to the smoker and his family. It causes swelling of the Eustachian tubes, which can lead to infection.

4. **Infection control during the cold and flu season.** Good hand-washing and flu shots for the family are helpful. The Prevnar vaccine for your child helps limit some (not all) infections.

5. **Reconsider your childcare options.** There is no question that children in daycare settings get more infections (and with drug-resistant bugs). When families have reached the end of their ropes, doctors may discuss this subject.

Q. Can we just start an antibiotic when my child has a cold? What about preventative antibiotics through the winter months?

Doctors used both of these methods in the past. And to a certain degree, they worked. However, the price paid is too great. This approach created drug-resistant bacteria.

Q. Can I prevent an ear infection from happening by using a decongestant or antihistamine to dry up all that snot?

No.

You would think that if you got rid of the fluid, the ear infection could be prevented. This idea was studied about 30 years ago and it didn't prevent ear infections. There is a reason it doesn't work. When there is infec-

DR B'S OPINION: WHEN TO CALL IN AN ENT

Here is how I would approach making a referral to an Ear/Nose/Throat (ENT) Specialist for a child with recurrent ear infections (other than the "too many" criteria above).

Scenario 1: If a child already has had three ear infections by Thanksgiving, that doesn't bode well for the rest of the season (cold and flu season will continue through March). Refer now to an ENT.

Scenario 2: If a child gets ear infections sporadically through the winter and gets his fourth infection in April, wait and see if the ear infections stop as the season ends.

Scenario 3: If a child gets two ear infections during the summer months and a third in September, the child gets one more chance before referring. But I prepare the family for the possibility.

tion, the Eustachian tubes are full of fluid *and* get swollen. This prevents them from draining effectively.

Q. What are "tubes"?

The official term is Pressure Equalization (PE) Tube.

The alternative to antibiotics for recurrent ear infections is to insert PE tubes into the eardrums. These tubes are the length of a pencil point and the diameter of angel hair pasta (i.e. really small). The procedure is relatively simple. An ENT Specialist makes a tiny hole in the eardrum, cleans out any fluid/pus, and inserts the tube. The tube falls out on its own after a lifespan of 6-18 months. The eardrum heals beautifully 99% of the time.

Children have this procedure done in a day-surgery facility. They do require anesthesia, but don't require an IV, breathing tube, or ventilator. Why anesthesia? It's helpful not to have a squirming child when someone is poking a hole into the eardrum. The procedure takes about five minutes. Kids are usually back to themselves again later that day.

Many parents are incredibly fearful of having PE tubes placed. They are afraid of the procedure, the anesthesia, or the risk of having an opening in the eardrum (you have to keep water out of the ear). Most of these concerns should be clearly addressed by your ENT doctor.

Helpful Hints: Understanding PE Tubes

Think of PE tube placement as a *procedure* and not surgery. I think the word surgery really freaks people out.

◆ This is a simple, quick procedure. For adults, it could be performed in an office setting.

◆ The risk of anesthesia is no greater than the risk of all the antibiotics your child has been taking.

◆ You'll stop needing to see the pediatrician. My frequent fliers stop visiting my office after they have PE tubes placed. I always enjoy seeing my patients, but I see some kids too often.

BOTTOM LINE

As a general rule, PE tubes are a life changing experience for the whole family. Even the most anxious parents report how "easy" the experience is, how much better their child feels, and wonder why they waited so long to do it.

Whew! That was a load of viruses and bacteria. Now, it's on to other medical problems that are NOT caused by infectious bugs. The next chapter explores the most common diseases that affect babies.

THE INFECTION HIT PARADE: VIRUSES AND BACTERIA

So, let's sum up this chapter. Here is a list of the top infections, as caused by viruses and bacteria:

Viruses That Cause Infection

Here is a list of the most common VIRUSES that cause infection in babies ages birth to age one.

Viral Respiratory Infections
1. The Common Cold or upper respiratory infection (Rhinovirus)
2. The Flu (Influenza)
3. Bronchiolitis (RSV)
4. Croup (numerous viruses)

Viral Mouth And Tonsil Infections
1. Hand-Foot-and-Mouth (Coxsackievirus)
2. Herpes Stomatitis (Herpes Type-1)
3. Sore throat virus (Adenovirus)

Gastrointestinal Viruses
1. Stomach virus, or "stomach flu" (Rotavirus)

Viral Exanthems (Viruses That Cause Skin Rashes)
1. Roseola (Herpesvirus-6)
2. Chickenpox (Varicella)
3. Slapped Cheek or Fifth Disease (Parvovirus)

Bacteria That Cause Infection

Here are some of the bacterial infections in babies birth to age one. For details, please see earlier in the chapter.

1. **Ear Infections** (Strep pneumoniae, H. Influenza, And others)
2. **Sinus Infections** (Strep pneumoniae H. Influenza, and others)
3. **Eye Infections** (H. Influenza, strep pneumoniae, and others)
4. **Throat Infections** (Group A strep)
5. **Lung Infections** (Strep pneumoniae, staph, and others)
6. **Food Poisoning** (E. Coli, Salmonella)
7. **Bladder Infections** (E. Coli, and others)
8. **Meningitis** (Group B strep, strep pneumoniae)
9. **Skin infections** (Staph, MRSA, strep)

Things That Make You Itchy Just Thinking About Them

1. **Fungus:** Ringworm, Thrush, Yeast diaper rash
2. **Mites:** Scabies, Lice
3. **Parasites:** Giardia
4. **Worms:** Pinworms

Notes

Common Diseases

Chapter 14

"Sooner or later we all quote our mothers."
~ Bern Williams

What's in this Chapter

- **Eyes: Lazy eye**
- **Lungs: Asthma, Bronchiolitis**
- **Heart: Murmurs**
- **Blood: Anemia, Sickle cell disease, Iron deficiency, Lead exposure**
- **Skin: Eczema**
- **Muscles/Bones: Intoeing, Bowed Legs, Flat feet, Torticollis**
- **Endocrine: Diabetes**
- **Allergies: Seasonal, Environmental**
- **Genitals: Penile, labial adhesions**
- **What's that smell? Unusual odors**

This chapter is devoted to the most common medical problems in infants ages birth to one. Some topics have been discussed in other chapters. (See the index if you can't find the disease you are looking for in this chapter). The common thread of these medical problems is that they are not caused by an infectious bug.

We've organized this discussion by body system—first up, it's the eyes.

Eyes

Q. I'm worried my baby has a lazy eye. How do you check for that?

By examining the eyes every time you visit your doctor.

Under three months of age, babies can looked cross-eyed occasionally. The muscles of both eyes aren't working together yet.

After three months, both eyes should move together. There are two medical reasons for why they don't:

1. **Strabismus.** The muscles that move the eye are weak.
2. **Amblyopia.** The eye itself is weak or injured.

Often a parent will notice this at home. Doctors check by covering up one eye and checking that the other eye can focus on an object. A child looks away or tries to remove the examiner's hand when the unaffected eye is covered.

Regardless of the reason, these kids need to see an eye specialist (ophthalmologist). If a lazy eye goes untreated, permanent problems can occur. Eye doctors prefer to assess these problems before three years of age.

Helpful Hint
There is a benign condition called **PSEUDOSTRABISMUS** where kids just have narrowly set eyes. This is not a medical problem.

RED FLAG
If your child has a dramatic new problem with an eye turning in, go see your doctor ASAP. This can be a sign of a brain tumor. Don't panic yet, just get it checked out.

Lungs

Q. What is asthma?

In short, it's like hay fever in the lungs.

Asthma is a process of swelling, muscle tightening, obstruction, destruction, and mucus production in the big and little airways of the lungs. This chain of events occurs due to a revved up immunologic/allergic response to *infections, allergies, weather, and emotions.*

The narrowed airways interfere with the air exchange (getting clean air in and dirty air out) that occurs with each breath. As a result, children are "air hungry." Their bodies try to get more air in by breathing fast and pulling the rib muscles in when breathing. The characteristic wheeze comes from air traveling through a narrowed passageway.

Asthma attacks (termed exacerbations) occur intermittently depending on what a child is hypersensitive to. Often, kids with asthma have flare ups with upper respiratory infections. This makes for a bad winter.

Q. How do you diagnose asthma?

Asthma is a diagnosis made by physical examination.

If a child is caught wheezing three or more times in his life, he carries a diagnosis of asthma. The first and second time a child wheezes, it might be bad luck. The third time, it's a trend.

There are reasons other than asthma that make children wheeze. Babies can get RSV Bronchiolitis (see more below) or another infection that results in wheezing. Older babies can get a raisin (or other small object) stuck in their airway and wheeze, too.

Your doctor can get a chest x-ray to rule out an infection or a foreign body in the airway. Blood tests aren't particularly helpful. Probably the best information to confirm a diagnosis is a child's response to asthma medication. If their lungs clear up with asthma medication, they likely have the diagnosis.

Q. My doctor said my child has "Reactive Airway Disease." Is that asthma?

Basically, yes. It's just a nicer term to use for a younger child who has not been diagnosed asthmatic.

Doctors tend to hedge on the diagnosis of asthma in a child before the first birthday. Some infants get hit really hard with an RSV infection and wheeze for what seems like months. By definition, they have airways that are "reacting" to infection—by getting swollen and full of mucus.

Still other babies with severe acid reflux (**GERD**) will wheeze when the airway gets irritated. This type of wheezing resolves when they outgrow their reflux.

Doctors use this term for little ones who haven't proven themselves to be true asthmatics yet.

Q. My husband had asthma as a child. What are the chances that my baby will have it?

There is definitely a genetic predisposition to asthma and other allergic disorders.

There is probably a 25% chance your child will have asthma. That means there is a 75% chance he won't. Given the odds, it doesn't pay to worry.

Q. My baby had RSV bronchiolitis this winter. What are the chances that he will have asthma?

Thirty to forty percent.

It is true that kids who wheeze with RSV tend to wheeze again (asthma) in their life times. This is a chicken or the egg dilemma. We just don't know which came first.

Interestingly, not all kids who get RSV wheeze. And of the kids who do wheeze with RSV, not all of them respond to asthma medication. So, there may be just a subset of kids who would have wheezed anyway who have trouble with RSV infection. See the RSV section in Chapter 13, "Infections," for more details.

Q. How do you treat asthma?

Are you old enough to remember those old Primatene mist commercials?

◆ *For immediate rescue:* A **BRONCHODILATOR** (albuterol) very quickly relaxes the airways. This can be administered by liquid taken by mouth or inhaled via an inhaler device or a nebulizer machine (a souped-up vaporizer). For infants, the nebulizer provides the most immediate, effective relief. This medication can be given for prolonged periods in an office or emergency room setting. It can be administered every four to six hours at home.

◆ *For prevention of attacks:* Kids who wheeze more than twice a week need a medication to keep their asthma in check. Persistent symptoms mean chronic destruction to the lungs, which we now know, can be permanent. An **INHALED STEROID** (Budesonide/Pulmicort) is administered via nebulizer daily for these high-risk kids.[1] An oral medication, called Singulair, is also used to prevent flare-ups (See common medications Appendix A for more info.)

Reality Check

Most insurance plans cover the cost of a nebulizer machine for a patient who needs one. They know it's less expensive to buy a $100 machine than to pay for an ER visit or hospitalization.

Q. What are the chances my child will outgrow asthma?

50/50.

Those odds aren't bad for a chronic illness. Unfortunately, no one can predict if and when your child will outgrow it. As a general rule, kids who have asthma before the age of five tend to outgrow it. Children who are diagnosed with asthma when they are older are more likely to have it in adulthood.[2]

Q. What are the long-term consequences of asthma?

Asthma can cause permanent airway damage. This is a recent discovery in the medical world.

Kids who have *occasional* asthma flare-ups do fine in the long term. If a child has *chronic* wheezing, normal parts of the lung can be damaged—and don't recover. So, doctors are more aggressive about treatment for a child with persistent symptoms. Chronic obstructed airways also decrease the amount of oxygen getting to the body on a daily basis.

Q. My child has eczema. My doctor told me he has a higher risk of developing asthma. Why?

Because allergic diseases can occur as a group. This particular problem is called **ATOPY**.

Atopy or atopic disease refers to a classic triad of asthma, eczema, and seasonal allergies. Of the kids who have eczema, 30% get either asthma or seasonal allergies (but 70% won't get either).[3]

Q. My child wheezes. Could he have Cystic Fibrosis?

Yes, but it is very unlikely. Cystic Fibrosis is a genetically inherited disorder that affects one in 1600 children. It causes an abnormality in body cells that impair absorption of chloride. The result of this is that the lungs pull in too much sodium. Normal airway secretions get thick and don't move. Chronic lung infections develop. Other body systems are affected by this cell abnormality, particularly the intestines, pancreas, and reproductive system.

If your baby wheezes chronically, and especially if he is having trouble gaining weight, a screening test for cystic fibrosis may be in order. A simple assessment of a baby's sweat will give the answer.[4]

Heart

Q. What is a heart murmur?

A murmur is an extra noise that is heard when your doctor listens to the heartbeat with a stethoscope. The normal heartbeat is actually a series of sounds best described as "lub-dub." A murmur is an extra noise that may sound like rushing water ("p-ssh") or a squeak ("eek"). The quality, duration, and location of that noise help your doctor determine what is producing it.

If the cause isn't obvious by simply listening, your doctor may recommend that a heart specialist (pediatric cardiologist) see the baby. Tests, such as an electrocardiogram (EKG) or echocardiogram ("echo" or ultrasound examination of the heart), may be recommended to gain additional information about your baby's heart.

Q. My doctor heard an "innocent" heart murmur in my baby. Should I be worried?

No.

We recruited one of our favorite pediatric cardiologists, Karen L. Wright, M.D., to field this one. She says, "An innocent murmur is the sound of normal blood flow passing through the heart chambers and blood vessels. These sounds are commonly heard in infants, and are no cause for alarm. If your baby is doing well and an innocent murmur is detected, your baby's doc will let you know and make a note to check on this during future visits. If there is any concern, or reassurance is needed, your baby's doctor can arrange for you to see a pediatric cardiologist."

Q. My baby has a heart murmur and is going to see a specialist. Should I be worried?

Be appropriately concerned, but not alarmed. Most heart murmurs are innocent (see above) and are not a problem.

Doctors err on the side of checking things out to be sure everything is okay. The term for a murmur caused by a defect in the heart is a **PATHOLOGIC MURMUR**. Most pathologic murmurs are caused by a problem with the way the heart developed before a baby was born (**CONGENITAL HEART DISEASE**). A congenital heart defect occurs in about one in 100 newborns.

Normal heart

According to Dr. Wright, "The vast majority of those defects are pretty mild, and do not significantly interfere with a child's life. In fact, some of these defects truly go away on their own. A common type of congenital heart defect is a hole between the pumping chambers of the heart, called a **VENTRICULAR SEPTAL DEFECT (VSD)**. Most of these holes are small, and will often close as the baby's heart grows."

VSD

Other, less common defects may require either a procedure or surgery to correct. These defects are beyond the scope of this book. But if you are looking for more information, check out www.cincinnatichildrens.org/heartcenter/encyclopedia

Q. Are there other types of heart problems seen in babies?

SUPRAVENTRICULAR TACHYCARDIA (SVT) is an abnormally fast heart rhythm and it can make babies pretty ill. Fortunately, it's rare.

A baby's normal heart rate is already fast (up to 180 beats/minute), so it can be difficult to tell what is *too* fast. But if a baby is unusually fussy, feeding poorly, or breathing rapidly, SVT is one thing to think about. Get it checked out by your doc.

DISEASES

Blood

Q. What is anemia?

Let's discuss what red blood cells are first.

Red blood cells carry oxygen to our body tissues and remove carbon dioxide. Hemoglobin is the name of the protein that performs this function in each red blood cell. The key ingredient of hemoglobin is iron.

"Anemia" means there are not enough red blood cells circulating in the bloodstream. The causes of anemia are either *excessive destruction* or *inadequate production of red blood cells*.

Examples of *excessive destruction* of red blood cells include:
- More blood is being lost than made (such as menstruating women).
- Abnormal red blood cells are made and destroyed (such as sickle cell disease).

Examples of *inadequate production* of red blood cells include:
- Bone marrow production slows (such as bone marrow suppression by virus).
- Iron deficiency limits production due to lack of a key ingredient (that is, iron-deficiency anemia).
- Lead poisoning (technically, this is competition for iron's place in the red blood cell).
- Poor nutritional intake of key vitamins like B12/Folate.

The number one cause of anemia in childhood is iron deficiency. Kids who are severely anemic are pale and fatigue easily. Anemia sometimes presents with odd symptoms, like breath-holding.

Q. My baby had an abnormal newborn screen. We found out he has "sickle cell trait." What does that mean?

Let's be geneticists for a moment. Babies get one set of genes/DNA from Mom, and one set from Dad. Some diseases require one defective gene to affect someone (**AUTOSOMAL DOMINANT**). Some diseases require *both* genes to be abnormal to manifest themselves (**AUTOSOMAL RECESSIVE**).

Sickle cell disease is an autosomal recessive disease. People with one defective gene and one normal gene are called carriers. They carry the trait (gene) for the disease but are not affected by it. About 8% of the African-American population are sickle cell carriers.

Both sickle cell trait and disease can be detected by that first newborn blood test sent to the state laboratory (see Newborn Screening Tests in Chapter 1). It's detected by the type of protein chain that makes up red blood cells.

This is only a problem when your child gets married. If he marries a woman who also has sickle cell trait, his children are at a high risk for having sickle cell disease.[5]

Q. My baby has sickle cell disease. Can you explain what that means and what I should worry about?

Sickle cell disease is caused by abnormal protein (hemoglobin) in red blood cells. This protein causes the red blood cell shape to be deformed. Instead of an oval shaped cell, these cells look like half moons (like the "sickle" on the old Soviet Union flag).

Sickle cells die more quickly, have trouble carrying oxygen, and clog up blood vessels. This blood vessel clogging kills the tissues that the blood vessel supplies (muscle, bones, spleen, lung, kidney, intestine).

The consequences in infancy and early childhood are the following:

1. **Chronic Anemia:** This shows up by age three months. Folate supplements are given to promote red blood cell formation.
2. **Dactylitis:** Infants get hand and foot swelling from clogged blood vessels.
3. **Non-functional spleen:** The spleen filters red blood cells as well as white blood cells (infection fighters). Because of the spleen's job, it takes the greatest hit as far as clogged vessels. We can't rely on the spleen being a functional organ in a child with sickle cell disease. This leaves children prone to infection, particularly with Strep pneumoniae and H. influenza bacteria. These kids need Prevnar vaccine, flu vaccine, and the Pneumonia (pneumococcal) vaccine that elderly people get.
4. **Failure to thrive:** Because of a chronic lack of oxygen to the tissues, these children are shorter and smaller than their peers.

There are a variety of medical problems associated with sickle cell disease as a child gets older. For more information, see www.sicklecelldisease.org.

Q. My nine month old had a routine blood test performed. He has iron-deficiency anemia. What did I do wrong?

You probably haven't done anything wrong.
However, there are some parent mistakes that can cause this problem:

1. **Exclusively breastfeeding** without introducing cereal after six months of age.
2. **Using low iron formula**—we have already warned you about this one.
3. **Replacing breast milk or iron-containing formula with regular cow's milk before the first birthday.**

Q. How is iron deficiency anemia treated?

With a high iron diet and an iron supplement (we discuss this in detail in Chapter 7, "Solids").

If your child is diagnosed with iron-deficiency anemia, your doctor will prescribe an iron supplement. Don't try to treat anemia by yourself without professional help. Why? Because iron, in high doses, can be toxic.

As a result, although vitamins containing iron are available without a prescription, the infant drops are located at the pharmacist's counter. The pharmacist dispenses these medications so he can counsel you on the correct dosage.

Also: there is a difference between the recommend daily allowance for iron (*maintenance iron dosage*) and the dose required for *replacement therapy* for those with low iron stores (iron-deficiency anemia). Doctors usually treat a child with iron-replacement therapy and then recheck their blood counts in three months.

Helpful Hints
Getting your child to take his iron supplement.
- Iron supplements universally taste bad. The brand name products taste a little better. Icar and Feostat brands taste best.
- It's okay to mix the medicine in juice. Just make sure your child drinks *all* the juice. Vitamin C actually helps the iron get absorbed into the bloodstream.
- DO NOT MIX WITH MILK. The calcium in milk competes with iron and can block absorption.
- Iron can cause a temporary gray/brown stain on the teeth. You can use baking soda on a toothbrush to remove it.
- Iron can make poop look black. It's not blood. Don't worry.

Q. **We live in an old house. I'm worried about lead exposure. When should I get my child tested?**

The appropriate time to get tested depends on when your child becomes mobile.

Most children who have lead poisoning live in homes built before 1978. These older homes have lead paint and lead pipes. Chipping paint is a very popular item for kids to pick up and eat. There is also lead in the soil surrounding these homes.

Screening for lead exposure is usually performed at nine to 12 months of age. In high-risk areas (urban, older homes), all children have a blood test done routinely. In low risk areas, doctors will screen with a risk-factor question list. If there is a possible exposure, a blood test is performed.

For more information, check out the Environmental Protection Agency's website at www.epa.gov/lead/index.html or call the National Lead Information Center (NLIC) at 800-424-5323.

While the Environmental Protection Agency recommends consumers turn to professionals to have their homes tested for lead, there are also a number of home tests available on the market. For under $10, you can purchase a lead test kit that includes swabs with a chemical that changes colors when it comes in contact with lead. Unfortunately, the accuracy of these tests has not been proven independently. If you're looking for a reputable professional testing lab in your state, check out the EPA's state-by-state listings of certification officers at epa.gov/safewater/privatewells/labs.html. Once you contact a certification officer in your state, he will be able to provide a list of certified labs.

Feedback from the Real World
I cared for a family who carefully de-leaded their home built in 1910 before moving in with their young children. Unfortunately, a central air conditioning unit was installed AFTER the move and it spewed old dust from the attic into all of the children's rooms. The children required medication to remove the lead from their bloodstreams. They are all doing fine now.

Skin

Q. What is eczema?

This falls into the allergic disease category. Eczema is a broad term to describe dry, scaly, itchy skin that appears in patches. It is often referred to as "the itch that rashes." In other words, kids have particularly sensitive, itchy skin. The itching is what produces the rash that you see.

The sensitive skin flares up with *dryness, exposure to perfumes/dyes,* or *allergies to metals/plants.*

The rash appears in different places depending on the age of the child. Younger kids tend to get it on their elbows, knees, and face. Older kids get it in their elbow and knee creases. We have more on managing eczema in Chapter 4, "Hygiene" and below.

LIVING WITH ECZEMA: 7 TIPS & TRICKS

As a parent of a child with severe eczema, we've been there, done that. Here are our tips:

1. Moisturizing soap: The cheapest in this category is good old Dove soap. Other options are Cetaphil, Aveeno, and Neutrogena. Avoid anti-bacterial soaps—the alcohol will sting cracked skin.

2. Avoid perfumes and dyes: If it smells good, don't use it on your child. That goes for laundry detergent too. Use All Free and Clear or an equivalent product.

3. The thicker and greasier the moisturizing cream, the better: My personal favorite is Creamy Vaseline. Eucerin cream, Aveeno, and Cetaphil are also popular choices among dermatologists. You need to lube your child up several times a day. As soon as you get your child out of the bathtub, apply the moisturizer (I'm serious—have the tube ready).

4. Apply 1% hydrocortisone cream to really red areas twice daily: 1% hydrocortisone cream is a low-potency steroid cream available without a prescription. It is very safe to use on a daily basis when flare-ups occur.

5. Give a sedating antihistamine like diphenhydramine (Benadryl) at bedtime, for babies over six months: it will help reduce the amount of scratching that goes on when you aren't watching your child.

6. No bubble bath—most contain dyes and perfumes that can aggravate eczema. Instead, consider oatmeal bath treatments (Aveeno makes one). If you bathe your child every night, do it in lukewarm water. Consider bathing every other night in winter. The combination of frequent baths and dry heated air can cause flare-ups.

7. If you have tried all of this and your child is still miserable, it's time to check in with your pediatrician. They can recommend prescription products that are safe and effective. Don't hesitate to see a dermatologist if you and your pediatrician can't keep your baby's eczema under control.

Q. How do you get rid of eczema?

You don't. You may win the battle, but you won't win the war.

The key to managing eczema is to keep the skin moist. Eczema always flares up in the wintertime because of cold, dry air.

Q. My baby has severe eczema. Should I be worried about using steroids all the time to treat eczema?

No, these are not the dangerous steroids our Major League Baseball friends use. Topical steroids are extremely good anti-inflammatory medicines. They act by reducing the irritation of the skin, thereby reducing the itching. Long-term use (for months or years), especially with high potency products, can cause unwanted side effects. It's always a good idea to use the lowest potency steroid creams and ointments for the least amount of time. Doctors move up on the strength level until they find one that works, and taper back down when the eczema improves. Ointments work best, followed by creams and lotions. High potency steroids should *not* be used on the face. And always use the product as prescribed. More is not better.

There is another alternative to topical steroids (approved for use in kids over age two) called immunoregulators. They are sold under the brand names Elidel and Protopic. They are an alternative for short-term or intermittent use to treat eczema. Because any medication has potential adverse effects, ask your doctor his/her opinion.

There is also a class of medications that are called essential fatty acid creams. They act by repairing the skin's top layer and reducing inflammation and itching. For details, see Appendix A.

Or, you can try the detergent-free household option. As we alluded to in the Hygiene chapter, this may really help improve your child's symptoms. The basic thesis here: some scientists have documented a rise in eczema along with increased use of household detergents (laundry, hair care products, hand soap, etc). So some parents have had positive results in reducing their kid's eczema by eliminating detergents and switching to soap-based products. Check our web site Baby411.com (click on Bonus Material) for a Detergent-Free How-To guide.

Finally, you may want to consider food allergy testing. You may improve the skin by eliminating an allergenic food.

Q. Is there a link between eczema and asthma?

Yes, for some people.

Eczema is an allergic disorder. About 70% of kids who have eczema have a parent, brother or sister who has some type of allergy (hay fever/seasonal allergies, eczema, asthma).

About 30% of kids with eczema will have the classic triad of **ATOPY** (eczema, seasonal allergies, and asthma). But 70% of kids have eczema without any other type of allergic disease.[6]

It's just something to pay particular attention to.

Q. Will my baby outgrow eczema?

Chances are, yes.

About 70% of kids will outgrow eczema. But no one can predict if and when your child will outgrow it. Chances are better if your child gets eczema as a baby. Kids who get eczema later in life have a greater chance of having it into adulthood.

Muscles/Bones

Q. My baby's feet turn in. Will he need to wear special shoes or a brace?

No.

The official term for this is called **INTOEING**. This is very common and usually corrects itself as your child becomes a good walker.

Old Wives Tale
Pigeon toed children need to wear corrective shoes.
The truth: It was trendy 30 to 40 years ago to have kids wear corrective shoes or braces (for example Forrest Gump) if they turned their feet in while walking. Since then, doctors discovered feet get better whether a child wears this apparatus or not—so why put a child through the trauma of special shoes or braces.

Q. My one year old is bow-legged. Will he always walk like this?

No.

Kids have some trouble finding their center of gravity. When they first start walking, they bend their knees to support their body weight. As they get older, they often go the opposite direction and look knock-kneed. It's nothing to worry about unless one leg is misshapen or both legs look severely deformed.

Q. My baby seems to have flat feet. My husband has flat feet, too. Do we need to see a podiatrist?

Your child can thank your husband for his feet. And no, you don't need to see a podiatrist yet.

The term "flat feet" refers to a lack of a natural arch in the bones of the feet. Some flat feet are flexible (the arch is seen when standing on tip-toe) and some are rigid (always flat). The feet that are always flat can cause some discomfort when kids become teenagers and adults. But placing a shoe insert (**ORTHOTIC**) into a toddler's shoes is not going to change the results down the line. The American Academy of Pediatrics feels orthotics are not necessary for kids with flat feet.

Q. My doctor says my baby has TORTICOLLIS. What is it and what do I do about it?

DISEASES

Here we go with the Latin again. This term literally means "twisted neck." It is caused by a tightening of a neck muscle (**STERNOCLEIDOMASTOID MUSCLE**) on one side of the neck. This neck muscle tightening occurs while the baby is still in the womb. The fetus may get stuck in one position for several weeks, forcing the baby's head to tilt towards the shoulder.

The muscle tightening gets worse after birth if babies sleep in the same position all the time. You may notice that your baby prefers to turn or tilt his head to one side. Babies who are at greater risk for this are boys, large birth weight babies, twins/multiples, breech, moms with uterus abnormalities, and first pregnancies.[10]

If your child has torticollis, his head and neck movements will be limited. And if you don't actively do something about it, his head and facial shape may be affected. See the next box for home exercises to work on. If you have no improvement in six to eight weeks, it's time to call in a physical therapist to help you.

EXERCISES FOR TORTICOLLIS

Here are two exercises you can do at home to fix this problem. It's easiest to remember if you do the exercises after each daytime diaper change. Your baby will respond best if he has a full tummy and is relaxed. You can do the exercises on the changing table or on your lap.

1. **Tilt the head, ear to shoulder, stabilizing the chest with one hand.** Hold for 10 seconds and repeat on the other side. Repeat three times on each side.

2. **Turn the baby's head, chin to shoulder, while stabilizing the chest with one hand.** Hold for 10 seconds. Then repeat in the other direction and hold for 10 seconds. Repeat three times on each side.

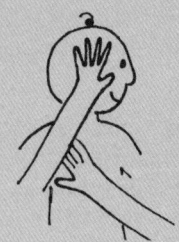

Source: Stellwagen L, et al. Look for the "stuck baby" to identify congenital torticollis. Contemporary Pediatrics May 2004;21:55.

Endocrine

Q. Diabetes runs in my family. How can I get my baby tested for it?

Let's discuss diabetes first.

Diabetes mellitus is a chronic disease due to impaired sugar metabolism. There are two types (Type 1 and Type 2). They are divided by the cause of the disorder and the treatment. Although both can be inherited diseases, Type 2 tends to "run in families" more often.

Here is a brief explanation of the malfunction:
Since a person with diabetes doesn't breakdown sugar properly, the sugar ends up in vast quantities in the bloodstream. The body tries to eliminate the sugar by filtering it through the kidneys and into the urine. The sugar pulls excessive amounts of water with it into the urine. The result?

◆ Elevated blood sugar level.
◆ Excessive urination (with sugar found in the urine).
◆ Excessive thirst to keep up with fluid loss in the urine.
◆ Weight loss (from poor metabolism and fluid losses).

Type 1 Diabetes is also known as *Juvenile Diabetes*, or *Insulin Dependent Diabetes*. This is an autoimmune disease—that means the cells in the pancreas that make insulin get killed off by a person's own body. Insulin is the chemical in our body that metabolizes sugars.

There are some genes that have been identified in people with Type 1 diabetes and genetic defects can be passed on to offspring. Treatment is life-long with insulin injections and dietary modifications. Onset of Type 1 Diabetes is usually around school age (six to seven years old). It is extraordinarily rare to be diagnosed with diabetes while a child is still in diapers.

Type 2 Diabetes is also known as *Adult Onset Diabetes*. This type of diabetes is caused by the body's impaired response to insulin—this impairment is related to obesity.

As you can tell by the name, this USED to be an adult disease. Unfortunately, there is a virtual "epidemic" today of Type 2 Diabetes in preteens and teens. Children at risk are obese (defined as a Body Mass Index greater than 85%—see Chapter 5, "Nutrition and Growth" for details on the BMI) as well as other family members with Type 2 diabetes. Treatment includes dietary modifications and medications taken by mouth. FYI: There is a higher risk of developing this disorder among African-Americans, Hispanics, and Native Americans.[7]

BOTTOM LINE

Diabetes is not a disorder of infancy. But if you have a family history of diabetes it's a good idea to watch your child's growth.

Eating a healthy diet and avoiding obesity is even more important in your family.

As your child gets older, a screening test for diabetes can be done by obtaining a urine and blood sample.

For more information, check out this web site: diabetes.org.

Allergies

Q. My husband and I both have seasonal allergies. What are the chances that our baby will have allergies?

50%.

For each parent who has allergies, a child has a 25% risk of developing them himself. This refers to seasonal allergies, asthma and eczema. Some doctors might also put food allergies on this list, too. The earliest manifestations of an allergic child are eczema and food allergies. Asthma is usually diagnosed after a year of age. Seasonal allergies come even later.

> **Reality Check**
> The hereditary patterns of allergies do *not* apply to *drug* allergies. Just because you have an allergy to Penicillin doesn't mean your child will have one too.

Q. My baby seems to have a runny nose all of the time. Does he have seasonal allergies?

No.

Allergies ("hay fever") that cause a runny nose can be divided into perennial (all year long) or seasonal categories.

- *Perennial allergies.* These are year round allergies caused by something a child is exposed to on a daily basis. This is something inside your house, not outside your house. The most common causes are dust mites or cat dander. Molds are found both inside and outside the house year round.

- *Seasonal allergies.* These are allergies caused by something that's in the air outside of your house. These pollens include weeds, trees, and grasses that come in seasonal patterns. Most children under one year of age do not get *seasonal* allergies. Allergies, by definition, are a body's hyper-response to an allergen they have seen before. In the first year of life, a child has never seen these pollens before so there is no response.

> **BOTTOM LINE**
> Newborns do not have seasonal allergies when they are congested for the first six weeks of life. Nor does a nine month old have a ragweed allergy.

FELINES ARE OUR FRIENDS

Although most people have heard that having a cat causes allergies, recent research shows that early exposure (first year of life) to cats and dogs may actually prevent allergies. Kids who grow up on farms have significantly less problems with allergies, presumably due to their constant exposure to animals and the germs they carry.[8]

Most of the time, a chronic runny nose is caused by one viral upper respiratory infection after another. Although there are conflicting viewpoints, some doctors feel that perennial allergies or food allergies may cause a chronic runny nose year round in kids under age two.

Helpful hint

For perennial allergies (for example, dust mites), allergists often recommend plastic bedding covers, air filters, etc. These products are available through medical supply companies. Check out the following resources for a product catalog: National Allergy Supply, Inc. (800-522-1448, web: natlallergy.com) or Allergy Asthma Technology Ltd. (800-621-5545, web: allergyasthmatech.com).

Genitals

Q. My son is circumcised, but he doesn't look circumcised anymore. What do I do?

See Chapter 4, "Hygiene" for a frank discussion on **PENILE ADHESIONS**. Some parents will comment that they see a white blister (called a bleb) on the skin, or a red swollen area, or that the penis just doesn't look right. These are usually all the same problem. The white blister is dead skin that has collected and is allowing the skin to stick together. The red swollen area may be the penis trying to unstick on its own. The penis doesn't look right because you can no longer see the helmet part.

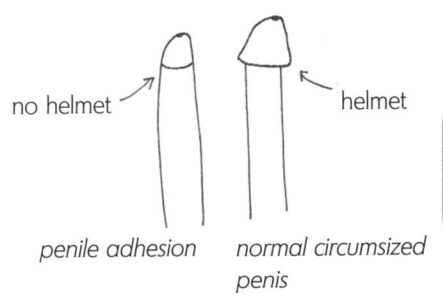

no helmet — *penile adhesion*

helmet — *normal circumsized penis*

Q. The skin of my daughter's genitals is sticking together. My doctor said not to worry about it . . . but I am worried.

Don't worry. This is a common problem called **LABIAL ADHESIONS**. The labia and vaginal areas stay lubricated and open when estrogen is being produced. Young women produce estrogen when they start menstruating. So prepubertal girls are prone to labrial adhesions until they go through puberty.

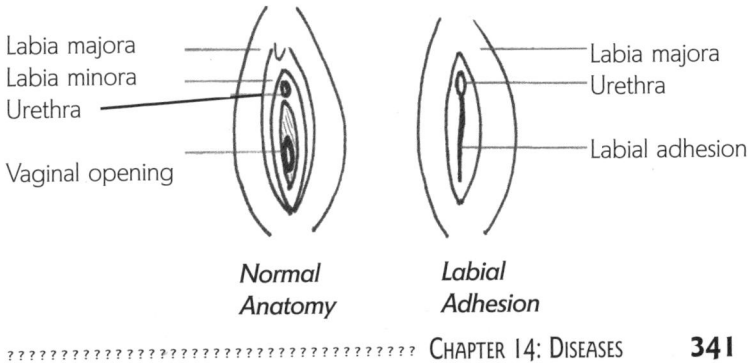

Labia majora
Labia minora
Urethra
Vaginal opening

Normal Anatomy

Labia majora
Urethra
Labial adhesion

Labial Adhesion

The only time this is a problem is when the labia are so fused together that the urethral opening is blocked too (that's where the urine comes out). See the graphic on the previous page to understand what we're talking about.

Labial adhesions are treated by using a prescription estrogen cream twice daily on the area for a couple of weeks. After that, apply petroleum jelly (Vaseline) on a daily basis to keep the area moist and open. Very rarely, a surgical procedure is necessary to open the area.

What's that smell?

Have you ever gone to a wine tasting and tried to describe the "nose" of a wine? When babies smell unusual, parents go to great lengths to come up with adjectives to explain the odor to their doctor.

We hesitate to explain this category of disorders in a chapter entitled "Common" diseases. But there are some very rare metabolic disorders that are associated with unusual body odors. It is important that you are aware of them, and seek medical care if you notice any of the following smells:

- ◆ *Body odors*: Barn-like, mousy, musty, horsey, wolf-like, sweaty socks, cheesy.
- ◆ *Breath odors:* fruity/sweet, fishy, ammonia-like, clover, musty fish, raw liver, foul.
- ◆ *Urine (pee) odors:* mousy, musty, horsey, wolf-like, barn-like, maple syrup, caramel, boiled Chinese Herbal medicine, yeast, celery, malt, brewery, sweaty feet/socks, ripe cheese, tomcat urine, dead fish, cabbage.
- ◆ *Stool (poop) odors:* foul, vile.

Note that other problems may cause you to turn your nose: poisonings and infections.

BOTTOM LINE: Bad odors are worth checking out.[9]

Now that you've been briefed on the most common diseases that affect children, let's talk First Aid. The next chapter covers the 12 most common calls that doctors get about babies—and what you can do to treat the problems.

Baby 411

Section 5

First Aid

Top 12 Problems & Solutions

First Aid

Problems & Solutions
Chapter 15

"It's no longer a question of staying healthy. It's a question of finding a sickness you like."
~ Jackie Mason

What's in this Chapter

1. Your First Aid Kit
2. Taking vital signs
3. The Top 12 Problems & Solutions.
   - Abdominal Pain
   - Allergic Reaction
   - Bleeding and Bruising
   - Breathing problems (Respiratory Distress)
   - Burns
   - Diarrhea and Vomiting
   - Fever
   - Poisoning
   - Rashes
   - Seizures
   - Does it need stitches?
   - Trauma (accidental injury)

Are you afraid your pediatrician will fire you for calling too much? Although doctors entertain this thought occasionally, we never act on it (well, almost never). Phone calls are a part of the job. Most phone calls come from new parents. You are not alone.

The purpose of this chapter is to help you troubleshoot the most common problems you will encounter on the front line of your baby's medical care. It should help you determine when to call the doctor. It also prepares you for what the doctor will ask when you call.

This chapter does not replace the need to check in with your doctor. Pick up the phone if you are worried. But being educated helps you worry less and trust your instincts more.

Helpful Hints
On Call Etiquette

How can you make the most of a call to your baby's doctor? As a doctor who has spent one third of her life on call, here are some important points to consider:

1. **The on-call doctor is not in the office.** Doctors leave the office at the end of the workday and carry a beeper to receive after hours calls. Doctors also go to sleep. (It's often disrupted sleep—but we try). If you call about your child's diaper rash at 2 am, the doctor won't be as perky as when you

call during office hours.

2 **TELL THE ON-CALL DOCTOR ABOUT PAST MEDICAL PROBLEMS.** Most pediatric and family doctor practices have SEVERAL doctors on staff. After hours, there is usually one doctor (who picks the short straw) that is on-call. This may or may NOT be your regular doctor. As a result, the on-call doctor may not know your child and does not have your child's medical chart. Explain any previous medical problems, surgeries, or hospitalizations. It might have a bearing on the particular problem at hand.

3 **TELL THE ON-CALL DOCTOR ABOUT ALLERGIES TO MEDICATIONS.** If your child has an allergic reaction to a medication, put it in YOUR family medical records. Don't rely on an on-call doctor or your pharmacy to know this information.

"The pink medicine" or "some antibiotic" is not adequate. Most doctors inquire about drug allergies before any medicine is prescribed—but we appreciate it if you tell us.

4 **HAVE A PHARMACY PHONE NUMBER READY.** True confession: I call patients back on my cell phone when I am driving. I don't have the yellow pages sitting in my glove compartment. And frequently, there is more than one Walgreen's on a major street in town. Please have a phone number of a pharmacy near you that is open when you are calling. That way, I can call in your prescription after I talk with you.

5 **DON'T CALL FOR REFILLS, REFERRALS, OR APPOINTMENTS AFTER HOURS.** Universal doctor rule—we don't do these things without patient charts or schedules available. Medical emergencies are the only exception to this rule.

6 **DON'T LEAVE YOUR HOUSE OR GET ON THE PHONE AFTER PAGING US.** Believe it or not, this happens. If it's truly an emergency, keep your phone line clear. During cold and flu season, it may take a while for the doctor to return your call (the on-call doctor may get several calls per hour). But we appreciate it if we can get through to you when we call you back.

7 **DON'T USE CALLER ID TO CALL THE ON-CALL DOCTOR BACK WITH ANOTHER QUESTION.** Okay, for the doctor, this is just creepy. If you call back through the appropriate answering service or voicemail system, you will always get your call returned. There is a protocol for a reason, folks—there is often a queue of patients who may need callbacks. If you use caller ID to find the doctor's home or cell phone number, don't use it.

8 **DON'T EXPECT OR DEMAND THAT ANTIBIOTICS BE PRESCRIBED OVER THE PHONE.** There is a good reason why antibiotics aren't available over the counter. A child needs to be seen to make a diagnosis of a bacterial infection. Remember the drug-resistant bacteria problem. (This is mentioned in Chapter 13, "Infections"). Doctors usually prescribe "supportive relief" (such as acetaminophen (Tylenol)) until your child can be evaluated.

9 **IF YOU HAVE A QUESTION ABOUT A MEDICATION, HAVE THE BOTTLE IN HAND WHEN YOU CALL.** Just common sense here. We will probably ask you to read the information on the bottle to us.

Q. What should I have in our first aid kit at home?

Here is your grocery list:

- Band-Aids (lots of them—they become badges of courage)
- sterile, non-stick dressing and tape
- "butterfly" bandages or thin adhesive strips
- Ace wrap
- a roll of gauze dressing
- rectal thermometer
- petroleum jelly
- acetaminophen (Tylenol)
- ibuprofen (Motrin, Advil)
- antibiotic ointment
- diphenhydramine liquid (Benadryl)
- saline nose drops (home made or store bought)
- decongestant nose spray (Afrin)
- 1% hydrocortisone cream
- A list of emergency phone numbers, including the National Poison Control Center (800-222-1222) or your local poison control number.
- baking soda
- tweezers
- measuring spoon, cup or dropper; you'll want one with cc/ml measurements for those tiny infant doses. (See Chapter 5, "Nutrition & Growth" for a list of common measurements)

Q. Should I take a CPR course?

Yes!

Learn how to handle emergencies before they happen. Even if you can't remember exactly what to do, you will be more prepared to take action if something bad happens.

It's also helpful to learn how to take your child's vital signs. This information is very useful for when you call your doctor for advice.

Q. How do I take my child's vital signs?

Vital signs include the heart rate (pulse), respiratory rate (breaths per minute), temperature, and blood pressure. The only thing you cannot do at home is the blood pressure.

1. **Temperature:** Know how to take a rectal temperature. (See fever section later in this chapter for details.)

2. **Pulse:** Feel your baby's pulse in the inner part of the elbow or in the groin. Count the number of pulsations for 15 seconds and multiply by four. This gives you the beats per minute. Below is a list of average heart rates for your baby's age:

FIRST AID

Average heart rates for babies, birth to three years of age:
Birth to one week: 95–160
One week to six months: 110–180
Six to 12 months: 110–170
One to three years: 90–150
(Compare these to an adult's heart rate of 60–100 beats per minute.)

3. **Respiratory Rate:** Watch your baby's chest as it moves in and out. Count one breath for each time he breathes in for 30 seconds and multiply by two. This gives you the number of breaths per minute. Babies have very erratic breathing, so you won't get an accurate count if you only look for ten or 15 seconds. Below are the details.

Average respiratory rates by age:
Newborns: 25–50
One week to one year: 24–38
One to three years: 22–30
(Compare to an adult's respiratory rates of 12–16 breaths per minute.)[1]

Helpful Hint
When a child runs a fever, all the other vital signs are elevated, too. Parents worry about the heart racing when children run a fever. That is to be expected and normal.

How Can Docs Make a Diagnosis Over the Phone Without Examining a Child?

Your doctor will rely on you to provide the signs and symptoms (the clues).

Doctors are very systematic in the way they make a diagnosis. A professor once told me that 90% of the time, a diagnosis can be made purely on the history of the problem. Only 10% of the time will the physical examination of the patient be necessary to make the diagnosis. It's true. I usually know what I will find when I examine the patient just by listening to the story. But this requires some detective work. I always ask the same questions for each complaint to get a history of signs and symptoms (that is, location/type of pain, length of fever, appetite or lack of, sleep disruption, runny nose, cough, vomiting, etc.) When you call, expect to be interrogated.

Nervous parents often focus on one particular aspect of a disease process while doctors are trying to figure out the big picture. (See fever section later in this chapter). Doctors need to know about various symptoms to put the puzzle together. Let the doctor help point you in the right direction!

The Most Frequent Phone Calls

First, here's some doctor lingo: ever heard the guys on the old M*A*S*H television series say a patient was "in triage?" Triage just means to sort out by severity of the condition. The point: phone calls are triaged by the doctor into the following categories:

- **Priority 1:** Needs immediate evaluation and treatment—NOW.
- **Priority 2:** Needs appointment the next day.
- **Priority 3:** Watch and wait. Needs appointment if there is no improvement or worsening of symptoms.
- **Red flags:** Denote symptoms that are medical emergencies.

We've adopted this system in this chapter to give you a general idea of how problems are managed. But every problem is unique. If you have concerns, call your doctor.

Abdominal Pain

Q. My baby has a stomachache. When do I need to worry?

It's hard to tell when an infant has a stomachache, unless he is vomiting or has diarrhea. Some reliable signs include irritability during/after feedings, pulling up of the legs, or a tense, full belly. There are also medical problems that have nothing to do with the stomach that cause abdominal pain (such as bladder infections).

Abdominal pain is divided into acute (a new event as of yesterday or today) or chronic pain (the problem has been going on for over a week). Acute issues *only* are discussed below.

Priority 1: Needs immediate evaluation and treatment—NOW:

The most serious problems are called surgical emergencies or an "acute abdomen." A piece of bowel may be kinked, blocked, or infected. Babies with these problems look sick and are often inconsolable. Concerning symptoms include: swollen and/or tender belly, lack of interest in eating, persistent vomiting, unusual looking diarrhea, and difficulty settling down. These problems need to be addressed quickly. See the Red Flags on the next page. Diagnoses include: **INTESTINAL OBSTRUCTION, INTUSSUSCEPTION, INCARCERATED HERNIA, APPENDICITIS, PYLORIC STENOSIS.**

Priority 2: Needs appointment the next day.

Most problems fall into the non-urgent category. These symptoms are less severe and babies are consolable. Symptoms include: gas, trouble settling after a feeding, crying/straining while attempting to poop, and one or two episodes of vomiting. Observation and medical evaluation is in order if things are not improving. NOTE: In babies under a year of age, it's better to be cautious and contact your doctor if you are worried.

Diagnoses include: **GAS, CONSTIPATION, EARLY VIRAL GASTROENTERITIS**

Helpful Hints
What the doctor will ask you about ABDOMINAL PAIN:
1. Does your baby have a fever?
2. Is your baby vomiting? What does the vomit look like?
3. Does your baby have diarrhea? Is it watery, bloody, mucousy, look like grape jelly?
4. Does your baby's tummy look like he is pregnant? Does it hurt to touch?
5. How long has the pain/vomiting/diarrhea been going on?
6. Does your baby have at least three wet diapers (urine) a day?
7. Is your son's scrotum swollen?

RED FLAGS
Call your doctor immediately if you see the following symptoms with abdominal pain:

- Fever and pain without diarrhea.
- Projectile vomiting or bright green/yellow vomit.
- Diarrhea that is bloody/mucousy/grape-jelly like.
- Tense, distended belly.
- Pain more than two hours in duration.
- Prolonged vomiting (see vomiting section later in this chapter).
- Prolonged diarrhea (see diarrhea section later in this chapter).
- Less than three wet diapers a day.
- Swollen scrotum.
- Crying with urination.

Feedback from the Real World
My four-year-old daughter slept for 12 hours once and awakened with the tensest belly I had ever seen. She was very uncomfortable and was having difficulty walking. She screamed when I tried to touch her belly. She had no interest in eating. Being quite convinced that she had an acute abdomen, I called one of my pediatric surgeon friends to evaluate her in the ER. As we drove to the hospital, she proclaimed that she needed to pee NOW. I pulled off the highway onto the shoulder. She urinated in my portable car trash can. She had had a full bladder. She felt much better and asked if we could go out to lunch after visiting the doctor. We sheepishly walked into the ER together. She skipped to the exam room. I apologized for calling my friend to look at my perfectly normal child. His comment was, "Well, she does have a *cute* abdomen!"

Lessons learned here:
1. Sometimes benign processes (like a full bladder, constipation, etc.) can look like an acute abdomen. Doctors prefer to check out suspicious patients rather than wait.
2. It's hard to be objective when dealing with your own child.

Allergic Reaction

Q. I think my child is having an allergic reaction. Do I need to go to the ER?

Clarify the reaction. Do you see a rash or is he having difficulty breathing?

Priority 1: Needs immediate evaluation and treatment—NOW:

RED FLAGS
Anaphylactic Reaction

Call 911 for a child who is drooling, anxious, having obvious labored breathing (stridor), lip swelling, sweating. Another serious allergic reaction is called Stevens Johnson Syndrome. This is an extensive rash accompanied by mouth ulcers. This requires immediate medical attention.

If your child is having an anaphylactic reaction, do not attempt to drive to the hospital. Unless you can see the hospital from your front door, call 911 and get immediate help. Most ambulances are equipped with medicine to handle these reactions immediately.

Diagnoses: **ANAPHYLACTIC REACTION, STEVENS-JOHNSON SYNDROME**

Priority 2: Needs appointment the next day.

Most rashes are less of an emergency. (See details of other rashes in the rash section later in this chapter). Allergic reaction rashes can have various configurations. They are all itchy. Rashes (except Stevens Johnson Syndrome, see above) can be evaluated by a doctor when their office is open. These include:

- *Hives:* raised mosquito bites with flat red circles around them or large flat red areas with raised edges (for example, a drug allergy).
- *Erythema multiforme:* extensive, small, flat, red patches with raised edges (for example, a drug allergy).
- *Eczema:* red plaques with a scaly rough appearance overlying it (for example, a food allergy).
- *Contact dermatitis:* red pimples or blisters in a patch or streak (for example, poison ivy).

See our web site at Baby411.com for a visual library of common rashes.

Reality Check

Have your child in front of you when you speak to the doctor on the phone. You will be asked to describe what you see over the phone.

What the doctor will ask you about ALLERGIC REACTIONS:
1. Is your baby having any trouble breathing?
2. What does the rash look like? Where is it on the body?
3. When did you first see the rash?
4. Is the rash itchy?
5. Is your baby currently taking any medication?
6. Has your baby been exposed to any new foods, laundry detergents, clothing, or soaps?

Helpful Hints

◆ Unless your child is having an anaphylactic reaction (see above), give diphenhydramine (Benadryl) and schedule an appointment.
◆ Stop any other medication until a doctor sees your child.
◆ Don't give diphenhydramine (Benadryl) in the morning before your appointment—otherwise the rash will be gone.
◆ Try to think of any new medication or food your child may have had recently.

Reality Check

FYI: An allergic reaction is caused by a release of a chemical called histamine. Diphenhydramine (Benadryl), an anti-histamine, effectively clears the results of histamine (the rash) until the medicine wears off (about six hours). Histamine levels stay elevated for several DAYS. So, don't be surprised to see the rash "come back" after the medicine wears off. You will need to use the antihistamine medicine for a few days.

Causes of allergic reactions: Food allergy, medication allergy, bug bites, poison ivy (rhus dermatitis).

Bleeding And Bruising

Q. My child bruises easily. Should I be worried?

No, not usually.

Bruising in high trauma areas is not worrisome (shins, knees, elbows, forehead). We worry much more about bruising on the torso—most falls do not cause bruising to this area.

Easy bruisability can be a sign of low platelet count (platelets help your blood clot). Bruising is much more worrisome when it is seen with **PETECHIAE**. (pe-teek-ee-eye). See box on the next page. Bruising accompanied by excessive bleeding can indicate a blood clotting disorder.

See our web site at Baby411.com (click on Bonus Material) for a picture.

Common Diagnoses include: Trauma/injury, temporary bone marrow suppression from a viral infection.

Uncommon Diagnoses include: Hemophilia, Von Willebrand's disease Leukemia, Idiopathic Thrombocytopenic Purpura, Henoch-Schonlein Purpura, Meningitis.

Priority 1: Needs immediate evaluation and treatment—NOW:

1. A fever with petechiae rash
2. Petechiae AND bruising, with or without a fever
3. Bruising and lethargy
4. Excessive bruising (beyond the knees/elbows)
5. Uncontrollable bleeding

Priority 2: Needs appointment the next day.

1. Bruising with no other symptoms
2. Recurrent nosebleeds

New Parent 411: All You Ever Wanted To Know About Petechiae But Were Afraid To Ask

Petechiae are flat, purplish, pinpoint dots that almost look like freckles. When you push down on them, they remain colored (that is, they do not blanch). Petechiae are caused by broken blood vessels. They arise for the following reasons:

1. **Pressure**: Straining while pooping, giving birth, coughing, or vomiting forcefully.
2. **Infection**: Strep, meningitis, Rocky Mountain Spotted Fever.
3. **Low platelet count**: Leukemia, Idiopathic Thrombocytopenic Purpura, temporary bone marrow suppression from a viral infection. If there is a good reason to have petechiae (such as repeated coughing), and they are located above the level of the chest only, you can relax a bit, but still call your doctor.

If there is not a good reason, your baby needs to be seen quickly to rule out the serious medical problems on this list.

What the doctor will ask you about BRUISING OR BLEEDING:
1. Where are the bruises?
2. Are there any other rashes on his body?
3. Does he bleed excessively? Does anyone in the family have bleeding problems?
4. Has he been unusually tired or been running a fever with no explanation?

Q. My child is having a nosebleed. What do I do about it?

Lean your child's head *forward*, not backwards. Apply pressure to the base (soft part) of the nose for ten minutes. If this doesn't work, you can spray some medicated decongestant nose drops into the nostrils (Little Noses or Children's Afrin are two brand names). This causes the blood vessels to shrink and stop bleeding.

Most nosebleeds stop in about ten minutes. If it goes beyond that, call your doctor.

Q. My child just vomited blood. Where is it coming from and should I be worried?

If it looks like fresh red blood, it can't be coming too far from the mouth. Blood that comes from the stomach is partially digested and will look like coffee grounds. Be prepared to describe the vomit. Lack of an obvious explanation for the blood needs an evaluation.

What the doctor will ask you about VOMITING BLOOD:
1. How old is your baby?
2. Are you breastfeeding? Are your nipples cracked and raw?
3. Have you been suctioning your baby's nose with a bulb syringe?

4. Has your baby been vomiting forcefully?
5. What does the vomit look like? Are there streaks of blood? Coffee grounds? Mucus?

The most common cause of *Upper GI Bleeding* (official term for vomiting blood) in a newborn is Mom's cracked nipples. The blood in the spit up is really Mom's. There is a test to prove it, but one look at Mom's nipples is a dead give-away.

The next likely culprit is that dreaded bulb syringe we told you to throw away in Chapter 4. It causes an irritation in the lining of the nose, making it raw to the point of bleeding. Nasal secretions are swallowed and then spit up.

As your baby gets older, he will explore his body. His finger will find his nostrils and cause trauma. The number one cause of bloody vomit in an older child is a nosepicker's nosebleed.

Now, for more serious causes. Forceful vomiting can cause a small tear in the lining of the esophagus. A child with persistent blood in vomit needs to be examined.

Vomit that looks like coffee grounds also needs to be evaluated. In older babies, doctors worry about a toxic ingestion/poison that irritates the esophagus or stomach, ulcers, gastritis, or esophagitis. If the vomit looks like Folger's coffee, call your doctor.

Diagnoses of an upper GI bleed include: Mom's cracked nipples, esophagitis, toxic ingestion/poisoning, gastritis, ulcers

Priority 1: Needs immediate evaluation and treatment—NOW:

1. No obvious source for bleeding
2. Vomit that looks like Folger's coffee.
3. Persistent bleeding.

Q. My baby has blood in his poop. Should I worry?

No, but Lower GI bleeding *always needs to be evaluated by a doctor*. If you see blood in the diaper, save the diaper. It's helpful to bring a fresh specimen to the office visit. If your baby doesn't cooperate, doctors have other ways to get what they need (via a rectal exam).

You will describe every detail of that poop to the On-Call Doctor. If the blood looks red and fresh, the source is close to the anus. If the blood looks darker or the poop looks like meconium, it comes from further up the pipes (small or large intestine). The age of the child partially determines the cause of the problem.

♦ ***Newborns:*** Bad *diaper rash* is often the explanation. Blood is usually found on the diaper wipe more than in the poop with an obvious raw bottom. Babies under four months of age with streaks of blood often have a *milk protein allergy.* Even exclusively breast fed babies can encounter this because the cow's milk protein can enter the breast milk. It often takes six weeks for the blood to clear once babies eliminate the cow's milk from their diets. Even if this is what the working diagnosis is, bacterial stool cultures are in order to rule out infection.

Diagnoses include: diaper rash, milk protein allergy, food poisoning (Bacterial gastroenteritis).

♦ **Older babies:** Babies who have started solids often get constipated. If your baby looks like he is giving birth when he pushes out a solid poop ball, he might bleed with it. An *anal tear or fissure* can be seen if you look for it. This is not serious. Put some Vaseline on the area and check out fiber facts in Chapter 8, "The Other End."

Now for more serious causes. Babies can get *food poisoning*—even those who aren't eating off the Chinese buffet line yet. Where do babies get it? Human carriers, pets, and food exposure. Babies in daycare are at higher risk of parasite infections. Your doctor can test for all of these bugs with cultures (see bacterial infections and parasites in Chapter 13, Infections). Symptoms include diarrhea with streaks of blood and mucus.

Finally, poop that looks like grape jelly (currant jelly stool) is a medical emergency. The diagnosis is *intussusception*, where the bowel telescopes on itself and creates an obstruction. Symptoms include abdominal pain (pulling up of the legs), irritability, and grape jelly stool.

Diagnoses: Anal fissure/tear (caused by constipation), food allergy, food poisoning (bacterial gastroenteritis), parasite infection, antibiotic induced colitis (C difficile infection), intussusception

What the doctor will ask you about BLOOD IN POOP:
1. How old is your baby? Was your baby premature?
2. What did you see in the diaper? Streaks of blood mixed in poop? Solid poop with blood on the diaper wipe? Explosive bloody diarrhea? Mucus also? Grape jelly?
3. Is there a diaper rash?
4. What is your baby eating?
5. Has anyone in the house had diarrhea?
6. Does your baby look sick or well? Fever?
7. Is your baby's belly full and distended?
8. Is your baby interested in eating? Is he vomiting?
9. Has your baby been on antibiotics recently?

Priority 1: Needs immediate evaluation and treatment—NOW:
♦ Bloody diarrhea
♦ Grape jelly poop
♦ No obvious diaper rash or anal tear
♦ Former premature baby

Priority 2: Needs appointment the next day.
♦ Streak of blood with normal looking stool and well appearing child

Priority 3: Watch and wait. Needs appointment if there is no improvement or worsening of symptoms:
♦ Obvious constipation
♦ Obvious diaper rash

Feedback from the Real World
Dr. Brown's TRUE STORIES about food poisoning:
1. One mother was a short order cook who discovered she was a carrier of Salmonella when her newborn had it. She truly was

"Typhoid Mary" (named for a woman who was a cook and a carrier of typhoid fever—a cousin of Salmonella). Sometimes parents are carriers who have had a previous infection and don't know it.

2. Unusual pets can be carriers of Salmonella. One of my patient's uncles had a pet iguana that roamed freely on the family's kitchen counter.

3. Raw eggs and chicken are also known to have Salmonella. I had a patient who acquired Salmonella when Grandma was preparing chicken gizzards next to Mom preparing a bottle for the baby.

Feedback from the Real World

There was an outbreak of the deadly E. coli 0157 bacteria (hemolytic uremic syndrome) on the East Coast several years back. It was traced to an apple cider producer in New Hampshire. It had been a bad apple season, so the producer used apples that had already fallen off the trees to press for cider. Unfortunately, the cows that lived on the farm pooped on those apples and contaminated them with the E.coli. There are new regulations for cider production now. Moral of the story: Never drink unpasteurized apple cider.

A similar outbreak happened with Odwalla apple juice in 1996—a small batch of unpasteurized juice contained E.coli bacteria, sickening more than a dozen children. This juice was blended with other products as well. Be sure to look for these products—make sure ALL the ingredients in a blended juice product are pasteurized.

How to avoid food poisoning

Many of these foods are off limits to infants under a year anyway, but they are good to know about. Remember to clean cutting boards, knives, and countertops when dealing with these products, too. Keep a spray bottle of bleach handy in the kitchen to clean these tools. Here are the foods to avoid for infants:

- unpasteurized dairy products
- unpasteurized juices (fresh squeezed OJ, apple cider)
- alfalfa sprouts
- raw shellfish
- oysters
- undercooked and raw meat or seafood
- unwashed fruit and vegetables
- undercooked eggs (sunny side up, raw cookie dough, fresh Caesar salad dressing, homemade ice cream, homemade mayonnaise)

Natural food warning: While it doesn't seem likely that you and your baby would come across the above items, think for a moment about unpasteurized juices. These are common in health food stores and some vegetarian/vegan restaurants. It can be easy to pick up a bottle of such juice without thinking about it. The same goes for unpasteurized dairy products—gourmet cheeses at health food stores sometimes fall into this category. While adults might be able to eat these products without a problem, they are much more dangerous to infants and children. Check the labels: raw milk cheese, for example, should be clearly labeled as such.

Burns: Water, Sun, Hot Drinks, Appliances, BBQ

Q. **My child got a burn from _____. What do I do? Does he need an appointment?**

Don't get out the butter . . . and yes, you may need a doctor visit.
First rule: If it blisters, it should be looked at.
Second rule: Apply cool water, not butter.
Third rule: Don't pop a blister.

Any type of burn damages the top layer of skin. This causes redness (first degree). Burns that go deeper than that create blisters (second degree) or damage to the full thickness of the skin. Your skin is your body's protection from foreign invaders such as infection. Without the skin, the body is defenseless. To help combat infection, it's always a good idea to use an antibiotic ointment (such as Neosporin) on a burn and cover it with a non-stick dressing.

For second-degree burns, a prescription product called Silvadene may be needed. Second degree burns (or worse) need to be seen by your doctor to assess the damage, look for infection, and clean away any dead skin (this debris inhibits healing and promotes infection). Any burns on the hands, genitals, and on large areas should also be seen.

Priority 1: Needs immediate evaluation and treatment—NOW:
- Extensive areas burned.
- Area looks infected (red, weeping pus, fever)

Priority 2: Needs appointment the next day.
- Second degree burns (blisters).
- Burns on the hands or genitals.

Priority 3: Watch and wait. Needs appointment if there is no improvement or worsening of symptoms:
- First degree burns.

Breathing Problems (Respiratory Distress)

Q. **My baby is having trouble breathing. What do I do?**

Knowing what true respiratory distress looks and sounds like is very important. Read the section below first. Then understand how calls like this are triaged. The short answer is—if your child is having labored breathing, call your doctor immediately.

Understanding the Respiratory System

Think of the respiratory system as one big tube. The opening of the tube starts at the nose. The bottom end branches into tiny tubes in the lungs. Air goes in and out of this tube with each breath.

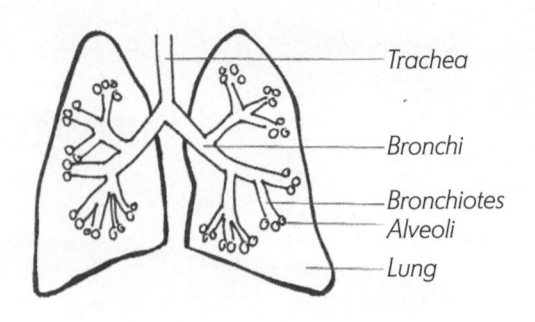

The Lungs

What is an UPPER respiratory infection?

The common cold or flu viruses live in the top of the tube (nose and sinuses). The body forms mucus or snot as a result of it. A person coughs because that mucus drips down the tube towards the lungs. Coughing protects our lungs. The cough brings the mucus up so it can be swallowed (into the stomach) instead of collecting in the lungs. Upper respiratory infections rarely cause labored breathing. They do cause noisy breathing, though, as air travels through the snot in the nasal passages.

Diagnoses include: Common cold, the flu (influenza)

What is a LOWER respiratory infection?

Bronchiolitis (RSV), bronchitis, or pneumonia are infections (viral or bacterial) that live in the lungs or tubes in the lungs. Because there is swelling or mucus in the tiny tubes and lung tissue, it is hard to exchange air effectively (remember that oxygen/carbon dioxide thing you learned about in science class). A person with a LOWER respiratory infection may become *air hungry*. We'll discuss this more in detail later in this section.

Rattling in the chest or **hearing wheezing** are NOT usually signs of a lower respiratory infection.

Diagnoses include: RSV Bronchiolitis, bronchitis, pneumonia

Any others?

There are also infections that attack the middle of the tube (larynx and trachea) where the voice box (vocal cords) is located. The tube swells in this area. Because children's tubes are smaller than adults, they are more compromised by these infections. The younger the child, the more problematic.

Diagnoses include: croup, whooping cough (pertussis)

WHAT AN AIR HUNGRY CHILD LOOKS LIKE: A MUST READ

The diagnosis of an air hungry child can be made without a stethoscope. It's not what is heard—it's what is seen. A baby or child who is air hungry breathes rapidly and shallowly (*elevated respiratory rate*), sucks in his rib cage (*retractions*), and flares his nostrils (*flaring*). A child may also make a grunting noise at the end of each breath. These are the body's way of using every muscle to pull in more air with each breath. The number of breaths taken per minute (respiratory rate) is much higher than normal. (See guide to vital signs earlier in this chapter). If a child is air hungry, call your doctor immediately.

Now that you understand the tube analogy, here is what you will encounter.

Think about the tube. You know how your pipes are all attached in your home? When you flush your toilet upstairs, you can hear it in the kitchen. Here is the analogy: nose is to toilet as lung is to kitchen. The water is in the nose, not the lung—but it can be heard and felt down there. This is called **transmitted upper airway noise.** The wheezing noise is *air passing through snot—it whistles.*

A child who is really wheezing enough to be audible to the naked ear is in such severe distress that you will *see it* in his chest (**AIR HUNGRY**).

Helpful Hints

♦ Sometimes your doctor can tell what the problem is just by listening to the baby breathing on the phone. If the breathing noises are dramatic, have the baby handy when you call.

♦ When a person lies down, the snot from the nose drips down the back of the throat. Our body's job is to cough and keep it out of the lungs. The cough is likely coming from nasal secretions when the "cough is worse at night."

Red Flags

♦ Air hungry.
♦ Croup under age two. (See below).
♦ Repeated coughing spasms, followed by reddening of face, possibly a "whoop," or vomiting.
♦ Episodes of not being able to catch one's breath.

What the doctor will ask you about RESPIRATORY DISTRESS:
1. How long has he been having trouble breathing?
2. Could he have swallowed something?
3. Does he have a fever?
4. Is he barking like a seal? Any high-pitched squeals?
5. Look at his chest. Is he sucking in his ribcage with each breath (retractions)? Is he panting or breathing fast? Are his nostrils flaring? Is he grunting at the end of each breath?
6. Has he wheezed before? Ever stayed in the hospital overnight for it?
7. Are there coughing spasms? Any gasping for breath? Vomiting or turning red with cough?

EVERYTHING YOU EVER WANTED TO KNOW ABOUT CROUP

A virus causes croup. It appears in epidemics every winter. A croup cough has a characteristic bark that sounds like a seal. Although impressive, this can be managed by quality time spent in your bathroom with a steamy shower running all night. When the airway tube is markedly swollen, the bark changes to a high-pitched squeal, called stridor. Stridor requires an emergency breathing treatment and steroids to reduce the swelling or the airway. FYI: Croup is always worse at night.

Priority 1: Needs immediate evaluation and treatment—NOW:

- Signs of air hunger.
- Any stridor noise (see croup box above).
- Trouble catching breath.
- Child who has asthma.
- Child who is a former premature infant.
- Choking (see choking emergencies on the next page).

Priority 2: Needs appointment the next day.

- Barking like a seal, but no squeal.

Priority 3: Watch and wait. Needs appointment if there is no improvement or worsening of symptoms:

- Chest rattling.
- Intermittent wheezing noises WITHOUT labored breathing.

Red Flag

When your child stops breathing. Call 911 immediately if your baby has any episode of true apnea (lack of breathing over 15 seconds).

Reality Check

There is a difference between apnea (not breathing) and **PERIODIC BREATHING**. Newborns frequently pause for several seconds between breaths. It is your child's job in life to give you grey hairs. Adults breathe 12 times a minute at a nice regular rate. Newborns breathe 30-60 times per minute at an irregular rate. *Newborns can pause for up to ten seconds and be feeling just fine.* To monitor the respiratory rate of a newborn, count the breaths for a whole minute.

What the doctor will ask about APNEA:
1. Is your child breathing okay now or is he having labored breathing?
2. Does he have a fever?
3. Has he had a problem with acid reflux?
4. Was he born prematurely?
5. Any recent trauma or injuries?

Babies with apnea get admitted to the hospital to be evaluated.

Diagnoses include:
1. Near Sudden Infant Death Syndrome (SIDS) event or acute life threatening event (ALTE).
2. Gastroesophageal reflux.
3. Infection (whooping cough, RSV bronchiolitis).
4. Metabolism problem.
5. Head trauma.

Choking Emergencies: 4 Tips

1 DO NOTHING IF YOUR CHILD IS ALERT AND MAKING NOISES (CRYING, GAGGING, COUGHING). He is effectively attempting to clear his airway.

2 **IF YOUR CHILD IS IN DISTRESS AND NOT MAKING ANY NOISE, ATTEMPT TO GET THE ITEM OUT OF HIS MOUTH.** Only put your finger in if you can see the item—do not blindly sweep his mouth with your finger; it can lodge the item in his throat.

3 **IF YOUR CHILD BECOMES UNCONSCIOUS,** put his belly on your forearm, face down (hold him like a football). Push forcefully between the shoulder blades with the lower part of your palm five times (called back blows). DO NOT PERFORM THE HEIMLICH MANEUVER ON INFANTS UNDER ONE YEAR OF AGE.

4 **IF THAT'S NOT WORKING, CALL 911.**

Feedback from the Real World
Another True Story from Dr. Brown

I was on-call and answering a page. While I was on the phone, my nine month old son crawled over to our dog's food bowl and did a taste test. In my panic, the first thing I did was to put my finger in his mouth to pull the food out. I ended up pushing it down and he swallowed it. He never touched the dog's food again! And I never made the mistake again of ignoring my own advice.

Cough And Congestion

Q. **My baby's nose is so congested that he can't eat or sleep. What do I do?**

This is the second most popular phone call. (Fever is number one). Nasal congestion happens for many reasons:

- Newborns all have nasal congestion for the first four to six weeks of life. They ALL sneeze and snort and snore. They do not have allergies (and rarely have a cold).
- Babies with acid reflux can have congestion from the milk that heads upwards behind the nose.
- Mucus pouring out the nose suggests an upper respiratory infection.

Diagnoses include: Common cold, the flu (influenza), RSV bronchiolitis

Tricks of the trade: How To Make (And Use) Saline Nose Drops

The most safe and effective way to clear the mucus is to flush the nostrils with saline nose drops. Saline is just a salt-water solution. You can't overdose on it. You can make your own concoction (1/2 tsp salt to eight oz water). Or you can buy it for about a dollar at the grocery store. Shoot several drops in each nostril before feedings. *You don't need to suck it out with a bulb syringe.* The saline will either make your baby sneeze or loosen the mucus enough to swallow it.

There are other methods of reducing the amount of mucus, but doctors always suggest saline first. Over the counter cough and cold medicines are *not recommended* under six months of age.

What the doctor will ask you about NASAL CONGESTION
1. Has he ever breathed through his nose?
2. Does he have a fever?
3. Is anyone else in the house sick? Is he in childcare?
4. Is he fussy or having disrupted sleep?
5. Does he have goopy eyes and/or green snot?

Helpful Hint
If a baby under age two has an upper respiratory infection, the flu, or especially RSV, he is at risk of getting an ear infection. Nasal discharge with fever, goopy eyes, and/or fussiness deserves a visit to the doctor to check for an ear infection.

Priority 1: Needs immediate evaluation and treatment—NOW:
- Has labored breathing or appears air hungry.
- Under four weeks of age and has a fever of 100.4 or greater (see fever section later in this chapter).
- Irritable and inconsolable.

Priority 2: Needs appointment the next day.
- Never breathes through the nose.
- Under four weeks of age, WITHOUT fever.
- Four weeks old to six months old, nasal congestion with or without fever.
- Fussy mood or disrupted sleep.
- Goopy eyes or red eyes.
- New appearance of green nasal discharge after clear discharge for at least one week.

Priority 3: Watch and wait. Needs appointment if there is no improvement or worsening of symptoms:
- Over six months of age with nasal congestion, runny nose, and cough for less than one week's duration (see fever section for other reasons to call).

Q. My child is keeping up the whole house with his cough! Make it go away.

Doctors are not miracle workers.

Nighttime coughs cause sleep deprivation for the child *and the parent*. Take a moment to review the respiratory system lecture. Coughing is a protective mechanism to keep the nasal discharge from collecting in the lungs. So for an upper respiratory infection (cold), let the cough happen during the day. The cough is worse at night because your baby is lying down. Always try saline nose drops first. Stopping the drip may stop the cough.

If the cough is keeping the baby awake, your doctor may recommend an infant cough suppressant—check first. Letting your baby sleep in an upright position (such as in a car seat) is also helpful.

If the cough is keeping YOU awake, turn off the baby monitor!

What the doctor will ask you about COUGHING:
1. How long has he had the cough? (Over three weeks deserves an appointment).
2. Is it worse at night or in the daytime?
3. Is he having any breathing difficulties? (See that section).
4. Is he barking like a seal? Squealing?
5. Is he panting or breathing shallowly?
6. Any apnea (no breathing for 15 seconds or more)?
7. Any concern for having swallowed a foreign body?
8. Any new fever?

Priority 1: Needs immediate evaluation and treatment—NOW:
- Breathing appears labored—grunting, flaring, retractions, stridor, or elevated respiratory rate.
- Trouble catching breath with coughing episodes.
- Foreign object known to be swallowed.
- Known asthma and not responding to medication.

Priority 2: Needs appointment the next day.
- Persistent cough.
- Cough sounds productive (wet or juicy).
- Vomiting or turning red with coughing episodes, but no apnea.
- Barking like a seal, but no squeal.
- New fever with a cough and NO labored breathing.

Priority 3: Watch and wait. Needs appointment if there is no improvement or worsening of symptoms:
- Cough under three weeks duration.
- Exposure to someone with a chronic cough.

Chronic Coughs

Not all coughs are caused by infection. Prolonged coughing (over three weeks) should be evaluated. Occasionally, we discover something interesting that has ended up in a branch of the lung airway. Mr. Dr. Brown (the Ear/Nose/Throat specialist) removes toy jacks, beads, peanuts, teeth, and popcorn kernels in the airways of small children on a regular basis.

The major causes of chronic cough include: foreign object in airway asthma, sinusitis, whooping cough, tuberculosis (rare).

Red Flags
- Cough with breathing difficulties.
- Chronic cough over three weeks.
- New fever with worsening cough.
- Possible foreign body (swallowed object).

Diarrhea

Q. My baby has diarrhea. What do I do ? When do I worry?

FIRST AID

Most of the time, diarrhea is a sign of a *stomach virus* (**VIRAL GASTROENTERITIS**). Some people call it the stomach flu. It's not THE flu. (The flu that we can get vaccinated for is influenza—a respiratory virus.) At best, your baby vomits once and the diarrhea continues for three to five days. At worst, your child vomits for 12-18 hours and has diarrhea 25 times a day for ten days (see rotavirus infection in Chapter 13, "Infections"). Those "24 hour bugs" don't really exist.

Food poisoning (**BACTERIAL GASTROENTERITIS**) is a concern when there is mucus or streaks of blood in the diarrhea. (See abdominal pain section earlier for details). Bacteria will cause only 10% of intestinal infections. Of those 10%, the most common culprit is **SALMONELLA**. *Other diagnoses include:* Shigella infection (bacteria), Yersinia infection (bacteria), Campylobacter infection (bacteria), C. difficile (bacteria, after an antibiotic) Giardia (parasite), Cryptosporidium (parasite), food allergy.

FYI: Chronic diarrhea (over two weeks duration) is a different problem More on this next.

Diarrhea for more than two weeks

If the diarrhea has been going on this long, your baby needs to see his doctor. Most commonly, chronic diarrhea is the result of an acute stomach virus.

Stomach viruses tear up the intestine's normal "flora" of good bacteria that help digest food. Stomach viruses can also break up a digestive enzyme called lactase, which helps the body digest milk sugar (lactose). Occasionally, infants and children can get a temporary lactose intolerance for up to six weeks after a stomach virus. Diarrhea results from repeated dairy intake and inability to digest it.

Another culprit is high juice intake. This is more of a problem with toddlers who become juice-a-holics. The high sugar content pulls water into the poop, causing increased frequency and watery stools.

Causes of chronic diarrhea include: Lactose intolerance (Post-stomach virus), high juice intake, food intolerance, celiac disease, parasite infection, Inflammatory Bowel Disease.

What the doctor will ask you about DIARRHEA:
1. How old is your baby?
2. How long has the diarrhea been going on?
3. Has there been vomiting or fever?
4. What does the diarrhea look like? Watery, bloody, mucus or blood streaked?
5. Is your baby still urinating?
6. Has your baby eaten any new foods?

Priority 1: Needs immediate evaluation and treatment—NOW:

- Under three months of age.
- Blood or mucus in diarrhea.
- Grape jelly diarrhea.
- Not urinating at least three times in 24 hours.
- Unsure about frequency of urination.
- Lethargy.

Priority 2: Needs appointment the next day.

- Diarrhea more than one week.
- Age over three months and fever more than three days.

Priority 3: Watch and wait. Needs appointment if there is no improvement or worsening of symptoms:

- Watery diarrhea for less than one week, with frequent wet diapers, and over three months of age.

Q. I'm worried about my baby getting dehydrated. Should I be?

Yes.

Babies under a year old are at higher risk of getting dehydrated. *Contrary to popular belief, dehydration is caused more by diarrhea than vomiting.* The vomiting part of an illness usually stops within about 12 hours. There is only a limited amount of fluid lost from vomiting (once the stomach is empty, there's not much left to throw up). As long as the vomiting is short lived, dehydration is not a problem. Diarrhea is another story. Frequent, explosive, watery diarrhea for a week causes a tremendous

---

HOW TO TELL IF YOUR BABY IS DEHYDRATED—A MUST READ

1 URINE OUTPUT: When our body needs fluid, less water is released as urine. If your baby pees (urinates) at least three times in 24 hours, he is doing okay. It's sometimes hard to tell if there is pee in the diaper, though, when there is explosive poop in it. (See helpful hint on the next page).

2 WEIGHT LOSS: If your baby has lost 10% of his body weight, he is severely dehydrated. This is an emergency.

3 SUNKEN FONTANELLE: Babies under a year still have a soft spot in their skull. That is their oil gauge equivalent. If the tank is low, the soft spot is sunken. That's the first place a doctor will touch when he examines your baby.

4 SKIN TURGOR: You know what your skin looks like when you have been in the bathtub too long? That prune like appearance is a clue to dehydration. Nice doughy skin has plenty of water in it.

5 DRY LIPS AND MOUTH: When you're dry, you stop making saliva.

6 CAPILLARY REFILL: Press down gently on your fingernail. You will see the pink color turn white. When you release the pressure, the pink color returns in less than two seconds. In severe dehydration, that refill will take more than two seconds because the blood supply is sluggish.

7 LETHARGY: This is a difficult one to assess. If your baby looks like a wet noodle, it's time to visit the doctor.

amount of water loss. Your baby needs to keep up with these losses with fluid intake.

BOTTOM LINE: Although vomiting is scary, persistent diarrhea is more likely to cause dehydration.

Helpful Hint
How to tell if there is urine in the diaper:
Put a tissue in the front part of the diaper. The urine looks yellow on the tissue because it is concentrated.

Q. What can I give my baby to eat and drink to prevent dehydration?

Start with liquids, then slowly add solids.

Presuming that vomiting has come first in this scenario, make sure that fluids stay down before going back to solid food (if baby is over four months old). *Liquids are much more important than solids.* It's the fluid that replaces the losses. Babies make up for lost time and will eat when they are feeling better.

Your doctor may recommend Pedialyte to treat dehydration—see the vomiting section later for details. Once your baby has kept Pedialyte down, return to regular formula or breast milk.

Here are some other suggestions:

1. *Try Isomil DF formula* for severe or prolonged diarrhea. (see formula section in liquid nutrition, Chapter 6) The DF stands for Diarrhea Formula. But it also stands for Dietary Fiber. The formula is lactose free and has a high fiber content that helps bulk up the poop.

2. *Try a high fat, high fiber diet* for babies over four months old. Resume solids when a baby is interested in food again. Depending on the age and what foods your baby has tried, look for high fiber foods (prunes, oatmeal, beans) and high fat foods (whole milk yogurt, avocados) to feed your baby.

3. *Try yogurt or probiotics.* Stomach viruses kill off the "good germs" that live in the intestines and help digest food. Replenishing the gut with good germs improves digestion. If your baby is over six months, offer four oz. yogurt daily during the illness. Another option: probiotic chewable tablets and powder packets are available over the counter. Use half of a packet or crush up a tablet daily and mix into food.

4. *Try a lactose (dairy) free diet* for diarrhea lasting over one or two weeks. If the diarrhea is prolonged, a secondary lactose intolerance may be the culprit (see chronic diarrhea section earlier).

BOTTOM LINE: Liquids are the priority in re-hydration. Your baby will eat solid food again when he is well.

Old Wives Tales

1. Avoid milk when your baby has diarrhea.
The truth: Your baby will have diarrhea no matter what he is eating or drinking. Give him what he is willing to drink. If the diarrhea has been going on for *over a week*, however, dairy restriction may be in order to avoid a lactose intolerance (see earlier section on chronic diarrhea).

2. Use the BRAT diet for a baby with diarrhea (Bananas, Rice, Applesauce, Toast).
The Truth: Fat and fiber are more effective in bulking up the poop than these foods. The *old* school of thought was called the BRAT diet. It was thought that a bland, carbohydrate diet was best for infants with diarrhea. The latest research suggests that fat and fiber are actually more effective in reducing water loss in diarrhea.

Q. Can I give my baby any anti-diarrhea medications?

No.

Some doctors feel uncomfortable using Pepto-Bismol and similar medications for babies under a year of age. Check with your doctor for her opinion.

These medicines slow down the intestines, which can actually prolong the length of some illnesses.

The American Academy of Pediatrics issued a policy statement in 1996 that advises against using anti-diarrhea medications in infants.[2] However, more recent studies suggest that these products are probably safe and somewhat beneficial for babies over four months of age.[3]

Vomiting

There is spit up, and then there is vomit. All babies spit up (see acid reflux in Chapter 8, "The Other End"). Vomiting is the forceful elimination of food and fluid that is in the stomach.

There is only a fixed amount of stomach contents. So, if a child is vomiting repeatedly, eventually he will have "dry heaves" (vomiting with nothing coming out). If a child is vomiting *bile* (fluorescent green/yellow fluid), that is coming from the small intestine and may be a concern for an intestinal blockage.

In the strictest sense, repeated vomiting causes dehydration. If your child is vomiting more than 18 hours straight, he is unable to maintain adequate fluid intake. *This rarely happens*. With most garden-variety stomach viruses, the vomiting stops within 12 hours and kids are drinking again. The greater risk of dehydration is the water lost in the diarrhea that accompanies the vomiting. Dehydration usually occurs later in the course of the illness.

All vomiting is not due to stomach upset. Babies and young children have active gag reflexes. *Forceful coughing* can result in vomiting (see **POST-TUSSIVE EMESIS**). So a baby with a common cold might vomit after coughing. Headaches can also be accompanied by vomiting. This category includes ear infections, head injury, brain tumors, meningitis. That's why unexplained vomiting needs to be checked out.

BOTTOM LINE: Persistent vomiting with no obvious cause should be evaluated.

Causes of vomiting include:

Gastroesophageal reflux	Early viral gastroenteritis
Pyloric stenosis	Intestinal obstruction (rare)
After coughing (post-tussive emesis)	Ear infection
Head injury	Brain tumor (rare)
Meningitis	Metabolic disorders (rare)
Bladder/ kidney infections	Food poisoning (bacterial gastroenteritis)

What the doctor will ask you about VOMITING

1. How old is your baby?
2. How long has he been vomiting?
3. Is it projectile (Exorcist-like) or just coming up effortlessly?
4. What does the vomit look like? Any fluorescent green or yellow color? Any blood or coffee grounds?
5. Does he have a fever?
6. Does he have diarrhea?
7. Is he around other children/anyone sick in the house?
8. Does he look like his stomach hurts?
9. Is he still urinating?
10. Any recent head injuries?

Priority 1: Needs immediate evaluation and treatment—NOW:

- Vomiting with a head injury.
- Vomiting bile (bright green or yellow).
- Vomiting over 12 hours straight.

WHAT TO DO WHEN YOUR BABY VOMITS

1. **While your baby is actively vomiting,** DO NOT GIVE HIM ANY FOOD OR DRINK. Parents are often so afraid that their baby will get dehydrated, they offer fluids immediately. And it comes right back at them. Don't give fluids on an unsettled stomach.

2. **If it has been at least one hour since your child has vomited, offer a few sips of Pedialyte (see below).** The goal is one teaspoon every five minutes for an hour. Do not offer a whole bottle to your child. He is thirsty and will drink the whole thing—only to vomit again because his stomach isn't ready for that much. If this plan fails (that is, your baby vomits again), call your doctor.

3. **If the Pedialyte stays down, you can add to the volume one to two ounces every time your baby wants to drink.** If this plan fails, call your doctor.

4. **If your child has four hours vomit free, return to breast-feeding or formula.**

5. **After eight hours of success,** babies who are already eating solid foods can return to eating again.

- ◆ Projectile vomiting more than three times in a row.
- ◆ Vomiting only in the mornings.
- ◆ Vomiting blood or coffee grounds.
- ◆ Appears dehydrated (see section earlier on this topic).

Priority 2: Needs appointment the next day.
- ◆ Large volume spit ups frequently.
- ◆ Recurrent vomiting.

Priority 3: Watch and wait. Needs appointment if there is no improvement or worsening of symptoms:
- ◆ Isolated episode of vomiting in well appearing child.

Q. What is Pedialyte?

Pedialyte is kind of a Gatorade equivalent for babies. It is made especially for babies ages birth to one year. Parents often ask if it's okay to use for babies that young—this is exactly who it is made for! It has a high salt and moderate sugar content and tastes like salt water. Usually babies under a year don't mind the flavor. (Kids over a year are pretty smart and will refuse it.) If you want to make your own Pedialyte, check out Appendix B for a recipe you can make at home.

Do NOT give plain water to babies when they have vomiting or diarrhea. Their body salts are already depleted and giving plain water messes up the delicate electrolyte balance even more.

For older kids, try Pedialyte popsicles, Sprite, or clear chicken broth.

> **Reality Check**
> Regular Pedialyte is a clear fluid. But it also comes in "flavored" varieties—which contain food coloring. Stick with the clear version. Why would you give a child who is vomiting a purple drink?

Eye Problems

Q. My newborn has goop draining from his eyes. Does he have pink eye?

No. It's a blocked tear duct.

Babies are born with narrow canals that let the tears flow out of them. Until the canals widen, the tears can get clogged. This can happen intermittently through the first year of life. (See glossary for **NASOLACRIMAL DUCT OBSTRUCTION**). Just wipe away the goop with warm water.

Call your doctor if the white of the eye is red, or if the eyelids are swollen.

Q. My nine month old has goop draining from his eyes and has a cold. Does he have pink eye?

Probably.

When the eye goop is accompanied by other symptoms (runny nose,

How to avoid having the whole family get pink eye

Pink eye is spread by the sick person touching the infected eye and leaving the germs for someone else to touch (doorknobs, hand towels, toys). The best approach if you have pink eye in your house is to wash hands frequently and make a concerted effort not to touch your face.

cough, fever), it's more likely to be an infection called conjunctivitis or pink eye.

Conjunctivitis can be caused by either a virus or bacteria. Bacterial infections cause goopy eye discharge (eye boogers) and viral infections cause watery eye discharge. Both are extremely contagious. Bacterial infections can be treated with antibiotic eye drops or oral antibiotics. Viruses cannot be treated and can last up to a week.

Children under age two years with bacterial conjunctivitis (goop) should see a doctor. About 30% have an ear infection or sinus infection to go along with it. The bug is usually Haemophilus influenza non-typable (a cousin of the HIB we vaccinate against). This is a smart bug often resistant to first line antibiotics.

BOTTOM LINE: A child under age two with goopy eyes needs to be seen by a doctor. There is an association of pink eye with ear infections and sinus infections.

Q. My baby's eye is red. Does he have allergies?

Unlikely.

As a general rule, babies under one year do not have seasonal allergies. A red eye is either caused by *trauma, irritation,* or *infection.* If just one eye is red, consider trauma (corneal abrasion—see below, foreign body) or irritation (soap, sun block). If it is bothersome to your baby, try flushing the eye with some lukewarm water.

If your baby looks uncomfortable, he needs to be evaluated.

Causes of red eyes: trauma, irritation, infection—viral or bacterial.

Q. My baby's eye is swollen shut. Should I worry?

Yes—if she has a fever.

Usually the cause of impressive swelling is a local allergic reaction. If a bug bite or poison ivy occurs on an eyelid, the reaction can be impressive. Proof of a bite or rash is helpful.

The concern is a serious infection called **ORBITAL CELLULITIS**. This is a sinus infection that extends into the area where the eye rests in the skull (orbit). It happens in stages, and the prognosis is obviously better if caught early. The first sign is redness and swelling of the eyelid. It then progresses to a bulging eye, with limited motion of the eye itself.

If you see this, call your doctor NOW. This is a medical emergency. See our web site at Baby411.com for a visual library picture (the picture titled "eyelid swelling" is the example you're looking for).

Q. My baby's eye is tearing constantly today. What is wrong?

Probably a corneal abrasion.

Babies can scratch their eyes accidentally. This is a superficial scratch that takes a day or two to heal. Foreign bodies (dust, etc.) can also cause similar symptoms. Doctors check for abrasions using a purple light and fluorescein dye. If a scratch is found, antibiotic eye drops are prescribed. If a foreign body is found, it can be flushed out.

What the doctor will ask you about RED EYES
1. How old is your baby?
2. Is there eye discharge? Is it watery or goopy?
3. Is there fever, runny nose, or fussiness?
4. If the eyelid is swollen, is there any bug bite or rash visible? Any fever?

Priority 1: Needs immediate evaluation and treatment—NOW:
- Eyelid swollen shut with fever.
- Question of foreign body in the eye.
- Very uncomfortable child with a red eye.

Priority 2: Needs appointment the next day.
- Goopy eyes with a cold, with or without fever

Priority 3: Watch and wait. Needs appointment if there is no improvement or worsening of symptoms:
- Newborn with eye that waters frequently, without redness.

Fever: Special Section

Fever is the number one reason pediatricians get called at night. At some point in your baby's life, he will have his first fever. And like every new parent that has come before you, you will have some anxiety. Read this section in its entirety! (Note: all temperatures are in degrees Fahrenheit).

Q. What is the definition of a fever?

Fever is an elevation of the body's regular temperature.

Contrary to what you learned in junior high science class, our body temperature is not 98.6 for 24 hours a day. It varies on a daily rhythm based on hormone levels. Our body is the coolest at 7 am (as low as 97.6) and the hottest at 7 pm (as high as 100). *The true definition of fever is a body temperature of 100.4 or higher taken rectally.*

When an infection (most common reason for fever) enters the body, the body mounts a defense via the immune system. The immune system revs up all other body systems into attack mode. This raises all vital signs (temperature, heart rate/pulse, respiratory rate, blood pressure). A warmer body temperature actually helps fight infection. FEVER IS NOT BAD.

Because the normal body temperature is lowest in the morning and highest at night, our fever will be lower in the morning and higher at night. With a typical viral infection, we may have a temperature of 99 in the morning and be 102 at night. This is why pediatricians get phone calls

> **DR B'S OPINION:**
> **FEVER-PHOBIC PARENTS**
>
> Here is a typical phone encounter on fevers:
>
> Parent: "Doctor, my baby has a fever."
> Doctor: "Yes, but what else is going on?"
> Parent: "But, doctor, he has a fever."
> Doctor: "I understand, but can you tell me if he has any other symptoms?"
>
> You get the picture. I heard you. I know your baby has a fever. I need to figure out WHY he has the fever. Help me. Don't fixate on the fever. *The fever is not the problem—it's a clue for the real problem.* Be a good detective and help me look for clues. It will make for a much more productive conversation!

about fever at night. *The fever doesn't go away and come back. It's always there. It's just lower in the morning. Fevers often last for three to four days for a viral infection.*

Fever, in and of itself, does not do any harm to the body. But it is an indicator that something (usually infection) is going on in the body. *Parents tend to focus and worry about the fever. Pediatricians worry about what the diagnosis/infection is.* Body temperatures over 108 cause brain damage. Infections do not cause body temperatures over the 106 range. (Hyperthermia, the term for body temperatures over 107, are usually caused accidentally—for example, someone locked in a car in the middle of August).

Fever is often the first sign of illness. It can take several hours to see the other symptoms blossom from the infection. So, unless a baby is under three months of age (see protocol below), you may need to watch and see how things evolve.

Fever Phobia

A recent study looked at parent misconceptions of fever:[4]
- 91% believed fever could cause harmful effects (death, brain damage).
- 44% believed that a fever over 102 was a "high" fever.
- 7% believed that a fever could rise to 110 if left untreated.
- 25% gave fever reducing medicine for temperatures less than 100.
- 85% said they awaken their child to give fever-reducing medicine.
- 44% dosed the fever reducing medicine incorrectly.
- 52% said they checked their child's temperature at least every hour when they had a fever.

BOTTOM LINE
The body is coolest at 7 am (as low as 97.6) and hottest at 7 pm (as high as 100). So, the true definition of fever is a body temperature of 100.4 or higher taken rectally.

Fever is the body's immune response to infection. The immune system revs up all other body systems and raises all vital signs. A warmer body temperature actually helps fight infection. Therefore, fever is *not* bad.

Remember, fever is not the problem, rather it is a clue to finding the problem. And fever is often the first sign of illness.

Don't be fooled that your child is fever-free in the morning if he had a fever the night before. It's just naturally lower in the morning. If you send him to childcare, you will get called to take him home when his fever spikes in the afternoon. Prepare to stay at home next day if your child has a fever at night.

Reality Check

Most of the time, newborns have a virus they picked up from a family member. But your doctor doesn't want to take any chances. Now you know why the standard advice is to limit visitors during the first four weeks after birth.

Helpful Hint

Newborns can also have problems if they have LOW body temperatures. If your newborn has a persistently low body temperature (under 97.6 taken rectally), it's best to check in with your doctor.

Q. At what temperature should I be worried?

Below is the protocol for fever in infants. The management plan is based on a child's age. The protocol is fairly universal for all babies under three months.

Priority 1: Needs Immediate Evaluation And Treatment—NOW:

◆ *Age zero to four weeks: any fever in this age group is an emergency!*
1. A rectal temperature of 100.4 or greater requires hospitalization ASAP.
2. Newborns have a unique risk of serious bacterial infections due to delivery and congenital urinary tract defects (Group B strep meningitis, pneumonia, sepsis, urinary tract infections/kidney infections). They are tested for all of these potential infections and treated with antibiotics until bacterial cultures are clear of growth. (see sepsis workup in Appendix C, "Lab Tests").
3. *Never give acetaminophen (Tylenol) to your feverish newborn. Call your doctor.*

◆ *Age four weeks to three months: any fever in this age group is an emergency!*
1. A rectal temperature 100.4 or greater requires examination and lab evaluation.
2. These infants need to be seen either in the doctor's office or in an emergency room depending on the hour. They still run the risk of having those bacterial infections that newborns get.
3. If there is an obvious source of infection (e.g. a cold), and the baby's lab work looks reassuring, hospitalization is unnecessary.
4. *Never give acetaminophen (Tylenol) without calling the doctor.* Exception: If your two-month-old baby received his vaccinations, and then starts running a fever within 24–48 hours, it's not a prob-

lem unless there are other symptoms going on. We expect your baby to run a fever after getting his shots. Review Chapter 12, "Vaccinations," for more information.

◆ **Age three months to six months: a fever AND these problems in this age group is an emergency.**
1. A fever over 102.
2. A fever lasting more than three days.
3. A new fever, after a recent illness.
4. No obvious symptoms of viral infection (cough, runny nose, diarrhea)
5. Fussy mood/inconsolable.
6. Petechiae rash (See bleeding section earlier).

◆ **Age six months to one year:**
1. A fever of 104 or above deserves a phone call. (We know—that's way beyond your comfort level.)
2. A fever lasting more than three days.
3. A new fever, after a recent illness.
4. No obvious symptoms of viral infection (cough, runny nose, diarrhea).
5. Fussy mood/inconsolable.
6. Petechiae rash (see bleeding section earlier in this chapter.)

Priority 2: Needs appointment the next day.

◆ *Age three months to six months*
1. If everyone in the house has the flu and your baby has the same symptoms, make an appointment if the fever persists longer than three days (or something else is concerning—i.e. dehydration, labored breathing).
2. *You can give acetaminophen (Tylenol) for the fever. Just make sure you have figured out why your baby has the fever first.*

Priority 3: Watch and wait. Needs appointment if there is no improvement or worsening of symptoms

◆ *Age six months to one year:*
1. Obvious symptoms of a virus (cough, runny nose, vomiting, diarrhea), you can probably manage the infection without a doctor's visit.
2. *You can give acetaminophen (Tylenol) or ibuprofen (Motrin) when your baby has a fever. Just make sure you know why your baby has the fever.*

Reality Check
After six months of age, it's not the degree of the fever that is concerning, it's what the baby looks like. Everyone looks sick when they are running a fever. If a baby still looks sick after taking a fever reducing medicine, it's time to call the doctor.

Insider Tip: Roseola
Children usually get the common childhood infection, **ROSEOLA**, between nine to 12 months of age. It causes a high fever (103 to 104) for about three days with no other symptoms. These kids look

perfectly happy and go about their daily routines. On day four, when they are fever free, the classic roseola rash (flat red patches on the chest and arms) comes out. They are not contagious with the rash. High fevers (104 or above) deserve to be evaluated, but roseola is often the culprit.

See our web site at Baby411.com (Bonus Material) for a visual library of rashes.

Q. My baby is running a "low grade" fever. Should I be worried?

Who started this urban legend? What is a low-grade fever? It's not in the doctor dictionary.

Parents worry about body temperatures of 99 to 100. This is not, by definition, a fever. It has no association with an infection unless your baby is 100 at 7am. In that case, it does not bode well for what the night will bring.

Q. My baby has had a fever "on and off" for several days. I thought he broke the fever. Why does it keep coming back?

Let's review. A typical viral infection will cause a fever for three or four days.

Remember, it may look like your baby doesn't have a fever in the morning, but it always comes back at night. If there is a fever at any point in a 24-hour day, your child still has fever on a daily basis. This is helpful when you are reporting symptoms to the doctor. Doctors want a record of how many days in a row your child has had a fever. It helps make diagnostic decisions.

Fever reducing medicine, acetaminophen (Tylenol) and ibuprofen (Motrin), will help bring the body temperature down for four to six hours. But once the medicine wears off, the fever will return. The medicine does not make the infection go away. (See later questions on fever-reducing medications).

BOTTOM LINE: A truly NEW fever after being fever free for a period of at least 24 hours is concerning for a bacterial infection that has capitalized on a sick person (such as ear infection, sinus infection, pneumonia). Make an appointment to see your doctor.

Helpful Hint
On Fever curves

Another important trend doctors watch is the fever curve over a period of days. At the beginning of an infection, the fever is the highest. As the body effectively fights off the infection, the maximum fever spikes should be lower. If a fever curve trends up instead of down (fevers are getting higher on a day to day basis), this is more concerning and may prompt an evaluation.

Q. How do you recommend taking a baby's temperature?

For the target age of this book (birth to age one), you need to take the temperature with a rectal thermometer.

Most parents cringe just thinking about this task. Are you cringing? Don't. Babies really don't mind. It does not hurt or make them feel like

> ### DR B'S OPINION: THERMOMETERS
>
> Ear thermometers are not my friend. Their reliability is based upon the ability of the user to line the tip up with the eardrum. If you compare your own two ears and get two different readings, you will understand what I mean. They are very pricey, too. Not to mention that they can also overestimate the degree of fever and create parent panic. I've received frantic calls regarding kids with fevers of 107F taken with an ear thermometer that turned out to be 102F or 103F when taken rectally.
>
> Except for the ear thermometers (which OVER estimate fever), alternative methods to check temperature UNDER estimate the degree of fever. Parents often ask, "Do you add or subtract a degree from the non-rectal measurement?" My response is, "If you ever get an actual reading that is 100F or over, you know your child has a fever. That is all the information I need."

you've invaded their space. In fact, it's a good trick to make them poop. But I digress.

Rectal temperatures are the most accurate way to check a human's body temperature. And for infants under three months of age, one tenth of a degree will make the difference between whether you stay at home in your nice warm bed or head out for an evening of fun at your local emergency room.

If you call the doctor at 2 am and tell her that your six week old has a fever, the first thing she will ask is, "How did you take the temperature?" If you took it any way other than rectally, we make you get a rectal thermometer and call us back. Invest in one now—digital rectal thermometers cost about $5.

After one year of age, there is more flexibility about how to take your child's temperature. Trendy products on the market for toddler temperatures include a pacifier thermometer, ear thermometer, temporal artery scanners, and plastic skin stickers. Using an oral thermometer in the armpit is also okay. None of these are as accurate as a rectal temperature. But after a year of age, the actual degree of fever is much less important to making a management plan for your child. That is, a child with 101 or 103 is managed based on the *other symptoms* they have in addition to the fever.

Mom Knows Best

There was a great study that tested Mom's method of temperature taking (placing the hand on the forehead). Guess what? Mom is usually right—at least 80% of the time—with this method. Some thoughts on this:

1. After six months of age, if you say your child "feels hot," that's often enough proof of fever.
2. Trust yourself! Parents think they need to take their baby's temperature periodically to make sure he is okay. You hold your baby 24 hours a day. You will know when he feels hot. Then you can get out the thermometer.

TREATING A FEVER: DR. B'S 10 COMMANDMENTS

1. **IF YOU HAVE YOUR DOCTOR'S BLESSING** (see age discussion earlier), **IT'S OKAY TO GIVE A FEVER REDUCING MEDICATION.**

2. **BABIES FROM THREE TO SIX MONTHS CAN USE ACETAMINOPHEN** (Tylenol).

3. **BABIES OVER SIX MONTHS OF AGE CAN USE IBUPROFEN** (Motrin/Advil) **OR ACETAMINOPHEN** (Tylenol).

4. **I PREFER IBUPROFEN FOR OLDER BABIES BECAUSE THE MEDICATION LASTS FOR SIX HOURS INSTEAD OF FOUR.** Since the fever will climb at night, this will buy everyone two extra hours of sleep.

5. **ACETAMINOPHEN IS PREFERRED IF A CHILD IS DEHYDRATED** or has a stomach virus (ibuprofen can upset an empty stomach).

6. **BE FOREWARNED: THESE MEDICATIONS ARE CALLED FEVER REDUCERS NOT FEVER ELIMINATORS.** At best, these medications will bring the body temperature down by two degrees. If your baby is cooking at 104F, he will be feeling more comfortable at 102F. That's as good as it gets.

7. **I DON'T ROUTINELY INSTRUCT PARENTS TO ALTERNATE ACETAMINOPHEN AND IBUPROFEN.** If a baby is old enough for the ibuprofen, stick with that. I only alternate medicines in babies prone to febrile seizures (see glossary for details). There is no proven benefit of alternating medicines.

8. **DON'T BOTHER PUTTING BABY IN A TEPID BATH.** If you had the chills, would you want to sit in cold water? This cooling technique is only necessary in an emergency situation (such as extreme hyperthermia, a 107F temperature). Bringing your child's temperature down with this technique is not only unpleasant, but a waste of time and effort.

9. **NEVER GIVE YOUR CHILD ASPIRIN.** It can cause liver failure when given with particular viral infections.

10. **ALWAYS USE THE MEDICINE DROPPER THAT COMES WITH THE PACKAGE.** The term "one dropperful" refers to the dropper that comes with the medicine.

New Parent 411:
How to take a baby's rectal temperature.

Don't be embarrassed. You've never done this before. Get out your digital rectal thermometer. Place some Vaseline on the tip. With one hand lift up your baby's feet, holding them together. With your other hand, insert the tip of the thermometer into his anus about one inch.

Leave the thermometer in there for one minute (or until it beeps at you). See, you and baby did just fine.

FYI: The American Academy of Pediatrics now recommends using digital (rectal/oral) thermometers as opposed to glass mercury thermometers. The latter are dangerous if broken.

Q. What is the correct dose of medication? It says on the box to consult a physician.

Ever wonder why it says this on the box? It's to make sure that you call the doctor when your newborn has a fever. Now that you know when you need to call, we will tell you how to dose these medicines. Both acetaminophen (Tylenol) and ibuprofen (Motrin) are dosed at five milligrams per pound per dose. See the dosing chart on page 379.

How to avoid overdosing your baby

1. Acetaminophen is the generic name for Tylenol, Feverall, and Tempra.
2. Ibuprofen is the generic name for Motrin and Advil.
3. Both acetaminophen and ibuprofen are effective fever reducers and pain medications.
4. Acetaminophen is dosed every four hours. Ibuprofen is dosed every six hours.
5. As we've said earlier, always use the medicine dropper that comes in the package. The dropper size varies between products. (The Tylenol dropper is a 0.8 ml one. The Motrin dropper is 1.875 ml.).
6. There is a difference in the concentration of medicine in the infant drops and the children's syrup. The infant drops are much more concentrated so you won't have to force a large volume of medicine into your baby.
7. Acetaminophen suppositories (medicine bullets inserted in the anus) are available for babies who resist taking medicine or are actively vomiting.
8. When your doctor tells you to use "one dropperful," it routinely means the dropper that comes with the package, with the medicine drawn up to the line marked on the dropper. A mother requested that we share this with you because she mistakenly thought it meant to fill the whole dropper up with medicine (look at a medicine dropper and you'll understand).
9. When you graduate to the syrup medicine, use a medicine cup to dispense. Silverware teaspoons are not an exact teaspoon measurement. They can be larger or smaller depending on your set. Medicine syringes are also helpful—they make it easier to measure and dispense medicine.

> **DR B'S OPINION**
>
> *"I have too many stories about Tylenol overdoses to share in this book. It's just not as easy to figure these medicines out as it should be."*

Dosing Chart

Acetaminophen:

Baby's weight in Lbs.	6-11LBS	12-17LBS	18-23LBS	24-35LBS
Dose in mg	40mg	80mg	120mg	160mg
Infant drops	0.4ml	0.8ml	0.8+0.4ml	0.8+0.8ml
(80mg per 0.8 ml)				
Children's syrup	*	1/2 tsp	3/4 tsp	1 tsp
(160 mg per tsp)				
Suppositories (80mg)	*	1 suppository	1 1/2	2
Suppositories (120mg)	*	*	1	1 1/3

Ibuprofen:

Baby's weight in Lbs.	6-11LBS	12-17LBS	18-23LBS	24-35LBS
Dose in mg	*	50mg	75mg	100mg
Infant drops				
(50mg per 1.25 ml)	*	1.25ml	1.25+0.625	1.25+1.25
1.875ml is a dropperful	*			
Children's syrup (100mg per tsp)		1/2 tsp	3/4 tsp	1 tsp

*Note: Ibuprofen is NOT for babies under six months of age

Q. Is it safe to give a fever reducing medicine longer than five days? It says on the box to consult a physician.

The medicine itself is safe to give. This warning is a way to make sure you have checked in with your doctor if your baby has a prolonged fever. A child with a fever more than four days straight should be seen by her doctor.

Q. I have given my baby acetaminophen (Tylenol) and he still has a fever.

This one is on the Top 10 List of most asked questions for any pediatrician.

The most common reason this happens is that your child has outgrown the dose of medicine you have given him. Fever reducing medicines (as well as most other types) are dosed based on the weight of a child. A few pounds can make a difference for the correct dosing.

Look at the chart above. When your doctor tells you the dose of acetaminophen (Tylenol) at your child's two-month well check, don't think that the dose will never change.

BOTTOM LINE: Acetaminophen and Ibuprofen are fever reducers (not eliminators). If your child has a high fever, it won't be completely eliminated by the medicine. The fact that the fever does not go down with medication has no implication on the severity of the illness.

Q. I've heard that fevers can cause seizures in babies. Is this true?

Yes, babies can have febrile seizures or convulsions.

A few children—less than 5% (ages six months to five years) are prone to having a seizure/convulsion as a fever is shooting up. "Febrile seizures" do not cause brain damage or lead to a seizure disorder such as epilepsy.

The seizure happens when the body temperature rises quickly. If your child's temperature is at 104, you don't have to worry about him having a seizure.

Yes, it is terrifying to watch a child have a full-blown seizure in your living room. Fortunately, febrile seizures last less than five minutes. And children are fine afterwards.

About 30% of children who are prone to febrile seizures have more than one episode in their lives. But after the first time, parents are much more comfortable about managing it. Parents will give fever medicine around the clock so that the temperature elevation can never rise rapidly during the course of an illness.

The first time a child has a febrile seizure, he needs to be evaluated thoroughly. Once this diagnosis is determined, treatment focuses on the cause of the fever.

Old Wives Tales

Don't give your baby a bath while he has a fever.
Don't let your baby drink milk while he has a fever.
Fevers cause brain damage.
Teething causes fever.

The Truth: None of these statements are remotely true. Keep feeding your baby breast milk or formula, go ahead and give him a bath, and unless his fever reaches the extreme temperatures mentioned earlier, relax a bit. Oh, and teething has *nothing* to do with fever; remember fever is caused by viral or bacterial invaders.

What the doctor will ask you about FEVER:
1. How old is your baby?
2. How did you take the temperature?
3. What other new symptoms are you seeing?
4. Is anyone else in the household sick?
5. Is your child exposed to other children?
6. How many days has the fever been going on?
7. Any recent illnesses prior to the fever?
8. Any rashes?
9. Have you given any fever reducing medicines?
10. What dose of medicine did you give?
11. What does your baby look like after giving the medicine?

Red Flags

- Fever under three months of age.
- Fever over 102 in three to six-month-old.
- Fever of 104 or above in six months and older.
- Fever lasting over three days.
- Fever without obvious source of infection.
- Fever with petechiae rash.
- Fever with irritability or lethargy.
- Febrile seizure.
- Fever with a limp or limb pain.

Poisonings/Ingestions

If your child accidentally swallows a household product, call poison control immediately.

Have the phone number at each of your telephones. It is no longer recommended to have ipecac, a medicine that induces vomiting, in your medicine cabinet. In fact, inducing vomiting with ipecac is used LESS as a treatment of poisonings today, as doctors have realized that other treatments are more effective (and vomiting can, in some cases, causes MORE harm than good).

Poison Control is an amazing resource of information on any product a curious child might ingest. They will tell you whether the product can do potential harm to the body or not. And they know the antidotes.

Occasionally, a parent is not even aware of the ingestion happening. They only know that their child is acting unusual. *Some clues to ingestion include: mouth burns, drooling, rapid or shallow breathing, vomiting without fever, seizures, extreme lethargy, or body/breath odor.*

THE MOST DANGEROUS HOUSEHOLD PRODUCTS

Here is a list of childhood favorites to keep out of reach. (Place items in high cabinets out of reach or in places with cabinet locks).

Chemicals
- cleaning products
- paint thinner
- dishwashing detergent
- gasoline

Medications
- especially Mom's prenatal vitamins (iron)
- especially visiting grandparents (heart or blood pressure medications)

Plants (some of these are common houseplants).
- Christmas favorites: poinsettias, mistletoe, holly
- wild mushrooms
- hyacinth, narcissus, daffodil, elephant ear, rosary pea, larkspur, Lily-of-the-Valley, iris, foxglove, bleeding heart, daphne, wisteria, golden chain, laurels, azaleas, jasmine, lantana

Hygiene products
- mouthwash
- nail polish remover
- rubbing alcohol
- hair dye

Food and wine
- liquor
- pottery from foreign countries (lead)

Helpful hint
If Poison Control directs you to an emergency room, take the poison/medication with you if you have it. It helps determine the ingredients and the amount that was swallowed.

Feedback from the Real World
Dr. B True Story

I cared for a patient once who ate part of a necklace a mother had brought back from traveling abroad. The beads were made of ricin, the active ingredient of poison darts (think Bond, James Bond). *Bottom Line:* Be careful. Babies are programmed to taste everything.

What the doctor will ask you about POISONING:
1. Is the product toxic vs. non-toxic?
2. Do you have the bottle/container?
3. Is your child having trouble breathing?

When to call:
All poisonings and ingestions are Priority 1: Needs immediate evaluation and treatment—NOW!

Rashes

Until we all have videophones, you need to be the eyes for your doctor. Trying to diagnose a rash over the phone is always a challenge. At best, we can figure out whether the rash fits into the worrisome or the non-worrisome categories. Worrisome rashes need prompt attention. Non-worrisome ones can wait until the office opens the next day. Causes of rashes include:
- **Infection:** viruses, bacteria, funguses, mites
- **Allergy:** eczema, contact allergy (poison ivy, sensitivity to a skin care product), food/medication allergy
- **Newborn rashes:** due to hormonal changes
- **Blood cell abnormalities**

See our website at Baby411.com (Bonus Material) for a visual library of rashes.

What the doctor will ask you about RASHES:
1. How long has the rash been there?
2. Where on the body did the rash start? Is it spreading? Where?
3. Is there a fever?
4. Is it itchy? Really really itchy?
5. Anyone else in the house with a rash?
6. Is the rash flat or raised? (Can you feel it with your eyes closed?)
7. Is it scaly on top?
8. What color is the rash?
9. How big are the spots?
10. When you press on the rash, does the color turn white? Or, does it remain discolored?
11. Is your child taking any medications?

12. Has your child eaten any new foods?
13. Have you used any new skin products? (sun block, lotion, soap, detergents)
14. How old is your child?

Q. Which rashes are worrisome?

Petechiae with or without bruising. (See bleeding section earlier for details on petechiae). Petechiae are small flat freckle or pinpoint dots, purplish in color, that stay purple when you push on them.

This is really the only rash that needs immediate attention. Petechiae can be caused by forceful coughing or vomiting. But this rash can also indicate meningitis, Rocky Mountain Spotted Fever, idiopathic thrombocytopenia purpura (ITP), or leukemia. Petechiae are *Priority 1: Needs immediate evaluation and treatment—NOW.*

Q. What are hives and what causes them?

A rash that appears due to release of a chemical called histamine. 20% of the population will get hives once in their lives. But 75% of the time, the cause is never found.[5]

Hives look like mosquito bites with red circles around them. Or, they look like a flat red area with a raised border. Hives vary in size and shape. They are itchy and occur anywhere on the body. The individual lesions come and go. See Chapter 14, "Diseases" for causes of hives.

What to do if your child breaks out in hives

- **Relax.** If your child is not having any trouble breathing, this can be managed at home.
- *Try to figure out what caused the hives* (foods, medications, illness).
- *Stop any medications until seeing the doctor.*
- **Give diphenhydramine (Benadryl).** Liquid Benadryl comes in 12.5mg per teaspoon syrup. A 20 lb. baby can have 3/4 tsp. If your baby is smaller than 20 lbs., call your doctor before giving it.

Q. What does a drug allergy rash look like?

True drug allergies will cause hives or erythema multiforme. Any other rash does not require avoidance of a particular medication.

Erythema multiforme basically means "redness in multiple forms." What you see is a full body rash of red flat patches and raised borders. Many of the patches run into each other.

If you see a concerning rash while your child is on medication, hold the dose of medicine and bring the child in to be seen. A particular medication class should not be avoided unless there is a documented allergy.

Q. What does a food allergy rash look like?

Food allergies can cause hives and lip swelling if the reaction is severe. But it can also cause a flare up of a rash called eczema. Eczema is an allergic skin disorder—the equivalent of hay fever. Eczema looks like a scaly plaque lying on top of a red base. With a food allergy, the eczema can cover huge body surface areas.

FIRST AID

RASH-O-RAMA: COMMON RASHES SEEN WITH

Viral exanthems: (rashes caused by viruses)

	Rash looks like	Where?
Chickenpox	fluid filled blisters come up in crops	all over avg. 350 lesions
Shingles	fluid filled blisters	1 patch
Measles	red, raised pimply	face to body
German measles	red, raised	face to body
Roseola	FLAT red ovals/ lace	chest, arms, neck, +/- face
Parvovirus (Fifth disease)	"slapped cheeks" Flat, red, lacy on body	chest, arms
Coxsackievirus (hand, foot, and mouth)	red dots or blisters +/- buttocks	palms, soles,
Unilateral Latero-thoracic Exanthem	raised red bumps, scaly on top	one armpit
Pityriasis rosea	raised red streaks a little scaly	back, angled like a fir tree

Special viral rashes:

Herpetic Whitlow	blister, red around	thumb, finger
Molluscum Contagiosum	pinpoint blisters	anywhere

Bacterial infections:

Impetigo*	red, raised with weeping golden crust	anywhere
Scarlet fever* (usually over 2 yrs old)	red, sandpaper feel, rough raised dots	armpit, groin, neck, body
Meningitis*	petechiae (purple freckles)	spreads head to toe

Fungal infections:

Ringworm*	circle, red raised edge +/- overlying scale	anywhere
Yeast diaper rash*	raw meat red with surrounding pimples	diaper area

Tick borne illness:

Lyme Disease*	bullseye with bite in the center	bite site
Rocky Mountain Spotted Fever*	starts out flat, red then petechiae (purple freckles)	wrist, ankles palms, soles

Mites:

Scabies*	lines of red raised bumps (burrows) blisters in babies	head, neck, palms, soles, armpits, finger webs

Other:

Kawasaki Disease*	red cracked lips peeling skin on fingers flat/mildly raised red spots	lips, palms, soles of feet

*Denotes an infection that needs treatment

Infections, How Long they Last and More!

Duration	Other symptoms
1 week	fever, itchy
1 week	painful
1 week	fever, pink eye
3 days	swollen glands
1 day	high fever that breaks then rash appears
2-40 days	mildly itchy, joint pains
1 week with ulcers	fever, sore throat
4-6 weeks	mildly itchy
6 weeks	mildly itchy
1 week	very painful
1-2 years	
gets worse until treated	very itchy
3-4 days	sore throat, fever
hours	fever, irritability, light sensitivity
gets worse until treated	very itchy
gets worse until treated	itchy
enlarging diameter	fever, fatigue
1-6 days	fever, vomiting irritability light sensitivity
worse until treated	**ITCHIEST RASH EVER!**
Over five days	fever for more than 5 days pink eye swollen lymph nodes in neck

Food allergies do NOT cause mild diaper rash, a few patches on the face, or heat rashes.

Q. My child has a scaly rash on his elbows and knees. What is it?

Eczema. It is sensitive skin. In infants, it likes the elbows and knees because these areas get chewed up from crawling. It also ends up in the skin folds of the elbows and knees from rubbing. See Chapter 14 "Common Diseases" for more details on this.

Q. Which rashes are likely to be contagious due to infection?

Most of them. Kids have wonderful immune systems (much better than ours). And rashes are created from an immune response to a particular infection.

The diseases listed on the previous pages are The Classics. There are also a variety of non-descript rashes that fit in the category of "viral and non-worrisome".

Q. I know that all newborns get rashes. Are there any I need to be worried about?

Yes. Herpes.

Moms with genital herpes have a chance of spreading it to their newborn during a vaginal delivery. (If Mom has an obvious outbreak a Caesarian section is performed.) A herpes rash in a newborn shows up within two weeks of life. The lesions look like little blisters either alone or in crops. This is *Priority 1: Needs immediate evaluation and treatment—NOW!*

Q. My four week old has a pimply rash all over his face and chest. What do I do?

It's acne, but don't break out the Oxy 10. This rash is caused by a hormonal change in the baby. Leave it alone and it goes away by eight weeks of age.

Feedback from the Real World
Dr. Brown True Story

My son woke up one morning with three distinct red circles on his chest. I thought he had ringworm until I realized the circles matched the snaps on his sleeper pajamas. He had an allergy to the metal snaps.

Necklaces, earrings, and snaps on jeans can cause a similar reaction in people with sensitive skin.

Q. My one year old looks like he has the measles! Does he?

No. Did he come in for his one year well check recently? That rash is the response to the MMR vaccination. (The same thing happens with the chickenpox vaccine). Be happy. This means he has formed a good response.

These rashes usually appear one to four weeks after being vaccinated.

Q. My baby has a diaper rash. What do I do about it?

See Chapter 4, "Hygiene" for details on how to treat diaper rash.

Priority 1: Needs immediate evaluation and treatment—NOW:
- Hives that occur while taking medication or trying a new food.
- Hives with difficulty breathing (**Call 911**).
- Petechiae rash.
- Newborn with a blistery rash.
- Any rash with a fever.

Priority 2: Needs appointment the next day.
- Rashes that are scaly, without fever.
- Rashes that are not going away after being treated by a doctor.

Priority 3: Watch and wait. Needs appointment if there is no improvement or worsening of symptoms:
- Newborn (birth to eight weeks) with a non-blistery rash, acting well.
- Diaper rashes.
- One year old with rash after being in for his one year well check.

Seizures

Seizures are scary to watch. If your child has a seizure, ***dial 911***. Once the episode is over, you can review this information.

Q. What is a seizure?

Involuntary muscle (motor) activity is the definition of a seizure. This is caused by an electrical brainwave that has fired incorrectly. In kids under age one, the most common type of seizure is associated with a fever that is rising quickly (See febrile seizure in the fever section of this chapter).

Causes of new onset seizures include: Febrile seizure (convulsion), head trauma/ injury, meningitis, poisoning/ingestion, metabolic disorder, seizure disorder

What To Do If Your Baby Has A Seizure
- *Call 911.*
- Put him in a safe place (a carpeted floor).
- Make sure he can breathe.
- Do not put anything in his mouth to hold his tongue (contrary to what you see on TV).
- Start CPR—do mouth-to-mouth resuscitation if baby looks blue.

What the doctor will ask you about SEIZURES:
1. Has your baby ever had a seizure before?
2. How old is your baby?
3. Does the baby have a fever?
4. Anyone in the family prone to febrile seizures as a child?

5. Any history of head trauma?
6. Any history of poisoning or ingestion?

Priority 1: Needs immediate evaluation and treatment—NOW:
- Known history of febrile seizures, with another episode
- Has a known seizure disorder.

Stitches (Sutures)

The key point to remember: *Stitches (sutures) need to be placed within 12 hours of the injury. So they are always considered Priority 1.* Any later than that, the wound has a much higher chance of getting infected. If your child has a wound that might need stitches, call your doctor now.

What the doctor will ask you about NEEDING STITCHES:
1. **What happened?** For example, animal bites usually are not stitched because of infection risk.
2. **How long ago did the injury happen?** If over 12 hours, wound can't be sutured.
3. **Where on the body is the cut (laceration)?** Location of the wound makes a difference because of cosmetic issues (face) and potential nerve damage (hands).
4. **If on the face, is it crossing the lip/skin line or the eyebrow line?** It may need stitches for better cosmetic result.
5. **How deep is it?** If you can see fat, it needs stitches—anything deeper than 1/4 inch.
6. **Is the bleeding under control?** If not, it needs stitches.
7. **For older wounds: Is there any pus, redness around the wound, streaks of red from the wound, or fever?** Needs

How to Clean and Care for Minor Wounds

It's not what you use, it's how you use it. Plain old soap and water is fine. You don't have to get high tech here. The key is to flush the wound and repeat this several times. Wash the wound every day until it heals. Here's how to care for minor wounds:

1. Apply pressure to the wound with a gauze pad or towel for ten minutes.
2. Thoroughly clean wound with soap and water. The most important part of the cleaning process is flushing with water repeatedly—especially with puncture wounds (bites, sharp objects). Your doctor will use a mechanism much like a Waterpik to clean "road rash" scrapes.
3. Apply antibiotic ointment for two or three days. This prevents infection and improves cosmetic results.
4. Look for signs of infection. (Redness, pus, fever).
5. For cuts in the mouth or tongue, try popsicles or ice cream (if age appropriate) to help control bleeding.

to be seen for possible wound infection.
8. **Are your child's immunizations current?** Needs tetanus shot if not up to date.
9. **Does your child have any bleeding disorders?** There is a risk of large volume of blood loss.

Q. Are there any body parts that always need stitches?

Yes. Eyebrows and lip lines. The lip line means the area where the lip meets the skin. If a wound crosses this line, the lip will not line up correctly without stitches. The same is true for the eyebrow line. Cosmetically, this is a big deal.

Q. Are there any body parts that never need stitches?

It is RARE to need stitches on the lip itself, tongue, or gums. The blood flow to these areas is tremendous (which is why they bleed so much). This blood flow allows very rapid healing.

Q. How can I tell if the wound is infected?

Pus (white/yellow/green discharge) will start to ooze out of the wound. There will be red and tender skin around the wound site, and maybe even a streak of redness starting from the wound. There may also be a fever.

Q. Is my child's tetanus shot up to date?

If your child is receiving his immunizations regularly at well baby checks, he is well protected. He gets a tetanus shot at two, four, six, fifteen months and again at five years old. Your child is probably better protected than you.

Q. Can I get water near the stitches?

YES!
This is a common misconception. Clean the wound, even if it has stitches in it. The not-cleaned ones have crust around them, making it a challenge for the doctor to remove the stitches.

Q. When should the stitches be removed?

It depends on the location. Skin heals at different rates on the body. The doctor who puts the stitches in will tell you when they need to come out. Try to do it when suggested— a delay in suture removal can not only impair the cosmetic result, but can also be very painful if the stitches are imbedded in the skin.

To give you an idea of the variability of suture removal, stitches on the face come out in four days. Stitches on the palm of the hand come out in 14 days.

Q. What is that new glue to close wounds? Can we use that instead of stitches?

It's called Dermabond. It's like superglue. It dissolves on its own and does not need any removal. Sounds great, right?

Well, it is only useful for a limited number of wounds. If the skin is under any tension (gets pulled frequently), the glue won't be able to hold the wound together. The glue is also not intended for use near the eyes.

Q. I've also heard about using staples instead of stitches. Is this better than stitches?

It's easier than stitches for placement, but they are painful to remove. For non-cosmetic areas such as the head, it is a reasonable option.

Helpful Hint

Cuts on the scalp and face bleed a lot. The blood flow to these body parts is much greater than any other areas. Don't be alarmed. It is only a problem if you can't get the bleeding under control.

Priority 1: Needs immediate evaluation and treatment—NOW:
- Any skin wound that you think might need stitches.
- Unable to control the bleeding after ten minutes of pressure to the wound.
- Wound in a cosmetically undesirable location.
- Looks like it is getting infected (redness, pus, fever).
- If immunizations are not current.

Priority 3: Watch and wait. Needs appointment if there is no improvement or worsening of symptoms:
- Make an appointment for suture removal.

Trauma (Accidental Injury)

No matter how good of a parent you are and how safety proofed your house is, your child will find a way to hurt himself. Welcome to parenthood—this is only one of the many reasons that your child will give you grey hairs.

This section is body part specific. The section on skin trauma/injury is covered in the Stitches section.

What the doctor will ask you about TRAUMA / ACCIDENTAL INJURIES
1. What happened?
2. Any loss of consciousness or did he cry immediately?
3. With head injury: Any vomiting or confusion?
4. With head injury: How far did the child fall and what surface did he fall onto?
5. Any bleeding or fluid draining from the nose or ears?
6. Are there any obvious broken bones—sticking out of the skin?
7. Any pain with touching or movement of a body part?
8. Any bruising or swelling?
9. Can you check the eye pupils. Are they equal?

Helpful Hint

The mechanism of injury (that is, what happened) is the most reliable factor in determining the severity of a body injury.

1. Head injury

Once babies are mobile, they run into things like the coffee table and fireplace hearth. The result is a big bruise (a.k.a. "goose egg") on the forehead. It is an impressive bump because of that vast blood supply to the head and face. Despite the appearance, goose eggs are not too worrisome.

The mechanism of injury is much more concerning. Here are the red flags for head injuries:

Priority 1: Needs immediate evaluation and treatment—NOW!

For injuries for a concussion or bleeding in the head.
- Child falls a distance greater than his own height.
- Child falls onto hardwood floors, tile, or concrete.
- Child loses consciousness (blacks out) after the injury.
- Child vomits more than once after the injury.
- Baby's soft spot is bulging.
- Seizure after head injury.
- Acting abnormal or confused.
- Bruising behind the ear or bleeding from the ear.
- Clear fluid draining from the nose.

Priority 2: Needs appointment the next day.

- Child falls a distance less than his height, onto a padded surface, no loss of consciousness.

Priority 3: Watch and wait. Needs appointment if there is no improvement or worsening of symptoms:

- Child has a minor accident resulting in a large bruise on the head (goose egg), no loss of consciousness, no vomiting, and is acting normally.

NEW PARENT 411: HANDLING MINOR HEAD INJURIES

- Put a bag of frozen vegetables on the goose egg, if your child lets you. It will be less swollen in the morning, but will change into a rainbow of colors for a week or two.
- Watch for signs of concussion for the next two days (vomiting, irritability from headache, confusion, lethargy)
- Let your child go to bed. Invariably, it's nap or bedtime when these events happen (probably because your child is tired and clumsy then). You can monitor him every few hours by watching his breathing and gently touching him to see if he stirs. Vomiting or seizure activity happens whether he is awake or asleep.

BOTTOM LINE

Every child who has rolled off a bed onto a carpeted floor does not need to be rushed to an emergency room. (And yes, this will happen to you!)

Which head injuries require a CAT scan?

When there is a concern for a severe head injury (bleeding inside the skull), a CT scan (Computer Tomography) is helpful to check it out. Here are the criteria:

- loss of consciousness for over one minute
- trauma (knife, bullet)
- abnormal neurologic examination (weakness, abnormal reflexes..)
- vomiting
- seizures
- bulging soft spot (fontanelle)
- bruising behind the ear or bleeding from the ear
- clear fluid draining from the nose
- depressed skull fracture (i.e. a break in the skull detected on a plain x-ray)

Reality Check

Walkers cause over 6000 head injuries in the U.S. annually. Yes, the newer models have more "safety features" that keep them from rolling down stairs. But we say save your money or buy some other really cool toy.

2. Neck and back injuries

CALL 911 and do not try to move your child. He will be immobilized on a straight board until x-rays can prove that no spine damage has occurred.

3. Eye injuries

All eye injuries should be evaluated by a doctor immediately. Here are the most common problems:

- **Corneal abrasion:** surface of the eye is scratched. It heals in a day or two. Frequent tearing is a clue to this diagnosis.
- **Hyphema:** bleeding that occurs beneath the surface of the eye (a doctor sees it with special equipment). If the blood is not removed, vision can be lost. This is fairly uncommon, but it is the reason that all eye injuries need a medical evaluation.
- **Subconjunctival hemorrhage:** bleeding occurs on the surface of the eye. It can be seen on the white part of the eye. Although it looks dramatic, it's not serious.

4. Ear injuries

Outer ear: (the part you can see) can be bruised and cause permanent cartilage damage. If you see bruising, this is a *Priority 1: Needs immediate evaluation and treatment* call—the blood might need to be drained.

Inner ear: (the inside) can be injured when curious kids put things in their ears. Usually they don't get anywhere near the eardrum. If you see bleeding, it's likely from scratching the lining of the canal. Doctors need to see these kids, but it can wait until the office opens (*a priority 2 call*). The only emergency is if your child had a head injury and you notice blood draining out of the ear or a bruise behind the outer ear. This is a sign of a skull fracture.

5. Nose injuries

Priority 1: Needs immediate evaluation and treatment—NOW:

◆ A nosebleed after a nose injury increases the chances of it being broken.
◆ A clear drainage or bloody nose after a head injury increases the chances of a skull fracture.
◆ Inability to breathe through the nose after an injury may mean a severe bruise in the nose (septal hematoma)
◆ Nose is obviously crooked (displaced nose fracture).

Priority 2: Needs appointment the next day.

◆ Nose injury without bleeding or obvious fracture.

6. Mouth injuries

See stitches section for details. The bottom line: Very few injuries to the mouth require stitches. They bleed a lot but heal quickly and beautifully. Injuries that go through the inside of the mouth to the outside of the skin, or full thickness through the tongue need to be seen *(Priority 1: Needs immediate evaluation and treatment–NOW)*.

7. Tooth injuries

Injuries to baby teeth rarely need intervention. Worry only if the tooth was "knocked out" and you can't find it anywhere. That is a sign of a tooth intrusion. The tooth can get pushed back into the gums *(Priority 1: Needs immediate evaluation and treatment–NOW; call the dentist)*.

FYI: You may know about the trick of placing a knocked out tooth in milk and rushing to the dentist to re-implant it. They only do this for permanent teeth, not baby teeth.

8. Bone injuries

Q. Is it BROKEN?

The best way to tell over the phone is to know the mechanism of injury and what your child is doing with the limb. The list of red flags is below.

If there is a break (fracture), your child needs a cast. Some specialists prefer to see kids with broken bones 48 hours after the injury so the swelling will be down before casting. As long as the bone is immobilized, it is fine. A temporary (splint) cast can be applied to keep the bone fixed and comfortable.

RED FLAGS
Does it need an x-ray?
All of these are *Priority 1: Needs immediate evaluation and treatment–NOW:*

1. Unable to move a limb without crying.
2. Limping or refusing to bear weight.
3. Impressive bruising or swelling.

BOTTOM LINE

Broken bones hurt. If you can distract your child and move or touch the area without pain, it may just be bruised.

Helpful hint

Kids have areas in their bones called growth plates. This area is located at the end of each bone that gives it growing room. These plates fuse when children go through puberty (hormone levels cause them to close). A normal x-ray of a child's bone shows a gap where the growth plate is. Occasionally, if there is a fracture along the line of the growth plate, it may not be seen when the x-ray is read. So, even if an x-ray is read as "no fracture," call the doctor if there is no improvement in your child's symptoms in five to seven days.

Q. My child was walking and put his hand out to break his fall. Is the wrist broken?

Probably. Your wrist joint is not intended to sustain your body weight. Your baby needs an x-ray.

Q. I was walking with my child and holding his hand. He pulled away from me and now he won't use his arm. Is it broken?

No—it's probably dislocated.

This is called a nursemaid's elbow. The elbow joint has gotten pulled out of its socket. Some children are repeat offenders. It can be easily fixed by your doctor in a matter of seconds. For frequent fliers, Mom and Dad can learn how to do it at home. It's a good idea not to pull your kids up by their arms, or jerk their arms when they resist motion. And obviously, kids with frequent dislocations shouldn't play on the monkey bars!

9. Fingers and toes

The classic injury here is the finger that gets slammed in a car door. If there is bruising or swelling, it needs an x-ray (*Priority 1: Needs immediate evaluation and treatment—NOW*). If there is a blood blister/collection of blood under the fingernail (subungual hematoma), it may need to be lanced by a doctor to relieve the pressure (*Priority 1 or 2*).

The fingers and toes are an exception for casting of broken bones. Some of these breaks only require stabilization (buddy taping) to the finger or toe next to it.

HOW TO IMMOBILIZE AN INJURED LIMB

- Use a scarf or large towel and wrap it around the shoulder to keep an arm in place. Pinning a long arm sleeve to the shoulder also works.
- Use a piece of cardboard and an Ace wrap to form a makeshift splint for an arm or leg.

So, how do you immobilize a finger or toe? Tape fingers or toes together (buddy tape) for an injured digit. The neighbor of the injured digit gets taped to it for support.

RED FLAGS

A recap:
- head injury with loss of consciousness
- head injury with vomiting
- head injury with confusion
- significant height of fall or to a hard surface
- any eye injury
- head injury with nosebleed or ear drainage
- ear injury with bruising
- limb injury with swelling/bruising and discomfort
- fall onto an outstretched arm
- jerked elbow
- neck or spine injury–call 911
- bone injury with exposed bone

BOTTOM LINE

If you are ever in doubt, call your doctor.

Notes

Baby 411

Section 6

The Reference Library

MEDICATIONS
Appendix A

Here's a look at the most common medications used by children.[1] Obviously, with the huge universe of possible medications, this chapter is by no means comprehensive. Instead, we focus on the most popular and widely used meds in children. We will cover both over the counter products and prescription medications. FYI: We have also designated products that are safe for moms who are breastfeeding. Let's begin with some general questions regarding administering medicine to your child.

Q. If my child throws up right after I give him medicine, do I re-dose the medicine or wait until the next dose is due?

If your child throws up less than 20 minutes after administering medicine, give the dose again. It didn't have time to get through the stomach and be absorbed into the blood stream.

Q. Is a generic medication as good as a brand name?

For the most part, yes.

When a pharmaceutical company develops a medication, the company obtains a patent for it, which lasts for 17 years. Because it takes several years of research before a medication is approved for use, a medication may be on the market for an average of eight years before the patent runs out. Once the patent runs out, any pharmaceutical company can make their own product, which is the exact duplicate of the original brand.

The potency is the same, but sometimes the taste is not. And the cost is definitely not the same. Generic medications are often much cheaper than the brand name.

Q. If my doctor prescribes an expensive antibiotic, can I ask for a generic brand at the pharmacy?

Yes, but it might not be available.

In the case of antibiotics, we have been forced to develop new medications to keep up with the drug resistant bacteria. If an antibiotic is less than 17 years old, only the brand name is available—which usually means it's pretty expensive.

MEDICATIONS

Helpful Hint

If you are paying out-of-pocket for prescription medications, speak up! Don't be shy about inquiring about the cost of the medication. Your doctor may have free samples available in the office. Or she will be able to prescribe a less-expensive generic drug if available.

Q. How do I get my baby to take her medicine?

Here are a few tricks to getting all the medicine down:

1. Give small amounts over several minutes, instead of the whole dose at once.
2. It is okay to mix certain medications in with formula or juice—but check with your pharmacist for the particulars. The only problem with this plan is that your child has to drink the whole thing. Be sure to mix the medicine in a small volume of fluid (less than an ounce).
3. Some pharmacies offer a service called Flavor RX (www.flavorx.com or 1-800-884-5771). For a relatively small fee (often worth it), a choice of 25 different flavorings is available—these can be added to your child's prescription to make it more palatable.
4. Taking a prescription medicine is not optional. It may take two parents to administer medicine to one strong-willed child.

Reality Check

Just a spoonful of sugar makes the medicine go down. Here are some tips from Edward Bell, Pharm.D., BCPS:

1. White grape juice or chocolate syrup masks a medicine's after taste.
2. Graham crackers get rid of the leftover drug particles in the mouth.
3. Strawberry jam mixed with a crushed chewable tablet disguises the flavor.

Q. Is it okay to use a medicine if it is past the expiration date?

No.

For the most part, medications start to lose their potency after the listed expiration date. So the medication may be less effective (for example, Albuterol for an asthma attack).

Q. The prescription medicine was supposed to be given for ten days. We ran out of it after eight days. What happened?

Most of the time, this happens when a "teaspoon" dose is administered with an actual teaspoon from your kitchen. Your silverware spoon may hold anywhere from 4-8 ml of fluid. Buy a medicine syringe that lists both cc/mls and teaspoons on it.

Q. I have some leftover antibiotic from a prescription. Can I save it and use it for another time?

No.

First of all, you should never have leftover antibiotics. Your doctor wanted your child to have a specific length of therapy for that medication. If your child stops taking an antibiotic "because he feels better," you run the risk of the bacteria growing back. This is particularly true of Group A Strep (of Strep throat fame). Yes, people often forget to give all of the doses of antibiotic—we're human. But try to finish a prescription as it was intended to be used.

Second of all, antibiotics that are in liquid form will only stay potent for about two weeks. They come as a powder from the manufacturer and the pharmacist mixes it with water when he fills the prescription order. If you have any medicine leftover—toss it.

Q. Are all medications administered to children of all ages?

No.

Many medications are not approved for infants under six months of age. Doctors' choices are more limited for these patients. There are also some medications that are purely for adult usage (for example, Tetracycline).

Q. How do I know if there is a problem taking more than one medicine at a time?

The official term is "drug interactions."

Your doctor or pharmacist can answer this question. Don't assume that your doctor knows all the medications your child is taking. If your child received a prescription from another doctor/specialist, it might not be recorded in your child's chart.

Reality Check

Tell your doctor if your child is taking any herbal remedies. There can be overlap in effects of herbal and over-the-counter products. For instance, a medical student made national news for taking ephedra (an herbal decongestant) and sudafed (a traditional decongestant) at the same time. He ended up in the ER with a heart rhythm disturbance. It pays to ask.

Q. Can you use Tylenol and an antibiotic at the same time?

It is okay to use Tylenol/Motrin, cough/cold medicine, and an antibiotic simultaneously.

Q. What does the term "off-label" mean?

It means that a pharmaceutical company has not received FDA (Food and Drug Administration) approval for a medication to be used for a particular problem or age group.

Medications are approved for use based on research studies for particular medical problems. Once a drug is available for use, doctors may find it useful to treat other ailments. In this case, a doctor might prescribe a medicine to a patient and explain that it is being used "off label."

What frequently happens in pediatric medicine is that clinical research studies are done on adults, so a medication is approved for use only in adults. When it appears to be a safe product, the medication is used in pediatric patients as well. Pediatricians feel relatively comfortable using these medications for children, but your doctor should always explain to you if he prescribes a medicine that does not have FDA approval for use in a particular age group. Good news: There is now a law requiring pharmaceutical companies to test medications in kids as part of their research.

Q. How can I find out if a generic equivalent is available for the medicine my doctor has prescribed?

Ask your doctor or pharmacist. For the medication tables below, generic availability is noted with an (*) asterisk. Note: while all medications have a generic name, not all of them are available to be purchased in generic form.

Q. How do I read a doctor's prescription? I've always wondered what they really mean.

It's written in medical abbreviations, so here's how to read it. You'll need this for the medication tables later in this appendix.

How often to take a medicine
   QD: once daily
   BID: twice daily
   TID: three times daily (preferably every eight hours)
   QID: four times daily (preferably every six hours)
   QHS: once daily, at bedtime
   QOD: every other day
   PRN: as needed

How medicine is given
   po: taken by mouth
   pr: insert in rectum
   ou: put into each eye
   au: put into each ear

How medicine is dosed
   1 cc (cubic centimeter): 1ml (milliliter)
   tsp: teaspoon (1 tsp is 5 cc or 5ml)
   T.: tablespoon (1 T. is 3 tsp or 15cc or 15 ml)
   tab: tablet
   gtt: drop

Q. How do I know which medications require a prescription?

We've included some handy tables later in this chapter with information on common medicines used for treating babies. In the tables, you'll note the following symbols.
- ◆ **Rx**: Denotes that a product is available with a doctor's prescription only. If nothing is designated, assume the product in question is prescription-only.
- ◆ **OTC**: Denotes that a product is available Over The Counter (that is, without a prescription).

MEDICATIONS

Q. How do I know if a medication is safe for me to take while I am pregnant or breast feeding?

Some information is listed in the medication tables later in this appendix. Your obstetrician, pediatrician, pharmacist, and lactation consultant all have reference books in their offices with this information—if you have doubts, call them.

Breastfeeding Categories
   Category 1: Okay to use while nursing.
   Category 2: Okay, but use with caution.
   Category 3: Unknown whether there is a risk.
   NO: Definitely harmful to baby.

Pregnancy Categories
   Category A: Studies have been done with first-trimester pregnancies and show no risk to fetus.
   Category B: Animal studies prove medicine to be safe, but not enough data in humans yet.
   Category C: Animal studies prove medicine to be harmful, but no data in humans.
   Category D: Known risk to fetus, but benefit of medicine to mother may outweigh the risk.
   NO: Known risk to fetus outweighs any benefit to the mother.

Drugs Of Abuse: Not To Be Used While Breastfeeding (And not recommended otherwise)
   Amphetamines, Cocaine, Heroin, Marijuana, Nicotine, Phenylcyclidine[2]

Category 3 Medications (Unknown Risk)[3]
   Medications in the following classes of drugs have potentially concerning effects on babies who are breastfed.
   Antianxiety drugs
   Antidepressant drugs
   Antipsychotic drugs

Category 2 Medications (Okay, But Use With Caution)[4]
   Acyclovir (Zovirax)
   Cetirizine (Zyrtec)
   Diphenhydramine (Benadryl)
   Fluconazole (Diflucan)
   Ketorolac (Toradol, Acular)
   Omeprazole (Prilosec)
   Ondansetron (Zofran)

Category 1 Medications (Okay To Use While Breastfeeding)
   Acetaminophen (Tempra, Tylenol)
   Albuterol (Proventil, Xopenex)
   Alcohol**
   Allergy injections
   Amoxicillin (Amoxil)

Amoxicillin + Clavulanate (Augmentin)
Cefadroxil (Duricef, Ultracef)
Cefazolin (Ancef, Kefzol)
Cefotaxime (Claforan)
Cefoxitin (Mefoxin)
Cefprozil (Cefzil)
Ceftazidime (Fortaz, Tazidime)
Ceftriaxone (Rocephin)
Cimetidine (Tagamet)
Cisapride (Propulsid)
Codeine (Tylenol #3, Empirin #3)**
Contraceptive pills
Dextromethorphan ("DM" products- Delsym, Robitussin DM)
Digoxin (Lanoxin)
Enalapril (Vasotec)
Erythromycin* (E-mycin, Ery-tab)
Hydralazine (Apresoline)
Ibuprofen (Advil, Ibuprofen, Motrin, Nuprin)
Loratadine (Claritin)
Magnesium sulfate
Prednisone (Deltasone, Meticorten, Orasone)
Propranolol (Inderal)
Valproic Acid (Depakote, Depakene)
Verapamil (Calan, Covera-HS)
Warfarin (Coumadin)

*Medication concentrates in breast milk, but is still acceptable to use while nursing.
**Acceptable in moderation.
Note: Pseudoephedrine (brand names: Sudafed, Actifed), a popular decongestant, may reduce milk supply by up to 25%. Use this product with caution, especially if milk supply is already low. [5]
FYI: Teeth whitening products are acceptable to use while breastfeeding.

Herbal Remedies and breastfeeding

Fenugreek and Blessed Thistle are both considered generally safe to use to improve milk production.

Herbal products that are unsafe while nursing include: Comfrey, Blue Cohosh, Sage, and Valerian Root. [6]

Medication Index

1. Allergies
2. Dental/Mouth
    ◆ fluoride
    ◆ teething products
3. Ear Problems
4. Eye Problems
5. Fever and pain
6. Gastrointestinal
    ◆ antacids/ gastroesophageal reflux
    ◆ constipation

- diarrhea
- gas/colic
- vomiting
- rehydration solutions

7. Infections
   - antibiotics (for bacterial infections)
   - antifungals (for fungal infections)
   - antihelminthics (for pinworms)
   - amebicides (for Giardia infection)
   - antivirals (for viral infections)

8. Nutrition
   - iron supplements
   - vitamins

9. Respiratory
   - asthma
   - cough and cold preparations

10. Skin
    - antibiotic creams
    - antifungal creams
    - scabies/ head lice medications
    - steroids
    - anti-inflammatory (immunomodulators)
    - diaper rash creams

Medications

1. Allergy Medicines

These medications are used for allergic reactions, itching, and nasal congestion. For skin allergy products, see skin section (10).

Antihistamines have been around for decades. They are classified by their "generation." The first generation products are very effective but also have more side effects (drowsiness, dry mouth). Second and third generation products do not cause nearly as much sedation and can be dosed once every 24 hours.

Under six months of age, doctors use all medications with caution. Antihistamines, which are usually sedating, can result in excitability in infants. Consult your doctor before using any of these products.

Generic	Brand	Dose	Rx?	Age limit	Breast
Brompheniramine	Dimetapp*	QID	OTC	over 2 years	1
Cetirizine	Zyrtec	QD	Rx	over 6 months	2
Clemastine	Tavist*	BID	Rx	over 6 months	2
Chlorpheniramine	Chlor-Trimeton*	QID	OTC	over 2 years	3—Observe for sedation
Desloratadine	Clarinex	QD	Rx	over 6 months	1
Diphenhydramine	Benadryl*	QID	OTC	Infants ok	2
Fexofenadine	Allegra	BID	Rx	over 6 months	1
Hydroxyzine	Atarax*	QID	Rx	Infants ok	1
Loratadine	Claritin, Alavert*	QD	OTC	over 6 months	1

KEY: Dose—see page 402 for an explanation of doses. Rx? Rx medications are available by prescription only; OTC is over-the-counter. Breast—see page 403 for an explanation of the safety of using these medications while breastfeeding. * A generic is available for this brand-name medicine.
Side effects: Drowsiness, dry mouth, headache, paradoxical excitability
Serious Adverse effects: tremors, convulsions

> **Feedback from the Real World**
> You may be tempted to use diphenhydramine (Benadryl) as a sleep aid for your child. A study, appropriately called the TIRED study—Trial of Infant Response to Diphenhydramine, showed there was no significant improvement in a baby's sleep when used in kids six to 15 months of age. Go back to Chapter 9, "Sleep," if you need tips that will actually work!

2. Dental/Mouth

Fluoride Supplements

Fluoride is a mineral well known to prevent cavities. But as we discussed back in Chapter 5, "Nutrition and Growth," the recommendations are confusing and a bit of a moving target when it comes to babies and young children.

Infants *under* six months of age should have little to no fluoride intake. Thus, the American Dental Association currently recommends that you prepare powdered or liquid concentrate formula with filtered tap water (reverse osmosis) or bottled water.

Infants *over* six months of age until age 16 years need a source of fluoride to significantly reduce cavities in both primary (baby) and secondary (adult) teeth. Fluoride is added to tap water in many cities and counties in the United States. Find out if your city has added fluoride to its water supply. Ideally, your water supply should have 0.7-1.2 ppm of fluoride. Once your baby is six months old, he should start drinking some water on a daily basis (about four to six ounces).

Who needs a fluoride supplement? There are just four specific situations where a fluoride supplement is recommended if baby is over six months of age AND:

1. In a household that has well water, and has no other source of fluoride-containing water.
2. Exclusively breast fed, and does not drink fluoride-containing water.
3. Formula is prepared with bottled water or uses ready-to-feed formula, and does not drink fluoride-containing water.
4. The local water supply does not contain added fluoride, and natural fluoride levels are less than 0.6ppm.

If you fall into one of those categories above, the American Academy of Pediatrics and American Dental Association recommends the following dosages of fluoride (these are based on age and the amount of fluoride in your drinking water):

How much extra fluoride does your baby need?

Age	Amt. of fluoride in community's water supply (in parts per million- ppm)		
	LESS THAN 0.3 PPM	0.3-0.6 PPM	GREATER THAN 0.6 PPM
0-6 months	None	None	None
6 months-3 yrs	0.25 mg	None	None
3-6 years	0.5 mg	0.25 mg	None
6-16 years	1 mg	0.5 mg	None

Fluoride supplements include: Luride*, Fluoritab, Pediaflor*, Poly-Vi-Flor*, Tri-Vi-Flor*. These are all available by prescription only and dosed once daily.

Possible side effects: Overuse of fluoride can cause white spots on the teeth (fluorosis). This occurs in daily doses of greater than 2 mg of fluoride/day.

Reality Check

Fluoride containing toothpaste has about 1 mg of fluoride per ribbon. Kids tend to eat toothpaste instead of spitting it out. For this reason, it is suggested NOT to use toothpaste until your child can spit (around age three). It's also a good idea to limit the volume to a pea-sized ration.

Q. Is fluoride safe? I've heard it can cause bone cancer in lab rats.

Yes it is safe. If you give toxic mega-doses of any product to rats, you will create medical problems. So just how much fluoridated water would you have to drink each day to equal the volume that the rats drank? Answer: 42 gallons a day!

Helpful Hint

Give fluoride drops on an empty stomach. Milk prevents the absorption of the medication.

3. Teething

Teething medications are topical numbing products. They are rubbed on the gums to provide temporary relief of gum pain due to tooth eruption. They are dosed four times daily. Their active ingredient is Benzocaine. The brand names are: Baby Anbesol, Baby Numz-it, Baby Orajel, and Zilactin Baby.

DR B'S OPINION: TEETHING PAIN

Tylenol (acetaminophen) is the most effective and safe medication available for teething pain. Teething gels may have unwanted side effects and provide very short-term relief (less than an hour). Homeopathic teething tablets are deemed safe by poison control, but do contain trace amounts of belladonna and caffeine.

4. Ear Medication

Antibiotic Ear Drops

For swimmer's ear (otitis externa) or for children who have ear infections with PE tubes, antibiotic eardrops are used. Because the medicine is not absorbed into the bloodstream, there are more antibiotic family choices. Below are the most popular antibiotic eardrops. Note: most products also contain a steroid. The steroid reduces the inflammation and swelling of the ear canal so the antibiotic can work more effectively.

GENERIC	BRAND	DOSE	RX
Acetic Acid	Vosol*	QID	yes
Acetic Acid + Hydrocortisone	Vosol-HC*	QID	yes
Chloroxylenol + Pramoxine + Hydrocortisone	Zoto-HC	QID	yes
Ciprofloxacin + Dexamethasone	Ciprodex	BID	yes
Ciprofloxacin + Hydrocortisone	Cipro HC	BID	yes
Ofloxin	Floxin Otic	BID	yes
Polymyxin B + Neomycin + + steroid	Cortisporin* Pediotic	TID	yes

KEY: Dose—see page 402 for an explanation of doses. Rx? Rx medications are available by prescription only; OTC is over-the-counter.
* A generic is available for this brand-name medicine.

Side Effects: Irritation of the ear canal such as itching and stinging.

Swimmer's Ear Prevention Drops

These drops dry up any left over water in the ear canal after swimming. Drops are placed in the ears immediately after swimming. These are used primarily for older kids, not infants.

You can make your own concoction: 2 drops of rubbing alcohol and 2 drops of vinegar per ear.

Brand names: Auro-Dri, Swim Ear. Both products are OTC. Active ingredient: Rubbing Alcohol.

Ear Pain Drops

These are topical numbing medications, in the same mindset as using teething gels for gum pain. They have a modest effect in pro-

> **DR B'S OPINION**
>
> "Yes, some doctors will prescribe numbing drops for ear pain. Know that these drops do not reach the real location of the pain (which is why many ear, nose, and throat specialists don't find these drops very helpful). I think Acetaminophen (Tylenol) or ibuprofen (Motrin) and a heating pad (low setting) placed on the ear are more effective pain relief."

viding temporary relief of pain in the ear canal. (Remember that middle ear infections occur behind the eardrum.)

Numbing drops are absolutely not intended for use if a child has PE tubes (see Chapter 11, "Infections," for more details) or has ruptured the eardrum with infection.

Brand names are: Americaine, Auralgan*, Tympagesic.* Active ingredient: Benzocaine *Dosing: 2-3 drops to affected ear, QID Rx only.*

Reality Check

Although we don't find them helpful, some doctors will prescribe numbing drops for pain relief. But do NOT use the drops prior to your doctor's appointment. It makes it hard for the doctor to see the eardrum!

Ear Wax Drops

These drops help loosen or dissolve earwax. Earwax rarely is a problem unless it is hard and stuck in the canal (impacted). If the earwax is impacted, earwax drops loosen up and break down the earwax.

Brand names are: Auro, Debrox, and Murine eardrops. OTC Active ingredient: carbamide peroxide *Dosing: 3 drops per ear, TID, for 3 days*

Colace, a stool softener, also works nicely to soften up earwax. It's available OTC.

BOTTOM LINE

We don't recommend routine cleaning with Q-tips. Q-tips can irritate the ear canal and push the earwax backwards, creating wax that is hard and stuck (impacted).

Helpful Hints

◆ Rub the eardrop bottle in your hands for a minute or two before administering the drops. Warm drops in the ear are less bothersome than cold ones.

◆ If a child has a perforated eardrum or PE tubes, many types of eardrops should NOT be used (exception: approved antibiotic drops). Check with your doctor.

Reality Check

ENT specialists frequently use antibiotic eye drops for the ears. If you get a prescription filled for your child's ear infection and it turns out to be eye drops, don't think we have lost our minds. One caveat here: It's okay to use *eye drops* for the ears, but you cannot use eardrops for the eyes!

6. Eye Problems

Antibiotic Eye Drops/Ointment

These are used primarily for conjunctivitis (pink eye) and corneal abrasions.

Medications

Generic	Family	Brand	Dose	Rx Only?
Ciprofloxacin	Quinolone	Ciloxan*	BID/QID	yes
Erythromycin	Erythromycin	(many)*	BID/QID	yes
Gatifloxacin	Quinolone	Zymar	QID	yes
Gentamicin	Aminoglycoside	(many)*	QID	yes
Moxifloxacin	Quinolone	Vigamox	TID	yes
Ofloxin	Quinolone	Ocuflox*	BID/QID	yes
Tobramycin	Aminoglycoside	Tobrex*	QID	yes

KEY: Dose—see page 402 for an explanation of doses. Rx? Rx medications are available by prescription only; OTC is over-the-counter. * A generic is available for this brand-name medicine.

Note: Although the quinolone based products are not FDA approved for under one year of age, your doctor may feel comfortable prescribing them.

Side effects: Burning, itching, local irritation

7. Fever And Pain Medications

Please keep in mind the following points about fever medication:

1. If your baby is less than four weeks old and has a fever, do NOT give a fever reducing medicine—call your doctor immediately.
2. Never give aspirin to a child unless directed by a doctor. Aspirin use is associated with Reye's syndrome (liver failure) when taken during an influenza or chickenpox infection.
3. Ibuprofen is not recommended for babies under six months of age.
4. Tylenol is the brand name. The generic name is acetaminophen (other brand names include Tempra, Feverall)
5. Ibuprofen: brand names are Motrin, Advil
6. Do not use more than one fever reducing medicine at a time, unless your doctor specifically recommends it.
7. REMEMBER TO USE THE DROPPER THAT COMES WITH THE PACKAGE OF MEDICINE. See Chapter 15, "First Aid," for details on fever and when to administer medication (as well as a dosing chart).

Reality Check

You may have heard the news about a child's family suing the makers of Children's Motrin, claiming their daughter had a severe aller-

DR B'S OPINION: ALTERNATING FEVER MEDS

Unless your child is prone to febrile seizures, I do not recommend alternating fever medications during the day to keep the body temperature down. I also prefer to use acetaminophen (Tylenol) for children who are dehydrated or not eating. Ibuprofen is more likely to cause stomach upset when taken on an empty stomach.

gic reaction (called Stevens Johnson Syndrome). While this does occur, it is extremely rare and can occur while taking several other types of medication, too. Bottom line: It is still okay to give ibuprofen to babies over six months. But realize that even over the counter medications can have side effects.

8. Gastrointestinal Problems

Antacids/Gastroesophageal Reflux

Generic	Brand	Dose	Rx?	Age limit	Breast
Aluminum Hydroxide	Gaviscon	QID	OTC	usually not recommended	
Calcium Carbonate	Mylanta Supreme	TID/QID	OTC	ask Dr.	
Cimetidine	Tagamet	BID	Rx	over 16 yr	2
Famotidine	Pepcid	BID	Rx	over 1 yr of age	1
Lansoprazole	Prevacid	QD	Rx	over 1 yr	3
Metoclopramide	Reglan*	QID	Rx	severe cases only	2
Nizatidine	Axid	BID	Rx	over 12 yr	2
Omeprazole	Prilosec	QD/BID	Rx	over 2 yr	2
Omeprazole+ Sodium bicarbonate	Zegerid	QD	Rx	over 18 yr	
Ranitidine	Zantac*	BID/QID	Rx	over 1 mo.	1

KEY: Dose—see page 402 for an explanation of doses. Rx? Rx medications are available by prescription only; OTC is over-the-counter. Breast—see page 361 for an explanation of the safety of using these medications while breastfeeding.
* A generic is available for this brand-name medicine.
Note: Of all the reflux medications, only Zantac is FDA approved for infants. Before 2004, pharmaceutical companies had no requirements to test products on infants. Despite the lack of FDA approval, gastroenterologists and pediatricians prescribe these effective medicines routinely.

Side effects:
◆ Aluminum hydroxide is generally *not* recommended for use in babies due to possible side effects.
◆ Most common side effects are headache, constipation, or diarrhea.
◆ Metoclopramide (Reglan) can cause rare but significant neurological problems, sedation, headaches, and diarrhea. Because of these adverse effects, Reglan is only used in very sick babies.

Helpful Hints
◆ It is more effective to give these medications 30 minutes before a meal if you can.
◆ Zantac is the cheapest choice, readily available at most pharmacies, with the longest track record. However, it takes like mouthwash. If your baby spits out the Zantac because it tastes bad, it won't work.

◆ Prilosec liquid has to be specially compounded at a pharmacy. It will become inactive within about two weeks. You will need to refill it frequently.
◆ Prevacid solutabs are a popular option because they can be cut into halves or quarters for smaller kids and suspended in a few drops of water. Once a day dosing is also convenient.
◆ Zegerid is a popular choice among pediatric gastroenterologists because the combination product seems to improve symptoms when nothing else has worked.
◆ As with other medications, dosing is based on a child's weight. Your baby may outgrow his therapeutic dose every few weeks/months. Ask your doctor to recalculate his dose based on his current weight.

Constipation

Generic	Brand Name	Dose	Rx?	Age limit	Breast
Docusate	Colace	QD/QID	OTC	over 1 year	2
Glycerin	(suppository)	1 dose	OTC	None	
Guar gum	Benefiber	QD	OTC	over 6 mos	
Lactulose	Duphalac, Chronulac*	QD	Rx	Ask Dr.	
Malt soup	Maltsupex	BID	OTC	over 1 month	
Mineral oil	Kondremul	QD/TID	OTC	over 5 years	
Polyethylene glycol	Miralax*	QD	OTC	Ask Dr.	3
Senna	Senokot	QD	OTC	over 1 mo	1

Side effects: diarrhea, bloating, gas, body salt (electrolyte) disturbances with excessive or prolonged use.

Diarrhea

Generic	Brand Name	Dose	Rx?	Age limit	Breast
Lactobacillus	Lactinex, Culturelle	QD	OTC	Ask Dr.	
Bismuth subsalicylate	Pepto-Bismol*	up to 6x day	OTC	Ask Dr.	2
Loperamide	Imodium AD*	QID	OTC	over 2 yrs	1

KEY: Dose—see page 402 for an explanation of doses. Rx? Rx medications are available by prescription only; OTC is over-the-counter. Breast—see page 403 for an explanation of the safety of using these medications while breastfeeding. *A generic is available for this brand-name medicine.

Helpful Hint
Fat and fiber intake both help bulk up the stools.

Reality Check
Pepto-Bismol has a common side effect of causing a temporary black-

DR B'S OPINION
"In general, the only product I recommend are probiotics (acidophilus/lactobacillus). The other meds have the potential to create problems by impairing the ability of the intestines to remove the infection."

ened tongue and black poop. Because it contains an ingredient similar to aspirin, some doctors have concerns about use when a child has chickenpox or an influenza-like illness (there is a risk of Reye's syndrome).

BOTTOM LINE

If diarrhea has been going on more than a week, check in with your doctor. Doctors also want to know about blood or mucus in the stools. (See Chapter 15 "First Aid" for more).

Gas/Colic

Generic	Brand Name	Dose	Rx?	Age limit
Ginger-Fennel	Gripe Water	QID	OTC	None
Lactobacillus	Lactinex, Culturelle	QD	OTC	None
Simethicone	Mylicon, Phazyme*	up to 12x day	OTC	None

Reality Check

Remember, there is no miracle cure for either gas or colic. These products are okay to try, but they may not work.

Vomiting

Generic	Brand	Dose	Rx?	Age limit	Breast
Dimenhydrinate	Dramamine*	QID	OTC	over 2 yrs	2
Diphenhydramine	Benadryl*	QID	OTC	over 6 mos.	2
Ondansetron	Zofran	TID	Rx	over 4 mos	2
Phosphorated-Carbohydrate	Emetrol*	QID	OTC	Ask Dr.	
Promethazine	Phenergan*	QID	Rx	over 2 yrs	2

KEY: Dose—see page 402 for an explanation of doses. Rx? Rx medications are available by prescription only; OTC is over-the-counter. Breast—see page 403 for an explanation of the safety of using these medications while breastfeeding.
* A generic is available for this brand-name medicine.

Helpful Hints

◆ Home remedy: The equivalent of Emetrol is to give 1-2 teaspoons of heavy fruit syrup (fruit cocktail juice) every 20-30 minutes. This occasionally works to relieve nausea.
◆ Phenergan has a black box warning from the FDA discouraging its use in kids under age two.
◆ Zofran is very popular for babies and kids under age two, but usually has a high price tag since a generic equivalent is not available at this time.

Rehydration Solutions

These products are the Gatorade equivalent for babies. They are designed to replace water, body salts, and sugar lost when a child has vomiting and diarrhea. They are most helpful in the early phase of a stomach virus when a child is just starting to take fluids after actively vomiting. Doctors prefer rehydration solutions instead of plain water, juice, milk, or soda for infants. Once a child is keeping down this clear fluid, we usually suggest that your child resume breastfeeding or formula. All products are available over the counter. See Chapter 15, "First Aid," for more information on using this product. See Appendix B, "Alternative Medicine," for a recipe you can make at home.

Brand Names: Enfalyte, Gerber Pediatric Electrolyte, Kao-electrolyte, Pedialyte.

9. Infections

Antibiotics (Bacterial infections)

This list contains the most popular choices of antibiotics (taken by mouth). There are basically four classes of medications approved for pediatric use. There are more classes available to adults. Take special note of the class or family each medicine belongs to. If a person develops an allergic reaction to a medication, ANY antibiotic that belongs to that class is to be avoided.

In this chart, we note what these medications are typically used for (usage): Ear and sinus infections (1), Pneumonia (2), Skin infections (3), Bladder infections-UTI (4), Strep throat (5).

Note: all products are available by prescription only.

GENERIC NAME	BRAND NAME	FORM	DOSE	USAGE	PREG/BREAST
PENICILLIN FAMILY					
Amoxicillin	Amoxil, Polymox, Trimox, Wymox*	Liq/Chew	BID	1,2,4,5	B, 1
Amoxicillin+ Clavulanate	Augmentin*, Augmentin ES-600*	Liq/Chew	BID	1,2,3,4,5	B, 1
(Clavulanate kills resistant bacteria strains)					
Dicloxacillin	Dycill, Dynapen, Pathocil	Liquid	QID	3, 5	B, 1
Penicillin V-K	Pen VeeK, V-cillinK*	Liquid	BID-QID	5	B, 1
CEPHALOSPORINS					
Cefaclor	Ceclor*	Liquid	BID	1,2,5	B, 2
Cefadroxil	Duricef, Ultracef	Liquid	BID	3, 5	B, 1
Cefdinir	Omnicef*	Liquid	QD/BID	1,2,3	B, 1
Cefpodoxime	Vantin	Liquid	QD/BID	1,2	B, 1
Cefprozil	Cefzil*	Liquid	BID	1,2,3,4,5	B, 1
Ceftibuten	Cedax	Liquid	QD	1,2,5	B, 1
Ceftriaxone	Rocephin	injection	QD	1,2,3,4,5	B, 1
Cefuroxime	Ceftin	Liquid	BID	1,2,3,5	B, 1
Cephalexin	Keflex*	Liquid	TID/QID	3,5	B, 1

MACROLIDES

Generic	Brand	Dose	Usage	Age Limit	RX/Breast
Azithromycin	Zithromax*	Liquid	QD	1,2,3,5	B, 2
Clarithromycin	Biaxin*	Liquid	BID	1,2,3,5	C, 2
Erythromycin	E.E.S., Eryped*	Liq/chew	BID/QID	2,3,5	B, 1
Erythromycin + Sulfisoxazole	Pediazole*	Liquid	TID	1,2	C, 1

SULFONAMIDES (SULFA)

Generic	Brand	Dose	Usage	Age Limit	RX/Breast
Sulfisoxazole	Gantrisin	Liquid	QD	1,4	B/D, 2
	Used as preventative therapy only				
Sulfamethoxazole + Trimethoprim	Bactrim, Septra*, Sulfatrim, TMP-SMX	Liquid	BID	1,4	C, 3

KEY: Dose—see page 402 for an explanation of doses. Rx? Rx medications are available by prescription only; OTC is over-the-counter. Breast—see page 403 for an explanation of the safety of using these medications while breastfeeding.
* A generic is available for this brand-name medicine.

Side Effects:
The most common side effects include:
1. *Diarrhea.* The antibiotic kills the bacteria causing infection, but also some normal bacterial "flora" that helps us digest food in our intestines. Lack of bacterial flora can cause malabsorption (i.e. upset stomach). ANY antibiotic can cause this problem.
2. *Yeast Infections.* Again, the antibiotic kills both bad bacteria and certain bacterial flora that live in our mouths and on our skin. Lack of normal bacteria predisposes a person to yeast infections in the mouth (thrush) and in the genital area (yeast diaper rash).

Allergic Reactions:
A true allergic reaction to these medications includes hives, lip swelling, or difficulty breathing. About 25% of patients who are allergic to the Penicillin family will also be allergic to the Cephalosporin family.

Rare Adverse Reactions:
1. Stevens-Johnson syndrome (severe allergic reaction)
2. C. difficile colitis (bacterial superinfection in intestines)

Antifungals:

Generic	Brand	Dose	Usage	Age Limit	RX	Breast
Fluconazole	Diflucan*	QD x 2 wks	Thrush	None	RX	1
Griseofulvin*	Fulvicin, Grifulvin, Grisactin	QD x 1 month	Scalp Ringworm	None	RX	2

Side effects: nausea, headache, rash, stomach upset
Griseofulvin can cause skin sensitivity to sunlight. Used with caution in patients with Penicillin allergy.

MEDICATIONS

Helpful Hint
Griseofulvin is absorbed better when taken with something rich in fat (milk, ice cream...)

Antihelminthics (For Pinworm Infections):

Generic	Brand	Dose	Age limit	Rx	Breast
Mebendazole	Vermox*	2 doses, 2 weeks apart	over 2 years	RX	1
Pyrantel	Pin-X	2 doses, 2 weeks apart	over 2 years	OTC	3

Side effects: stomach upset, headache

KEY: Dose—see page 402 for an explanation of doses. Rx? Rx medications are available by prescription only; OTC is over-the-counter. Breast—see page 403 for an explanation of the safety of using these medications while breastfeeding.
* A generic is available for this brand-name medicine.

Reality Check
Often the whole family gets treated when one child has pinworms.

Amebicides (For Giardia Infection):

Generic	Brand	Dose	Age limit	Rx	Breast
Metronidazole	Flagyl*	TID for 10 days	None	RX	3

Side effects: nausea, diarrhea, hives, metallic taste, dizziness

Antivirals:

Generic	Brand	Dose	Used for	Age limit	Rx	Breast
Acyclovir	Zovirax*	4-5x daily	Varicella Oral herpes, Zoster	None	RX	1
Amantadine*		BID	Influenza A	over 1 year	RX	1
Oseltamivir	Tamiflu	BID	Influenza	over 1 year	RX	3

Side effects: stomach upset, insomnia, headache. Case reports of children acting strangely while taking Tamiflu currently are being investigated.
Adverse reactions: kidney failure with acyclovir—patient needs to be well hydrated

KEY: Dose—see page 402 for an explanation of doses. Rx? Rx medications are available by prescription only; OTC is over-the-counter. Breast—see page 403 for an explanation of the safety of using these medications while breastfeeding.
* A generic is available for this brand-name medicine.

BOTTOM LINE
Because antiviral medications work by preventing replication of the virus, the medication must be started within 48 hours of when the illness began. Otherwise, it will have no effect on the course of the illness.

10. Nutrition

Vitamin supplements for children aged birth to one are used for specific situations. These include Vitamin D for exclusively breastfed infants, and iron for children with iron-deficiency anemia. A multivitamin for general well being of infants is not routinely prescribed.

Vitamins

Vitamin D supplements:

BRAND NAME	INGREDIENTS	DOSE	RX?
Tri-Vi-Sol	Vitamins A, D, C	1 ml/day	OTC
Vi-Daylin	Vitamins A, D, C	1 ml/day	OTC

*Other products containing Vitamin D are multivitamins and you should consult your doctor before purchasing.

Iron Supplements:

Iron is a necessary ingredient to carry oxygen on red blood cells. Babies are born with a stockpile of iron from their mothers. However, by six months of age, they need to consume iron in their diets to meet their daily needs (11mg/day for ages six to 12 months). Some babies need an iron supplement in addition to their food intake (see Chapter 5, Nutrition & Growth, for details of iron containing foods).

Multivitamins often contain iron (see chart above). The dose of iron in multivitamins made for infants is 9–10 mg of iron per daily dose. This meets the daily nutritional needs of a six to 12 month old. If a child has iron deficiency anemia, he needs daily nutritional iron requirements PLUS an additional amount to fill back up his depleted iron stores. The only way to get the higher dose of iron is to use the specific products listed below.

Iron Replacement Therapy

Brand Names: Fer-In-Sol*, Feosol*, Icar, Niferex
Dose: Comes in drops 15mg iron per 0.6 ml. Dose is based on weight. Your doctor will calculate it for you. There are also syrups for older kids, which can be confusing!
Rx: These drugs are OTC, but are behind your pharmacist's counter so they can help you select the appropriate product.
Side effects: constipation, black looking poop, nausea, stomachache, temporary teeth staining

Helpful Hints

◆ You can avoid staining the teeth by shooting the medicine in the back of the throat. If the teeth do become stained, use baking soda on a toothbrush to remove the stains.
◆ Vitamin C improves the absorption of iron. Calcium interferes with the absorption of iron. So if you are offering a drink with the iron medicine, offer juice—not milk.
◆ If you give the iron AFTER a meal, there is less stomach upset.

11. Respiratory Problems

Asthma

Asthma medications are divided into rescue medications and preventative/long term control medications. The rescue medicines are used as needed (with a certain interval between doses). A child is placed on preventative medicine if he:

1. needs rescue medicine more than twice a week
2. has his activity affected by asthma flare-ups
3. has problems at night more than twice a month

The idea is to get the asthma under control, then cut back on the amount of medications needed to minimize flare ups.

For information on asthma and home nebulizers, see the common diseases chapter.

Rescue medicines

GENERIC	BRAND	DOSE	RX	BREAST
Albuterol	Proventil, Ventolin Accuneb* Nebulizer Inhaler	Syrup TID Q4 hrs Q4 hrs	Rx	1
Levalbuterol	Xopenex	Nebulizer solution TID	Rx	2

This class of medication is called a Beta agonist. There can be effects on the body similar to caffeine. More side effects are seen with the dose given orally (syrup) than with the doses that are inhaled (nebulizer machine, inhaler). Levalbuterol is a newer product that seems to have fewer side effects than the older albuterol product.

Side effects: Increased heart rate, palpitations, nervousness, insomnia, nausea, headache.

Preventative/Long term control medicines

GENERIC	BRAND	DOSE	RX	AGE LIMIT	BREAST
Mast cell stabilizer					
Cromolyn	Intal*	Nebulizer TID	Rx	None	1
Inhaled corticosteroid					
Budesonide	Pulmicort	Nebulizer BID	Rx	over 1yr/ask Dr.	2
Fluticasone	FloventHFA	Inhaler BID	Rx	over 4yrs	3
Leukotriene antagonist					
Montelukast	Singulair	Chew tab QHS	Rx	over 1 yr	3

Long acting beta agonist
Salmeterol	Serevent	Diskus BID	Rx	over 4 yrs	2

Combination product
Fluticasone + Salmeterol	Advair	Diskus BID	Rx	over 4yrs	3

KEY: Dose—see page 402 for an explanation of doses. Rx—Rx medications are available by prescription only; OTC is over-the-counter. Breast—see page 403 for an explanation of the safety of using these medications while breastfeeding.
* A generic is available for this brand-name medicine.

Side effects:
1. Mast cell stabilizer: bad taste, cough, nasal congestion, wheezing.
2. Inhaled corticosteroid: sore throat, nosebleeds, cough, thrush (see below for more information).
3. Leukotriene antagonist: stomach upset, headache, dizziness.

Helpful Hint
◆ In the past, there were no inhaled steroid options for children under four years of age. We would use oral steroids (Prednisone) to get a severe flare up under control. We now have Pulmicort respules (a grainy substance dissolved in liquid), which can be administered in a nebulizer machine. Pulmicort is very effective for younger children and has significantly fewer side effects than its oral counterpart. Many doctors feel comfortable using this product in infants even though the product is approved for ages one year and up.

◆ Always rinse your child's mouth after he has taken an inhaled steroid. It reduces the incidence of thrush.

◆ Steroid medications are always used cautiously. Steroids given by mouth (liquid/pill) are more likely to cause systemic side effects if given for a long

MAKE THE CALL: ASTHMA CONCERNS

If your child needs his rescue medicine more frequently than it has been prescribed, CALL YOUR DOCTOR. Here are some important points to consider:
1. Your child is air hungry and needs to be evaluated by a doctor See Chapter 15, "First Aid."
2. Administering asthma medicine more frequently than recommended can be dangerous. A doctor's office or hospital can administer asthma medicine more often than prescribed because a medical provider can be monitoring a patient for side effects of the medicine.
3. If a child is having that much trouble breathing, it is likely that he needs to receive oxygen in addition to medication, which is only available in a medical facility.

time (more than one to two weeks). Inhaled steroids (nebulizer or inhaler) have significantly fewer side effects because only a small amount is absorbed into the bloodstream. As with any medication, the risks of taking these medications are weighed against the potential benefit of therapy for the disease.

Risks of long-term steroid use:
1. Mood change
2. Stomach upset
3. Intestinal bleeding
4. Impaired body's stress responses (HPA axis suppression: hypothalamic-pituitary-adrenal)
5. Bone demineralization (Osteopenia)
6. Weight gain, hair growth (Cushingoid features)
7. Cataracts
8. Growth suppression. There is data which shows some evidence of decreased height curves while a pre-pubertal child is taking steroids chronically. However, children with chronic problems with asthma also have poor growth. Studies have not concluded whether or not these children have "catch up growth" when steroids are discontinued.[7]

Preventing RSV infection in premature babies

If you have a baby who has graduated from a Neonatal Intensive Care Unit, you may already know that RSV (bronchiolitis) can be a serious lung infection for a premature infant.

A new product to prevent RSV infection is called Synagis (generic name is palivizumab). This is a synthetic antibody given by a monthly injection during the peak of RSV season (November to April). The antibody provides immunity for a period of 30 days.

Children who are at risk for more severe cases of RSV are:
1. Babies born prematurely, prior to 35 weeks gestation.
2. Children with chronic lung disease under age two years.
3. Children with congenital heart disease.
4. Children with certain immune deficiencies.
5. Weight under ten pounds.
6. Children of lower socioeconomic status.
7. Males.

Children who are more likely to get RSV infection include:
1. Babies under age six months when RSV season begins.
2. Babies in daycare.
3. Multiple births.
4. Babies with school age siblings.
5. Babies exposed to smoking.

The American Academy of Pediatrics recommends monthly Synagis injections during RSV season for the following babies:
1. Children under age two years with chronic lung disease (requiring treatment within six months of RSV season)
2. Babies born at or less than 28 weeks gestation and at or less than one year of age at the start of RSV season.

3. Babies born at 29-32 weeks gestation and at or less than six months of age at the start of RSV season.
4. Babies born 32-35 weeks gestation, at or less than six months of age at the start of RSV season, AND another risk factor for likelihood of infection.

Cough And Cold Medicines

Decongestant

These medications reduce or relieve congestion in the nose. They can be taken by mouth (absorbed into bloodstream) or sprayed into the nose.
Oral decongestants: Pseudoephedrine, phenylephrine, ephedrine.
Side effects: Insomnia, restlessness, dizziness, high blood pressure, heart rhythm disturbances.

Nasal spray: Oxymetazoline (Afrin), Phenylephrine (Neosynephrine)
Side effects: stinging, burning, nosebleed, rebound nasal congestion with prolonged use (more than 4 days)

Nasal spray: Saline
Side effects: None! Saline is salt water. It is effective in loosening mucus and can be used as often as needed.

FYI: A very effective decongestant, phenylpropanolamine or PPA, was taken off the market a few years back because it was similar to a product used in diet pills that was also taken off the market. There are no products containing PPA available today.

Pseudoephedrine, another popular decongestant, has been replaced by phenylephrine in many over the counter and prescription products. The reason? Methamphetamine (Meth) labs use pseudoephedrine to produce illegal drugs. Federal legislation in 2006 now requires products containing pseudoephedrine to be purchased from behind the pharmacy counter (not "over-the-counter"), thus limiting supplies. Pharmaceutical companies responded by just changing their formulations, to improve access to their products and their bottom line.

Antihistamine

These medications combat the effect of histamine in the body. Histamine is released as an allergy response and causes nasal congestion.

DR B'S OPINION: COUGH & COLD MEDICINE

I don't like to use any of these products (decongestants, etc.) in children under six months of age because there is a higher chance of side effects. I usually stick with saline nose drops.

I am also not very excited about the combination products that contain a fever reducing medication. Your child may not need all of the ingredients in a particular product. Sometimes it's better to get single-ingredient medication and use what you need.

Antihistamines are frequently found in cough and cold medicines because they are sedating, improve the cough suppressant effect, and dry up a runny nose.

Common ingredients: brompheniramine, chlorpheniramine, diphenhydramine, (promethazine— Rx only), carbinoxamine

Side effects: sedation, dry mouth, blurred vision, stomach upset, paradoxical excitement in infants

Expectorant

These medications make thick mucus looser. By doing this, the mucus in the bronchial tubes (lungs) can be coughed up more easily. These medications do not suppress the cough.

Common ingredients: guaifenesin
Side effects: sedation, stomach upset, headache

Cough Suppressant

These medications reduce the brain's "cough center" activity. These products are not recommended when someone has pneumonia. For common cold and flu bugs, this is the type of cough medicine you want to give for your child to stop coughing at night.

Common ingredients: Dextromethorphan, codeine (Rx only), carbetapentane

Side effects: drug interactions with psychiatric medications.

Helpful Hints

A study published in the journal, Pediatrics, looked at 100 children who took over-the-counter cough medicines and whether they slept better or not. The verdict: nobody slept better (child or parent). Since kids do about the same with or without cough medicine, you might want to think twice about using these products.

The Centers for Disease Control issued a warning in 2007 regarding use of cough and cold remedies in children under age two. This came after three deaths of infants under six months of age who had about 14 times the recommended dose of pseudoephedrine decongestant in their bloodstream. Bottom line: these medications don't work very well. And don't guess what dose is right for your baby. Time is the best remedy for a cold.

Cold Medicines For Breastfeeding Moms

Cold medicines and breastfeeding: Decongestant nose sprays (like Afrin) are usually okay as are antihistamines. Some cough medicines are NOT okay. Pseudoephedrine, a popular decongestant, may reduce milk supply by 25%.

12. Skin (Dermatologic) Products

1. Antibiotic creams are used for wound care and minor bacterial infections (impetigo, mild cellulitis).
2. Antifungal creams are used for fungus infections (ringworm, yeast infection, jock itch, athlete's foot) on the skin.

3. Scabicides and pediculocides are used for scabies and head lice.
4. Steroids are used for contact irritations (bug bites, poison ivy, local allergic reactions), seborrhea, cradle cap, and eczema. Steroids are divided into classes by their potency. Doctors always try to use the lowest potency if possible. The higher the potency, the more the risk of side effects (the high potency products can get absorbed into the bloodstream).
5. Anti-inflammatories are FDA approved for kids over age twp with eczema.
6. Diaper rash creams form a barrier between the irritated skin and recurrent insults caused by pee and poop.

Antibiotic Cream

GENERIC	BRAND	RX
Bacitracin, Polymyxin B	Polysporin	OTC

Used for minor cuts, scrapes, irritations

Mupirocin	Bactroban*, Centany	Rx

Used for impetigo and cellulitis

Neomycin, Polymixin, Bacitracin	Neosporin*	OTC

Used for minor cuts, scrapes, irritations, and superficial burns

Silver Sulfadiazine	Silvadene*	Rx

Antibiotic salve used for second-degree burns

Side effects: Burning, stinging, itching.

Antifungal Cream

Uses:
1. Yeast diaper rash (monilial dermatitis)
2. Ringworm of skin (tinea corporis)
3. Athlete's foot (tinea pedis)
4. Jock itch (tinea cruris)

GENERIC	BRAND	USED FOR	AGE LIMIT	RX
Clotrimazole 1%	Lotrimin AF*	1, 2, 3, 4	None	OTC
Ketoconazole 2%	Nizoral*	1,2,3,4	Over 2 yrs	Rx
Miconazole	Vusion*	1	Over 4 wks old	Rx
Nystatin	Mycostatin, Nilstat*	1	None	Rx
Econazole	Spectazole*	1,2,3,4	None	Rx

KEY: Rx—Rx medications are available by prescription only; OTC is over-the-counter. * A generic is available for this brand-name medicine.

Reality Check

Ringworm of the scalp (called tinea capitis) requires an antifungal medication by mouth for four to eight weeks. The fungus gets imbedded in the hair follicles and will not respond to an antifungal cream.

Scabicides And Pediculocides

Generic	Brand	Dose	Used for	Age limit	Rx
Acetic acid	Klout	No limit	Head lice	None	OTC
Lindane 1%**	Lindane	1 dose	Head lice, scabies	Over 1 yr	RX
Malathion	Ovide	2 doses, 1 week apart	Head lice	Over 6 yrs	RX
Permethrin 1%	NIX*	1-2 doses, 1 week apart	Head lice	None	OTC
Permethrin 5%	Elimite*, Acticin	1-2 doses 1 week apart	Head lice scabies	None	RX
Pyrethrum***	A-200* Pyrinyl* RID, Pronto*	2 doses, 1 week apart	Head Lice	None	OTC

* A generic is available for this brand-name medicine.
**Medication has significant side effects/potential for seizures. Other medications are better alternatives.
***Medication is derived from the chrysanthemum flower. Avoid use with a ragweed allergy.

Side effects: burning, itching, redness, rash

Helpful Hints for Head Lice

1. Use OTC products as directed. I know you are grossed out, but don't overdose the medicine.
2. Don't use more than one medicine at a time.
3. Use the nit combs every three days.
4. Wash clothing and bed linens in hot water and dry on the hot cycle.
5. Soak combs and hairbrushes in rubbing alcohol for one hour.
6. See Appendix B, Alternative Medications, for other possible remedies.

Reality Check

◆ When head lice enters your home, treat any family member who has an itchy scalp.

◆ When scabies enters your home, treat *all* family members, regardless of whether they have symptoms or not.

Steroids

◆ Low potency: can be used for longer periods (months) of time without side effects, okay to use on the face
◆ Mid potency: okay to use for short periods (weeks) of time without side effects, use with doctor's recommendation on the face
◆ High potency: okay to use for limited period (days) of time without side effects, do not use on the face

Note: None of these steroid creams are FDA approved for use under age two years. But they are used routinely by medical providers who feel that they are safe and efficacious.

MEDICATIONS

GENERIC	BRAND	POTENCY	DOSE	Rx/OTC
Hydrocortisone 0.5%	Cortaid, etc*	Low	BID	OTC
Hydrocortisone 1%	Cortaid, etc*	Low	BID	OTC
Hydrocortisone 2.5%	Hytone*	Low	BID	Rx
Triamcinolone 0.025%	Aristocort, Kenalog*	Low	BID	Rx
Desonide 0.05%	Desowen*	Mid	BID	Rx
Hydrocortisone valerate	Westcort*	Mid	BID	Rx
Hydrocortisone butyrate	Locoid*	Mid	BID	Rx
Mometosone furoate	Elocon*	Mid	QD	Rx
Triamcinolone 0.1%	Aristocort, Kenalog*	Mid	BID	Rx
Betamethasone	Diprolene*	High	BID	Rx
Diflorasone diacetate	Psorcon*	High	BID	Rx
Fluocinonide	Lidex*	High	BID	Rx
Triamcinolone 0.5%	Aristocort, Kenalog*	High	BID	Rx

KEY: Dose—see page 402 for an explanation of doses. Rx? Rx medications are available by prescription only; OTC is over-the-counter. * A generic is available for this brand-name medicine.

Side effects: skin irritation, decreased pigmentation, thinning of skin
Rare adverse reactions:
HPA axis (adrenal gland suppression)—only with high potency steroids

Anti-inflammatory cream

GENERIC	BRAND	DOSE	Rx/OTC
Pimecrolimus	Elidel	BID	Rx
Tacrolimus -.03%, 0.1 %	Protopic	BID	Rx

Side effects: burning, redness, itching
Rare adverse reactions: worsens warts, herpes, and chicken pox infections
Note: FDA approved for use in kids over the age of two years.

Essential Fatty Acid Creams

There is a new class of eczema medications that repairs the skin's top layer and reduce inflammation and itching. Brand names include Mimyx and Atopiclair. Both are Rx only (and pretty pricey).

Side effects: burning, redness, itching
Rare adverse reactions: Atopiclair is derived from the shea nut, so allergic reactions are possible.

Diaper rash creams

The idea behind all of the products listed below is to provide a barrier between the skin and moisture (pee and poop). When applying these creams and ointments, it is key to apply liberally and frequently.

Dr. B's opinion: I prefer creams to powders. When powder is applied, there is a risk that the baby will inhale the powder.

Diaper rash creams

A+D ointment	OTC
Boudreaux's Butt Paste	OTC
Dr. Smith's Diaper Ointment	OTC
Silvadene	Available by Rx only. Used for rash that looks like a burn.
Triple Paste	OTC
Vaseline	OTC
Zinc Oxide (brands: Desitin, Balmex)	OTC

BOTTOM LINE

Many pediatricians have a secret recipe of salves and barrier creams that pharmacies will make especially for them. If none of these over the counter products are working, it's time to visit your pediatrician for some help.

ALTERNATIVE MEDICINES
Appendix B

After reading the last section, you can see that the pharmaceutical industry is big business. And the list in Appendix A only included medications used for babies, which is a mere fraction of the total number of medications on the market.

But while it seems there is a drug for just about every malady, sometimes there's not. That may leave you frustrated as a parent. And some families fear that medications will have harmful side effects. This leads some to search out a "natural" or "alternative" remedy for their children.

That's why we wrote this appendix.

Alternative and complementary therapies are also big business (over $7 billion annually in the U.S.). Some of these treatment options have real merit and the science to back them up. Those are the therapies we will present to you. While there are many more choices in your local organic grocer's aisle, we are sticking to our comfort zone and our mantra: show us the science.

As a consumer, you also need to know a few things about natural or herbal remedies:

1. **Are they effective?** There are very few scientific studies that prove with statistical significance that herbal remedies work. The National Center for Complementary and Alternative Medicine, part of the National Institutes of Health, is starting to investigate many of these products.
2. **Are they safe?** There are no required clinical research trials that test herbal products on humans to prove that they are safe before they are sold to the public. Herbal remedies fall into the category of "foods" by the FDA (Food and Drug Administration). This is

> **DR B'S OPINION: A SIDE NOTE**
>
> Disclaimer: I admit that my medical training did not include acupuncture, spinal manipulations, homeopathy, or herbal supplements. So I have a certain degree of skepticism in complementary therapies—particularly when used in children. But I am always open to trying new remedies if they are proven beneficial and safe.

a convenient loophole for herbal product manufacturers. This means that they do not need to do any of the scientific research that a pharmaceutical company does to market their medications. This is based on federal legislation from 1994. Attempts to revise this act have failed in the past due to political pressure (and money) from the dietary supplements lobbying group.[1]

3. **Are production standards uniform?** Production is not standardized. The potency and purity of the product may vary tremendously. This is especially true for products that contain expensive herbs (e.g. ginseng). In fact, herbs produced in China are often laced with unlabeled products such as steroids and antibiotics to make them more potent. Also know that developing countries may sell products that are contaminated with mercury, arsenic, and lead.[2] And, in the United States, researchers found that only 7% of the studied Echinacea supplements complied with FDA labeling standards and some of the supplements contained no measurable amounts of Echinacea![3]

4. **Can I trust the label?** The claims on the label for marketing purposes do not require scientific evidence that the information is accurate. Bottom line: consumers don't have any protection against misleading information.

Compare herbs to traditional medicine. Many traditional medications are based on naturally occurring products. Penicillin is derived from a mold. Digoxin, a popular heart drug, is based on the digitalis plant. It is true that certain naturally occurring products have medical value. The difference between herbs and medications is *how they are tested and regulated*. Some herbs have absolutely no therapeutic value. And some herbs are so potent, they can be harmful. Just because it's natural, doesn't mean it is safe.

Consider alcohol and tobacco. Both have known effects on the body. Both are legal for use. But long term, chronic use of these products also can cause problems. These products are as natural as the herbs you are trying. No one knows what long-term problems *some* herbs can create.

Herbs: A review of uses and precautions

Aloe Vera
Uses: Minor burns, eczema, constipation
Scientific Data: Good evidence that it promotes wound healing. Not enough data to prove it works as a laxative, treats asthma, or diabetes.
Precautions: Overusing aloe as a laxative has been linked to increased cancer risk.
Not safe for use as a laxative in children under 12 yrs of age.[4]

Calendula
(calendula officinalis)
Uses: Skin irritation, wounds/burns, numbing drops for earaches
Scientific Data: Some evidence that it promotes wound healing in rats. Virtually no studies in humans.
Precautions: Allergic reactions can occur, and can cause eye irritation. Not

> ## DR B'S OPINION: TELL YOUR DOCTOR
>
> A recent article in a parenting magazine stated that 12% of all children have been given alternative therapies. Patients are using these products—most of the time without their doctor's knowledge. Parents don't tell the doctor they are trying herbals because:
>
> a) they fear that their decision will not be respected or
> b) think the doctor won't know anything about the product.
>
> The truth is, I respect parents' decisions even though I may not agree with them. As far as my knowledge about herbal remedies, I am learning as I go along. *But it is very important to tell your doctor if you are giving your child an herbal remedy. Some herbal products have significant drug interactions with other medications your doctor might be prescribing.*

recommended for use in the eye.[5] *Not recommended in children under 18.*

Chamomile
(anthemis nobilis)
Uses: acne, allergies, colds, colic, diaper rash, ear infections, eczema, sleep problems, sore throats, vomiting.
Scientific Data: Some data shows 3-4 oz per day of a combination (chamomile, fennel, vervain, licorice, balm mint) herbal tea improves symptoms of colic. Some evidence of improved wound healing.
Precautions: Infant botulism has been reported from contaminated home-grown chamomile tea. *Allergic reactions can be severe including shortness of breath, throat swelling, and anaphylaxis.*[6] The National Library of Medicine/National Institute of Health discourages its use during pregnancy and in children.

Echinacea
Uses: allergies, prevention of colds, sore throats
Scientific data: Study results are conflicting whether or not Echinacea prevents cold symptoms in adults. However, research shows no significant benefit in reducing length and severity of cold symptoms in children under 11 years of age.
Precautions: It can cause allergic reactions.[7] When taken at recommended doses, there are few side effects. These include: stomachache, nausea, sore throat, rash, liver inflammation.

Evening Primrose Oil
(Oenothera biennis)
Uses: allergies, eczema, attention deficit disorder
Scientific Data: Approved in several countries outside of U.S for eczema and atopic dermatitis. Several studies show benefit.
Precautions: Stomachache, headaches reported.[8]

ALT MEDS

Fennel
(foeniculum vulgare)
Uses: colic, gas, diarrhea, colds, conjunctivitis
Scientific Data: Only one study has been done which shows some benefit for colic, in combination with other herbs.
Precautions: None[9]

Ginger
(Zingiber officinale)
Uses: colds, diarrhea, headaches, nausea, vomiting, colic
Scientific Data: Some evidence for use in vomiting with pregnancy. No studies done in children.
Precautions: heartburn. Not for use if prone to gallstones.[10]

Licorice
(glycyrrhiza glabra)
Uses: allergies, asthma, cough, eczema, sore throats, canker sores
Scientific Data: Minimal data on canker sores done on 20 patients, one study on eczema.
Precautions: Long-term use has similar effects to steroids (high blood pressure, altered body salts). Heart rhythm disturbances possible. Not for use during pregnancy, or if patient has diabetes, liver, kidney disease.[11]

Peppermint
(Mentha piperita)
Uses: decongestant, cough, irritable bowel syndrome, indigestion, headaches, itching
Scientific Data: Research shows positive effects on irritable bowel syndrome and indigestion. Peppermint actually INCREASES nasal congestion but people subjectively report that they can breathe better.
Precautions: Heartburn. Peppermint oil should not be placed in nasal passages of babies as it increases risk of apnea (they stop breathing)[12]
National Institute of Health does not recommend use of peppermint leaf or oil in young children because of side effect risks.

Tea Tree oil
(Melaleuca alternifolia)
Uses: dandruff, head lice, fungal infections
Scientific Data: Some research shows benefit for mild to moderate dandruff.
Precautions: Toxic if taken by mouth. May mimic effects of estrogen and cause pre-pubertal boys to have breast enlargement.[13]

Zinc
Uses: common cold, diarrhea, malnutrition, gastric ulcers, acne
Scientific Data: Positive effect seen in malnourished kids with diarrhea, gastric ulcers. Contradictory results for reducing duration of common cold symptoms.
Precautions: Unpleasant or "distorted" taste. Occasional nausea, vomiting, diarrhea.[14]

BOTTOM LINE

Just because it's natural doesn't mean it's safe. Get educated about these products before using them.

What is *probably* safe to use on your baby (with several disclaimers via our attorneys):

1. Calendula based diaper rash cream (although Lanolin cream is just as "natural").
2. Baby's Bliss Gripe Water (made of ginger and fennel) for gas and colic.
3. Probiotic supplements for babies with diarrhea.

Insider Secret

Probiotics (good germs that live in your intestines and help digest food) are becoming an increasingly popular supplement in traditional medicine. These "good germs" seem to reduce antibiotic-associated diarrhea and diarrhea from stomach viruses. Probiotics may also be useful for eczema, colic intestinal problems of premature babies.

Probiotic products are mostly bacteria from the Lactobacillus or Bifidobacterium families that are similar to the germs that naturally live in our guts. A few probiotics are actually yeast-based, like Saccaromyces. Specific products include: Lactinex (Lactobacillus acidophilus and Lactobacillus bulgaricus), Culturelle (Lactobacillus GG), Lactobacillus reuteri, and Florastor (Saccaromyces).

Do all probiotics have the same effectiveness? Frankly, we don't really know. Probiotics research is really in its infancy. We do know that Lactinex, Culturelle, and Florastor have been studied in children with positive results. Lactobacillus reuteri is the probiotic that was specifically used in the study done on reduction of colic in infants (see Chapter 11 for details). We also know that these products appear to be relatively safe. But data is still lacking to dispel any theoretical safety concerns—particularly with young children and those with immune deficiencies.

So, will your local warehouse club version of probiotics prevent your child's diarrhea or colic? We don't have the answers yet—the research is still evolving. Watch our blog or sign up for our eNewsletter for the latest updates at Baby411.com.

And, what dose do you give to a baby to achieve these miraculous results? Well, we're kinda shooting from the hip here since there are no official recommendations. But, based on what we do know, your baby could take half teaspoon of L. reuteri powder per day to help with colic symptoms. Or the powder contained in one capsule of Culturelle a day may be used to combat diarrhea.

DR B'S OPINION: NEW STUDIES MAY SHED LIGHT ON ALT MEDS

The NIH (National Institutes of Health) has numerous scientific trials ongoing to study the effects and safety of herbal medicines. Hopefully, this will provide the data that physicians need to feel comfortable prescribing these products to their patients.

ALT MEDS

Homeopathic Remedies

These are products containing diluted ingredients that are listed in the *Homeopathic Pharmacopeia of the United States* (HPUS). But according to the National Center for Complementary and Alternative Medicine, "A product's compliance with requirements of the HPUS, ...does not establish that it has been shown by appropriate means to be safe, effective, and not mis-branded for its intended use."

For more information on herbal and homeopathic remedies, check out *The Holistic Pediatrician*, by Kathi J. Kemper, M.D. (see Appendix F). She is a well-respected pediatrician who has done a great deal of research on alternative therapies.

The National Center for Complementary and Alternative Medicine, a branch of the National Institute of Health, also has a useful website at nccam.nih.gov/health/herbsataglance.htm.

Home Remedies

Not every ailment requires a trip to the pharmacy. Here is a list of household items and remedies that often provide symptomatic relief for various problems.

Abdominal pain/gas/colic

Give your child a bath. The warm water is soothing. Playing in the bathtub is also a nice distraction technique.

Bruises

Pull out a bag of frozen vegetables and place on the site.

Common Cold (URI)

Make your own saline (salt water) nose drops. Take 1/2 teaspoon of salt and add to 8 oz. of water. Use as much as needed.

Chicken soup. Every culture has their own recipe, and for good reason. The high salt and water content is good for hydrating a child with a fever.

Pull out the humidifier. This moistens the air your child breathes, and loosens the mucus in his nose.

Cradle cap

Massage olive oil into the scalp. Then lift off the plaques.

Croup

Take your child into the bathroom. Close the door. Turn on the shower for ten to 15 minutes. The warm mist will help relax the airway.

If this technique doesn't work, walk outside with your child. The cold night air will often shrink up the swollen airway. It also changes the scenery for your child, which has a therapeutic effect too.

Croup usually occurs in the wintertime. If you live in a warm climate, this might not work for you.

Diaper rash

Good old petroleum jelly (Vaseline) works well. It provides a barrier between the skin and moisture.

Leave your baby open to air (diaper-less) in a safe place inside or outside your house.

Use a blow dryer on the lowest setting to dry baby's bottom.

Some doctors recommend applying liquid antacids (milk of magnesia, kaopectate) to the diaper rash. It might be worth a try.

Vomiting and Diarrhea

Make your own Pedialyte solution. Here is the recipe:
4 cups of water
1/2 tsp of salt
2 Tbsp. of sugar
1/2 tsp of instant Jell-O powder for flavor

Ear infections

Use a heating pad on low setting up to the ear.

Want to prevent your child's ear infections? Stop smoking.

To prevent swimmer's ear, you can make your own "Swim-ear" drops. The alcohol will dry up the water left in the ear canal. The vinegar changes the pH of the ear canal so bugs won't want to grow there. Here's the recipe:
2 drops rubbing alcohol
2 drops of vinegar

Eczema

Keeping the skin moist is the key. The best moisturizer (although not very practical) is good old petroleum jelly (Vaseline). Lube your child up head to toe.

Eye stye

Place a warm tea bag over the eyelid. It is soothing and reduces the swelling.

Lice

Put mayonnaise on your child's hair at bedtime. Cover with a shower cap. Rinse off in the morning. There seems to be limited success in smothering the lice with this technique. I used to tell people to use Vaseline instead of mayonnaise until I received too many phone calls about getting the Vaseline out!

Another alternative: Lice Ice. This is a product that contains tea tree oil as it active ingredient.

Sore throat

Make a milkshake or smoothie (depending on the age of your child). Cold drinks feel good and are a nice way to get the fluid intake in. This idea makes me very popular

> **DR B'S OPINION**
>
> *"I think that infant, child, and spouse massage all have therapeutic benefits. The laying on of hands, for most people, is very soothing and comforting. But doing acupuncture and spinal manipulations on a baby just makes me nervous!"*

ALT MEDS

with my patients.

Warts

Try duct tape. A study showed that smothering the warts suppresses the growth of the virus that causes them. Apply a new piece of duct tape to the wart nightly and leave on for the day. It takes about six weeks.

Lab Work & Tests
Appendix C

When The Parent Wants Tests Done

Parents frequently ask their doctor to order lab work on their child. Doctors are less interested in getting lab work done if they are comfortable in making a diagnosis. But doctors also know that a parent may bring their child in for the common cold and are actually concerned that the child has leukemia or some other devastating diagnosis. In medical terms, this is called "The Hidden Agenda." It's perfectly fine to have that agenda—you are a parent. But don't keep it a secret. Your doctor won't laugh at you. What we will do is make sure that your child does not have the problem that is keeping you up at night worrying.

What you need to know is that there is no one "test" that will uncover every disease that you have concerns about (like a total body CAT scan or a comprehensive blood test panel). In the past, doctors would perform annual blood metabolic panels on adults to go on a fishing expedition for abnormalities. This is out of vogue for adults and has never been standard practice for children.

What we might do is order a particular test that would help to diagnose or rule out the concern you have.

When The Doctor Wants Tests Done

Pediatricians can frequently make a correct diagnosis of illness in a child without any tests. I wish I could say it's because we are so much smarter than our other doctor colleagues. The truth is, childhood illnesses are often infections that follow classic patterns. And rashes, which occur more in kids than adults, are helpful in determining the cause of illness.

When do doctors order a test?
1. When there is something about the child's illness history or examination that may indicate a bacterial infection.
2. When there is a concern infection is bacterial and cultures are needed to know what bug the patient has (so it can be treated appropriately).
3. When a child has a fever with no obvious source.
4. When a baby under three months has a fever.
5. When your doctor thinks your child has a broken bone.

Lab Work

6. When your doctor feels a hip "click" in a newborn. Testing will verify he doesn't have a congenitally dislocated hip.
7. When a child is vomiting bile or has intractable vomiting.
8. When a child has blood in his poop.
9. When a child has pain when he urinates.
10. When a child's head size is enlarging across percentiles (in other words, the head is growing much faster than the rest of the body).
11. When a child's head size is *not* enlarging.
12. When a child is failing to thrive (not gaining weight).
13. When a child wheezes for the first time and it doesn't sound like RSV bronchiolitis.
14. If an abnormality is found during a regular exam (such as distended abdomen, swollen testes).
15. When a child is drinking or urinating excessively.
16. When a child has excessive bruising.
17. When a child has petechiae.
18. When a child has a persistent fever (five days or more).
19. When a newborn is jaundiced to the level below the belly button.
20. When a child is disoriented.
21. When a child has a seizure for the first time.
22. When a child appears dehydrated and the doctor needs to decide how dehydrated he is (that is, does he need to be admitted to the hospital and get IV fluids).
23. When a child bleeds excessively—with cuts or nosebleeds.
24. When a mother has Blood Type O. Your doctor needs to know the baby's blood type so the doctor can be prepared for potential newborn jaundice problems.
25. When your doctor thinks a child has pneumonia and want to confirm it.
26. When a parent is worried.
27. When a child is limping.
28. When a child has recurrent bacterial infections (not just ear infections) such as pneumonia, sinus infections, skin infections.
29. When a child has chronic or severe problems with wheezing.
30. Anytime a child is jaundiced out of the newborn period.
31. When a child has a heart murmur that does not sound like an innocent heart murmur.
32. When a child has an irregular heartbeat.
33. When a child has a bladder or kidney infection.
34. When a child has swallowed a non-food object.

With that said, here are the most common tests we order and what they mean.

Imaging Studies

Ultrasound

The beauty of ultrasonography is that no radiation is used. The technology involves use of sonar waves and computer imaging. Doppler flow studies in addition to ultrasound pictures are helpful in looking at blood flow.

Ultrasound pictures can be limited, however. Gas and fat obstructs the view.

Abdominal. Looks at the anatomy of the liver, gallbladder, spleen. Not as good at looking at intestines. Detects pyloric stenosis, intussusception, gallstones, masses.

Head. Looks for bleeding inside the skull. Wand is placed on top of the anterior fontanelle (soft spot) to see inside. Not used once fontanelle has closed. Detects intraventricular hemorrhage (IVH), a problem that can occur in babies born prematurely.

Hip. Looks at the hip joint. Detects congenital hip dislocations in infants under four months of age.

Heart (echocardiogram with Doppler). Looks at the anatomy of the heart and the great blood vessels coming off of the heart. Detects heart defects.

Kidney (renal). Looks at the anatomy of the kidneys. Detects evidence of enlargement, fluid collection (hydronephrosis), and infection.

Pelvic. Looks at anatomy of the ovaries, uterus, bladder. Detects ovarian cysts, masses. Also detects location of a testes if it has not descended into the scrotum.

Spine. Looks for spina bifida, an abnormal formation of the spine

Testicular, with Doppler flow. Looks at the anatomy of the testes. Detects a twisted testes and can assess blood flow to the testes. Also detects some hernias.

Plain x-rays

X-rays use diffraction of low doses of high-speed electrons (radiation) to project an image. Solid or fluid filled objects appear white and air appears clear. As a general rule, plain x-rays are better at detecting bone problems, and less helpful at assessing problems with "soft tissues."

Abdomen. Looks at the anatomy of the intestines, liver, spleen. Detects intestinal obstructions, malrotations, constipation. Can detect some foreign bodies (swallowed objects that are metal).

Chest. Looks at the anatomy of the heart, lungs, ribs. Detects fluid (blood, pus) in lungs, masses in lungs, enlargement of the heart, rib fractures, foreign inhaled objects.

Extremities. Looks at the bones of the arms and legs. Detects fractures (broken bones), fluid or swelling occasionally. Less helpful in detecting problems with muscles, tendons, and joints.

Neck. Looks at the anatomy of the throat (epiglottis, tonsils, adenoid, trachea). Detects swelling of these areas, location of some swallowed objects.

Skull. Looks at the anatomy of the skull bones. Detects craniosynostosis, fractures.

Sinus. Looks at the anatomy of the sinus cavities of the face. Detects *acute* sinus infections by identifying an air/fluid level. Not helpful in detecting chronic sinus infections.

Spine. Looks at the anatomy of the vertebrae from the neck to the buttocks. Detects fractures, slipped discs, scoliosis.

CT/MRI with or without contrast

Computerized Tomography (CT) uses x-ray technology (radiation) to look at cross sectional slices of the body in a two-dimensional picture. Magnetic Resonance Imaging (MRI) uses a magnetic field to detect the body's electromagnetic transmissions. MRI's produce narrow slices of the body without radiation.

As a general rule, these studies are better at detecting abnormalities with soft body tissues and less helpful with bone problems. The decision to perform a CT versus an MRI is based on the particular problem that is being assessed.

Abdomen. Looks at the anatomy of the liver, spleen, pancreas, gallbladder, intestines, kidneys. Detects masses, tumors, abscesses—including appendicitis, fluid collections, trauma.

Chest. Looks at the anatomy of the lungs and heart. Detects masses, tumors, fluid collections, congenital abnormalities, trauma.

Extremity. Looks at the anatomy of the arm or leg. Detects fractures, torn ligaments, masses, tumors, osteomyelitis (infection).

Head. Looks at the anatomy of the brain. Detects masses, tumors, obstruction of spinal fluid flow (hydrocephalus), evidence of stroke (cerebrovascular accident), evidence of trauma, bleeding.

Lymph node. Looks at the anatomy of a concerning (swollen) lymph node. Detects pus (infection), masses, congenital cysts.

Pelvic. Looks at the anatomy of the ovary, uterus, bladder. Detects masses, tumors, fluid collections.

Sinus. Looks at the anatomy of the sinus cavities. More helpful imaging study than plain x-rays. Detects obstruction to flow in the sinuses, chronic sinus infections, masses/polyps.

Special studies

Barium swallow/Upper GI. Looks at the anatomy of the upper gastrointestinal tract (esophagus, stomach, upper small intestine). Detects anatomic abnormalities, hiatal hernias, pyloric stenosis, ulcerations, narrowings. Although gastroesophageal reflux may be seen (barium goes backwards), it doesn't tell you the severity of the reflux. It also does not rule out reflux as a diagnosis.

Bone scan. Nuclear medicine study (uses a radio-isotope to be visualized on x-ray). Looks at the all of the bones of the body in one study. Hot and cold "spots" detect areas of inflammation. Detects: infection, tumors, avascular necrosis, child abuse.

Voiding Cystourethrogram. Looks at the flow of urine from kidney to ureters to bladder to urethra. Detects vesicoureteral reflux in children prone to bladder infections.[1]

Laboratory Tests

Blood tests

Amylase. This test looks at the level of an enzyme that the pancreas makes. Detects: pancreatitis

Basic Metabolic Panel. This is a battery of tests that includes *sodium, potassium, chloride, bicarbonate, blood urea nitrogen, creatinine, glucose.* This combination of tests assesses body fluid and salt (electrolyte) balance as well as kidney and adrenal function.
Detects: Dehydration, kidney dysfunction, diabetes, hypoglycemia, adrenal dysfunction

Bilirubin. This test assesses the level of this substance circulating in the bloodstream. Newborns uniquely have higher levels than any other time in life because:
    1. Newborn metabolism is not functioning at 100%
    2. Newborns are not eliminating bilirubin in their stool yet
    3. Newborns have bilirubin load due to prematurity, birth trauma, or blood type incompatibility.
    A total level is assessed as well as *direct* and *indirect* levels. These indicate the cause of the total elevation. Beyond the newborn period, any evidence of jaundice prompts a lab evaluation.
Detects: Hyperbilirubinemia, Hepatitis, Biliary Atresia, gallstones, hemolytic anemia

Blood culture. see below

Blood sugar (glucose). This test assesses the body's metabolism of sugar. A random level above 110 is concerning for diabetes. In newborns, a level less than 40 is concerning for hypoglycemia. Levels less than 60 in children is concerning for hypoglycemia.
Detects in newborns: Hypoglycemia in large birth weights, babies whose mothers have gestational diabetes or diabetes, body temperature irregularities, lethargy
Detects in children: Diabetes, hypoglycemia
Blood type. This test determines what proteins sit on the surface of a patient's red blood cells. There are A and B proteins. The AB blood type means both A and B protein are present. The O blood type means there are no proteins present. Rh typing refers to the presence (+) or absence (-) of another type of protein that sits on the red blood cell surface. These

tests are necessary when a blood transfusion is needed. In an emergency situation, however, everyone gets O (-) negative blood. Most hospitals no longer test a newborn's blood type on a routine basis.

Cholesterol level. See lipid panel

Complete Blood Count (CBC). This refers to a test that looks at the number of white blood cells, red blood cells, and platelets that are circulating in the bloodstream.

1. *White blood cell count (WBC).* These cells fight infection, but also rise with inflammation. An elevated count is concerning for a bacterial infection. A depressed count is due to decreased bone marrow production (where white blood cells are made)—usually caused by viral infections (e.g. influenza, mononucleosis).

2. *White blood cell count differential.* Not only is the number of white blood cells counted, but the types of white blood cells are identified in a CBC. The types of cells also give your doctor clues as to the disease process going on.
- *Neutrophils (PMN's)-* Cells that fight bacteria. If more than 50% of the WBC's are this type, the likelihood of a bacterial infection is greater.
- *Lymphocytes*: Cells that fight viruses. If more than 50% of the WBC's are this type, the likelihood of viral infection is greater.
- *Eosinophils*: Cells that fight parasites. Also revved up by allergies. If more than 10-15% of these cells are present, it prompts an investigation.*

3. *Hematocrit/Hemoglobin.* These measurements assess the amount of red blood cells in the circulation. Low levels detect anemia.

4. *Platelet count.* These cells help clot the blood. A low level detects a cause for bleeding problems. A low level can also suggest bone marrow suppression (where platelets are made) or an autoimmune disorder. Platelet counts can be elevated with infection or inflammation.

*When all thee cell lines (white, red, platelet) are depressed, there is a concern for leukemia.
Uses: infection, inflammation, leukemia, anemia, bleeding disorder

Comprehensive Metabolic Panel. This is a large battery of tests that assesses adrenal, kidney, liver, gallbladder, fluid and electrolyte balance, and a measure of general nutrition. Many physicians pick a select number of these tests and not the whole panel. These tests include:
Albumin
Alkaline phospatase
Alanine Aminotransferase (ALT)
Aspartate Aminotransferase (AST)
Bicarbonate
Bilirubin
Blood Urea Nitrogen (BUN)

Calcium
Chloride
Creatinine
Glucose
Phosphorous
Potassium
Sodium
Total Protein
Detects: Liver dysfunction, hepatitis, gallbladder dysfunction, kidney dysfunction, dehydration, diabetes, adrenal dysfunction, malnutrition.

Chromosome analysis. This test assesses a patient's chromosomes, the part of each cell that contains genes. Blood, tissue, or an amniotic fluid sample can be tested.
Detects: Chromosomal abnormalities related to developmental delays/congenital defects; determines the sex of a baby born with ambiguous genitalia.

Coagulation studies. These tests detect an abnormality in the clotting "cascade" or chain of events that allow blood to clot. These tests include:
Bleeding Time, Factor levels, Prothrombin time (PT), Partial thromboplastin time (PTT)
Detects: Bleeding disorders—such as Hemophilia, von Willebrand's disease

Coombs test. This test looks for antibodies (reaction) to a person's blood type. In newborns whose mothers have O Blood type, many hospitals perform a Coombs test on the baby routinely. There is some mixing of mother's and fetus's blood in the placenta, which can cause a Type O mother's blood to create antibodies to a type A or B baby. These antibodies can potentially kill some of the baby's red blood cells creating an extra bilirubin load in the newborn.
Detects: Blood type incompatibility in newborns

Electrolytes. See Basic Metabolic Panel

Erythrocyte Sedimentation Rate (ESR). This test looks at how fast it takes for red blood cells to settle at the bottom of a test tube. It is a very nonspecific test, but an elevated level suggests further testing. It is a non-specific sign of inflammation.
Detects: inflammation, infection, pregnancy, malignancy, anemia

Liver function tests. This is a battery of tests that evaluates how the liver is working. It looks at products the liver is in charge of metabolizing and producing. Some tests look at the breakdown product of liver cells (but these products are also seen in muscle breakdown) so they are not specific in detecting liver disorders.
Alanine Aminotransferase (ALT)
Albumin
Aspartate Aminotransferase (AST)
Bilirubin
Total protein

Detects: Hepatitis, liver failure, drug toxicity, heart attack.

Monospot/EBV titers. For monospot, see rapid assays below.
Epstein-Barr Virus (EBV) titers detect a person's immune response (antibodies) to an EBV infection (mononucleosis). Because different types of antibodies are formed through the course of infection, this test differentiates a recent infection and a prior one.
Detects: Acute mononucleosis, prior mononucleosis.

Lipid panel/cholesterol. This battery of tests looks at how the body metabolizes fat. Poor fat metabolism is associated with coronary artery disease (heart disease) in later life. In children, often a random (non-fasting) cholesterol level is obtained for those at risk (family history, obesity). If that level is elevated, a full panel is done with the child fasting prior to the test.
Cholesterol
HDL
LDL
Triglyceride level
Detects: Hypercholesterolemia, hepatitis, metabolic disorders, bile duct obstruction, nephrotic syndrome, pancreatitis, hypothyroidism

Reticulocyte count. Reticulocytes are baby red blood cells. They circulate in the bloodstream while they mature. This test looks at the number of these present in the blood. A high level suggests good bone marrow production in response to anemia.
Detects: Body's response to anemia

Thyroid function tests. This is a battery of tests that assesses the function of the thyroid gland. An indirect way of testing thyroid gland function is to look at a Thyroid Stimulating Hormone (TSH) level, a hormone produced by the pituitary gland. If the thyroid gland is not functioning well (hypothyroidism), the TSH level is elevated to stimulate the gland to work harder. This is a test included in all state metabolic screens to detect congenital hypothyroidism.
T3 (triiodothyronine) level
Thyroxine Binding Globulin
T4 (thyroxine) level
Free T3, Free T4 levels
TSH
Detects: Hypothyroidism, Hyperthyroidism

Viral titers. There are a few viruses for which a patient's antibody response can be detected. These tests are useful to make a diagnosis or confirm immunity to a particular virus.
CMV
Hepatitis A, B, C
HIV
Parvovirus
Rubella
Syphilis
Toxoplasmosis
Varicella

Urine tests

Urinalysis. This is a test that looks at the components of urine and detects any abnormal components. Urine is normally a sterile fluid, thus should not contain any bacteria or white blood cells (which fight infection). Urine does not breakdown sugar or protein, so it should not contain any of those substances. Urine is produced in the kidneys, so some abnormalities will point to a kidney dysfunction.

In children, obtaining a urine specimen can be a challenge. A urine specimen needs to be clean to be able to make any decisions based on its findings. The preferred method of obtaining this specimen is to insert a small catheter in the urethra of a non-toilet trained child. If the reason for testing urine is not to look for infection, a collection bag may be placed over the urethra.

Specific gravity
pH
Color, odor
White Blood Cells
Red Blood Cells
Glucose
Protein
Nitrite
Microscopic analysis for bacteria

Detects: Bladder infection, dehydration, kidney disease, diabetes, adrenal dysfunction, metabolic disorder, kidney stones

Skin tests

PPD. This is the preferred test for exposure to tuberculosis. PPD stands for purified protein derivative, which refers to a synthetic protein "signature" that belongs to the tuberculosis bacteria. If a person has had an exposure to tuberculosis, their antibodies will also respond to this skin test. A positive test requires further evaluation and testing.

Stool tests

Occult blood. This test detects blood in the stool. A small amount of stool (poop) is placed on a special developing card. When a processing fluid is added to the specimen, it turns blue in the presence of blood.

Detects: Gastrointestinal bleeding (e.g. food allergy, infection, ulcer, inflammatory bowel disease, polyp)

Spinal fluid (CSF) tests

Cerebrospinal fluid (CSF) is a liquid that bathes the brain and spinal cord. It transports important chemicals through the central nervous system. A specimen of this fluid helps diagnose viral infection, bacterial infection, tuberculosis meningitis (infection of the tissues protecting the brain), brain infection, and obstruction of the spinal fluid collecting system.

CSF is obtained by performing a lumbar puncture or "spinal tap." This sounds scary, but it is a similar concept to having an epidural placed in childbirth. A small needle is inserted between two vertebrae in the back. A small amount of fluid is collected, and then the needle is removed.

We look at the pressure of the fluid, the appearance of the fluid (should be clear/watery), the sugar/protein levels, and if there are any cells in the fluid (white, red, bacteria).

A culture of the fluid is also done (see below).

Sweat test

A specimen of sweat is obtained by warming the skin on the arm or thigh and obtaining a small amount of sweat.
Detects: Cystic Fibrosis

Cultures

This group of tests takes a particular body fluid and incubates it (creates ideal growing conditions for bugs). If there is a germ in a specimen, there is a chance to identify it. Germs that grow are very accurate for infection growing in the patient (except for contaminated/dirty specimens). But, lack of growth in culture does not necessarily rule out an infection.

Most germs will grow out in a culture within three days. Fungus infections, however, may take up to one month to grow.

Blood. Detects BACTERIAL infections
Urine. Detects bacterial infections
Spinal fluid. Detects primarily BACTERIAL infections, some VIRAL infections
Stool. Detects BACTERIAL, PARASITE, AMOEBA infections
Throat. Detects BACTERIAL infection
Sputum. Detects BACTERIAL infection
Abscess. Detects BACTERIAL infection
Viral. Detects limited number of VIRAL infections (such as Herpes, Varicella, Chlamydia)
Fungal. Detects FUNGUS infections

Rapid Antigen Assays

As a group, these tests identify responses that infections have to certain chemicals. You might think of them in a similar way to a home pregnancy test. A positive test accurately confirms infection. But a negative test does not rule *out* infection. These "assay kits" also look like a home pregnancy test. The earlier these tests are done in the course of an illness, the less accurate they are.

Strep. Throat swab specimen
Monospot. Blood specimen
Influenza. Nasal secretion specimen (not covered on some insurance plans)
RSV. Nasal secretion specimen. Not offered in pediatric offices. Used routinely in a hospital setting to isolate and treat patients who have this infection.
Rotavirus. Stool specimen[2]

GLOSSARY
REALLY BIG LATIN WORDS
Appendix D

Abdominal tumors. There are some solid tumors that occur more frequently in children than adults. These include Wilm's tumor and neuroblastoma. Patients with these tumors may (not always) have enlarged, firm bellies with a mass that can be felt. Other symptoms include weight loss, lack of appetite, or unexplained fevers.

ABO incompatibility. See Coombs test in Lab section.

Acholic stool. Official term for a clay colored poop. In isolation, it may have no significance. But, it can indicate a problem with the biliary system (liver, gallbladder, pancreas) if it is associated with other symptoms—particularly jaundice (yellowing) of the skin. Diagnoses can include hepatitis infection and biliary atresia. If you see this, check in with your doctor.

Acne (neonatal). Skin inflammation due to hormonal changes in the newborn period. Onset is usually by four weeks of age and lasts until about eight weeks of age.

Acute abdomen. Term that refers to an emergency requiring surgical intervention to alleviate an intestinal problem. Examples of these problems include: appendicitis, intussusception, intestinal obstruction.

Acute life threatening event (ALTE). The term that describes an episode of lack of breathing (apnea) that requires intervention to resume spontaneous breathing. If an event like this happens, a thorough evaluation is done to determine the cause of the event.

Acute otitis media. Infection in the middle ear space. This is primarily caused by bacteria. When the infection comes up quickly, it is called "acute." Symptoms include fever, cranky mood, and vomiting. Occasionally, children may also seem dizzy. Ear infections that smolder for a long period of time are called "chronic" and do not have the same symptoms.

Acrocyanosis. The blue discoloration frequently seen on the hands and feet of newborns. This is due to the body circulation transitioning from fetal to newborn. It doe not indicate any problem with the heart or circulatory system. Blue discoloration only on the feet or legs (not hands) can be a sign of a circulation problem (Coarctation of the Aorta) and needs to be evaluated.

Air hungry. The inability of a person to get enough oxygen in with each breath. The person then tries to get more air in with each breath by using chest wall muscles and increasing the number of breaths taken per minute. This is also known as **respiratory distress**.

Ambiguous Genitalia. It's hard to tell whether the baby has boy parts or girl parts. We'll test chromosomes, hormone levels, and get an ultrasound to look for internal genitalia (ovaries/uterus or undescended testes).

Amblyopia. (Known as lazy eye). A reduction of vision in an eye that is not correctable with glasses. This problem can be caused by a weakness of an eye muscle (strabismus). It is important to detect this eye problem early (under age two or three years) so it can be treated.

Anal fissure. A crack in the anus opening usually due to passage of a hard poop. The crack causes discomfort and occasionally blood in the diaper or on a diaper wipe.

Anaphylactic reaction. An allergic response to exposure to a particular item (that is, medication, food). The response is extremely serious and life-threatening. These body responses include: difficulty breathing, heart failure, loss of blood pressure.

Anemia. A reduced amount of hemoglobin that carries oxygen on red blood cells. Because the body is less capable of getting oxygen, symptoms include tiredness, pale appearance, and quick fatigue.

Ankyloglossia (tongue tie). The tongue is attached to the base of the mouth too close to the tip. Not all babies with tongue tie need intervention. If it is so tight that it interferes with feeding or talking, the tissue band can be clipped. This is more likely to be a problem if the tip of the tongue is forked.

Anomaly. Fancy word for abnormality, usually malformed prior to birth (congenital anomaly).

Antibiotic induced colitis. Inflammation of the lower part of the intestine which, rarely, can be caused by antibiotics. Symptoms of colitis include blood and mucus in the poop, diarrhea, and cramping. If someone has been on an antibiotic just prior to the onset of these symptoms, a specimen of poop can be checked for this problem.

Apnea. Pause, or temporary absence in breathing. Frequently babies born prematurely have these events when they just plain forget to breathe. This is called **apnea of prematurity**. Preemies eventually outgrow this problem. Until they do, they are placed on an apnea monitor which alarms when breathing stops. Some babies also need caffeine (in medication form) to stimulate them to breathe.

Appendicitis. Inflammation of a small piece of the intestine called the appendix. The appendix is usually located in the lower RIGHT side of the belly, but this varies occasionally. When the appendix gets swollen, symptoms include: vomiting, diarrhea, fever, and abdominal pain that worsens over time. Appendicitis is extremely rare in the birth age one group.

Asperger's Syndrome. A developmental disorder that is part of the Autism Spectrum Disorders. Children with Asperger's have more social and language skills than those more severely affected.

Asthma. The swelling of the big and little airways in the lungs. The swelling can occur due to allergic response. The episodes happen intermittently. Symptoms include: coughing and labored breathing (respiratory distress).

Atopy. A classic triad of allergic disorders: eczema, asthma, and seasonal allergies (termed "allergic rhinitis"). Not everyone is unlucky enough to have all three problems, but some people are.

Atresia. Means that something is completely absent or is significantly narrowed
   Anal atresia. anus (opening of the intestines to the outside)
   Biliary atresia. Bile ducts
   Choanal atresia. Nasal/throat
   Duodenal atresia. Small intestine
   Esophageal atresia. Esophagus
   Ileal atresia. Small intestine
   Tricuspid atresia. Heart valve

Autism. A developmental disorder that is characterized by poor or no language development, lack of normal social skills and repetitive self-soothing behaviors. The disorder likely has a genetic basis, as seen by research done on twins. There is a broad range of this disorder from mild to severely affected. Thus, Autism Spectrum Disorder is a new term used to describe it.

Autosomal dominant. A genetically inherited trait that requires only one parent to have an abnormal gene to pass it on to a child. If one parent carries an autosomal dominant gene, the chances are 50% that a child inherits the gene.

Autosomal recessive. A genetically inherited trait that requires both parents to have the gene to pass it on to a child. If both parents are carriers of the autosomal recessive gene, the chances are 25% that they will have an affected child. If both parents have the disease, chances are nearly 100% that they will have an affected child.

Bacterial gastroenteritis. (See gastroenteritis)

GLOSSARY

BAER. Brainstem Audio Evoked Response. An objective hearing test that measures the electrical activity of the inner ear in response to sound. This is a universal screening test done on newborns. It is recommended by the American Academy of Pediatrics and currently mandated by law in 37 states.

Bladder infection (see UTI)

Blood in stool. A symptom that may be caused by a variety of reasons. Blood can be found in poop due to skin irritation (diaper rash), a crack or tear in the anus (see anal fissure), inflammation in the intestine (milk protein allergy), intestinal infection (see gastroenteritis), or intestinal obstruction (intussusception). As you can see, the problem may be a minor or serious one. It always should be checked out by your doctor.

Brain tumor. Abnormal mass of cells that grow in the brain tissue. Although not all tumors are malignant (fast growing, aggressive), even benign tumors can be life threatening depending on the location that it arises. Symptoms in infants and young children include morning headaches accompanied by vomiting, increasing head size, behavior changes, imbalance, seizures, and new onset eye abnormalities.

Branchial cleft cyst. An abnormality in fetal development of the throat that results in a cyst that occurs on the neck

Breath-holding spell. An episode where a child holds his breath when upset or angry. Usually occurs after one year of age. The episode ultimately results in a child losing consciousness and regaining normal breathing. Rarely, these episodes are due to anemia—but worth checking out if the episodes occur frequently.

Bronchiolitis. Swelling in the tiny airways in the lungs (bronchioles). In children, this is caused primarily by a virus called RSV (respiratory syncytial virus). When the little airways are swollen, it can be difficult to exchange oxygen poor air with oxygen rich air. In severe cases, particularly infants under a year of age or those born prematurely, some children need medication to reduce the swelling (see bronchodilators in medication appendix) and supplemental oxygen.

Bronchitis. Swelling in the larger airways of the lungs (bronchi). In children, this swelling is usually caused by a virus or bacterial infection.

Broncopulmonary dysplasia (BPD). Term used to describe chronic lung disease that occurs primarily in babies who are born prematurely who require prolonged breathing assistance with a mechanical ventilator. The longer the baby is dependent on mechanical ventilation, the poorer the prognosis. Babies with BPD may have poor lung function, wheezing, and higher risk of severe complications with respiratory syncytial virus (RSV) infection. Lung function, however, usually improves over the first several years of life.

Cafe au lait spots. As the name implies, these are light brown (coffee with milk) colored birthmarks. They occur in babies of all races. Most of the time, there is no significance to these marks. When a child has more than five of these birthmarks, there may be an association with a disorder called **neurofibromatosis**.

Carotinemia. A benign yellow discoloration of the skin due to a large dietary intake of carotene containing foods (carrots, sweet potatoes). The whites of the eyes remain white, as opposed to what is seen with jaundice—**see jaundice**.

Cataracts. A clouding of the eye's lens. This can occur at birth (congenital cataracts). If a newborn has cataracts, it can be detected by the lack of a 'red reflex' on an eye examination. A referral to a pediatric ophthalmologist is made.

Celiac disease. A disorder of the intestines which causes poor digestion and absorption of foods. The underlying problem is due to an abnormal response to 'gluten' containing foods (e.g. wheat, oat, rye grains). The classic symptoms of this disorder include foul smelling, chronic diarrhea and failure to thrive (lack of weight gain). Treatment is a lifelong gluten-free diet.

Cephalhematoma. Literally, a head bruise. This often occurs in newborns as a result of birth trauma. Some of these bruises are quite large and take one to two months to completely go away. In the process of healing, these areas can become very hard and firm. Since the bruise is a collection of blood, it sometimes creates an additional bilirubin load and can lead to jaundice in some newborns.

Cerebral palsy. An abnormality of the brain center that controls muscle tone and movement. Cerebral palsy does not cause any abnormalities in IQ. However, there are children who have *both* mental retardation AND cerebral palsy.

Choanal atresia. Lack of communication between the back of the nasal passages and the throat. This can occur in one or both sides of the nose. If both sides are blocked, a newborn will have severe breathing problems. Newborns only know how to breathe through their noses for the first four months of life.

Clavicle (collar bone) fracture. When Mom is small and baby is big, it can be difficult to get the baby out of the birth canal. The baby's shoulder pulls out and can break the clavicle (collar bone) in the process. It heals nicely without a cast. The area can feel crunchy under the skin, then it feels like a hard lump. The lump is healing bone and goes away after several weeks.

Cleft lip and palate. The roof of the mouth and/or the upper lip does not completely form in a fetus. These defects can occur together or separately in 1 in 1000 births. There is some hereditary predisposition. Rarely, this defect is associated with other congenital defects. Frequently, a team of providers manage babies with these defects (Ear, Nose, and Throat doctors, Plastic Surgeons, Dentist, and Occupational Therapists). See Appendix F for web sites on this issue.

Club foot. An abnormality in the formation of the foot of the fetus. The result is a stiff foot that turns markedly inwards. Pediatric orthopedic surgeons are consulted and a cast is made to correct the position of the foot.

Coarctation of the Aorta. A narrowing or kink in the great artery (aorta) that leaves the heart and supplies the body with oxygen rich blood. This is a defect that occurs during fetal development (prior to birth). If the abnormality is severe, it is diagnosed in newborns who have weakened/no pulse in the legs. If the abnormality is small, it may go undetected until later in life. It is repaired by surgery.

Colostrum. A first "milk" that a mother produces. This product is rich in antibodies and cells. It has fewer calories than mature milk which arrives on about the fourth day after birth.

Conductive hearing loss. Difficulty hearing due to a problem with the transmission of sound waves to the part of the ear that controls hearing. Sound waves can be blocked due to fluid sitting behind the eardrum (see serous obits media) or a significant amount of earwax sitting in the ear canal. The good news about conductive hearing loss is that the problem can usually be fixed and normal hearing is restored.

Congenital. This refers to an abnormality in the *formation* of a certain organ/body part that occurs in the development of an unborn fetus. These abnormalities may be due to either hereditary problems or environmental exposures during pregnancy. The lay term for these disorders is **birth defect.**

Congenital Adrenal Hyperplasia. An abnormality in the gland that produces steroids in the body (adrenal gland). This can cause severe metabolism problems of body salts. This abnormality is routinely tested in the newborn metabolic screen.

Congenital heart disease. A defect in the structural development of the heart or the great vessels that attach to the heart. Because heart development occurs in the first trimester of pregnancy, many congenital defects can be identified on a prenatal ultrasound. Some abnormalities will resolve on their own. Some require surgical repair. The disease incidence is 1:1000. The most common defects are the least serious ones. Remember, there is a difference between an innocent heart murmur (no defect) and a pathologic murmur (caused by congenital heart disease).

Congenital nevus. (Known as moles, birthmarks) A mark on the skin which is present at birth, or appears within the first year of life. The most concerning moles are ones larger than 10 to 20 cm (really big) that are present at birth. These have more potential risk of skin cancer and removal is usually advised.

Congestive heart failure. When the heart is unable to perform adequately, the blood flow accumulates in the lungs and liver. So, symptoms of heart failure include shortness of breath and enlarged liver size. In children, symptoms include failure to thrive, sweating with feedings, shortness of breath, and excessive fatigue.

Conjunctivitis. An inflammation of the lining of the eyelid. Otherwise known as "pink eye." The inflammation can be caused by a virus, bacteria, allergies, or irritation. All types of conjunctivitis cause redness and some discomfort. Here are the major types of conjunctivitis:
Allergic. An allergic response usually due to a sensitivity to something in the air (e.g. pollens). Usually causes watery, somewhat itchy eyes. Antihistamines treat the symptoms.
Bacterial. A bacterial infection in the eye (often accompanied by ear and sinus infection). Causes thick yellowish eye discharge and may even cause the eyes to be caked over or "matted." Antibiotic eye drops treat the infection.
Viral. A viral infection in the eye (that may be accompanied by a sore throat). Causes watery and very itchy eyes.
Irritation. Eyes become inflamed because of a chemical irritant (e.g. shampoo).

Constipation. The texture of poop is significantly hard, and is passed either in small pieces or in a very large mass of small pieces stuck together. Contrary to popular belief, constipation is NOT defined by the infrequency of poop (although this can contribute to the problem). There is no defined length of interval for which a person needs to poop—it can vary considerably. If the poop is soft when it comes out, your baby is unlikely to be constipated.

Craniosynostosis. A baby's skull bones have gaps that allow for the brain's growth in the first one to two years of life. This abnormality is a premature closure of the gaps (sutures) which occurs in about 1 in 1800 children. The reason why this occurs is unknown, but is not due to any birth trauma or complication. Early closure can cause deformities in the skull and facial shape, inhibition of brain growth, and increased pressure within the skull.

Cystic Fibrosis (CF). This is a genetic disease that causes body glands to produce abnormal secretions. Lung, sinus, pancreas, intestine, and reproductive organ problems occur because of it. One in 20 Caucasians are carriers of this genetic abnormality. The disease incidence is 1:1600 for Caucasian babies (it is much less common in other races). Many women now receive genetic testing during pregnancy for CF, although it is not a routine screening test.

Diarrhea. Frequent passage of watery or very soft poop. In a breast fed baby, diarrhea is defined more by the dramatic increase in frequency of poop than by the texture.

Duodenal atresia. Congenital abnormality of the first part of the small intestine to form. It's often associated with other abnormalities. Babies are diagnosed with this disorder before birth by an abnormal ultrasound (extra amniotic fluid found) or shortly after birth when they start vomiting bile. This requires surgical repair.

Eczema. A skin disorder that causes redness and scaling. The underlying problem seems to be allergic in nature, and children with eczema have flare-ups with exposure to perfumed products and certain chemicals. Eczema can be associated with other allergic disorders such as asthma, seasonal allergies, and food allergies but it can also occur without any other problems.

Egocentric. The inability to see things from someone else's point of view. This is a child's view of the world from age two to about seven years.

Emesis. The technical term for vomit.

Enamel hypoplasia. A thinning of the enamel of the teeth found in babies who are born prematurely. And, there appears to be less "catch up" growth of that enamel in babies born prematurely compared to their full term peers. This may result in increased risk of cavities.

Encephalitis. Brain inflammation usually caused by a virus or a bacterial infection.

Engorgement. The Milkman Cometh. Period of excessive breast milk production around three to five days after childbirth. Women's breasts feel full and often uncomfortable until milk demand and milk supply equilibrate.

Epispadias. Congenital abnormality of the formation of a boy's urethra (tube connecting the bladder to the outside). The hole is located on the top side of the penis, instead of in the center. This requires surgical repair.

Epstein's pearls. Tiny cysts (white bumps) found on the roof of the mouth in newborns. These are common, non-problematic, and go away on their own.

Erb's palsy. An injury to the nerves that supply the arm. This occurs as a result of a difficult delivery requiring the baby's head to be pulled forcefully. On examination, the arm will hang limp. The nerve injury usually heals in a year, but may require surgery or physical therapy.

Erythema toxicum. A normal newborn rash that looks like flea bites (white pimple with red around it). These tiny bumps come and go.

Esophagitis. The inflammation of the upper part of the gastrointestinal system (esophagus).

Expressive language delays. A child whose ability to speak words is behind his peers. A child with this delay may have completely normal ability to understand and process language that he hears (see receptive language).

Failure to thrive. When a baby or child falls below the 3rd percentile on the weight curve. When the problem is a chronic one, height and head size also drop on the growth curves. Failure to thrive prompts a thorough medical evaluation.

Fat necrosis. An occasional complication from vaccination injection. As a needle goes through the fat under the skin, it can injure it and create a firm lump. This lump may be present for several weeks after the injection is given. It is painless and not harmful.

Flaring (nostrils). When an infant or young child is having trouble breathing (respiratory distress), he will use any additional methods his body can to get in more air. Nostrils will flare with each breath to try to capture more air. Thus, this is a red flag for respiratory distress.

Flat angiomata. Official term for an "angel kiss" birthmark on the forehead or eyelids. These are flat, reddish colored marks that eventually fade. The color becomes more dramatic with crying or anger.

Fomites. Objects handled by a person with an infection that subsequently allows passage of the germs to someone else.

Fontanelle. A space between the bones of the skull that allows room for the baby's head to pass through the birth canal and room for the baby's brain to grow after birth. The main fontanelle is on top of the head (anterior) and is sometimes called the baby's "soft spot." There is a smaller fontanelle in the back of the head (posterior). The anterior fontanelle closes between nine to 18 months of age.

Food poisoning (see gastroenteritis)

Foreign body/object. Term used to describe an object which has no place being where it is in someone's body. Kids have a way of putting objects like small toys in their noses, ears, etc. as well as swallowing them.

Foremilk. A breastfeeding term used to describe the milk that is released in the first several minutes of nursing. It is less fatty than what comes out later (see **hindmilk**). If your breastfed baby is a snacker, he may not be getting the richer milk. For these babies, its better to nurse on one breast per feeding.

Frenulum. The tissue that connects the tongue to the base of the mouth. (see **ankyloglossia**).

Frenulectomy. The process of clipping the tissue at the tongue base to correct a 'tongue tie' or ankyloglossia. This procedure can be performed in an office setting if the baby is less than a few weeks old.

GLOSSARY

Galactosemia. A rare metabolic disorder that makes a baby unable to digest galactose, a milk sugar. Newborns are routinely tested for this disorder in the state metabolic screen. If present, a baby needs a special formula diet. Breastmilk contains galactose, so it is not possible to breastfeed. Babies who have galactosemia and continue a normal diet can become mentally retarded.

Gastroenteritis. An inflammation of the stomach and intestines caused by either a virus or bacteria. The inflammation can cause both vomiting and diarrhea. Viral gastroenteritis is commonly known as the "stomach flu" and tends to cause watery diarrhea. Bacterial gastroenteritis is commonly known as "food poisoning" and tends to cause diarrhea mixed with blood or mucus.

Gastroesophageal reflux (GER, acid reflux). The backflow of food and liquids from the stomach into the esophagus (and often all the way to the mouth). This is a common problem for newborns up to age one year. The muscle that separates the esophagus and the stomach (lower esophageal sphincter) is relatively loose in infants, allowing food to travel down to the stomach (good) and back up to the esophagus (not good). Once food contents make it to the stomach, they are mixed with stomach acid. So, when this partially digested food goes backwards, the stomach acid can irritate the esophagus, cause discomfort, and sometimes wheezing or coughing (GERD–Gastroesophageal Reflux Disease). Most babies outgrow this problem by age one.

Gingivostomatitis. Inflammation and irritation of the gums and lining of the mouth caused by the Oral Herpes virus. The amount of inflammation is usually extensive and may lead to refusal to eat or drink anything.

Glaucoma. Increased pressure behind the eye. Babies with hemangiomas near the eye need to be evaluated by an ophthalmologist because they are at risk for glaucoma.

Heart murmur. A noise heard in addition to the normal heart sounds audible with a stethoscope. The murmur can be due to normal heart function (termed innocent, benign, or transitional). Or, it can be due to a structural defect of the heart or great blood vessels coming off of the heart (termed pathologic). The type of noise, location of the noise, and other abnormalities found on physical examination help determine the cause of the murmur. All murmurs do not require an echocardiogram and a cardiologist evaluation to determine the cause.

Hemangioma. See Strawberry Hemangioma.

Hemolytic Uremic Syndrome. (Also known as HUS). A group of medical problems caused by some food poisoning (E coli, Shigella) infections. The problems include severe anemia, low platelet count, and kidney failure. HUS typically occurs in children ages four months to four years of age.

Hemophilia. A genetically inherited blood clotting disorder. People with this disorder lack a chemical clotting "factor" that impairs the body's chain reaction to clot blood when bleeding occurs. In general, this is a disease of males and women are only carriers (i.e. not affected) because the gene for the disorder is on the "X" chromosome.

Henoch-Schonlein Purpura. (Also known as HSP) Inflammation of the blood vessels (vasculitis) after a viral illness. Symptoms include a dramatic rash of raised bruised areas on the legs. Joint pain, abdominal pain, and blood in the urine also occur. Although the disease sounds and looks serious, 90% of children recover completely without any treatment. Occurs mostly in children aged four to 10 years.

Hernia. The term used to describe a bulging out of tissue or organ where it is not supposed to be. It occurs due to a weakness of a muscle wall. The most common types include:
Diaphragmatic hernia—abdominal organs protrude into chest
Femoral hernia—intestines protrude into thigh
Inguinal hernia—intestines protrude into groin
Umbilical hernia—intestines protrude into belly button
The risk of all hernias is that the organ that is bulging out will get stuck in that position and cut off the blood supply to it. Umbilical hernias rarely get stuck (incarcerate), thus rarely require any treatment.

Hemorrhagic disease of the newborn. A relatively common (one in 200) problem of newborns who have a Vitamin K deficiency. Infants with this disorder can have severe bleeding. Because of this risk, all newborns receive a shot of Vitamin K shortly after they are born.

Hindmilk. Another breastfeeding term. This refers to the fattier milk that comes out after several minutes of nursing. This milk can actually look yellow (like fat). Don't be alarmed—it's good stuff.

Hip dysplasia. Also known as congenital hip dyplasia, or developmental dysplasia of the hip. This is a congenital abnormality where the leg bone is out of its socket at the hip. It is easily treated with a brace if detected in the first few months of life. Babies who are **breech** have a slightly higher risk of having this disorder.

Hirschprung's disease. A congenital abnormality where the nerves of the rectum (intestinal exit) don't form. As a result, newborns cannot poop (stool) without assistance. Infants with severe constipation may have a partial defect and are also tested for this disorder. Treatment is surgical.

Histamine. A chemical compound the body produces in an allergic response. Histamine causes the characteristic "allergy symptoms" that people experience such as hives, itchy eyes, and congestion.

Human Papilloma Virus (HPV). A virus that is transmitted through sexual contact. HPV can live in the undersurface of the foreskin of an uncircumcised man. HPV is also a known factor in the development of cervical cancer in women.

GLOSSARY

Hydrocele. A fluid collection in a boy's scrotum. Rarely, it is associated with a **hernia**. Most of the time, the fluid is present at birth and goes away on its own by six months of life. It makes the boy's scrotum look unusually large.

Hydrocephalus. An abnormally large collection of cerebrospinal fluid (CSF), the fluid that bathes the brain and spinal cord. This can be caused by excessive production, blockage of the collection pathway, or decreased absorption in the body. Symptoms include: bulging fontanelle (soft spot), headache, vomiting, enlarged head size, loss of developmental milestones, and abnormal neurologic exam.

Hypospadias. A congenital abnormality where the urethra (tube that connects the bladder to the outside) opening is on the underside of the penis instead of in the middle. This requires surgical repair, usually after six months of age. Because the foreskin is used to perform the repair, these babies are not circumcised.

Hypothyroidism. A poorly functioning thyroid gland produces a suboptimal level of thyroid hormone. Thyroid hormone is an essential chemical needed for body metabolism. Babies with congenital hypothyroidism can become mentally retarded (cretins) if they are not treated. This is one of the screening tests performed in the state metabolic screen. The incidence of congenital hypothyroidism is one in 4000 newborns.

Idiopathic Thrombocytopenic Purpura (ITP). The destruction of platelets due to an autoimmune response in the body. Can occur after a viral illness. Because platelets are needed to clot blood, a low count causes bruising and **petechiae**. Some children need medication to help the body increase platelet production in the body, others bounce back on their own. The good news is that almost 90% of kids do beautifully and have no further problems after the one episode.

Imperforate Anus. A congenital abnormality where the anus (opening of the intestines to the outside) does not form completely. This abnormality is often associated with a combination of abnormalities called VATER syndrome. It is repaired surgically.

Inflammatory Bowel Disease (IBD). Chronic swelling of the intestinal lining that results in bloody diarrhea. Crohn's Disease and Ulcerative Colitis are types of IBD. It is rare for a child under age two years to be diagnosed with this disorder.

Inguinal hernia. (see **hernia**)

Inhaled steroid. Medication used to control chronic asthma symptoms. The medication is administered via a machine that aerosolizes it (nebulizer) or via a hand-held "inhaler." The inhaled method is preferable because most of the medication goes to the location it is intended to help (i.e. the lungs). Very little of the medicine gets absorbed into the bloodstream—this means there is less of the unwanted side effects and more therapeutic benefit.

Intestinal obstruction. This is a general term to describe the blockage of the intestine. The gastrointestinal tract is like a big pipe, and in these terms, obstruction is a clogged pipe. This can occur due to intussusception, volvulus, malrotation (congenital defect), and hernias. Because the area is blocked, blood flow to the intestines decreases and may cause death of that tissue. This is a surgical emergency or an "acute abdomen." Symptoms include distended belly, vomiting bile.

Intraventricular hemorrhage (IVH). Bleeding within the brain area called the ventricles due to a weak, fragile matrix of blood vessels and blood pressure changes in premature babies. Premature babies born before 32 weeks gestation or less than three pounds are at risk for IVH, which most often occurs in the first five days of life. Some bleeds may be minor and have no significant long term consequences. Severe bleeds can be potentially fatal or have significant neurologic effects.

Intussusception. When a piece of intestine telescopes upon itself creating an intestinal obstruction. The most common time this occurs is between six and 18 months of age. Symptoms include intermittent abdominal pain with pulling up of the legs. Vomiting, and poop that looks like "currant jelly" also occur. This is an emergency. Diagnosis (and treatment) can be done with a special radiological study.

Jaundice. Yellowing of the skin and the whites of the eyes due to a collection of body garbage called bilirubin. The newborn period is a unique time in life that causes a "normal" jaundice. Outside of the newborn period, jaundice is NOT normal. It requires a thorough medical evaluation to look for the cause.

Kawasaki Disease. An illness that causes the body's blood vessels to swell (vasculitis). The cause is unknown. Occurs mostly in children under two years of age. Symptoms include: fever for five or more days straight, rash on the palms and soles, peeling skin on the fingertips, pink eye, bright red lips/tongue, swollen lymph nodes in the neck, general body rash, and irritable mood. The most severe complication is swelling of the arteries that supply the heart (coronary artery aneurysm). This disease is one of the reasons that doctors want to see a child who has had a fever for five consecutive days or more.

Kernicterus. A serious consequence of jaundice. Bilirubin collects in the brain, causing permanent damage.

Labial adhesion. A condition where the labia minora (smaller lips) of the vaginal opening get stuck together. This happens in little girls because they do not make estrogen hormone yet (pre-puberty). The amount of tissue that is stuck can vary. The problem is that the urethra (opening for the bladder) is located beneath the labia. If the lips are almost completely fused shut, estrogen cream (RX) is applied so that the urine can flow out more easily. Once the labia are unstuck, it is prudent to put Vaseline on the area at diaper changes to prevent them from re-sticking. All girls outgrow this condition once they hit puberty.

GLOSSARY

Laryngomalacia. A floppy airway. Some babies are born with relaxed throat tissue. When they breathe in, they make a high pitched squeaky noise (**stridor**). Babies outgrow this condition, often by age one. These babies get evaluated by an ear, nose, and throat specialist just to confirm the diagnosis. It does not affect their breathing and no treatment is needed.

Leukemia. Abnormal production of body's blood cells which then leads to failure of the bone marrow to produce normal blood cells necessary for body functioning. Symptoms include: fever, fatigue, paleness of the skin, excessive bruising, **petechiae**, and joint pain.

Macrocephaly. Official term to describe a big head. Most of the time, a child's big head is due to his genes (i.e. someone else in the family has a big head). But, if the head size percentile is enlarging or if there are other concerning symptoms, a doctor may evaluate the head with an imaging study to rule out **hydrocephalus** or a **brain tumor**.

Malabsorption. When the intestine is not performing its job of digesting food. The result is a watery, foul smelling diarrhea. Some causes of chronic malabsorption are **celiac disease** and **cystic fibrosis**. This deserves to be checked out.

Malrotation. A congenital abnormality in the development of the intestines. The abnormal position creates a problem with blood flow to the intestines as well as potential for obstruction of food transit. Newborns with this problem have vomiting, constipation, and abdominal pain. Treatment is surgical.

Masturbation. A normal behavior of exploring one's sexual organs. Both boys and girls do it.

Meconium. The first poop a newborn passes. Black, tarry, sticky. Some babies will pass this first poop before birth during a stressful labor. If the meconium is seen prior to birth, a baby will have his nose, mouth, and throat suctioned at delivery to prevent passage of this stuff into the lungs (called **meconium aspiration syndrome**).

Meconium ileus. A failure of the newborn's poop (**meconium**) to pass because of abnormally thick intestinal secretions. This condition is associated with **cystic fibrosis**.

Meconium plug. A delay in passing of the newborn's first poop (**meconium**). This usually responds to rectal stimulation (e.g. taking a rectal temperature).

Meningitis. Inflammation of the tissues that line the brain and the spinal cord. This can be caused by a virus, bacteria, or by tuberculosis. Symptoms include: headache, vomiting, TRUE IRRITABILITY (i.e. inconsolable), bulging fontanelle (soft spot), fever, neck stiffness, seizures, **petechiae**. This is a medical emergency.

Metabolic disorder. A broad term that describes disorders in breaking down foods (see metabolic storage disease below). These disorders are different than endocrine disorders, which involve abnormal levels of body hormones (e.g. thyroid disease, diabetes, adrenal disease).

Metabolic Storage Disease (Inborn Errors of Metabolism). A group of diseases that all cause an inability to break down certain food products. As a result, byproducts of metabolism accumulate. In some of these disorders this accumulation goes to body parts (liver, heart, brain, kidney, eye) causing permanent damage or even death. The more common storage diseases are tested for on the state metabolic screens (**PKU, galactosemia**). Some of the less common disorders can be tested in the optional **supplemental newborn screens**.

Microcephaly. The technical term for a small head. Head size is often hereditary. Families with small heads have small headed babies. However, if a child's head size percentile is plateauing or decreasing, an imaging study may be done to look for **craniosynostosis**.

Milk protein allergy. Milk contains protein, sugar, and fat. Some babies (about 2%) have an allergy to the protein component that causes inflammation and irritation of the intestine lining. This leads to diarrhea that can be mixed with blood or mucus. A significant percentage of babies who are allergic to milk protein are also allergic to soy protein. The good news—most kids outgrow this problem.

Milia. A normal newborn rash on the nose that look like pinpoint white dots. These go away on their own.

Miliaria. A normal newborn rash that looks like prickly heat. This goes away on its own.

Mongolian Spots. A bruise like discoloration found on the buttocks of darker pigmented newborns. These spots fade over several years. No treatment is needed.

Murmur. (see heart murmur)

Nasolacrimal Duct Obstruction (blocked tear duct). Babies have narrow tear ducts that lead out to the corner of the eyes. Occasionally, the tube gets clogged. Tears, which are usually watery, get thick from being backed up. The result—goopy fluid that comes out of the eyes. This can happen intermittently for the first year of life. You can help open up the duct by massaging gently just below the corner of the eye near the nose. I usually refer patients to an eye doctor if this is happening beyond a year of age. The difference between blocked tear ducts and pink eye (infection) is that the eye is not red or irritated.

Nevus Flammeus (Stork bite, angel kiss). These are newborn birthmarks located at the nape of the neck, eyelids, and forehead. They are bright pink in color. The marks on the face fade over the first year of life. The marks on the neck can last forever. These marks are not associated with cancer.

GLOSSARY

Neural tube defects. A congenital abnormality of the brain/spinal cord development. Many of these disorders can be detected prenatally via an abnormal AFP test or an ultrasound. These disorders vary in severity. The most severe form is lack of brain formation (anencephaly). The least severe form is **spina bifida occulta** (see **sacral dimple**), where there is completely normal nerve function.

Neurofibromatosis (NF). A genetic disorder (gene defect) that causes tumors of the tissue covering nerves. Babies are often born without symptoms, although some will have three or more **cafe au lait spots** at birth. As a child grows, he develops numerous (more than five) cafe au lait spots and freckles in the armpit and groin areas. The tumors on the nerves grow later and can be seen as large bumps under the skin. Most of these tumors are benign (not cancerous), but can occur in dangerous places (e.g. eye, ear, brain, kidney). Children with this disorder are seen regularly by a number of doctors. FYI: The diagnosis of NF is not made on the presence of cafe au lait spots alone—this is only one of several symptoms and signs. Most children with a few cafe au lait spots do not have NF.

Newborn acne. (see acne)

Newborn nasal congestion. All newborns have snotty noses. They will sneeze, snort, cough, and snore. This lasts for four to six weeks. If it does not interfere with feedings or sleep, do nothing. If it is causing a problem, use saline nose drops to flush the nose before feedings or bedtime.

Omphalitis. A belly button infection. The umbilical stump and skin surrounding it looks red and swollen. There is a foul odor coming from it. If this occurs in a newborn, it usually requires admission to a hospital for intravenous (IV) antibiotics.

Orbital cellulitis. A serious infection that involves the tissue surrounding the eye. It is caused by a sinus infection that spreads into the area. Symptoms include: limited eye motion, bulging of the eyeball, eyelid swelling, eye pain, and fever. This is the reason that doctors want to see children who have eyelid swelling and a fever.

Orthotic. A custom made shoe insert designed by a podiatrist to provide arch support for people who are flat-footed. The AAP does not currently recommend orthotics for babies and young children.

Otitis media. Literally, middle ear inflammation. Acute otitis media refers to an active infection that came up shortly before it is diagnosed in the office. Serous otitis media (or otitis media with effusion) refers to residual fluid that remains after the active infection is over.

Otitis externa. (Otherwise known as swimmer's ear) Literally, external ear inflammation. This is really an infection of the skin that lines the ear canal. It is caused by water that pools in the ear canal and allows germs to grow. Symptoms include pain with touching the ear itself, swelling and redness of the canal, and sometimes a fever. This is uncommon in the under one age group.

Paraphimosis. The foreskin gets stuck behind the head of the penis in an uncircumcised boy. This causes lots of swelling and pain.

Pathologic Heart Murmur. (see Heart Murmur)

Penile adhesions. The head of the penis sticks to the shaft skin. In boys who are circumcised, it is important to visualize the edge of the head at diaper changes and clean the area of any debris (smegma). If the skin starts to get stuck together, try gently pulling down at the base of the penis to separate the area.

Perforated eardrum. Occurs with severe middle ear infection. A small hole in the eardrum lets the pus drain. It is the equivalent of a pimple popping and draining. Pus and blood will be seen draining out of the ear canal.

Periodic breathing. Newborns do not breathe in a regular pattern. They breathe 30 to 60 times a minute, but very erratically. There may be a stretch of several pants in a row, then a long p-a-u-s-e, then a big breath. That is normal, as long as that pause is less than ten seconds.

Pervasive Developmental Delay (PDD). A disorder of development that falls into the category of Autism Spectrum Disorders. Children with PDD are higher functioning and capable of limited social interactions. They may also have more language skills than those who are severely affected.

Phenylketonuria (PKU). A metabolic disorder routinely tested on the state metabolic screen. It is a genetic defect in an enzyme that breaks down phenylalanine. The incidence is one in 10,000. People with this disorder need to have a special diet. See **metabolic storage disease**.

Phimosis. Inability to pull the foreskin of an uncircumcised boy's penis back. In severe cases, circumcision is necessary to fix the problem.

Phototherapy. The term used for treatment of moderate-severe jaundice (hyperbilirubinemia). A jaundiced baby is placed in a blue light source (either via "bili" blanket or bank of lights). The lights help to breakdown the bilirubin. For babies who are mildly jaundiced, we do NOT recommend placing an undressed baby near a sunny window in the house. It doesn't help and makes the baby uncomfortable.

Pneumonia. Lung inflammation caused primarily by infection. Both viruses and bacteria can cause pneumonia. The tiny air sacs (alveoli) fill up with pus and prevent air exchange. Symptoms include fever, cough, chest pain, and respiratory distress.

Polydactyly. When there are more than five fingers or toes on a hand or a foot. The extra digit can be removed.

Port wine stain. This is a large, red/purple, flat birthmark that occurs on one side of the face or limb. These do not fade over time and are mostly a cosmetic issue. If the birthmark covers the eyelid, a child is evaluated for glaucoma. Any time it occurs on the forehead or eye, a child is also evaluated for a brain abnormality (**Sturge-Weber syndrome**).

Posterior urethral valves. A congenital defect of the formation of the urethra (tube that connects the bladder to the outside). There are valves that normally push the urine (pee) outwards. In this condition, the valves push the urine backwards into the urinary tract. This is rare, and only occurs in boys.

Post-tussive emesis. The Latin words for "after-cough" vomiting. Babies and young children have overactive gag reflexes. So a forceful cough might bring up lunch. All vomiting in children is not due to an upset stomach.

Preauricular pits and tags. Minor congenital defects of the formation of the external ear. The pits are due to remnants of a cyst that occurred prior to birth. Pits are rarely associated with hearing disorders. The tags are extra pieces of skin. If severe, these can be removed for cosmetic reasons.

Pseudostrabismus. The false appearance that a child looks cross-eyed or has a lazy eye due to the child's facial structure. Babies and young children are often referred to a pediatric ophthalmologist for concerns of a lazy eye (**esotropia, amblyopia**) and are ultimately diagnosed with this benign entity. But, it is better to be on the safe side and check out any concerns.

Pustular melanosis. A normal newborn rash found in darker pigmented babies. The original rash looks like little pimples. As the lesions fade, they leave a temporary brown freckle. Some babies have hundreds of these freckles. They go away on their own.

Pyelonephritis. An infection of the kidneys. In an acute infection, a child has fever, back pain, and pain with urination. Infants under six months of age with a bladder infection routinely get admitted to the hospital because there is a greater risk of the infection extending into the kidneys.

Pyloric stenosis. A narrowing of the outlet from the stomach to the small intestine due to a congenital abnormality in the muscle (pylorus). Babies (more commonly males) will have projectile (REALLY IMPRESSIVE) vomiting at every feeding starting between two and four weeks of life. The vomiting may start out in a small way, but progressively gets worse and more projectile. Delay in seeking medical attention results in dehydration. Treatment is surgical, by making a cut in the muscle.

Refractive errors. This fancy term means that one cannot focus an image perfectly in the eye (retina). It includes near-sightedness, far-sightedness, astigmatism, and amblyopia.

Respiratory Distress. This is the term used to describe a child who is air-hungry. If a child cannot successfully get enough oxygen in with each breath, he will breathe faster, heavier, and use chest wall muscles to get as much air in as possible. This equates to a child who is panting, grunting, flaring his nostrils, and retracting (sucking in of the ribcage).

Respiratory Syncytial Virus (RSV). This is a virus that causes different symptoms depending on the age, and health status of the person. Healthy adults may have an RSV infection and feel like they have a cold. A premature baby may have complete respiratory collapse and need hospitalization. A healthy six month old may have a ton of nasal secretions, wheeze, and breathe at twice his normal respiratory rate but not have any distress. RSV shows up every year between November and April in the northern hemisphere.

Retinoblastoma. A malignant tumor of the eye that occurs in babies. Fortunately, this is quite rare. This is one of the important reasons we do an eye exam in the nursery.

Retinopathy of Prematurity (ROP). Incomplete growth of blood vessels in the eyes due to premature birth. Babies born at less than 32 weeks gestation are at the greatest risk of ROP. The growth of the blood vessels need to be monitored regularly by a pediatric ophthalmologist to head off any abnormalities, such as retinal folding/detachment, or permanent vision defects.

Retractions. The term used to describe the sucking in of the ribcage when a child has **respiratory distress**. Retractions occur when the body starts using the chest wall muscles to pull more air in with each breath. With phone encounters, we will ask you to look at how your child is breathing to tell us if he has retractions.

Rickets. Malformation of growing bones in children most commonly due to Vitamin D deficiency. Vitamin D is necessary for calcium to be deposited into the bone (which makes them hard). Bones will form with a bent shape because they are softer than they should be.

Ringworm. (see fungal infections in Chapter 13, "Infections")

Rooting reflex. This is a newborn 'primitive' reflex that causes a baby to turn his head if you stroke his cheek. It is an instinctive mechanism that encourages eating. Babies lose this primitive reflex by three to six months of age.

Sacral dimple. This is a tiny divot, or dimple in the lower portion of the back. These can be associated with a minor abnormality of neural tube development called spina bifida occulta. The L5-S1 vertebrae bone is slightly abnormal but the spinal cord (nerve) is formed normally. Most babies with sacral dimples are unaffected and do not need evaluation or treatment.

Seborrhea. (Also known as dandruff, cradle cap) A skin problem that causes greasy, flaky, and sometimes red skin in areas where 'sebaceous glands' reside—typically the scalp, ears, beside the nose, eyebrows. Many babies are afflicted with this and outgrow it. Teenagers can also get seborrhea and have it for a lifetime. Treatment includes anti-dandruff shampoos, low potency steroid creams/lotions, and vegetable oil to loosen up the flakes in the scalp.

Sensory Integration Disorder. A constellation of behaviors stemming from an inability to process and adapt to stimuli of the five senses. Children with this disorder have trouble with activities of daily living and social encounters (aversion to textured foods, dislike of socks and tags on clothing, avoidance of messy activities, avoidance of being touched...) Diagnosis occurs most frequently in pre-school or school aged children.

Serous otitis media. Fluid in the middle ear space. This fluid can be present several weeks to months after an acute infection (i.e. ACUTE otitis media). This fluid is sterile (free of bugs), but has the potential to get re-infected. Antibiotics are not usually necessary or helpful to clear the fluid.

Shoulder dystocia. This refers to a difficult delivery where the shoulders are forcefully pulled to get the baby out. This happens to a mom with a small pelvis or a big baby. Occasionally, the collar bone (clavicle) breaks during delivery. It heals nicely without any residual problems.

Sickle cell anemia. A hereditary abnormality of the red blood cell structure, causing impaired oxygen carrying capacity and increased destruction of the red blood cells.

Sinusitis. (see Chapter 13, "Infections")

Skin tags. These are tiny pieces of raised skin that can occur anywhere on the body. In the newborn, they are most frequently found in front of the ear (**preauricular tag**) or on the vagina. They are not problematic and require no intervention.

Spina Bifida. A congenital abnormality of the spinal cord development. There is a spectrum of severity of the defect. Most severe defects cause paralysis of the legs and body parts supplied by the affected nerves (bowel, bladder function). The incidence of spina bifida is decreasing as more women are taking pre-natal vitamins (folic acid) during pregnancy. See **neural tube defects.**

Stevens-Johnson Syndrome. A serious allergic reaction that can be fatal.

Strabismus. An abnormal alignment of the eyes.

Strawberry Hemangioma. A birthmark made of a collection of blood vessels. The vessels grow and enlarge for the first few years of life. So, the birthmark gets bigger. The good news—the vessels shrink up and disappear, usually by age five years. Surgery is usually not done to remove these. However, laser therapy may be helpful for lesions on the eyes, nose, or lips.

Stridor. A squeaky, high pitched noise with breathing in that can be heard without a stethoscope. In newborns, it is usually caused by **laryngomalacia**. In any other situation, it is a sign of respiratory distress at the level of the throat. Children with severe **croup** infection have a very swollen airway if they have stridor. If your child has stridor, call your doctor immediately.

Stork Bites see Nevus Flammeus

Sturge Weber syndrome. A serious disorder that includes brain abnormalities in combination with a port wine stain on the face. Brain atrophy, seizures, and paralysis can occur.

Supranumerary nipple (accessory nipple). These are extra, nonfunctional nipples found along the same vertical line as the nipples themselves. They are not problematic. They can be removed for cosmetic reasons.

Supraventricular Tachycardia (SVT). The heart beats at an extraordinarily faster pace (over 200 beats per minute) because a faulty electrical circuitry in the heart. The abnormality may be detected if a baby appears pale, has trouble feeding, or is extremely irritable.

Syndactyly. Two or more fingers or toes are fused either partially or fully together. The severity of the defect determines whether treatment is required.

Thrush. (see Chapter 13, "Infections")

Tongue-tied (see ankyloglossia)

TORCH infections. This is an acronym for the standard tests that are done in Mom's prenatal evaluation. They include: Toxoplasmosis, Syphilis, Rubella, Cytomegalovirus (CMV), Hepatitis B, HIV, and Herpes. In certain situations, Varicella (chickenpox) and Parvovirus are also tested. If Mom has been infected, or is a carrier of the Hepatitis B virus, her baby receives not only the Hepatitis B vaccine at birth, but also a shot of medicine to prevent passage of infection.

Torticollis. Literally means, "twisted neck." When it occurs in newborns, (about 1 in 100 babies), it is called congenital torticollis. It occurs more commonly in babies who are born in breech presentation. It usually becomes noticeable by two to four weeks of age, when the baby's head appears tilted to one side. Occasionally, a knot is felt in the neck where the neck muscle is tensed and tightened. Rarely, these babies have other associated issues like hip dysplasia or strabismus. If left untreated, babies can develop asymmetry of the face and skull. Treatment includes muscle stretching exercises and encouraging the baby turn his head in the opposite direction.

GLOSSARY

Transient Tachypnea of the Newborn (TTN). A common cause of mild respiratory distress in the newborn. Fetuses swallow amniotic fluid while in the womb. When a baby is born vaginally, that fluid gets squeezed out as the baby passes through the birth canal and cries for the first time. Rarely, some of that fluid remains in babies delivered vaginally. More commonly, babies delivered by C-section have this problem. The good news is that the babies all do just fine. They breath faster than normal and may need a little oxygen for the first hour of life.

Transitional heart murmur. The term for a benign, flow murmur heard in the first 24 hours of life. As a baby is born, the fetal heart circulation changes over to the newborn circulation. There are a series of valves that close off the fetal blood pathways and open pathways to the lungs. We often hear the turbulence of blood flow as this is happening. It's nothing to worry about. If a murmur is heard after 24 hours of life, or has a different quality or location that it is heard, your doctor will evaluate it further.

Transmitted upper airway noise. Noise that comes from the nose that is heard and felt in the lungs. When there is a moderate amount of nasal congestion (snot) in the nose, the air going through it makes a loud noise as it passes through. Since babies and young children don't know how to blow their noses, this is often a unique occurrence in this age group.

Tuberculosis. (Known as TB. Previously known as "consumption"). Infectious lung disease that causes nodules in the lungs, but can spread to the lymph nodes and brain. The scary part of the disease is that people can be infected or be "carriers" of the infection without showing symptoms. People 0with active infection classically have fever, cough, weight loss, night sweats, and blood in the mucus they cough up. Although TB is less common than it used to be, it occurs in urban populations and immigrants from Asia, Africa, and Latin America. Recommendations for TB screening (PPD) varies among communities, but is usually required for public school entry.

Umbilical hernia. See **hernia**. These are very common in newborns, particularly African American babies. The size of the hernia can be quite large, but the intestine almost never (I've had one patient) gets stuck (incarcerated). These are caused by weak abdominal muscles which will get stronger as the baby starts using them. Most of these hernias resolve on their own. If the hernia is still present by age two, I'll refer a child to a pediatric surgeon for repair. Old Wives Tale: You do not need to bandage the hernia or place a coin on it to make it go away. Your baby will fix the problem himself when he starts doing Ab crunches.

Undescended testes. Failure of the male sex organs to descend into the scrotum in the newborn male. (In fetal development, they grow in the pelvic area, then travel down to the scrotum.) Often, the testes will come down on their own by six months of life. If they don't, a surgical procedure is performed to affix the testes in the scrotum. Testes in the pelvis are at slightly higher risk for testicular cancer, and make it awfully difficult to perform a monthly self-testicular exam in that location.

Uric acid crystals. A waste product found in the urine. When the urine is concentrated (low water volume), the uric acid will pull itself out of the urine solution and can be found in crystal form in the diaper. It looks like brick dust and tends to alarm parents who think it is blood. It is an indication of mild dehydration—so aggressive feeding is the only treatment.

Urinary tract infections (UTI). An infection in the urinary bladder. It is difficult to diagnose a bladder infection in babies because they do not complain that it burns when they urinate. Sometimes fever and irritability are the only symptoms. It is a good idea to obtain a urine specimen on babies who have a fever with no obvious source of infection.

Vaginal discharge. Newborn girls often have vaginal discharge due to fluctuating hormone levels. Older girls who have vaginal discharge prior to puberty need to be evaluated for infection.

Ventricular Septal Defect (VSD). The most common type of congenital heart defect (abnormal formation of the heart in the fetus). In this defect, a hole is present in either the muscle wall or tissue between the two large chambers (ventricles) of the heart. A murmur is detected due to the blood flow that crosses between the chambers. Most of these holes close on their own with no medical intervention. Children with VSD's are followed by pediatric cardiologists until the hole closes.

Vernix. A cheesy, greasy white coating found on the skin of newborns. The nursery nurses will wash it off nicely at your baby's first bath.

Vesicles. Pinpoint, fluid filled blisters seen classically with chickenpox, shingles, and herpes infections. In chickenpox, these lesions appear in crops over a period of a few days.

Vesicoureteral reflux (VUR). An abnormality in the urinary tract system that causes urine to track backwards towards the bladder and kidneys. This urine is not sterile, thus these children are predisposed to bladder and kidney infections. Any boy and any pre-pubertal girl with a bladder infection for the first time needs to be tested for this disorder. Many children outgrow this disorder, but it can take several years (up to age seven). Children with severe reflux (Grades 3-4) may need surgical repair to prevent scarring and permanent kidney damage. Children with milder forms (Grades 1-2) remain on preventative doses of antibiotics until they outgrow it. There is a hereditary predisposition to this disorder. If a parent has VUR, their children should be tested. Some doctors will test siblings of affected individuals as well.

von Willebrand Disease. A genetically inherited bleeding disorder that affects both the platelets and the blood clotting chain reaction. People with this disorder have frequent, excessive nosebleeds, easy bruising, and heavy periods.

GLOSSARY

Whooping Cough. (See pertussis in Chapter 12, "Vaccines.")

Yeast infection. (See thrush, yeast diaper rash in Chapter 13, "Infections.")

References for this section are footnoted in Appendix F, "Footnotes."

REFERENCES

RECOMMENDED READING, WEB SITES & MORE

Appendix E

Q. How do I know if an Internet site has reliable medical information?

Here are a few thoughts:
1. Find out who has created the website. Is there contact information?
2. What is the purpose of the website?
3. Who are the experts giving the advice?
4. What references are cited? Citations should be listed from scientific journals.
5. Be suspicious of information that is opinionated or seems biased.
6. Be suspicious of products that are touted as cure-alls or miracles.

Source: ImmunizationInfo.org

Good books to have in the house

Alternative Therapies
Kemper, K. *The Holistic Pediatrician*. New York: HarperCollins, 2002.

Breastfeeding
Hale, T. *Medications and Mother's Milk*. 12th Edition. Amarillo: Pharmasoft Publishing, 2006.
Huggins, K. *The Nursing Mother's Companion*. Boston: Harvard Common Press, 1990.

Child Development/Behavior
Brazelton, T. *Touchpoints*. Revised edition. Cambridge MA: DeCapo Press 2006.
Lerner, C. *Bringing Up Baby*. Washington, D.C.: Zero To Three Press, 2005.
Davis, L. *Becoming The Parent You Want to Be*. New York: Broadway Books, 1997.

Medical Information
Woolf, A. *Children's Hospital Guide to Your Child's Health and Development*. Persens 2002.

Multiples
Luke, B. *When You're Expecting Twins, Triplets, or Quads*. New York: Harper Perennial, 1999.

References

Nutrition
Swinney, B. *Baby Bites*. New York: Meadowbrook Press, 2007.

Prematurity
Garcia-Prats, J, etal. *What To Do When Your Baby is Premature*. New York: Three Rivers Press, 2000.
Linden, DW, etal. *Preemies: The Essential Guide for Parents of Premature Babies*. New York: Pocket Books, 2000.

Sleep
Ferber, R. *Solve Your Child's Sleep Problems*. 2nd Ed. New York: Simon and Schuster, 2006.
Mindell, J. *Sleeping Through the Night: How Infants, Toddlers, and Their Parents Can Get a Good Night's Sleep*. Revised Edition. New York: Harper Collins, 2005.
Weissbluth, M. *Healthy Sleep Habits, Happy Child*. New York: Fawcett Books, 2003.

Vaccinations
Humiston, S. *Vaccinating Your Child. Questions and Answers for the Concerned Parent*. Atlanta: Peachtree, 2000.
Offit, P. *Vaccines: What You Should Know*. 3rd Ed. New York: Macmillan, 2003.

Reliable web sites

For starters, go to our website at baby411.com for a wealth of useful information, a visual library of rashes and diseases (see Bonus Material), parent chat room, and links to reliable websites (several of which are listed below). We also suggest you sign up for our free e-newsletter for updates on infant health news.

Adoption

University of Minnesota, Adoption Clinic	peds.umn.edu/IAC/
International Adoption Alliance	i-a-a.org
Association for Research in International Adoption	adoption-research.org
Centers for Disease Control	cdc.gov/ncidod/dq/
U.S. Dept. of State	travel.state.gov/adopt.html

Allergies

American Academy of Allergy, Asthma, and Immunology	aaaai.org
Food Allergy Network	foodallergy.org
Allergy and Asthma Network	aanma.org
Asthma and Allergy Foundation of America	aafa.org
The Allergy Group	immunecom/allergy/index

Alternative Therapies/Herbal remedies

National Center for Complementary and Alt. Medicine	http://nccam.nih.gov/
UCSF Complementary- Alt. Med	library.ucsf.edu/collres/reflinks/cam/

Breastfeeding

iBreastfeeding Bookstore	ibreastfeeding.com
Breastfeeding.com	breastfeeding.com

Cancer

National Cancer Institute	cancer.gov/cancer_information/
Johns Hopkins	hopkinscancercenter.org

Carseats

Children's Hospital of Philadelphia	chop.edu/carseat
National Highway Traffic Safety Administration	nhtsa.gov
American Academy of Pediatrics	aap.org
National Safe Kids Campaign	safekids.org

Childcare

National Association for the Education of Young Children	NAEYC.org
Child Care Aware	childcareaware.org

Child Development

Centers for Disease Control	cdc.gov/actearly
Reach Out and Read	reachoutandread.org
Zero to Three	zerotothree.org
National Institute of Health (cerebral palsy)	ninds.nih.gov
Learning Disabilities Association of America	ldanatl.org
Easter Seals	easterseals.org
Autism Society of America	autism-society.org

Cord blood banking

General info	parentsguidecordblood.com
National Marrow Donor	marrow.org
Lifebank	lifebankusa.com
CBR	cordblood.com
New England Cord Blood Bank	cordbloodbank.com
California Cryobank, Inc.	cryobank.com

Diabetes

American Diabetes Association	diabetes.org
Juvenile Diabetes Research Foundation International	jdrf.org

Emergency Care

Emergency Medical Services for Children	emscmn.org

Gastrointestinal problems (stomach/intestine)

North American Society for Pediatric Gastroenterology and Nutrition	naspgn.org

References

General medical information

American Academy of Pediatrics	aap.org
Food and Drug Administration	fda.gov
Keep Kids Healthy	keepkidshealthy.com
Kids Health	kidshealth.org
Mayo Clinic	mayoclinic.com
National Institutes of Health	ncbi.nlm.nih.gov
Medscape	medscape.com
Parents Magazine	parents.com
Centers for Disease Control	cdc.gov

Heart defects

American Heart Association	americanheart.org
Cincinnati Children's Hospital	cincinnatichildrens.org/heartcenter/encyclopedia/

HIV in children

U.S. Dept. of Health and Human Services	aidsinfo.nih.gov/

Lung Problems

American Lung Association	lungusa.org
Cystic Fibrosis Foundation	cff.org
Stanford University CF Center	cfcenter.stanford.edu
American Academy of Allergy, Asthma, and Immunology	aaaai.org

Nervous System/Seizure disorders

American Academy of Neurology	aan.com
Epilepsy Foundation	epilepsyfoundation.org

Nutrition

Centers for Disease Control	cdc.gov
American Dietetic Association	eatright.org
Mead Johnson	meadjohnson.com
Nestle	nestle.com
Ross	rosspediatrics.com

Parenting

Baby Center	babycenter.com
Baby Corner	thebabycorner.com
Baby Zone	babyzone.com
Parenthood.com	parenthood.com

Sickle Cell Disease

Sickle Cell Disease Association of America, Inc.	sicklecelldisease.org

Skin Disorders

Johns Hopkins Hospital	med.jhu.edu/peds/dermatlas

National Eczema Association — nationaleczema.org

Supplemental Newborn Screening

Baylor	Baylorhealth.com/medicalspecialties/metablicdisease/newbornscreening.htm
March of Dimes	Marchofdimes.com
Mayo	mayoclinic.com
National Newborn Screen	genes-r-us.uthscsa.edu
Pediatrix	pediatrix.com
Save The Babies	savebabies.org
CBR	cordblood.com
National Coalition for PKU	pku-allieddisorders.org

Travel Health

Centers for Disease Control — cdc.gov/travel/index.htm

Vaccinations

Johns Hopkins:	vaccinesafety.edu
World Health Organization	who.int/gpv
Immunofacts	immunofacts.com
Immunization Action Coalition	immunize.org
National Network for immunization info	immunizationinfo.org
Vaccine Adverse Event Reporting System	fda.gov/cber/vaers/vaers.htm
Centers for Disease Control	cdc.gov/nip
Children's Hospital of Philadelphia	vaccine.chop.edu

National Organizations

*There is a support group for virtually every medical disease and syndrome. The organizations below should be able to link you to a specific organization to meet your particular needs.

American Academy of Pediatrics, 141 Northwest Point Blvd., Elk Grove Village, IL 60007. Phone: (847) 434-4000; Web: www.aap.org

Centers for Disease Control and Prevention, 1600 Clifton Road, Atlanta, GA 30333. Phone: (800) 311-3435; Web: www.cdc.gov

Easter Seals, 230 West Monroe St., Suite 1800, Chicago, IL 60606 Phone: (800) 221-6827 x7153; Web: www.easter-seals.org

March of Dimes Birth Defects Foundation, 1275 Mamroneck Ave., White Plains, NY 10605 Phone: (888) 663-4637; Web: www.modimes.org

National Center on Birth Defects and Developmental Disabilities, 4770 Buford Highway, N.E., Atlanta, GA 30341, Phone: (770) 488-7150; Web: www.cdc.gov/ncbddd

ZERO to THREE: National Center for Infants, Toddlers, and Families. 2000 M Street NW, Suite 200, Washington, DC 20036, Phone: (202) 638-0851; Web: www.zerotothree.org

References

Growth Chart: Boys (Birth to 36 months)

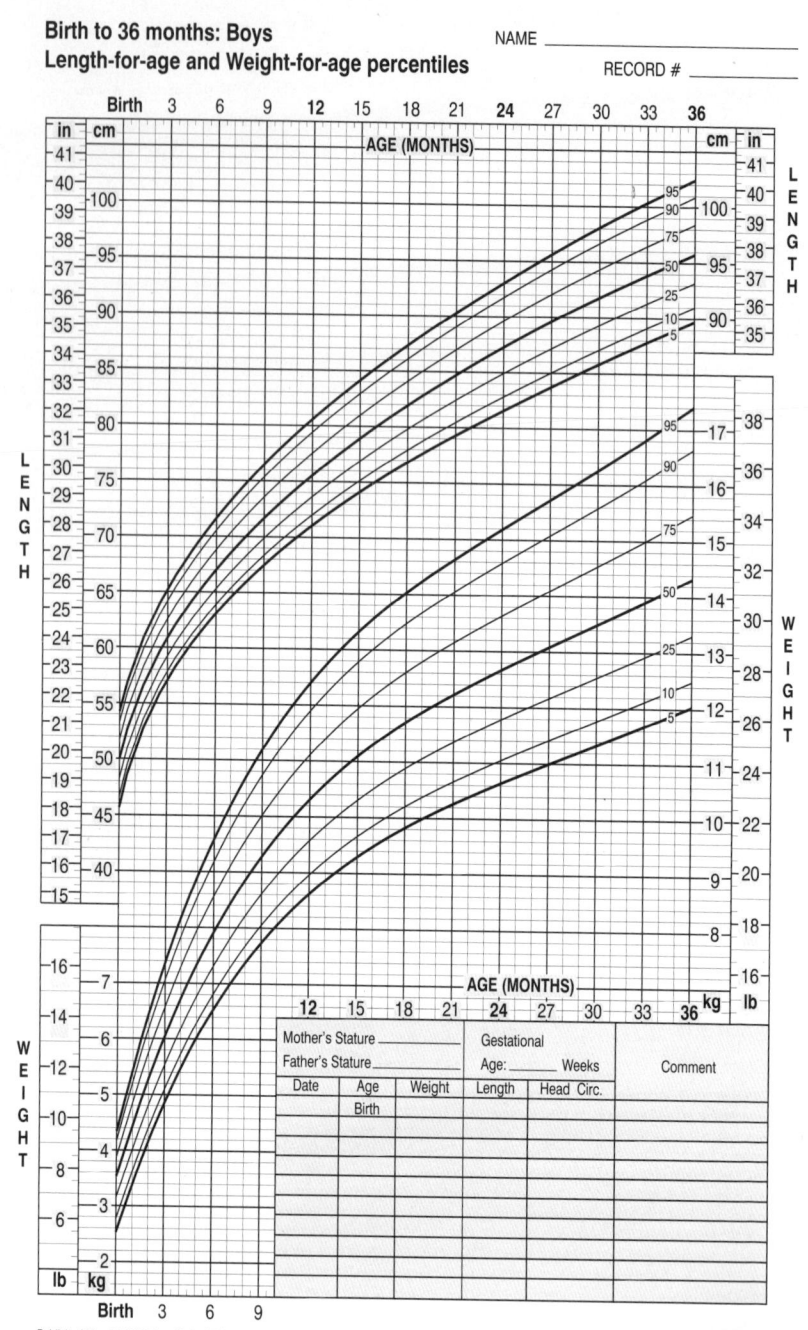

Birth to 36 months: Boys
Length-for-age and Weight-for-age percentiles

NAME _____
RECORD # _____

Growth Chart: Girls (Birth to 36 months)

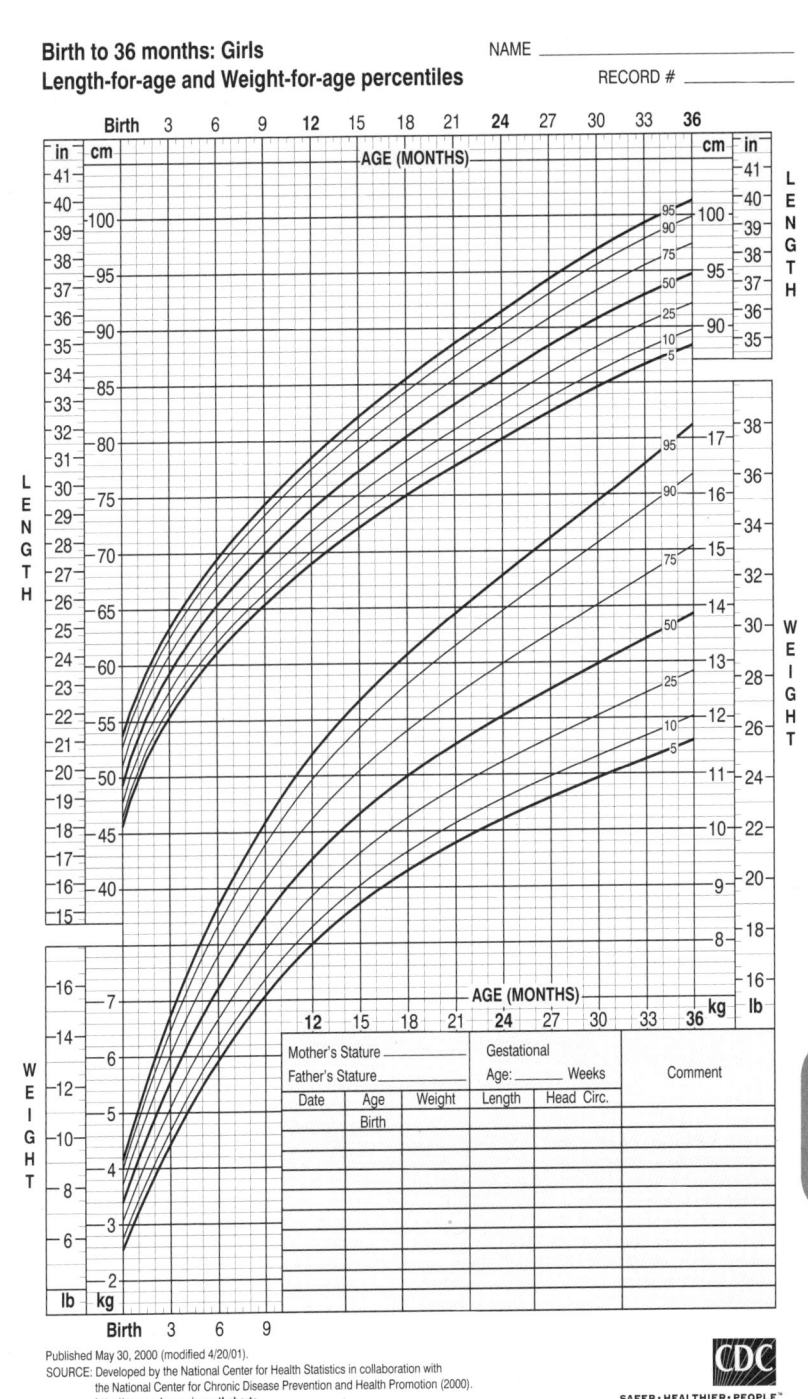

Birth to 36 months: Girls
Length-for-age and Weight-for-age percentiles

NAME _____
RECORD # _____

Published May 30, 2000 (modified 4/20/01).
SOURCE: Developed by the National Center for Health Statistics in collaboration with
the National Center for Chronic Disease Prevention and Health Promotion (2000).
http://www.cdc.gov/growthcharts

SAFER · HEALTHIER · PEOPLE™

REFERENCES

Head Circumference: boys

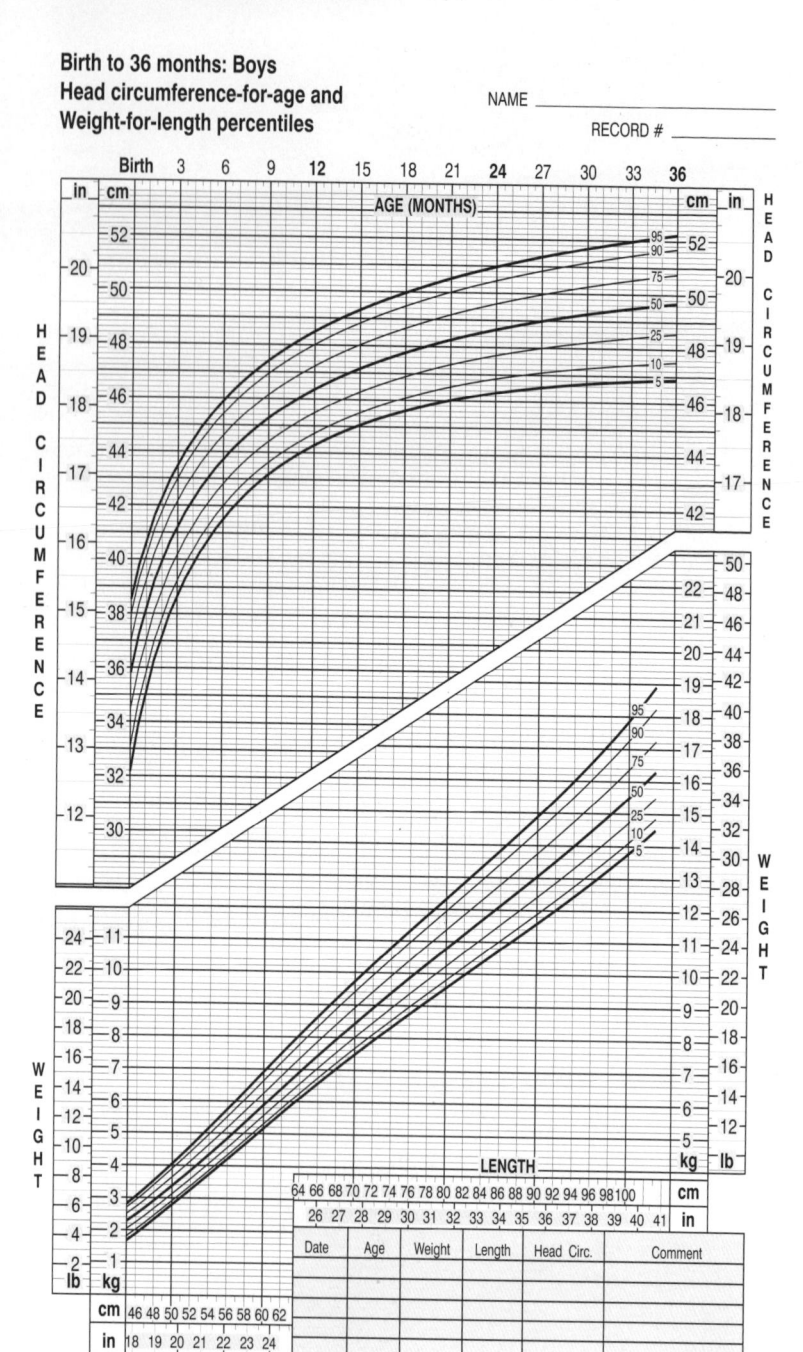

Birth to 36 months: Boys
Head circumference-for-age and
Weight-for-length percentiles

NAME _____

RECORD # _____

Published May 30, 2000 (modified 10/16/00).
SOURCE: Developed by the National Center for Health Statistics in collaboration with
the National Center for Chronic Disease Prevention and Health Promotion (2000).
http://www.cdc.gov/growthcharts

CDC
SAFER · HEALTHIER · PEOPLE™

Head Circumference: girls

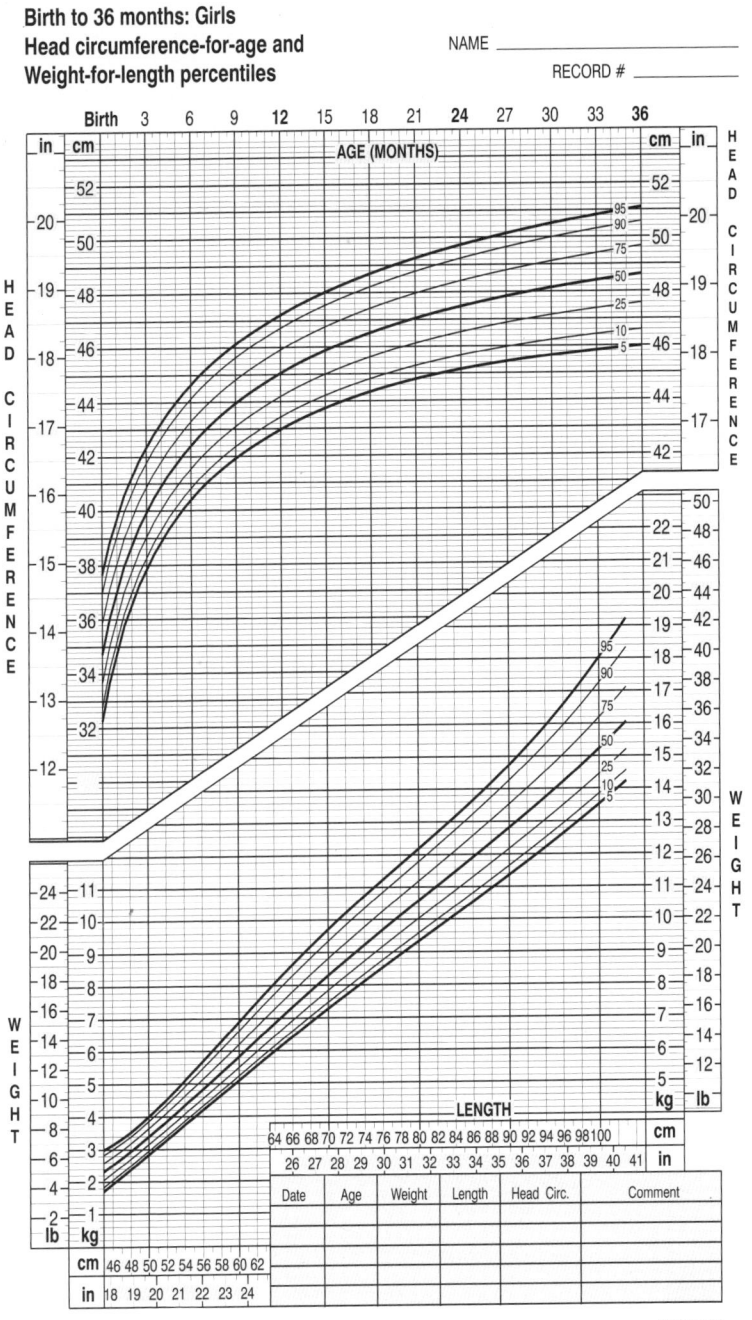

Birth to 36 months: Girls
Head circumference-for-age and
Weight-for-length percentiles

NAME _____
RECORD # _____

Published May 30, 2000 (modified 10/16/00).
SOURCE: Developed by the National Center for Health Statistics in collaboration with
the National Center for Chronic Disease Prevention and Health Promotion (2000).
http://www.cdc.gov/growthcharts

REFERENCES

Preemie growth chart

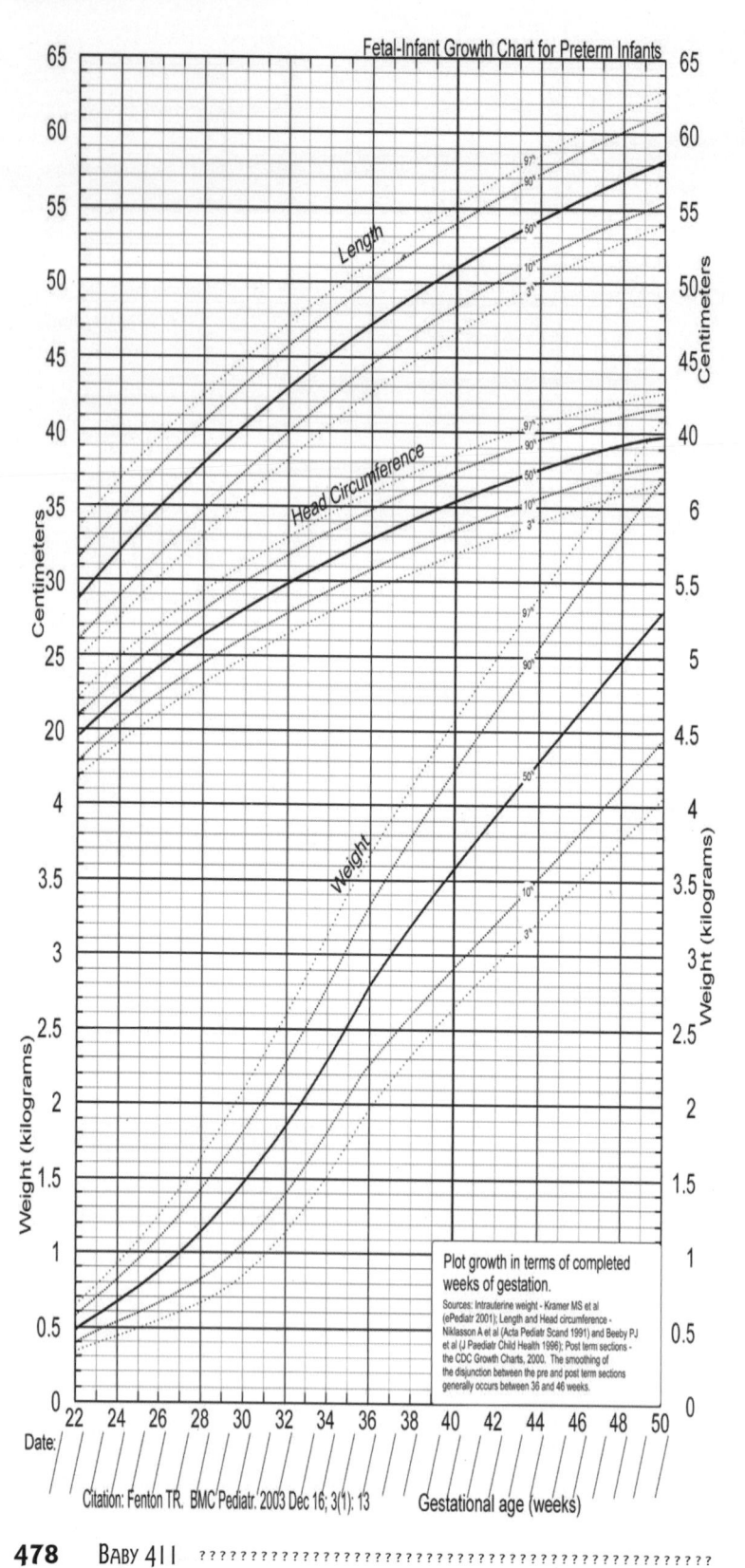

Fetal-Infant Growth Chart for Preterm Infants

Plot growth in terms of completed weeks of gestation.

Sources: Intrauterine weight - Kramer MS et al (ePediatr 2001); Length and Head circumference - Niklasson A et al (Acta Pediatr Scand 1991) and Beeby PJ et al (J Paediatr Child Health 1996); Post term sections - the CDC Growth Charts, 2000. The smoothing of the disjunction between the pre and post term sections generally occurs between 36 and 46 weeks.

Citation: Fenton TR. BMC Pediatr. 2003 Dec 16; 3(1): 13

Gestational age (weeks)

Chapter 1: Decisions

1. *Child Development* 2004;75(4):1254-1267.
2. *New England Journal of Medicine* 2003; 348 (11): 977-985
3. Curr Opin Infect Dis. 2007 Feb;20(1):33-8
4. Castellsague, X., et al: Male circumcision, penile human papillomavirus, and cervical cancer in female patients. *New England Journal of Medicine* 2002 Apr 11; 346 (15): 1105-12.
5. a) Collins S, etal. Effects of circumcision on male sexual function:debunking a myth? J Urol 2002 May; 167 (5): 2111-12. b) Masood S, etal. Penile sensitivity and sexual satisfaction after circumcision: are we informing men correctly? Urol Int. 2005:75 (1): 62-6 3. Kim D, etal. The effect of male circumcision on sexuality. BJU Int. 2006 Nov 28, PMID 17155977
6. American Academy of Pediatrics policy statement. *Pediatrics* 1999 July; 104 (1): 116. Pasquini, et al: The Likelihood of Hematopoietic Stem Cell Transplantation (HCT) in the United States: Implications for Umbilical Cord Blood Storage.
7. See footnote #6.
8. AAP, Section on hematology/oncology and section on allergy/immunology. Cord blood banking for potential future transplantation. Pediatrics 2007;119;165-170.
9. Huston, AC, Aronson, SR: Mothers' Time With Infant and Time in Employment as Predictors of Mother-Child Relationships and Children's Early Development. *Child Development* 2005;76 (2):467-482.
10. See footnote #9.
11. Celedon, et al: Day care attendance, respiratory tract illnesses, wheezing, asthma, and total serum IgE level in early childhood. *Archives of Pediatric and Adolescent Medicine* 2002; 156: 241-245.
12. Kamper-Jorgensen M, etal. Population-based study of the impact of childcare attendance and hospitalizations for acute respiratory infections. Pediatrics 2006;118;1439-1446.
13. Martinez, F: The "coming of age" of the hygiene hypothesis. Respiratory Sciences Center, University of Arizona, Respiratory Research, April 2001.
14. American Academy of Pediatrics Policy Statement: Initial medical evaluation of an adopted child. *Pediatrics* 1991; 88(3): 642-44.

Chapter 3: Labor Day

1. American Academy of Pediatrics Policy Statement: Newborn and Infant Hearing Loss: Detection and Intervention. *Pediatrics* 1999; 103(2): 527-530.

2. American Academy of Pediatrics, American College of Obstetrics and Gynecology, and the Centers for Disease Control as of 2002.
3. Hovert DL, etal. Annual summary of vital statistics: 2004. Pediatrics. 2006 Jan;117(1):168-83
4. Sturgeon PE. Care of the neonatal intensive care graduate. In Rose BD (Ed), UptoDate, Waltham, MA, 2007.
5. Abrams SA. Calcium and phosphorus requirements in newborn infants. In Rose BD (Ed), UptoDate, Waltham, MA, 2007.
6. Shaheed K. Monitoring growth of preterm NICU graduates. In Rose BD (Ed), UptoDate, Waltham, MA, 2007.

Chapter 4: Hygiene

1. AAP. Guidelines for Perinatal Care. 5th Ed. Elk Grove Village, IL: 2002
2. Palazzi DL, etal. Care of the umbilicus and management of umbilical disorders. In Rose BD (Ed), UptoDate, Waltham, MA, 2007.
3. Zupan J, etal. Topical umbilical cord care at birth. Cochrane Database Syst Rev. 2004;(3):CD001057.
4. Fradin, MS: Comparative efficacy of insect repellant against mosquito bites. *New England Journal of Medicine* 2002; 347: 13-18.
5. Wall Street Journal May 20, 2003. PD8.
6. American Academy of Pediatrics Policy Statement: Oral Hygiene. *Pediatrics* 2003; 111(5): 1113-1116.

Chapter 5: Nutrition &Growth

1. Kim J. etal. *Growing up to a new standard*. WHO growth charts make breastfeeding the norm. In *Pediatric Basics, The Journal of Pediatric Nutrition and Development*. 116. 2007, p 16-20.
2. Behrman, RE. Editor: *Nelson Essentials of Pediatrics*. Philadelphia: WB Saunders, 1990.
3. Behrman, RE. See footnote 1.
4. Bernbaum, J.C: *Primary Care of the Preterm Infant*. St. Louis: Mosby,1993.
5. Behrman, RE. See footnote 1.
6. American Academy of Pediatrics Clinical Report. Persing J, etal. prevention and management of positional skull deformities in infants. Pediatrics 112 (1) 2003. pp199-202.
7. a) Nield LS, etal. Odd skull shapes: head's up on diagnosis and therapy. Consultation for Pediatricians. November 2006;701-709. b) Persing J, etal. See footnote #6.
8. American Academy of Pediatrics Committee on Nutrition: *Pediatric Nutrition Handbook*, 4th Ed. Elk Grove Village, IL, 1999.
9. Gartner, LM, et al: American Academy of Pediatrics. Prevention of rickets and Vitamin D deficiency. New guidelines for Vitamin D intake. *Pediatrics* 2003; 111(4): 908-910.
10. Taylor SN, etal. Vitamin D: benefits for bone, and beyond. Contemporary Pediatrics: 23 (11); 70-82.
11. ADA.org, Fluoride and Infant Formula Frequently Asked Questions, indexed 3/22/07

Chapter 6: Liquids

1. Danner, SC, Cerutti ER: *Nursing your neurologically impaired baby*. Waco, TX: Childbirth Graphics.
2. Barnes, GR, Lethin, AN, Jackson EB et al: Management of breastfeeding. *JAMA* 1953; 151:192.

3. Huggins, K: *The Nursing Mother's Companion*. Third Revised Ed. Boston: The Harvard Common Press, 1995.
4. Pediatrics, 111 (3): March 2003; 511-518
5. Lawrence, RA: *Breastfeeding: A Guide for the Medical Profession*, 5th ed. St. Louis: Mosby, 1999.
6. Riordan, J, Auerbach, KG: *Breastfeeding and Human Lactation*. Sudbury: Jones and Bartlett Publishers, 1999.
7. Suitor CW: Nutrition care during pregnancy and lactation: new guidelines from the IOM. *J Am Diet Assoc* 1993; 93: 478.
8. Sampson, HA: Food Allergy, Part 1. Immunopathogenesis and clinical disorders. *J Allergy Clin Immunol* 1999; 103: 717-28.
9. FDA, Press release Jan 12, 2001
10. Lawrence, RA. See footnote 5.
11. Lawrence, RA. See footnote 5.
12. Lawrence, RA. See footnote 5.
13. Lawrence, RA. See footnote 5.
14. Adapted with permission from Physician's Breastfeeding Triage Tool Kit, developed by Diana West, IBCLC, for International Lactation Consultant Association, Copyright August 2006.
15. Schuman, AJ: A concise history of infant formula (twists and turns included). *Contemporary Pediatrics* 2003; 20 (2): 91-103.
16. American Academy of Pediatrics Committee on Nutrition: Soy protein-based formulas: recommendations for use in infant feeding. *Pediatrics* 1998;101:148-153.
17. Chandran, L: Is there a role for long-chain polyunsaturated fatty acids in infant nutrition? *Contemporary Pediatrics* 2003; 20 (2): 107-124.
18. Wall St. Journal, June 24, 2003 p. D4
19. Tran TT, et al: Effect of high dietary manganese intake of neonatal rats on tissue mineral accumulation, striatal dopamine levels, and neurodevelopmental status. *Neurotoxicology* 2002; 23: 635-643.
20. American Academy of Pediatrics Committee on Nutrition: Iron-fortified infant formulas. *Pediatrics*. 1989; 84 (6): 1114-1115.
21. AAP. See footnote 20.
22. Weizman Z, etal. Effect of a probiotic infant formula on infections in child care centers: comparison of two probiotic agents. Pediatrics. 115(1); 2005; pp. 5-9.
23. Georgieff, M. Taking a rational approach to the choice of formula. *Contemporary Pediatrics* 2001; 18(8):112-130.
24. CDC E. sakazakii infections associated with the use of powdered infant formula- Tennessee 2001. MMWR 2002;51;297-300.
25. Gibson R. Toxic Baby Bottles: Scientific study finds leaching in chemicals in clear plastic baby bottles. Environment California Research and Policy Center, 2007
26. Onn Wong K, etal. Dietary exposure assessment of infants to bisphenol A from the use of polycarbonate baby milk bottles. Food Addit Contam. 2005 Mar;22(3):280-8.
27. http://www.stats.org/stories/2007/euro_safety_bpa_feb01_07.htm
28. National Institute of Health, March, 2007.
29. cerhr.niehs.nih.gov/chemicals/bisphenol/MEETING_SUMMARY_BPA.pdf

Chapter 7: Solids

1. Sampson, HA: Food allergy. *J Allergy Clin Immunol* 2003; 111(12): 540-547.
2. Eigenmann, PA, et al: Prevalence of IgE mediated food allergy among children with atopic dermatitis. *Pediatrics* 1998;101(3): E8.

3. Mofidi, S: Nutritional management of pediatric food hypersensitivities. *Pediatrics* 2003; 111(6): 1645-1653.
4. American Academy of Pediatrics, Committee on Nutrition: Hypoallergenic infant formulas. *Pediatrics* 2000; 106(2): 346-349.
5. Sampson, HA. See footnote 1.
6. Wood, RA: The natural history of food allergy. *Pediatrics* 2003; 111(6): 1631-1637.

Chapter 8: The Other End

1. McClung HJ, et al: Constipation and dietary fiber intake in children. *Pediatrics* 1995; 96: 999-1001.
2. Edmunds A. Gastroesophageal reflux disease in the pediatric patient. Therapeutic Spotlight. August 2005;p4-13.
3. Orenstein SR, etal. Reflux symptoms in 100 normal infants: diagnostic validity of the infant gastroesophageal reflux questionnaire. Clinical Pediatrics. 1996. 35(12); 607-614. Reprinted with permission from the American Academy of Pediatrics.
4. Nelson SP, etal. One-year followup of gastroesophageal reflux during infancy. Pediatrics. 1998;102 (6);e67.
5. American Urological Association: Pediatric VUR Clinical Practice Guidelines Panel. Report on the Management of VUR in Children. 1996.
6. See footnote 5.

Chapter 9: Sleep

1. Kleitman, N.: *Sleep and Wakefulness*, 2nd Ed. Chicago: University of Chicago Press,1963.
2. Paterson DS, etal. Multiple serotonergic brainstem abnormalities in sudden infant death syndrome. JAMA. 2006; 296 (17); 2124-2132.
3. American Academy of Pediatrics, SIDS Task Force, press conference, October 10, 2005.
4. American Academy of Pediatrics (aap.org/family/inffurn.htm) Accessed March 28, 2007.
5. Hunt, CE, etal: Infant sleep position and associated health outcomes. *Arch Pediatr Adolesc Med* 2003; 157: 469-474.
6. Data from McKenna, JJ. Mother-Baby Behavioral Sleep Laboratory, University of Notre Dame.
7. Willinger, M, etal: Trends in infant bed sharing in the United States, 1993-2000: the National Infant Sleep Position study. *Arch Ped Adol Med* 2003; 157(1): 43-49.
8. Okami, P, et al: Outcome correlates of parent-child bed sharing: an eighteen-year longitudinal study. *Dev and Behav Pediatrics* 2002; (23) 4: 244-253.
9. Owens, JA. Culture and Sleep in Children. *Pediatrics*, 115 (1), 2005: 201-203.
10. Touchette, E: Annual meeting of the Associated Professional Sleep Societies, 2003.
11. Ferber, R: *Solve Your Child's Sleep Problems*. New York: Simon &Schuster, 1985.
12. Ferber, R. See footnote 11.

Chapter 10: Development

1. Maestro S. Psychopathology. 32(6) :292-300, 1999 Nov-Dec.
2. Fombonne E., Pediatrics 2001;108; e58
3. Archives of Pediatrics and Adolescent Medicine 2005;159 (1):37-44

4. Croen LA, etal. Maternal and paternal age and risk of autism spectrum disorders. Arch Ped Adol Med. 2007 Apr 161(4): 334-40.
5. Jamain S, etal. Mutations of the X-linked genes encoding neuroligins NLGN3 and NLGN4 are associated with autism. Nature Genetics. 2003;34:27-29
6. Institute of Medicine, 2004
7. Brainerd, C: *Piaget's Theory of Intelligence*. Englewood, NJ: Prentice-Hall, 1978.
8. psychology.about.com
9. Dehaene-Lambertz G, etal. Functional organization of perisylvian activation during presentation of sentences in preverbal infants. Proceedings of the National Academy of Sciences, France, 2006. Pnas.org/cgi/doi/10.1073/pnas.0606302103
10. American Academy of Pediatrics, Committee on Public Education. Children, Adolescents, and television. Pediatrics. 2001;107:423-426.
11. Kaiser Family Foundation, 2003
12. Anderson DR, Pempek TA. Television and very young children. American Behavioral Scientist. 2005: 48 (5): 505-522.
13. Vandewater EA, Bickham DS, etal. Time well spent? Relating television use to children's free-time activities. Pediatrics. 2006:117:181-191.
14. American Academy of Pediatrics, Committee on Public Education. Children, Adolescents, and television. Pediatrics. 2001;107:423-426.
15. Goodwyn SW, etal. Impact of symbolic gesturing on early language development. 2000;24;81-103.

Chapter 11: Discipline & Temperament

1. Adapted from Thomas A, Chess S: *Temperament and Development*. New York, Brunner/Mazel 1977.
2. Adapted from Kurcinka MS. Raising your Spirited Child: A Guide for Parents Whose Child is More Intense, Sensitive, Perceptive, Persistent, Energetic. Harper, 1998.
3. High, P: Data compiled at Infant Development Center, Brown University, 2003.
4. Viggiano D. Arch Dis Child 2004;89:1121-1123
5. www.msn.com, April, 17, 2003.

Chapter 12: Vaccinations

1. http://www.library.ucla.edu/libraries/biomed/smallpox/
2. Fenn, EA: Biological warfare in eighteenth century North America: beyond Jeffrey Amherst. *Journal of American History* 2000; (86) 4: 1552-1580.
3. cdc.gov/nip/publications/pink/appendices/G/cases&deaths. pdf. Accessed April 2, 2007.
4. Offit P: Addressing parents' concerns: Do multiple vaccines overwhelm or weaken the infants' immune system? Pediatrics 2002;109:124.
5. Reis EC, et al: Taking the sting out of shots: control of vaccination-associated pain and adverse reactions. *Pediatric Annals* 1998; 27(6): 375-386.
6. Schuval, S: Avoiding allergic reactions to childhood vaccines (and what to do when they occur). *Contemporary Pediatrics* 2003; 20(4): 29-53.
7. Pickering, LK, editor: *Red Book: 2003 Report of the Committee of Infectious Diseases*. 26th ed. Elk Grove Village, IL: American Academy of Pediatrics, 2003.
8. See footnote 7.
9. www.immunizeinfo.org
10. JAMA 10/11/06 issue.

11. National Public Radio news service.
12. Zeiger, RS. Current issues with influenza vaccine in egg allergy. *Journal Allergy Clin Immunol* 2002; 110; 834.
13. Smith PJ. Pediatrics. 2004;114:187-195.
14. cdc.gov/nip/publications/pink/appendices/G/cases&deaths.pdf. Accessed April 2, 2007.
15. cdc.gov/nip/recs/2007 Accessed April 2, 2007.
16. Wakefield, A.J., et al: Ileal-lymphoid-nodular hyperplasia, non-specific colitis, and pervasive developmental disorder in children. *Lancet* 1998; 351: 637-641.
17. Lancet 363:747-50, 820-824; 2004.
18. American Academy of Pediatrics Technical Report: Mercury in the environment: implications for pediatricians. *Pediatrics* 2001; 108 (1): 197-205.
19. EPA. Mercury study report to Congress: Vol 4: An assessment of exposure to mercury in the US; 1997. www.epa.gov/mercury.
20. Reference: Communicable Disease Surveillance Center, London
21. Offit P. Pediatrics: 112 (6):2003; 1394-1401.

Chapter 13: Infections

1. Dowell, SF: Seasonal variations in host susceptibility and cycles of certain infectious diseases. *Emerg Infect Dis* 2001; 7 (3): 369-74.
2. Mangione-Smith, RM, et al: The relationship between perceived parental expectations and pediatrician antimicrobial prescribing behavior. *Pediatrics* 1999;103: 711-718.
3. Donowitz, L: Infection control in the office: keeping germs at bay. *Contemporary Pediatrics* 2000; 17(9): 47.
4. Pickering, LK, editor. *Red Book: 2003 Report of the Committee of Infectious Diseases,* 26th ed. Elk Grove Village, IL: American Academy of Pediatrics, 2003.
5. Ped Inf Dz J. 2002:21:629.
6. Pickering, LK. See footnote 1.
7. Pickering, LK. See footnote 1.
8. Pickering, LK. See footnote 1.
9. Pickering, LK. See footnote 1.
10. Pickering, LK. See footnote 1.
11. Centers for Disease Control 2007.
12. Pickering, LK. See footnote 1.
13. Pickering, LK. See footnote 1.
14. Pickering, LK. See footnote 1.
15. Pickering, LK. See footnote 1.
16. Data from Centers for Disease Control. www.cdc.gov.
17. Rosenfeld, RM, etal: Clinical efficacy of antimicrobial drugs for acute otitis media: metaanalysis of 5400 children from thirty-three randomized trials. *Journal of Pediatrics* 1994; 124: 355-67.
18. Baker, RB: Is ear pulling associated with ear infection? *Pediatrics* 1992; 90: 1006-7.
18. Peter, G: Bacterial resistance in office practice: the need for judicious antimicrobial therapy. Lecture at 25th Annual Pediatric Postgraduate Symposium, Houston, 2003.
19. Post JC, et al: Is pacifier use a risk factor for otitis media? *Lancet* 2001; 357: 823-4.

Chapter 14: Diseases

1. Expert Panel Report II: *Guidelines of the Diagnosis and Management of Asthma.* 1997.

2. Behrman, RE. Editor: *Nelson Essentials of Pediatrics*. Philadelphia: WB Saunders, 1990.
3. Behrman. RE. See footnote 2.
4. Behrman. RE. See footnote 2.
5. Behrman. RE. See footnote 2.
6. Behrman. RE. See footnote 2.
7. Behrman. RE. See footnote 2.
8. Ownby, D. et al: Exposure to dogs and cats in the first year of life and risk of allergic sensitization at six or seven years of age. *JAMA* 2002; 288(8): 963-972.
9. Fleisher, G., Ludwig, S, editors: *Pediatric Emergency Medicine*, 3rd Ed. Baltimore: Williams and Wilkins, 1993.
10. Stellwagen L, etal. Look for the "stuck baby" to identify congenital torticollis. Contemporary Pediatrics May 2004;21:55.

Chapter 15: First Aid

1. Gunn, VL, Nechyba, C, editors: *The Harriet Lane Handbook: A Manual for Pediatric House Officers*, 16th ed. Philadelphia: Mosby, 2002.
2. American Academy of Pediatrics: The management of acute gastroenteritis in young children. *Pediatrics* 1996; 97 (3): 424-35.
3. Chowdhury HR, et al: The efficacy of bismuth salicylate in the treatment of acute diarrhea and the prevention of persistent diarrhea. *Acta Pediatrica* 2001: 90 (6): 605-610.
4. Crocetti, M: Fever phobia revisited: have parental misconceptions about fever changed in 20 years? *Pediatrics* 2001;107 (6): 1241-6.
5. Fleisher, G., Ludwig, S, editors: *Pediatric Emergency Medicine*, 3rd Ed. Baltimore: Williams and Wilkins, 1993.

Appendix A: Medications

1. Murphy JL, editor: *Prescribing Reference for Pediatricians: Spring-Summer 2007*. New York: Prescribing Reference, Inc., 2007.
2. American Academy of Pediatrics Committee on Nutrition: *Pediatric Nutrition Handbook*, 4th ed. Elk Grove Village, IL: American Academy of Pediatrics, 1998.
3. AAP Committee on Nutrition. See footnote 2.
4. AAP Committee on Nutrition. See footnote 2.
5. (1) Hale, T: Medications and Mother's Milk. *A Manual of Lactational Pharmacology*, 12th ed. Amarillo: Pharmasoft Publishing, 2006. (2) AAP Committee on Nutrition. See footnote 2.
6. Thomas Hale, see footnote 5.
7. Shared PJ, Berfman DA: The effect of inhaled steroids on the linear growth of children with asthma: A meta-analysis. *Pediatrics* 2000;106 (1): E8.

Appendix B: Alternative Medicines

1. Politics and lobbying in the US nutritional and dietary supplements industry. National Public Radio, All Things Considered, June 23, 2003.
2. Kemper, KJ: *The Holistic Pediatrician. A pediatrician's comprehensive guide to safe and effective therapies for the 25 most common ailments of infants, children, and adolescents*, 2nd ed. New York: HarperCollins, 2002.
3. Gilroy CM, Steiner, JF, Byers T, Shapiro H, Georgian W: Echinacea and truth in labeling. *Archives of Internal Medicine* 2003;163: 699-704.
4. a) Rodriguez-Bigas, M: A comparative evaluation of aloe vera in the

management of burn wounds in guinea pigs. *Plastic Reconst Surg* 1988; 81: 386-9. b) National Library of Medicine, Medline Plus. nlm.nih.gov/medlineplus accessed April 17, 2007.
5. a) Kemper KJ, ee footnote 1. b) National Library of Medicine, see footnote 4.
6. a) Weizman Z. et al: Efficacy of herbal tea preparation in infantile colic. *Journal of Pediatrics* 1993; 122: 650-2. b) National Library of Medicine, see footnote 4.
7. a) Barrett, BP, et al: Treatment of the common cold with unrefined Echinacea. A randomized, double blind, placebo-controlled trial. *Annals of Int Medicine* 2002;137(12): 939-46. b) Kemper KJ, see footnote 1. c) National Library of Medicine, see footnote 4.
8. a) Horrobin, DF: Essential fatty acid metabolism and its modification in atopic eczema. *American Journal Clin Nutrition* 2000; 71 (supp): 367s-372. b) Hederos, C. Berg, A: Epogram evening primrose oil treatment in atopic dermatitis and asthma. *Archives of Dz in Childhood* 1996; 75: 494-7. c) National Library of Medicine, see footnote 4.
9. Weizman, Z. See footnote 6.
10. a) Schmid, R. et al: Comparison of seven commonly used agents for prophylaxis of seasickness. *Jnl Travel Med* 1994; 1; 203-6. b) Motion sickness, ginger, and psychophysics. *Lancet* 1982; 91: 655-7.
11. a) Das SK, et al: Deglycyrrhizinated liquorice in aphthous ulcers. *J Assoc Physicians India* 1989; 37(10): 647. b) Teelucksingh S: Potentiation of hydrocortisone activity in skin by glycyrrhetinic acid. *Lancet* 1990; 335 (8697): 1060-3. c) Gardiner P. Longwood Herbal Task Force website:www.mcp.edu/herbal/
12. a) Fox N: Effect of camphor, eucalyptol, and menthol on the vascular state of the mucous membrane. *Arch Oto HNS* ; 1027 (6):112-122. b) Eeles R: The effect of menthol on nasal resistance to airflow. *J Laryng Otol* 1983; 97: 705-9. c) Gardiner, P. Longwood Herbal Task Force website: www.mcp.edu/herbal/. d) National Library of Medicine, see footnote 4.
13. National Library of Medicine, Medline Plus. Nlm.nih.gov/medlineplus.druginfo/natural/patient-teatreeoil.html. Accessed April 14, 2007.
14. National Library of Medicine, see footnote 4.

Appendix C: Lab Tests

1. Gunn, VL, Nechyba, C, editors: *The Harriet Lane Handbook: A Manual for Pediatric House Officers*,16th ed. Philadelphia: Mosby, 2002.
2. Loeb, S., editor: *Clinical Laboratory Tests: Values and Implications*. Springhouse, Pennsylvania: Spring House, 1991.

Appendix D: Glossary

1. Behrman RE, Kliegman R. *Nelson Essentials of Pediatrics*. W.B. Saunders, 1990, Philadelphia.
2. Urdang Associates. *The Bantam Medical Dictionary*. Bantam, 1981, New York.
3. Cloherty JP, Stark AR. *Manual of Neonatal Care*, 3rd ed. Little Brown, 1992, Boston.
4. Shelov, SP. *Your Baby's First Year*. Bantam, 1998, New York

INDEX

AABB. See American Association of Blood Banks
AAFP. See American Academy of Family Physicians
AAP. See American Academy of Pediatrics
Abacavir, 295
Abdomen
    acute, 174, 349, 350, 445
    checking, 46
    CT/MRI for, 438
    distended, 350, 436
    x-rays for, 437
    ultrasound for, 437
Abdominal pain, 349-50
    home remedy for, 432
ABO incompatibility, 50, 445
Abstract reasoning, 226
Accidental injuries, 390-95
Acetaminophen, 80, 127, 346, 347, 410
    antibiotics and, 401
    breastfeeding and, 114
    dosing for, 378, 379
    fever and, 373, 374, 375, 377
    giving, 379
    suppositories, 378
    teething and, 407
    vaccinations and, 269, 272
Acholic stools, 167, 445
Acid reflux, xxi, 92, 168, 360, 361
    crying and, 213
    delaying, 173
    outgrowing, 173
    red flags with, 169
    sleep and, 198, 213
    testing for, 171
    thickened formula and, 141
    treating, 170
    wheezing and, 173
Acidophilus, 82, 123, 366, 412, 431
ACIP. See Advisory Committee on Immunization Practices
Acne, 73, 445
    neonatal, 49, 460
Acrocyanosis, 46, 445-46
Acupuncture, 427
Acute life threatening event (ALTE), 360, 445
Acylovir, 295
ADA. See American Dental Association
Adair, Steven: on baby's mouth, 80
ADD. See Attention Deficit Disorder

Adenovirus, 325
Adoption
    breast milk stimulation and, 32, 124
    immunization status and, 33
    screening tests and, 33
    web site on, 470
Adrenal gland insufficiency, 49
Advil, 347, 377
    dosing, 378
Advisory Committee on Immunization Practices (ACIP), 270, 273
Agency for Toxic Substances and Disease Registry, 286
Agenesis of the corpus callosum, 224
AIDS, 300
Air hungry, 328, 359, 360, 419
    described, 358, 446
Albuterol, 329, 400, 418
Alcohol, 428
    breastfeeding and, 121
Alimentum Advance, 134
All Free and Clear, 74, 335
Allergies, 350-52, 361
    asthma and, 156
    breast milk, 104
    breastfeeding and, 156, 157
    cats/dogs and, 340
    cocoa, 154
    drug, 274, 283, 346, 351, 352, 382, 383
    eczema and, 121, 157
    egg, 153 156, 157, 158, 270, 283
    fish, 153, 156, 157, 158
    food, 5, 8, 75, 90, 119, 134, 148, 151, 153, 155-56, 157, 270, 273, 336, 340, 341, 351, 352, 355, 364, 382, 383, 386
    fruit, 154
    genetic predisposition for, 329, 340
    IgE-mediated, 135
    medications for, 405-6
    metal snap, 79, 386
    milk, 100, 119, 133, 134, 151, 153, 154, 156, 157, 171, 354, 459
    nut, 153, 154, 156, 157, 158
    outgrowing, 157
    peanut, 101, 121, 153, 154, 155-56, 157, 158
    perennial, 340, 341
    poops and, 167
    ragweed, 340
    rashes and, 382, 386

red eyes and, 370
runny nose and, 340, 341
seasonal, 330, 336, 340, 370
shellfish, 153, 156, 157, 158
soy, 154, 156, 157
vaccine, 270, 272, 273
web site on, 470
wheat, 153, 157
See also Intolerance
Allergy Asthma Technology Ltd., 341
Aloe vera, 428
ALTE. *See* Acute life threatening event
Alternative medicine, 11, 297, 429
    books on, 469
    effectiveness of, 427
    production standards for, 428
    safety with, 427-28
    studies on, 431
    traditional medicine and, 12
    web site on, 470
Amantadine, 295
Ambecides, 416
Ambiguous genitalia, 47, 446
Amblyopia, 56, 229, 327-28, 446
Ameda Purely Yours, 117
American Academy of Family Physicians (AAFP), 270, 273
American Academy of Pediatrics (AAP), 5, 37
    adoption and, 33
    allergies and, 154, 157
    anti-diarrhea medications and, 367
    autism and, 224
    Babywise method and, 208
    brain damage and, 54
    breastfeeding and, 104-5, 107, 109, 127, 192
    car seats and, 55
    circumcision and, 15
    contact information for, 473
    cord blood and, 22
    dental visits and, 81
    DHA supplements and, 121
    ear infections and, 319
    family beds and, 105, 193
    feedings and, 91
    flat feet and, 337
    fluoride and, 406
    formula and, 135, 137-38
    Hepatitis A and, 279
    juice and, 144
    milk and, 145
    Prevnar and, 281
    rooming-in and, 53
    screens and, 36, 45
    SIDS and, 191
    sleep and, 192, 194
    solid foods and, 90, 147
    soy formula and, 137
    sunscreen and, 74
    Synagis and, 420
    television and, 238
    thermometers and, 378
    vaccinations and, 270, 273, 284, 289
    varicella vaccine and, 281
    vitamin D supplements and, 93
    walkers and, 231
    well-child appointments and, 35
American Academy of Pediatrics (AAP) Committee on Nutrition, 139, 149
American Association of Blood Banks (AABB), 20, 21
American Association of Poison Control Centers, 238
American College of Obstetrics and Gynecology, 5, 15, 121
American Dental Association (ADA), 81
    fluoride and, 95, 139, 406
American Urological Association, 15
Amniotic fluid, 51, 73
Amoxicillin, 302, 320, 321
Amphetamines, 403
Amylase, blood test for, 439
Anal fissures, 355, 446
Anaphylactic reaction, 153, 155, 351, 352, 446
Anemia, 94, 446
    breath-holding and, 332
    chronic, 333
    iron-deficiency, 93, 333-34, 259, 417
    testing, 33
Anesthetic cream, 269-70
Angel kiss, 459
Anger, physical release of, 254
Ankyloglossia, 45, 114, 446
Anomaly, defined, 446
Antacids, 170, 411-12
Antibiotic creams, 131, 423, 442
Antibiotic ointment, 49, 357, 388
Antibiotics, 50, 70, 123, 131, 297, 299, 428
    abuse of, 302
    bacteria and, 302
    broader spectrum, 302
    function of, 267-68
    generic, 399
    leftover, 400-401
    limiting use of, 319
    Motrin and, 401
    organic foods and, 152
    preventative, 323
    resistance to, 269, 301, 303
    secondary infections and, 304
    Strep infections and, 303

too many courses of, 322
Tylenol and, 401
using, 82, 123, 301, 320, 321, 324, 346, 414-15
viruses and, 302
Antibodies, 104, 107, 116, 123, 293
Antifungal creams, 124, 131, 422, 423
Antifungals, 71, 124, 415-16, 423
Antihelminthics, 416
Antihistamines, 296, 352, 405, 421-22
  ear infections and, 323-24
  eczema and, 335
Anti-inflammatories, 336, 423, 425
Antimicrobials, 292, 293, 302
Antiseptics, 70
Antivirals, 295, 416
Anxiety
  nine to twelve months, 234-35
  separation, 233, 244, 253, 257
  stranger, 257
AOP. See Apnea of Prematurity
Apgar tests, 51, 52
Apnea, 45, 191, 360, 363, 446-47
Apnea of Prematurity (AOP), 57
Appendicitis, 349, 447
Appointments
  consultation, 7-8, 11, 38
  during cold and flu season, 39
  initial, 38
  problem-focused, 217
  running late for, 39
  scheduling, 10-11, 39-40, 109
  sick-child, 8, 9, 10, 11-12, 37, 39
  well-child, 8, 10, 35-37, 38, 39, 215, 217, 274
Arachonic Acid (ARA), 5, 104, 133, 136
Arachis oil, 73
Arching back, spells of, 172
Arsenic, 428
Artificial sweeteners, 158
ASD. See Autism spectrum disorder
Asperger's Syndrome, 220, 447
Aspirin, 377, 410
Association of Women's Health Obstetric and Neonatal Nurses, 72
Asthma, 283, 340, 360, 363
  bronchiolitis and, 329
  concerns about, 419
  coughing and, 363
  described, 328-29, 447
  diagnosing, 173, 328, 329
  eczema and, 330, 336
  flare-ups of, 330, 418
  food allergies and, 156
  genetic predisposition for, 329
  long-term consequences of, 330
  medications for, 418, 419
  outgrowing, 330
  respiratory infections and, 328
  treating, 329, 418
  vaccines and, 284
Atopy, 330, 336, 447
Atresia
  anal, 46, 447
  biliary, 447
  choanal, 447, 449
  duodenal, 46, 447, 451-52
  esophageal, 447
  ileal, 447
  tricuspid, 447
Attachment parenting, 5
  family beds and, 207, 208
Attention Deficit Disorder (ADD), 246, 286
  manganese and, 137
  soy formula and, 137
  television and, 238
AuPairAmerica.com, 32
Au pairs, 27, 28-29, 32
Auditory processing disorder, 216
Autism Genome Project, 223
Autism Society of America, 224
Autism spectrum disorder (ASD), xxi, 220-24, 286, 447
  concerns for, 287
  developmental delays and, 221, 222, 223, 224
  diagnosing, 222, 223
  and mercury poisoning compared, 288
  MMR vaccine and, 221, 222, 284, 287
  television and, 238
  therapy for, 223-24
  thimerosal and, 287, 288
Autonomy, doubt versus, 227
Autosomal dominant, 332, 447
Autosomal recessive, 332, 447
Aveeno, 75, 335
Avent
  bottles from, 141, 142
  BPA and, 142
  nipples from, 140-41
Axid, 170
AZT, 295

Babblesoft, Baby Manager by, 65
Baby Anbesol, 407
Baby Bargains (Fields and Fields), xvii
  bottles and, 142
  breast pumps and, 117
  breastfeeding pillows and, 112
  bumpers and, 189
  car seats and, 55

humidifiers/vaporizers and, 298
laundry tips and, 74
nannies and, 28
nipples and, 141
pediatricians and, 10
safety and, 59, 237
Baby Bjorn, 228
Baby blues, 63, 64
Baby Book, The (Sears), 206-7
Baby carriers, head control and, 228-29
Baby food, 83
 store-bought, 142, 160
 cereal-based, xxi
Baby Manager, 65
Baby monitors, 195, 210, 362
Baby Numz-it, 407
Baby Orajel, 407
Baby's Bliss Gripe Water, 431
Babysitting, 3, 32
Babywise method, 208, 209
Back injuries, 392
"Back to Sleep" Campaign, 187, 192, 231
Bacteria, 49, 139, 291, 299-304, 324
 antibiotics and, 302, 321
 detecting, 295
 drug-resistant, 301, 302, 322, 323, 346, 399
 good, 299, 364
 gut, 299
 intestinal, 299
 mouth, 79, 299
 nostril, 299
 rashes and, 382
 skin, 299
 vaginal, 299
Bacterial enteritis, 174
Bacterial infections, 266, 298, 325, 355, 370, 435, 436
 contagiousness of, 300-301
 described, 309-13
 medications for, 414-15
 primary, 299
 secondary, 299, 300, 303, 304, 322
BAERS, 36, 44, 448
Balanitis, 16
Balmex, 71
Barium swallow, 171, 438
Barnes, Sarah: story of, 224
Barracuda, 112
Barrier creams, 426
Basic Metabolic Panel, 439
Bassinets, 185, 194, 212
Baths, 72
 eczema and, 75
 fever and, 377
 seizures and, 380
 steps for, 73

Baylor University Medical Center, screening and, 19
Bedding, SIDS and, 188, 189, 192
Bedtime, 195, 202
 routine for, 196-97, 210
Bedwetting, 204
Behavior, 38
 aggressive, 244
 attention-seeking, 255
 autistic, 221, 224
 books on, 469
 categorizing, 255
 changing, 209
 focusing on, 255
 ignoring, 256
 inappropriate, 253, 256
 limiting, 258
 noticing good, 255
 redirecting, 256
 repetitive, 221
 self-control of, 252-53
 television and, 239
Bell, Edward: on taking medications, 400
Belladonna, 80, 407
Belly buttons, 436
 care for, 46, 69, 70-72
 infection of, 70, 71
Benadryl. *See* Diphenhydramine
Benzocaine, 407
Beta agonists, 418
Beta Strep test, 50
Bifidobacterium, 431
Bifidus lactis, 138
Big beds, sleeping in, 212
Bile, vomiting, 173, 368, 436
Bilirubin, 63, 109, 152, 280
 blood test for, 439
 break down of, 54
 getting rid of, 55
Birth control, 104, 193
Birth plan, 4, 33-34, 51
Birth weight, 84, 107, 130
 loss of, 109, 111
 regaining, 143
 soy formula and, 135
Birthmarks, 48
Bisphenol A (BPA), 141, 142
Bite position, 249
Bites
 animal, 388
 bug, 352
Bladder infections, 47, 78, 123, 299, 325, 349, 436, 448
 boys/girls and, 176
 circumcision and, 16
 described, 311
 diagnosing, 176

medications for, 414
preventing, 175-76
vomiting and, 368
Bladders, 47, 78, 350
Bleeding, 392, 393, 394
controlling, 388, 389, 390
excessive, 353, 436
head, 391
persistent, 354
problems with/solutions to, 352-55
upper GI, 354
Blessed thistle, 125
Blisters, 357, 387, 394
Blood
in diapers, 53, 175
in diarrhea, 119, 355, 364, 413
loss of, 389
in pee, 175
in poop, 119, 167, 354, 355, 436, 448
problems with, 332-34
vomiting, 173-74, 353-54, 369
Blood count, 300
Blood culture, 439
Blood pressure, 347
Blood sugar, 51, 339, 439
Blood tests, 18, 435, 439-40
Blood type, 50, 436, 439-40
Body Mass Index (BMI), 84, 96-99, 339
Body odor, 342, 381
Bonding, 56, 126
Bone injuries, 45, 393, 395, 435, 449
Bone marrow
production of, 332
temporary suppression of, 353
transplants, 20
Bone scan, CT/MRI for, 439
Bones
broken, 390, 393, 394
problems with, 337-38
Books
on alternative medicine, 469
on behavior, 469
on breastfeeding, 469
children's, 241-42
on development, 241
on multiples, 469
on nutrition, 470
on preemies, 470
on sleep, 202, 470
on vaccinations, 289, 470
Booster seats, 55
Born Free, bottles from, 142
Bottles, 140-42
introducing, 118
recommended, 140-41
refusing, 118
safety with, 141, 142

toxic, xxi
Botulism, 158, 164
Boudreaux's Butt Paste, 71
Boulder Weekly, on vaccines, 276
Bouncer seats, colic and, 251
Bowel obstruction, 285
Bowleggedness, 229, 337
Boy parts, caring for, 77
BPA. *See* Bisphenol A
BPD. *See* Bronchopulmonary dysplasia
Bra pads, 124
Brain abnormalities
autism and, 224
SIDS and, 188
vaccinations and, 270
Brain damage, 54
fever and, 380
temperature and, 372
Brain development, 85, 230
autism and, 222
breastfeeding and, 104
cow's milk and, 145
environmental exposure for, 223
stages of, 225
Brainwaves, 387
Branchial cleft cyst, 45, 448
BRAT diet, 367
Brazelton, T. Berry, xvii, 6, 241
Breast implants, breastfeeding and, 115
Breast milk, 61, 83, 90, 102, 103, 104-5,
144, 151, 154, 156
antibodies in, 104, 107, 116, 123
arrival of, 107, 109, 110, 125
bottle feeding, 107, 128
buying, 125
calories in, 89, 160
casein ratio of, 135
color of, 117
environmental toxins and, 104
expressed, 58, 89, 114, 116
fiber and, 165
formula and, 128
hypoallergenic, 104, 132
mature, 107, 108, 109, 111
and milk compared, 132, 134, 354
nutrition from, 93
offering, 117, 126, 152
pasteurizing, 125
poops and, 162, 163, 165
pumping, 106, 111, 114, 122, 123
replacing, 127, 333
rice cereal and, 92, 170
sour tasting, 122
stimulating, 32-33, 124
storing, 116, 117, 118, 123, 126
supply of, 88, 106, 111, 113, 116, 128
vitamin D and, 129

INDEX **491**

weaning from, 126-27
Breast pumps, 106, 122, 123, 131
   electric, 117, 126
   hospital-grade, 114, 117, 130
   insurance companies and, 118
   manual, 117
   renting/buying, 117, 126
   using, 107, 111, 125
Breast shells, 108, 131
Breast surgery, breastfeeding and, 106
Breastfeeding, xxi, xx, 5, 51, 60, 103, 333
   advantages of, 104, 133
   alcohol and, 121
   comfort during, 112, 128
   continuing, 90, 105
   diet and, 118-19
   drug abuse and, 403
   etiquette for, 107
   exercise and, 122
   fever and, 123
   for first year, 128-29
   fluoride and, 95
   food allergies and, 156, 157
   formula and, 104
   frequency of, 108, 129
   groups, 41
   growth and, 84
   herbal remedies and, 404
   high fiber foods and, 178
   hygiene with, 114
   infection with, 79
   jaundice and, 54
   learning, 43, 104
   medications and, 121-22, 403-4, 422
   multiples and, 125-26
   pacifiers and, 105, 115, 249
   pillows, 112
   poops and, 130, 165
   positions for, 105, 112, 113, 114, 126
   preemies and, 58, 59, 126
   prenatal vitamins and, 120, 121
   problems with, 106, 107, 111-12, 129, 130-31
   references for, 115
   rooming-in and, 53, 105
   science of, 107
   sleep and, 126, 183, 192
   solid food and, 127
   solutions for, 130-31
   starting, 107-11
   stopping, 104-5, 119, 127, 128, 129
   support for, 106
   technique for, 105, 109
   tips on, 108
   troubleshooting with, 113
   urination and, 175
   vitamin D deficiency and, 94
   vomiting and, 368
   web site on, 471
   work and, 116, 122, 129
Breasts
   changes in, 110-11
   massaging, 115, 123, 131
Breath-holding spells, 259, 448
   anemia and, 332
Breath odor, 342, 381
Breathing, 34, 169
   checking, 44, 46
   erratic, 348
   labored, 51, 351, 357, 360, 362, 363, 374
   periodic, 45, 61, 461
   problems with, 61, 172, 357-61, 381, 382, 387, 419
Breathing motion detectors, 190-91
Bronchiolitis, 325, 328, 358, 360, 361, 362, 436, 463
   asthma and, 329
   described, 304-5, 448
   preemies and, 57
   preventing, 420
Bronchitis, 358, 448
Bronchodilator, 329
Bronchopulmonary dysplasia (BPD), 57, 448
Bruising, 48, 390, 391, 392
   ear injuries and, 395
   excessive, 436
   home remedy for, 432
   limb injuries and, 395
   problems with/solutions to, 352-55
Bucknam method, 203, 208
Buddy tape, 395
Bulb syringes, 81, 353, 354, 361
Bumpers, 189, 192, 237
Burns, problems with/solutions to, 357
Burping, 126, 161, 162
   efficient, 176-77
Burrito Wrap, 190, 247

C. difficile, 355, 364
Caffé au lait spots, 48, 449
Caffeine, 119, 407
Cal-Ben's products, 75
Calcium, 83, 100-101
   iron and, 94, 417
   requirements for, 90
Calendula, 428-29, 431
Calories, 93, 138, 160
   need for, 88-89
   preemies and, 89
Campylobacter infection, 364
Cancer
   bone, 407

breast, 16, 104
breastfeeding and, 104
cervical, 16
circumcision and, 15
cord blood and, 19
fluoride and, 407
government conspiracy and, 266
liver, 280
penile, 16
skin, 16, 76
soy formula and, 136
web site on, 471
Capillary refill, 365
CAP-RAST test, 157
Car seats, 55, 106, 190, 245
head control and, 235
head shape and, 87
inspecting, 56
preemies and, 59
web site on, 471
Carbohydrate diet, diarrhea and, 367
Careers. *See* Work
Carnation Instant Breakfast, 146
Carotinemia, 152, 449
Casein ratio, 135
CAT scans, 392, 435
Cataracts, 44, 449
Catch-up growth, 58, 84, 149, 217, 225, 287
night feedings and, 213
Cavities, 81, 201
CBC. *See* Complete Blood Count
CDC. *See* Centers for Disease Control
Celiac disease, 159, 364, 449
Cellulitis, 309-10
Center care, 30
churches and, 32
finding, 29
Center for Evaluation of Risks to Human Reproduction, 136
Centers for Disease Control (CDC), 99
antibacterial soap and, 292-93
autism and, 221, 224
contact information for, 473
cough and cold remedies and, 422
growth chart by, 84, 92
Rotavirus and, 285
rubella and, 279
vaccinations and, 270, 273-74, 284
VAERS and, 272
varicella vaccine and, 281
Cephalhematoma, 44, 86, 449
Cephalosporins, 414
Cereal, xxi, 158
fiber in, 166
See also Rice cereal
Cerebral palsy, 48, 449

Cerebrospinal fluid (CSF), 443-44
Cetaphil, 335
CF. *See* Cystic fibrosis
Chamomile, 429
Chemotherapy, 282, 300
Chest
checking, 45
CT/MRI for, 438
rattling in, 358, 360
x-rays for, 437
Chickenpox, 265, 270, 271, 325, 410
deadliness of, 281
described, 280, 308
preventing, 295
rash with, 384-85
vaccine for, 267, 268, 272, 279, 280, 281
Chiggers, 314
Child, Sears in, 206
Child development, 5-6, 469
web site on, 471
Child Development, 28
Childcare, xx, xvii
costs of, 27, 30
ear infections and, 317, 323
feedback on, 23-24
finding, 4, 23, 30-31, 32
internet sources for, 25-26, 471
licensed, 27
naps and, 211
options for, 4, 22-32
out-of-the-home, 24
referral services for, 31
sick children and, 23, 24, 303
Strep pneumoniae and, 282
See also Day care
Child-centered school, 5, 208
Childrearing, 5, 28
Children's Afrin, 353
Children's Hospital of Philadelphia, 56, 289
Children's Motrin, 410-11
Chloride, absorption of, 330
Choices, xx, 257
Choking, 158, 360
Cholesterol, 37, 440
Chromosome analysis, 441
Chromosome 11, autism and, 223
Chronic airway reactivity, 330
Chronic obstructed airways, 330
Circadian rhythms, 182-83
Circulation, checking, 46
Circumcision, xv, 4
arguments against, 16-17
arguments for, 15-16
caring for, 77
hygiene and, 15-16

medical benefits of, 15, 17
pain meds for, 18
problems with, 341
Clavicle fracture, 45, 449
Cleft lip and palate, 45, 317, 449-50
Clitoris, checking, 47
Clostridium botulinum spores, 158
Club foot, 48, 450
Coagulation studies, 441
Coarctation of aorta, 46, 450
Cognitive development, 217, 225
four to six months, 231
six to nine months, 233
Cold and flu season
appointments during, 39
ear infections and, 323
phone calls during, 346
vaccinations during, 275
Cold medications, 296, 361, 421-22
breastfeeding and, 422
Cold sores, 306
Cold viruses, exposure to, 61
Colds. See Common colds
Colic, xxi, 169, 171, 244, 247, 431
crying and, 251
dealing with, 138, 250-52
gas and, 178
heartburn and, 249
home remedy for, 432
medications for, 413
outgrowing, 249
probiotics and, 249, 250, 431
white noise and, 249-50
Colitis, 355, 446
Colostrum, 61, 107, 109, 111, 450
Comfort objects, 201, 221
Common colds, 296-98, 325, 358, 361, 435
breastfeeding and, 104
contagiousness of, 297
ear infections and, 317
fevers and, 298
home remedy for, 432
diagnosing, 296-97
and sinus infections compared, 298
symptoms of, 296
traveling with, 260
treating, 296-97
vaccinations and, 270
Communication skills, 219, 235
Complete Blood Count (CBC), 440
Comprehensive Metabolic Panel, 440-41
Computerized Tomography (CT), 438
Comvax, 278
Concussion, 391
Conflicts, 65, 255

Confusion, 390, 391
Congenital, 450
Congenital adrenal hyperplasia, 450
Congenital heart disease, 46, 331, 450
Congenital nevus, 48, 450
Congestion, 81
nasal, 45, 61, 81, 361-63, 460
Congestive heart failure, 46, 451
Conjunctivitis, 370, 451
bacterial, 310
viral, 306
Consciousness, loss of, 361, 390, 391, 392, 395
Constipation, 62, 163, 178, 247, 349, 350, 355, 451
fiber and, 138
formula and, 164
iron and, 138, 164
medications for, 412
relieving, 164-65
rice cereal and, 165-66
Consumer Product Safety Commission (CPSC), 189, 238
guide by, 242
walkers and, 231
Consumer Reports, 75
Convulsions, 387
Cooking, 26, 151
Coombs test, 441
CorCell, 21
Cord blood banking, xvi, 4, 19-22
web site on, 471
Cord Blood Registry, 21
Corneal abrasion, 371, 392
Corrected age, 91, 149
Co-sleepers, 186, 191
Co-sleeping, 192, 207
hybrid method of, 193
SIDS and, 191
study on, 194
Coughing, 293, 294, 296, 303, 348, 353, 359, 360
chronic, 363
forceful, 367
mucus and, 358
nighttime, 362
persistent, 363
problems with/solutions to, 361-63
vomiting and, 368
Cowpox virus, 264, 266
Coxsackievirus, 294, 305-6, 325
rash with, 384-85
CPR courses, 59, 159, 238, 347, 387
Cradle cap, 69, 74
home remedy for, 432
Cradle hold, 112, 125
Craniosynostosis, 44, 85, 86-87, 451

Crawling, walking and, 233
Creamy Vaseline, 73, 335
Cribs
  borrowing/buying, 189, 212
  sharing, 212
  sleeping in, 5, 212
Cross-bite, 249
Crossed-eyes, 44, 229
Croup, 305, 325, 358, 359
  home remedy for, 432
Crying, 350, 360
  acid reflux and, 213
  colic and, 251
  feedings and, 172
  listening to, 209, 210
  management approach for, 246, 248, 251
  medical causes for, 247
  spoiling and, 247
Cryobanks International, 21
Cryo-Cell International, 21
Cryovials, 22
Cryptosporidium, 364
C-sections, 34, 51, 86, 112
CSF. *See* Cerebrospinal fluid
CT. *See* Computerized Tomography
Culturelle, diarrhea and, 431
Cultures, 301, 435, 444
Cups, 145
  sippy, 143, 146
Cutter Advanced, 76
Cystic fibrosis (CF), 46, 330, 451

Dactylitis, 333
Dairy, 143
  alternative, 145
  calcium from, 100
  elimination of, 171
  food poisoning and, 356
  guidelines for, 101
  iron supplements and, 94
  reintroducing, 120
  requirements for, 90
  Stage 1, 150
Day care
  biting at, 259
  commuting and, 31
  competition for, 23
  cost of, 27
  home, 29, 31, 32
  licensed, 29
  naps and, 211
  options for, 4
  sick child policies of, 29
  See also Childcare
Day-Night Reversal, 183
Decongestants, 296, 422
  ear infections and, 323-24
  oral, 421
DEET, 76, 77
Dehydration, 44, 83, 85, 174, 282, 369, 374, 377, 410, 436
  Babywise method and, 208
  diarrhea and, 365-66
  jaundice and, 55
  preventing, 366
  signs of, 174, 365
  vomiting and, 365, 366, 367
Dental, 69
  juice and, 144
  medications for, 406-7
  preemies and, 59
Denver Developmental Checklist, 217, 232
Depression
  postpartum, 41, 63, 64
  struggling with, 41
Dermabond, 389-90
Dermatitis, 352
  contact, 351
Dermatologic products, using, 422-26
Desitin, 71
Desperation move, 192
Detergents
  eczema and, 75, 336
  thoughts on, 73-74
Development
  birth to two months, 227-29
  two to four months, 229-30
  four to six months, 230-31
  six to nine months, 232-34
  nine to twelve months, 234-36
  books on, 241
  catching up in, 217
  concerns about, 217, 287
  described, 216
  discipline and, 243
  DVDs and, 241
  milestones of, 33, 217
  pacifiers and, 248
  preemies and, 57, 59, 225
  reviewing, 253
  television and, 238
  toys and, 241
Developmental delays, 215, 217
  autism and, 223, 224
  global, 220
  help with, 221, 224
  identifying, 218
  isolated, 219
  preemies and, 57
  white noise and, 249
DHA. *See* Docosahexaenoid Acid
Diabetes mellitus, 156, 283
  breastfeeding and, 104

diet and, 339
formula and, 136
gestational, 51
obesity and, 339
testing for, 339
vaccines and, 284
web site on, 471
Diaper changes, 70, 176, 245, 247, 338
number of, 161, 165
sleep and, 185
Diaper rash, xvi, 69, 110, 345, 354, 355
food allergies and, 153, 386
home remedy for, 433
severe, 71
treating, 71, 387
yeast, 79, 313, 314, 325, 384-85
Diaper rash creams, 423, 426, 431
Diaper wipes, 70
Diapers, 51, 52
blood in, 53, 175
Diarrhea, 138, 163, 167, 176, 282, 303, 349, 374, 451
antibiotic-associated, 431
blood in, 119, 355, 364, 413
Celiac Disease and, 159
chronic, 364
dehydration and, 365-66
diet and, 339
fat/fiber and, 366, 367
food allergies and, 153
grape jelly, 355, 364
home remedy for, 433
juice and, 144
medications for, 412-13
mucus in, 413
persistent, 350, 364
probiotics and, 431
problems with/solutions for, 363-67
stomach virus and, 431
vomiting and, 175, 368, 369, 413
watery, 365
Diet
breastfeeding and, 118-19
diabetes and, 339
elimination, 157, 178
healthy, 94, 98
high calorie, 93
liquid, 147
needs in, 89
toddler, 102
Dietary supplements, 146, 428
Difficult child, 244-45
Digitalis plant, 428
Digoxin, 428
Diphenhydramine, 127, 347, 352, 406
hives and, 383
travel and, 260

Diphtheria, 275, 277
booster for, 271
vaccine for, 267, 268
Discipline, 3, 5
age-appropriate, 255
center care, 29
conflicts and, 254
consistency in, 253
developing style of, 255
development and, 243
goal of, 254
management plan for, 253
planting seeds of, 235, 243, 252-57
problems in, 258
teachers and, 259
techniques for, 256-57
temperament-appropriate, 255
Diseases
exposure to, 270
specifics about, 275-82
vaccine-preventable, 268, 271, 277, 289
Dislocations, 394, 436
DNA, xxi, 267, 292
Docosahexaenoid Acid (DHA), 104, 133, 136
breastfeeding and, 121
taking, 5
Dr. Brown, bottles from, 141
Doctor-parent relationships, 12, 14
Dr. Smith's Diaper Ointment, 71
Dosing, 378, 379, 412
Doubt, autonomy versus, 227
Dove soap, 72, 75, 293, 335
Downtime, 211, 259
Dream feeds, 198, 206
Dressing, 60
heat rash and, 70
SIDS and, 192
Drinking
excessive, 436
urination and, 175
vomiting and, 174
Drool, 80, 351, 381
Drug abuse, 33, 403
Drug interactions, 401
Dry skin, 75
lotion on, 73
soaps and, 293
DTaP vaccine, 269, 272, 277, 278
DTP vaccine, 277
Dust mites, 314, 340, 341
DVDs, 240, 241

E. coli, 310-11, 325, 356
Ear drops, 408, 409
Ear infections, 60, 80, 301, 303, 316-24,

325, 362, 436
  antibiotics for, 316, 318-20
  bacterial, 319
  bath water and, 318
  complications from, 319
  home remedy for, 433
  medications for, 408-9, 414
  outgrowing, 322
  pacifiers and, 249
  pink eye and, 370
  preventing, 322-24
  Prevnar and, 323
  proneness to, 316
  risk factors for, 317
  and swimmer's ear compared, 316-17
  travel and, 260, 321
  viral, 319
  vomiting and, 368
  wind and, 300
Ear injuries, 392-93, 395
Ear piercing, 78-79
Ear pulling, 80, 320
Eardrums, 44, 316, 392
  infected, 317
  perforated, 317, 318, 321, 409, 461
Early Childhood Intervention, 59, 224
Early Head Start, 220
Earth's Best, 133, 138
Earwax, dissolving, 409
Easter Seals, 224
  contact information for, 473
Easy child, 244
Eating, ebbs/flows in, 98-99
EC. *See* Elimination Communication
Echinacea, 428, 429
Echocardiogram, 331
Eczema, 293, 340, 351, 386, 431
  asthma and, 330, 336
  dealing with, 75
  described, 335, 452
  foods and, 75, 157
  home remedy for, 433
  managing, 335, 336
  outgrowing, 337
  peanut allergies and, 121
  rashes and, 382, 383
  steroids and, 336
EFSA. *See* European Union Food Safety Authority
Ego, development of, 235
Egocentric perspective, 225, 253, 256, 452
Electrocardiogram (EKG), 331
Electrolytes, 369, 441
Elidel, 336
Elimination, 61, 62
Elimination chart, 65, 66

Elimination Communication (EC), 168
Emergencies, 13, 14
  dental, 81
  handling, 347
  Labor Day, 43-44
  pediatricians and, 41
  phone calls and, 13, 346, 349
  web site on, 471
Emesis, 452
Emetrol, 413
EMLA, 269-70
Emotional development, 225, 226-27, 244
Emotional health, 41, 209
Enamel hypoplasia, 59, 452
Encephalitis, 279, 280, 452
  vaccinations and, 270, 272
Endocrine, 339
Enfamil, 133, 134, 135
Engerix B, 286, 287
Engorgement, 105, 113, 114-15, 130
  described, 108, 452
  surviving, 116
Enterobacter sakazakii, 139
Enterocolitis, 135
Enteropathy, 135
Enteroviruses, 294
Entrapment, 189, 191
Environment California Research and Policy Center, 141
Environmental Protection Agency (EPA)
  BPA and, 141
  lead and, 334
  mercury and, 5, 286
Ephedra, sudafed and, 401
Epidemics, 266, 277, 294
  immunization rates and, 271
  protection from, 289-90
  vaccines and, 267
Epidurals, 34
Epiglotitis, 278
Epilepsy, 380
Epi-Pens, 156
Epispadias, 47, 452
Epstein's Pearls, 45, 452
Erb's Palsy, 48, 452
Erikson, Erik: influence of, 226
Erythema infectiosum, 308-9
Erythema multiforme, 351, 383
Erythema toxicum, 49, 452
Erythrocyte Sedimentation Rate (ESR), 441
Esophageal pH probes, 171
Esophageal sphincter, 168
Esophagitis, 171, 354, 452
Esophagus, 174, 354
  heartburn and, 171
  spit ups and, 168

ESR. *See* Erythrocyte Sedimentation Rate
Essential fatty acid cream, 325, 336
Estradiol, 141
Estrogen, 136, 341
Estrogen cream, 342
Ethylmercury, 286
Eucerin cream, 335
European Union Food Safety Authority (EFSA), 141
Eustachian tubes, 299, 316, 324
   dysfunction of, 317
   ear infections and, 323
Evenflo, bottles from, 141
Evening Primrose Oil, 429
Excited Ineffective, 112-13
Exercise, breastfeeding and, 122
Expectorants, 422
Extremities
   bruising and, 395
   checking, 48
   CT/MRI for, 438
   deformed, 337
   immobilizing, 394
   x-rays for, 437
Eye contact, lack of, 221
Eye drops, antibiotic, 371, 409-10
Eye exams, 56-57, 59
Eye infections, 49, 301, 310, 325
   CMV, 295
Eye injuries, 392, 395
Eye ointment, 49, 409-10
Eye stye, home remedy for, 433
Eye virus, 294
Eyebrows, stitches for, 389
Eyes
   checking, 44
   problems with, 327-28, 369-71
   red, 370, 371
   swollen shut, 370, 371
Ezzo method, 203, 208, 209

FACT. *See* Foundation for the Accreditation of Cellular Therapy
Failure to thrive, 93, 333, 436, 453
   Babywise method and, 208
Family
   balancing work with, 24-25, 26
   nurturing, 208
Family beds, 5, 105
   advantages of, 192-93
   attachment parenting and, 207, 208
   bassinets and, 194
   disadvantages of, 193
   safety with, 191, 193
   SIDS and, 193
   solitary sleep versus, 192-94

Family caretakers, considering, 27-28
Family Cord Blood Services, 21
Family Medical Leave Act (FMLA), 26
Fat, diarrhea and, 366, 367, 412
Fat necrosis, 272, 453
Fatty acid supplements, 5
FDA. *See* Food and Drug Administration
Febrile seizures, 379-80, 387, 388, 410
Feeding chart, 65, 66
Feeding patterns, 163
   breastfeeding and, 106
   regular, 195
   sleep patterns and, 128
Feedings, xvi, xvii, 5, 83, 92, 247, 322
   behaviors for, 112-13
   challenges of, 159
   cluster, 128, 183
   crying and, 172
   dream, 198, 206
   on-demand, 5, 91, 125
   distractions during, 127
   ear infections and, 323
   first morning, 208
   first year, 143
   frequency of, 108, 109, 111, 128, 129, 143
   length of, 109, 111, 114
   parent directed, 91
   poops and, 164
   poor routines with, 93
   preemies and, 59
   red flags with, 61-62
   refusing, 172
   scheduling, 92, 208
   sleep and, 61, 109, 112, 127, 145, 195, 196, 199, 201, 203
   sleeping through the night and, 143, 197-98
   See also Night feedings
Feet
   controlling, 216
   flat, 337
   purple, 46
Fennel, 178, 430
Fenugreek, 125
Feostat, 334
Ferber method, 196, 202, 206, 207
   described, 203-4
   naps and, 211
   night wakenings and, 209
   sleep training and, 205
   success for, 208-9
Fever, 51, 176, 247
   brain damage and, 380
   breastfeeding and, 123
   common colds and, 298
   curves, 375

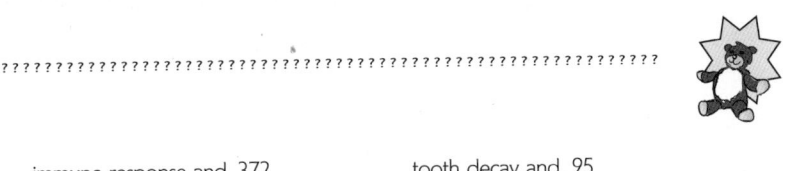

immune response and, 372
infections and, 300, 303, 372
maximum spikes in, 375
milk and, 380
persistent, 298, 436
problems with/solutions to, 371-80
rash and, 387
red flags with, 64, 380
seizures and, 379-80
teething and, 380
treating, 377
vaccinations and, 274-75
vomiting and, 174, 368
Fever reducing medications, 64, 375, 410-11, 421
alternating, 377, 410
giving, 377, 379
Feverall, 378
Fiber, 83
breast milk and, 165
breastfeeding and, 178
constipation and, 138
diarrhea and, 366, 367, 412
eating, 100-101
importance of, 165-66
Fifth Disease, 308-9, 325
rash with, 384-85
Financial Post, xxi-xxi
Fine motor skills
two to four months, 229
four to six months, 230, 232
six to nine months, 232, 233
nine to twelve months, 234, 236
achieving, 216, 219
delays in, 218
foods and, 148
toys for, 242
Fingers, broken, 394, 395
First Aid, 342, 347
Fish
eating, 121, 160
food poisoning and, 356
mercury in, 286, 287
Fish oils, 5, 121
Flaring (nostrils), 46, 61, 358, 359, 453
Flat angiomata, 48, 453
Flat heads, xxi, 85
sleep positions and, 191
tummy time and, 86-87
Flavor RX, 400
Flora, 299
Florastor, 431
Flu. *See* Influenza
Flumist, 283
Fluoride, 81, 144, 407
breastfeeding and, 95
in formula, 139
tooth decay and, 95
Fluoride supplements, 95, 96, 406-7
milk and, 407
Fluorosis, 95
Flushield, 270
Fluvirin, 270
Fluzone, 270
FMLA. *See* Family Medical Leave Act
Fomites, 292, 453
Fontanelle, 44, 453
bulging of, 392
closing of, 85, 86
dehydration and, 365
Food Allergy Network, 156, 157
FoodAllergy.org, 119
Food and Drug Administration (FDA), 402, 427
antacids and, 170
cord blood banks and, 20
fish consumption and, 121, 160
Flumist and, 283
labeling standards by, 428
mercury and, 5, 286
off-label and, 401
Rotavirus and, 282, 285
soy formula and, 137
thimerosal and, 285, 287
vaccinations and, 268, 269, 273-74, 284
VAERS and, 272
Food challenge, 157
Food poisoning, 325, 354, 364
described, 310-11, 453
stories about, 355-56
vomiting and, 368
Foods
allergy-causing, 153-54
avoiding, 158
choices of, 5, 102
choking hazards with, 158
complementary, 105, 149
eczema and, 75
eliminating, 156, 157
ethnic, 158
fiber, 165-67
finger, 148, 158-59
guidelines for, 101
healthy, 99
introducing, 129, 148, 149
junk, 98
making, 152, 153, 158
malabsorption of, 93
natural, 356
offering, 149, 151, 152, 381
organic, 152-53
poops and, 165-66, 167
sleeping through the night and, 148

solid, 80, 83, 90, 92, 102, 105, 142, 147, 148, 149, 151, 152, 157, 159, 368
Stage 1, 147, 148, 149-50, 151, 153, 158, 160, 165
Stage 2, 147, 149, 153, 158, 159, 160
Stage 3, 148, 150, 153, 158, 160
table, 148, 159, 160
teething and, 159
texture, 159
yellow skin and, 152
Football hold, 112, 113, 125, 126
Foreign body/object, 238, 453
Foremilk, 108, 163, 453
Foreskin, 17, 78
Formula, 83, 90, 102, 103, 106, 129, 151
brand name, 133
breast milk and, 128
breastfeeding and, 104
calcium in, 139
calories in, 89, 138, 160
commercial, 133
concentrate, 139
constipation and, 164
cost of, 104, 132
cow's milk based, 134, 135, 136
cow's milk based, with iron, 132, 133
diabetes and, 136
feeding, 53, 132, 152
fluoride and, 95, 96, 139
generic, 137
history of, 132-33
iron-rich, 94, 137, 333
lactose free, 137
lipids in, 136
liquid concentrate, 144
low-iron, 137-38, 333
medications and, 400
organic, 138
poops and, 162, 163
powder, 139, 144
premature, 58, 59
with probiotics, 138, 139
protein hydrolysate, with iron, 133-34
ready-to-feed, 139, 140, 144
recommended, 132-33
rice cereal and, 92, 170
soy, 133, 134, 135, 136, 137
supplementing with, 55, 123, 126
switching, 134
toddler, 139
vitamin D deficiency and, 94
vomiting and, 368
Formvirisen, 295
Foundation for the Accreditation of Cellular Therapy (FACT), 20
Four C's, avoiding, 97, 98, 99

Fragile X Syndrome, 222
Frenulectomy, 114, 453
Frenulum, 453
Frist, Lewis: on formula, 132-33
Fruits, 158
fiber in, 166
food poisoning and, 356
organic, 153
Stage 1, 150
Stage 2, 150
vegetables and, 152
Fungus, 303, 313-17, 325
rashes and, 382
Fussiness, 122, 169, 213, 272, 371
breastfeeding and, 120
formula and, 134
questions about, 172

Gagging, 190, 360
Galactosemia, 49, 454
Gas, 133, 161, 247, 349, 431
breastfeeding and, 120
colic and, 178
formula and, 134
home remedy for, 432
intestines and, 162
medications for, 413
sleeping and, 177
Gas drops, 250
Gastritis, 354
Gastroenteritis, 163, 174, 454
bacterial, 354, 364, 368, 447
vomiting and, 368
viral, 307, 349, 364, 368
vomiting and, 368
Gastroesophageal problems, 58
colic and, 249
medications for, 411-14
web site on, 471
Gastroesophageal reflux (GER), 93, 138, 143, 168, 213, 247, 249, 360, 454
evaluation for, 173
outgrowing, 329
preemies and, 58
sleep positions and, 190
suffering from, 169, 171
treating, 169, 411-12
Gastrointestinal virus, 307, 325
Gatorade, 174, 369, 413
Gauze pads, 70, 77, 388
Gene therapy, 20
Genetics, 222, 223
Genital mutilation, 17
Genitals
burns on, 357
checking, 47
playing with, 258

problems with, 341-42
GER. *See* Gastroesophageal reflux
Gerber, 141, 153
German measles, 278
    rash with, 384-85
    vaccine for, 279, 281
    See also Measles
Germs, 60, 264, 291
    exposure to, 140, 269, 293
    good, 123, 250, 366, 431
    mouth, 79
Giardia infections, 315, 325, 364
    medications for, 416
Ginger, 178, 430
Gingivostomatitis, 454
Ginseng, 428
Girl parts, caring for, 78-79
Glaucoma, 454
Glycerine bullets, 166
Goat's milk, 128
Goop, eye, 369-70, 371
Gourmet, 113
Government conspiracy, 266, 273
Grains, 150
    fiber in, 166
Grimace, 52
Griseofulvin, 416
Gross motor skills
    two to four months, 229
    four to six months, 230, 232
    six to nine months, 232, 233
    nine to twelve months, 234, 236
    achieving, 216, 218
    delays in, 218, 220
    toys for, 242
Group A Strep, 301, 320, 325, 401
Group B Strep, 50, 51, 312, 325, 373
Growth, 83, 216
    breastfeeding and, 84
    catch-up, 58, 84, 149, 213, 217, 225, 287
    consistent, 84
    newborn, 88
    preemies and, 58, 84
    spurts of, 88, 91
Growth charts, 83-84, 163
    boys, birth to 36 months, 474
    dropping off, 93
    girls, birth to 36 months, 475
    preemie, 478
Growth percentiles, drop in, 92-93
Growth plates, 394
Grunting Baby Syndrome, 163
Guilt, 25
    initiative versus, 227
Gums, 45, 80
Guns, safety with, 237

Gymboree, 27, 241

Haemophilus influenza B (HIB), 265, 267, 269, 278, 325, 333
    non-typable, 320, 370
    vaccine for, 268
HALO Innovations, 189
Hand-foot-and-mouth virus, 294, 305-6, 325
    rash with, 384-85
Hand gestures, 239
Hand sanitizers, 70
Hands
    burns on, 357
    purple, 46
    washing, 60
Happiest Baby on the Block (Karp), 251
Hay fever, 336, 340
Head and Shoulders, 74
Head banging, 221
Head control, 216, 228-29, 235
Head injuries, 360, 387, 388
    CAT scans and, 392
    confusion and, 395
    handling, 391
    nosebleeds and, 395
    seizures and, 391
    vomiting and, 368, 390, 391, 395
    walkers and, 392
Head shapes
    car seats and, 87
    changes in, 191
    odd, 86, 87
    sleep position and, 87
Head size
    autism/mercury poisoning and, 288
    enlarging, 436
    measuring, 85
Head Start, help from, 220
Heads
    checking, 44
    circumference of, 477
    CT/MRI for, 438
    holding up, 87
    ultrasound for, 437
Health Canada, xxi
Health care, xx, 3, 35
    scrutiny for, 11
Health insurance, 11
    alternative medicine and, 12
    breast pumps and, 118
    changing, 14, 38
    circumcision and, 17
    hearing screens and, 45
    nebulizers and, 330
Healthy Sleep Habits, Happy Child (Weissbluth), 205

Hearing, 225
　birth to two months, 228
Hearing loss, 36, 57, 318, 319, 321
Hearing screens, 33, 44
　health insurance and, 45
　preemies and, 57
Heart
　checking, 46
　problems with, 44, 330-31
　ultrasound for, 437
Heart defects, web site on, 472
Heart disease, 46, 283, 451
　fiber and, 100
Heart murmurs, 436, 459
　benign, 46
　described, 330-31, 454, 461
　innocent, 331
　pathologic, 331, 461
　transitional, 46, 466
Heart rate, 52
　average, 348
　checking, 44, 347
　fast/slow, 46
Heartbeats
　irregular, 46, 436
　listening to, 330
Heartburn, 92, 138, 143, 190, 213
　colic and, 249
　crying, 247
　esophagus and, 171
　treating, 170
Heat rash, 70
Height, predicting, 84, 85
Heimlich maneuver, 238, 361
Helmets, 85, 86, 191
Hemangioma, 454
Hematocrit, 36, 440
Hemoglobin, 332, 440
　sickle cell disease and, 333
Hemolytic Uremic Syndrome (HUS), 356, 454
Hemophilia, 352, 454-55
Hemorrhagic disease of the newborn, 49, 455
Hemphill, Jim, 224
Hemphill, Meredith, 224
Henoch-Schonlein Purpura (HSP), 352, 455
Hepatitis A, 279
　vaccine for, 267, 268
Hepatitis B, 269, 278
　breast milk and, 125
　carriers of, 280
　preventing, 295
　screening for, 33
　transmission of, 280
　vaccine for, 52, 267, 268
Herbal remedies
　breastfeeding and, 404
　drug interactions with, 429
　expensive, 428
　knowledge about, 429
　OTC products and, 401
　precautions with, 428-29
　studies on, 431
　traditional medicine and, 428
　web site on, 470
Herbal supplements, 125, 427
Herd immunity, 266
Hernias, 455
　hiatal, 173
　incarcerated, 349
　inguinal, 47, 456
　intestinal, 47
　umbilical, 46, 466
Herpes, 295, 307-8, 325, 386
Herpetic Withrow, rash with, 384-85
HIB. See Haemophilus influenza B
Hiccups, 162, 172, 177
High-maintenance babies, 245, 247
Hill, Linda
　breastfeeding tips from, 108, 112, 124
　on yeast infections, 82
Hindmilk, 108, 111, 163, 455
Hip dysplasia, 48, 455
HIPAA, 41
Hips
　congenitally dislocated, 436
　ultrasound for, 437
Hirschsprung's disease, 46, 455
Histamine 2 Receptor Antagonists, 170
Histamines, 153, 352, 383, 421, 455
HIV, 292, 295
　breast milk and, 125
　circumcision and, 16, 17
　screening for, 33
　web site on, 472
Hives, 155, 351, 383
Hoag Hospital, immersion baths at, 72
Hogg method, 203, 206
Holistic Pediatrician, The (Kemper), 431
Home remedies, 296, 432-34
Homeopathic Pharmacopeia of the United States (HPUS), 432
Homeopathy, 427, 432
Hormones, 64, 65, 105, 175, 386
　breastfeeding and, 106
　organic foods and, 152
　rashes and, 382
　supporting, 63
House Rules, 96, 253
Household products, ingesting, 381
Housekeepers, hiring, 32
HPUS. See Homeopathic Pharmacopeia of the United States
HPV. See Human Papilloma Virus

HSP. *See* Henoch-Schonlein Purpura
Human milk fortifier, 58, 59
Human Papilloma Virus (HPV), 455
    circumcision and, 15-16
Hume, Mary C.: vaccination and, 264
Humidifiers, 297, 298
Hunger strikes, 102
HUS. *See* Hemolytic Uremic Syndrome
Hydrocele, 47, 456
Hydrocephalus, 85, 174, 456
Hygiene, 69
    bladder infections and, 175-76
    breastfeeding, 114
Hygiene Hypothesis, 31
Hygiene products, ingesting, 381
Hyperthermia, 372
Hyphema, 392
Hypospadias, 47, 456
Hypothyroidism, 49, 93, 456

IBD. *See* Inflammatory bowel disease
Ibuprofen, 115, 130, 347, 410-11
    antibiotics and, 401
    dosing for, 378, 379
    fever and, 374, 375, 377
Icar, 334
Identity, role confusion versus, 227
Idiopathic thrombocytopenic purpura (ITP), 352, 353, 456
    rash with, 383
I-GERQ score, 171
Illnesses
    bizarre, 30
    daycare and, 29, 31
    evening/weekend, 40
    frequency of, 28, 30
    patterns of, 435
    sleep etiquette and, 197
    sleep patterns and, 202, 205
Imagination, evolution of, 263
Imaging studies, 436-39
Imitation, 221, 235
Immune compromised people, 267, 270, 299
Immune systems, 277, 294, 300, 303
    children's, 269
    compromised, 282
    fever and, 372
    infections and, 371
    rashes and, 386
    vaccines and, 266, 272
Immunization Action Coalition, 289
Immunization rates
    disease/mortality rates and, 267
    drop in, 277
    epidemics and, 271
Immunization records, 274

Immunizations, 52, 280, 389, 390
    adoption and, 33
    delay in, 38
    described, 37
    schedule for, 36
    sick children and, 38
Imperforate anus, 456
Impetigo, 309-10
    rash with, 384-85
Inborn Errors of Metabolism, 459
Independence, 227, 252, 253, 254, 256
Independent play, 239, 240
Industry, inferiority versus, 227
Infant Formula Act (1986), 135
Infant scales, 58, 59
Infections, 44, 293
    bacteria and, 325
    breastfeeding and, 104
    common, 291
    controlling, 30
    exposure to, 31, 265
    fever and, 303
    immune system and, 371
    invasive, 313
    localized, 300
    looking for, 388
    medications for, 414-16
    opportunistic, 313
    preemies and, 57
    rashes and, 382, 384-85
    serious, 274
    temperature and, 372
    viruses and, 325
Inferiority, industry versus, 227
Inflammatory bowel disease, 364, 456
    breastfeeding and, 104
Influenza, 295, 325, 358, 361, 364, 410
    described, 304
    exposure to, 61
    strains of, 283
    symptoms of, 296
    wintertime and, 294
Influenza vaccine, 267, 270, 282-83, 333
    optional, 286
    preemies and, 57, 59
    thimerosal-free, 286
Ingestions, 381-82, 387
Inhalers, 329, 420
Initiative, guilt versus, 227
Insect repellents, 76-77
Instincts, xx, 4, 26
Institute of Medicine (IOM)
    autism/thimerosal and, 287
    diet recommendations by, 119
    mercury question and, 285
    MMR/autism and, 284, 285
    vaccine safety and, 269

Insulin, 339
Intellectual development, 225
  achieving, 217, 219
  delays in, 218
  preemies and, 225
International Committee on Taxonomy of Viruses, 292
International Pediatric Sleep Education Task Force, 198
Interventions
  naps and, 211
  cutting back on, 210
Intestinal obstruction, 349, 457
  vomiting and, 367, 368
Intestines, 165, 177
  gas and, 162
  infections of, 364
  problems with, 93
Intoeing, 337
Intolerance
  food, 153, 364
  formula, 133
  lactose, 137, 364, 366, 367
  milk, 132, 171, 247
  See also Allergies
Intraventricular hemorrhage (IVH), 56, 457
Intussusception, 163, 167, 282, 285, 349, 355, 457
IOM. See Institute of Medicine
IPV, 269
Iron, 83
  calcium and, 94, 417
  constipation and, 138, 164
  poop and, 334
  sources of, 100-101
  teeth and, 334
  vitamin C and, 101, 334, 417
Iron deficiency, 93, 259, 332, 333-34, 417
Iron supplements, 334, 417
  dairy and, 94
  preemies and, 59, 94
Isomil Advance, 133
Isomil DF, 137, 366
ITP. See Idiopathic thrombocytopenic purpura
IV fluids, 436
IVH. See Intraventricular hemorrhage

Jaundice, 48, 50, 51, 53-54, 63, 152, 436, 457
  breastfeeding and, 54, 109
  normal/abnormal, 53
  treating, 54-55
Jenner, Edward, 264
Jerked elbows, 395
Johnson and Johnson shampoo, 72

Juice, 83, 103
  diarrhea and, 364
  medications and, 400
  nutritional, 165
  problems with, 96, 97, 144, 364
Just Tomatoes, 99

Karo cocktails, 164
Karp, Harvey: on colic, 251
Karyotyping, 222
Kawasaki Disease, 457
  rash with, 384-85
Kernicterus, 54, 457
Kidney infections, 47, 176, 436
  vomiting and, 368
Kidneys, 47
  mercury and, 286
  ultrasound for, 437
Knee control, 216
Knock-kneedness, 337

L.V.N.s. See Licensed vocational nurses
La Leche League, 115, 125
Lab work, 300, 303, 439-44
  doctor-requested, 435-36
  parent-requested, 435
Labia, 78, 176, 341
Labial adhesion, 47, 341, 342, 457
Labor Day, 43-44, 69
Lactase, 135, 137, 364
Lactation consultants (LCs), 108, 130
  contacting, 106, 110, 115, 116
  help from, 55, 63, 126
  nipple recommendations from, 140-41
Lactic acid, 122
Lactinex, 431
Lactobacillus, 123, 412, 431
  diarrhea and, 366
Lactobacillus acidophilus, 431
Lactobacillus bulgaricus, 431
Lactobacillus GG, 431
Lactobacillus reuteri, 139, 250, 431
  colic and, 431
Lactose, 136, 137
Lactose intolerance, 137, 364
  diarrhea and, 366, 367
Language delays, 57, 218, 284
  expressive, 220, 321, 322, 452-53
Language skills, 322
  birth to two months, 228
  two to four months, 230
  four to six months, 231, 232
  six to nine months, 232-33, 233-34
  nine to twelve months, 235, 236
  achieving, 219
  autism and, 222
  expressive, 216

receptive, 216, 236
tantrums and, 256
Languages, 226
speaking multiple, 236
understanding, 239
Lanolin, 71, 108, 110, 114, 431
Lansinoh, 108, 110
Lansoprazole, 170
Larson, Elaine, 292
Laryngomalacia, 45, 458
Latching, 105, 107, 109, 126, 130, 131
help with, 114
problems with, 113, 123
technique for, 110
Lawrence, Ruth, 122
Lazy eye, 229, 327
LCs. *See* Lactation consultants
Leach, Penelope, 6
Lead exposure, 37, 332, 334, 428
"Learn the Signs, Act Early" (CDC), 221
Learning, 225-26, 240
Learning curve, 217
Learning delays, 57
Learning disabilities, 220, 224
Lethargy, 174, 273, 364, 391
dehydration and, 365
extreme, 381
Leukemia, 352, 353, 435, 458
rash with, 383
Levalbuterol, 418
Lice, 314-15, 325
home remedy for, 433
treating, 314, 424
Licensed vocational nurses (L.V.N.s), 40
Licorice, using, 430
Lieus, 163
LifebankUSA, 21
LifeLine Cryogenics, 21
Limits
setting, 206, 209, 227, 235, 244
testing, 253
Lipids, 136, 442
Liquids, 90, 143-44
Little Gym, 241
Little Noses, 353
Liver failure, 410
Liver function tests, 441-42
Logical thinking, 226
Lotions, 73, 121
Lotrimin, 82
Lotrimin AF, 71
Low-maintenance babies, 245
Lower respiratory infection, 358
Lung infections, 301, 309, 325
Lung problems, 328-30
chronic, 57
web site on, 472

Lyme Disease, 76
rash with, 384-85
Lymph nodes, 297, 298
CT/MRI for, 438
Lymphocytes, 295

Macrocephaly, 85, 458
Macrolides, 415
Mad Hatter's Disease, 286, 287
Magnetic Resonance Imaging (MRI), 438
Malabsorption, 167, 458
Malnutrition, 92-93
Malrotation, 46, 458
Manganese, ADD and, 137
March of Dimes Birth Defects Foundation, 19, 473
Massage
breast, 115, 123, 131
colic and, 251-52
infant, 178, 248
Mastitis, 82, 123, 131
Mastoiditis, 319
Masturbation, 15, 238, 458
Maternity leave, 118, 123
Mattresses, 192, 212
Mayo Clinic, screening and, 19
Measles, 272, 278-79, 386
epidemic of, 271
preventing, 295
rash with, 384-85
vaccine for, 268, 271, 279, 281
See also German measles
Measurements, 38
common conversions for, 89
Meconium, 46, 51, 52, 62, 70, 112, 162, 163, 167, 354, 458
Meconium ileus, 458
Meconium plug, 458
Medela Lactina, 117
Medela Pump In Style, 117
Medela Symphony, 117
Medical problems, xvi, 7, 38, 327
Labor Day, 43
MedicAlert bracelets, 156
Medication index, 404-5
Medications, xxi, 405-26
anti-diarrhea, 367
antiviral, 295
breastfeeding and, 121-22, 403-4, 422
cold, 296, 361, 421-22
control, 418-19
correct dosage with, 378
cough, 361, 362, 421-22
fever-reducing, 64, 375, 377, 379, 410, 421

formula and, 400
generic/brand name, 399, 400, 402
herbs and, 428
juice and, 400
leftover, 400-401
multiple at once, 401
off-label, 401
pain, 33-34, 410-11
pregnancy and, 403-4
preventative, 418-19
questions about, 347
rescue, 418
safety with, 237
side effects of, 346, 427
taking, 381, 400, 401
vomiting and, 399
Medications and Mother's Milk (Hale), 122
Melanin, 76
Melatonin, 182
Meningitis, 85, 174, 176, 271, 278, 279, 319, 325, 352, 353, 387
described, 311, 458
developing, 289
HIB, 265
meningococcal, 289
rash with, 384-85
vomiting and, 368
Menstruation, 341
Mental retardation, 18, 220, 223, 287
Menthols, 297
Mercury, 160
avoiding, 5
contamination with, 428
controversy over, 285
in fish, 286, 287
Mercury poisoning, 286, 287
and autism compared, 288
Metabolic disorders, 93, 222, 342, 387, 459
testing for, 18
vomiting and, 368
Metabolic screening, 4, 33, 36
thoughts on, 18-19
Metabolic Storage Disease, 46, 459
Metabolism, 208, 360
Methanol, 286
Methylmercury, 286
Metoclopramide, 124, 125
Microcephaly, 85, 459
Middle ear bones, 316
Middle ear infections, 317, 318, 321, 409
Milestones, 168
achieving, 215, 217, 218, 231
autism and, 222
failing in, 218-19
MMR vaccine and, 222

preemies and, 225
Milia, 49, 459
Miliaria, 49, 459
Milk, 79, 102, 103, 160
and breast milk compared, 132, 134
avoiding, 73
contents of, 134, 145
diarrhea and, 367
evaporated, 133
fever and, 380
fluoride supplements and, 407
hypersensitivity to, 119
organic, 145
skim, 145
transition to, 128, 145
whole, 90, 128
Milk banks, 125
Milk ducts, clogged, 127
Milley, Frankie: story from, 289-90
Mindell method, 203, 206
Minor care centers, 40
Miracle Blanket, 189
Mistrust, trust versus, 226
Mites, 303, 314, 325
rashes and, 382
MMR vaccine, 267, 270, 272, 279
autism and, 221, 222, 284, 287
milestones and, 222
questions about, 285
rashes from, 386
MMR-V vaccine, 279, 281
Moisturizing, 75
Moisturizing cream, 335
Moki, 428
Molluscum contagiosum, rash with, 384-85
"Mommy and Me" program, 240
Mommy Wars, 23
Moms Day Out programs, 25, 27
Mongolian spots, 48, 459
Monistat, 82
Monospot/EBV titers, 442
Montagu, Lady Mary Wortly, 264
Moraxella, 320
Moro, 48
Mortality rates, 273
decrease in, 265
immunization rates and, 267
Mother's Milk Banks, 125
Mother's Milk Plus, 125
Motor skills, 253
birth to two months, 227
two to four months, 230
autism/mercury poisoning and, 288
tantrums and, 256
Motrin. *See* Ibuprofen
Mouth

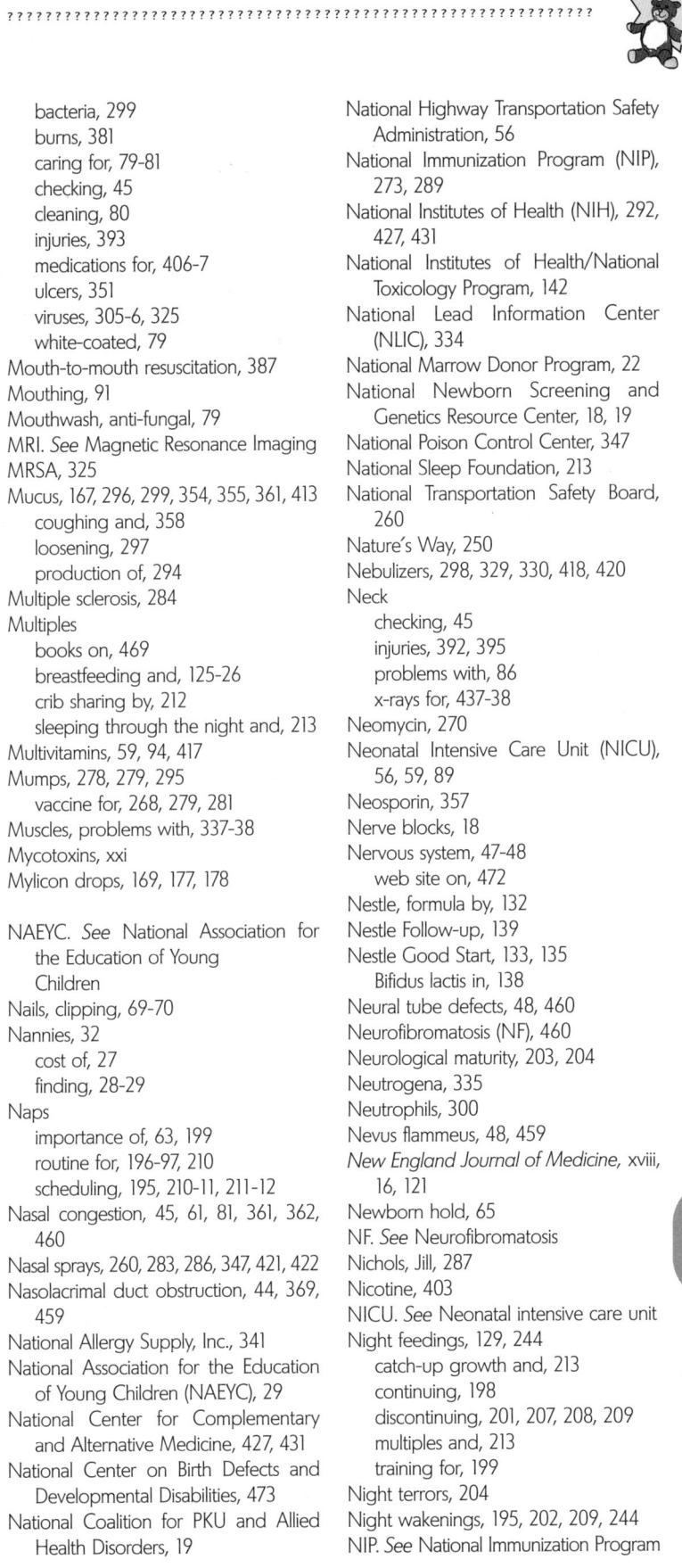

bacteria, 299
burns, 381
caring for, 79-81
checking, 45
cleaning, 80
injuries, 393
medications for, 406-7
ulcers, 351
viruses, 305-6, 325
white-coated, 79
Mouth-to-mouth resuscitation, 387
Mouthing, 91
Mouthwash, anti-fungal, 79
MRI. *See* Magnetic Resonance Imaging
MRSA, 325
Mucus, 167, 296, 299, 354, 355, 361, 413
coughing and, 358
loosening, 297
production of, 294
Multiple sclerosis, 284
Multiples
books on, 469
breastfeeding and, 125-26
crib sharing by, 212
sleeping through the night and, 213
Multivitamins, 59, 94, 417
Mumps, 278, 279, 295
vaccine for, 268, 279, 281
Muscles, problems with, 337-38
Mycotoxins, xxi
Mylicon drops, 169, 177, 178

NAEYC. *See* National Association for the Education of Young Children
Nails, clipping, 69-70
Nannies, 32
cost of, 27
finding, 28-29
Naps
importance of, 63, 199
routine for, 196-97, 210
scheduling, 195, 210-11, 211-12
Nasal congestion, 45, 61, 81, 361, 362, 460
Nasal sprays, 260, 283, 286, 347, 421, 422
Nasolacrimal duct obstruction, 44, 369, 459
National Allergy Supply, Inc., 341
National Association for the Education of Young Children (NAEYC), 29
National Center for Complementary and Alternative Medicine, 427, 431
National Center on Birth Defects and Developmental Disabilities, 473
National Coalition for PKU and Allied Health Disorders, 19

National Highway Transportation Safety Administration, 56
National Immunization Program (NIP), 273, 289
National Institutes of Health (NIH), 292, 427, 431
National Institutes of Health/National Toxicology Program, 142
National Lead Information Center (NLIC), 334
National Marrow Donor Program, 22
National Newborn Screening and Genetics Resource Center, 18, 19
National Poison Control Center, 347
National Sleep Foundation, 213
National Transportation Safety Board, 260
Nature's Way, 250
Nebulizers, 298, 329, 330, 418, 420
Neck
checking, 45
injuries, 392, 395
problems with, 86
x-rays for, 437-38
Neomycin, 270
Neonatal Intensive Care Unit (NICU), 56, 59, 89
Neosporin, 357
Nerve blocks, 18
Nervous system, 47-48
web site on, 472
Nestle, formula by, 132
Nestle Follow-up, 139
Nestle Good Start, 133, 135
Bifidus lactis in, 138
Neural tube defects, 48, 460
Neurofibromatosis (NF), 460
Neurological maturity, 203, 204
Neutrogena, 335
Neutrophils, 300
Nevus flammeus, 48, 459
New England Journal of Medicine, xviii, 16, 121
Newborn hold, 65
NF. *See* Neurofibromatosis
Nichols, Jill, 287
Nicotine, 403
NICU. *See* Neonatal intensive care unit
Night feedings, 129, 244
catch-up growth and, 213
continuing, 198
discontinuing, 201, 207, 208, 209
multiples and, 213
training for, 199
Night terrors, 204
Night wakenings, 195, 202, 209, 244
NIP. *See* National Immunization Program

Nipple shields, 108, 110, 114
Nipples
　accessory, 465
　boiling, 124
　bottle, 131
　burning, 124
　cracked, 108, 109, 110, 123, 130, 131, 174, 353, 354
　cross cut, 141
　infection on, 79, 130
　newborn, 141
　older baby, 141
　recommended, 140-41
　relief for, 114
　rubber, 138
　sore, 105, 110, 112, 113, 114, 124, 130
Nizatidine, 170
Nizoral AD shampoo, 74
No Cry Sleep Solution, The (Pantley), 207
Nose injuries, 393
Nosebleeds, 352, 354, 393
　head injuries and, 395
　treating, 353
NPs. *See* Nurse practitioners
Numbing drops, 409
Numzit, 80
Nurse practitioners (NPs), 40
Nursemaid's elbow, 394
Nursing Mother's Companion, The (Huggins), 115
Nursing staff, 40
Nutramigen Lipil, 134
Nutrition, 83, 93, 102, 103, 129, 165
　books on, 470
　deficiency, 139
　first-year, 90
　information on, 99
　liquid, 92, 147, 149, 160
　medications for, 417-18
　needs for, 88
　poor, 332
　preemies and, 58
　solid, 160
　status, screening for, 33
　web site on, 472
Nutrition Committee (AAP), 149

Obesity, 83, 96-99
　diabetes and, 339
　television and, 238, 239
OB-GYN, pediatricians and, 7
Object permanence, 226, 252
Obstetricians
　circumcision and, 17
　Labor Day and, 43
Occupational therapists, autism and, 224

Odwalla apple juice, *e. coli* and, 356
Off-label, 401
Oil of Lemon Eucalyptus, 76
Omega 3 fatty acids, 121
Omeprazole, 170
Omphalitis, 63, 460
On Becoming Babywise (Ezzo and Bucknam), 91, 208
1% hydrocortisone cream, 74, 335, 347
100 Day Cough, 276
Oppenheimer Toy Portfolio, 236, 240
Oragel, 80
"Oral exploration" phase, 249
Oral Herpes Stomatitis, 306
Oral motor skills
　four to six months, 231
　six to nine months, 232
　nine to twelve months, 234
　foods and, 148
　preemies and, 149
Orbital cellulitis, 370, 460
Organic, 152
Organization, 25, 26
Orthotics, 337, 460
Otitis externa, 317, 318, 460
　ear drops for, 408
Otitis media, 460
　acute, 316, 317, 445
Otoscopes, 318
Outlet safety covers, 237
Over The Counter (OTC), 402
Overdosing, 297
Overeating, 96-99
Overproduction, problems with, 130
Overtiredness, 197, 199, 205, 210, 211

Pacifiers, 128, 131, 196, 248, 322
　boiling, 124
　breastfeeding and, 105, 115, 249
　development and, 248
　ear infections and, 249, 317, 323
　glow-in-the-dark, 200-201
　orthotic, 249
　prolonged use of, 206
　removing, 115-16, 197
　SIDS and, 188-89, 191
　sleep and, 199, 200-201, 204
　withdrawing, 248, 249
Palmar Grasp, 48
Pantley method, 203, 207
Paraphimosis, 16, 78, 461
Parasites, 303, 315, 325
　infection with, 355, 364
Parent-centered school, 5
Parenting
　attachment, 5, 192, 207, 208
　guidelines for, xxi-xx, 28

questions about, 7
stay-at-home, 27
web site on, 220, 472
Parenting styles, 3-6, 15, 65, 205
Parent's Choice, 135, 138
Parent's Guide to Private Cord Blood Banks, A, 21, 22
Partial wakenings, 182, 199
Parvovirus, 308-9, 325
rash with, 384-85
Pasteurization, 132, 356
PDD. See Pervasive developmental disorder
PE tubes. See Pressure equalization tubes
"Peanut challenge" test, 156
Peanuts, 73, 154
breastfeeding and, 121
Pedialyte, 174, 366, 368, 369
Pediasure, 146
Pediatricians
adoption and, 33
confiding in, 41
delays for, 8-9
diagnosis by, 435
emergencies and, 41
Labor Day and, 43
on-call, 13, 345-46
philosophy of, 11-12
questions for, 8-13, 14
selecting, xvi, 4, 6-7, 10, 14-15
speaking with, 14, 41, 345-46
switching from, 38
time with, 11, 35
Pediatrics (journal), 250, 422
Pediatrix, 269, 286, 287
screening and, 19
Pediculocides, 424
Pee, 44, 47, 62, 78, 161, 162, 175-76
blood in, 175
odors, 342
urge to, 168
See also Urine
Pelvic
CT/MRI for, 438
ultrasound for, 437
Penicillin, 320, 340, 414, 428
Penile adhesions, 16, 77, 78, 342, 461
Penis
caring for, 78
hidden, 16-17
swollen, 78
uncircumcised, 78
Peppermint, 297, 430
Pepto-Bismol, 167, 367
side effects of, 412-13
Personality
two to four months, 230

four to six months, 232
six to nine months, 234
nine to twelve months, 234
development, 218, 219, 226
predicting, 246
Pertussis, 275-76, 277, 358
vaccine for, 267, 268
Pervasive developmental disorder (PDD), 159, 220, 461
Pesticides, organic foods and, 152
Petechiae rash, 352, 353, 374, 383, 387, 436
Petroleum jelly, 71, 73
Pharmaceutical industry, 427, 428
Phenergan, 413
Phenylcyclidine, 403
Phenylketonuria (PKU), 33, 49, 461
Phimosis, 78, 461
Phone calls
cold and flu season, 346
consultation, 14
diagnoses and, 348
emergency, 13, 346, 349
etiquette for, 345-46
handling, 13, 14
most frequent, 349
Phototherapy, 55, 461
Physician assistants, 40
Physician's Breastfeeding Triage Tool Kit (West), 131
Phytoestrogens, 136
Piaget, Jean, 225
Picarding, 76, 77
Pigeon toeing, 337
Pigmentation, 76
Pincer grasp, 158-59, 232
Pink eye, 278, 310, 320, 369-70
avoiding, 370
ear infections and, 370
sinus infections and, 370
Pinworms, 315, 325, 416
Pirate Booty, 99
Pityriasis rosea, rash with, 384-85
PKU. See Phenylketonuria
Platelet count, 440
Playpens, bassinet inserts with, 185
Playtex
bottles from, 141, 142
nipples from, 140
Pleasure zones, exploring, 258
Plugged ducts, 108, 113, 114, 123, 131
Pneumococcal, 289
Pneumonia, 60, 70, 279, 280, 358, 375, 436
described, 309, 461
medications for, 414
rain and, 300

vaccine for, 333
See also Strep pneumoniae
Point and grunt, 239
Poison control, 238, 381, 382
Poison ivy, 351, 352, 382
Poisoning, 387
   food, 310-11, 325, 354, 355-56, 364, 368, 453
   mercury, 286, 287, 288
   problems with/solutions to, 381-82
Polio, 270, 273, 295
   vaccine for, 267, 268, 271, 278
Polychlorinated biphenyls (PCBs), 286
Polydactyly, 48, 461
Polyethylene, 142
Polymyxin B, 270
Polypropylene, 142
Poops, 44, 110, 161, 175
   bacteria in, 78
   black tar, 52
   blood in, 119, 163, 167, 354, 355, 436, 448
   breast milk and, 162, 163, 165
   breastfeeding and, 130, 165
   color of, 54, 62, 112, 167
   consistency of, 164
   described, 161, 162
   feedings and, 164
   firmness of, 164
   first, 63
   floating, 167
   food allergies and, 167
   food coloring and, 168
   foremilk and, 163
   formula and, 162, 163
   frequency of, 62, 162, 163
   grape jelly, 167, 282
   iron and, 334
   jaundice and, 54
   mucus in, 167
   newborn, 162-64
   odor of, 392
   red faces and, 163
   solid, 355
   solid foods and, 165-66, 167
   texture of, 62
   washing out, 164
   worrisome, 163, 167
Port wine stains, 48, 461-62
Positional plagiocephaly, 85, 86, 191, 228
Posterior urethral valves, 47, 462
Post-tussive emesis, 367, 368, 462
PPD, described, 36-37, 443
Preauricular pits and tags, 44, 462
Precocious puberty, milk and, 145
Prednisone, 419

Preemies
   books on, 470
   breastfeeding and, 58, 59, 126
   calorie needs of, 89
   catch-up growth by, 84
   development and, 225
   feeding for, 91
   formula for, 138
   growth chart for, 478
   iron supplements and, 94
   milestones and, 225
   primer for, xxi, 56-59
   sleeping through the night and, 213
   solid foods and, 149
Preemies: The Essential Guide for Parents of Premature Babies (Linden), 56
Pregnancy, 5
   medications and, 403-4
   tests during, 50
Prenatal care, 92
Prenatal consultations, 7-8, 10
Prenatal vitamins, 59, 93
   breastfeeding and, 120, 121
Preschool, 23, 27, 30
Prescriptions, 400, 402
Preservatives, 286, 288
Pressure equalization (PE) tubes, 324, 408, 409
Prevacid, 170, 412
"Preventing or Delaying the Onset of Food Allergies in Infants" (brochure), 156
Prevnar, 269, 281, 302, 333, 367
   ear infections and, 323
   shortage of, 289
   Strep pneumoniae and, 320
Prilosec, 170, 412
Primary care providers, 40
Probiotics, 131, 412, 431
   colic and, 249, 250
   formulas with, 138, 139
Problem solving, 217, 226
Procrastinator, 113
Prolactin hormone level, 125
Prosobee Lipil, 133
Proton pump inhibitors, 170
Protopic, 336
Prune juice cocktails, 164
Pseudostrabismus, 328, 462
Psychiatric, autism/mercury poisoning and, 288
Public health, 265
Pulmicort, 419
Pulse, 52
   checking, 44, 347
   femoral, 46

Purell, 293
Pur-lan, 108
Pustular melanosis, 49, 462
Pyelonephritis, 47, 462
Pyloric sphincter, 173
Pyloric stenosis, 169, 173, 349, 462
   vomiting and, 368

Quality time, 28
Quiet zone, 258

RabAvert, 270
Rabies, vaccine for, 270
Ragweed, 340
Ranitidine, 170
Rapid antigen assays, 444
Rapid Eye Movement (REM), 182, 193
Rashes, 48-49, 303, 335, 351, 352, 382-87, 435,
   allergies and, 153, 382
   blistery/non-blistery, 387
   causes of, 382
   contagious, 386
   diagnosing, 382
   fever and, 387
   immune systems and, 386
   infections and, 382, 384-85
   MMR vaccine and, 386
   newborn, 382
   non-descript, 386
   pimply, 386
   questions about, 382
   scaly, 386
   viruses causing, 307-9, 325
   worrisome, 383, 386
Reach Out and Read program, 229
Reactive Airway Disease, 328-29
Reading, 228, 229
Red blood cells, 332
   sickle cell disease and, 333
Reflexes, 44, 48, 227
Refractive errors, 56, 462
Registered nurses (RNs), 40
Reglan, 124, 125
Regularity, 245
Regurgitation, 168-74
Rehydration, 366, 413-14
Reinforcement, positive, 257
Relaxation, sleep and, 184, 204
REM. *See* Rapid Eye Movement
Replacement therapy, 334
Residuals, 288
Respiratory distress, 45, 46, 462-63
   medications for, 418-22
   problems with/solutions to, 357-61
Respiratory infections
   acute, 30

   asthma and, 328
   viral, 325
Respiratory rate, 52, 348, 363
   checking, 44, 347, 360
   elevated, 358
Respiratory Syncytial Virus (RSV), 325, 328, 358, 360, 361, 362, 436, 463
   asthma and, 329
   described, 304-5, 448
   preemies and, 57
   preventing, 420
Respiratory system, 57, 357-59
Respiratory viruses, 294, 303-4, 364
Rester, 113
Reticulocyte count, 442
Retinoblastoma, 44, 463
Retinopathy of Prematurity (ROP), 56, 463
Retractions, 46, 463
Reye's syndrome, 410
Rhinoviruses, 297, 325
Rice cereal, 148, 151, 152, 158
   adding, 138
   breast milk and, 92, 170
   constipation and, 165-66
   formula and, 92, 170
   sleeping through the night and, 184
Rice milk, 128, 145
Ricin, 382
Rickets, 93, 94, 463
Ringworm, 325, 386, 463
   diagnosing, 313
   infection with, 314
   rash with, 384-85
   treating, 313, 423
RNs. *See* Registered nurses
Robeez, 237
Robert's American Gourmet, 99
Rocky Mountain Spotted Fever, 353
   rash with, 383, 384-85
Role confusion, identity versus, 227
Role models, 97, 98, 234, 254
Rolling over, 215, 231
Room sharing, SIDS and, 191
Room temperature, SIDS and, 188, 192
Rooming-in, 53, 105
Rooting, 48, 91, 463
ROP. *See* Retinopathy of Prematurity
Roseola, 307-8, 325, 374-75
   rash with, 384-85
Rotarix, 282
Rotateq, 282
Rotavirus, 288, 307, 325
   vaccine for, 267, 282, 284-85
Routines, 25, 26, 93
   See also Sleep routines

RSV. See Respiratory Syncytial Virus
Rubella, 278
   congenital, 268, 279
   preventing, 295
   vaccine for, 268, 279, 281
Rule of Threes, 249
Runny nose, 297, 303, 348, 362
   allergies and, 340, 341
   hay fever and, 340
Rx, 402

Saccaromyces, 431
Sacral dimple, 48, 463
Safety, 141, 142, 187-89, 191, 192, 193, 253, 390
   gates, 237
   natural products and, 431
   preemies and, 59
   tips on, 237
Sage tea, 127
Saline drops, 81, 296, 297, 361-62, 421
Salivary glands, 80
Salmonella, 310-11, 325, 364
   carriers of, 355-56
Salves, 426
SARS. See Sudden Acute Respiratory Syndrome
Scabicides, 423, 424
Scabies, 314, 325, 424
   rash with, 384-85
Scarlet fever, rash with, 384-85
Science
   junk, xviii
   showing, xviii-xxi, 11, 12, 153, 427
Science (journal), 249
Screening tests, xv, 5, 36-37, 49, 442
   adoption and, 33
   hearing, 33, 44, 45, 57
   metabolic, 4, 18-19, 33, 36
   performing, 40
   web site for, 473
Scrotum, swollen, 47, 350
Sears, William, 6, 203
Sears method, 203, 206-7
Seborrhea, 74, 463-64
Sebulex, 74
Secrets of the Baby Whisperer (Hogg), 206
Seizures, 273, 381, 392, 436
   baths and, 380
   febrile, 272, 379-80, 387, 388, 410
   head injuries and, 391
   temperature and, 380
   web site on, 472
Self-control, 252-53, 256
Self-soothing, 185, 196, 198, 200, 202, 203, 206, 209, 248, 258, 259
   allowing for, 199
   autism and, 220
Selsun Blue, 74
Sensory Integration Disorder, 159, 464
Sensory-motor development
   autism/mercury poisoning and, 288
   birth to two years, 225-26, 228
Septal hematoma, 393
Serous fluid, 321
Serous otitis media, 320, 464
Sexually transmitted infections, 15
Shampoos, 72, 74
   antidandruff, 84
Shigella, 310-11, 364
Shingles, 295
   rash with, 384-85
Shoes, 236-37
Shoulder dystonia, 45, 464
Shoulder/trunk support, 216
Shoulders, checking, 45
Shrinking baby phenomenon, 52
Sick child policies, 29, 30
Sick leave policy, 26
Sick-child appointments, 8, 9, 10, 37
   problem-oriented, 11-12
   scheduling around, 39
   well-child appointments and, 39
Sickle cell anemia, 49, 464
Sickle cell disease, 33, 332-33
   web site on, 472
Side-lying, 112
SIDS. See Sudden infant death syndrome
Sign language, 239
Silvadene, 357
Simethicone drops, 177, 178, 250
Similac, 133, 134, 138
Singulair, 329
Sinus
   CT/MRI for, 438
   x-rays for, 438
Sinus infections, 296, 303, 325, 375, 436
   and common colds compared, 298
   described, 309
   medications for, 414
   pink eye and, 370
Sinusitis, 363, 464
Sitting up, 231
Skills, 4, 217
Skin, 61
   checking, 48
   dry, 73, 75, 293
   problems with, 62-63, 335-37
   sensitive, 335, 386
   web site on, 472-73
   yellow, 48, 53-54, 152
Skin infections, 309-10, 318, 325, 436

medications for, 414
Skin products, 422-26
    rashes and, 382, 383
Skin stickers, 376
Skin tags, 44, 464
Skin testing, 157, 443
Skin turgor, dehydration and, 365
Skin virus, 294
Skull, 86
    fractures, 392, 393
    x-rays for, 438
Slapped cheek, 308-9, 325
Sleep
    acid reflux and, 198, 213
    back, 187, 192
    books on, 202, 470
    breastfeeding and, 126, 183, 192
    in cars, 211
    changes in, 183
    cluster feedings and, 183
    decisions about, 5
    diaper changes and, 185
    feedings and, 61, 109, 112, 127, 145, 195, 196, 198, 199, 201, 203
    gassiness and, 177
    help falling to, 195, 196, 210
    importance of, 63
    inclined position, 170
    nighttime, 187
    noisy, 53
    parental behavior and, 198, 200
    preemies and, 59
    red flags with, 62
    regular, 29
    relaxation and, 174
    REM, 182, 193
    safety with, 187-89, 192
    science of, 181-82
    uninterrupted, 184
    See also Solitary sleep
Sleep aids, 186
Sleep associations, 202, 206, 207, 194
Sleep crutches, 203, 206, 248, 296
Sleep cycles, 182, 195, 196, 200, 210
Sleep deprivation, 64, 65, 181, 208, 362
Sleep disorders, 194, 203, 204, 348
Sleep habits, 181
    setting up, 194-98, 205, 207
    undoing bad, 184, 186, 187, 198, 200, 202
Sleep issues, 38, 183, 204, 244, 247
    addressing, 208
    cross-cultural, 198
    persistent, 200
    preventing, 205
Sleep patterns, 198, 204
    changes in, 186-87
    disrupted, 197, 199, 201-2, 205
    feedings and, 128, 197
    improving, 184, 196
    newborn, 182, 183
    regular, 195
SLEEP PLAN, 210
Sleep positions
    bald spots and, 191
    flat heads and, 191
    GER and, 190
    head shape and, 87
    recommendations on, 187
    rolling over and, 190
    SIDS and, 191
    vomiting/choking and, 188
Sleep routines, 185, 200
    consistency in, 196-97, 204, 206
    deciding on, 192-94
    establishing, 196, 207-8, 210
    following, 197, 203, 211
    healthy, 186
    mistakes with, 199
    multiples and, 213
    positive, 202
Sleep theories, 203
"Sleep Tight," 251
Sleep training, 205, 207
Sleep walking, 204
Sleeping through the night, 129, 200, 208
    acid reflux and, 213
    adjusting time for, 202
    expectations about, 184
    feedings and, 143, 197-98
    foods and, 148
    multiples and, 213
    preemies and, 213
    rice cereal and, 184
Sleeping Through the Night (Mindell), 206
SleepSack, 189
Slow to warm up child, 244, 257
Smallpox, 273, 295
    elimination of, 264, 271
    vaccination for, 264, 266, 267, 268, 283
Smegma, 16, 77, 78
Smells, 225, 342
Smoking
    ear infections and, 317, 323
    SIDS and, 188, 192
Snacks, 25, 125
    healthy, 97, 98, 99
Snoring, 81, 361
Snot, 81, 296, 297, 359
    green, 298, 302, 303, 362
    prolonged, 298

Snugli, 228
Soaps
    antibacterial, 292-93, 335
    antimicrobial, 292-93
    Dove, 72, 75, 293, 335
    dry skin and, 293
    moisturizing, 335
Social growth, 216, 225, 226-27
Social skills
    birth to two months, 228
    two to four months, 230
    four to six months, 231, 232
    six to nine months, 233, 234
    nine to twelve months, 234, 236
    lack of, 221
    learning, 216-17
Soft spots, 85, 86, 392
Solitary sleep, 192-94
Solve Your Child's Sleep Problems (Ferber), 202
Soothing, 106
    autism and, 220
    need for, 246
    self-, 185, 196, 198, 199, 200, 202, 203, 206, 209, 220, 248, 258, 259
    tricks for, 247-48
Sore throats, 302, 325
    home remedy for, 433-34
    viral, 306-7, 325
Soy milk, 128, 145
Spanking, 254
Special education, autism and, 223
Speech, autism/mercury poisoning and, 288
Speech therapists, autism and, 224
Spina bifida, 48, 464
Spinal fluid, 300
Spinal fluid (CSF) tests, 443-44
Spinal manipulations, 427
Spine
    checking, 47-48
    injuries, 395
    ultrasound for, 437
    x-rays for, 438
Spit up, 161, 168-74
    concerns about, 169, 172
Spleen, non-functional, 333
Spock, Benjamin, 6
Spoiling, 185, 247
Staph, 325
Stem cells, 19, 20
Sternocleidomastoid muscles, 338
Steroid creams, 16, 424
Steroids, 423, 428
    eczema and, 336
    inhaled, 329, 419, 420, 456
    oral, 419
    topical, 336
    using, 424-25
Stevens-Johnson Syndrome, 351, 411, 464
Stitches, 388-90
Stomach acid, 171
Stomach ulcers, 354
Stomach virus, 174, 294, 325, 364, 367
    breastfeeding and, 104
Stomachaches, 173, 349
Stool cultures, 33, 354
Stool odors, 342
Stool rules, 62
Stool tests, 443
Stools. *See* Poops
Stork bites, 459, 465
Strabismus, 56, 327, 464
Strawberry hemangioma, 48, 464
Strep infection, 265, 281, 325, 353
    antibiotics and, 303
Strep pneumoniae, 289, 301, 302, 325, 333
    described, 281, 312-13
    Prevnar and, 320
    treating, 282
    See also Pneumonia
Strep throat, 281, 301, 302
Streptomycin, 270
Stress response, 18
Stridor, 351, 359, 360, 363, 465
Sturge Weber syndrome, 48, 465
Subconjunctival hemorrhage, 392
Sucking, 48, 109, 115, 126, 128, 146, 185
    breastfeeding and, 127
    sleep and, 204
    soothing by, 247, 248
    thumb, 248, 258, 259
Sudafed, 127
    ephedra and, 401
Sudden Acute Respiratory Syndrome (SARS), 265
Sudden infant death syndrome (SIDS), xxi, 85, 187-89, 360
    bedding and, 188, 189, 192
    potential for, 193
    preventing, 189, 190, 191, 192, 231
    rate of, in U.S., 187
    risk factors for, 188
    sleep positions and, 191
    tummy time and, 189, 190, 191
    vaccines and, 284
    vomiting and, 190
Suffocation hazards, 191
Sulfonamides, 415
Sunscreen, 69, 74-75, 76
Super-ego, 252
Suppositories, 165

Supraventricular tachycardia (SVT), 331, 465
Sutures, 388-90
Swaddling, 186, 189, 190, 192
Sweat test, 444
Swimmer's ear, 318, 408
   and ear infections compared, 316-17
Symbolic play, 221
Symbols, concept of, 226
Symmetrel, 295
Synagis, 59, 420
Synapese, 223
Syndactyly, 48, 465
Syrup of Ipecac, 238, 381

Tachypnea of newborn, 46, 51, 466
Talking, walking and, 235
Tamiflu, 295
Target, formula from, 132, 133
TB, screening for, 33
Tea Tree oil, 430
Teachers, 29, 259
Tear ducts
   blocked, 459
   checking, 44
Tearing, 370-71
Teeth, 393
   cleaning, 80, 86, 145, 201
   eruption of, 79, 85-86
   iron and, 334
Teething
   breastfeeding and, 127
   drool and, 80
   fever and, 380
   foods and, 159
   medications for, 407
   relief for pain of, 80
   sleep etiquette and, 197
   sleep patterns and, 202, 205
   toys for, 131, 234, 241
Teething gels, 80
Teething tablets, 80, 407
Television
   ADD and, 238
   autism and, 238
   behavior and, 239
   educational, 238, 239, 240
   inappropriate programs on, 239
   limiting, 238, 239
   meal times and, 240
   obesity and, 238, 239
Temper tantrums, 254, 256
Temperament
   learning, 244-46
   resources for, 243
   travel and, 260
Temperature, 371
   brain damage and, 372
   concerns about, 373
   infections and, 372
   rectal, 377-78
   room, 188, 192
   seizures and, 380
   taking, 44, 347, 375-76
   rectal, 376
Temporal artery scanners, 376
Tempra, 378
Terrible Two's, 254
Testes
   swollen, 436
   ultrasound for, 437
   undescended, 47, 466-47
Tetanus, 275, 277, 389
   booster for, 271, 289
   vaccine for, 267, 268
Tetracycline, 401
Texture aversion, 159
Texture complexity, 148
Thermometers
   ear, 376
   glass mercury, 378
   oral, 376, 378
   pacifier, 376
   rectal, 164, 376, 377-78
Thimerosal, 283, 285, 286
   autism and, 287, 288
Throat
   checking, 45
   infections, 325
   See also Strep throat; Sore throats
Thrush, 79, 124, 325, 419, 465
   diagnosing, 313
   infection with, 314
   treating, 79, 82, 313
Thumb sucking, 248, 258, 259
Thyroid, screening for, 33, 442
Tide Free, 74
Time out, 256, 260
Tinea capitis, 423
TIRED. *See* Trial of Infant Response to Diphenhydramine
Tiredness cues, 206
TNX-901, 156
Tobacco, 428
Toddler 411 (Fields and Fields), 241
Toddler Bargains (Fields and Fields), xvii, 75
Toes
   broken, 394
   controlling, 216
   immobilizing, 395
Toilet lid locks, 237
Toilet training, 168
Tongue, checking, 45

Tongue-tied, 114, 465
Tonsil viruses, 305-6, 325
Tooth decay, 80, 81
    fluoride and, 95
    sippy cups and, 146
Toothpaste, 79
    fluoride in, 80-81, 407
Torch infections, 50, 465
Torticollis, 45, 86, 87, 337-38, 465
Touchpoints (Brazelton), 241
Toxins, 267, 299, 354
Toxoplasmosis screening, 5
Toys, 131, 234, 242
    age-appropriate, 240, 241
    cause and effect, 236
    classic, 236
    developmental stimulation and, 241
    favorite, 252
    safety with, 237, 238
    teething, 241
Transient Tachypnea of the Newborn (TTN), 51, 466
Transitional objects, 201, 252
Transitions, setting up, 196
Transmitted upper airway noise, 466
Trauma, 370, 390-95
Travel
    ear infections and, 321
    sleep etiquette and, 197
    sleep patterns and, 202, 205
    temperament and, 260
    web site for, 473
Trial of Infant Response to Diphenhydramine (TIRED), 406
Trihibit, 278
Triple Paste, 71
Triple-dye, 70
Tri-Vi-Sol, 93
Tropicana Health Kids Orange Juice, 144
Trust, mistrust versus, 226
TTN. *See* Transient Tachypnea of the Newborn
Tuberculosis, 466
    coughing and, 363
    vaccine for, 267
Tucker Sling, 190
Tummy time, 230
    flat heads and, 86-87
    SIDS and, 189, 190, 191
Tumors
    abdominal, 46, 445
    brain, 85, 324, 328, 368, 448
    vomiting and, 368
"Two stop" rule, 26
Tylenol. *See* Acetaminophen

Ulcers, 354
Ultrasound, 43, 46, 48, 436-37
Umbilical cord
    blood from, 19
    caring for, 63, 71-72
UNICEF, vaccination by, 271
Unilateral laterothoracic exanthem, rash with, 384-85
U.S. Department of Health and Human Services, 273
U.S. News and World Report, on obesity, 96
University of Colorado Health Sciences Center, 19
Upper respiratory infection (URI), 123, 296, 325, 358, 361, 362
    antibiotics for, 302
    ear infections and, 317
    home remedy for, 432
Urethra, 78, 175, 176, 342
URI. *See* Upper respiratory infection
Uric acid crystals, 52, 175, 467
Urinalysis, 36, 443
Urinary tract infection (UTI), 47, 78, 311, 467
    circumcision and, 16
    medications for, 414
Urination, 47, 62, 364
    breastfeeding and, 175
    crying with, 350
    drinking and, 175
    excessive, 339, 436
    pain with, 436
Urine, 161-62, 175-76, 300
    abnormal stream of, 78
    cloudy, 176
    dehydration and, 365, 366
    foul smelling, 176, 342
    normal flow of, 176
    tests, 443
    See also Pee
Urologists, circumcision and, 17
UTI. *See* Urinary tract infection
UVB rays, 93
Uvula, 45

Vaccinations
    benefits of, 289
    books on, 289, 470
    booster, 271, 274, 277, 289
    decision making about, 270-71
    development of, 264, 269
    exemptions for, 271, 276
    fever and, 64, 272, 274-75
    less pain with, 269-70
    life expectancy and, 264
    protection from, 267-68

records, 274
red flags with, 272, 273
required/optional, 274
responsibility with, 263-64, 265
schedule, 275, 276
schools and, 271
web site for, 473
well-child appointments and, 38
Vaccine Adverse Event Reporting System (VAERS), 272, 284, 285, 288
Vaccine Education Center, 289
Vaccine Injury Compensation Program (VICP), 273
Vaccines, xv, xxi, 33
acellular, 277
additives in, 288
allergies to, 270, 273
combination, 269
controversies over, 263, 265, 266, 283-89
effectiveness of, 268
epidemics and, 267
inactivated, 266, 267, 272
live attenuated, 266, 267, 272
nasal spray, 283
preservatives/stabilizers in, 283, 286
questions about, 266-75
safety with, 267, 268, 269, 277, 284
shortage of, 288-89
side effects of, 268, 276, 284
specifics about, 275-82
thimerosal-free, 285-86
VAERS. See Vaccine Adverse Event Reporting System
Vagina, 78, 341
Vaginal discharge, 47, 467
Vapocoolant sprays, 270
Vaporizers, 298
Vapo-rubs, 297
Varicella, 272, 280, 308, 325
deadliness of, 281
economic impact of, 281
vaccine for, 267, 279, 280, 281
Variolation, 264
Vaseline, 71, 73, 342, 355
Vegetables, 150, 158
fiber in, 167
food poisoning and, 356
fruits and, 152
organic, 153
Veggie Booty, 99
Ventricular septal defect (VSD), 331, 467
Vernix, 467
Very low birth weight (VLBW), 58
Vesicles, 467
Vesicoureteral reflux (VUR), 47, 176, 467
ViaCord, 21

VICP. See Vaccine Injury Compensation Program
Vioxx, 268
Viral exanthems, 307-9, 325
Viral infections, 266, 268, 269, 299, 303-9, 370
bacterial infections and, 300
fever and, 372
typical, 375
Viral titers, 442
Viruses, 291, 296, 299, 324
antibiotics and, 302
described, 292-95
drug-resistant, 282
garden-variety, 294
infection from, 294, 325
length of, 295
protection from, 267, 295
rashes and, 307-9, 325, 382
Vision
birth to two months, 228
two to four months, 230
six to nine months, 233
autism/mercury poisoning and, 288
defects, 211
screening for, 33, 37
Vital signs, 44, 347, 348
Vitamin A, 119, 144, 152
Vitamin C, 144
iron and, 101, 334, 417
Vitamin D, 143
breast milk and, 129
taking, 93-94, 417
Vitamin E, 49, 144
Vitamins, 94, 100, 332, 417
preemies and, 58
prenatal, 59, 93, 120, 121
using, 93-96, 417
VLBW. See Very low birth weight
Voiding Cystourethrogram, CT/MRI for, 439
Vomiting, 61, 96, 168-74, 238, 282
bile, 173, 368, 436
blood, 173-74, 353-54, 369
breastfeeding and, 368
coffee ground, 173-74, 354, 369
coughing and, 368
dehydration and, 365, 366, 367
diarrhea and, 175, 368, 369, 413
drinking and, 174
fever and, 174, 368
food allergies and, 153
forceful, 353, 354
formula and, 368
head injuries and, 390, 391, 395
home remedy for, 433
medications and, 399, 413

persistent, 174, 350, 368, 369
problems with/solutions to, 367-69
projectile, 169, 350, 368, 369
red flags with, 173-74
rehydration and, 414
SIDS and, 190
sleep positions and, 188
Von Willebrand Disease, 352, 467
Vruit, 97, 144
VSD. *See* Ventricular septal defect
VUR. *See* Vesicoureteral reflux

Waiting rooms, delays in, 8-10, 14
Walkers, 231, 392
Walking, 216, 394
   crawling and, 233
   talking and, 235
Wall Street Journal, 136
Wal-Mart, 108
   formula from, 132, 133, 135
Warts, home remedy for, 434
Water, 103, 143-44
   bottled, 140, 144
   breastfeeding and, 120
   fluoride in, 95, 96
   loss of, 366
   purification, 265
WBC. *See* White blood cell count
Weaning, 123, 126-27
Weight
   bearing, 229
   checking, 44
   See also Birth weight
Weight gain, 84, 88, 140
   Babywise method and, 208
   juice and, 144
   problems with, 172
Weight loss, 88, 107, 109, 339
   dehydration and, 365
Weight percentiles, drop in, 92
Weissbluth method, 196, 203, 206, 207
   described, 205
Well-child appointments, 38, 215
   development and, 217
   for multiple children, 39
   schedule of, 35-37
   sick-child appointments and, 39
   vaccinations and, 38, 274
West Nile Virus, 76
Wet nurses, 125, 132
What to Do When Your Baby is Premature (Garcia-Prats and Hornfischer), 56
Wheezing, 329, 359
   acid reflux and, 173
   chronic, 330, 436
Whey protein, 135-36

Which Toys for Which Child: A Consumer's Guide for Selecting Suitable Toys, Ages Birth Through Five (CPSC), 241
White blood cell count (WBC), 295, 300, 440
White noise, 249-50
WHO. *See* World Health Organization
Whole Foods, bottles at, 142
Whooping cough, 265, 271, 275, 276, 277, 358, 359, 360, 468
   coughing and, 363
   epidemics of, 277
   vaccine for, 267
Womanly Art of Breastfeeding, The (La Leche League), 115
Womb infections, 123
Work, xx
   balancing family with, 24-25, 26
   breastfeeding and, 106, 122, 129
World Health Organization (WHO)
   complementary foods and, 149
   growth chart by, 84, 92
   smallpox and, 264, 283
Worms, 325
Wounds
   cleaning/caring for, 388
   closing, 389-90
   infected, 389
Wright, Karen L., 331
Wrists, broken, 394

X-rays, 303, 437-48

Yeast diaper rash, 314, 325
   rash with, 384-85
   treatment of, 313
Yeast infection, 124, 131, 468
   treating, 71, 79, 82
Yellow fever, vaccine for, 270
Yersinia infection, 364
YF-VAX, 270
YWCA, child care and, 31

Zantac, 89, 170, 411
Zegerid, 170, 412
ZERO to THREE: National Center for Infants, Toddlers, and Families, contact information for, 473
Zilactin Baby, 407
Zinc, 430
Zinc oxide, 71
Zofran, 413
Zovirax, 295
Zwiener, R. Jeff, 168

TODDLER 411

If you liked Baby 411 . . . you'll love Toddler 411!

Toddler 411

Clear Answers & Smart Advice For Your Toddler
$12.95
As seen on the Dr. Phil show!
Inside you'll learn:

- The truth about **The Terrible Twos**—and how to raise a well-behaved child without going insane.
- **Picky Eaters**—learn how to cope . . . and convince your child to eat something besides Goldfish crackers.
- **Toilet train your toddler in just one day.** No, that's not a typo—learn the Zen of Toilet Training, when to start and how to make it work.
- **What's normal**—and what's not when it comes to your toddler's growth and development.
- Simple steps and smart advice to **avoid environmental hazards.**
- The most up-to-date, **evidence-based health info** for you and your toddler.

Call toll-free to order!
1-800-888-0385
Or order online
Toddler411.com

Additional information on all our books is available online at
www.WindsorPeak.com

What's on Baby411.com?

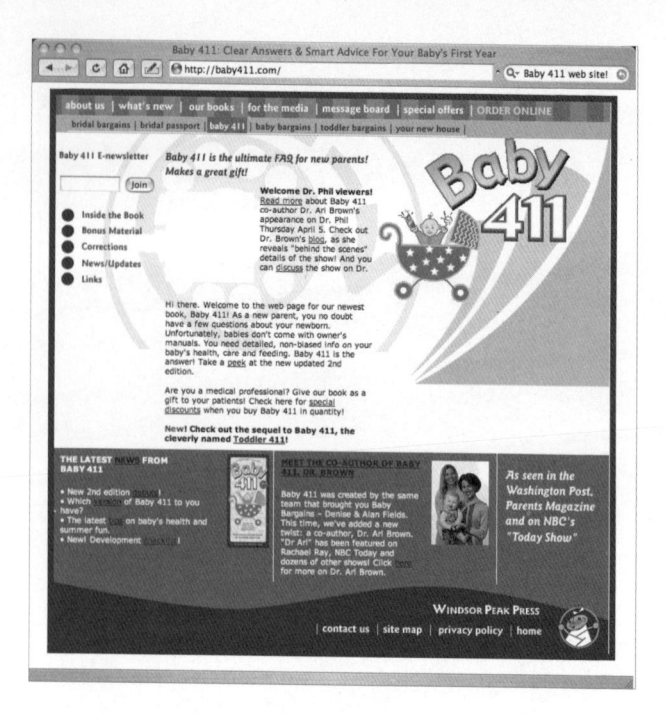

Come visit us at Baby411.com!

What's online?

◆ *Rash-o-rama!* Check out pictures of common rashes, birth marks and more. Click on Bonus Material.

◆ Updates on this book between editions.

◆ THE LATEST NEWS on medical research for babies.

◆ MESSAGE BOARDS with in-depth reader feedback.

◆ CORRECTIONS and clarifications.

◆ Sign up for a FREE E-NEWSLETTER!

How to Reach the Authors

Have a question about
Baby 411?

Want to make a suggestion?

*Discovered a great tip
you'd like to share?*

Contact the authors, Denise Fields and Ari Brown
in one of four flavorful ways:

1. By email:
authors@Baby411.com

2. On our web page:
www.Baby411.com

3. By phone:
(303) 442-8792

4. By mail:
436 Pine Street, Suite 600,
Boulder, CO 80302

If this address isn't active, try one of our other URL's:
www.WindsorPeak.com or
www.BabyBargainsBook.com
Or call our office at 1-800-888-0385
if you're having problems accessing the page.

More Books by the Fields

Baby Bargains
Secrets to saving 20% to 50% on baby furniture, equipment, clothes, toys, maternity wear and much, much more!
$17.95 (7th Edition)
As seen on Oprah and the NBC Today Show
Over 500,000 copies sold

Toddler Bargains
Secrets to saving 20% to 50% on toddler furniture, clothing; shoes, travel gear, toys and more!
$14.95 (2nd Edition)

Bridal Bargains
Secrets to throwing a fantastic wedding on a realistic budget
$14.95 (7th Edition)
Over 500,000 copies sold!
As seen on Oprah!

Call toll-free to order!
1-800-888-0385
Or order online
WindsorPeak.com

Additional information on all our books is available online at
www.WindsorPeak.com
Mastercard, VISA, American Express and Discover Accepted!
Shipping to any U.S. address is $3.